CODE OF FEDERAL
REGULATIONS

I0046269

Title 24
Housing and Urban Development

Part 1700 to End

Revised as of April 1, 2019

Containing a codification of documents
of general applicability and future effect

As of April 1, 2019

Published by the Office of the Federal Register
National Archives and Records Administration
as a Special Edition of the Federal Register

Table of Contents

Cite this Code: CFR

To cite the regulations in this volume use title, part and section number. Thus, 24 CFR 2002.1 *refers to title 24, part 2002, section 1.*

Explanation

The Code of Federal Regulations is a codification of the general and permanent rules published in the Federal Register by the Executive departments and agencies of the Federal Government. The Code is divided into 50 titles which represent broad areas subject to Federal regulation. Each title is divided into chapters which usually bear the name of the issuing agency. Each chapter is further subdivided into parts covering specific regulatory areas.

Each volume of the Code is revised at least once each calendar year and issued on a quarterly basis approximately as follows:

Title 1 through Title 16...as of January 1
Title 17 through Title 27 ....as of April 1
Title 28 through Title 41 ....as of July 1
Title 42 through Title 50...as of October 1

The appropriate revision date is printed on the cover of each volume.

LEGAL STATUS

The contents of the Federal Register are required to be judicially noticed (44 U.S.C. 1507). The Code of Federal Regulations is prima facie evidence of the text of the original documents (44 U.S.C. 1510).

HOW TO USE THE CODE OF FEDERAL REGULATIONS

The Code of Federal Regulations is kept up to date by the individual issues of the Federal Register. These two publications must be used together to determine the latest version of any given rule.

To determine whether a Code volume has been amended since its revision date (in this case, April 1, 2019), consult the "List of CFR Sections Affected (LSA)," which is issued monthly, and the "Cumulative List of Parts Affected," which appears in the Reader Aids section of the daily Federal Register. These two lists will identify the Federal Register page number of the latest amendment of any given rule.

EFFECTIVE AND EXPIRATION DATES

Each volume of the Code contains amendments published in the Federal Register since the last revision of that volume of the Code. Source citations for the regulations are referred to by volume number and page number of the Federal Register and date of publication. Publication dates and effective dates are usually not the same and care must be exercised by the user in determining the actual effective date. In instances where the effective date is beyond the cut-off date for the Code a note has been inserted to reflect the future effective date. In those instances where a regulation published in the Federal Register states a date certain for expiration, an appropriate note will be inserted following the text.

OMB CONTROL NUMBERS

The Paperwork Reduction Act of 1980 (Pub. L. 96–511) requires Federal agencies to display an OMB control number with their information collection request.

Many agencies have begun publishing numerous OMB control numbers as amendments to existing regulations in the CFR. These OMB numbers are placed as close as possible to the applicable recordkeeping or reporting requirements.

PAST PROVISIONS OF THE CODE

Provisions of the Code that are no longer in force and effect as of the revision date stated on the cover of each volume are not carried. Code users may find the text of provisions in effect on any given date in the past by using the appropriate List of CFR Sections Affected (LSA). For the convenience of the reader, a "List of CFR Sections Affected" is published at the end of each CFR volume. For changes to the Code prior to the LSA listings at the end of the volume, consult previous annual editions of the LSA. For changes to the Code prior to 2001, consult the List of CFR Sections Affected compilations, published for 1949-1963, 1964-1972, 1973-1985, and 1986-2000.

"[RESERVED]" TERMINOLOGY

The term "[Reserved]" is used as a place holder within the Code of Federal Regulations. An agency may add regulatory information at a "[Reserved]" location at any time. Occasionally "[Reserved]" is used editorially to indicate that a portion of the CFR was left vacant and not accidentally dropped due to a printing or computer error.

INCORPORATION BY REFERENCE

What is incorporation by reference? Incorporation by reference was established by statute and allows Federal agencies to meet the requirement to publish regulations in the Federal Register by referring to materials already published elsewhere. For an incorporation to be valid, the Director of the Federal Register must approve it. The legal effect of incorporation by reference is that the material is treated as if it were published in full in the Federal Register (5 U.S.C. 552(a)). This material, like any other properly issued regulation, has the force of law.

What is a proper incorporation by reference? The Director of the Federal Register will approve an incorporation by reference only when the requirements of 1 CFR part 51 are met. Some of the elements on which approval is based are:

(a) The incorporation will substantially reduce the volume of material published in the Federal Register.

(b) The matter incorporated is in fact available to the extent necessary to afford fairness and uniformity in the administrative process.

(c) The incorporating document is drafted and submitted for publication in accordance with 1 CFR part 51.

What if the material incorporated by reference cannot be found? If you have any problem locating or obtaining a copy of material listed as an approved incorporation by reference, please contact the agency that issued the regulation containing that incorporation. If, after contacting the agency, you find the material is not available, please notify the Director of the Federal Register, National Archives and Records Administration, 8601 Adelphi Road, College Park, MD 20740-6001, or call 202-741-6010.

CFR INDEXES AND TABULAR GUIDES

A subject index to the Code of Federal Regulations is contained in a separate volume, revised annually as of January 1, entitled CFR INDEX AND FINDING AIDS. This volume contains the Parallel Table of Authorities and Rules. A list of CFR titles, chapters, subchapters, and parts and an alphabetical list of agencies publishing in the CFR are also included in this volume.

An index to the text of "Title 3—The President" is carried within that volume.

The Federal Register Index is issued monthly in cumulative form. This index is based on a consolidation of the "Contents" entries in the daily Federal Register.

A List of CFR Sections Affected (LSA) is published monthly, keyed to the revision dates of the 50 CFR titles.

REPUBLICATION OF MATERIAL

There are no restrictions on the republication of material appearing in the Code of Federal Regulations.

INQUIRIES

For a legal interpretation or explanation of any regulation in this volume, contact the issuing agency. The issuing agency's name appears at the top of odd-numbered pages.

For inquiries concerning CFR reference assistance, call 202–741–6000 or write to the Director, Office of the Federal Register, National Archives and Records Administration, 8601 Adelphi Road, College Park, MD 20740-6001 or e-mail *fedreg.info@nara.gov*.

SALES

The Government Publishing Office (GPO) processes all sales and distribution of the CFR. For payment by credit card, call toll-free, 866-512-1800, or DC area, 202-512-1800, M-F 8 a.m. to 4 p.m. e.s.t. or fax your order to 202-512-2104, 24 hours a day. For payment by check, write to: US Government Publishing Office – New Orders, P.O. Box 979050, St. Louis, MO 63197-9000.

ELECTRONIC SERVICES

The full text of the Code of Federal Regulations, the LSA (List of CFR Sections Affected), The United States Government Manual, the Federal Register, Public Laws, Public Papers of the Presidents of the United States, Compilation of Presidential Documents and the Privacy Act Compilation are available in electronic format via *www.govinfo.gov*. For more information, contact the GPO Customer Contact Center, U.S. Government Publishing Office. Phone 202-512-1800, or 866-512-1800 (toll-free). E-mail, *ContactCenter@gpo.gov*.

The Office of the Federal Register also offers a free service on the National Archives and Records Administration's (NARA) World Wide Web site for public law numbers, Federal Register finding aids, and related information. Connect to NARA's web site at *www.archives.gov/federal-register*.

The e-CFR is a regularly updated, unofficial editorial compilation of CFR material and Federal Register amendments, produced by the Office of the Federal Register and the Government Publishing Office. It is available at *www.ecfr.gov*.

OLIVER A. POTTS,
Director,
Office of the Federal Register
April 1, 2019.

THIS TITLE

Title 24—HOUSING AND URBAN DEVELOPMENT is composed of five volumes. The first four volumes containing parts 0–199, parts 200–499, parts 500–699, parts 700–1699, represent the regulations of the Department of Housing and Urban Development. The fifth volume, containing part 1700 to end, continues with regulations of the Department of Housing and Urban Development and also includes regulations of the Board of Directors of the Hope for Homeowners Program, and the Neighborhood Reinvestment Corporation. The contents of these volumes represent all current regulations codified under this title of the CFR as of April 1, 2019.

For this volume, Michele Bugenhagen was Chief Editor. The Code of Federal Regulations publication program is under the direction of John Hyrum Martinez, assisted by Stephen J. Frattini.

Title 24—Housing and Urban Development

(This book contains part 1700 to end)

1

Subtitle B—Regulations Relating to Housing and Urban Development (Continued)

.

CHAPTER X—OFFICE OF ASSISTANT SECRETARY FOR HOUSING—FEDERAL HOUSING COMMISSIONER, DEPARTMENT OF HOUSING AND URBAN DEVELOPMENT (INTERSTATE LAND SALES REGISTRATION PROGRAM) [RESERVED]

PARTS 1700–1799 [Reserved]

CHAPTER XII—OFFICE OF INSPECTOR GENERAL, DEPARTMENT OF HOUSING AND URBAN DEVELOPMENT

PARTS 2000–2001 [RESERVED]

PART 2002—AVAILABILITY OF INFORMATION TO THE PUBLIC

AUTHORITY: 5 U.S.C. 552; 5 U.S.C. App. 3; 42 U.S.C. 3535(d); Delegation of Authority, 46 FR 2389.

SOURCE: 83 FR 7391, Feb. 21, 2018, unless otherwise noted.

§ 2002.1 Scope of this part and applicability of other HUD regulations.

(a) *General.* This part contains the regulations of the Office of Inspector General (OIG) that implement the Freedom of Information Act (FOIA) (5 U.S.C. 552). It informs the public how to request records and information from the OIG and explains the procedure to use if a request is denied. Requests made by individuals for records about themselves under the Privacy Act of 1974, 5 U.S.C. 552a, are processed in accordance with 24 CFR part 2003 as well as this part. Requests for documents made by subpoena or other demands of courts or other authorities are governed by procedures contained in part 2004 of this chapter. These rules should be read in conjunction with the text of the FOIA and the Uniform Freedom of Information Fee Schedule and Guidelines published by the Office of Management and Budget. This policy does not create any right enforceable in court.

(b) *Applicability of HUD's FOIA regulations.* In addition to the regulations in this part, §§ 15.2 and 15.106 of this title apply to the production or disclosure of information in the possession of the OIG, except as limited in paragraph (c) of this section or otherwise expressly stated in this part.

(c) *Limited applicability of §§ 15.2 and 15.106 of this title.* The OIG has different people and entities involved in the FOIA process than those defined in § 15.2 and these people and entities are specifically identified in this part. For purposes of this part, when the words "HUD" or "Department" are used in § 15.2 or § 15.106, the term means the OIG. The OIG will follow the fee schedule at § 15.106 except as otherwise provided in this part. Where § 15.106 references § 15.103, the OIG reference in this part is § 2002.15.

§ 2002.3 OIG's overall policy concerning disclosable records.

(a) The OIG will administer its FOIA program with a presumption of openness. This policy does not create any right enforceable in court. The OIG will fully and responsibly disclose its identifiable records and information consistent with competing public interests, such as national security, personal privacy, grand jury and investigative secrecy, complainant confidentiality, and agency deliberative process, as are recognized by FOIA and other Federal statutes. The OIG will apply the FOIA exemptions if release could foreseeably harm an interest protected by a FOIA exemption. Release of records will be made as promptly as possible.

(b) The OIG FOIA Public Liaison is the Deputy Counsel to the Inspector General. Requesters who have questions or comments concerning their FOIA request may contact the FOIA Public Liaison at 202–708–1613, or through the FOIA email at *FOIARequests@hudoig.gov.*

§ 2002.5 How to make a request for OIG records; records produced.

(a) Any request for OIG records must be made in writing. The easiest way to make a FOIA request is electronically through our public website at *www.hudoig.gov.* A request may also be made by submitting the written request to The Office of Inspector General; Department of Housing and Urban Development; 451 Seventh Street SW, Suite 8260, Washington, DC 20410. The envelope should indicate it is a FOIA request. A request for OIG records may also be made in person during normal business hours at any office where OIG employees are permanently stationed.

(b) Each request must reasonably describe the desired record, including the title or name, author, subject matter, and number or date, where possible, so that the record may be identified and located. The more specific the FOIA request for records, the more likely OIG officials will be able to locate the records requested. The request should also include the name, address and telephone number of the requester, the fee category that the requester believes applies to the request, and the form or format in which the requester would like the desired record to be reproduced, if the requester has a preference. In order to enable the OIG to comply with the time limitations set forth in § 2002.15, both the envelope containing a written request and the letter itself should clearly indicate that the subject is a Freedom of Information Act request.

(c) The request must be accompanied by the fee or an offer to pay the fee as determined in § 15.106 of this title and § 2002.13.

(d) The OIG may require information verifying the requester's identity, if the requester requests agency records pertaining to the requester, a minor, or an individual who is legally incompetent. Failure to provide the information when requested will result in the request being found insufficient and closed. It will not prevent the future refiling of the request.

(e) Duplication of available records will be made as promptly as possible. Such duplication can take the form of paper copy, audiovisual materials, or machine-readable documentation (e.g., electronic documents on CD, DVD, flash drive, etc.). Records that are published or available for sale will not be reproduced.

(f) The OIG shall honor a requester's specified preference of form or format of disclosure if the record is readily re-producible with reasonable efforts in the requested form or format by the office responding to the request.

(g) If the requester makes a request for expedited processing, the request must provide a detailed explanation of the basis for the request. The requester should also include a statement certifying the truth of the circumstances supporting the requester's compelling need. Requests for expedited processing that simply recite the statutory language are generally not granted.

§ 2002.7 OIG processing of requests, multi-tracking, and expedited processing.

(a) *Tracking number.* FOIA requests will be logged in the order that they are received and be assigned a tracking number, except as provided in paragraph (c) of this section. A requester should use the tracking number to identify his or her request when contacting the FOIA office for any reason. An acknowledgement of receipt of the request, with the assigned tracking number, will be sent to the requester by the FOIA office.

(b) *Multi-track processing—(1) Types of tracks.* For requests that do not qualify for expedited processing, the OIG places each request in one of two tracks, simple or complex, based on the amount of work and time involved in processing the request. In doing so, the OIG will consider whether the request involves the processing of voluminous documents or responsive documents from more than one organizational unit. Within each track, the OIG processes requests in the order in which they are received.

(2) *Unusual circumstances.* Requests for audit work papers are considered complex requests and generally qualify as an unusual circumstance under 5 U.S.C. 552(a)(6)(B)(iii), taking longer than 20 working days to process. Requests for "all" specified records over a span of time, if they are accepted as reasonably describing a specific group of records, are considered complex requests and usually qualify as an unusual circumstance under 5 U.S.C. 552(a)(6)(B)(iii), taking longer than 20 working days to process. Requesters who make requests qualifying as unusual circumstances will be offered an

opportunity to narrow the scope of their request or arrange for an alternative time period.

(3) *Misdirected requests.* For requests that have been sent to the wrong office, the OIG will assign the request within each track using the earlier of either:

(i) The date on which the request was referred to the appropriate office; or

(ii) The end of the 10 working-day period in which the request should have been referred to the appropriate office.

(c) *Expedited processing.* (1) The OIG may take your request or appeal out of normal order if the OIG determines that you have a compelling need for the records or in other cases as determined by the OIG. Any requester may ask for expedited processing at any time. If expedited processing is requested, the OIG will notify the requester within 10 working days whether it will grant expedited processing.

(2) The OIG will grant requests for expedited processing if it finds a compelling need under 5 U.S.C. 552(a)(6)(E). Evidence of a compelling need by a person making a request for expedited processing must be made in a statement certified by such person to be true and correct to the best of such person's knowledge and belief. A compelling need exists if:

(i) Your failure to obtain the requested records on an expedited basis could reasonably be expected to pose an imminent threat to the life or physical safety of an individual;

(ii) You are primarily engaged in disseminating information and there is an urgency to inform the public concerning actual or alleged Federal Government activity; or

(iii) Your failure to obtain the requested records on an expedited basis could result in the loss of substantial due process rights.

(3) If the OIG grants the request for expedited processing, the OIG will give the request priority and will process it as soon as practicable.

§ 2002.9 Proactive disclosures of records.

(a) You may review records that section 552(a)(2) of FOIA requires the OIG to make available to the public in the electronic reading rooms identified in paragraph (b) of this section. That is the preferable method; however, you may also ask to review those documents that are in hardcopy at the Headquarters offices at HUD's Library, 451 Seventh Street SW, Suite 8141, Washington, DC 20410. This request should be coordinated through Office of Legal Counsel, Office of Inspector General, Suite 8254. Local offices may coordinate local requests for hardcopy reviews.

(b) As required by 5 U.S.C. 552(a)(2), the OIG makes records created on or after November 1, 1996, available through its Electronic FOIA Reading Room, located at *https://www.hudoig.gov/foia*. These records include:

(1) Copies of all records, regardless of form or format that have been released to any person under this part: and

(i) Because of the nature of their subject matter, the agency determines that the records have become or are likely to become the subject of subsequent requests for substantially the same records; or

(ii) Have been requested three or more times.

(2) Report for the preceding fiscal year submitted to the U.S. Attorney General and the Director of the Office of Government Information Services as required by 5 U.S.C. 552(e) and the raw statistical data used in each report. This report will be made available:

(i) Without charge, license, or registration requirement;

(ii) In an aggregated, searchable format; and

(iii) In a format that may be downloaded in bulk.

(c) The OIG also makes other documents, such as audits and semiannual reports, available to the public at *https://www.hudoig.gov/*.

§ 2002.11 Agency review of records and aggregating requests.

(a) *Review of records.* Only requesters who are seeking documents for commercial use may be charged for the time the OIG spends reviewing records to determine whether the records are exempt from mandatory disclosure. Charges will be assessed only for the initial review; *i.e.,* the review undertaken the first time the OIG reviews a particular record or portion of a record to apply an exemption. The OIG will not charge for review at the administrative appeal level of an exemption already applied. However, records or portions of records withheld under an exemption that is subsequently determined not to apply may be reviewed again to determine the applicability of other exemptions not previously considered. The costs for such a subsequent review would be properly assessable. Review time will be assessed at the same rates established for search time in §§ 2002.13 and 15.106 of this title.

(b) *Aggregating requests.* (1) The OIG may aggregate multiple requests in cases where unusual circumstances exist and the OIG determines that:

(i) Certain requests from the same requester or from a group of requesters acting in concert actually constitute a single request; and

(ii) The requests involve clearly related matters.

(2) Aggregation of requests for this purpose will be conducted independent of aggregation of requests for fee purposes under § 15.106(h) of this title.

§ 2002.13 Fee schedule, advance payment, interest charges, and waiving or reducing fees.

The OIG will charge for processing requests under the FOIA in accordance with § 15.106 of this title, except where those provisions conflict with provisions of this part; more specifically, where § 15.106 references § 15.103 of this title replace such reference with § 2002.15.

§ 2002.15 Time limitations.

(a) *General.* Upon receipt of a request for records, the appropriate Assistant Inspector General or an appointed designee will generally make a determination whether to comply with a FOIA request within 20 working days. The Assistant Inspector General or designee will immediately notify the requestor in writing of the determination and the reason(s) for such determination and the right of the person to request assistance from the FOIA Public Liaison. The 20-day period will begin on the day the request is received by the OIG, but in any event not later than 10 working days after the request

is received by any component designated to receive FOIA requests, and after any fees or advance payment of fees under § 2002.13 has been made.

(b) *Scope of responsive records.* In determining which records are responsive to a request, an agency ordinarily will include only records in its possession as of the date that it begins its search. If any other date is used, the agency must inform the requester of that date. A record that is excluded from the requirements of the FOIA pursuant to 5 U.S.C. 552(c) is not considered responsive to a request.

(c) *Unusual circumstances.* Under unusual circumstances, as specified in this paragraph (c), the OIG may extend the time period for processing a FOIA request. In such circumstances, the OIG will provide the requester with written notice setting forth the unusual circumstances for the extension and the date on which a determination is expected to be made. This date will not exceed 10 working days beyond the general time established in paragraph (a) of this section. If processing a request would require more than 10 working days beyond the general time limit established in paragraph (a) of this section, the OIG will offer the requester an opportunity to reduce or limit the scope of the request in order to allow the OIG to process it within the extra 10-day working period or arrange an alternative time period within which the FOIA request will be processed. To aid the requester, the OIG shall make available its FOIA Public Liaison, who shall assist in the resolution of any disputes between the requester and the OIG, and notify the requester of the right of the requester to seek dispute resolution services from the Office of Government Information Services. Unusual circumstances mean that there is a need:

(1) To search for and collect the requested records from field facilities or other establishments that are separate from the office processing the request;

(2) To search for, collect, and appropriately examine a voluminous amount of separate and distinct records that are demanded in a single request (*e.g.* audit work papers); or

(3) For consultation, which shall be conducted with all practicable speed,

with another agency having a substantial interest in the determination of the request or among two or more offices of the Office of Inspector General having a substantial interest in the subject matter of the request.

§2002.17 Authority to release records or duplications.

Any Assistant Inspector General or an appointed designee is authorized to release any record (or duplication) pertaining to activities for which he or she has primary responsibility, unless disclosure is clearly inappropriate under this part. No authorized person may release records for which another officer has primary responsibility without the consent of the officer or his or her designee.

§2002.19 Authority to deny requests for records and form of denial, exemptions, and exclusions.

(a) *Process for denying requests.* An Assistant Inspector General or the Counsel to the Inspector General, or their designees, may deny a request for a record. Any denial will:

(1) Be in writing;

(2) State simply the reasons for the denial;

(3) Provide an estimate of the volume of records or information withheld, when appropriate, in number of pages or in some other reasonable form of estimation. This estimate does not need to be provided if the volume is otherwise indicated through deletions on records disclosed in part, or if providing an estimate would harm an interest protected by an applicable exemption;

(4) Identify the person(s) responsible for the denial by name and title;

(5) Provide notice of the right of the requester to appeal to the Deputy Inspector General, within a period determined by the head of the agency that is not less than 90 days after the date of such adverse determination, consistent with §2002.23; and

(6) Provide notice of the right of the requester to seek dispute resolution services from the FOIA Public Liaison of the agency or the Office of Government Information Services.

(b) *Denying requests generally.* The OIG shall withhold information only if the OIG reasonably foresees that disclosure would harm an interest protected by an exemption as provided in this section, or disclosure is prohibited by law. The OIG will consider whether partial disclosure of information is possible whenever the OIG determines that a full disclosure of a requested record is not possible and will take reasonable steps necessary to segregate and release nonexempt information. Nothing in this section requires disclosure of information that is otherwise prohibited from disclosure by law or otherwise exempted from disclosure as provided in this section.

(c) *FOIA exemptions.* The FOIA contains nine exemptions (5 U.S.C. 552(b)) that authorize agencies to withhold various records from disclosure, and two exclusions to the statute that may be used by the OIG. With regard to the records normally requested, the OIG generally applies the exemptions and exclusions as follows:

(1) *Classified documents.* Exemption 1 (5 U.S.C. 552(b)(1)) protects classified national defense and foreign relations information. The OIG seldom relies on this exception to withhold documents. However, where applicable, the OIG will refer a request for records classified under Executive Order 13526 and the pertinent records to the originating agency for processing. The OIG may refuse to confirm or deny the existence of the requested information if the originating agency determines that the fact of the existence of the information itself is classified.

(2) *Internal agency rules and practices.* Exemption 2 (5 U.S.C. 552(b)(2)) protects records relating to internal personnel rules and practices.

(3) *Information prohibited from disclosure by another statute.* Exemption 3 (5 U.S.C. 552(b)(3)) protects information that is prohibited from disclosure by another Federal law. Some investigative records contain information that could reveal grand jury proceedings, which are protected from disclosure by Federal Rule of Criminal Procedure 6(e). Section 7 of the Inspector General Act of 1978 prohibits the OIG from disclosing the identity of employees who make protected disclosures. The OIG generally will not disclose competitive

proposals prior to contract award, competitive proposals that are not set forth or incorporated by reference into the awarded contract, (see 41 U.S.C. 4702), or, during the selection process, any covered selection information regarding such selection, either directly or indirectly (see 42 U.S.C. 3537a).

(4) *Commercial or financial information.* Exemption 4 (5 U.S.C. 552(b)(4)) protects trade secrets and commercial or financial information obtained from a person that is privileged and confidential. The OIG frequently obtains this information through its audits. The OIG will process the release of this category of information pursuant to Executive Order 12600 and give notice to the affected business and an opportunity for the business to present evidence of its confidentiality claim. If the OIG is sued by a requester under the FOIA for nondisclosure of confidential business information, the OIG expects the affected business to cooperate to the fullest extent possible in defending such a decision.

(5) *Certain interagency or intra-agency communications.* Exemption 5 (5 U.S.C. 552(b)(5)) protects interagency or intra-agency communications that are protected by legal privileges, such as the attorney-client privilege, attorney work-product privilege, or communications reflecting the agency's deliberative process. These communications may include communications with the Department of Justice and with HUD. The deliberative process privilege shall not apply to records created 25 years or more before the date on which the records were requested.

(6) *Personal privacy.* Exemption 6 (5 U.S.C. 552(b)(6)) protects information involving matters of personal privacy. This information may be found in personnel, medical, and similar files the disclosure of which would constitute a clearly unwarranted invasion of personal privacy. Names, addresses, telephone numbers, and email addresses of persons identified in audits or complaints generally will not be disclosed. The OIG has learned through experience that some of its employees (*i.e.* Hotline employees) will be harassed if their identities are known, and the OIG will protect the identities of these employees. As a law enforcement agency, the OIG finds individuals generally have a heightened privacy interest for not having their identities associated with the OIG.

(7) *Law enforcement records.* Exemption 7 (5 U.S.C. 552(b)(7)) protects certain records or information compiled for law enforcement purposes. This exemption protects records where the production could reasonably be expected to interfere with enforcement proceedings. The protection of this exemption also encompasses, but is not limited to, information in law enforcement files that could reasonably be expected to constitute an unwarranted invasion of personal privacy; the names of confidential informants; and techniques and procedures for law enforcement investigations, or guidelines for law enforcement investigations if such disclosure could reasonably be expected to risk circumvention of the law. It is the policy of the OIG in responding to all FOIA requests for investigative records pertaining to specifically named individuals to refuse to confirm or deny the existence of such records. Lacking the subject individuals consent, proof of death, an official acknowledgement of an investigation, or an overriding public interest, even to acknowledge the existence of such records could reasonably be expected to constitute an unwarranted invasion of personal privacy.

(8) *Supervision of financial institutions.* Exemption 8 (5 U.S.C. 552(b)(8)) protects information relating to the supervision of financial institutions. It is unlikely that the OIG will have these documents.

(9) *Wells.* Exemption 9 (5 U.S.C. 552(b)(9)) protects geological information on wells. It is unlikely that the OIG will have these documents.

(d) *FOIA exclusion.* Some law enforcement records are excluded from the FOIA. 5 U.S.C. 552(c)(1) permits a law enforcement agency to exclude a document from the FOIA if there is reason to believe that:

(1) The subject of the investigation or proceeding is not aware of its pendency; and

(2) Disclosure of the existence of the records could reasonably be expected to interfere with enforcement proceedings, in which case the agency

may, during only such time as that circumstance continues, treat the records as not subject to the requirements of the FOIA. Section 552(c)(2) of FOIA allows the exclusion of informant records, unless the existence of the informant has been officially confirmed.

§ 2002.21 Effect of denial of request.

Denial of a request shall terminate the authority of the Assistant Inspector General or his or her designee to release or disclose the requested record, which thereafter may not be made publicly available except with express authorization of the Inspector General, Deputy Inspector General, or Counsel to the Inspector General.

§ 2002.23 Administrative review.

(a) Review is available only from a written determination denying a request for a record and only if a written request for review is filed within 90 days after issuance of the written determination. If mailed, the requester's letter of appeal must be postmarked within 90 calendar days of the date of the letter of determination. If the letter of appeal is transmitted electronically or by a means other than the United States Postal Service, it must be received in the appropriate office by the close of business on the 90th calendar day after the date of the letter of determination. Before seeking court review of an adverse determination, a requester must exhaust their administrative remedies under this section.

(b) A review may be initiated by sending a request for review to the Office of Inspector General; Department of Housing and Urban Development; 451 Seventh Street SW, Room 8256, Washington, DC 20410 or to *FOIArequests@hudoig.gov*. In order to enable the OIG to comply with the time limitations set forth in § 2002.17, both the envelope containing the request for review and the letter itself should clearly indicate that the subject is a Freedom of Information Act request for review. Each request for review must contain the following:

(1) A copy of the original request;

(2) A copy of the written denial; and

(3) A statement of the circumstances, reasons, or arguments advanced in support of disclosure of the original records requested.

(c) Review will be made promptly by the Deputy Inspector General, or designee, on the basis of the written record. The OIG will decide an appeal of a denial of a request to expedite processing of a FOIA request within 10 working days of receipt of the appeal. The OIG will make a determination on all other appeals within 20 working days of receipt, unless unusual circumstances require the OIG to extend the time for an additional 10 working days.

(d) The time of receipt for processing of a request is the time it is received by the Inspector General. If a request is misdirected by the requester and is received by one other than the Inspector General, the OIG official who receives the request will forward it promptly to the Inspector General and will advise the requester about the delayed time of receipt.

(e) The decision after review will be in writing, will constitute final agency action on the request, and, if the denial of the request for records is in full or in part upheld, the Inspector General will notify the person making the request of his or her right to seek judicial review under 5 U.S.C. 552(a)(4).

(f) Adverse decisions will include the name and contact information of dispute resolution services that offer mediation services to resolve disputes between FOIA requesters and Federal agencies as a nonexclusive alternative to litigation.

PART 2003—IMPLEMENTATION OF THE PRIVACY ACT OF 1974

Sec.

15

AUTHORITY: 5 U.S.C. 552a; 5 U.S.C. App. 3 (Inspector General Act of 1978); 42 U.S.C. 3535(d).

SOURCE: 57 FR 62142, Dec. 29, 1992, unless otherwise noted.

§ 2003.1 Scope of the part and applicability of other HUD regulations.

(a) *General.* This part contains the regulations of the Office of Inspector General ("OIG") implementing the Privacy Act of 1974 (5 U.S.C. 552a). The regulations inform the public that the Inspector General has the responsibility for carrying out the requirements of the Privacy Act and for issuing internal OIG orders and directives in connection with the Privacy Act. These regulations apply to all records that are contained in systems of records maintained by the OIG and that are retrieved by an individual's name or personal identifier.

(b) *Applicability of part 16.* In addition to these regulations, the provisions of 24 CFR part 16 apply to the OIG, except that appendix A to part 16 is not applicable. The provisions of this part shall govern in the event of any conflict with the provisions of part 16.

§ 2003.2 Definitions.

For purposes of this part:

Department means the OIG, except that in the context of §§ 16.1(d); 16.11(b) (1), (3), and (4); and 16.12(e), when those sections are incorporated by reference, the term means the Department of Housing and Urban Development.

Privacy Act Officer means an Assistant Inspector General.

Privacy Appeals Officer means the Inspector General.

[59 FR 14098, Mar. 25, 1994]

§ 2003.3 Requests for records.

(a) A request from an individual for an OIG record about that individual which is not contained in an OIG system of records will be considered to be a Freedom of Information Act (FOIA) request and will be processed under 24 CFR part 2002.

(b) A request from an individual for an OIG record about that individual which is contained in an OIG system of records will be processed under both the Privacy Act and the FOIA in order to ensure maximum access under both statutes. This practice will be undertaken regardless of how an individual characterizes the request.

(1) The procedures for inquiries and requirements for access to records under the Privacy Act are more specifically set forth in 24 CFR part 16, except that appendix A to part 16 does not apply to the OIG.

(2) An individual will not be required to state a reason or otherwise justify his or her request for access to a record.

§ 2003.4 Officials to receive requests and inquiries.

Officials to receive requests and inquiries for access to, or correction of, records in OIG systems of records are the Privacy Act Officers described in § 2003.2 of this part. Written requests may be addressed to the appropriate Privacy Act Officer at: Office of Inspector General, Department of Housing and Urban Development, Washington, DC 20410.

[57 FR 62142, Dec. 29, 1992, as amended at 59 FR 14098, Mar. 25, 1994]

§ 2003.5 Initial denial of access to records.

(a) Access by an individual to a record about that individual which is contained in an OIG system of records will be denied only upon a determination by the Privacy Act Officer that:

(1) The record was compiled in reasonable anticipation of a civil action or proceeding; or the record is subject to a Privacy Act exemption under § 2003.8 or § 2003.9 of this part; and

(2) The record is also subject to a FOIA exemption under § 2002.21(b) of this chapter.

(b) If a request is partially denied, any portions of the responsive record that can be reasonably segregated will be provided to the individual after deletion of those portions determined to be exempt.

(c) The provisions of 24 CFR 16.6(b) and 16.7, concerning notification of an initial denial of access and administrative review of the initial denial, apply to the OIG, except that:

(1) The final determination of the Inspector General, as Privacy Appeals Officer for the OIG, will be in writing and

will constitute final action of the Department on a request for access to a record in an OIG system of records; and

(2) If the denial of the request is in whole or in part upheld, the final determination of the Inspector General will include notice of the right to judicial review.

§2003.6 Disclosure of a record to a person other than the individual to whom it pertains.

(a) The OIG may disclose an individual's record to a person other than the individual to whom the record pertains in the following instances:

(1) Upon written request by the individual, including authorization under 24 CFR 16.5(e);

(2) With the prior written consent of the individual;

(3) To a parent or legal guardian of the individual under 5 U.S.C. 552a(h); or

(4) When permitted by the provisions of 5 U.S.C. 552a(b) (1) through (12).

(b) [Reserved]

§2003.7 Authority to make law enforcement-related requests for records maintained by other agencies.

(a) The Inspector General is authorized by written delegation from the Secretary of HUD and under the Inspector General Act to make written requests under 5 U.S.C. 552a(b)(7) for transfer of records maintained by other agencies which are necessary to carry out an authorized law enforcement activity under the Inspector General Act.

(b) The Inspector General delegates the authority under paragraph (a) of this section to the following OIG officials:

(1) Deputy Inspector General;

(2) Assistant Inspector General for Audit;

(3) Assistant Inspector General for Investigation; and

(4) Assistant Inspector General for Management and Policy.

(c) The officials listed in paragraph (b) of this section may not redelegate the authority described in paragraph (a) of this section.

§2003.8 General exemptions.

(a) The systems of records entitled "Investigative Files of the Office of Inspector General," "Hotline Complaint Files of the Office of Inspector General," "Name Indices System of the Office of Inspector General," and "AutoInvestigation of the Office of Inspector General" consist, in part, of information compiled by the OIG for the purpose of criminal law enforcement investigations. Therefore, to the extent that information in these systems falls within the scope of exemption (j)(2) of the Privacy Act, 5 U.S.C. 552a(j)(2), these systems of records are exempt from the requirements of the following subsections of the Privacy Act, for the reasons stated in paragraphs (a)(1) through (6) of this section.

(1) From subsection (c)(3), because release of an accounting of disclosures to an individual who is the subject of an investigation could reveal the nature and scope of the investigation and could result in the altering or destruction of evidence, improper influencing of witnesses, and other evasive actions that could impede or compromise the investigation.

(2) From subsection (d)(1), because release of investigative records to an individual who is the subject of an investigation could interfere with pending or prospective law enforcement proceedings, constitute an unwarranted invasion of the personal privacy of third parties, reveal the identity of confidential sources, or reveal sensitive investigative techniques and procedures.

(3) From subsection (d)(2), because amendment or correction of investigative records could interfere with pending or prospective law enforcement proceedings, or could impose an impossible administrative and investigative burden by requiring the OIG to continuously retrograde its investigations attempting to resolve questions of accuracy, relevance, timeliness and completeness.

(4) From subsection (e)(1), because it is often impossible to determine relevance or necessity of information in the early stages of an investigation. The value of such information is a question of judgment and timing; what appears relevant and necessary when collected may ultimately be evaluated and viewed as irrelevant and unnecessary to an investigation. In addition,

the OIG may obtain information concerning the violation of laws other than those within the scope of its jurisdiction. In the interest of effective law enforcement, the OIG should retain this information because it may aid in establishing patterns of unlawful activity and provide leads for other law enforcement agencies. Further, in obtaining evidence during an investigation, information may be provided to the OIG which relates to matters incidental to the main purpose of the investigation but which may be pertinent to the investigative jurisdiction of another agency. Such information cannot readily be identified.

(5) From subsection (e)(2), because in a law enforcement investigation it is usually counterproductive to collect information to the greatest extent practicable directly from the subject thereof. It is not always feasible to rely upon the subject of an investigation as a source for information which may implicate him or her in illegal activities. In addition, collecting information directly from the subject could seriously compromise an investigation by prematurely revealing its nature and scope, or could provide the subject with an opportunity to conceal criminal activities, or intimidate potential sources, in order to avoid apprehension.

(6) From subsection (e)(3), because providing such notice to the subject of an investigation, or to other individual sources, could seriously compromise the investigation by prematurely revealing its nature and scope, or could inhibit cooperation, permit the subject to evade apprehension, or cause interference with undercover activities.

(b) [Reserved]

[57 FR 62142, Dec. 29, 1992, as amended at 65 FR 50904, Aug. 21, 2000]

§ 2003.9 Specific exemptions.

(a) The systems of records entitled "Investigative Files of the Office of Inspector General," "Hotline Complaint Files of the Office of Inspector General," "Name Indices System of the Office of Inspector General," and "AutoInvestigation of the Office of Inspector General" consist, in part, of investigatory material compiled by the OIG for law enforcement purposes.

Therefore, to the extent that information in these systems falls within the coverage of exemption (k)(2) of the Privacy Act, 5 U.S.C. 552a(k)(2), these systems of records are exempt from the requirements of the following subsections of the Privacy Act, for the reasons stated in paragraphs (a) (1) through (4) of this section.

(1) From subsection (c)(3), because release of an accounting of disclosures to an individual who is the subject of an investigation could reveal the nature and scope of the investigation and could result in the altering or destruction of evidence, improper influencing of witnesses, and other evasive actions that could impede or compromise the investigation.

(2) From subsection (d)(1), because release of investigative records to an individual who is the subject of an investigation could interfere with pending or prospective law enforcement proceedings, constitute an unwarranted invasion of the personal privacy of third parties, reveal the identity of confidential sources, or reveal sensitive investigative techniques and procedures.

(3) From subsection (d)(2), because amendment or correction of investigative records could interfere with pending or prospective law enforcement proceedings, or could impose an impossible administrative and investigative burden by requiring the OIG to continuously retrograde its investigations attempting to resolve questions of accuracy, relevance, timeliness and completeness.

(4) From subsection (e)(1), because it is often impossible to determine relevance or necessity of information in the early stages of an investigation. The value of such information is a question of judgment and timing; what appears relevant and necessary when collected may ultimately be evaluated and viewed as irrelevant and unnecessary to an investigation. In addition, the OIG may obtain information concerning the violation of laws other than those within the scope of its jurisdiction. In the interest of effective law enforcement, the OIG should retain this information because it may aid in

establishing patterns of unlawful activity and provide leads for other law enforcement agencies. Further, in obtaining evidence during an investigation, information may be provided to the OIG which relates to matters incidental to the main purpose of the investigation but which may be pertinent to the investigative jurisdiction of another agency. Such information cannot readily be identified.

(b) The systems of records entitled "Investigative Files of the Office of Inspector General," "Hotline Complaint Files of the Office of Inspector General," "Name Indices System of the Office of Inspector General," and "Autoinvestigation of the Office of Inspector General" consist in part of investigatory material compiled by the OIG for the purpose of determining suitability, eligibility, or qualifications for Federal civilian employment or Federal contracts, the release of which would reveal the identity of a source who furnished information to the Government under an express promise that the identity of the source would be held in confidence. Therefore, to the extent that information in these systems fall within the coverage of exemption (k)(5) of the Privacy Act, 5 U.S.C. 552a(k)(5), these systems of records are exempt from the requirements of subsection (d)(1), because release would reveal the identity of a source who furnished information to the Government under an express promise of confidentiality. Revealing the identity of a confidential source could impede future cooperation by sources, and could result in harassment or harm to such sources.

[57 FR 62142, Dec. 29, 1992, as amended at 65 FR 50904, Aug. 21, 2000]

PART 2004—SUBPOENAS AND PRODUCTION IN RESPONSE TO SUBPOENAS OR DEMANDS OF COURTS OR OTHER AUTHORITIES

Subpart A—General Requirements

Subpart B—Office of Inspector General Subpoenas

Subpart C—Requests for Testimony and Production of Documents

AUTHORITY: Inspector General Act of 1978, as amended (5 U.S.C. app.) and 42 U.S.C. 3535(d).

SOURCE: 68 FR 3366, Jan. 23, 2003, unless otherwise noted.

Subpart A—General Requirements

§2004.1 Scope and purpose.

(a) This part sets forth the policy for service of a subpoena issued by the Office of Inspector General (OIG), and policies and procedures that you must follow when you submit a demand or request to an employee of the OIG to produce official records and information, or provide testimony relating to official information, in connection with a legal proceeding. You must comply with these requirements when you request the release or disclosure of official records and information.

(b) The OIG intends these provisions to:

(1) Promote economy and efficiency in its programs and operations;

(2) Minimize the possibility of involving OIG in controversial issues not related to OIG's functions;

(3) Maintain OIG's impartiality among private litigants where OIG is not a named party; and

(4) Protect sensitive, confidential information and the deliberative processes of OIG.

(c) In providing for these requirements, OIG does not waive the sovereign immunity of the United States.

(d) This part provides guidance for the internal operations of OIG. This part does not create any right or benefit, substantive or procedural, that a party may rely upon in any legal proceeding against the United States.

§ 2004.2 Applicability.

This subpart applies to demands and requests to employees for factual or expert testimony relating to official information, or for production of official records or information, in legal proceedings in which HUD or OIG is not a named party. However, this subpart does not apply to:

(a) Demands upon or requests for an OIG employee to testify as to facts or events that are unrelated to his or her official duties or that are unrelated to the functions of OIG;

(b) Requests for the release of records under the Freedom of Information Act, 5 U.S.C. 552, or the Privacy Act, 5 U.S.C. 552a; and

(c) Congressional demands and Congressional requests for testimony or records.

§ 2004.3 Definitions.

Counsel means the Counsel to the Inspector General.

Demand means a subpoena, or an order or other command of a court or other competent authority, for the production, disclosure, or release of records or for the appearance and testimony of an OIG employee that is issued in a legal proceeding.

Legal proceeding means any matter before a court of law, administrative board or tribunal, commission, administrative law judge, hearing officer, or other body that conducts a legal or administrative proceeding. Legal proceeding includes all phases of litigation.

OIG means the Office of Inspector General, U.S. Department of Housing and Urban Development.

OIG employee or *employee means:*
(1) Any current or former officer or employee of OIG;
(2) Any other individual hired through contractual agreement by or on behalf of OIG or who has performed or is performing services under such an agreement for OIG; and

(3) Any individual who served or is serving in any consulting or advisory capacity to OIG, whether formal or informal.

Records or official records or information means:
(1) All documents and materials that are OIG agency records under the Freedom of Information Act, 5 U.S.C. 552;
(2) All other documents and materials contained in OIG files; and
(3) All other information or materials acquired by an OIG employee in the performance of his or her official duties or because of his or her official status.

Request means any informal request, by whatever method, for the production of records and information or for testimony that has not been ordered by a court or other competent authority.

Testimony means any written or oral statements, including depositions, answers to interrogatories, affidavits, declarations, recorded interviews, and statements made by an individual in connection with a legal proceeding.

Subpart B—Office of Inspector General Subpoenas

§ 2004.10 Service of an Office of Inspector General subpoena.

Service of a subpoena issued by OIG may be accomplished as follows:

(a) *Personal service.* Service may be made by delivering the subpoena to the person to whom it is addressed. If the subpoena is addressed to a corporation or other business entity, it may be served upon an employee of the corporation or entity. Service made to an employee, agent, or legal representative of the addressee shall constitute service upon the addressee.

(b) *Service by mail.* Service may also be made by mailing the subpoena, certified mail—return receipt requested, to the addressee at his or her last known business or personal address.

Subpart C—Requests for Testimony and Production of Documents

§ 2004.20 General prohibition.

No employee may produce official records and information or provide any testimony relating to official information in response to a demand or request without the prior, written approval of the Inspector General or the Counsel.

§2004.21 Factors OIG will consider.

The Counsel or Inspector General, in their discretion, may grant an employee permission to testify on matters relating to official information, or produce official records and information, in response to a demand or request. Among the relevant factors that the Inspector General or the Counsel may consider in making this decision are whether:

(a) The purposes of this part are met;

(b) OIG has an interest in the decision that may be rendered in the legal proceeding;

(c) Allowing such testimony or production of records would assist or hinder OIG in performing its statutory duties or use OIG resources where responding to the request will interfere with the ability of OIG employees to do their work;

(d) The records or testimony can be obtained from other sources;

(e) The demand or request is unduly burdensome or otherwise inappropriate under the applicable rules of discovery or the rules of procedure governing the case or matter in which the demand or request arose;

(f) Disclosure would violate or be inconsistent with a statute, Executive Order, or regulation;

(g) Disclosure would reveal confidential or privileged information, trade secrets, or similar, confidential commercial, or financial information;

(h) Disclosure would impede or interfere with an ongoing law enforcement investigation or proceedings, or compromise constitutional rights;

(i) Disclosure would result in OIG appearing to favor one litigant over another;

(j) Disclosure relates to documents that were produced by another agency;

(k) The demand or request is in conformance with all other applicable rules;

(l) The demand or request is sufficiently specific to be answered; and

(m) For any other good cause.

§2004.22 Filing requirements for demands or requests for documents or testimony.

You must comply with the following requirements whenever you issue demands or requests to an OIG employee for official records and information or testimony.

(a) Your request must be in writing and must be submitted to the Counsel. If you serve a subpoena on OIG or on an OIG employee before submitting a written request and receiving a final determination from the Counsel, OIG will oppose the subpoena on grounds that your request was not submitted in accordance with this subpart.

(b) Your written request must contain the following information:

(1) The caption of the legal proceeding, docket number, and name and address of the court or other authority involved;

(2) A copy of the complaint or equivalent document setting forth the assertions in the case and any other pleading or document sufficient to show relevance;

(3) A list of categories of records sought, a detailed description of how the information sought is relevant to the issues in the legal proceeding, and a specific description of the substance of the testimony or records sought;

(4) A statement as to how the need for the information outweighs the need to maintain any confidentiality of the information and outweighs the burden on OIG to produce the records or provide testimony;

(5) A statement indicating that the information sought is not available from another source, from other persons or entities, or from the testimony of someone other than an OIG employee, such as a retained expert;

(6) If testimony is requested, the intended use of the testimony, a general summary of the desired testimony, and a showing that no document could be provided and used in lieu of testimony;

(7) A description of all prior decisions, orders, or pending motions in the case that bear upon the relevance of the requested records or testimony;

(8) The name, address, and telephone number of counsel to each party in the case; and

(9) An estimate of the amount of time that the requester and other parties will require with each OIG employee for time spent by the employee to prepare for testimony, in travel, and for attendance in the legal proceeding.

(c) The OIG reserves the right to require additional information to complete your request where appropriate.

(d) Your request should be submitted at least 30 days before the date that records or testimony are required. Requests submitted less than 30 days before records or testimony are required must be accompanied by a written explanation stating the reasons for the late request and the reasons for expedited processing.

(e) Failure to cooperate in good faith to enable the Counsel to make an informed decision may serve as the basis for a determination not to comply with your request.

§ 2004.23 Service of subpoenas or requests.

Subpoenas or requests for official records or information or testimony must be served on the Counsel to the Inspector General, Office of Inspector General, U.S. Department of Housing and Urban Development, 451 Seventh Street, SW, Room 8260, Washington, DC 20410–4500.

§ 2004.24 Processing demands or requests.

(a) After service of a demand or request to testify, the Counsel will review the demand or request and, in accordance with the provisions of this subpart, determine whether, or under what conditions, to authorize the employee to testify on matters relating to official information and/or to produce official records and information.

(b) The OIG will process requests in the order in which they are received. Absent exigent or unusual circumstances, OIG will respond within 30 days from the date that we receive all information necessary to the evaluation of the demand or request. The time for response will depend upon the scope of the request.

(c) The Counsel may grant a waiver of any procedure described in this subpart where a waiver is considered necessary to promote a significant interest of OIG, HUD, and the United States, or for other good cause.

§ 2004.25 Final determination.

The Counsel makes the final determination on demands and requests to employees for production of official records and information or testimony. All final determinations are within the sole discretion of the Counsel. The Counsel will notify the requester of the final determination, the reasons for the grant or denial of the demand or request, and any conditions that the Counsel may impose on the release of records or information, or on the testimony of an OIG employee.

§ 2004.26 Restrictions that apply to testimony.

(a) The Counsel may impose conditions or restrictions on the testimony of OIG employees including, for example, limiting the areas of testimony or requiring the requester and other parties to the legal proceeding to agree that the transcript of the testimony will be kept under seal or will only be used or made available in the particular legal proceeding for which testimony was requested. The Counsel may also require a copy of the transcript of testimony at the requester's expense.

(b) The OIG may offer the employee's written declaration in lieu of testimony.

(c) If authorized to testify pursuant to this part, an employee may testify as to facts within his or her personal knowledge, but, unless specifically authorized to do so by the Counsel, the employee shall not:

(1) Disclose confidential or privileged information;

(2) Testify as to facts when the Counsel determines such testimony would not be in the best interest of OIG, HUD and the United States; or

(3) Testify as an expert or opinion witness with regard to any matter arising out of the employee's official duties or the functions of OIG. This provision does not apply to requests from the United States for expert or opinion testimony.

§ 2004.27 Restrictions that apply to released records.

(a) The Counsel may impose conditions or restrictions on the release of official records and information, including the requirement that parties to the proceeding obtain a protective order or execute a confidentiality agreement to limit access and any further disclosure. The terms of the protective order or of a confidentiality agreement must be acceptable to the Counsel. In cases where protective orders or confidentiality agreements have already been executed, OIG may condition the release of official records and information on an amendment to the existing protective order or confidentiality agreement.

(b) If the Counsel so determines, original OIG records may be presented for examination in response to a demand or request, but they are not to be presented as evidence or otherwise used in a manner by which they could lose their identity as official OIG records, nor are they to be marked or altered. In lieu of the original records, certified copies will be presented for evidentiary purposes.

§ 2004.28 Procedure in the event of an adverse ruling.

(a) *Opportunity to review adverse ruling.* Any person aggrieved by a decision made by the Counsel under this part denying a request for documents or testimony, or restricting the release of documents or testimony, may seek review of that decision pursuant to paragraph (c) of this section.

(b) *Procedure in the event of conflicting court order.* If the Inspector General or Counsel declines to approve a demand for records or testimony and a court or other authority rules that the demand must be complied with irrespective of the instructions from the OIG not to produce the material or disclose the information sought, the employee or former employee upon whom the demand has been made shall respectfully decline to comply with the demand, citing *United States ex rel. Touhy* v. *Ragen*, 340 U.S. 462 (1951).

(c) *Procedure*—(1) *Notice of intention to petition for review.* A party or any person aggrieved by the decision made pursuant to this part denying or re-

stricting the release of documents or testimony may seek review of the decision by filing a written Notice of Intention to Petition for Review (Notice) within five business days of the date of this decision. The Notice shall identify the petitioner, the adverse decision, and any dates (such as deposition, hearing, or court dates) that are significant to the party. The Notice shall be served in accordance with § 2004.23.

(2) *Petition for review.* Within five business days of the filing of a Notice, the person or party seeking review shall file a Petition for Review (Petition) containing a clear and concise statement of the issues to be reviewed and the reasons why the review is appropriate. The petition shall include exceptions to any findings of fact or conclusions of law made, together with supporting reasons and arguments for such exceptions based on appropriate citations to such record or law as may exist. These reasons may be stated in summary form. Decisions on the Petition may be made by either the Inspector General or the Counsel and shall become the final decisions of the OIG. The Petition will be served in accordance with § 2004.23.

(d) *Prerequisite to judicial review.* Pursuant to Section 704 of the Administrative Procedure Act, 5 U.S.C. 704, a petition to the agency for review of a decision made under the authority of this part is a prerequisite to the seeking of judicial review of the final decision.

[70 FR 36791, June 24, 2005]

§ 2004.29 Fees.

(a) *Generally.* The Counsel may condition the production of records or appearance for testimony upon advance payment of a reasonable estimate of the costs to OIG.

(b) *Fees for records.* Fees for producing records will include fees for searching, reviewing, and duplicating records, costs of attorney time spent in reviewing the demand or request, and expenses generated by materials and equipment used to search for, produce, and copy the responsive information. Costs for employee time will be calculated on the basis of the hourly pay of the employee (including all pay, allowance, and benefits). Fees for duplication will be the same as those charged by OIG in its Freedom of Information Act Regulations at 24 CFR part 2002.

(c) *Witness fees.* Fees for attendance by a witness will include fees, expenses, and allowances prescribed by the court's rules. If no such fees are prescribed, witness fees will be determined based upon the rule of the federal district court closest to the location where the witness will appear. Such fees will include cost of time spent by the witness to prepare for testimony, in travel, and for attendance in the legal proceeding.

(d) *Payment of fees.* You must pay any applicable witness fees for current OIG employees and any records certification fees by submitting to the Counsel a check or money order for the appropriate amount made payable to the Treasury of the United States. In the case of testimony by former OIG employees, you must pay applicable fees directly to the former employee in accordance with applicable statutes.

(e) *Waiver or reduction of fees.* The Counsel, in his or her sole discretion, may, upon a showing of reasonable cause, waive or reduce any fees in connection with the testimony or production of records. Additionally, fees will not be assessed if the total charge would be $10.00 or less.

PARTS 2005–2099 [RESERVED]

CHAPTER XV—EMERGENCY MORTGAGE INSURANCE AND LOAN PROGRAMS, DEPARTMENT OF HOUSING AND URBAN DEVELOPMENT [RESERVED]

PARTS 2700–2799 [Reserved]

CHAPTER XX—OFFICE OF ASSISTANT SECRETARY FOR HOUSING—FEDERAL HOUSING COMMISSIONER, DEPARTMENT OF HOUSING AND URBAN DEVELOPMENT

AUTHORITY: 42 U.S.C. 3535(d), 5403, and 5424.

SOURCE: 40 FR 58752, Dec. 18, 1975, unless otherwise noted. Redesignated at 44 FR 20679, Apr. 6, 1979.

Subpart A—General

§ 3280.1 Scope.

This standard covers all equipment and installations in the design, construction, transportation, fire safety, plumbing, heat-producing and electrical systems of manufactured homes which are designed to be used as dwelling units. This standard seeks to the maximum extent possible to establish performance requirements. In certain instances, however, the use of specific requirements is necessary.

[58 FR 55002, Oct. 25, 1993]

§ 3280.2 Definitions.

Definitions in this subpart are those common to all subparts of the standard and are in addition to the definitions provided in individual parts. The definitions are as follows:

Approved, when used in connection with any material, appliance or construction, means complying with the requirements of the Department of Housing and Urban Development.

Bay window—a window assembly whose maximum horizontal projection is not more than two feet from the plane of an exterior wall and is elevated above the floor level of the home.

Certification label means the approved form of certification by the manufacturer that, under § 3280.8, is permanently affixed to each transportable section of each manufactured home manufactured for sale in the United States.

Dwelling unit means one or more habitable rooms which are designed to be occupied by one family with facilities for living, sleeping, cooking and eating.

Equipment includes materials, appliances, devices, fixtures, fittings or accessories both in the construction of, and in the fire safety, plumbing, heat-producing and electrical systems of manufactured homes.

Federal manufactured home construction and safety standard means a reasonable standard for the construction, design, and performance of a manufactured home which meets the needs of the public including the need for quality, durability, and safety.

Installations means all arrangements and methods of construction, as well as fire safety, plumbing, heat-producing and electrical systems used in manufactured homes.

Labeled means a label, symbol or other identifying mark of a nationally recognized testing laboratory, inspection agency, or other organization concerned with product evaluation that maintains periodic inspection of production of labeled equipment or materials, and by whose labeling is indicated compliance with nationally recognized standards or tests to determine suitable usage in a specified manner.

Length of a manufactured home means its largest overall length in the traveling mode, including cabinets and other projections which contain interior space. Length does not include bay windows, roof projections, overhangs, or eaves under which there is no interior space, nor does it include drawbars, couplings or hitches.

Listed or certified means included in a list published by a nationally recognized testing laboratory, inspection agency, or other organization concerned with product evaluation that maintains periodic inspection of production of listed equipment or materials, and whose listing states either that the equipment or material meets nationally recognized standards or has been tested and found suitable for use in a specified manner.

Manufacturer means any person engaged in manufacturing or assembling manufactured homes, including any person engaged in importing manufactured homes for resale.

Manufactured home means a structure, transportable in one or more sections, which in the traveling mode is 8 body feet or more in width or 40 body feet or more in length or which when erected on-site is 320 or more square feet, and which is built on a permanent chassis and designed to be used as a dwelling with or without a permanent foundation when connected to the required utilities, and includes the plumbing, heating, air-conditioning, and electrical systems contained in the structure. This term includes all structures that meet the above requirements except the size requirements and with respect to which the manufacturer voluntarily files a certification pursuant to § 3282.13 of this chapter and complies with the construction and safety standards set forth in this part 3280. The term does not include any self-propelled recreational vehicle. Calculations used to determine the number of square feet in a structure will include the total of square feet for each transportable section comprising the completed structure and will be based on the structure's exterior dimensions measured at the largest horizontal projections when erected on site. These dimensions will include all expandable rooms, cabinets, and other projections containing interior space, but do not include bay windows. Nothing in this definition should be interpreted to mean that a manufactured home necessarily meets the requirements of HUD's Minimum Property Standards

(HUD Handbook 4900.1) or that it is automatically eligible for financing under 12 U.S.C. 1709(b).

Manufactured home construction means all activities relating to the assembly and manufacture of a manufactured home including, but not limited to, those relating to durability, quality and safety.

Manufactured home safety means the performance of a manufactured home in such a manner that the public is protected against any unreasonable risk of the occurrence of accidents due to the design or construction of such manufactured home, or any unreasonable risk of death or injury to the user or to the public if such accidents do occur.

Registered Engineer or Architect means a person licensed to practice engineering or architecture in a state and subject to all laws and limitations imposed by the state's Board of Engineering and Architecture Examiners and who is engaged in the professional practice of rendering service or creative work requiring education, training and experience in engineering sciences and the application of special knowledge of the mathematical, physical and engineering sciences in such professional or creative work as consultation, investigation, evaluation, planning or design and supervision of construction for the purpose of securing compliance with specifications and design for any such work.

Secretary means the Secretary of Housing and Urban Development, or an official of the Department delegated the authority of the Secretary with respect to title VI of Pub. L. 93–383.

State includes each of the several States, the District of Columbia, the Commonwealth of Puerto Rico, Guam, the Virgin Islands, the Canal Zone, and American Samoa.

Width of a manufactured home means its largest overall width in the traveling mode, including cabinets and other projections which contain interior space. Width does not include bay windows, roof projections, overhangs, or eaves under which there is no interior space.

[40 FR 58752, Dec. 18, 1975, as amended at 42 FR 960, Jan. 4, 1977. Redesignated at 44 FR 20679, Apr. 6, 1979, as amended at 47 FR 28092, June 29, 1982; 58 FR 55002, Oct. 25, 1993; 61 FR 5216, Feb. 9, 1996; 72 FR 27228, May 14, 2007]

§ 3280.3 Manufactured home procedural and enforcement regulations and consumer manual requirements.

A manufacturer must comply with the requirements of this part 3280, part 3282 of this chapter, and 42 U.S.C. 5416.

[61 FR 18250, Apr. 25, 1996]

§ 3280.4 Incorporation by reference.

(a) The specifications, standards, and codes of the following organizations are incorporated by reference in 24 CFR part 3280 (this Standard) pursuant to 5 U.S.C. 552(a) and 1 CFR part 51 as though set forth in full. The incorporation by reference of these standards has been approved by the Director of the Federal Register. Incorporated standards have the same force and effect as this Standard (24 CFR part 3280), except that whenever reference standards and this Standard are inconsistent, the requirements of this Standard prevail to the extent of the inconsistency. The Department will enforce the listed editions of material incorporated by this section. Where two or more incorporated standards are equivalent in application, the manufacturer may use either standard. If a later edition is to be enforced, the Department will publish a notice of change in the FEDERAL REGISTER. These incorporated standards are available for purchase from the organization that developed the standard at the corresponding addresses noted below. Incorporated standards are available for inspection at the Office of Manufactured Housing Program, Manufactured Housing and Construction Standards Division, U.S. Department of Housing and Urban Development, 451 Seventh Street SW., Room B–133, Washington, DC 20410. Copies of incorporated standards that are not available from their producer organizations may be obtained from the Office of Manufactured Housing Programs. These standards are also available for inspection at the National Archives and Records Administration (NARA). For more information on the availability of this material at NARA, call 202–741–6030 or go to *http:// www.archives.gov/federal_register*.

(b) Air Conditioning & Refrigeration Institute (ARI), 4100 North Fairfax Drive, Suite 200, Arlington, VA 22203, telephone number 703–524–8800, fax number 703–528–3816, Web site: *http:// www.lightindustries.com/ARI/*.

(1) ANSI/ARI Standard 210/240–89, Unitary Air-Conditioning and Air-Source Heat Pump Equipment, IBR approved for §§ 3280.511(b), 3280.703, and 3280.714(a),

(2) [Reserved]

(c) Aluminum Association (AA), 1525 Wilson Blvd., Suite 600, Arlington, VA 22209; telephone number 703–358–2960, fax number 703–358–3921; Web site: *http://www.aluminum.org*.

(1) Aluminum Design Manual, Specifications and Guidelines for Aluminum Structures, Part 1–A, Sixth Edition, October 1994, IBR approved for § 3280.304(b).

(2) Aluminum Design Manual, Specifications and Guidelines for Aluminum Structures, Part 1–B, First Edition, October 1994, IBR approved for § 3280.304(b).

(d) American Architectural Manufacturers Association (AAMA), 1827 Walden Office Square, Suite 550, Schaumburg, IL 60173, telephone number 847–303–5664, fax number 847–303–5774, Web site: *http://www.aamanet.org*.

(1) AAMA 1503.1–88, Voluntary Test Method for Thermal Transmittance and Condensation Resistance of Windows, Doors, and Glazed Wall Sections, IBR approved for § 3280.508(e).

(2) AAMA 1600/I.S.7–00, Voluntary Specification for Skylights, 2003 IBR approved for § 3280.305(c).

(3) AAMA 1701.2–95, Voluntary Standard Primary Window and Sliding Glass Door for Utilization in Manufactured Housing, IBR approved for §§ 3280.403(e) and 3280.404(b).

(4) AAMA 1702.2–95, Voluntary Standard Swinging Exterior Passage Door for Utilization in Manufactured Housing, IBR approved for § 3280.405(b) and (e).

(5) AAMA Standard 1704–1985, Voluntary Standard Egress Window Systems for Utilization in Manufactured Housing, IBR approved for § 3280.404(b).

(6) AAMA/WDMA/CSA/101/I.S.2/A440–08 North American Fenestration Standard/Specification for Windows, Doors and Skylights, January 2008, IBR approved for § 3280.403(b) and (e).

(7) ANSI/AAMA/NWWDA 101/I.S.2–97,Voluntary Specifications for Aluminum, Vinyl (PVC) and Wood Windows and Glass Doors, IBR approved for § 3280.304(b).

(e) American Forest and Paper Association (AFPA), 1111 Nineteenth Street, Suite 800, Washington, DC 20036 (previously named National Forest Products Association (NFPA), telephone number 1–800–878–8878, Web site: *http://www.afandpa.org.*

(1) AFPA, Design Values for Joists and Rafters 1992, IBR approved for § 3280.304(b).

(2) AFPA PS–20–70, Span Tables for Joists and Rafters, 1993, IBR approved for § 3280.304(b).

(3) ANSI/AFPA NDS–2001, National Design Specifications for Wood Construction, 2001 Edition, with Supplement, Design Values for Wood Construction, November 30, 2001, IBR approved for § 3280.304(b).

(4) AFPA, Wood Structural Design Data, 1986 Edition with 1992 Revisions, IBR approved for § 3280.304(b).

(f) American Gas Association (AGA), 400 North Capitol Street NW., Washington, DC 20001, telephone number 202–824–7000, Web site: *http://www.aga.org/Pages/default.aspx.*

(1) AGA No. 3–87, Requirements for Gas Connectors for Connection of Fixed Appliances for Outdoor Installation, Park Trailers, and Manufactured (Mobile) Homes to the Gas Supply, IBR approved for § 3280.703.

(2) [Reserved]

(g) American Hardboard Association (AHA), 1210 West NW Highway, Palatine, IL 60067, Web site: *http://hardboard.org.*

(1) ANSI/AHA A135.4–1995, Basic Hardboard, IBR approved for § 3280.304(b).

(2) ANSI/AHA A135.5–1995, Prefinished Hardboard Paneling, IBR approved for § 3280.304(b).

(3) ANSI/AHA A135.6–1998, Hardboard Siding, IBR approved for § 3280.304(b).

(h) American Institute of Steel Construction (AISC), One East Wacker Drive, Chicago, IL 60601, telephone number 312–670–2400, fax number 312–670–5403, Web site: *http://www.aisc.org/.*

(1) AISC–S335, 1989. Specification for Structural Steel Buildings—Allowable Stress Design and Plastic Design (except for the following parts of this standard which are not incorporated by reference: 1.3.3, 1.3.4, 1.3.5, 1.3.6, 1.4.6, 1.5.1.5, 1.5.5, 1.6, 1.7, 1.8, 1.9, 1.10.4 through 1.10.7, 1.10.9, 1.11, 1.13, 1.14.5, 1.17.7 through 1.17.9, 1.19.1, 1.19.3, 1.20, 1.21, 1.23.7, 1.24, 1.25.1 through 1.25.5, 1.26.4, 2.3, 2.4, 2.8 through 2.10), June 1, 1989, IBR approved for §§ 3280.304(b) and 3280.305(j).

(2) [Reserved]

(i) American Iron and Steel Institute (AISI), 25 Massachusetts Ave., NW., Suite 800, Washington, DC 20001, telephone number 202–452–7100, Web site: *http://www.steel.org.*

(1) AISI, Specification for the Design of Cold-Formed Steel Structural Members, 1996, IBR approved for §§ 3280.304(b) and 3280.305(j).

(2) [Reserved]

(j) American National Standards Institute (ANSI), 25 West 43rd Street, 4th floor, New York, NY 10018, telephone number 212–642–4900, fax number 212–398–0023, Web site: *http://www.ansi.org.*

(1) ANSI A112.14.1–1975, Backflow Valves, IBR approved for § 3280.604(b).

(2) ANSI A112.19.5–1979, Trim for Water Closet, Bowls, Tanks, and Urinals, IBR approved for § 3280.604(b).

(3) ANSI/AITC A190.1–1992, For wood products—Structural Glued Laminated Timber, IBR approved for § 3280.304(b).

(4) ANSI A208.1–1999, Particleboard, IBR approved for § 3280.304(b).

(5) ANSI A208.2–2002, Medium Density Fiberboard (MDF) For Interior Applications, approved May 13, 2002, IBR approved for § 3280.304(b).

(6) ANSI B16.18–1984, Cast Copper Alloy Solder-Joint Pressure Fittings, IBR approved for § 3280.604(b).

(7) ANSI C72.1–1972, section 4.3.1, Household Automatic Electric Storage Type Water Heaters, IBR approved for § 3280.707(d).

(8) ANSI/IAS LC 1–1997, Fuel Gas Piping Systems Using Corrugated Stainless Steel Tubing (CSST), approved October 28, 1996, IBR approved for § 3280.705(b).

(9) ANSI Z21.1–2000, Household Cooking Gas Appliances, IBR approved for § 3280.703.

(10) ANSI Z21.5.1–1999, Gas Clothes Dryers Volume 1, Type 1 Clothes Dryers, with Addendum Z21.5.1a–1999, IBR approved for § 3280.703.

(11) ANSI Z21.10.1–1998, Gas Water Heaters—Volume 1, Storage Water Heaters with Input Ratings of 75,000 BTU per hour or Less, with Addendum Z21.10.1a–2000, IBR approved for §§ 3280.703 and 3280.707(d).

(12) ANSI Z21.15–1997, Manually Operated Gas Valves for Appliances, Appliance Connector Valves and Hose End Valves, IBR approved for §§ 3280.703 and 3280.705(c).

(13) ANSI Z21.19–1990, with Addendum ANSI Z21.19a–1992 and Z21.19b–1995, Refrigerators Using Gas Fuel, IBR approved for § 3280.703.

(14) ANSI Z21.20 with Addendum Z21.20a–2000, Automatic Gas Ignition Systems and Components, IBR approved for § 3280.703.

(15) ANSI Z21.21–2000, Automatic Valves for Gas Appliances, IBR approved for § 3280.703.

(16) ANSI Z21.22–1999, Relief Valves for Hot Water Supply Systems, IBR approved for §§ 3280.604(b) and 3280.703.

(17) ANSI Z21.23–1993, Gas Appliance Thermostats, approved August 10, 1993, IBR approved for § 3280.703.

(18) ANSI Z21.24–1997/CGA 6.10–M97, Connectors for Gas Appliances, IBR approved for § 3280.703.

(19) ANSI Z21.40.1–1996/CGA 2.91–M96, Gas-Fired, Heat Activated Air Conditioning and Heat Pump Appliances, IBR approved for §§ 3280.703 and 3280.714(a).

(20) ANSI Z21.47–1990 with Addendum Z21.47a–1990 and Z21.47b–1992, Gas-Fired Central Furnaces (Except Direct Vent System Central Furnaces), IBR approved for § 3280.703.

(21) ANSI Z34.1–1993, Third-Party Certification Programs for Products, Processes, and Services, IBR approved for §§ 3280.403(e) and 3280.405(e).

(22) ANSI Z97.1–2004, Standard for Safety Glazing Materials used in Buildings—Safety Performance Specifications and Methods of Test, copyright 2004, IBR approved for §§ 3280.113(c), 3280.304(b), 3280.403(d)(1), 3280.604(b), and 3280.607(b).

(23) ANSI Z124.1–1987, Plastic Bathtub Units with Addendum Z124.1a–1990 and Z124.1b–1991, IBR approved for § 3280.604(b).

(24) ANSI Z124.2–1987, Plastic Shower Receptors and Shower Stalls with Addendum Z124.2a–1990, IBR approved for § 3280.604(b).

(25) ANSI Z124.3–1986, Plastic Lavatories with Addendum Z124.3a–1990, IBR approved for § 3280.604(b).

(26) ANSI Z124.4–1986, Plastic Water Closets, Bowls, and Tanks with Addenda Z124.4a–1990, IBR approved for § 3280.604(b).

(27) ANSI Z124.5–1997, Plastic Toilet (Water Closets) Seats, IBR approved for § 3280.604(b).

(28) ANSI Z124.7–1997, Prefabricated Plastic Spa Shells, IBR approved for § 3280.604(b).

(29) ANSI Z–124.9–1994, Plastic Urinal Fixtures, IBR approved for § 3280.604(b).

(k) The Engineered Wood Association (APA) (formerly the American Plywood Association), 7011 South 19th Street, Tacoma, WA 98411, telephone number 253–565–6600, fax number 253–565–7265, Web site: *http://www.apawood.org.*

(1) APA D410A–2004, Panel Design Specification, IBR approved for § 3280.304(b).

(2) APA E30P–1996, APA Design/Construction Guide, Residential and Commercial Structures, IBR approved for § 3280.304(b).

(3) APA E30R, Engineered Wood Construction Guide, revised January 2001, IBR approved for § 3280.304(b).

(4) APA H815E–1995 (PDS Supplement #5), Design and Fabrication of All-Plywood Beams, IBR approved for § 3280.304(b).

(5) APA S 811M–1990 (PDS Supplement 1), Design and Fabrication of Plywood Curved Panels, IBR approved for § 3280.304(b).

(6) APA S 812R, Design and Fabrication of Glued Plywood-Lumber Beams, revised November 1998, Supplement #2, July 1992 IBR approved for § 3280.304.

(7) APA U 813L, Design and Fabrication of Plywood Stressed-Skin Panels,

revised April 1996, Supplement # 3, August 1992, IBR approved for § 3280.304(b).

(8) APA U 814H, Design and Fabrication of Plywood, Sandwiched Panels, revised September 1993, Supplement #4, March 1990, IBR approved for § 3280.304(b).

(l) American Society of Civil Engineers (ASCE), 1801 Alexander Bell Drive, Reston, VA 20191, telephone number 800–548–2723, Web site: *http://www.asce.org*.

(1) ANSI/ASCE 7–88, Minimum Design Loads for Buildings and Other Structures, IBR approved for §§ 3280.5(f), 3280.304(b), and 3280.305(c).

(2) SEI/ASCE 8–02, Specification for the Design of Cold-Formed Stainless Steel Structural Members, 2002, IBR approved for §§ 3280.304(b) and 3280.305(j).

(3) ASCE 19–96, Structural Applications of Steel Cables for Buildings, IBR approved for § 3280.304(b).

(m) American Society of Heating, Refrigeration and Air Conditioning Engineers (ASHRAE), 1791 Tullie Circle NE., Atlanta, GA 30329, telephone number 404–636–8400, fax number 404–321–5478, Web site: *https://www.ashrae.org/home/*.

(1) 1997 ASHRAE Handbook of Fundamentals, Inch-Pound Edition (1997), chapters 22 through 27, (except for the following parts of this standard that are not incorporated by reference: 23.1 Steel Frame Construction; 23.2 Masonry Construction; 23.3 Foundations and Floor Systems; 23.15 Pipes; 23.17 Tanks, Vessels, and Equipment; 23.18 Refrigerated Rooms and Buildings; 24.18 Mechanical and Industrial Systems; 25.19 Commercial Building Envelope Leakage; 27.9 Calculation of Heat Loss from Crawl Spaces). IBR approved for §§ 3280.508(a), 3280.508(e), and 3280.511(a).

(2) [Reserved]

(n) ASME (formally the American Society of Mechanical Engineers), Two Park Avenue, New York, NY 10016–5990, telephone number 800–843–2763, Web site: *http://www.asme.org/*.

(1) ASME A112.1.2–1991, Air Gaps in Plumbing Systems, IBR approved for § 3280.604(b).

(2) ANSI/ASME A112.4.1–1993, Water Heater Relief Valve Drain Tubes, IBR approved for § 3280.604(b).

(3) ANSI/ASME A112.4.3–1999, Plastic Fittings for Connecting Water Closets to the Sanitary Drainage System, IBR approved for § 3280.604(b).

(4) ASME/ANSI A112.18.1M–1989, Plumbing Fixture Fittings, IBR approved for § 3280.604(b).

(5) ASME A112.18.3M–1996, Performance Requirements for Backflow Protection Devices and Systems in Plumbing Fixture Fittings, IBR approved for § 3280.604(b).

(6) ASME A112.18.6–1999, Flexible Water Connectors, IBR approved for § 3280.604(b).

(7) ASME A112.18.7–1999, Deck Mounted Bath/Shower Transfer Valves with Integral Backflow Protection, IBR approved for § 3280.604(b).

(8) ANSI/ASME A112.19.1M–1987, Enameled Cast Iron Plumbing Fixtures, IBR approved for § 3280.604(b).

(9) ANSI/ASME A112.19.2(M)–1990, Vitreous China Plumbing Fixtures, IBR approved for § 3280.604(b).

(10) ANSI/ASME A112.19.3M–1987, Stainless Steel Plumbing Fixtures (Designed for Residential Use), IBR approved for § 3280.604(b).

(11) ANSI/ASME A112.19.4(M)–1984, Porcelain Enameled Formed Steel Plumbing Fixtures, IBR approved for § 3280.604(b).

(12) ASME A112.19.6–1995, Hydraulic Performance Requirements for Water Closets and Urinals, IBR approved for § 3280.604(b).

(13) ASME/ANSI A112.19.7M–1987, Whirlpool Bathtub Appliances, IBR approved for § 3280.604(b).

(14) ASME/ANSI A112.19.8M–1989, Suction Fittings for Use in Swimming Pools, Wading Pools, Spas, Hot Tubs, and Whirlpool Bathtub Appliances, IBR approved for § 3280.604(b).

(15) ASME A112.19.9M–1991, Non-Vitreous Ceramic Plumbing Fixtures, IBR approved for § 3280.604(b).

(16) ASME A112.19.10–1994, Dual Flush Devices for Water Closets, IBR approved for § 3280.604(b).

(17) ANSI/ASME A112.21.3M–1985, Hydrants for Utility and Maintenance Use, IBR approved for § 3280.604(b).

(18) ANSI/ASME B1.20.1–1983, Pipe Threads, General Purpose (Inch), IBR approved for §§ 3280.604(b), 3280.703, 3280.705(e), and 3280.706(d).

(19) ANSI/ASME B16.3–1992, Malleable Iron Threaded Fittings, IBR approved for § 3280.604(b).

(20) ANSI/ASME B16.4–1992, Gray Iron Threaded Fittings, IBR approved for § 3280.604(b).

(21) ANSI/ASME B16.15–1985, Cast Bronze Threaded Fittings, Classes 125 and 250, IBR approved for § 3280.604(b).

(22) ASME/ANSI B16.22–1973, Wrought-Copper and Copper Alloy Solder-Joint Pressure Fitting, IBR approved for § 3280.604(b).

(23) ASME B16.23–1992, Cast Copper Alloy Solder-Joint Drainage Fittings-DWV, IBR approved for § 3280.604(b).

(24) ASME/ANSI B16.26–1988, Cast Copper Alloy Fittings for Flared Copper Tubes, IBR approved for § 3280.604(b).

(25) ASME/ANSI B16.29–1986, Wrought Copper and Wrought Copper Alloy Solder-Joint Drainage Fittings-DWV, IBR approved for § 3280.604(b).

(26) ANSI/ASME B36.10–1979, Welding and Seamless Wrought Steel Pipe, IBR approved for §§ 3280.604(b), 3280.703, 3280.705(b), and 3280.706(b).

(o) American Society of Sanitary Engineering (ASSE), 901 Canterbury, Suite A, Westlake, OH 44145, phone number 440–835–3040, fax number 440–835–3488, Web site: *http://www.asse-plumbing.org*.

(1) ASSE 1001 (ANSI Approved 1990), Performance Requirements for Pipe Applied Atmospheric Type Vacuum Breakers, IBR approved for § 3280.604(b).

(2) ASSE 1002 Revision 5–1986 (ANSI/ASSE–1979), Performance Requirements for Water Closet Flush Tank Fill Valves (Ballcocks), IBR approved for § 3280.604(b).

(3) ASSE 1006 (ASSE/ANSI–1986), Plumbing Requirements for Residential Use (Household) Dishwashers, IBR approved for § 3280.604(b).

(4) ASSE 1007–1986, Performance Requirements for Home Laundry Equipment, IBR approved for § 3280.604(b).

(5) ASSE 1008–1986, Performance Requirements for Household Food Waste Disposer Units, IBR approved for § 3280.604(b).

(6) ASSE 1011–1981 (ANSI–1982), Performance Requirements for Hose Connection Vacuum Breakers, IBR approved for § 3280.604(b).

(7) ASSE 1014–1989 (ANSI–1990), Performance Requirements for Hand-held Showers, IBR approved for § 3280.604(b).

(8) ASSE 1016–2005, Performance Requirements for Automatic Compensating Values for Individual Shower and Tub/Shower Combinations, approved January 2005, IBR approved for §§ 3280.604(b) and 3280.607(b).

(9) ASSE 1017–1986, Performance Requirements for Temperature Activated Mixing Valves for Primary Domestic Use, IBR approved for § 3280.604(b).

(10) ANSI/ASSE 1019–1978, Performance Requirements for Wall Hydrants, Frost Proof Automatic Draining, Anti-Backflow Types, IBR approved for § 3280.604(b).

(11) ASSE 1023 (ANSI/ASSE–1979), Performance Requirements for Hot Water Dispensers, Household Storage Type Electrical, IBR approved for § 3280.604(b).

(12) ASSE 1025 (ANSI/ASSE–1978), Performance Requirements for Diverters for Plumbing Faucets with Hose Spray, Anti-Siphon Type, Residential Applications, IBR approved for § 3280.604(b).

(13) ASSE 1037–1990 (ANSI–1990), Performance Requirements for Pressurized Flushing Devices (Flushometers) for Plumbing Fixtures, IBR approved for § 3280.604(b).

(14) ASSE 1051 Revised 1996 (ANSI 1998), Performance Requirements for Air Admittance Valves for Plumbing Drainage Systems—Fixture and Branch Devices, IBR approved for § 3280.604(b).

(15) ASSE 1070–2004, Performance Requirements for Water Temperature Limiting Devices, IBR approved for §§ 3280.604(b) and 3280.607(b).

(p) American Society for Testing and Materials (ASTM), 100 Barr Harbor Drive, West Conshohocken, PA 19428, (610) 832–9500, fax number 610–832–9555, Web site: *http://www.astm.org*.

(1) ASTM A53–93. Standard Specification for Pipe, Steel, Black and Hot-Dipped, Zinc-Coated, Welded and Seamless, IBR approved for §§ 3280.604(b) and 3280.703.

(2) ASTM A74–92, Standard Specification for Cast Iron Soil Pipe and Fittings, IBR approved for § 3280.604(b).

(3) ASTM A539–99, Standard Specification for Electric-Resistance-Welded Coiled Steel Tubing for Gas and Fuel

Oil Lines, IBR approved for §§ 3280.703, 3280.705(b), and § 3280.706(b).

(4) ASTM B42–93, Standard Specification for Seamless Copper Pipe, Standard Sizes, IBR approved for §§ 3280.604 and 3280.703.

(5) ASTM B43–91, Standard Specification for Seamless Red Brass Pipe, Standard Sizes, IBR approved for §§ 3280.604(b) and 3280.705(b).

(6) ASTM B88–93, Standard Specification for Seamless Copper Water Tube, IBR approved for §§ 3280.604, 3280.703, 3280.705(b), and 3280.706(b).

(7) ASTM B251–93, Standard Specification for General Requirements for Wrought Seamless Copper and Copper-Alloy Tube, IBR approved for §§ 3280.604 and 3280.703.

(8) ASTM B280–95a, Standard Specification for Seamless Copper Tube for Air Conditioning and Refrigeration Field Service, IBR approved for §§ 3280.703, 3280.705(b), and 3280.706(b).

(9) ASTM B306–92, Standard Specification for Copper Drainage Tube (DWV), IBR approved for § 3280.604(b).

(10) ASTM C 36/C 36M–99, Standard Specification for Gypsum Wallboard, 1999, IBR approved for § 3280.304.

(11) ASTM C564–97, Standard Specification for Rubber Gaskets for Case Iron Soil Pipe and Fittings, approved December 10, 1997, IBR approved for §§ 3280.604(b) and 3280.611(d).

(12) ASTM C920–02, Standard Specification for Elastomeric Joint Sealants, approved January 10, 2002, IBR approved for § 3280.611(d).

(13) ASTM D781–68 (Reapproved 1973), Standard Test Methods for Puncture and Stiffness of Paperboard, and Corrugated and Solid Fiberboard, IBR approved for §§ 3280.304(b), and 3280.305(g).

(14) ASTM D2235–88, Standard Specification for Solvent Cement for Acrylonitrile-Butadiene-Styrene (ABS) Plastic Pipe and Fittings, IBR approved for § 3280.604(b).

(15) ASTM D2564–91a, Standard Specification for Solvent Cements for Poly (Vinyl Chloride) (PVC) Plastic Piping Systems, IBR approved for § 3280.604(b).

(16) ASTM D2661–91, Standard Specification for Acrylonitrile-Butadiene-Styrene (ABS) Schedule 40 Plastic Drain, Waste, and Vent Pipe and Fittings, IBR approved for § 3280.604(b).

(17) ASTM D2665–91b, Standard Specification for Poly (Vinyl Chloride) (PVC) Plastic Drain, Waste, and Vent Pipe and Fittings, IBR approved for § 3280.604(b).

(18) ASTM D2846–92, Standard Specification for Chlorinated Poly (Vinyl Chloride) (CPVC) Plastic Hot- and Cold-Water Distribution Systems, IBR approved for § 3280.604(b).

(19) ASTM D3309–92a, Standard Specification for Polybutylene (PB) Plastic Hot- and Cold-Water Distribution Systems, IBR approved for § 3280.604(b).

(20) ASTM D3311–92, Standard Specification for Drain, Waste, and Vent (DWV) Plastic Fittings Patterns, IBR approved for § 3280.604(b).

(21) ASTM D3953–97, Standard Specification for Strapping, Flat Steel, and Seals, approved April 10, 1997, IBR approved for §§ 3280.306(b) and 3280.306(g).

(22) ASTM D4442–92 (Reapproved 1997), Standard Test Methods for Direct Moisture Content Measurement of Wood and Wood-Base Materials, IBR approved for § 3280.304(b).

(23) ASTM D4444–92, Standard Test Methods for Use and Calibration of Hand-Held Moisture Meters, IBR approved for § 3280.304(b).

(24) ASTM D4635–01, Standard Specification for Polyethylene Films Made from Low-Density Polyethylene for General Use and Packaging Applications, approved June 10, 2001, IBR approved for § 3280.611(d).

(25) ASTM E84–01, Standard Test Method for Surface Burning Characteristics of Building Materials, 2001, IBR approved for § 3280.203(a).

(26) ASTM E 96–95 Standard Test Methods for Water Vapor Transmission of Materials, IBR approved for § 3280.504(a).

(27) ASTM E 162–94, Standard Test Method for Surface Flammability of Materials Using a Radiant Heat Energy Source, IBR approved for § 3280.203(a).

(28) ASTM E 773–97, Standard Test Methods for Accelerated Weathering of Sealed Insulating Glass Units, IBR approved for § 3280.403(d).

(29) ASTM E 774–97, Standard Specification for the Classification of the Durability of Sealed Insulating Glass Units, IBR approved for § 3280.403(d).

(30) ASTM E 1333–96, Standard Test Method for Determining Formaldehyde

Concentrations in Air and Emission Rates from Wood Products Using a Large Chamber, approved March 10, 1996, IBR approved for § 3280.406(b).

(31) ASTM F628–91, Standard Specification for Acrylonitrile-Butadiene-Styrene (ABS) Schedule 40, Plastic Drain, Waste, and Vent Pipe with a Cellular Core, IBR approved for § 3280.604(b).

(32) ASTM F876–10, Standard Specification for Crosslinked Polyethylene (PEX) Tubing, approved February 10, 2010, IBR approved for § 3280.604(b).

(33) ASTM F877–07, Standard Specification for Crosslinked Polyethylene (PEX) Plastic Hot- and Cold-Water Distribution Systems, approved February 1, 2007, IBR approved for § 3280.604(b).

(q) Cast Iron Soil Pipe Institute (CISPI), 1064 Delaware Avenue SE, Atlanta, GA 30316, telephone number 404–622–0073, fax number 404–973–2845, Web site: http://www.cispi.org/.

(1) CISPI–301–90, Standard Specification for Hubless Cast Iron Soil Pipe and Fittings for Sanitary and Storm Drain, Waste, and Vent Piping Applications, IBR approved for § 3280.604(b).

(2) CISPI–HSN–85, Specification for Neoprene Rubber Gaskets for HUB and Spigot Cast Iron Soil Pipe and Fittings, IBR approved for §§ 3280.604, 3280.611(d).

(r) FS—Federal Specifications, General Services Administration, Specifications Branch, Room 6039, GSA Building, 7th and D Streets, SW., Washington, DC 20407.

(1) FS WW–P–541E/GEN–1980, Plumbing Fixtures (General Specifications), IBR approved for § 3280.604(b).

(2) FS ZZ–R–765B–1970, Silicone Rubber, (with 1971 Amendment), IBR approved for § 3280.611(d).

(s) HPVA (previously HPMA)—Hardwood Plywood and Veneer Association (HPVA) (previously named Hardwood Plywood Manufacturers Association (HPMA), 1825 Michael Faraday Drive, Reston, VA 22090, telephone number 703–435–2900, fax number 703–435–2537, Web site: http://www.hpva.org/.

(1) ANSI/HPVA HP–1–1994 (Approved 1995), American National Standard for Hardwood and Decorative Plywood, IBR approved for § 3280.304(b).

(2) HP–SG–96, Structural Design Guide for Hardwood Plywood Wall Panels, revised 1996, IBR approved for § 3280.304(b).

(t) HUD User, 11491 Sunset Hills Road, Reston, VA 20190–5254.

(1) HUD User No. 0005945, Overall U-values and Heating/Cooling Loads—Manufactured Homes, February 1992. IBR approved for § 3280.508(b).

(2) [Reserved]

(u) IIT Research Institute (IITRI), 10 West 35th Street, Chicago, IL 60616, telephone number 312–567–4000, Web site: http://www.iitri.org/.

(1) IITRI Fire and Safety Research Project J–6461 "Development of Mobile Home Fire Test Methods to Judge the Fire-Safe Performance of Foam Plastic Sheathing and Cavity Insulation", 1979, IBR approved for § 3280.207(a).

(2) [Reserved]

(v) International Association of Plumbing and Mechanical Officials (IAPMO), 4755 East Philadelphia Street, Ontario, CA 91716, telephone number 909–472–4100, fax number 909–472–4150, Web site: http://www.iapmo.org.

(1) IAPMO PS 2–89, Material and Property Standard for Cast Brass and Tubing P-Traps, IBR approved for § 3280.604(b).

(2) IAPMO PS 4–90, Material and Property Standard for Drains for Prefabricated and Precast Showers, IBR approved for § 3280.604(b).

(3) IAPMO PS 5–84, Material and Property Standard for Special Cast Iron Fittings, IBR approved for § 3280.604(b).

(4) IAPMO PS 9–84, Material and Property Standard for Diversion Tees and Twin Waste Elbow, IBR approved for § 3280.604(b).

(5) IAPMO PS 14–89, Material and Property Standard for Flexible Metallic Water Connectors, IBR approved for § 3280.604(b).

(6) IAPMO PS 23–89, Material and Property Standard for Dishwasher Drain Airgaps, IBR approved for § 3280.604(b).

(7) IAPMO PS 31–91, Material and Property Standards for Backflow Prevention Assemblies, IBR approved for § 3280.604(b).

(8) IAPMO TSC 9–97, Standard for Gas Supply Connectors for Manufactured Homes, IBR approved for § 3280.703.

(9) IAPMO TSC 22–85, Standard for Porcelain Enameled Formed Steel Plumbing Fixtures, IBR approved for § 3280.604(b).

(w) Military Specifications and Standards, Naval Publications and Forms Center (MIL), 5801 Tabor Avenue, Philadelphia, PA 19120.

(1) MIL–L–10547E–1975, Liners, Case, and Sheet, Overwrap; Water-Vapor Proof or Waterproof, Flexible, IBR approved for § 3280.611(d).

(2) [Reserved]

(x) National Electrical Manufacturers Association (NEMA), 1300 North 17th Street, Suite 1752, Arlington, VA 22209, telephone number 703–841–3200, fax number 703–841–5900, Web site: *http://www.nema.org/Pages/default.aspx*.

(1) ANSI/NEMA WD–6–1997 Wiring Devices–Dimensional Specifications, IBR approved for § 3280.803(f).

(2) [Reserved]

(y) International Code Council Evaluation Service (NER), (previously known as National Evaluation Service), 5360 Workman Mill Road, Whittier, CA 90601–0543, telephone number 1–800–423–6587, ext. 66546, fax number 562–695–4694, Web site: *http://www.icc-es.org*.

(1) NER–272, National Evaluation Report, Power Driven Staples, Nails, and Allied Fasteners for Use in All Types of Building Construction, Reissued September 1, 1997, IBR approved for § 3280.304(b).

(2) [Reserved]

(z) National Fenestration Rating Council (NFRC), 6305 Ivy Lane, Suite 140, Greenbelt, MD 20770, telephone number 301–589–1776, fax number 301–589–3884, Web site: *http://www.nfrc.org*.

(1) NFRC 100, Procedure for Determining Fenestration Product U-factors, 1997 Edition, IBR approved for § 3280.508(e).

(2) [Reserved]

(aa) National Fire Protection Association (NFPA), 1 Batterymarch Park, Quincy, MA 02269, phone number 617–770–3000, fax number 617–770–0700, Web site: *http://www.nfpa.org*.

(1) NFPA 31, Standard for the Installation of Oil Burning Equipment, 2001, IBR approved for §§ 3280.703 and 3280.707(f).

(2) NFPA 54–2002, National Fuel Gas Code, IBR approved for § 3280.703.

(3) NFPA 58, Liquefied Petroleum Gas Code, 2001 Edition, IBR approved for §§ 3280.703 and 3280.704(b).

(4) NFPA No. 70–2005, National Electrical Code, IBR approved as follows:

(i) Article 110.22, IBR approved for §§ 3280.803(k) and 3280.804(k).

(ii) Article 210.12(A) and (B), IBR approved for § 3280.801(b).

(iii) Article 220.61, IBR approved for § 3280.811(b).

(iv) Article 230, IBR approved for §§ 3280.803(k) and 3280.804(k).

(v) Article 250.24, IBR approved for §§ 3280.803(k) and 3280.804(k).

(vi) Article 250.26, IBR approved for §§ 3280.803(k) and 3280.804(k).

(vii) Article 250.28, IBR approved for §§ 3280.803(k) and 3280.804(k).

(viii) Article 312.2(A), IBR approved for §§ 3280.803(k) and 3280.804(k).

(x) Table 314.16(A), IBR approved for §§ 3280.808(m) and 3280.808(q).

(ix) Article 314.23(B), IBR approved for §§ 3280.808(m) and 3280.808(q).

(xi) Article 406.3, IBR approved for § 3280.807(d).

(xii) Article 410.4(D), IBR approved for § 3280.805(a).

(xiii) Article 440, IBR approved for § 3280.805(a).

(xiv) Article 440.65, IBR approved for § 3280.801(b).

(xv) Part II of Article 550, IBR approved for §§ 3280.801(a) and 3280.801(b).

(xvi) Article 550.25(a), IBR approved for § 3280.801(b).

(xvii) Article 680.70, IBR approved for §§ 3280.607(c) and 3280.801(a).

(xviii) Article 680.71, IBR approved for §§ 3280.607(c) and 3280.801(a).

(xix) Articles 680.72, IBR approved for §§ 3280.607(c) and 3280.801(a).

(5) NFPA 90B, Warm Air Heating and Air Conditioning Systems, 1996 Edition, IBR approved for § 3280.703.

(6) NFPA 220, Standard on Types of Building Construction, Chapter 2: definitions of "limited combustible" and "noncombustible material", 1995 Edition, IBR approved for § 3280.202.

(7) NFPA 253, Standard Method of Test for Critical Radiant Flux of Floor Covering Systems Using a Radiant Heat Energy Source, 2000, IBR approved for § 3280.207(c).

39

(8) NFPA 255, Standard Method of Test of Surface Burning Characteristics of Building Materials, 1996, IBR approved for §§ 3280.203(a) and 3280.207(a).

(bb) U.S. Department of Commerce, National Institute of Standards and Technology (NIST), Office of Engineering Standards, Room A–166, Technical Building, Washington, DC 20234 and Voluntary Product Division, 100 Bureau Drive, Stop 2100, Gaithersburg, MD 20899–2100, telephone number 301–975–4000, fax number 301–975–4715, Web site: *http://www.nist.gov.*

(1) PS 1–95, Construction and Industrial Plywood (With Typical APA Trademarks), IBR approved for § 3280.304(b).

(2) Voluntary Product Standard PS 2–04, Performance Standard for Wood-Based Structural-Use Panels, December 2004, IBR approval for § 3280.304(b).

(cc) National Sanitation Foundation (NSF), 789 North Dixboro Road, Ann Arbor, MI 48105, telephone number 734–769–8010, fax number 734–769–0109, Web site: *http://www.nsf.org.*

(1) ANSI/NSF 14–1990, Plastic Piping Components and Related Materials, IBR approved for § 3280.604(b).

(2) ANSI/NSF 24–1988, Plumbing System Components for Manufactured Homes and Recreational Vehicles, IBR approved for § 3280.604(b).

(3) ANSI/NSF 61–2001, Drinking Water System Components–Health Effects, IBR approved for § 3280.604(b).

(dd) Resources, Applications, Designs, & Controls (RADCO), 3220 East 59th Street, Long Beach, CA 90805, telephone number 562–272–7231, fax number 562–529–7513, Web site: *http://www.radcoinc.com.*

(1) RADCO DS–010–91, Decorative Gas Appliances for Installation in Solid Fuel Burning Fireplaces, May 1991, IBR approved for § 3280.703.

(2) [Reserved]

(ee) Society of Automotive Engineers (SAE), 400 Commonwealth Drive, Warrendale, PA 15096, telephone number 724–776–0790, Web site: *http://www.sae.org/.*

(1) SAE–J533b–1992, Flares for Tubing, IBR approved for §§ 3280.703 and 3280.705(f).

(2) [Reserved]

(ff) Steel Joist Institute (SJI), 234 West Cheves Street, Florence, SC 29501, telephone number 843–407–4091, Web site: *http://steeljoist.org.*

(1) Standard Specifications Load Tables and Weight Tables for Steel Joists and Joist Girders, SJI 1994, Fortieth Edition, IBR approved for § 3280.304(b).

(2) [Reserved]

(gg) Truss Plate Institute (TPI), 218 North Lee Street, Suite 312, Alexandria, VA 22314, telephone number 703–683–1010, fax number 866–501–4012, Web site: *http://www.tpinst.org/index.html.*

(1) TPI–85, Design Specifications for Metal Plate and Wood Connected Trusses, IBR approved for § 3280.304(b).

(2) [Reserved]

(hh) Underwriters' Laboratories, Inc. (UL), 333 Pfingsten Road, Northbrook, IL 60062, telephone number 847–272–8800, fax number 847–509–6257, Web site: *http://www.ul.com.*

(1) UL 94–1996, with 2001 revisions, Test for Flammability of Plastic Materials for Parts in Devices and Appliances, Fifth Edition, IBR approved for § 3280.715(e).

(2) UL 103–1995, with 1999 revisions, Factory-Built Chimneys for Residential Type and Building Heating Appliances, Ninth Edition, IBR approved for § 3280.703.

(3) UL 109–1997, with 2001 revisions, Tube Fittings for Flammable and Combustible Fluids, Refrigeration Service, and Marine Use, Sixth Edition, IBR approved for § 3280.703.

(4) UL 127–1996, with 1999 revisions, Factory-Built Fireplaces, Seventh Edition, IBR approved for § 3280.703.

(5) UL 174–1996, with 1997 revisions, Household Electric Storage Tank Water Heaters, Tenth Edition, IBR approved for § 3280.703.

(6) UL 181 Factory-Made Air Ducts and Air Connectors, Ninth Edition, April 4, 1996, with revisions through May 15, 2003, IBR approved for §§ 3280.702, 3280.703 and 3280.715(a).

(7) UL 181A, 1994, with 1998 revisions, Standard for Safety Closure Systems for use with Rigid Air Ducts and Air Connectors, Second Edition, IBR approved for §§ 3280.703 and 3280.715(c).

(8) UL 181B, 1995, with 1998 revisions, Standard for Safety Closure Systems for use with Flexible Air Ducts and Air Connectors, First Edition, IBR approved for §§ 3280.703 and 3280.715(c).

(9) UL 217, Single and Multiple Station Smoke Alarms, Fifth Edition, dated January 4, 1999, IBR approved for § 3280.208(a).

(10) UL 268, Smoke Detectors for Fire Protective Signaling Systems, Fourth Edition, dated January 4, 1999, IBR approved for § 3280.208(a).

(11) UL 307A–1995, Liquid Fuel-Burning Heating Appliances for Manufactured Homes and Recreational Vehicles, Seventh Edition, with 1997 revisions, IBR approved for §§ 3280.703 and 3280.707(f).

(12) UL 307B–1995, Gas Burning Heating Appliances for Manufactured Homes and Recreational Vehicles, Fourth Edition, with 1998 revisions, IBR approved for § 3280.703.

(13) UL 311, 1994, with 1998 revisions, Roof Jacks for Manufactured Homes and Recreational Vehicles, Eighth Edition, IBR approved for § 3280.703.

(14) UL 441, 1996 with 1999 revisions, Gas Vents, Ninth Edition, IBR approved for § 3280.703.

(15) UL 569, 1995 with 2001 revisions, Pigtails and Flexible Hose Connectors for LP-Gas, Seventh Edition, IBR approved for §§ 3280.703 and 3280.705(k).

(16) UL 737, 1996, Fireplace Stoves, Eight Edition, with 2000 revisions, IBR approved for § 3280.703.

(17) UL 923 Microwave Cooking Appliances, Fifth Edition, May 23, 2002, IBR approved for § 3280.204(c).

(18) UL 1042–1994, Electric Baseboard Heating Equipment, Fourth Edition, with 1998 revisions, IBR approved for § 3280.703.

(19) UL 1096, 1986, Electric Central Air Heating Equipment, Fourth Edition with revisions July 16, 1986, and January 30, 1988, IBR approved for § 3280.703.

(20) UL 1482, 1996, with 2000 revisions, Solid-Fuel Type Room Heaters, Fifth Edition, IBR approved for § 3280.703.

(21) UL 1995, 1995, Heating and Cooling Equipment, Second Edition, with 1999 revisions, IBR approved for § 3280.703.

(22) UL 2021–1997. Fixed and Location-Dedicated Electric Room Heaters, Second Edition, with 1998 revisions, IBR approved for § 3280.703.

(ii) Underwriters' Laboratories of Canada (ULC), 7 Underwriters Road, Toronto, Ontario, Canada M1 R 3A9, telephone number 866-937-3852, fax number 416–757–8727, Web site: *http:// www.ul.com/canada/eng/pages/*.

(1) CAN/ULC S102.2–M88, Standard Method of Test for Surface Burning Characteristics of Floor Coverings and Miscellaneous Materials and Assemblies, Fourth Edition, April 1988, IBR approved for § 3280.207(b).

(2) [Reserved]

(jj) Window and Door Manufacturers Association (WDMA) (Previously known as the National Wood Window and Door Association, (NWWDA)), 2025 M Street, NW., Suite 800, Washington, DC 20036–3309, telephone number 202–367–1157, Web site: *https:// www.wdma.com*.

(1) NWWDA I.S.4–81, Water Repellent Preservative Non-Pressure Treatment for Millwork, IBR approved for § 3280.405(b).

(2) [Reserved]

[78 FR 73976, Dec. 9, 2013, as amended at 79 FR 31863, June 3, 2014]

§ 3280.5 Data plate.

Each manufactured home shall bear a data plate affixed in a permanent manner near the main electrical panel or other readily accessible and visible location. Each data plate shall be made of material what will receive typed information as well as preprinted information, and which can be cleaned of ordinary smudges or household dirt without removing information contained on the data plate; or the data plate shall be covered in a permanent manner with materials that will make it possible to clean the data plate of ordinary dirt and smudges without obscuring the information. Each data plate shall contain not less than the following information:

(a) The name and address of the manufacturing plant in which the manufactured home was manufactured.

(b) The serial number and model designation of the unit, and the date the unit was manufactured.

(c) The applicable statement:

This manufactured home is designed to comply with the Federal Manufactured Home Construction and Safety Standards in force at the time of manufacture.or

This manufactured home has been substantially completed in accordance with an approved design and has been inspected (except for the components specifically identified in

41

the instructions for completion on-site) in accordance with the Federal Manufactured Home Construction and Safety Standards and the requirements of the Department of Housing and Urban Development (HUD) in effect on the date of manufacture.

(d) A list of the certification label(s) number(s) that are affixed to each transportable manufactured section under § 3280.8.

(e) A list of major factory-installed equipment, including the manufacturer's name and the model designation of each appliance.

(f) Reference to the roof load zone and wind load zone for which the home is designed and duplicates of the maps as set forth in § 3280.305(c). This information may be combined with the heating/cooling certificate and insulation zone map required by §§ 3280.510 and 3280.511. The Wind Zone Map on the Data Plate shall also contain the statement:

This home has not been designed for the higher wind pressures and anchoring provisions required for ocean/coastal areas and should not be located within 1500′ of the coastline in Wind Zones II and III, unless the home and its anchoring and foundation system have been designed for the increased requirements specified for Exposure D in ANSI/ASCE 7–88.

(g) The statement:

This home has—has not—(appropriate blank to be checked by manufacturer) been equipped with storm shutters or other protective coverings for windows and exterior door openings. For homes designed to be located in Wind Zones II and III, which have not been provided with shutters or equivalent covering devices, it is strongly recommended that the home be made ready to be equipped with these devices in accordance with the method recommended in the manufacturers printed instructions.

(h) The statement: "Design Approval by", followed by the name of the agency that approved the design.

[59 FR 2469, Jan. 14, 1994, as amended at 80 FR 53727, Sept. 8, 2015]

§ 3280.6 Serial number.

(a) A manufactured home serial number which will identify the manufacturer and the state in which the manufactured home is manufactured, must be stamped into the foremost cross member. Letters and numbers must be ⅜ inch minimum in height. Numbers must not be stamped into hitch assembly or drawbar.

§ 3280.7 Excluded structures.

Certain structures may be excluded from these Standards as modular homes under 24 CFR 3282.12.

[52 FR 4581, Feb. 12, 1987]

§ 3280.8 Waivers.

(a) Where any material piece of equipment, or system which does not meet precise requirements or specifications set out in the standard is shown, to the satisfaction of the Secretary, to meet an equivalent level of performance, the Secretary may waive the specifications set out in the Standard for that material, piece of equipment, or system.

(b) Where the Secretary is considering issuing a waiver to a Standard, the proposed waiver shall be published in the FEDERAL REGISTER for public comment, unless the Secretary, for good cause, finds that notice is impractical, unnecessary or contrary to the public interest, and incorporates into the waiver that finding and a brief statement of the reasons therefor.

(c) Each proposed and final waiver shall include:

(1) A statement of the nature of the waiver; and

(2) Identification of the particular standard affected.

(d) All waivers shall be published in the FEDERAL REGISTER and shall state their effective date. Where a waiver has been issued, the requirements of the Federal Standard to which the waiver relates may be met either by meeting the specifications set out in the Standard or by meeting the requirements of the waiver published in the FEDERAL REGISTER.

[58 FR 55003, Oct. 25, 1993]

§ 3280.9 Interpretative bulletins.

Interpretative bulletins may be issued for the following purposes:

(a) To clarify the meaning of the Standard; and

(b) To assist in the enforcement of the Standard.

[58 FR 55003, Oct. 25, 1993]

§3280.10 Use of alternative construction.

Requests for alternative construction can be made pursuant to 24 CFR 3282.14 of this chapter.

[58 FR 55003, Oct. 25, 1993]

§3280.11 Certification label.

(a) A permanent label shall be affixed to each transportable section of each manufactured home for sale or lease in the United States. This label shall be separate and distinct from the data plate which the manufacturer is required to provide under §3280.5 of the standards.

(b) The label shall be approximately 2 in. by 4 in. in size and shall be permanently attached to the manufactured home by means of 4 blind rivets, drive screws, or other means that render it difficult to remove without defacing it. It shall be etched on 0.32 in. thick aluminum plate. The label number shall be etched or stamped with a 3 letter designation which identifies the production inspection primary inspection agency and which the Secretary shall assign. Each label shall be marked with a 6 digit number which the label supplier shall furnish. The labels shall be stamped with numbers sequentially.

(c) The label shall read as follows:

As evidenced by this label No. ABC 000001, the manufacturer certifies to the best of the manufacturer's knowledge and belief that this manufactured home has been inspected in accordance with the requirements of the Department of Housing and Urban Development and is constructed in conformance with the Federal manufactured home construction and safety standards in effect on the date of manufacture. See date plate.

(d) The label shall be located at the tail-light end of each transportable section of the manufactured home approximately one foot up from the floor and one foot in from the road side, or as near that location on a permanent part of the exterior of the manufactured home unit as practicable. The road side is the right side of the manufactured home when one views the manufactured home from the tow bar end of the manufactured home.

[42 FR 960, Jan. 4, 1977. Redesignated at 44 FR 20679, Apr. 6, 1979, as amended at 52 FR 47553, Dec. 15, 1987. Redesignated and amended at 58 FR 55003, Oct. 25, 1993]

Subpart B—Planning Considerations

§3280.101 Scope.

Subpart B states the planning requirements in manufactured homes. The intent of this subpart is to assure the adequacy of architectural planning considerations which assist in determining a safe and healthful environment.

§3280.102 Definitions.

(a) *Gross floor area* means all space, wall to wall, including recessed entries not to exceed 5 sq. ft. and areas under built-in vanities and similar furniture. Where the ceiling height is less than that specified in §3280.104, the floor area under such ceilings shall not be included. Floor area of closets shall not be included in the gross floor area.

(b) *Habitable room* means a room or enclosed floor space arranged for living, eating, food preparation, or sleeping purposes not including bathrooms, foyers, hallways, and other accessory floor space.

(c) *Laundry area* means an area containing or designed to contain a laundry tray, clothes washer and/or clothes dryer.

§3280.103 Light and ventilation.

(a) *Lighting.* Each habitable room shall be provided with exterior windows and/or doors having a total glazed area of not less than 8 percent of the gross floor area.

(1) Kitchens, bathrooms, toilet compartments, laundry areas, and utility rooms may be provided with artificial light in place of windows.

(2) Rooms and areas may be combined for the purpose of providing the required natural lighting provided that at least one half of the common wall area is open and unobstructed, and the open area is at least equal to 10 percent of the combined floor area or 25 square feet whichever is greater.

(b) *Whole-house ventilation.* Each manufactured home must be provided with whole-house ventilation having a minimum capacity of 0.035 ft³/min/ft² of interior floor space or its hourly average equivalent. This ventilation capacity must be in addition to any openable window area. In no case shall the installed ventilation capacity of the system be less than 50 cfm nor more than 90 cfm. The following criteria must be adhered to:

(1) The ventilation capacity must be provided by a mechanical system or a combination passive and mechanical system. The ventilation system or provisions for ventilation must not create a positive pressure in Uo Value Zone 2 and Zone 3 or a negative pressure condition in Uo Value Zone 1. Mechanical systems must be balanced. Combination passive and mechanical systems must have adequately sized inlets or exhaust to release any unbalanced pressure. Temporary pressure imbalances due to gusting or high winds are permitted.

(2) The ventilation system or provisions for ventilation must exchange air directly with the exterior of the home, except the ventilation system, or provisions for ventilation must not draw or expel air with the space underneath the home. The ventilation system or provisions for ventilation must not draw or expel air into the floor, wall, or ceiling/roof systems, even if those systems are vented. The ventilation system must be designed to ensure that outside air is distributed to all bedrooms and main living areas. The combined use of undercut doors or transom grills connecting those areas to the room where the mechanical system is located is deemed to meet this requirement.

(3) The ventilation system or a portion of the system is permitted to be integral with the home's heating or cooling system. The system must be capable of operating independently of the heating or cooling modes. A ventilation system that is integral with the heating or cooling system is to be listed as part of the heating and cooling system or listed as suitable for use with that system.

(4) A mechanical ventilation system, or mechanical portion thereof, must be provided with a manual control, and must be permitted to be provided with automatic timers or humidistats.

(5) A whole-house ventilation label must be attached to the whole-house ventilation control, must be permanent, and must state: "WHOLE-HOUSE VENTILATION".

(6) Instructions for correctly operating and maintaining whole-house ventilation systems must be included with the homeowner's manual. The instructions must encourage occupants to operate these systems whenever the home is occupied, and must refer to the labeled whole-house ventilation control.

(c) *Additional ventilation.* (1) At least half of the minimum required glazed area in paragraph (a) of this section shall be openable directly to the outside of the manufactured home for unobstructed ventilation. These same ventilation requirements apply to rooms combined in accordance with § 3280.103(a)(2).

(2) Kitchens shall be provided with a mechanical ventilation system that is capable of exhausting 100 cfm to the outside of the home. The exhaust fan shall be located as close as possible to the range or cook top, but in no case farther than 10 feet horizontally from the range or cook top.

(3) Each bathroom and separate toilet compartment shall be provided with a mechanical ventilation system capable of exhausting 50 cfm to the outside of the home. A separate toilet compartment may be provided with 1.5 square feet of openable glazed area in place of mechanical ventilation, except in Uo value Zone 3.

[58 FR 55003, Oct. 25, 1993, as amended at 70 FR 72042, Nov. 30, 2005]

§ 3280.104   Ceiling heights.

(a) Every habitable room and bathroom shall have a minimum ceiling height of not less than 7 feet, 0 inches for a minimum of 50 percent of the room's floor area. The remaining area may have a ceiling with a minimum height of 5 feet, 0 inches. Minimum height under dropped ducts, beams, etc. shall be 6 feet, 4 inches.

(b) Hallways and foyers shall have a minimum ceiling height of 6 feet, 6 inches.

§3280.105 Exit facilities; exterior doors.

(a) *Number and location of exterior doors.* Manufactured homes shall have a minimum of two exterior doors located remote from each other.

(1) Required egress doors shall not be located in rooms where a lockable interior door must be used in order to exit.

(2) In order for exit doors to be considered *remote* from each other, they must comply with all of the following:

(i) Both of the required doors must not be in the same room or in a group of rooms which are not defined by fixed walls.

(ii) *Single wide units.* Doors may not be less than 12 ft. c-c from each other as measured in any straight line direction regardless of the length of path of travel between doors.

(iii) *Double wide units.* Doors may not be less than 20 ft. c-c from each other as measured in any straight line direction regardless of the length of path of travel between doors.

(iv) One of the required exit doors must be accessible from the doorway of each bedroom without traveling more than 35 feet. The travel distance to the exit door must be measured on the floor or other walking surface along the center-line of the natural and unobstructed path of travel starting at the center of the bedroom door, curving around any corners or permanent obstructions with a one-foot clearance from, and ending at, the center of the exit door.

(b) *Door design and construction.* (1) Exterior swinging doors shall be constructed in accordance with §3280.405 the "Standard for Swinging Exterior Passage Doors for Use in Manufactured Homes". Exterior sliding glass doors shall be constructed in accordance with §3280.403 the "Standard for Windows and Sliding Glass Doors Used in Manufactured Homes".

(2) All exterior swinging doors must provide a minimum 28-inch wide × 74-inch high clear opening. Door seals are permitted to reduce the opening, either vertically or horizontally, a maximum of one inch. All exterior sliding glass doors must provide a minimum 28-inch wide × 72-inch high clear opening.

(3) Each swinging exterior door other than screen or storm doors shall have a key-operated lock that has a deadlocking latch or a key-operated dead bolt with a passage latch. Locks shall not require the use of a key for operation from the inside.

(4) All exterior doors, including storm and screen doors, opening outward shall be provided with a safety door check.

[40 FR 58752, Dec. 18, 1975. Redesignated at 44 FR 20679, Apr. 6, 1979, as amended at 50 FR 9269, Mar. 7, 1985; 78 FR 73981, Dec. 9, 2013]

§3280.106 Exit facilities; egress windows and devices.

(a) Every room designed expressly for sleeping purposes, unless it has an exit door (*see* §3280.105), shall have at least one outside window or approved exit device which meets the requirements of §3280.404, the "Standard for Egress Windows and Devices for Use in Manufactured Homes."

(b) The bottom of the window opening shall not be more than 36 inches above the floor.

(c) Locks, latches, operating handles, tabs, and any other window screen or storm window devices which need to be operated in order to permit exiting, shall not be located in excess of 54 inches from the finished floor.

(d) Integral rolled-in screens shall not be permitted in an egress window unless the window is of the hinged-type.

[49 FR 58752, Dec. 18, 1975. Redesignated at 44 FR 20679, Apr. 6, 1979, as amended at 49 FR 36086, Sept. 14, 1984; 52 FR 4581, Feb. 12, 1987]

§3280.107 Interior privacy.

Bathroom and toilet compartment doors shall be equipped with a privacy lock.

§3280.108 Interior passage.

(a) Interior doors having passage hardware without a privacy lock, or with a privacy lock not engaged, shall open from either side by a single movement of the hardware mechanism in any direction.

(b) Each manufactured home interior door, when provided with a privacy lock, shall have a privacy lock that has an emergency release on the outside to permit entry when the lock has been locked by a locking knob, lever, button, or other locking device on the inside.

§ 3280.109   **Room requirements.**

(a) Every manufactured home shall have at least one living area with not less than 150 sq. ft. of gross floor area.

(b) Rooms designed for sleeping purposes shall have a minimum gross square foot floor area as follows:

(1) All bedrooms shall have at least 50 sq. ft. of floor area.

(2) Bedrooms designed for two or more people shall have 70 sq. ft. of floor area plus 50 sq. ft. for each person in excess of two.

(c) Every room designed for sleeping purposes shall have accessible clothes hanging space with a minimum inside depth of 22 inches and shall be equipped with a rod and shelf.

[40 FR 58752, Dec. 18, 1975. Redesignated at 44 FR 20679, Apr. 6, 1979, and further redesignated at 58 FR 55004, Oct. 25, 1993]

§ 3280.110   **Minimum room dimensions.**

The gross floor area required by § 3280.110 (a) and (b) shall have no clear horizontal dimension less than 5 feet except as permitted by § 3280.102(a).

[40 FR 58752, Dec. 18, 1975. Redesignated at 44 FR 20679, Apr. 6, 1979, and further redesignated at 58 FR 55004, Oct. 25, 1993]

§ 3280.111   **Toilet compartments.**

Each toilet compartment must have a minimum width of 30 inches, with a minimum clear space of 21 inches in front of each toilet. A toilet located adjacent to a wall must have the center-line of the toilet located a minimum of 15 inches from the wall. A toilet located adjacent to a tub must have the center-line of the toilet located a minimum of 12 inches from the outside edge of the tub.

[78 FR 73981, Dec. 9, 2013]

§ 3280.112   **Hallways.**

Hallways shall have a minimum horizontal dimension of 28 inches measured from the interior finished surface to the interior finished surface of the opposite wall. When appliances are installed in a laundry area, the measurement shall be from the front of the appliance to the opposite finished interior surface. When appliances are not installed and a laundry area is provided, the area shall have a minimum clear depth of 27 inches in addition to the 28 inches required for passage. In addition, a notice of the available clearance for washer/dryer units shall be posted in the laundry area. Minor protrusions into the minimum hallway width by doorknobs, trim, smoke alarms or light fixtures are permitted.

[40 FR 58752, Dec. 18, 1975. Redesignated at 44 FR 20679, Apr. 6, 1979, and further redesignated at 58 FR 55004, Oct. 25, 1993; 67 FR 12817, Mar. 19, 2002]

§ 3280.113   **Glass and glazed openings.**

(a) *Windows and sliding glass doors.* All windows and sliding glass doors shall meet the requirements of § 3280.403 the "Standard for Windows and Sliding Glass Doors Used in Manufactured Homes".

(b) *Hazardous locations requiring safety glazing.* Except as provided in paragraph (d) of this section, the following locations and areas require the use of safety glazing conforming to the requirements of paragraph (c) of this section:

(1) Glazing in all entrance or exit doors;

(2) Glazing in fixed and sliding panels of sliding glass doors;

(3) Glazing in storm-type doors;

(4) Glazing in unframed side-hinged swinging doors;

(5) Glazing in doors and fixed panels less than 60 inches above the room floor level that enclose bathtubs, showers, hydromassage tubs, hot tubs, whirlpools, saunas;

(6) Glazing within 12 inches horizontally, as measured from the edge of the door in the closed position, and 60 inches vertically as measured from the room floor level, adjacent to and in the same plane of a door;

(7) Glazing within 36 inches of an interior room walking surface when the glazing meets all of the following:

(i) Individual glazed panels exceed 9 square feet in area in an exposed surface area;

(ii) The bottom edge of the exposed glazing is less than 19 inches above the room floor level; and

(iii) The top edge of the exposed glazing is greater than 36 inches above the room floor level.

(8) Glazing in rails and guardrails; and

(9) Glazing in unbacked mirrored wardrobe doors (i.e., mirrors that are not secured to a backing that is capable of being the door itself).

(c) Safety glazing material is considered to be any glazing material capable of meeting the requirements of Consumer Product Safety Commission 16 CFR part 1201, or Standard for Safety Glazing Materials used in Buildings —Safety Performance Specifications and Methods of Test, ANSI Z97.1–2004 (incorporated by reference, see § 3280.4).

(d) Glazing in the following locations is not required to meet the requirements in paragraph (b) of this section:

(1) Openings in doors through which a 3-inch sphere is unable to pass;

(2) Leaded and decorative glazed panels;

(3) Glazing in jalousie-type doors;

(4) Glazing as described in paragraph (b)(6) of this section when an intervening wall or other permanent barrier exists between the door and the glazing;

(5) Glazing as described in paragraph (b)(7) of this section when a protective bar or member is installed horizontally between 34 inches and 38 inches above the room floor level, as long as the bar or member is a minimum of 1½ inches in height and capable of resisting a horizontal load of 50 pounds per lineal foot; and

(6) Mirrors mounted on a flush door surface or solid wall surface.

[40 FR 58752, Dec. 18, 1975. Redesignated at 44 FR 20679, Apr. 6, 1979, as amended at 52 FR 4581, Feb. 12, 1987. Redesignated at 58 FR 55004, Oct. 25, 1993; 78 FR 73981, Dec. 9, 2013]

Subpart C—Fire Safety

Source: 49 FR 32008, Aug. 9, 1984, unless otherwise noted.

§ 3280.201 Scope.

The purpose of this subpart is to set forth requirements that will assure reasonable fire safety to the occupants by reducing fire hazards and by providing measures for early detection.

§ 3280.202 Definitions.

The following definitions are applicable to subparts C, H, and I of the Standards:

Combustible material: Any material not meeting the definition of limited-combustible or non-combustible material.

Flame-spread rating: The measurement of the propagation of flame on the surface of materials or their assemblies as determined by recognized standard tests conducted as required by this subpart.

Interior finish: The surface material of walls, fixed or movable partitions, ceilings, columns, and other exposed interior surfaces affixed to the home's structure including any materials such as paint or wallpaper and the substrate to which they are applied. Interior finish does not include:

(1) Trim and sealant 2 inches or less in width adjacent to the cooking range and in furnace and water heater spaces provided it is installed in accordance with the requirements of § 3280.203(b)(3) or (4), and trim 6 inches or less in width in all other areas;

(2) Windows and frames;

(3) Single doors and frames and a series of doors and frames not exceeding 5 feet in width;

(4) Skylights and frames;

(5) Casings around doors, windows, and skylights not exceeding 4 inches in width;

(6) Furnishings which are not permanently affixed to the home's structure;

(7) Baseboards not exceeding 6 inches in height;

(8) Light fixtures, cover plates of electrical receptacle outlets, switches, and other devices;

(9) Decorative items attached to walls and partitions (i.e., pictures, decorative objects, etc.) constituting no more than 10% of the aggregate wall surface area in any room or space not more than 32 square feet in surface area, whichever is less;

(10) Plastic light diffusers when suspended from a material which meets the interior finish provisions of § 3280.203(b);

(11) Coverings and surfaces of exposed wood beams; and

(12) Decorative items including the following:

(i) Non-structural beams not exceeding 6 inches in depth and 6 inches in width and spaced not closer than 4 feet on center;

(ii) Non-structural lattice work;

(iii) Mating and closure molding; and

(iv) Other items not affixed to the home's structure.

Limited combustible: A material meeting:

(1) The definition contained in Chapter 2 of NFPA 220–1995, Standard on Types of Building Construction; or

(2) 5/16-inch or thicker gypsum board.

Noncombustible material: A material meeting the definition contained in Chapter 2 of NFPA 220–1995, Standard on Types of Building Construction.

Smoke alarm: An alarm device that is responsive to smoke.

Tactile notification appliance: A notification appliance that alerts by the sense of touch or vibration.

[58 FR 55004, Oct. 25, 1993, as amended at 67 FR 12817, Mar. 19, 2002; 70 FR 72042, Nov. 30, 2005]

§ 3280.203 Flame spread limitations and fire protection requirements.

(a) *Establishment of flame spread rating.* The surface flame spread rating of interior-finish material must not exceed the value shown in § 3280.203(b) when tested by Standard Test Method for Surface Burning Characteristics of Building Materials, ASTM E84–01, 2001, or Standard Method of Test of Surface Burning Characteristics of Building Materials NFPA 255, 1996, except that the surface flame spread rating of interior-finish materials required by § 3280.203(b)(5) and (6) may be determined by using the Standard Test Method for Surface Flammability of Materials Using a Radiant Heat Energy Source, ASTM E 162–94. However, the following materials need not be tested to establish their flame spread rating unless a lower rating is required by the standards in this part:

(1) Flame-spread rating—76 to 200.

(i) .035-inch or thicker high pressure laminated plastic panel countertop;

(ii) 1/4-inch or thicker unfinished plywood with phenolic or urea glue;

(iii) Unfinished dimension lumber (1-inch or thicker nominal boards);

(iv) 3/8-inch or thicker unfinished particleboard with phenolic or urea binder;

(v) Natural gum-varnished or latex- or alkyd-painted:

(A) 1/4-inch or thicker plywood, or

(B) 3/8-inch or thicker particleboard, or

(C) 1-inch or thicker nominal board;

(vi) 5/16-inch gypsum board with decorative wallpaper; and

(vii) 1/4-inch or thicker unfinished hardboard,

(2) Flame-spread rating-25 to 200,

(i) Painted metal;

(ii) Mineral-base acoustic tile;

(iii) 5/16-inch or thicker unfinished gypsum wallboard (both latex- or alkyd-painted); and

(iv) Ceramic tile.

(The above-listed material applications do not waive the requirements of § 3280.203(c) or § 3280.204 of this subpart.)

(b) Flame-spread rating requirements.

(1) The interior finish of all walls, columns, and partitions shall not have a flame spread rating exceeding 200 except as otherwise specified herein.

(2) Ceiling interior finish shall not have a flame spread rating exceeding 75.

(3) Walls adjacent to or enclosing a furnace or water heater and ceilings above them shall have an interior finish with a flame spread rating not exceeding 25. Sealants and other trim materials 2 inches or less in width used to finish adjacent surfaces within these spaces are exempt from this provision provided that all joints are completely supported by framing members or by materials having a flame spread rating not exceeding 25.

(4) Exposed interior finishes adjacent to the cooking range shall have a flame spread rating not exceeding 50, except that backsplashes not exceeding 6 inches in height are exempted. Adjacent surfaces are the exposed vertical surfaces between the range top height and the overhead cabinets and/or ceiling and within 6 horizontal inches of the cooking range. (Refer also to § 3280.204(a), Kitchen Cabinet Protection.) Sealants and other trim materials 2 inches or less in width used to finish adjacent surfaces are exempt from this provision provided that all

joints are completely supported by a framing member.

(5) Kitchen cabinet doors, countertops, backsplashes, exposed bottoms, and end panels shall have a flame spread rating not to exceed 200. Cabinet rails, stiles, mullions, and top strips are exempted.

(6) Finish surfaces of plastic bathtubs, shower units, and tub or shower doors shall not exceed a flame spread rating of 200.

(c) Fire protective requirements.

(1) Materials used to surface the following areas shall be of limited combustible material (e.g., 5/16-inch gypsum board, etc.):

(i) The exposed wall adjacent to the cooking range (see §3280.203(b)(4));

(ii) Exposed bottoms and sides of kitchen cabinets as required by §3280.204;

(iii) Interior walls and ceilings enclosing furnace and/or water heater spaces; and

(iv) Combustible doors which provide interior or exterior access to furnace and/or water heater spaces. The surface may be interrupted for louvers ventilating the enclosure. However, the louvers shall not be constructed of a material of greater combustibility than the door itself (e.g., plastic louvers on a wooden door).

(2) No burner of a surface cooking unit shall be closer than 12 horizontal inches to a window or an exterior door with glazing.

[49 FR 32008, Aug. 9, 1984, as amended at 58 FR 55005, Oct. 25, 1993; 70 FR 72042, Nov. 30, 2005]

§3280.204 Kitchen cabinet protection.

(a) The bottom and sides of combustible kitchen cabinets over cooking ranges to a horizontal distance of 6 inches from the outside edge of the cooking range shall be protected with at least 5/16-inch thick gypsum board or equivalent limited combustible material. One-inch nominal framing members and trim are exempted from this requirement. The cabinet area over the cooking range or cooktops shall be protected by a metal hood (26-gauge sheet metal, or .017 stainless steel, or .024 aluminum, or .020 copper) with not less than a 3-inch eyebrow projecting horizontally from the front cabinet face.

The 5/16-inch thick gypsum board or equivalent material which is above the top of the hood may be supported by the hood. A 3/8-inch enclosed air space shall be provided between the bottom surface of the cabinet and the gypsum board or equivalent material. The hood shall be at least as wide as the cooking range.

(b) The 3-inch metal eyebrow required by paragraph (a) of this section will project from the front and rear cabinet faces when there is no adjacent surface behind the range, or the 5/16-inch thick gypsum board or equivalent material shall be extended to cover all exposed rear surfaces of the cabinet.

(c) *Alternative compliance.* When all exposed surfaces along the bottoms and sides of combustible kitchen cabinets are protected as described in paragraph (a) of this section, the metal hood, the 5/16-inch thick gypsum board or equivalent material, and the 3/8-inch airspace required by paragraph (a) of this section can be omitted, provided that:

(1) A microwave oven is installed between the cabinet and the range; and

(2) The microwave oven is equivalent in fire protection to the metal range hood required by paragraph (a) of this section; and

(3) The microwave oven is certified to be in conformance with Microwave Cooking Appliances, UL 923–2002 (incorporated by reference, see §3280.4).

(d) When a manufactured home is designed for the future installation of a cooking range, the metal hood and cabinet protection required by paragraph (a) of this section and the wall-surfacing protection behind the range required by §3280.203 shall be installed in the factory.

(e) Vertical clearance above cooking top. Ranges shall have a vertical clearance above the cooking top of not less than 24 inches to the bottom of combustible cabinets.

[49 FR 32008, Aug. 9, 1984, as amended at 78 FR 73982, Dec. 9, 2013]

§3280.205 Carpeting.

Carpeting shall not be used in a space or compartment designed to contain only a furnace and/or water heater. Carpeting may be used in other areas where a furnace or water heater is installed, provided that it is not located under the furnace or water heater.

§ 3280.206 Fireblocking.

(a) *General.* Fireblocking must comply with the requirements of this section. The integrity of all fireblocking materials must be maintained.

(b) *Fireblocking materials.* Fireblocking must consist of the following materials:

(1) Minimum one inch nominal lumber, ⁵⁄₁₆ inch thick gypsum board, or equivalent fire resistive materials; or

(2) Other Listed or Approved Materials;

(c) *Fireblocking locations.* (1) Fireblocking must be installed in concealed spaces of stud walls, partitions, and furred spaces at the floor and ceiling levels. Concealed spaces must not communicate between floor levels. Concealed spaces must not communicate between a ceiling level and a concealed roof area, or an attic space.

(2) Fireblocking must be installed at the interconnection of a concealed vertical space and a concealed horizontal space that occurs:

(i) Between a concealed wall cavity and the ceiling joists above; and

(ii) At soffits, drop ceilings, cover ceilings, and similar locations.

(3) Fireblocking must be installed around the openings for pipes, vents, and other penetrations in walls, floors, and ceilings of furnace and water heater spaces. Pipes, vents, and other penetrations that cannot be moved freely within their opening are considered to be fireblocked. Materials used to fireblock heat producing vent penetrations must be noncombustible or limited combustible types.

[71 FR 72042, Nov. 30, 2005]

§ 3280.207 Requirements for thermal insulating materials.

(a) *General.* Except for foam plastic materials and as provided in this section, exposed and concealed thermal insulating materials, including any facings, must be tested in accordance with NFPA 255-96, Standard Method of Test of Surface Burning Characteristics of Building Materials (incorporated by reference, see § 3280.4) and must have a flame spread index of 25 or

less and a smoke developed index of 450 or less. The flame spread and smoke developed limitations do not apply to:

(1) Coverings and facings of insulation batts or blankets installed in concealed spaces when the facings are in substantial contact with the unexposed surface of wall, floor, or ceiling finish; or

(2) Cellulose loose-fill insulation that complies with paragraph (b) of this section.

(b) *Loose-fill insulation.* (1) Cellulose loose-fill insulation that is not spray-applied or self-supporting must comply with, and each package must be labeled in accordance with the Consumer Product Safety Commission requirements in 16 CFR parts 1209 and 1404.

(2) Other loose-fill insulation that cannot be mounted in the NFPA 255-96, test apparatus without a screen or other artificial support must be tested in accordance with CAN/ULC S102.2-M88, Standard Method of Test for Surface Burning Characteristics of Floor Coverings and Miscellaneous Materials and Assemblies (incorporated by reference, see § 3280.4), and must have a flame spread index of 25 or less and a smoke developed index of 450 or less.

(c) *Attic locations.* Exposed insulation installed on the floor or ceiling forming the lower boundary of the attic must be tested in accordance with NFPA 253-2000, Standard Method of Test for Critical Radiant Flux of Floor Covering Systems Using a Radiant Heat Energy Source (incorporated by reference, see § 3280.4) and must have a critical radiant flux of not less than 0.12 watt/cm².

§ 3280.208 Requirements for foam plastic thermal insulating materials.

(a) *General.* Foam plastic thermal insulating materials shall not be used within the cavity of walls (not including doors) or ceilings or be exposed to the interior of the home unless:

(1) The foam plastic insulating material is protected by an interior finish of ⁵⁄₁₆-inch thick gypsum board or equivalent material for all cavities where the material is to be installed; or

(2) The foam plastic is used as a sheathing or siding backerboard, and it:

(i) Has a flame spread rating of 75 or less and a smoke-developed rating of 450 or less (not including outer covering of sheathing);

(ii) Does not exceed ⅜-inch in thickness; and

(iii) Is separated from the interior of the manufactured home by a minimum of 2 inches of mineral fiber insulation or an equivalent thermal barrier; or

(3) The foam plastic insulating material has been previously accepted by the Department for use in wall and/or ceiling cavities of manufactured homes, and it is installed in accordance with any restrictions imposed at the time of that acceptance; or

(4) The foam plastic insulating material has been tested as required for its location in wall and/or ceiling cavities in accordance with testing procedures described in the Illinois Institute of Technology Research Institute (IIT) Report, "Development of Mobile Home Fire Test Methods to Judge the Fire-Safe Performance of Foam Plastic Sheathing and Cavity Insulation, IITRI Fire and Safety Research Project J–6461, 1979" or other full-scale fire tests accepted by HUD, and it is installed in a manner consistent with the way the material was installed in the foam plastic test module. The materials must be capable of meeting the following acceptance criteria required for their location:

(i) *Wall assemblies.* The foam plastic system shall demonstrate equivalent or superior performance to the control module as determined by:

(A) Time to reach flashover (600 °C in the upper part of the room);

(B) Time to reach an oxygen (O_2) level of 14% (rate of O_2 depletion), a carbon monoxide (CO) level of 1%, a carbon dioxide (CO_2) level of 6%, and a smoke level of 0.26 optical density/meter measured at 5 feet high in the doorway; and

(C) Rate of change concentration for O_2, CO, CO_2 and smoke measured 3 inches below the top of the doorway.

(ii) *Ceiling assemblies.* A minimum of three valid tests of the foam plastic system and one valid test of the control module shall be evaluated to determine if the foam plastic system demonstrates equivalent or superior performance to the control module. In-

dividual factors to be evaluated include intensity of cavity fire (temperature-time) and post-test damage.

(iii) *Post-test damage assessment for wall and ceiling assemblies.* The overall performance of each total system shall also be evaluated in determining the acceptability of a particular foam plastic insulating material.

(b) All foam plastic thermal insulating materials used in manufactured housing shall have a flame spread rating of 75 or less (not including outer covering or sheathing) and a maximum smoke-developed rating of 450.

[49 FR 32008, Aug. 9, 1984, as amended at 70 FR 72043, Nov. 30, 2005. Redesignated at 78 FR 73982, Dec. 9, 2013]

§3280.209 Smoke alarm requirements.

(a) *Labeling.* Each smoke alarm required under paragraph (b) of this section must conform with the requirements of UL 217, Single and Multiple Station Smoke Alarms, dated January 4, 1999 (incorporated by reference, see §3280.4), or UL 268, Smoke Detectors for Fire Protective Signaling Systems, dated January 4, 1999 (incorporated by reference, see §3280.4), and must bear a label to evidence conformance.

(b) *Required smoke alarm locations.* (1) At least one smoke alarm must be installed in each of the following locations:

(i) To protect both the living area and kitchen space. Manufacturers are encouraged to locate the alarm in the living area remote from the kitchen and cooking appliances. A smoke alarm located within 20 feet horizontally of a cooking appliance must incorporate a temporary silencing feature or be of a photoelectric type.

(ii) In each room designed for sleeping.

(iii) On the ceiling of the upper level near the top or above each stairway, other than a basement stairway, in any multistory home completed in accordance with this part or part 3282 of this chapter. The alarm must be located so that smoke rising in the stairway cannot be prevented from reaching the alarm by an intervening door or obstruction.

(2) For each home designed to be placed over a basement, the manufacturer must provide a smoke alarm for

51

the basement and must install at the factory an electrical junction box for the installation of this smoke alarm and for its interconnection to other smoke alarms required by this section. The instructions for installers and information for homeowners required in paragraph (f) of this section must clearly indicate that a smoke alarm should be installed and is to be located on the basement ceiling near the stairway.

(3) A smoke alarm required under this section must not be placed in a location that impairs its effectiveness or in any of the following locations:

(i) Within 3 feet horizontally from any discharge grille when a home is equipped or designed for future installation of a roof-mounted evaporative cooler or other equipment discharging conditioned air through a ceiling grille into the living space; and

(ii) In any location or environment that is prohibited by the terms of its listing, except as permitted by this section.

(c) *Mounting requirements.* (1) Except in rooms with peaked sloping or shed sloping ceilings with a slope of more than 1.5/12 or as permitted pursuant to paragraph (e) of this section, smoke alarms must be mounted either:

(i) On the ceiling at least 4 inches from each wall; or

(ii) On a wall with the top of the alarm not less than 4 inches below the ceiling, and not farther from the ceiling than 12 inches or the distance from the ceiling specified in the smoke alarm manufacturer's listing and instructions, whichever is less.

(2) Except as permitted pursuant to paragraph (e) of this section, in rooms with peaked sloping ceilings with a slope of more than 1.5/12, smoke alarms must be mounted on the ceiling within 3 feet, measured horizontally, from the peak of the ceiling; at least 4 inches, measured vertically, below the peak of the ceiling; and at least 4 inches from any projecting structural element.

(3) Except as permitted pursuant to paragraph (e) of this section, in rooms with shed sloping ceilings with a slope of more than 1.5/12, smoke alarms must be mounted on the ceiling within 3 feet, measured horizontally, of the high side of the ceiling, and not closer than

4 inches from any adjoining wall surface and from any projecting structural element.

(d) *Connection to power source.* (1) Each smoke alarm must be powered from:

(i) The electrical system of the home as the primary power source and a battery as a secondary power source; or

(ii) A battery rated for a 10-year life, provided the smoke alarm is listed for use with a 10-year battery.

(2) Each smoke alarm whose primary power source is the home electrical system must be mounted on an electrical outlet box and connected by a permanent wiring method to a general electrical circuit. More than one smoke alarm is permitted to be placed on the same electrical circuit. The wiring circuit for the alarm must not include any switches between the overcurrent protective device and the alarm, and must not be protected by a ground fault circuit interrupter.

(3) Smoke alarms required under this section must be interconnected such that the activation of any one smoke alarm causes the alarm to be triggered in all required smoke alarms in the home.

(e) *Visible and tactile notification appliances.* (1) In addition to the smoke alarms required pursuant to this section, the manufacturer must provide visible and listed tactile notification appliances if these appliances are ordered by the purchaser or retailer before the home enters the first stage of production. These appliances are required to operate from the primary power source, but are not required to operate from a secondary power source.

(2) A visible notification appliance in a room designed for sleeping must have a minimum rating of 177 candela, except that when the visible notification appliance is wall-mounted or suspended more than 24 inches below the ceiling, a minimum rating of 110 candela is permitted.

(3) A visible notification appliance in an area other than a room designed for sleeping must have a minimum rating of 15 candela.

(f) *Testing and maintenance.* (1) Each required smoke alarm installed at the factory must be operationally tested, after conducting the dielectric test specified in §3280.810(a), in accordance with the alarm manufacturer's instructions. A smoke alarm that does not function as designed during the test and is not fixed so that it functions properly in the next retest must be replaced. Any replacement smoke alarm must be successfully tested in accordance with this paragraph.

(2) Home manufacturers must provide specific written instructions for installers on how to inspect and test the operation of smoke alarms during installation of the home. These instructions must indicate that any smoke alarm that does not meet the inspection or testing requirements needs to be replaced and retested.

(3) Home manufacturers must provide the homeowner with the alarm manufacturer's information describing the operation, method and frequency of testing, and proper maintenance of the smoke alarm. This information must be provided in same manner and location as the consumer manual required by §3282.207 of this chapter, but does not have to be incorporated into the consumer manual. No dealer, distributor, construction contractor, or other person shall interfere with the distribution of this information

[67 FR 12817, Mar. 19, 2002, as amended at 67 FR 49795, July 31, 2002. Redesignated at 78 FR 73982, Dec. 9, 2013]

§3280.210 Fire testing.

All fire testing conducted in accordance with this subpart shall be performed by nationally recognized testing laboratories which have expertise in fire technology. In case of dispute, the Secretary shall determine if a particular agency is qualified to perform such fire tests.

[49 FR 32011, Aug. 9, 1984. Redesignated at 78 FR 73982, Dec. 9, 2013]

Subpart D—Body and Frame Construction Requirements

§3280.301 Scope.

This subpart covers the minimum requirements for materials, products, equipment, and workmanship needed to assure that the manufactured home will provide the following:

(a) Structural strength and rigidity;

(b) Protection against corrosion, decay, insects, rodents, and other similar destructive forces;

(c) Protection against wind hazards;

(d) Resistance to the elements; and

(e) Durability and economy of maintenance.

[78 FR 73982, Dec. 9, 2013]

§3280.302 Definitions.

The following definitions are applicable to subpart D only:

Anchor assembly means any device or other means designed to transfer home anchoring loads to the ground.

Anchoring equipment means ties, straps, cables, turnbuckles, chains, and other approved components, including tensioning devices that are used to secure a manufactured home to anchor assemblies.

Anchoring system means a combination of anchoring equipment and anchor assemblies that will, when properly designed and installed, resist the uplift, overturning, and lateral forces on the manufactured home and on its support and foundation system.

Diagonal tie means a tie intended to resist horizontal or shear forces, but which may resist vertical, uplift, and overturning forces.

Footing: means that portion of the support system that transmits loads directly to the soil.

Foundation system means a system of support that is capable of transferring all design loads to the ground, including elements of the support system as defined in this section, or a site-built permanent foundation that meets the requirements of 24 CFR 3282.12.

Ground anchor means a specific anchoring assembly device designed to transfer home anchoring loads to the ground.

Loads: (1) *Dead load:* means the weight of all permanent construction including walls, floors, roof, partition, and fixed service equipment.

(2) *Live load:* means the weight superimposed by the use and occupancy of the manufactured home, including wind load and snow load, but not including dead load.

(3) *Wind load:* means the lateral or vertical pressure or uplift on the manufactured home due to wind blowing in any direction.

Main frame: means the structural component on which is mounted the body of the manufactured home.

Pier: means that portion of the support system between the footing and manufactured home exclusive of caps and shims.

Sheathing: means material which is applied on the exterior side of a building frame under the exterior weather resistant covering.

Stabilizing devices means all components of the anchoring and support systems, such as piers, footings, ties, anchoring equipment, anchoring assemblies, or any other equipment, materials, and methods of construction that support and secure the manufactured home to the ground.

Support system: means a combination of footings, piers, caps, and shims that will, when properly installed, support the manufactured home.

Support system means any pilings, columns, footings, piers, foundation walls, shims, and any combination thereof that, when properly installed, support the manufactured home.

Tie: means straps, cable, or securing devices used to connect the manufactured home to ground anchors.

Vertical tie: means a tie intended to resist the uplifting or overturning forces.

[58 FR 55005, Oct. 25, 1993; 59 FR 15113, Mar. 31, 1994, as amended at 72 FR 59361, Oct. 19, 2007]

§ 3280.303   General requirements.

(a) *Minimum requirements.* The design and construction of a manufactured home shall conform with the provisions of this standard. Requirements for any size, weight, or quality of material modified by the terms of *minimum, not less than, at least,* and similar expressions are minimum standards. The manufacturer or installer may exceed these standards provided such deviation does not result in any inferior installation or defeat the purpose and intent of this standard.

(b) *Construction.* All construction methods shall be in conformance with accepted engineering practices to insure durable, livable, and safe housing and shall demonstrate acceptable workmanship reflecting journeyman quality of work of the various trades.

(c) *Structural analysis.* The strength and rigidity of the component parts and/or the integrated structure shall be determined by engineering analysis or by suitable load tests to simulate the actual loads and conditions of application that occur. (See subparts E and J.)

(d) [Reserved]

(e) *New materials and methods.* (1) Any new material or method of construction not provided for in this standard and any material or method of questioned suitability proposed for use in the manufacture of the structure shall nevertheless conform in performance to the requirements of this standard.

(2) Unless based on accepted engineering design for the use indicated, all new manufactured home materials, equipment, systems or methods of construction not provided for in this standard shall be subjected to the tests specified in paragraph (g) of this section.

(f) *Allowable design stress.* The design stresses of all materials shall conform to accepted engineering practice. The use of materials not certified as to strength or stress grade shall be limited to the minimum allowable stresses under accepted engineering practice.

(g) *Alternative test procedures.* In the absence of recognized testing procedures either in the Standards in this part or in the applicable provisions of those standards incorporated in this part by reference, the manufacturer electing this option must develop or cause to be developed testing procedures to demonstrate the structural properties and significant characteristics of the material, assembly, sub-assembly component, or member, except for testing methods involving one-piece metal roofing as would be required in § 3280.305(c)(1)(iii). Such testing procedures become part of the manufacturer's approved design. Such tests must be witnessed by an independent licensed professional engineer or architect or by a recognized testing organization. Copies of the test results must be kept on file by the manufactured home manufacturer.

[40 FR 58752, Dec. 18, 1975. Redesignated at 44 FR 20679, Apr. 6, 1979, as amended at 58 FR 55005, Oct. 25, 1993; 59 FR 2469, Jan. 14, 1994; 70 FR 72043, Nov. 30, 2005]

§ 3280.304 Materials.

(a) Dimension and board lumber shall not exceed 19 percent moisture content at time of installation.

(b)(1) Standards for some of the generally used materials and methods of construction are listed in the following table:

Aluminum

Aluminum Design Manual, Specifications and Guidelines for Aluminum Structures, Part 1-A, Sixth Edition, October 1994, and Part 1-B, First Edition, October 1994.

Steel

Specification for Structural Steel Buildings—Allowable Stress Design and Plastic Design—AISC–S335, 1989. The following parts of this reference standard are not applicable: 1.3.3, 1.3.4, 1.3.5, 1.3.6, 1.4.6, 1.5.1.5, 1.5.5, 1.6, 1.7, 1.8, 1.9, 1.10.4 through 1.10.7, 1.10.9, 1.11, 1.13, 1.14.5, 1.17.7 through 1.17.9, 1.19.1, 1.19.3, 1.20, 1.21, 1.23.7, 1.24, 1.25.1 through 1.25.5, 1.26.4, 2.3, 2.4, 2.8 through 2.10.
Specification for the Design of Cold-Formed Steel Structural Members—AISI–1996.
Specification for the Design of Cold-Formed Stainless Steel Structural Members—SEI/ASCE 8–02, 2002.
Standard Specifications Load Tables and Weight Tables for Steel Joists and Joist Girders, SJI, Fortieth Edition, 1994.
Structural Applications of Steel Cables for Buildings—ASCE19, 1996.
Standard Specification for Strapping, Flat Steel and Seals—ASTM D3953, 1991.

Wood and Wood Products

Basic Hardboard—ANSI/AHA A135.4–1995.
Prefinished Hardboard Paneling—ANSI/AHA A135.5–1995.
Hardboard Siding—ANSI/AHA A135.6–1998.
American National Standard for Hardwood and Decorative Plywood—ANSI/HPVA HP–1–1994 (Approved 1995).
Structural Design Guide for Hardwood Plywood Wall Panels—HPVA Design Guide HP–SG–96, 1996.
For wood products—Structural Glued Laminated Timber—ANSI/AITC A190.1–1992.
Construction and Industrial Plywood (With Typical APA Trademarks)—PS 1–95.
APA Design/Construction Guide, Residential and Commercial—APA E30-P–1996.
Design Specifications for Metal Plate and Wood Connected Trusses—TPI–85.
Design and Fabrication of All-Plywood Beams—APA H–815E (PDS Supplement #5), 1995.
Panel Design Specification—APA D410A, 2004.
Design and Fabrication of Glued Plywood-Lumber Beams, Supplement# 2—APA S 812R, 1992 (incorporated by reference, see § 3280.4).
Design and Fabrication of Plywood Curved Panels—APA–S 811M, Suppl. 1, 1990.
Design and Fabrication of Plywood Sandwich Panels, Supplement #4—APA U 814H, 1990 (incorporated by reference, see § 3280.4).
Performance Standard for Wood-Based Structural Use Panels—NIST PS 2–04, 2004 (incorporated by reference, see § 3280.4).
Design and Fabrication of Plywood Stressed-Skin Panels, Supplement 3—APA–U 813L, 1992 (incorporated by reference, see § 3280.4).
National Design Specifications for Wood Construction, 2001 Edition, with Supplement, Design Values for Wood Construction, NDS–2001, ANSI/AFPA.
Wood Structural Design Data, 1986 Edition with 1992 Revisions, AFPA.
Span Tables for Joists and Rafters—PS–20–70, 1993, AFPA.
Design Values for Joists and Rafters 1992, AFPA.
Particleboard—ANSI A208.1–1999.
Voluntary Specifications for Aluminum, Vinyl (PVC) and Wood Windows and Glass Doors—ANSI/AAMA/NWWDA 101/I.S.2–97.
Standard Test Methods for Puncture and Stiffness of Paperboard, and Corrugated and Solid Fiberboard—ASTM D781, 1973.
Standard Test Methods for Direct Moisture Content Measurement of Wood and Wood-Base Materials—ASTM D 4442–92 (Re-approved 1997), 1997.
Standard Test Methods for Use and Calibration of Hand-Held Moisture Meters—ASTM D4444, 1992.
Engineered Wood Construction Guide—APA E30R 2001 (incorporated by reference, see § 3280.4).
Medium Density Fiberboard (MDF) For Interior Applications—ANSI A208.2–2002 (incorporated by reference, see § 3280.4).

Other

Standard Specification for Gypsum Wallboard—ASTM C 36/C 36M–99, 1999.

Fasteners

National Evaluation Report, Power Driven Staples, Nails, and Allied Fasteners for Use in All Types of Building Construction—NER–272, 1997.

Unclassified

Minimum Design Loads for Buildings and Other Structures—ASCE 7–1988.
Standard for Safety Glazing Materials used in Buildings—Safety Performance Specifications and Methods of Test, ANSI Z97.1–2004 (incorporated by reference, see § 3280.4).

(2) Materials and methods of construction utilized in the design and

construction of manufactured homes which are covered by the standards in the following table, or any applicable portion thereof shall comply with these requirements.

(3) Engineering analysis and testing methods contained in these references shall be utilized to judge conformance with accepted engineering practices required in § 3280.303(c).

(4) Materials and methods of installation conforming to these standards shall be considered acceptable when installed in conformance with the requirements of this part.

(5) Materials meeting the standards (or the applicable portion thereof) are considered acceptable unless otherwise specified herein or unless substantial doubt exists as to conformance.

(c) Wood products shall be identified as complying with the appropriate standards.

[40 FR 58752, Dec. 18, 1975, as amended at 42 FR 961, Jan. 4, 1977. Redesignated at 44 FR 20679, Apr. 6, 1979, as amended at 58 FR 55006, Oct. 25, 1993; 59 FR 15113, Mar. 31, 1994; 70 FR 72043, Nov. 30, 2005; 78 FR 73982, Dec. 9, 2013]

§ 3280.305 Structural design requirements.

(a) *General.* Each manufactured home shall be designed and constructed as a completely integrated structure capable of sustaining the design load requirements of this standard, and shall be capable of transmitting these loads to stabilizing devices without exceeding the allowable stresses or deflections. Roof framing shall be securely fastened to wall framing, walls to floor structure, and floor structure to chassis to secure and maintain continuity between the floor and chassis, so as to resist wind overturning, uplift, and sliding as imposed by design loads in this part. Uncompressed finished flooring greater than 1/8 inch in thickness shall not extend beneath load-bearing walls that are fastened to the floor structure.

(b) *Design loads*—(1) *Design dead loads.* Design dead loads shall be the actual dead load supported by the structural assembly under consideration.

(2) *Design live loads.* The design live loads and wind and snow loads shall be as specified in this section and shall be considered to be uniformly distributed.

The roof live load or snow load shall not be considered as acting simultaneously with the wind load and the roof live or snow load and floor live loads shall not be considered as resisting the overturning moment due to wind.

(3) When engineering calculations are performed, allowable unit stresses may be increased as provided in the documents referenced in § 3280.304 except as otherwise indicated in §§ 3280.304(b)(1) and 3280.306(a).

(4) Whenever the roof slope does not exceed 20 degrees, the design horizontal wind loads required by § 3280.305(c)(1) may be determined without including the vertical roof projection of the manufactured home. However, regardless of the roof slope of the manufactured home, the vertical roof projection shall be included when determining the wind loading for split level or clerestory-type roof systems.

(c) *Wind, snow, and roof loads*—(1) *Wind loads—design requirements.* (i) *Standard wind loads (Zone I).* When a manufactured home is not designed to resist the wind loads for high-wind areas (Zone II or Zone III) specified in paragraph (c)(1)(ii) of this section, the manufactured home and each of its wind-resisting parts and portions must be designed for horizontal wind loads of not less than 15 psf and a net uplift roof load of not less than 9 psf. The net uplift roof load must not be reduced by the dead load of the roof structure for the purposes of engineering design or structural load testing.

(ii) *Wind loads for high wind areas (Zone II and Zone III).* When designed for high wind areas (Zone II and Zone III), the manufactured home, each of its wind resisting parts (including, but not limited to, shear walls, diaphragms, ridge beams, and their fastening and anchoring systems), and its components and cladding materials (including, but not limited to, roof trusses, wall studs, exterior sheathing, roofing and siding materials, exterior glazing, and their connections and fasteners) shall be designed by a Professional Engineer or Architect to resist:

(A) The design wind loads for Exposure C specified in ANSI/ASCE 7-88, "Minimum Design Loads for Buildings and Other Structures," for a fifty-year recurrence interval, and a design wind speed of 100 mph, as specified for Wind Zone II, or 110 mph, as specified for

Wind Zone III (Basic Wind Zone Map); or

(B) The wind pressures specified in the following table:

TABLE OF DESIGN WIND PRESSURES

Element	Wind zone II design wind speed 100 MPH	Wind zone III design wind speed 110 MPH
Anchorage for lateral and vertical stability (See §3280.306(a)):		
Net Horizontal Drag [1] [2]:	[3] ±39 PSF	[3] ±47 PSF
Uplift [4]:	[5] − 27 PSF	− 32 PSF
Main wind force resisting system:		
Shearwalls, Diaphragms and their Fastening and Anchorage Systems [1] [2]	±39 PSF	±47 PSF
Ridge beams and other Main Roof Support Beams (Beams supporting expanding room sections, etc.)	− 30 PSF	− 36 PSF
Components and cladding:		
Roof trusses [4] in all areas; trusses shall be doubled within 3′-0′ from each end of the roof	[5] − 39 PSF	[5] − 47 PSF
Exterior roof coverings, sheathing and fastenings [4],[6],[7] in all areas except the following	[5] − 39 PSF	[5] − 47 PSF
Within 3′-0′ from each gable end (overhang at end wall) of the roof or endwall if no overhang is provided [4],[6],[7]	[5] − 73 PSF	[5] − 89 PSF
Within 3′-0′ from the ridge and eave (overhang at sidewall) or sidewall if no eave is provided [4],[6],[7]	[5] − 51 PSF	[5] − 62 PSF
Eaves (Overhangs at Sidewalls) [4],[6],[7]	[5] − 51 PSF	[5] − 62 PSF
Gables (Overhangs at Endwalls) [4],[6],[7]	[5] − 73 PSF	[5] − 89 PSF
Wall studs in sidewalls and endwalls, exterior windows and sliding glass doors (glazing and framing), exterior coverings, sheathing and fastenings [8]:		
Within 3′-0′ from each corner of the sidewall and endwall	±48 PSF	±58 PSF
All other areas	±38 PSF	±46 PSF

NOTES:

[1] The net horizontal drag of ±39 PSF to be used in calculating Anchorage for Lateral and Vertical Stability and for the design of Main Wind Force Resisting Systems is based on a distribution of wind pressures of + 0.8 or + 24 PSF to the windward wall and − 0.5 or − 15 PSF to the leeward wall.

[2] Horizontal drag pressures need not be applied to roof projections when the roof slope does not exceed 20 degrees.

[3] + sign would mean pressures are acting towards or on the structure; − sign means pressures are acting away from the structure; ±sign means forces can act in either direction, towards or away from the structure.

[4] Design values in this "Table" are only applicable to roof slopes between 10 degrees (nominal 2/12 slope) and 30 degrees.

[5] The design uplift pressures are the same whether they are applied normal to the surface of the roof or to the horizontal projection of the roof.

[6] Shingle roof coverings that are secured with 6 fasteners per shingle through an underlayment which is cemented to a 3/8″ structural rated roof sheathing need not be evaluated for these design wind pressures.

[7] Structural rated roof sheathing that is at least 3/8″ in thickness, installed with the long dimension perpendicular to roof framing supports, and secured with fasteners at 4″ on center within 3′-0′ of each gable end or endwall if no overhang is provided and 6″ on center in all other areas, need not be evaluated for these design wind pressures.

[8] Exterior coverings that are secured at 6″ o.c. to a 3/8″ structural rated sheathing that is fastened to wall framing members at 6″ on center need not be evaluated for these design wind pressures.

(iii) One-piece metal roofing capable of resisting the design wind pressures for "Components and Cladding: (Exterior roof coverings)" in the Table for Design Wind Pressures in this section is allowed to be used without structural sheathing, provided the metal roofing is tested using procedures that have been approved by HUD and that meet all requirements of §§ 3280.303(c) and (g) and 3280.401.

(2) *Wind loads—zone designations.* The Wind Zone and specific wind design load requirements are determined by the fastest basic wind speed (mph) within each Zone and the intended location, based on the Basic Wind Zone Map, as follows:

(i) *Wind Zone I.* Wind Zone I consists of those areas on the Basic Wind Zone Map that are not identified in paragraphs (c)(2)(ii) or (iii) of this section as being within Wind Zone II or III, respectively.

(ii) *Wind Zone II.....100 mph.* The following areas are deemed to be within Wind Zone II of the Basic Wind Zone Map:

Local governments: The following local governments listed by State (counties, unless specified otherwise):

Alabama: Baldwin and Mobile.

Florida: All counties except those identified in paragraph (c)(1)(i)(C) of this section as within Wind Zone III.

Georgia: Bryan, Camden, Chatham, Glynn, Liberty, McIntosh.

Louisiana: Parishes of Acadia, Allen, Ascension, Assumption, Calcasieu, Cameron, East Baton Rouge, East Feliciana, Evangeline, Iberia, Iberville, Jefferson Davis, La-Fayette, Livingston, Pointe Coupee, St. Helena, St. James, St. John the Baptist, St. Landry, St. Martin, St. Tammany, Tangipahoa, Vermillion, Washington, West Baton Rouge, and West Feliciana.

Maine: Hancock and Washington.

Massachusetts: Barnstable, Bristol, Dukes, Nantucket, and Plymouth.

Mississippi: George, Hancock, Harrison, Jackson, Pearl River, and Stone.

North Carolina: Beaufort, Brunswick, Camden, Chowan, Columbus, Craven, Currituck, Jones, New Hanover, Onslow, Pamlico, Pasquotank, Pender, Perquimans, Tyrrell, and Washington.

South Carolina: Beaufort, Berkeley, Charleston, Colleton, Dorchester, Georgetown, Horry, Jasper, and Williamsburg.

Texas: Aransas, Brazoria, Calhoun, Cameron, Chambers, Galveston, Jefferson, Kenedy, Kleberg, Matagorda, Nueces, Orange, Refugio, San Patricio, and Willacy.

Virginia: Cities of Chesapeake, Norfolk, Portsmouth, Princess Anne, and Virginia Beach.

(iii) *Wind Zone III.....*110 mph. The following areas are considered to be within Wind Zone III of the Basic Wind Zone Map:

(A) *States and Territories:* The entire State of Hawaii, the coastal regions of Alaska (as determined by the 90 mph isotach on the ANSI/ASCE 7-88 map), and all of the U.S. Territories of American Samoa, Guam, Northern Mariana Islands, Puerto Rico, Trust Territory of the Pacific Islands, and the United States Virgin Islands.

(B) *Local governments:* The following local governments listed by State (counties, unless specified otherwise):

Florida: Broward, Charlotte, Collier, Dade, Franklin, Gulf, Hendry, Lee, Martin, Manatee, Monroe, Palm Beach, Pinellas, and Sarasota.

Louisiana: Parishes of Jefferson, La Fourche, Orleans, Plaquemines, St. Bernard, St. Charles, St. Mary, and Terrabonne.

North Carolina: Carteret, Dare, and Hyde.

(iv) *Consideration of local requirements.* For areas where wind mapping data or records or the requirements of the State or local authority indicate wind speeds in excess of those identified in this section, the Department may establish, through rulemaking, more stringent requirements for manufactured homes to be installed in such areas.

(3) *Snow and roof loads.* (i) Flat, curved and pitched roofs shall be designed to resist the following live loads, applied downward on the horizontal projection as appropriate for the design zone marked on the manufactured home:

Zone (see Map in § 3280.305(c)(4))	Pounds per square foot
North Zone	40
Middle Zone	30
South Zone	20

(A) *North Roof Load Zone.* The following counties in each of the following states are deemed to be within the North Roof Load Zone:

Maine—Aroostook, Piscataquis, Somerset, Penobscot, Waldo, Knox, Hancock, and Washington.

Alaska—All Counties

(B) *Middle Roof Load Zone.* The following counties in each of the following states are deemed to be within the Middle Roof Load Zone:

States	Counties			
South Dakota	Grant	Brookings	Hanson	Lincoln
	Codington	Miner	Minnehaha	Yankton
	Deuel	Lake	Hutchinson	Union
	Hamlin	Moody	Turner	Clay
	Kingsbury	McCook		
Minnesota	Koochiching	Stearns	Renville	Sibley
	Itasca	Swift	McLeod	Nicollet
	Hubbard	Kandiyohi	Carver	Blue Earth
	Cass	Meeker	Dakota	Martin
	Crow Wing	Wright	Goodhue	Watonwan
	Aitkin	Lac qui Parle	Wabasha	Brown
	St. Louis	Chippewa	Winona	Redwood
	Lake	Yellow Medicine	Fillmore	Lyon
	Cook	Mille Lacs	Mower	Lincoln

States	Counties			
	Carlton	Kanabec	Olmsted	Pipestone
	Pine	Benton	Dodge	Murray
	Wadena	Isanti	Rice	Cottonwood
	Todd	Sherburne	Steele	Jackson
	Morrison	Anoka	Freeborn	Nobles
	Douglas	Chisapo	Faribault	Rock
	Grant	Washington	Waseca	
	Stevens	Hennepin	Le Sueur	
	Pope	Ramsey	Scott	
Iowa	Hancock	Mitchell	Hamilton	Buena Vista
	Lyon	Howard	Webster	Cherokee
	Osceola	Chickasaw	Calhoun	Plymouth
	Dickinson	Butler	Sac	Sioux
	Emmet	Floyd	Ida	O'Brien
	Kossuth	Cerro Gordo	Humboldt	Clay
	Winnebago	Franklin	Pocahontas	Wright
	Worth	Hardin	Palo Alto	
Wisconsin	Douglas	Oconto	Pepin	Lincoln
	Bayfield	Menominee	Pierce	Oneida
	Ashland	Langlade	Dunn	Polk
	Iron	Marathon	Eau Claire	Burnett
	Vilas	Clark	Chippewa	Washburn
	Forest	Jackson	Rusk	Sawyer
	Florence	Trempealeau	Barron	Price
	Marinette	Buffalo	Taylor	Door
	St. Croix			
Michigan	Houghton	Iron	Presque Isle	Wexford
	Baraga	Dickinson	Charlevoix	Benzie
	Marquette	Menominee	Montmorency	Grand Traverse
	Alger	Delta	Alpena	Kalkaska
	Luce	Schoolcraft	Alcona	Oscoda
	Chippewa	Mackinac	Ogemaw	Otsego
	Keweenaw	Cheyboygan	Roscommon	Leelanau
	Ontonagon	Emmet	Missaukee	Antrim
	Gogebic	Crawford		
New York	St. Lawrence	Herkimer	Onondaga	Genesee
	Franklin	Lewis	Madison	Orleans
	Clinton	Oswego	Cayuga	Niagara
	Essex	Jefferson	Seneca	Erie
	Hamilton	Oneida	Wayne	Wyoming
	Warren	Fulton	Ontario	Monroe
	Saratoga	Montgomery	Yates	
	Washington	Schenectady	Livingston	
Massachusetts	Essex			
Maine	Franklin	Kennebec	Lincoln	Cumberland
	Oxford	Androscoggin	Sagadahoc	York
Montana	All Counties			
Idaho	All Counties			
Colorado	All Counties			
Wyoming	All Counties			
Utah	All Counties			
Vermont	Franklin	Orleans	Caledonia	Addison
	Grand Isle	Essex	Washington	Rutland
	Lamoille	Chittenden	Orange	Windsor
New Hampshire	All Counties			

(C) *South Roof Load Zone.* The states and counties that are not listed for the North Roof Load Zone in paragraph

59

(c)(3)(i)(A) of this section, or the Middle Roof Load Zone in paragraph (c)(3)(i)(B) of this section, are deemed to be within the South Roof Load Zone.

(ii) *Consideration of local requirements.* For exposures in areas (mountainous or other) where recognized snow records, wind records, or the requirements of the State or local authority indicate significant differences from the loads stated in this paragraph (c)(3), the Department may establish, through rulemaking, more stringent requirements for manufactured homes to be installed in such areas. For snow loads, such requirements must be based on a roof snow load of 0.6 of the ground snow load for areas exposed to wind and a roof snow load of 0.8 of the ground snow load for sheltered areas.

(iii) Eaves and cornices shall be designed for a net uplift pressure of 2.5 times the design uplift wind pressure cited in § 3280.305(c)(1)(i) for Wind Zone I, and for the design pressures cited in § 3280.305(c)(1)(ii) for Wind Zones II and III.

(iv) Skylights must be capable of withstanding roof loads as specified in paragraphs (c)(3)(i) or (c)(3)(ii) of this section. Skylights must be listed and tested in accordance with AAMA 1600/I.S.7–00, 2003, Voluntary Specification for Skylights.

(4) *Data plate requirements.* The Data Plate posted in the manufactured home (see § 3280.5) shall designate the wind and roof load zones or, if designed for higher loads, the actual design external snow and wind loads for which the home has been designed. The Data Plate shall include reproductions of the Load Zone Maps shown in this paragraph (c)(4), with any related information. The Load Zone Maps shall be not less than either 3½ in. by 2¼ in., or one-half the size illustrated in the Code of Federal Regulations.

Basic Wind Zone Map for Manufactured Housing

NOTE: See Section 3280.305(c)(2) for areas included in each Wind Zone.

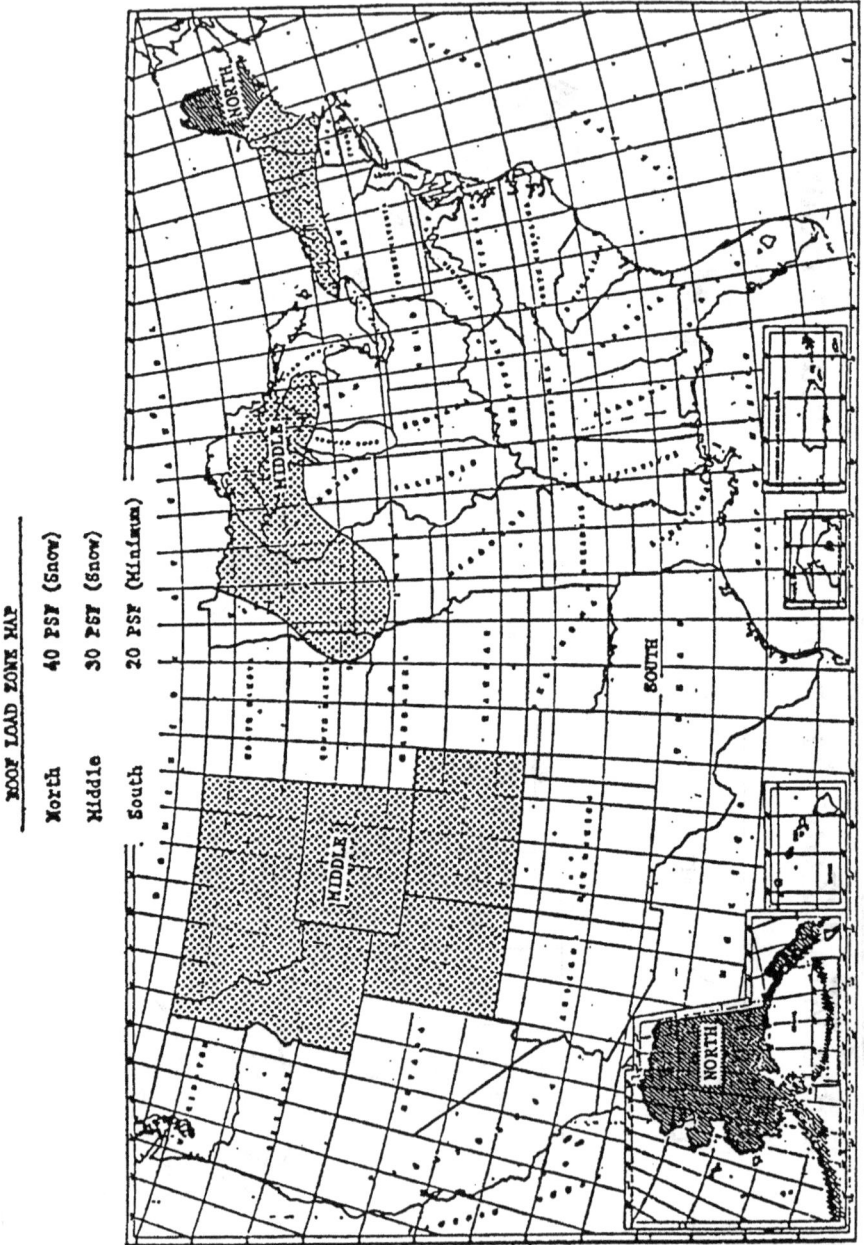

ROOF LOAD ZONE MAP

North   40 PSF (Snow)
Middle   30 PSF (Snow)
South   20 PSF (Minimum)

(d) *Design load deflection.* (1) When a structural assembly is subjected to total design live loads, the deflection for structural framing members shall not exceed the following (where L equals the clear span between supports or two times the length of a cantilever):

Floor—L/240
Roof and ceiling—L/180
Headers, beams, and girders (vertical load)—L/180
Walls and partitions—L/180

(2) The allowable eave or cornice deflection for uplift is to be measured at the design uplift load of 9 psf for Wind Zone I, and at the design uplift pressure cited in paragraph (c)(1)(ii) of this section for Wind Zones II and III. The allowable deflection shall be (2 × Lc)/180, where Lc is the measured horizontal eave projection from the wall.

(e) *Fastening of structural systems.* (1) Roof framing must be securely fastened to wall framing, walls to floor structure, and floor structure to chassis, to secure and maintain continuity between the floor and chassis in order to resist wind overturning, uplift, and sliding, and to provide continuous load paths for these forces to the foundation or anchorage system. The number and type of fasteners used must be capable of transferring all forces between elements being joined.

(2) For Wind Zone II and Wind Zone III, roof framing members must be securely fastened at the vertical bearing points to resist design overturning, uplift, and sliding forces. When engineered connectors are not installed, roof framing members must be secured at the vertical bearing points to wall framing members (studs), and wall framing members (studs) must be secured to floor framing members, with 0.016 inch base metal, minimum steel strapping or engineered connectors, or by a combination of 0.016 inch base metal, minimum steel strapping or engineered connectors, and structural-rated wall sheathing that overlaps the roof and floor system if substantiated by structural analysis or by suitable load tests. Steel strapping or engineered connectors are to be installed at a maximum spacing of 24 inches on center in Wind Zone II, and 16 inches on center in Wind Zone III. *Exception:* Where substantiated by structural analysis or suitable load tests, the 0.016 inch base metal minimum steel strapping or engineered connectors may be omitted at the roof to wall and/or wall to floor connections, when structural rated sheathing that overlaps the roof and wall and/or wall and floor is capable of resisting the applicable design wind loads.

(f) *Walls.* The walls shall be of sufficient strength to withstand the load requirements as defined in § 3280.305(c) of this part, without exceeding the deflections as specified in § 3280.305(d). The connections between the bearing walls, floor, and roof framework members shall be fabricated in such a manner as to provide support for the material used to enclose the manufactured home and to provide for transfer of all lateral and vertical loads to the floor and chassis.

(1) Except where substantiated by engineering analysis or tests, studs shall not be notched or drilled in the middle one-third of their length.

(2) Interior walls and partitions shall be constructed with structural capacity adequate for the intended purpose and shall be capable of resisting a horizontal load of not less than five pounds per square foot. An allowable stress increase of 1.33 times the permitted published design values may be used in the design of wood framed interior partitions. Finish of walls and partitions shall be securely fastened to wall framing.

(g) *Floors.* (1) Floor assemblies shall be designed in accordance with accepted engineering practice standards to support a minimum uniform live load of 40 lb/ft^2 plus the dead load of the materials. In addition (but not simultaneously), floors shall be able to support a 200–pound concentrated load on a one-inch diameter disc at the most critical location with a maximum deflection not to exceed one-eighth inch relative to floor framing. Perimeter wood joists of more than six inches depth shall be stabilized against overturning from superimposed loads as follows: at ends by solid blocking not less than two-inch thickness by full depth of joist, or by connecting to a continuous header not less than two-inch thickness and not less than the depth of the joist with connecting devices; at eight-feet maximum intermediate spacing by solid blocking or by wood cross-bridging of not less than one inch by three inches, metal cross-bridging of equal strength, or by other approved methods.

(2) Wood, wood fiber or plywood floors or subfloors in kitchens, bathrooms (including toilet compartments), laundry areas, water heater compartments, and any other areas subject to excessive moisture shall be moisture resistant or shall be made moisture resistant by sealing or by an overlay of nonabsorbent material applied with water-resistant adhesive. Use of one of the following methods would meet this requirement:

(i) Sealing the floor with a water-resistant sealer; or

(ii) Installing an overlay of a non-absorbent floor covering material applied with water-resistant adhesive; or

(iii) Direct application of a water-resistant sealer to the exposed wood floor area when covered with a non-absorbent overlay; or

(iv) The use of a non-absorbent floor covering which may be installed without a continuous application of a water-resistant adhesive or sealant when the floor covering meets the following criteria:

(A) The covering is a continuous membrane with any seams or patches seam bonded or welded to preserve the continuity of the floor covering; and

(B) The floor is protected at all penetrations in these areas by sealing with a compatible water-resistant adhesive or sealant to prevent moisture from migrating under the nonabsorbent floor covering; and

(C) The covering is fastened around the perimeter of the subfloor in accordance with the floor covering manufacturer's instructions; and,

(D) The covering is designed to be installed to prevent moisture penetration without the use of a water-resistant adhesive or sealer except as required in this paragraph (g). The vertical edges of penetrations for plumbing shall be covered with a moisture-resistant adhesive or sealant. The vertical penetrations located under the bottom plates of perimeter walls of rooms, areas, or compartments are not required to be sealed; this does not include walls or partitions within the rooms or areas.

(3) Wood panel products used as floor or subfloor materials on the exterior of the home, such as in recessed entryways, must be rated for exterior exposure and protected from moisture

by sealing or applying nonabsorbent overlay with water resistant adhesive.

(4) Carpet or carpet pads shall not be installed under concealed spaces subject to excessive moisture, such as plumbing fixture spaces, floor areas under installed laundry equipment. Carpet may be installed in laundry space provided:

(i) The appliances are not provided;

(ii) The conditions of paragraph (g)(2) of this section are followed; and

(iii) Instructions are provided to remove carpet when appliances are installed.

(5) Except where substantiated by engineering analysis or tests:

(i) Notches on the ends of joists shall not exceed one-fourth the joist depth.

(ii) Holes bored in joists shall not be within 2 inches of the top or bottom of the joist, and the diameter of any such hole shall not exceed one-third the depth of the joist.

(iii) Notches in the top or bottom of the joists shall not exceed one-sixth the depth and shall not be located in the middle third of the span.

(6) Bottom board material (with or without patches) shall meet or exceed the level of 48 inch-pounds of puncture resistance as tested by the Beach Puncture Test in accordance with Standard Test Methods for Puncture and Stiffness of Paperboard, and Corrugated and Solid Fiberboard, ASTM D–781–1968 (73). The material shall be suitable for patches and the patch life shall be equivalent to the material life. Patch installation instruction shall be included in the manufactured home manufacturer's instructions.

(h) *Roofs.* (1) Roofs shall be of sufficient strength to withstand the load requirements as defined in § 3280.305 (b) and (c) without exceeding the deflections specified in § 3280.305(d). The connections between roof framework members and bearing walls shall be fabricated in such a manner to provide for the transfer of design vertical and horizontal loads to the bearing walls and to resist uplift forces.

(2) Roofing membranes shall be of sufficient rigidity to prevent deflection which would permit ponding of water or separation of seams due to wind, snow, ice, erection or transportation forces.

(3) Cutting of roof framework members for passage of electrical, plumbing or mechanical systems shall not be allowed except where substantiated by engineering analysis.

(4) All roof penetrations for electrical, plumbing or mechanical systems shall be properly flashed and sealed. In addition, where a metal roof membrane is penetrated, a wood backer shall be installed. The backer plate shall be not less than 5/16 inch plywood, with exterior glues, secured to the roof framing system beneath the metal roof, and shall be of a size to assure that all screws securing the flashing are held by the backer plate.

(i) *Frame construction.* The frame shall be capable of transmitting all design loads to stabilizing devices without exceeding the allowable load and deflections of this section. The frame shall also be capable of withstanding the effects of transportation shock and vibration without degradation as required by subpart J.

(1) [Reserved]

(2) *Protection of metal frames against corrosion.* Metal frames shall be made corrosion resistant or protected against corrosion. Metal frames may be protected against corrosion by painting.

(j) *Welded connections.* (1) All welds must be made in accordance with the applicable provisions of the Specification for Structural Steel Buildings, Allowable Stress Design and Plastic Design, AISC–S335, 1989; the Specification for the Design of Cold-Formed Steel Structural Members, AISI, 1996; and the Specification for the Design of Cold-Formed Stainless Steel Structural Members, SEI/ASCE 8–02, 2002.

(2) Regardless of the provisions of any reference standard contained in this subpart, deposits of weld slag or flux shall be required to be removed only from welded joints at the following locations:

(i) Drawbar and coupling mechanisms;

(ii) Main member splices, and

(iii) Spring hanger to main member connections.

(k) *Attics.* (1) For roofs with slopes 7:12 or greater, the area of the attic floor that meets the ceiling-height/living-space requirements of these construction and safety standards must be designed to resist a minimum design live load of 40 pounds per square foot (psf) in accordance with paragraph (g) of this section.

(2) For roofs with slopes less than 7:12 that contain an attic area or for portions of roofs with slopes 7:12 or greater that do meet the ceiling height/living space requirements of the standards, the attic floor must be designed for a storage live load of 20 pounds per square foot (psf).

[40 FR 58752, Dec. 18, 1975. Redesignated at 44 FR 20679, Apr. 6, 1979, as amended at 44 FR 66195, Nov. 19, 1979; 52 FR 4582, Feb. 12, 1987; 58 FR 55006, Oct. 25, 1993; 59 FR 2469, Jan. 14, 1994; 59 FR 15113, 15114, Mar. 31, 1994; 62 FR 54547, Oct. 20, 1997; 70 FR 72043, Nov. 30, 2005; 71 FR 19638, Apr. 17, 2006; 78 FR 73983, Dec. 9, 2013; 80 FR 53727, Sept. 8, 2015]

§ 3280.306 Windstorm protection.

(a) *Provisions for support and anchoring systems.* Each manufactured home shall have provisions for support/anchoring or foundation systems that, when properly designed and installed, will resist overturning and lateral movement (sliding) of the manufactured home as imposed by the respective design loads. For Wind Zone I, the design wind loads to be used for calculating resistance to overturning and lateral movement shall be the simultaneous application of the wind loads indicated in § 3280.305(c)(1)(i), increased by a factor of 1.5. The 1.5 factor of safety for Wind Zone I is also to be applied simultaneously to both the vertical building projection, as horizontal wind load, and across the surface of the full roof structure, as uplift loading. For Wind Zones II and III, the resistance shall be determined by the simultaneous application of the horizontal drag and uplift wind loads, in accordance with § 3280.305(c)(1)(ii). The basic allowable stresses of materials required to resist overturning and lateral movement shall not be increased in the design and proportioning of these members. No additional shape or location factors need to be applied in the design of the tiedown system. The dead load of the structure may be used to resist these wind loading effects in all Wind Zones.

(1) The provisions of this section shall be followed and the support and anchoring systems shall be designed by a Registered Professional Engineer or Architect.

(2) The manufacturer of each manufactured home is required to make provision for the support and anchoring systems but is not required to provide the anchoring equipment or stabilizing devices. When the manufacturer's installation instructions provide for the main frame structure to be used as the points for connection of diagonal ties, no specific connecting devices need be provided on the main frame structure.

(b) *Contents of instructions.* (1) The manufacturer must provide printed instructions with each manufactured home that specify the location and required capacity of stabilizing devices on which the home's design is based. The manufacturer must identify by paint, label, decal stencil, or other means: the location of each column support pier location required along the marriage line(s) of multi-section manufactured homes; each pier location required along the perimeter of the home; each required shear wall pier support; and any other special pier support locations specified in the manufacturer's printed instructions. Such identifications must be visible after the home is installed. The manufacturer must provide drawings and specifications, certified by a registered professional engineer or architect, that indicate at least one acceptable system of anchoring, including the details or required straps or cables, their end connections, and all other devices needed to transfer the wind loads from the manufactured home to an anchoring or foundation system.

(2) For anchoring systems, the instructions shall indicate:

(i) The minimum anchor capacity required;

(ii) That anchors should be certified by a professional engineer, architect, or a nationally recognized testing laboratory as to their resistance, based on the maximum angle of diagonal tie and/or vertical tie loading (see paragraph (c)(3) of this section) and angle of anchor installation, and type of soil in which the anchor is to be installed;

(iii) That ground anchors are to be embedded below the frost line, unless the foundation system is frost-protected in accordance with §§ 3285.312(b) and 3285.404 of the Model Manufactured Home Installation Standards in this chapter.

(iv) That ground anchors must be installed to their full depth, and stabilizer plates must be installed in accordance with the ground anchor listing or certification to provide required resistance to overturning and sliding.

(v) That anchoring equipment should be certified by a registered professional engineer or architect to resist these specified forces in accordance with testing procedures in ASTM D3953–97, Standard Specification for Strapping, Flat Steel and Seals (incorporated by reference, see § 3280.4).

(c) *Design criteria.* The provisions made for anchoring systems shall be based on the following design criteria for manufactured homes.

(1) The minimum number of ties provided per side of each home shall resist design wind loads required in § 3280.305(c)(1).

(2) Ties shall be as evenly spaced as practicable along the length of the manufactured home, with not more than two (2) feet open-end spacing on each end.

(3) Vertical ties or straps shall be positioned at studs. Where a vertical tie and a diagonal tie are located at the same place, both ties may be connected to a single anchor, provided that the anchor used is capable of carrying both loadings, simultaneously.

(4) Add-on sections of expandable manufactured homes shall have provisions for vertical ties at the exposed ends.

(d) *Requirements for ties.* Manufactured homes in Wind Zone I require only diagonal ties. These ties shall be placed along the main frame and below the outer side walls. All manufactured homes designed to be located in Wind Zones II and III shall have a vertical tie installed at each diagonal tie location.

(e) *Protection requirements.* Protection shall be provided at sharp corners where the anchoring system requires the use of external straps or cables. Protection shall also be provided to minimize damage to siding by the cable or strap.

(f) *Anchoring equipment—load resistance.* Anchoring equipment shall be capable of resisting an allowable working load equal to or exceeding 3,150 pounds and shall be capable of withstanding a 50 percent overload (4,725 pounds total) without failure of either the anchoring equipment or the attachment point on the manufactured home.

(g) *Anchoring equipment—weatherization.* Anchoring equipment exposed to weathering shall have a resistance to weather deterioration at least equivalent to that provided by a coating of zinc on steel of not less than 0.30 ounces per square foot of surface coated, and in accordance with the following:

(1) Slit or cut edges of zinc-coated steel strapping do not need to be zinc coated.

(2) Type 1, Finish B, Grade 1 steel strapping, 1¼ inches wide and 0.035 inches in thickness, certified by a registered professional engineer or architect as conforming with ASTM D3953–97, Standard Specification for Strapping, Flat Steel and Seals (incorporated by reference, see § 3280.4).

[40 FR 58752, Dec. 18, 1975. Redesignated at 44 FR 20679, Apr. 6, 1979, as amended at 52 FR 4583, Feb. 12, 1987; 59 FR 2473, Jan. 14, 1994; 70 FR 72045, Nov. 30, 2005; 72 FR 59362, Oct. 19, 2007; 78 FR 73983, Dec. 9, 2013]

§ 3280.307 Resistance to elements and use.

(a) Exterior coverings shall be of moisture and weather resistive materials attached with corrosion resistant fasteners to resist wind, snow and rain. Metal coverings and exposed metal structural members shall be of corrosion resistant materials or shall be protected to resist corrosion. All joints between portions of the exterior covering shall be designed, and assembled to protect against the infiltration of air and water, except for any designed ventilation of wall or roof cavity.

(b) Joints between dissimilar materials and joints between exterior coverings and frames of openings shall be protected with a compatible sealant suitable to resist infiltration of air or water.

(c) Where adjoining materials or assemblies of materials are of such nature that separation can occur due to expansion, contraction, wind loads or other loads induced by erection or transportation, sealants shall be of a type that maintains protection against infiltration or penetration by air, moisture or vermin.

(d) Exterior surfaces shall be sealed to resist the entrance of rodents.

§ 3280.308 Formaldehyde emission controls for certain wood products.

(a) *Formaldehyde emission levels.* All plywood and particleboard materials bonded with a resin system or coated with a surface finish containing formaldehyde shall not exceed the following formaldehyde emission levels when installed in manufactured homes:

(1) Plywood materials shall not emit formaldehyde in excess of 0.2 parts per million (ppm) as measured by the air chamber test method specified in § 3280.406.

(2) Particleboard materials shall not emit formaldehyde in excess of 0.3 ppm as measured by the air chamber test specified in § 3280.406.

(b) *Product certification and continuing qualification.* All plywood and particleboard materials to be installed in manufactured homes which are bonded with a resin system or coated with a surface finish containing formaldehyde, other than an exclusively phenol-formaldehyde resin system or finish, shall be certified by a nationally recognized testing laboratory as complying with paragraph (a) of this section.

(1) Separate certification shall be done for each plant where the particleboard is produced or where the plywood or particleboard is surface-finished.

(2) To certify plywood or particleboard, the testing laboratory shall witness or conduct the air chamber test specified in § 3280.406 on randomly selected panels initially and at least quarterly thereafter.

(3) The testing laboratory must approve a written quality control plan for each plant where the particleboard is produced or finished or where the plywood is finished. The quality control plan must be designed to assure that

67

all panels comply with paragraph (a) of this section. The plan must establish ongoing procedures to identify increases in the formaldehyde emission characteristics of the finished product resulting from the following changes in production.

(i) In the case of plywood:

(A) The facility where the unfinished panels are produced is changed;

(B) The thickness of the panels is changed so that the panels are thinner; or

(C) The grooving pattern on the panels is changed so that the grooves are deeper or closer together.

(ii) In the case of particleboard:

(A) The resin formulation is changed so that the formaldehyde-to-urea ratio is increased;

(B) The amount of formaldehyde resin used is increased; or

(C) The press time is decreased.

(iii) In the case of plywood or particleboard:

(A) The finishing or top coat is changed and the new finishing or top coat has a greater formaldehyde content; or

(B) The amount of finishing or top coat used on the panels is increased, provided that such finishing or top coat contains formaldehyde.

(4) The testing laboratory shall periodically visit the plant to monitor quality control procedures to assure that all certified panels meet the standard.

(5) To maintain its certification, plywood or particleboard must be tested by the air chamber test specified in § 3280.406 whenever one of the following events occurs:

(i) In the case of particleboard, the resin formulation is changed so that the formaldehyde-to-urea ratio is increased; or

(ii) In the case of particleboard or plywood, the finishing or top coat is changed and the new finishing or top coat contains formaldehyde; or

(iii) In the case of particleboard or plywood, the testing laboratory determines that an air chamber test is necessary to assure that panels comply with paragraph (a) of this section.

(6) In the event that an air chamber test measures levels of formaldehyde from plywood or particleboard in ex-

cess of those permitted under paragraph (a) of this section, then the tested product's certification immediately lapses as of the date of production of the tested panels. No panel produced on the same date as the tested panels or on any day thereafter may be used or certified for use in manufactured homes.

(i) Provided, however, that a new product certification may be obtained by testing randomly selected panels which were produced on any day following the date of production of the tested panels. If such panels pass the air chamber test specified in § 3280.406, then the plywood or particleboard produced on that day and subsequent days may be used and certified for use in manufactured homes.

(ii) Provided further, that plywood or particleboard produced on the same day as the tested panels, and panels produced on subsequent days, if not certified pursuant to paragraph (b)(4)(i) of this section, may be used in manufactured homes only under the following circumstances:

(A) Each panel is treated with a scavenger, sealant, or other means of reducing formaldehyde emissions which does not adversely affect the structural quality of the product; and

(B) Panels randomly selected from the treated panels are tested by and pass the air chamber test specified in § 3280.406.

(c) *Panel identification.* Each plywood and particleboard panel to be installed in manufactured homes which is bonded or coated with a resin system containing formaldehyde, other than an exclusively phenol-formaldehyde resin system, shall be stamped or labeled so as to identify the product manufacturer, date of production and/or lot number, and the testing laboratory certifying compliance with this section.

(d) *Treatment after certification.* If certified plywood or particleboard subsequently is treated with paint, varnish, or any other substance containing formaldehyde, then the certification is no longer valid. In such a case, each stamp or label placed on the panels pursuant to paragraph (c) of this section must be obliterated. In addition, the treated panels may be recertified and reidentified in accordance with paragraphs (b) and (c) of this section.

[49 FR 32011, Aug. 9, 1984]

§ 3280.309 Health Notice on formaldehyde emissions.

(a) Each manufactured home shall have a Health Notice on formaldehyde emissions prominently displayed in a temporary manner in the kitchen (i.e., countertop or exposed cabinet face). The Notice shall read as follows:

IMPORTANT HEALTH NOTICE

Some of the building materials used in this home emit formaldehyde. Eye, nose, and throat irritation, headache, nausea, and a variety of asthma-like symptoms, including shortness of breath, have been reported as a result of formaldehyde exposure. Elderly persons and young children, as well as anyone with a history of asthma, allergies, or lung problems, may be at greater risk. Research is continuing on the possible long-term effects of exposure to formaldehyde.

Reduced ventilation resulting from energy efficiency standards may allow formaldehyde and other contaminants to accumulate in the indoor air. Additional ventilation to dilute the indoor air may be obtained from a passive or mechanical ventilation system offered by the manufacturer. Consult your dealer for information about the ventilation options offered with this home.

High indoor temperatures and humidity raise formaldehyde levels. When a home is to be located in areas subject to extreme summer temperatures, an air-conditioning system can be used to control indoor temperature levels. Check the comfort cooling certificate to determine if this home has been equipped or designed for the installation of an air-conditioning system.

If you have any questions regarding the health effects of formaldehyde, consult your doctor or local health department.

(b) The Notice shall be legible and typed using letters at least ¼ inch in size. The title shall be typed using letters at least ¾ inch in size.

(c) The Notice shall not be removed by any party until the entire sales transaction has been completed (refer to part 3282—Manufactured Home Procedural and Enforcement Regulations for provisions regarding a sales transaction).

(d) A copy of the Notice shall be included in the Consumer Manual (refer to part 3283—Manufactured Home Consumer Manual Requirements).

[49 FR 32012, Aug. 9, 1984, as amended at 54 FR 46049, Nov. 1, 1989; 58 FR 55007, Oct. 25, 1993]

Subpart E—Testing

§ 3280.401 Structural load tests.

Every structural assembly tested shall be capable of meeting the Proof Load Test or the Ultimate Load Test as follows:

(a) *Proof load tests.* Every structural assembly tested must be capable of sustaining its dead load plus superimposed live loads equal to 1.75 times the required live loads for a period of 12 hours without failure. Tests must be conducted with loads applied and deflections recorded in ¼ design live load increments at 10-minute intervals until 1.25 times design live load plus dead load has been reached. Additional load shall then be applied continuously until 1.75 times design live load plus dead load has been reached. Assembly failure shall be considered as design live load deflection (or residual deflection measured 12 hours after live load removal) that is greater than the limits set in § 3280.305(d), rupture, fracture, or excessive yielding. Design live load deflection criteria do not apply when the structural assembly being evaluated does not include structural framing members. An assembly to be tested shall be of the minimum quality of materials and workmanship of the production. Each test assembly, component, or subassembly shall be identified as to type and quality or grade of material. All assemblies, components, or subassemblies qualifying under this test shall be subject to a continuing qualification testing program acceptable to HUD.

(b) *Ultimate load tests.* Ultimate load tests must be performed on a minimum of three assemblies or components to generally evaluate the structural design. Every structural assembly or component tested must be capable of sustaining its total dead load plus the design live load increased by a factor of safety of at least 2.5. A factor of safety greater than 2.5 shall be used when required by an applicable reference standard in § 3280.304(b)(1). Tests shall be conducted with loads applied and deflections recorded in 1/4 design live load increments at 10-minute intervals until 1.25 times design live load plus dead load has been reached. Additional loading shall then be applied continuously until failure occurs, or the total of the factor of safety times the design live load plus the dead load is reached. Assembly failure shall be considered as design live load deflection greater than the limits set in § 3280.305(d), rupture, fracture, or excessive yielding. Design live load deflection criteria do not apply when the structural assembly being evaluated does not include structural framing members. Assemblies to be tested shall be representative of average quality of materials and workmanship of the production. Each test assembly, component, or subassembly shall be identified as to type and quality or grade of material. All assemblies, components, or subassemblies qualifying under this test shall be subject to a periodic qualification testing program acceptable to HUD.

[40 FR 58752, Dec. 18, 1975. Redesignated at 44 FR 20679, Apr. 6, 1979, as amended at 58 FR 55007, Oct. 25, 1993; 70 FR 72045, Nov. 30, 2005]

§ 3280.402 Test procedures for roof trusses.

(a) *Roof load tests.* This section provides the roof truss test procedure for vertical loading conditions. Where roof trusses act as support for other members, have eave or cornice projections, or support concentrated loads, roof trusses must also be tested for those conditions. These test procedures are required for new truss designs in all three wind zones and for existing truss designs used in Wind Zones II and III.

(b) *General.* Trusses must be tested in a truss test fixture that replicates the design loads, and actual support points, and does not restrain horizontal movement. When tested singly or in groups of two or more trusses, trusses shall be mounted on supports and positioned as intended to be installed in the manufactured home in order to give the required clear span distance (L) and eave or cornice distance (Lo), if applicable, as specified in the design.

(1) When trusses are tested singly, trusses shall be positioned in a test fixture, with supports properly located and the roof loads evenly applied. See Figure 3280.402(b)(1).

Figure 3280.402(b)(1) – Test fixture for testing trusses singly

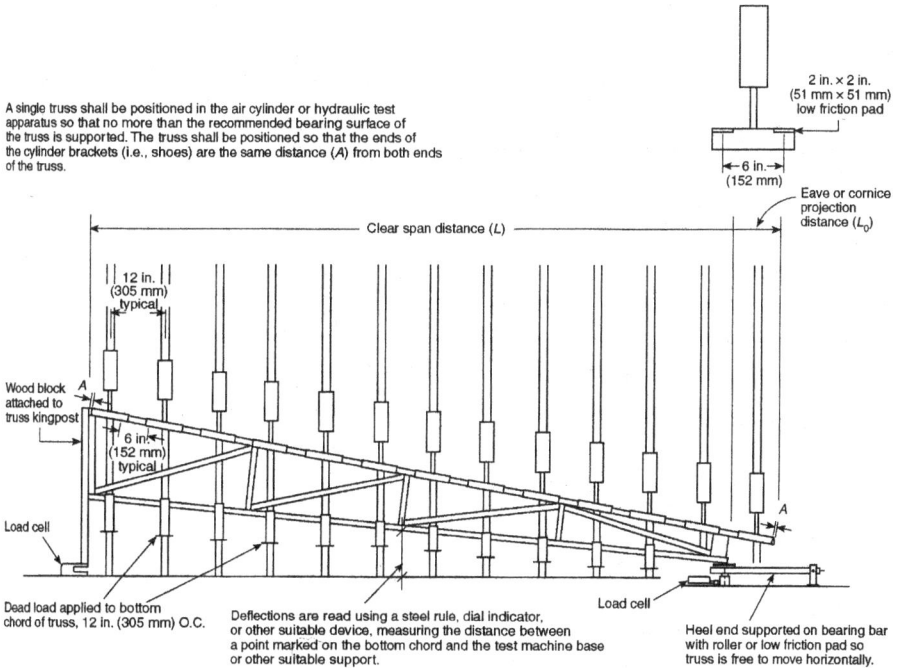

A single truss shall be positioned in the air cylinder or hydraulic test apparatus so that no more than the recommended bearing surface of the truss is supported. The truss shall be positioned so that the ends of the cylinder brackets (i.e., shoes) are the same distance (A) from both ends of the truss.

2 in. × 2 in. (51 mm × 51 mm) low friction pad

←6 in.→ (152 mm)

Eave or cornice projection distance (L₀)

Clear span distance (L)

12 in. (305 mm) typical

Wood block A attached to truss kingpost

6 in. (152 mm) typical

Load cell

Dead load applied to bottom chord of truss, 12 in. (305 mm) O.C.

Deflections are read using a steel rule, dial indicator, or other suitable device, measuring the distance between a point marked on the bottom chord and the test machine base or other suitable support.

Load cell

Heel end supported on bearing bar with roller or low friction pad so truss is free to move horizontally.

(2) When tested in groups of two or more, the top chords are permitted to be sheathed with nominal 1/4-inch × 12-inch plywood strips. The plywood strips shall be at least long enough to cover the top chords of the trusses at the designated design truss spacing. Adjacent plywood strips shall be separated by at least 1/8-inch. The plywood strips shall be nailed with 4d nails or equivalent staples no closer than 8 inches on center along the top chord. The bottom chords of the adjacent trusses shall be permitted to be one of the following:

(i) Unbraced; or

(ii) Laterally braced together (not cross-braced) with 1-inch × 2-inch stripping no closer than 24 inches on center, nailed with only one 8d nail at each truss. See Figure 3280.402(b)(2).

71

Figure 3280.402(b)(2) – Test set-up for roof trusses tested in groups of two or more

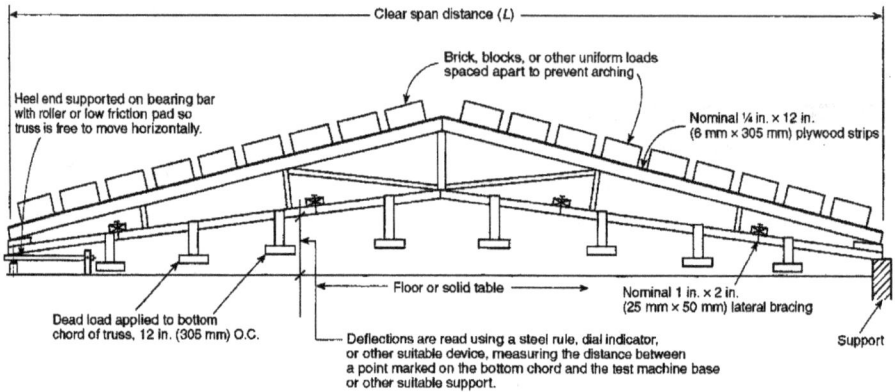

(c) *Measuring and loading methods.* Deflections must be measured at the free end of an eave or cornice projection and at least at the truss mid-span and quarter points. Scissors or other unique truss configurations are to be measured at as many additional bottom chord panel points as necessary to obtain an accurate representation of the deflected shape of the truss so as to be able to locate and record the point(s) of maximum deflection. Deflections must be read and recorded relative to a fixed reference datum. Deflections must be read and recorded to the nearest 1/32-inch. Dead load must be applied to the top and bottom chord, and live load must be applied to the top chord through a suitable hydraulic, pneumatic, or mechanical system or weights to simulate design loads. Load unit weights for uniformly distributed top chord loads must be separated so that arch action does not occur and be spaced not more than 12 inches on center so as to simulate uniform loading. Bottom chord loading must be spaced as uniformly as practical. Truss gravity loads must be calculated based on the overall truss length (horizontal projection), including eave or cornice projections.

(d) *Testing procedures.* Either the testing method in paragraph (d)(1) or (d)(2) of this section may be used, however, the testing method in paragraph (d)(3) of this section must be used, to test trusses to establish compliance with the provisions of these standards.

(1) *Proof load truss test procedure.* At least three average quality/consecutively tested trusses must pass all requirements of the test, for initial qualification of the truss design. All tests for initial qualification of the truss designs evaluated by this procedure must be certified by a Registered Engineer or Architect, or by a nationally recognized testing laboratory. An in-house quality control and follow-up testing program (see paragraphs (e) and (f) of this section) must be approved prior to entering production of any truss design evaluated by this procedure.

(i) *Dead load.* Measure and record initial elevation of the truss or trusses in the test position at no load. Apply to the top and bottom chords of the truss dead loads that are representative of the actual weights of materials to be supported by the truss. However, the dead load may only be applied as indicated in paragraph (e)(4) of this section for ongoing follow-up testing. Dead loads to be applied to the truss test assembly are permitted to include only the weights of materials supported by the truss and not the weight of the truss itself. However, readings from load cells (when used) on which the test truss rests must reflect the sum of the applied load plus the weight of the truss. Apply dead loads and hold for 5 minutes. Measure and record the deflections.

(ii) *Live load.* Maintaining the dead loads, apply live load to the top chord in approximate ¼ live load increments until dead load plus the live load is reached. Measure and record the deflections no sooner than one minute after each ¼ live load increment has been applied and 5 minutes after the full live load has been reached.

(iii) *Initial recovery phase.* Remove the design live load but not the dead load. Measure and record the deflections 5 minutes after the total live load has been removed.

(iv) Continue to load the truss to:

(A) Dead load plus 2.0 times the design live load. Maintain this loading for 6 hours and inspect the truss for failure. Failure is rupture, fracture, or excessive yielding; or

(B) Dead load plus 1.75 times the design live load. Maintain this loading for 12 hours and inspect the truss for failure. Failure is rupture, fracture, or excessive yielding.

(v) *Final recovery phase.* Remove 2.0 times the design live load, but not the dead load or 1.75 times the design live load, but not the dead load. Measure and record deflections within 4 hours after removing 2.0 times the design live load or 1.75 times the design live load.

(vi) *Acceptance criteria.* The truss design is acceptable if all of the following conditions are met:

(A) The maximum deflection between no load and dead load must be L/480 or less for simply supported clear spans and Lo/180 or less for eave and cornice projections; and

(B) The maximum deflection between dead load and design live load must be L/180 or less for simply supported clear spans and Lo/90 or less for eave and cornice projections; and

(C) After the design live load is removed, and with the dead load still applied, the maximum recovery deflection must be L/360 or less for simply supported spans and Lo/180 or less for eave and cornice projections; and

(D) The truss must maintain the overload condition for 6 hours without rupture or fracture, or excessive yielding; and

(E) After 2.0 times the design live load has been removed, and with the dead load still applied, the maximum recovery deflection must be L/180 or less for simply supported clear spans and Lo/90 or less for eave and cornice projections; and

(F) As applicable, each truss design must also meet all requirements for uplift loads required by paragraph (d)(3) of this section. For Wind Zone I uplift load requirements, see paragraph (d)(3)(i) of this section. For Wind Zones II and III uplift load requirements, see paragraph (d)(3)(ii) of this section.

(2) *Ultimate load truss test procedure.* (i) At least two average quality/consecutively tested trusses must pass all requirements of the test, for initial qualification of the truss design. All tests for initial qualification of the truss designs evaluated by this procedure must be certified by a Registered Engineer or Architect, or by a nationally recognized testing laboratory. An in-house quality control and follow-up testing program (see paragraph (e) and (f) of this section) must be approved prior to entering production of any truss design evaluated by this procedure.

(ii) *Dead load.* Measure and record initial elevation of the truss or trusses in the test position at no load. Apply to the top and bottom chords of the truss dead loads that are representative of the actual weights of materials to be supported by the truss. However, the dead load may only be applied as indicated in paragraph (e)(4) of this section for ongoing follow-up testing. Dead loads to be applied to the truss test assembly shall be permitted to include only the weights of materials supported by the truss, and not the weight of the truss itself. However, readings from load cells (when used) on which the test truss rests must reflect the sum of the applied load plus the weight of the truss. Apply dead loads and hold for 5 minutes. Measure and record the deflections.

(iii) *Live load.* Maintaining the dead loads, apply live load at a uniform rate to the top chord in approximate ¼ live load increments until the dead load plus the live load is reached. Measure and record the deflections no sooner than one minute after each ¼ live load increment has been applied and 5 minutes after the full live load has been reached.

(iv) *Initial recovery phase*. Remove the design live load but not the dead load. Measure and record the deflections 5 minutes after the design live load has been removed.

(v) *Overload phase*. After the recovery phase is completed, reapply the full live load to the truss assembly. Additional loading shall then be applied continuously until the dead load plus 2.5 times the design live load is reached. This overload condition must be maintained for at least 5 minutes.

(vi) *Final recovery phase*. Remove 2.5 times the design live load but not the dead load. Measure and record deflections within 4 hours after 2.5 times the design live load has been removed.

(vii) *Acceptance criteria*. The truss design is acceptable if all of the following conditions are met:

(A) The maximum deflection between no load and dead load must be L/480 or less for simply supported clear spans and Lo/180 or less for eave and cornice projections; and

(B) Dead load to design live load deflections shall be L/180 or less for simply supported clear spans and Lo/90 or less for eave and cornice projections; and

(C) After the design live load is removed and with the dead load still applied, the maximum recovery deflection must be L/360 or less for simply supported spans and Lo/180 or less for eave and cornice projections; and

(D) The truss shall maintain the overload condition for 5 minutes without rupture, fracture, or excessive yielding; and

(E) After 2.5 times the design live load is removed, and with the dead load still applied, the truss must recover to at least L/180 for simply supported clear spans and Lo/90 for eave and cornice within 4 hours after the total live load has been removed; and

(F) As applicable, each truss design must also meet all requirements for uplift loads in Wind Zone I or Wind Zone II and III, as required by paragraph (d)(3) of this section. For Wind Zone I uplift load requirements, see paragraph (d)(3)(i) of this section. For Wind Zones II and III uplift load requirements, see paragraph (d)(3)(ii) of this section.

(3) *Uplift load tests*. Each truss design must also pass all requirements of the uplift load test, as applicable, in paragraph (d)(3)(i) or (d)(3)(ii) and paragraphs (d)(3)(iii) and (d)(3)(iv) of this section.

(i) *Wind Zone I uplift load test*. Where there are engineered connectors between the top chord and web members of the truss, such as metal connector plates or wood gussets or their equivalents, uplift testing in Wind Zone I is at the discretion of the Registered Engineer or Architect or nationally recognized testing laboratory certifying the truss design. When testing is deemed necessary by the Registered Engineer or Architect or nationally recognized testing laboratory certifying the truss design, a minimum of one average quality uplift load test is to be conducted for each such truss design and must pass all requirements of the test for initial qualification of the truss design. The net uplift load for trusses designed for use in Wind Zone I is 9 psf for the clear span of the truss and 22.5[1]psf for eave or cornice projections.

(ii) *Wind Zones II and III uplift loads test*. This test is required for all trusses designed for use in Wind Zones II and III. A minimum of three average quality/consecutive uplift load tests are to be conducted for each truss design when tested in the inverted position and a minimum of two average quality/consecutive uplift load tests are to be conducted for trusses in the upright position. The trusses must pass all requirements of the test for initial qualification of the truss design. The uplift load for trusses designed to be used in Wind Zones II and III for the clear span or eave cornice projections is to be determined by subtracting the dead load applied to the truss from the uplift load provided in the Table of Design Wind Pressures in § 3280.305(c)(1)(ii)(B).

(iii) Trusses designed for use in Wind Zone I, when tested (see paragraph (d)(3)(i) of this section), must be tested in either the inverted position to 2.5 times the net wind uplift load or in the upright position to 1.75 times the net wind uplift load. Trusses designed for use in Wind Zones II and III (see paragraph (d)(3)(ii) of this section) must be tested to 2.0 times the uplift load minus the dead load in the inverted position and to 1.75 times the uplift load minus the dead load in the upright position. See Figure 3280.402(b)(3).

(iv) The following describes how to conduct the uplift test with the truss in the upright position. Similar proce-

dures must be used if conducting the test in the inverted position.

(A) Place the truss in the test fixture and position as it is intended to be installed in the manufactured home. See Figure 3280.402(b)(3).

Figure 3280.402(b)(3) – Test setup for roof trusses tested for uplift in the upright position

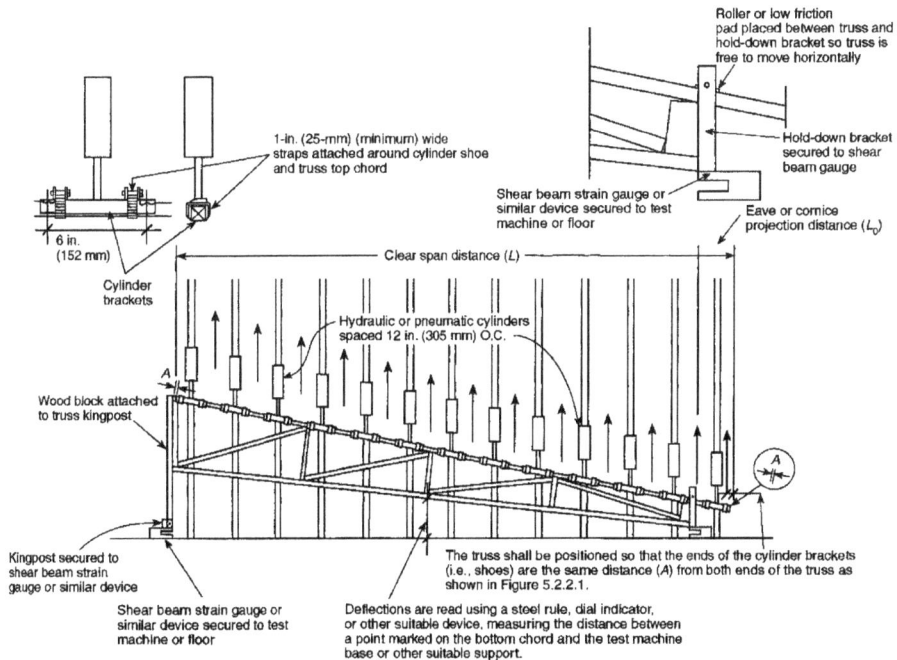

(B) Position the load measurement devices to register the wind uplift loads that will be applied to the top chord of the truss. The uplift loads shall be applied through tension devices not wider than one inch and spaced not greater than approximately 12 inches on center and shall be applied as uniform as possible, so as to simulate uniform loading. Gravity and wind uplift load tests may be performed on the same truss in this single setup mode. For the wind uplift test, it is permissible to stabilize the bottom chord of the truss in the test fixture to simulate ceiling materials or purlin supports. Measure and record the initial elevation of the bottom chord of the truss in the test posi-

tion at the mid-span and quarter points of the truss, and at the free end of an eave or cornice projection greater than 12 inches. Scissors or other unique truss configurations are to be measured at as many additional bottom chord panel points as necessary to obtain an accurate representation of the deflected shape of the truss, so as to be able to locate and record the point(s) of maximum deflection. Eave or cornice projection loads are applied separately for eaves or cornice projections greater than 12 inches. For eave or cornice projections greater than 12 inches, the additional required load must be applied to the eave simultaneously with the main body load. For eave or cornice projections of 12 inches or less, add the additional required load to the main body load and apply it to the entire top chord.

(C) Measure and record the deflection 5 minutes after the net uplift load has been applied. Design load deflection shall be L/180 or less for a simply supported clear span and Lo/90 or less for eave or cornice projections.

(D) For trusses tested in the upright position, continue to load the truss to 1.75 times the net uplift load in paragraph (d)(3)(i) of this section for Wind Zone I and 1.75 times the uplift load in paragraph (d)(3)(ii) for Wind Zones II and III, and maintain the load for one minute. For trusses tested in the inverted position, continue to load the truss to 2.50 times the net uplift load in paragraph (d)(3)(i) for Wind Zone I and to 2.0 times the uplift load minus the dead load in paragraph (d)(3)(ii) for Wind Zones II and III, and maintain the full load for one minute. Regardless of the test position of the truss, upright or inverted, trusses must maintain the overload for the specified time period without rupture, fracture, or excessive yielding.

(e) *Follow-up testing.* Follow-up testing procedures must include the following:

(1) All trusses qualifying under these test procedures must be subject to a quality control and follow-up testing program.

(i) Manufacturers of listed or labeled trusses must follow an in-house quality control program with follow-up testing approved by a nationally recognized testing program as specified in paragraph (e)(3) of this section. The in-house quality control program must include, at a minimum, procedures for quality of materials including, but not limited to, grade(s) of materials, allowable splits, knots, and other applicable lumber qualities; workmanship including, but not limited to, plate placement and embedment tolerances; other manufacturing tolerances; description and calibration of test equipment; truss retesting criteria; and procedures in the event of noncomplying results.

(ii) Those home manufacturers producing trusses for their own use, and which are not listed or labeled, must have an in-house quality control program (see paragraph (i) of this section) that includes follow-up testing, as specified in this section, and is approved by their Design Approval Primary Inspection Agency (DAPIA).

(2) Truss designs that are qualified but not in production are not subject to follow-up testing until produced. When the truss design is brought into production, a follow-up test is to be performed if the truss design has been out of production for more than 6 months.

(3) The frequency of truss manufacturer's quality control follow-up testing for trusses must be at least:

(i) One test for the first 100 trusses produced, with a subsequent test for every 2,500 trusses for trusses qualified under the proof load truss test procedure or inverted uplift test procedure for trusses used in Wind Zones II and III or once every 6 months, whichever is more frequent, for every truss design produced; or

(ii) One test for every 4,000 trusses produced for trusses qualified under the ultimate load truss test procedure or upright uplift test procedure for trusses used in Wind Zones II and III or once every 6 months, whichever is more frequent, for every truss design produced.

(4) For follow-up testing only, the full dead load may be applied to the top chord of the truss, when the bottom chord dead load is 5 psf or less.

[78 FR 4065, Jan. 18, 2013]

§ 3280.403 Requirements for windows, sliding glass doors, and skylights.

(a) *Scope.* This section establishes the requirements for prime windows and sliding glass doors, except that windows used in an entry door are components of the door and are excluded from these requirements.

(b)(1) *Standard.* All primary windows and sliding glass doors shall comply with AAMA 1701.2–95, Voluntary Standard Primary Window and Sliding Glass Door for Utilization in Manufactured Housing, except the exterior and interior pressure tests must be conducted at the design wind loads required for components and cladding specified in § 3280.305(c)(1).

(2) All skylights must comply with AAMA/WDMA/CSA/101/I.S.2/A440–08:

North American Fenestration Standard/Specifications for Windows, Doors and Skylights (incorporated by reference, see §3280.4). Skylights must withstand the roof loads for the applicable Roof Load Zone specified in §3280.305(c)(3), and the following wind loads:

(i) For Wind Zone I, the wind loads specified in §3280.305(c)(1)(i); and

(ii) For Wind Zones II and III, the wind loads specified for exterior roof coverings, sheathing, and fastenings in §3280.305(c)(1)(ii).

(c) *Installation.* All primary windows, sliding glass doors, and skylights must be installed in a manner that allows proper operation and provides protection against the elements, as required by §3280.307.

(d) *Glass.* (1) Safety glazing materials, where used shall meet Standard for Safety Glazing Materials used in Buildings—Safety Performance Specifications and Methods of Test, ANSI Z97.1-2004 (incorporated by reference, see §3280.4).

(2) Sealed insulating glass, where used, must meet all performance requirements for Class C in accordance with ASTM E 774-97, Standard Specification for the Classification of the Durability of Sealed Insulating Glass Units. The sealing system must be qualified in accordance with ASTM E 773-97, Standard Test Methods for Accelerated Weathering of Sealed Insulating Glass Units. Each glass unit must be permanently identified with the name of the insulating glass manufacturer.

(e) *Certification.* All primary windows and sliding glass doors to be installed in manufactured homes must be certified as complying with AAMA 1701.2-95. This certification must be based on tests conducted at the design wind loads specified in §3280.305(c)(1).

(1) All such windows and doors must show evidence of certification by affixing a quality certification label to the product in accordance with ANSI Z34.1-1993, Third-Party Certification Programs for Products, Processes, and Services.

(2) In determining certifiability of the products, an independent quality assurance agency shall conduct preproduction specimen tests in accordance with AAMA 1701.2-95. Further, such agency must inspect the product manufacturer's facility at least twice per year.

(3) All skylights installed in manufactured homes must be certified as complying with AAMA/WDMA/CSA 101/I.S.2/A440-08: North American Fenestration Standard/Specifications for Windows, Doors, and Skylights (incorporated by reference, see §3280.4). This certification must be based on applicable loads specified in paragraph (b) of this section.

(f) *Protection of primary window and sliding glass door openings in high wind areas.* For homes designed to be located in Wind Zones II and III, manufacturers shall design exterior walls surrounding the primary window and sliding glass door openings to allow for the installation of shutters or other protective covers, such as plywood, to cover these openings. Although not required, the Department encourages manufacturers to provide the shutters or protective covers and to install receiving devices, sleeves, or anchors for fasteners to be used to secure the shutters or protective covers to the exterior walls. If the manufacturer does not provide shutters or other protective covers to cover these openings, the manufacturer must provide to the homeowner instructions for at least one method of protecting primary window and sliding glass door openings. This method must be capable of resisting the design wind pressures specified in §3280.305 without taking the home out of conformance with the standards in this part. These instructions must be included in the printed instructions that accompany each manufactured home. The instructions shall also indicate whether receiving devices, sleeves, or anchors, for fasteners to be used to secure the shutters or protective covers to the exterior walls, have been installed or provided by the manufacturer.

[52 FR 4583, Feb. 12, 1987, as amended at 52 FR 35543, Sept. 22, 1987; 58 FR 55009, Oct. 25, 1993; 59 FR 2474, Jan. 14, 1994; 70 FR 72046, Nov. 30, 2005; 78 FR 73983, Dec. 9, 2013]

§ 3280.404 Standard for egress windows and devices for use in manufactured homes.

(a) *Scope and purpose.* The purpose of this section is to establish the requirements for the design, construction, and installation of windows and approved devices intended to be used as an emergency exit during conditions encountered in a fire or similar disaster.

(b) *Performance.* Egress windows including auxiliary frame and seals, if any, shall meet all requirements of AAMA 1701.2–95, Voluntary Standard Primary Window and Sliding Glass Door for Utilization in Manufactured Housing and AAMA Standard 1704–1985, Voluntary Standard Egress Window Systems for Utilization in Manufactured Housing, except the exterior and interior pressure tests for components and cladding must be conducted at the design wind loads required by § 3280.305(c)(1).

(c) *Installation.* (1) The installation of egress windows or devices shall be installed in a manner which allows for proper operation and provides protection against the elements. (*See* § 3280.307.)

(2) An operational check of each installed egress window or device must be made at the manufactured home factory. All egress windows and devices must be capable of being opened to the minimum required dimensions by normal operation of the window without binding or requiring the use of tools. Any window or device failing this check must be repaired or replaced. A repaired window must conform to its certification. Any repaired or replaced window or device must pass the operational check.

(3) Windows that require the removal of the sash to meet egress size requirements are prohibited.

(d) *Operating instructions.* Operating instructions shall be affixed to each egress window and device and carry the legend "Do Not Remove."

(e) *Certification of egress windows and devices.* Egress windows and devices shall be listed in accordance with the procedures and requirements of AAMA Standard 1704–1985. As of January 17, 1995, this certification must be based on tests conducted at the design wind loads specified in § 3280.305(c)(1).

(f) *Protection of egress window openings in high wind areas.* For homes designed to be located in Wind Zones II and III, manufacturers shall design exterior walls surrounding the egress window openings to allow for the installation of shutters or other protective covers, such as plywood, to cover these openings. Although not required, the Department encourages manufacturers to provide the shutters or protective covers and to install receiving devices, sleeves, or anchors for fasteners to be used to secure the shutters or protective covers to the exterior walls. If the manufacturer does not provide shutters or other protective covers to cover these openings, the manufacturer must provide to the homeowner instructions for at least one method of protecting egress window openings. This method must be capable of resisting the design wind pressures specified in § 3280.305 without taking the home out of conformance with the standards in this part. These instructions must be included in the printed instructions that accompany each manufactured home. The instructions shall also indicate whether receiving devices, sleeves, or anchors, for fasteners to be used to secure the shutters or protective covers to the exterior walls, have been installed or provided by the manufacturer.

[52 FR 4583, Feb. 12, 1987, as amended at 59 FR 2474, Jan. 14, 1994; 70 FR 72046, Nov. 30, 2005; 78 FR 73983, Dec. 9, 2013]

§ 3280.405 Standard for swinging exterior passage doors for use in manufactured homes.

(a) *Introduction.* This standard applies to all exterior passage door units, excluding sliding doors and doors used for access to utilities and compartments. This standard applies only to the door frame consisting of jambs, head and sill and the attached door or doors.

(b) *Performance requirements.* The design and construction of exterior door units must meet all requirements of AAMA 1702.2–95, Voluntary Standard Swinging Exterior Passage Door for Utilization in Manufactured Housing.

(c) *Materials and methods.* Any material or method of construction shall conform to the performance requirements as outlined in paragraph (b) of this section. Plywood shall be exterior type and preservative treated in accordance with NWWDA I.S.4–81, Water Repellent Preservative Non-Pressure Treatment for Millwork.

(d) *Exterior doors.* All swinging exterior doors shall be installed in a manner which allows proper operation and provides protection against the elements (see §3280.307).

(e) *Certification.* All swinging exterior doors to be installed in manufactured homes must be certified as complying with AAMA 1702.2–95, Voluntary Standard Swinging Exterior Passage Door for Utilization in Manufactured Housing.

(1) All such doors must show evidence of certification by affixing a quality certification label to the product in accordance with ANSI Z34.1–1993, Third Party Certification Programs for Products, Processes, and Services.

(2) In determining certifiability of the products, an independent quality assurance agency must conduct a pre-production specimen test in accordance with AAMA 1702.2–95, Voluntary Standard Swinging Exterior Passage Door for Utilization in Manufactured Housing.

(f) *Protection of exterior doors in high wind areas.* For homes designed to be located in Wind Zones II and III, manufacturers shall design exterior walls surrounding the exterior door openings to allow for the installation of shutters or other protective covers, such as plywood, to cover these openings. Although not required, the Department encourages manufacturers to provide the shutters or protective covers and to install receiving devices, sleeves, or anchors for fasteners to be used to secure the shutters or protective covers to the exterior walls. If the manufacturer does not provide shutters or other protective covers to cover these openings, the manufacturer must provide to the homeowner instructions for at least one method of protecting exterior door openings. This method must be capable of resisting the design wind pressures specified in §3280.305 without taking the home out of conformance with the standards in this part. These instructions must be included in the printed instructions that accompany each manufactured home. The instruc-

tions shall also indicate whether receiving devices, sleeves, or anchors, for fasteners to be used to secure the shutters or protective covers to the exterior walls, have been installed or provided by the manufacturer.

[40 FR 58752, Dec. 18, 1975. Redesignated at 44 FR 20679, Apr. 6, 1979, as amended at 52 FR 4583, Feb. 12, 1987; 52 FR 35543, Sept. 22, 1987; 58 FR 55009, Oct. 25, 1993; 59 FR 2474, Jan. 14, 1994; 70 FR 72046, Nov. 30, 2005]

§3280.406 Air chamber test method for certification and qualification of formaldehyde emission levels.

(a) *Preconditioning.* Preconditioning of plywood or particleboard panels for air chamber tests shall be initiated as soon as practicable but not in excess of 30 days after the plywood or particleboard is produced or surface-finished, whichever is later, using randomly selected panels.

(1) If preconditioning is to be initiated more than two days after the plywood or particleboard is produced or surface-finished, whichever is later, the panels must be dead-stacked or airtight wrapped until preconditioning is initiated.

(2) Panels selected for testing in the air chamber shall not be taken from the top or bottom of the stack.

(b) *Testing.* Testing must be conducted in accordance with the Standard Test Method for Determining Formaldehyde Levels from Wood Products Under Defined Test Conditions Using a Large Chamber, ASTM E 1333–96, with the following exceptions:

(1) The chamber shall be operated indoors.

(2) Plywood and particleboard panels shall be individually tested in accordance with the following loading ratios:

(i) Plywood—0.29 Ft2/Ft3, and

(ii) Particleboard—0.13 Ft2/Ft3.

(3) Temperature to be maintained inside the chamber shall be 77° plus or minus 2 °F.

(4) The test concentration (C) shall be standardized to a level (C_O) at a temperature (t_O) of 77 °F and 50% relative humidity (H_O) by the following formula:

$$C = C_O \times [1 + Ax (H - H_O)] \times e^{-R(1/t - 1/t_O)}$$

where:

C = Test formaldehyde concentration

C_O = Standardized formaldehyde concentration

e = Natural log base

R = Coefficient of temperature (9799)

t = Actual test condition temperature (^{O} K)

t_O = Standardized temperature (^{O} K)

A = Coefficient of humidity (0.0175)

H = Actual relative humidity (%)

H_O = Standardized relative humidity (%)

The standardized level (C_O) is the concentration used to determine compliance with § 3280.308(a).

(5) The air chamber shall be inspected and recalibrated at least annually to insure its proper operation under test conditions.

[49 FR 32012, Aug. 9, 1984, as amended at 58 FR 55009, Oct. 25, 1993; 70 FR 72046, Nov. 30, 2005]

Subpart F—Thermal Protection

§ 3280.501 Scope.

This subpart sets forth the requirements for condensation control, air infiltration, thermal insulation and certification for heating and comfort cooling.

§ 3280.502 Definitions.

(a) The following definitions are applicable to subpart F only:

(1) *Pressure envelope* means that primary air barrier surrounding the living space which serves to limit air leakage. In construction using ventilated cavities, the pressure envelope is the interior skin.

(2) *Thermal envelope area* means the sum of the surface areas of outside walls, ceiling and floor, including all openings. The wall area is measured by multiplying outside wall lengths by the inside wall height from floor to ceiling. The floor and ceiling areas are considered as horizontal surfaces using exterior width and length.

§ 3280.503 Materials.

Materials used for insulation shall be of proven effectiveness and adequate durability to assure that required design conditions concerning thermal transmission are attained.

§ 3280.504 Condensation control and installation of vapor retarders.

(a) *Ceiling vapor retarders.* (1) In U_o Value Zones 2 and 3, ceilings must have a vapor retarder with a permeance of not greater than 1 perm (as measured by ASTM E 96–95 Standard Test Methods for Water Vapor Transmission of Materials) (incorporated by reference, see § 3280.4) installed on the living space side of the roof cavity.

(2) For manufactured homes designed for Uo Value Zone 1, the vapor retarder may be omitted.

(b) *Exterior walls.* (1) Exterior walls must have a vapor retarder with a permeance no greater than 1 perm (dry cup method) installed on the living space side of the wall; or

(2) Unventilated wall cavities must have an external covering and/or sheathing that forms the pressure envelope. The covering and/or sheathing must have a combined permeance of not less than 5.0 perms. In the absence of test data, combined permeance is permitted to be computed using the following formula: P total = $(1/[(1/P_1) + (1/P_2)])$, where P_1 and P_2 are the permeance values of the exterior covering and sheathing in perms. Formed exterior siding applied in sections with joints not caulked or sealed, are not considered to restrict water vapor transmission; or

(3) Wall cavities must be constructed so that ventilation is provided to dissipate any condensation occurring in these cavities; or

(4) Homes manufactured to be sited in "humid climates" or "fringe climates" as shown on the Humid and Fringe Climate Map in this paragraph are permitted to have a vapor retarder specified in paragraph (b)(1) of this section installed on the exterior side of the wall insulation or be constructed with an external covering and sheathing with a combined permeance of not greater than 1.0 perms, provided the interior finish and interior wall panel materials have a combined permeance of not less than 5.0 perms. The following need not meet the minimum combined permeance rating of not less than 5.0 perms for interior finish or wall panel materials:

(i) Kitchen back splash materials, less than 50 square feet in area installed around countertops, sinks, and ranges;

(ii) Bathroom tub areas, shower compartments;

(iii) Cabinetry and built-in furniture;

(iv) Trim materials;

(v) Hardboard wall paneling of less than 50 square feet in area under chair rails.

Humid and Fringe Climate Map

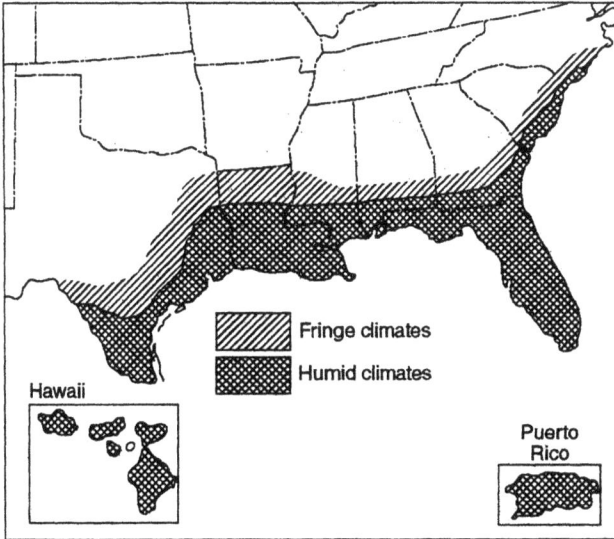

(5) The following areas of local governments (counties or similar areas, unless otherwise specified), listed by state are deemed to be within the humid and fringe climate areas shown on the Humid and Fringe Climate Map in paragraph (b)(4) of this section, and the vapor retarder or construction methods specified in paragraph (b)(4) of this section may be applied to homes built to be sited within these jurisdictions:

ALABAMA

Baldwin, Barbour, Bullock, Butler, Choctaw, Clarke, Coffee, Conecuh, Covington, Crenshaw, Dale, Escambia, Geneva, Henry, Houston, Lowndes, Marengo, Mobile, Monroe, Montgomery, Pike, Washington, Wilcox.

FLORIDA

All counties and locations within the State of Florida.

GEORGIA

Appling, Atkinson, Bacon, Baker, Ben Hill, Berrien, Brantley, Brooks, Bryan, Calhoun, Camden, Charlton, Chatham, Clay, Clinch, Coffee, Colquitt, Cook, Crisp, Decatur, Dougherty, Early, Echols, Effingham, Evans, Glynn, Wayne, Grady, Irwin, Jeff Davis, Lanier, Lee, Liberty, Long, Lowndes, McIntosh, Miller, Mitchell, Pierce, Quitman, Randolph, Seminole, Tattnall, Terrell, Thomas, Tift, Turner, Ware, Worth.

HAWAII

All counties and locations within the State of Hawaii.

LOUISIANA

All counties and locations within the State of Louisiana.

MISSISSIPPI

Adams, Amite, Claiborne, Clarke, Copiah, Covington, Forrest, Franklin, George, Greene, Hancock, Harrison, Hinds,

Issaquena, Jackson, Jasper, Jefferson, Jefferson Davis, Jones, Lamar, Lawrence, Lincoln, Marion, Pearl River, Perry, Pike, Rankin, Simpson, Smith, Stone, Walthall, Warren, Wayne, Wilkinson.

NORTH CAROLINA

Brunswick, Carteret, Columbus, New Hanover, Onslow, Pender.

SOUTH CAROLINA

Jasper, Beaufort, Colleton, Dorchester, Charleston, Berkeley, Georgetown, Horry.

TEXAS

Anderson, Angelina, Aransas, Atascosa, Austin, Bastrop, Bee, Bexar, Brazoria, Brazos, Brooks, Burleson, Caldwell, Calhoun, Cameron, Camp, Cass, Chambers, Cherokee, Colorado, Comal, De Witt, Dimmit, Duval, Falls, Fayette, Fort Bend, Franklin, Freestone, Frio, Galveston, Goliad, Gonzales, Gregg, Grimes, Guadalupe, Hardin, Harris, Harrison, Hays, Henderson, Hidalgo, Hopkins, Houston, Jackson, Jasper, Jefferson, Jim Hogg, Jim Wells, Karnes, Kaufman, Kennedy, Kinney, Kleberg, La Salle, Lavaca, Lee, Leon, Liberty, Limestone, Live Oak, Madison, Marion, Matagorda, Maverick, McMullen, Medina, Milam, Montgomery, Morris, Nacogdoches, Navarro, Newton, Nueces, Orange, Panola, Polk, Rains, Refugio, Robertson, Rusk, Sabine, San Augustine, San Jacinto, San Patricio, Shelby, Smith, Starr, Titus, Travis, Trinity, Tyler, Upshur, Uvalde, Val Verde, Van Zandt, Victoria, Walker, Waller, Washington, Webb, Wharton, Willacy, Williamson, Wilson, Wood, Zapata, Zavala.

(c) *Liquid applied vapor retarders.* Each liquid applied vapor retarder must be tested by a nationally recognized testing agency for use on the specific substrate to which it is applied. The test report must include the perm rating, as measured by ASTM E 96–95, Standard Test Methods for Water Vapor Transmission of Materials, and associated application rate for each specific substrate.

(d) *Attic or roof ventilation.* (1) Attic and roof cavities shall be vented in accordance with one of the following:

(i) A minimum free ventilation area of not less than 1/300 of the attic or roof cavity floor area. At least 50 percent of the required free ventilation area shall be provided by ventilators located in the upper portion of the space to be ventilated. At least 40 percent shall be provided by eave, soffit or low gable vents. The location and spacing of the vent openings and ventilators shall provide cross-ventilation to the entire attic or roof cavity space. A clear air passage space having a minimum height of 1 inch shall be provided between the top of the insulation and the roof sheathing or roof covering. Baffles or other means shall be provided where needed to insure the 1 inch height of the clear air passage space is maintained.

(ii) A mechanical attic or roof ventilation system may be installed instead of providing the free ventilation area when the mechanical system provides a minimum air change rate of 0.02 cubic feet per minute (cfm) per sq. ft. of attic floor area. Intake and exhaust vents shall be located so as to provide air movement throughout space.

(2) Single section manufactured homes constructed with metal roofs and having no sheathing or underlayment installed, are not required to be provided with attic or roof cavity ventilation provided that the air leakage paths from the living space to the roof cavity created by electrical outlets, electrical junctions, electrical cable penetrations, plumbing penetrations, flue pipe penetrations and exhaust vent penetrations are sealed.

(3) Parallel membrane roof section of a closed cell type construction are not required to be ventilated.

(4) The vents provided for ventilating attics and roof cavities shall be designed to resist entry of rain and insects.

[40 FR 58752, Dec. 18, 1975. Redesignated at 44 FR 20679, Apr. 6, 1979, as amended at 58 FR 55009, Oct. 25, 1993; 70 FR 72046, Nov. 30, 2005; 71 FR 19639, Apr. 17, 2006; 78 FR 73984, Dec. 9, 2013]

§ 3280.505　Air infiltration.

(a) *Envelope air infiltration.* The opaque envelope shall be designed and constructed to limit air infiltration to the living area of the home. Any design, material, method or combination thereof which accomplishes this goal may be used. The goal of the infiltration control criteria is to reduce heat loss/heat gain due to infiltration as much as possible without impinging on health and comfort and within the limits of reasonable economics.

(1) *Envelope penetrations.* Plumbing, mechanical and electrical penetrations of the pressure envelope not exempted by this part, and installations of window and door frames shall be constructed or treated to limit air infiltration. Penetrations of the pressure envelope made by electrical equipment, other than distribution panel boards and cable and conduit penetrations, are exempt from this requirement. Cable penetrations through outlet boxes are considered exempt.

(2) *Joints between major envelope elements.* Joints not designed to limit air infiltration between wall-to-wall, wall-to-ceiling and wall-to-floor connections shall be caulked or otherwise sealed.

When walls are constructed to form a pressure envelope on the outside of the wall cavity, they are deemed to meet this requirement.

§3280.506 Heat loss/heat gain.

The manufactured home heat loss/heat gain shall be determined by methods outlined in §§3280.508 and 3280.509. The Uo (Coefficient of heat transmission) value zone for which the manufactured home is acceptable and the lowest outdoor temperature to which the installed heating equipment will maintain a temperature of 70 F shall be certified as specified in §3280.510 of this subpart. The Uo value zone shall be determined from the map in figure 506.

U/O Value Zone Map for Manufactured Housing

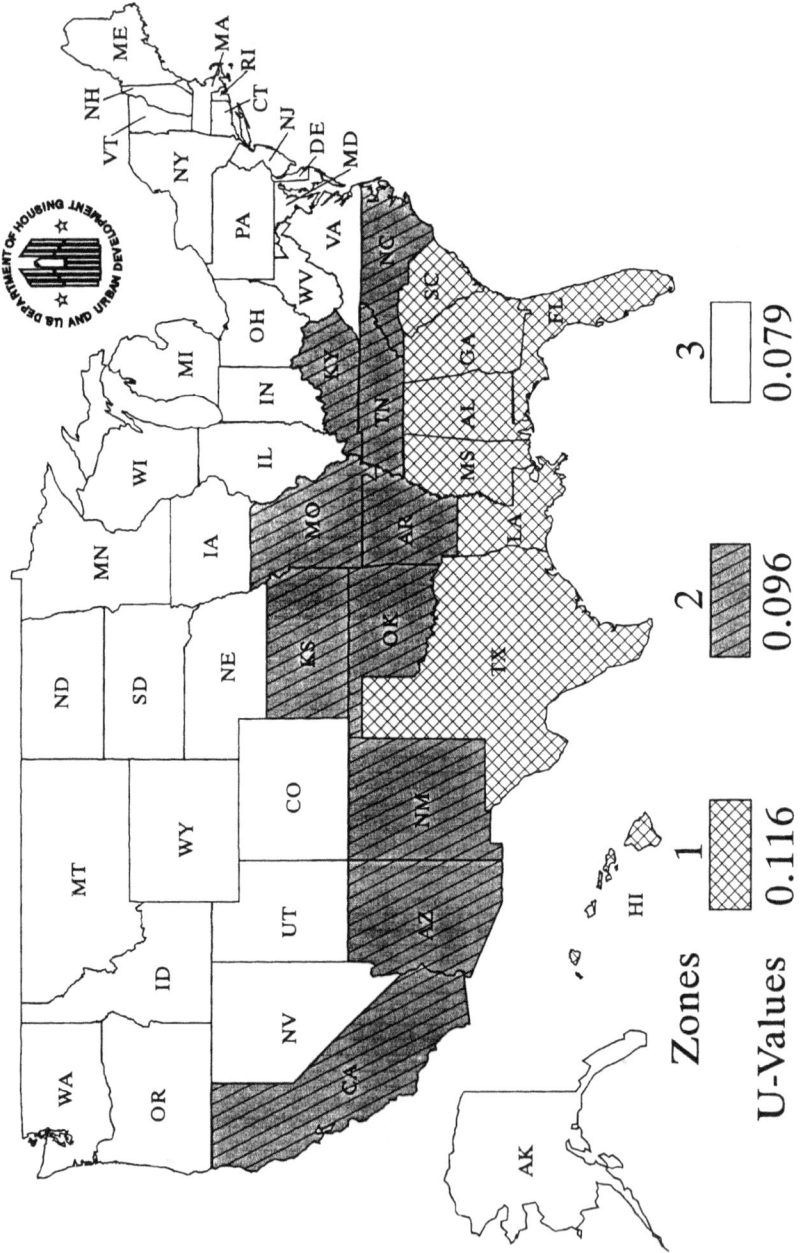

Zones	U-Values
3	0.079
2	0.096
1	0.116

(a) *Coefficient of heat transmission.* The overall coefficient of heat transmission (Uo) of the manufactured home for the respective zones and an indoor design temperature of 70 F, including internal and external ducts, and excluding infiltration, ventilation and condensation control, shall not exceed the Btu/(hr.) (sq. ft.) (F) of the manufactured home envelope are as tabulated below:

Uo value zone	Maximum coefficient of heat transmission
1	0.116 Btu/(hr.) (sq. ft.) (F).
2	0.096 Btu/(hr.) (sq. ft.) (F).
3	0.079 Btu/(hr.) (sq. ft.) (F).

(b) To assure uniform heat transmission in manufactured homes, cavities in exterior walls, floors, and ceilings shall be provided with thermal insulation.

(c) Manufactured homes designed for Uo Value Zone 3 shall be factory equipped with storm windows or insulating glass.

[58 FR 55009, Oct. 25, 1993; 59 FR 15113, Mar. 31, 1994]

§3280.507   Comfort heat gain.

Information necessary to calculate the home cooling load shall be provided as specified in this part.

(a) *Transmission heat gains.* Homes complying with this section shall meet the minimum heat loss transmission coefficients specified in §3280.506(a).

§3280.508   Heat loss, heat gain and cooling load calculations.

(a) Information, values and data necessary for heat loss and heat gain determinations must be taken from the 1997 ASHRAE Handbook of Fundamentals, Inch-Pound Edition, chapters 22 through 27. The following portions of those chapters are not applicable:

23.1   Steel Frame Construction
23.2   Masonry Construction
23.3   Foundations and Floor Systems
23.15   Pipes
23.17   Tanks, Vessels, and Equipment
23.18   Refrigerated Rooms and Buildings
24.18   Mechanical and Industrial Systems
25.19   Commercial Building Envelope Leakage
27.9   Calculation of Heat Loss from Crawl Spaces

(b) The calculation of the manufactured home's transmission heat loss coefficient (Uo) must be in accordance with the fundamental principles of the 1997 ASHRAE Handbook of Fundamentals, Inch-Pound Edition, and, at a minimum, must address all the heat loss or heat gain considerations in a manner consistent with the calculation procedures provided in the document, Overall U-values and Heating/Cooling Loads—Manufactured Homes—February 1992–PNL 8006, HUD User No. 0005945.

(c) Areas where the insulation does not fully cover a surface or is compressed shall be accounted for in the U-calculation (see §3280.506). The effect of framing on the U-value must be included in the Uo calculation. Other low-R-value heat-flow paths ("thermal shorts") shall be explicitly accounted for in the calculation of the transmission heat loss coefficient if the aggregate all types of low-R-value paths amount to more than 1% of the total exterior surface area. Areas are considered low-R-value heat-flow paths if:

(1) They separate conditioned and unconditioned space; and

(2) They are not insulated to a level that is at least one-half the nominal insulation level of the surrounding building component.

(d) *High efficiency heating and cooling equipment credit.* The calculated transmission heat loss coefficient (Uo) used for meeting the requirement in §3280.506(a) may be adjusted for heating and cooling equipment above that required by the National Appliance Energy Conservation Act of 1987 (NAECA) by applying the following formula:

Uo adjusted = Uo standard × [1 + (0.6) (heating efficiency increase factor) + (cooling multiplier) (cooling efficiency increase factor)]

where:

Uo standard = Maximum Uo for Uo Zone required by §3280.506(a)

Uo adjusted = Maximum Uo standard adjusted for high efficiency HVAC equipment

Heating efficiency increase factor = The increase factor in heating equipment efficiency measured by the Annual Fuel Utilization Efficiency (AFUE), or the Heating Seasonal Performance Factor (HSPF) for heat pumps, above that required by NAECA (indicated as "NAECA" in formula). The formula is heating efficiency increase factor = AFUE (HSPF) home − AFUE (or HSPF) NAECA divided by AFUE (HSPF) NAECA.

Cooling efficiency increase factor = the increase factor in the cooling equipment efficiency measured by the Seasonal Energy Efficiency Ratio (SEER) above that required by NAECA.

The formula being cooling equipment = SEER home—SEER NAECA divided by SEER NAECA.

The cooling multiplier for the Uo Zone is from the following table:

Uo zone	Cooling multiplier (Cm)
1	0.60 (Florida only).
1	0.20 (All other locations).
2	0.07.
3	0.03.

(e) U values for any glazing (e.g., windows, skylights, and the glazed portions of any door) must be based on tests using AAMA 1503.1–1988, Voluntary Test Method for Thermal Transmittance and Condensation Resistance of Windows, Doors, and Glazed Wall Sections, or the National Fenestration Rating Council 100, 1997 Edition, Procedure for Determining Fenestration Product U-factors. In the absence of tests, manufacturers are to use the residential window U values contained in Chapter 29, Table 5 of the 1997 ASHRAE Handbook of Fundamentals, Inch-Pound Edition. In the event that the classification of the window type is indeterminate, the manufacturer must use the classification that gives the higher U value. Where a composite of materials from two different product types is used, the product is to be assigned the higher U value. For the purpose of calculating U_o values, storm windows are treated as an additional pane.

(f) *Annual energy used based compliance.* As an alternative, homes may demonstrate compliance with the annual energy used implicit in the coefficient of heat transmission (Uo) requirement. The annual energy use determination must be based on generally accepted engineering practices. The general requirement is to demonstrate that the home seeking compliance approval has a projected annual energy use, including both heating and cooling, less than or equal to a similar "base case" home that meets the standard. The energy use for both homes must be calculated based on the same assumptions; including assuming the same dimensions for all boundaries between conditioned and unconditioned

spaces, site characteristics, usage patterns and climate.

[58 FR 55011, Oct. 25, 1993, as amended at 70 FR 72047, Nov. 30, 2005]

§ 3280.509 **Criteria in absence of specific data.**

In the absence of specific data, for purposes of heat-loss/gain calculation, the following criteria shall be used:

(a) *Infiltration heat loss.* In the absence of measured infiltration heat loss data, the following formula shall be used to calculate heat loss due to infiltration and intermittently operated fans exhausting to the outdoors. The perimeter calculation shall be based on the dimensions of the pressure envelope.

Infiltration Heat-Loss = 0.7 (T) (ft. of perimeter), BTU/hr.

where: T = 70 minus the heating system capacity certification temperature stipulated in the Heating Certificate, in F.

(b) *Framing areas.*

Wall .... 15 percent of wall area less windows and doors.
Floor and Ceiling .... 10 percent of the area.

(c) *Insulation compression.* Insulation compressed to less than nominal thickness and loose-fill insulation in sloping cavities must have its nominal R-values reduced in compressed areas in accordance with the following table:

TABLE TO PARAGRAPH (C)—EFFECT OF INSULATION COMPRESSION AND RESTRICTION ON R-VALUES

Original thickness (%)	Non-uniform (a) restriction		Uniform (b) compression batt (%)
	Batt (%)	Blown (%)	
0	20	15	0
1	26	21	1
2	32	25	2
3	36	28	4
4	38	30	5
5	41	32	7
6	43	33	8
7	45	35	10
8	46	36	11
9	48	38	13
10	49	39	14
11	51	40	15
12	52	42	17
13	53	43	18
14	54	44	20
15	55	45	21
16	57	46	22
17	58	47	24
18	59	48	25
19	59	49	26

TABLE TO PARAGRAPH (C)—EFFECT OF INSULATION COMPRESSION AND RESTRICTION ON R-VALUES—Continued

Original thickness (%)	Non-uniform (a) restriction		Uniform (b) compression batt (%)
	Batt (%)	Blown (%)	
20	60	50	28
21	61	51	29
22	62	52	30
23	63	52	31
24	64	53	33
25	65	54	34
26	65	55	35
27	66	56	36
28	67	57	37
29	68	57	39
30	68	58	40
31	69	59	41
32	70	60	42
33	70	60	43
34	71	61	44
35	72	62	45
36	72	63	47
37	73	63	48
38	74	64	49
39	74	65	50
40	75	65	51
41	75	66	52
42	76	67	53
43	76	68	54
44	77	68	55
45	78	69	56
46	78	70	57
47	79	70	58
48	79	71	59
49	80	71	60
50	80	72	61
51	81	73	62
52	81	73	63
53	82	74	64
54	82	75	65
55	83	75	65
56	83	76	66
57	84	76	67
58	84	77	68
59	84	78	69
60	85	78	70
61	85	79	71
62	86	79	72
63	86	80	73
64	87	81	74
65	87	81	74
66	88	82	75
67	88	82	76
68	88	83	77
69	89	84	78
70	89	84	78
71	90	85	79
72	90	85	80
73	90	86	81
74	91	86	82
75	91	87	82
76	92	87	83
77	92	88	84
78	92	89	85
79	93	89	85
80	93	90	86
81	93	90	87
82	94	91	88
83	94	91	88
84	95	92	89
85	95	92	90

TABLE TO PARAGRAPH (C)—EFFECT OF INSULATION COMPRESSION AND RESTRICTION ON R-VALUES—Continued

Original thickness (%)	Non-uniform (a) restriction		Uniform (b) compression batt (%)
	Batt (%)	Blown (%)	
86	95	93	91
87	96	93	91
88	96	94	92
89	96	94	93
90	97	95	93
91	97	95	94
92	97	96	95
93	98	96	95
94	98	97	96
95	98	97	97
96	99	98	97
97	99	98	98
98	99	99	99
99	100	99	99
100	100	100	100

Note: To use this table, first compute the restricted insulation thickness as a fraction of the uncompressed (full) insulation thickness. Then look up the R-value remaining from the appropriate column (Non-uniform Restriction, Batt Non-uniform Restriction, Blown or Uniform Compression, Batt). Example: Assume a section of loose-fill ceiling insulation went from R-25 insulation at a height of 10 inches to a minimum height of 2 inches at the edge of the ceiling. The ratio of minimum to full thickness is 0.20 (2 divided by 10). Look up 0.20 (20 percent), read across to column 3 (Non-uniform Restriction, Blown), and read 50 percent. Therefore, the R-value of the loose-fill insulation over the restricted area would be R-12.5 (50 percent of 25).

(a) Non-uniform restriction is that which occurs between non-parallel planes, such as in the ceiling near the eaves.

(b) Uniform compression is compression between parallel planes, such as that which occurs in a wall.

(d) *Air supply ducts within floor cavity.* Air supply ducts located within a floor cavity shall be assumed to be heating or cooling the floor cavity to living space temperatures unless the duct is structurally isolated by the framing system or thermally insulated from the rest of the floor cavity with a thermal insulation at least equal to R-4.

(e) *Air supply ducts within ceiling cavity.* Where supply ducts are located in ceiling cavities, the influence of the duct on cavity temperatures shall be considered in calculating envelope heat loss or heat gain.

(f) The supply duct loss (and/or heat gain where applicable—See § 3280.511) shall be calculated using the actual duct surface area and the actual thickness of insulation between the duct and outside of the manufactured home. If there is an air space of at least ½ inch between the duct and the insulation, heat loss/gain need not be calculated if the cavity in which the duct is located is assumed to be at living space temperature. The average temperature inside the supply duct, including ducts installed outside the manufactured home, shall be assumed to be 130 F for purposes of calculation of heat loss and 60 F for heat gain.

(g) *Return air cavities.* Cavities used as return air plenums shall be considered to be at living space temperature.

[40 FR 58752, Dec. 18, 1975. Redesignated at 44 FR 20679, Apr. 6, 1979, as amended at 78 FR 73984, Dec. 9, 2013]

§ 3280.510 Heat loss certificate.

The manufactured home manufacturer shall permanently affix the following "Certificate" to an interior surface of the home that is readily visible to the homeowner. The "Certificate" shall specify the following:

(a) *Heating zone certification.* The design zone at which the manufactured home heat loss complies with § 3280.506(a).

(b) *Outdoor certification temperature.* The lowest outdoor temperature at which the installed heating equipment will maintain a 70 °F temperature inside the home without storm sash or insulating glass for Zones 1 and 2, and with storm sash or insulating glass for Zone 3 and complying with § 3280.508 and § 3280.509.

(c) *Operating economy certification temperature.* The temperature to be specified for operating economy and energy conservation shall be 20 °F or 30% of the design temperature difference, whichever is greater, added to the temperature specified as the heating system capacity certification temperature without storm windows or insulating glass in Zones 1 and 2 and with storm windows or insulating glass in Zone 3. Design temperature difference is 70° minus the heating system capacity certification temperature in degrees Fahrenheit.

HEATING CERTIFICATE

Home Manufacturer _____
Plant Location _____
Home Model _____

(Include Uo Value Zone Map)

This manufactured home has been thermally insulated to conform with the requirements of the Federal Manufactured Home Construction and Safety Standards for all locations within Uo Value Zone ____.

Heating Equipment Manufacturer _____
Heating Equipment Model _____

The above heating equipment has the capacity to maintain an average 70F temperature in this home at outdoor temperatures of [see paragraph (b) of this section] F. To maximize furnace operating economy and to conserve energy, it is recommended that this home be installed where the outdoor winter design temperature (97 1/2%) is not higher than [see paragraph (c) of this section] F degrees Fahrenheit.

The above information has been calculated assuming a maximum wind velocity of 15 MPH at standard atmospheric pressure.

(d) The following additional statement must be provided on the heating certificate and data plate required by § 3280.5 when the home is built with a vapor retarder of not greater than one perm (dry cup method) on the exterior side of the insulation: "This home is designed and constructed to be sited only in humid or fringe climate regions as shown on the Humid and Fringe Climate Map." A reproduction of the Humid and Fringe Climate Map in § 3280.504 is to be provided on the heating certificate and data plate. The map must be not less than 3½ inch × 2¼ inch in size and may be combined with the U₀ Value Zone Map for Manufactured Housing in § 3280.506.

[40 FR 58752, Dec. 18, 1975. Redesignated at 44 FR 20679, Apr. 6, 1979, as amended at 58 FR 55011, Oct. 25, 1993; 70 FR 72048, Nov. 30, 2005]

§ 3280.511 Comfort cooling certificate and information.

(a) The manufactured home manufacturer shall permanently affix a "Comfort Cooling Certificate" to an interior surface of the home that is readily visible to the home owner. This certificate may be combined with the heating certificate required in § 3280.510. The manufacturer shall comply with one of the following three alternatives in providing the certificate and additional information concerning the cooling of the manufactured home:

(1) *Alternative I.* If a central air conditioning system is provided by the home manufacturer, the heat gain calculation necessary to properly size the air conditioning equipment shall be in accordance with procedures outlined in

chapter 22 of the 1989 ASHRAE Handbook of Fundamentals, with an assumed location and orientation. The following shall be supplied in the Comfort Cooling Certificate:

Air Conditioner Manufacturer _____
Air Conditioner Model _____

Certified Capacity _____ BTU/Hr. in accordance with the appropriate Air Conditioning and Refrigeration Institute Standards

The central air conditioning system provided with this home has been sized, assuming an orientation of the front (hitch) end of the home facing _____ and is designed on the basis of a 75 °F indoor temperature and an outdoor temperature of _ °F dry bulb and _ °F wet bulb.

EXAMPLE ALTERNATE I

COMFORT COOLING CERTIFICATE

Manufactured Home Mfg _____
Plant Location _____
Manufactured Home Model _____
Air Conditioner Manufacturer _____

Certified Capacity _____ BTU/Hr. in accordance with the appropriate Air Conditioning and Refrigeration Institute Standards.

The central air conditioning system provided with this home has been sized assuming an orientation of the front (hitch end) of the home facing _____. On this basis, the system is designed to maintain an indoor temperature of 75 °F when outdoor temperatures are _ °F dry bulb and _ °F wet bulb.

The temperature to which this home can be cooled will change depending upon the amount of exposure of the windows to the sun's radiant heat. Therefore, the home's heat gains will vary dependent upon its orientation to the sun and any permanent shading provided. Information concerning the calculation of cooling loads at various locations, window exposures and shadings are provided in chapter 22 of the 1989 edition of the ASHRAE Handbook of Fundamentals.

(2) *Alternative 2.* For each home suitable for a central air cooling system, the manufacturer shall provide the following statement: "This air distribution system of this home is suitable for the installation of a central air conditioning system."

EXAMPLE ALTERNATE 2

COMFORT COOLING CERTIFICATE

Manufactured Home Manufacturer _____
Plant Location _____
Manufactured Home Model _____

This air distribution system of this home is suitable for the installation of central air conditioning.

The supply air distribution system installed in this home is sized for Manufactured Home Central Air Conditioning System of up to _____ B.T.U./Hr. rated capacity which are certified in accordance with the appropriate Air Conditioning and Refrigeration Institute Standards. When the air circulators of such air conditioners are rated at 0.3 inch water column static pressure or greater for the cooling air delivered to the manufactured home supply air duct system.

Information necessary to calculate cooling loads at various locations and orientations is provided in the special comfort cooling information provided with this manufactured home.

(3) *Alternative 3.* If the manufactured home is not equipped with an air supply duct system, or if the manufacturer elects not to designate the home as being suitable for the installation of a central air conditioning system, the manufacturer shall provide the following statement: "This air distribution system of this home has not been designed in anticipation of its use with a central air conditioning system."

EXAMPLE ALTERNATE 3

COMFORT COOLING CERTIFICATE

Manufactured Home Mfg _____
Plant Location _____
Manufactured Home Model _____

The air distribution system of this home has not been designed in anticipation of its use with a central air conditioning system.

(b) For each home designated as suitable for central air conditioning the manufacturer shall provide the maximum central manufactured home air conditioning capacity certified in accordance with the ARI Standard 210/240–89 Unitary Air-Conditioning and Air-Source Heat Pump Equipment and in accordance with § 3280.715(a)(3). If the capacity information provided is based on entrances to the air supply duct at other than the furnace plenum, the manufacturer shall indicate the correct supply air entrance and return air exit locations.

(c) *Comfort cooling information.* For each manufactured home designated, either "suitable for" or "provided with" a central air conditioning system, the manufacturer shall provide comfort cooling information specific to the manufactured home necessary to complete the cooling load calculations. The comfort cooling information shall include a statement to read as follows:

To determine the required capacity of equipment to cool a home efficiently and economically, a cooling load (heat gain) calculation is required. The cooling load is dependent on the orientation, location and the structure of the home. Central air conditioners operate most efficiently and provide the greatest comfort when their capacity closely approximates the calculated cooling load. Each home's air conditioner should be sized in accordance with chapter 22 of the American Society of Heating, Refrigerating and Air Conditioning Engineers (ASHRAE) Handbook of Fundamentals, 1989 Edition, once the location and orientation are known.

INFORMATION PROVIDED BY THE MANUFACTURER NECESSARY TO CALCULATE SENSIBLE HEAT GAIN

Walls (without windows and doors)	U
Ceilings and roofs of light color	U
Ceilings and roofs of dark color	U
Floors	U
Air ducts in floor	U
Air ducts in ceiling	U
Air ducts installed outside the home	U

Information necessary to calculate duct areas.

[40 FR 58752, Dec. 18, 1975. Redesignated at 44 FR 20679, Apr. 6, 1979, as amended at 58 FR 55012, Oct. 25, 1993]

Subpart G—Plumbing Systems

§ 3280.601   Scope.

Subpart G of this standard covers the plumbing materials, fixtures, and equipment installed within or on manufactured homes. It is the intent of this subpart to assure water supply, drain, waste and vent systems which permit satisfactory functioning and provide for health and safety under all conditions of normal use.

§ 3280.602   Definitions.

The following definitions are applicable to subpart G only:

Accessible, when applied to a fixture, connection, appliance or equipment, means having access thereto, but which may require removal of an access panel or opening of a door.

Air gap (water distribution system) means the unobstructed vertical distance through the free atmosphere between the lowest opening from any pipe or faucet supplying water to a tank, plumbing fixture, water supplied appliances, or other device and the flood level rim of the receptacle.

Backflow means the flow of water or other liquids, mixtures, or substances into the distributing pipes of a potable supply of water from any source or sources other than its intended sources.

Backflow connection means any arrangement whereby backflow can occur.

Backflow preventer means a device or means to prevent backflow.

Branch means any part of the piping system other than a riser, main or stack.

Common vent means a vent connecting at the junction of fixture drains and serving as a vent for more than one fixture.

Continuous vent means a vertical vent that is a continuation of the drain to which it connects.

Continuous waste means a drain from two or more fixtures connected to a single trap.

Critical level means a point established by the testing laboratory (usually stamped on the device by the manufacturer) which determines the minimum elevation above the flood level rim of the fixture or receptacle served on which the device may be installed. When a backflow prevention device does not bear a critical level marking, the bottom of the vacuum breaker, combination valve, or of any such approved or listed device shall constitute the critical level.

Cross connection means any physical connection or arrangement between two otherwise separate systems or sources, one of which contains potable water and the other either water, steam, gas or chemical of unknown or questionable safety whereby there may be a flow from one system or source to the other, the direction of flow depending on the pressure differential between the two systems.

Developed length means that length of pipe measured along the center line of the pipe and fittings.

Diameter, unless otherwise specifically stated, means the nominal (inside) diameter designated commercially.

Drain means a pipe that carries waste, water, or water-borne waste in a drainage system.

Drain connector means the removable extension, consisting of all pipes, fittings and appurtenances, from the drain outlet to the drain inlet serving the manufactured home.

Drain outlet means the lowest end of the main or secondary drain to which a sewer connection is made.

Drainage system means all piping within or attached to the structure that conveys sewage or other liquid waste to the drain outlet, not including the drain connector.

Fixture drain means the drain from the trap of a fixture to the junction of that drain with any other drain pipe.

Fixture supply means the water supply pipe connecting a fixture to a branch water supply pipe or directly to a main water supply pipe.

Flood-level means the level in the receptacle over which water would overflow to the outside of the receptacle.

Flooded means the condition which results when the liquid in a container or receptacle rises to the flood-level.

Flush tank means that portion of a water closet that is designed to contain sufficient water to adequately flush the fixture.

Flush valve means a device located at the bottom of a flush tank for flushing a water closet.

Flushometer tank: means a device integrated within an air accumulator vessel which is designed to discharge a predetermined quantity of water to fixtures for flushing purposes.

Flushometer valve means a device which discharges a predetermined quantity of water to a fixture for flushing purposes and is closed by direct water pressure.

Grade means the fall (slope) of a pipe in reference to a horizontal plane expressed in inches per foot length.

Horizontal branch means any pipe extending laterally, which receives the discharge from one or more fixture drains and connects to the main drain.

Horizontal pipe means any pipe or fitting which makes an angle of not more than 45 degrees with the horizontal.

Individual vent means a pipe installed to vent a fixture drain.

Inlet coupling means the terminal end of the water system to which the water service connection is attached. It may be a swivel fitting or threaded pipe end.

Main means the principal artery of the system to which branches may be connected.

Main drain means the lowest pipe of a drainage system which receives sewage from all the fixtures within a manufactured home and conducts these wastes to the drain outlet.

Main vent means the principal artery of the venting system to which vent branches may be connected.

Mechanical trap vent device means a device that automatically opens to admit air to a fixture drain above the connection of the trap arm so as to prevent siphonage, and closes tightly when the pressure within the drainage system is equal to or greater than atmospheric pressure, so as to prevent the escape of gases from the drainage system into the manufactured home.

Offset means a combination of pipe and/or fittings that brings one section of the pipe out of line but into a line parallel with the other section.

Pitch. See *Grade.*

Plumbing appliance: means any one of a special class of plumbing fixture which is intended to perform a special plumbing function. Its operation and/or control may be dependent upon one or more energized components, such as motors, control, heating elements, or pressure or temperature-sensing elements. Such fixture may operate automatically through one or more of the following actions: A time cycle, a temperature range, a pressure range, a measured volume or weight, or the fixture may be manually adjusted or controlled by the user or operator.

Plumbing appurtenance: means a manufactured device, or a prefabricated assembly, or an on-the-job assembly of component parts, and which is an adjunct to the basic piping system and plumbing system and plumbing fixtures. An appurtenance demands no additional water supply, nor does it add any discharge load to a fixture or the drainage system.

Plumbing fixtures means receptacles, devices, or appliances which are supplied with water or which receive liquid or liquid-borne wastes for discharge into the drainage system.

Plumbing system means the water supply and distribution pipes; plumbing fixtures, faucets and traps; soil, waste and vent pipes; and water-treating or water-using equipment.

Primary vent. See *main vent.*

Relief vent means an auxiliary vent which permits additional circulation of air in or between drainage and vent systems.

Secondary vent means any vent other than the main vent or those serving each toilet.

Sewage means any liquid waste containing animal or vegetable matter in suspension or solution, and may include liquids containing chemicals in solution.

Siphonage means the loss of water seal from fixture traps resulting from partial vacuum in the drainage system which may be of either of the following two types, or a combination of the two:

(a) Self-siphonage resulting from vacuum in a fixture drain generated solely by the discharge of the fixture served by that drain, or,

(b) Induced siphonage resulting from vacuum in the drainage system generated by the discharge of one or more fixtures other than the one under observation.

Trap means a fitting or device designed and constructed to provide a liquid seal that will prevent the back passage of air without materially affecting the flow of liquid waste through it.

Trap arm means the portion of a fixture drain between a trap and its vent.

Trap seal means the vertical depth of liquid that a trap will retain.

Vacuum breaker. See *backflow preventer.*

Vent cap means the device or fitting which protects the vent pipe from foreign substance with an opening to the atmosphere equal to the area of the vent it serves.

Vent system means that part of a piping installation which provides circulation of air within a drainage system.

Vertical pipe means any pipe or fitting which makes an angle of not more than 45 degrees with the vertical.

Water closet drain means that part of the drainage piping which receives the discharge from each individual water closet.

Water connection means the fitting or point of connection for the manufactured home water distribution system designed for connection to a water supply.

Water connector means the removable extension connecting the manufactured home water distribution system to the water supply.

Water distribution system means potable water piping within or permanently attached to the manufactured home.

Wet vent means a vent which also serves as a drain for one or more fixtures.

Wet vented drainage system means the specially designed system of drain piping that also vents one or more plumbing fixtures by means of a common waste and vent pipe.

Whirlpool bathtub means a plumbing appliance consisting of a bathtub fixture which is equipped and fitted with a circulation piping system, pump, and other appurtenances and is so designed to accept, circulate, and discharge bathtub water upon each use.

[40 FR 58752, Dec. 18, 1975. Redesignated at 44 FR 20679, Apr. 6, 1979, as amended at 52 FR 4584, Feb. 12, 1987; 52 FR 47553, Dec. 15, 1987; 58 FR 55012, Oct. 25, 1993; 78 FR 73984, Dec. 9, 2013]

§ 3280.603 General requirements.

(a) *Minimum requirements.* Any plumbing system installed in a manufactured home shall conform, at least, with the provisions of this subpart.

(1) *General.* The plumbing system shall be of durable material, free from defective workmanship, and so designed and constructed as to give satisfactory service for a reasonable life expectancy.

(2) *Conservation.* Each water closet must not use more than 1.6 gallons of water per flush.

(3) *Connection to drainage system.* All plumbing, fixtures, drains, appurtenances, and appliances designed or used to receive or discharge liquid waste or sewage shall be connected to the manufactured home drainage system in a manner provided by this standard.

(4) *Workmanship.* All design, construction, and workmanship shall be in conformance with accepted engineering practices and shall be of such character as to secure the results sought to be obtained by this standard.

(5) *Components.* Plumbing materials, devices, fixtures, fittings, equipment, appliances, appurtenance, and accessories intended for use in or attached to a manufactured home shall conform to one of the applicable standards referenced in § 3280.604. Where an applicable standard is not referenced, or an alternative recognized standard is utilized, the plumbing component shall be listed by a nationally recognized testing laboratory, inspection agency or other qualified organization as suitable for the intended use.

(6) *Prohibited fittings and practices.* (i) Drainage or vent piping shall not be drilled and tapped for the purpose of making connections.

(ii) Except as specifically provided elsewhere in this standard, vent pipes shall not be used as waste or drain pipes.

(iii) Fittings, connections, devices, or methods of installation that obstruct or retard the flow of sewage, or air in the drainage or venting systems in an amount greater than the normal frictional resistance to flow shall not be used unless their use is acceptable in this standard or their use is accepted as having a desirable and acceptable function of ultimate benefit to the proper and continued functioning of the plumbing system.

(iv) Cracks, holes, or other imperfections in materials shall not be concealed by welding, brazing, or soldering or by paint, wax, tar, or other leak-sealing or repairing agents.

(v) Piping, fixtures or equipment shall be located so as not to interfere with the normal use or with the normal operation and use of windows, doors or other required facilities.

(vi) Galvanized pipe shall not be bent or welded.

(7) *Alignment of fittings.* All valves, pipes, and fittings shall be installed in correct relationship to the direction of flow.

(b) *Protective requirements.* (1) Cutting structural members. Structural members shall not be unnecessarily or carelessly weakened by cutting or notching.

(2) *Exposed piping.* All piping, pipe threads, hangers, and support exposed to the weather, water, mud, and road hazard, and subject to damage therefrom, shall be painted, coated, wrapped, or otherwise protected from deterioration.

(3) *Road damage.* Pipes, supports, drains, outlets, or drain hoses shall not extend or protrude in a manner where they could be unduly subjected to damage during transit.

(4) *Freezing.* All piping and fixtures subject to freezing temperatures shall be insulated or protected to prevent freezing, under normal occupancy. The manufacturer shall provide:

(i) Written installation instructions for the method(s) required for compliance to this section;

(ii) A statement in the installation instructions required by § 3280.306(b), stating that if the heat tape or pipe heating cable is used, it must be listed for use with manufactured homes.

(iii) A receptacle outlet complying with § 3280.806(d)(10).

(5) All piping, except the fixture trap, shall be designed to allow drainage.

(6) *Rodent resistance.* All exterior openings around piping and equipment shall be sealed to resist the entrance of rodents.

(7) Piping and electrical wiring shall not pass through the same holes in walls, floors or roofs. Plastic piping shall not be exposed to heat in excess of manufacturers recommendation or radiation from heat producing appliances.

[40 FR 58752, Dec. 18, 1975, as amended at 42 FR 54383, Oct. 5, 1977. Redesignated at 44 FR 20679, Apr. 6, 1979, as amended at 58 FR 55012, Oct. 25, 1993; 78 FR 73985, Dec. 9, 2013]

§ 3280.604 **Materials.**

(a) *Minimum standards.* Materials, devices, fixtures, fittings, equipment, appliances, appurtenances and accessories shall conform to one of the standards in the following table and be free from defects. Where an appropriate standard is not indicated in the table or a standard not indicated in the table is preferred, the item may be used if it is listed. A listing is also required when so specified in other sections of this subpart.

(b) Where more than one standard is referenced for a particular material or component, compliance with only one of those standards is acceptable. Exceptions:

(1) When one of the reference standards requires evaluation of chemical, toxicity or odor properties which are not included in the other standard, then conformance to the applicable requirements of each standard shall be demonstrated;

(2) When a plastic material or component is not covered by the Standards in the following table, it must be certified as non-toxic in accordance with ANSI/NSF 61–2001, Drinking water system components—Health effects.

FERROUS PIPE AND FITTINGS

Gray Iron Threaded Fittings—ANSI/ASME B16.4–1992.
Malleable Iron Threaded Fittings—ANSI/ASME B16.3–1992.
Material and Property Standard for Special Cast Iron Fittings—IAPMO PS 5–84.
Welding and Seamless Wrought Steel Pipe—ANSI/ASME B36.10–1979.
Standard Specification for Pipe, Steel, Black and Hot-Dipped, Zinc-Coated, Welded and Seamless—ASTM A53–93.
Pipe Threads, General Purpose (Inch)—ANSI/ASME B1.20.1–1983.
Standard Specification for Cast Iron Soil Pipe and Fittings—ASTM A74–92.
Standard Specification for Hubless Cast Iron Soil Pipe and Fittings for Sanitary and Storm Drain, Waste, and Vent Piping Applications—CISPI-301–90.

NONFERROUS PIPE AND FITTINGS

Standard Specification for Seamless Copper Pipe, Standard Sizes—ASTM B42–93.
Standard Specification for General Requirements for Wrought Seamless Copper and Copper-Alloy Tube—ASTM B251–93.
Standard Specification for Seamless Copper Water Tube—ASTM B88–93.
Standard Specification for Copper Drainage Tube (DWV)—ASTM B306–92.
Wrought Copper and Copper Alloy Solder-Joint Pressure Fitting—ASME/ANSI B16.22–1989.
Wrought Copper and Wrought Copper Alloy Solder-Joint Drainage Fittings-DWV—ASME/ANSI B16.29–1986.
Cast Copper Alloy Solder-Joint Pressure Fittings—ANSI B16.18–1984.
Cast Copper Alloy Solder-Joint Drainage Fittings-DWV—ASME B16.23–1992.
Cast Copper Alloy Fittings for Flared Copper Tubes—ASME/ANSI B16.26–1988.

Standard Specification for Seamless Red Brass Pipe, Standard Sizes—ASTM B43–91.
Cast Bronze Threaded Fittings, Classes 125 and 250—ANSI/ASME B16.15–1985.

PLASTIC PIPE AND FITTINGS

Standard Specification Acrylonitrile-Butadiene-Styrene (ABS) Schedule 40 Plastic Drain, Waste, and Vent Pipe and Fittings—ASTM D2661–91.
Standard Specification for Poly (Vinyl Chloride) (PVC) Plastic Drain, Waste, and Vent Pipe and Fittings—ASTM D2665–91b.
Standard Specification for Drain, Waste, and Vent (DWV) Plastic Fittings Patterns—ASTM D3311–92.
Standard Specification for Acrylonitrile-Butadiene-Styrene (ABS) Schedule 40, Plastic Drain, Waste, and Vent Pipe With a Cellular Core—ASTM F628–91.
Standard Specification for Chlorinated Poly (Vinyl Chloride) (CPVC) Plastic Hot- and Cold-Water Distribution Systems—ASTM D2846–92.
Standard Specification for Polybutylene (PB) Plastic Hot- and Cold-Water Distribution Systems—ASTM D3309–92a.
Plastic Piping Components and Related Materials—ANSI/NSF 14–1990.
Standard Specification for Crosslinked Polyethylene (PEX) Tubing—ASTM F876–10 (incorporated by reference, see § 3280.4).
Standard Specification for Crosslinked Polyethylene (PEX) Plastic Hot- and Cold-Water Distribution Systems—ASTM F877–07 (incorporated by reference, see § 3280.4).

MISCELLANEOUS

Standard Specification for Rubber Gaskets for Cast Iron Soil Pipe and Fittings, ASTM C564–97 (incorporated by reference, see § 3280.4).
Backflow Valves—ANSI A112.14.1–1975.
Plumbing Fixture Setting Compound—TTP 1536A–1975.
Material and Property Standard for Cast Brass and Tubing P-Traps—IAPMO PS 2–89.
Relief Valves for Hot Water Supply Systems, ANSI Z21.22–1999 (incorporated by reference, see § 3280.4).
Standard Specification for Solvent Cement for Acrylonitrile-Butadiene-Styrene (ABS) Plastic Pipe and Fittings—ASTM D2235–88.
Standard Specification for Solvent Cements for Poly (Vinyl Chloride) (PVC) Plastic Piping Systems—ASTM D2564–91a.
Specification for Neoprene Rubber Gaskets for HUB and Spigot Cast Iron Soil Pipe and Fittings—CISPI-HSN–85.
Plumbing System Components for Manufactured Homes and Recreational Vehicles—ANSI/NSF 24–1988.
Material and Property Standard for Diversion Tees and Twin Waste Elbow—IAPMO PS 9–84.

Material and Property Standard for Flexible Metallic Water Connectors—IAPMO PS 14–89.

Material and Property Standard for Dishwasher Drain Airgaps—IAPMO PS 23–89.

Material and Property Standards for Backflow Prevention Assemblies—IAPMO PS 31–91.

Performance Requirements for Air Admittance Valves for Plumbing Drainage Systems, Fixture and Branch Devices—ASSE Standard #1051, 1990 Revised: 1996/ANSI 1998.

Drinking Water System Components–Health Effects—ANSI/NSF 61–2001.

PLUMBING FIXTURES

Plumbing Fixtures (General Specifications)—FS WW–P–541E/GEN–1980.

Vitreous China Plumbing Fixtures—ANSI/ASME A112.19.2(M)–1990.

Enameled Cast Iron Plumbing Fixtures—ANSI/ASME A112.19.1M–1987.

Porcelain Enameled Formed Steel Plumbing Fixtures—ANSI/ASME A112.19.4(M)–1984.

Plastic Bathtub Units with Addenda Z124.1a–1990 and Z124.16–1991—ANSI Z124.1–1987.

Standard for Porcelain Enameled Formed Steel Plumbing Fixtures—IAPMO TSC 22–85.

Plastic Shower Receptors and Shower Stalls with Addendum Z124.2a–1990—ANSI Z124.2–1987.

Stainless Steel Plumbing Fixtures (Designed for Residential Use)—ANSI/ASME A112.19.3M–1987.

Material and Property Standard for Drains for Prefabricated and Precast Showers—IAPMO PS 4–90.

Plastic Lavatories with Addendum Z124.3a–1990—ANSI Z124.3–1986.

Standard for Safety Glazing Materials used in Buildings—Safety Performance Specifications and Methods of Test, ANSI Z97.1–2004 (incorporated by reference, see §3280.4).

Water Heater Relief Valve Drain Tubes—ASME A112.4.1–1993.

Flexible Water Connectors—ASME A112.18.6–1999.

Performance Requirements for Backflow Protection Devices and Systems in Plumbing Fixture Fittings—ASME A112.18.3M–1996.

Non-Vitreous Ceramic Plumbing Fixtures—ASME A112.19.9M–1991.

Dual Flush Devices for Water Closets—ASME A119.19.10–1994.

Deck Mounted Bath/Shower Transfer Valves with Integral Backflow Protection—ASME A112.18.7–1999.

Plastic Fittings for Connecting Water Closets to the Sanitary Drainage System—ASME A112.4.3–1999.

Hydraulic Performance Requirements for Water Closets and Urinals, ASME A112.19.6–1995.

Plumbing Fixture Fittings—ASME/ANSI A112.18.1M–1989.

Trim for Water Closet, Bowls, Tanks, and Urinals—ANSI A112.19.5–1979.

Plastic Water Closets, Bowls, and Tanks with Addenda Z124.4a-1990—ANSI Z124.4–1986.

ANSI Z124.5, Plastic Toilet (Water Closets) Seats, 1997.

ANSI Z124.7, Prefabricated Plastic Spa Shells, 1997.

Whirlpool Bathtub Appliances—ASME/ANSI A112.19.7M–1987.

ANSI Z–124.9, Plastic Urinal Fixtures, 1994.

Performance Requirements for Individual Thermostatic Pressure Balancing and Combination Control for Bathing Facilities—ASSE 1016–1988 (ANSI 1990).

Performance Requirements for Pressurized Flushing Devices (Flushometers) for Plumbing Fixtures—ASSE 1037–1990 (ANSI–1990).

Performance Requirements for Water Closet Flush Tank Fill Valves (Ballcocks)—ASSE 1002 Revision 5–1986 (ANSI/ASSE–1979).

Performance Requirements for Hand-held Showers—ASSE 1014–1989 (ANSI–1990).

Hydrants for Utility and Maintenance Use—ANSI/ASME A112.21.3M–1985.

Performance Requirements for Home Laundry Equipment—ASSE 1007–1986.

Performance Requirements for Hot Water Dispensers, Household Storage Type Electrical—ASSE 1023, (ANSI/ASSE–1979).

Plumbing Requirements for Residential Use (Household) Dishwashers—ASSE 1006, (ASSE/ANSI–1986).

Performance Requirements for Household Food Waste Disposer Units—ASSE 1008–1986.

Performance Requirements for Temperature Activated Mixing Valves for Primary Domestic Use—ASSE 1017–1986.

Water Hammer Arresters—ANSI A112.26.1–1969 (R 1975).

Suction Fittings for Use in Swimming Pools, Wading Pools, Spas, Hot Tubs, and Whirlpool Bathtub Appliances—ASME/ANSI A112.19.8M–1989.

Air Gaps in Plumbing Systems—ASME A112.1.2–1991.

Performance Requirements for Diverters for Plumbing Faucets with Hose Spray, Anti-Siphon Type, Residential Applications—ASSE 1025 (ANSI/ASSE–1978).

Performance Requirements for Pipe Applied Atmospheric Type Vacuum Breakers—ASSE 1001 (ASSE/ANSI–1990).

Performance Requirements for Hose Connection Vacuum Breakers—ASSE 1011–1981 (ANSI–1982).

Performance Requirements for Wall Hydrants, Frost Proof Automatic Draining, Anti-Backflow Types—ANSI/ASSE 1019–1978.

Performance Requirements for Automatic Compensating Values for Individual Shower and Tub/Shower Combinations, approved January 2005 ASSE 1016–2005 (incorporated by reference, see § 3280.4).

Performance Requirements for Water Temperature Limiting Devices, approved February 2004, ASSE 1070–2004 (incorporated by reference, see § 3280.4).

[58 FR 55013, Oct. 25, 1993, as amended at 70 FR 72048, Nov. 30, 2005; 78 FR 73985, Dec. 9, 2013; 79 FR 31863, June 3, 2014]

§ 3280.605 Joints and connections.

(a) *Tightness.* Joints and connections in the plumbing system shall be gas-tight and watertight for the pressures required under testing procedures.

(b) *Assembling of pipe.* All joints and connections shall be correctly assembled for tightness. Pipe threads shall be fully engaged with the threads of the fitting. Plastic pipe and copper tubing shall be inserted to the full depth of the solder cup or welding sockets of each fitting. Pipe threads and slip joints shall not be wrapped with string, paper, putty, or similar fillers.

(c) *Threaded joints.* Threads for screw pipe and fittings shall conform to the approved or listed standard. Pipe ends shall be reamed out to size of bore. All burrs, chips, cutting oil and foreign matter shall be removed. Pipe joint cement or thread lubricant shall be of approved type and applied to male threads only.

(d) *Solder joints.* Solder joints for tubing shall be made with approved or listed solder type fittings. Surfaces to be soldered shall be cleaned bright. The joints shall be properly fluxed with noncorrosive paste type flux and, for manufactured homes to be connected to a public water system, made with solder having not more than 0.2 percent lead.

(e) *Plastic pipe, fittings and joints.* Plastic pipe and fittings shall be joined by installation methods recommended by the manufacturer or in accordance with the provisions of a recognized, approved, or listed standard.

(f) *Union joints.* Metal unions in water piping shall have metal-to-metal ground seats.

(g) *Flared joints.* Flared joints for soft-copper water tubing shall be made with approved or listed fittings. The tubing shall be expanded with a proper flaring tool.

(h) *Cast iron soil pipe joints.* Approved or listed cast iron pipe may be joined as follows:

(1) Approved or listed hub-less pipe and fittings must be permitted to be joined with listed couplings or adapters, per the manufacturer's recommendations.

(2) Hub and plain-end soil pipe may be joined by compression fittings per the manufacturer's recommendation.

[40 FR 58752, Dec. 18, 1975. Redesignated at 44 FR 20679, Apr. 6, 1979, as amended at 53 FR 23611, June 23, 1988; 78 FR 73985, Dec. 9, 2013]

§ 3280.606 Traps and cleanouts.

(a) *Traps*—(1) *Traps required.* Each plumbing fixture, except listed toilets, shall be separately trapped by approved water seal "P" traps. All traps shall be effectively vented.

(2) *Combination Fixtures.* For the purposes of drainage and ventilation requirements, a two- or three-compartment sink, up to three single sinks, or up to three lavatories may be connected to one "P" trap and considered as a single fixture, so long as the sinks and lavatories are in the same room, have waste outlets not more than 30 inches apart, and have flood level rims at the same level. The "P" trap must be installed at the center fixture when three such fixtures are installed.

(3) *Prohibited traps.* A trap which depends for its seal upon concealed interior partitions shall not be used. Full "S" traps, bell traps, drum traps, crown-vented traps, and running traps are prohibited. Fixtures shall not be double-trapped.

(4) *Material and design.* Each trap shall be self-cleaning with a smooth and uniform interior waterway. Traps shall be manufactured of cast iron, cast brass, or drawn brass tubing of not less than No. 20 Brown and Sharpe gage, or approved or listed plastic, or other approved or listed material. Union joints for a trap shall be beaded to provide a shoulder for the union nut. Each trap shall have the manufacturer's name stamped or cast in the body of the trap, and each tubing trap shall show the gage of the tubing.

(5) *Trap seal.* Each "P" trap shall have a water seal of not less than 2 inches and not more than 4 inches and shall be set true to its seal.

(6) *Size.* Traps shall be not less than 1¼ inches in diameter. A trap shall not be larger than the waste pipe to which it is connected.

(7) *Location.* Each trap shall be located as close to its vent and to its fixture outlet as structural conditions will permit.

(8) *Length of tailpiece.* The vertical distance from a trap to the fixture outlet shall not exceed 24 inches.

(9) *Installation.* (i) *Grade of trap arm.* The piping between a "P" trap and the fixture tee or the vented waste line shall be graded ¼ inch per foot towards the vent and in no event shall have a slope greater than its diameter. The vent opening at fixture tees shall not be below the weir of the "P" trap outlet.

(ii) *Trap arm offset.* The piping between the "P" trap and vent may change direction or be offset horizontally with the equivalent of no more than 180 degrees total change in direction with a maximum of 90 degrees by any one fitting.

(iii) *Concealed traps.* Traps with mechanical joints shall be accessible for repair and inspection.

(iv) *Removability of traps, etc.* Traps shall be designed and installed so the "U" bend is removable without removing the strainers from the fixture. Continuous waste and tail pieces which are permanently attached to the "U" bend shall also be removable without removing the strainer from the fixture.

(b) *Cleanout openings—*(1) *Location of cleanout fittings.* (i) Cleanouts shall be installed if the drainage system cannot be cleaned through fixtures, drains, or vents. Cleanouts shall also be provided when fittings of more than 45 degrees are used to affect an offset except where long turn ells are used which provide sufficient "sweep" for cleaning.

(ii) A full size cleanout shall be installed at the upper end of any section of drain piping which does not have the required minimum slope of ¼ inch per foot grade.

(iii) A cleaning tool shall not be required to pass through more than 360 degrees of fittings, excluding removable "P" traps, to reach any part of the drainage system. Water closets may be removed for drainage system access.

(2) *Access to cleanouts.* Cleanouts shall be accessible through an unobstructed minimum clearance of 12 inches directly in front of the opening. Each cleanout fitting shall open in a direction opposite to the flow or at right angles to the pipe. Concealed cleanouts that are not provided with access covers shall be extended to a point above the floor or outside of the manufactured home, with pipe and fittings installed, as required, for drainage piping without sags and pockets.

(3) *Material.* Plugs and caps shall be brass or approved or listed plastic, with screw pipe threads.

(4) *Design.* Cleanout plugs shall have raised heads except that plugs at floor level shall have counter-sunk slots.

[40 FR 58752, Dec. 18, 1975. Redesignated at 44 FR 20679, Apr. 6, 1979, as amended at 58 FR 55014, Oct. 25, 1993; 78 FR 73985, Dec. 9, 2013]

§ 3280.607 Plumbing fixtures.

(a) *General requirements—*(1) *Quality of fixtures.* Plumbing fixtures shall have smooth impervious surfaces, be free from defects and concealed fouling surfaces, be capable of resisting road shock and vibration, and shall conform in quality and design to listed standards. Fixtures shall be permanently marked with the manufacturer's name or trademark.

(2) *Strainers.* The waste outlet of all plumbing fixtures, other than toilets, shall be equipped with a drain fitting that will provide an adequate unobstructed waterway.

(3) *Fixture Connections.* Fixture tailpieces and continuous wastes in exposed or accessible locations must be of not less than No. 20 Brown and Sharpe gauge seamless drawn-brass tubing or other approved pipe or tubing materials. Inaccessible fixture connections must be constructed according to the requirements for drainage piping. The diameter of each fixture tailpiece, continuous waste, or waste and overflow must be not less than:

(i) 1½ inches, for sinks of two or more compartments, dishwashers, clothes washing machines, laundry tubs, bathtubs, and showers; and

(ii) Not less than 1¼ inches for lavatories or single compartment sinks having a 2-inch maximum drain opening.

(4) *Concealed connections.* Concealed slip joint connections shall be provided with adequately sized unobstructed access panels and shall be accessible for inspection and repair.

(5) *Directional fitting.* An approved or listed "Y" or other directional-type branch fitting shall be installed in every tailpiece or continuous waste that receives the discharge from food waste disposal units, dishwashing, or other force-discharge fixture or appliance. (See also § 3280.607(b)(4)(ii).)

(6) *Water conservation.* All lavatory faucets, showerheads, and sink faucets must not exceed a flow of 2.5 gallons per minute (gpm).

(b) *Fixtures—*(1) *Spacing.* All plumbing fixtures shall be so installed with regard to spacing as to be reasonably accessible for their intended use.

(2) *Water closets.* (i) Water closets shall be designed and manufactured according to approved or listed standards and shall be equipped with a water flushing device capable of adequately flushing and cleaning the bowl at each operation of the flushing mechanism.

(ii) Water closet flushing devices shall be designed to replace the water seal in the bowl after each operation. Flush valves, flushometer valves, flushometer tanks and ballcocks shall operate automatically to shut off at the end of each flush or when the tank is filled to operating capacity.

(iii) All water closets must be low consumption (1.6 gallons per flush (gpf)) closets.

(iv) Flush tanks shall be fitted with an overflow pipe large enough to prevent flooding at the maximum flow rate of the ball cock. Overflow pipes shall discharge into the toilet, through the tank.

(v) *Floor Connection.* Water closets must be securely bolted to an approved flange or other approved fitting that is secured to the floor by means of corrosion-resistant screws. The bolts must be of solid brass or other corrosion-resistant material and must not be less than ¼ inch in diameter. A watertight seal must be made between the water closet and flange or other approved fitting by use of a gasket, sealing compound, or listed connector device.

(vi) *Floor connection.* Water closets shall be securely bolted to an approved flange or other approved fitting which is secured to the floor by means of corrosion-resistant screws. The bolts shall be of solid brass or other corrosion-resistant material and shall be not less than one-fourth inch in diameter. A watertight seal shall be made between the water closet and flange or other approved fitting by use of a gasket or sealing compound.

(3) *Shower compartment.* (i) Each compartment stall shall be provided with an approved watertight receptor with sides and back extending at least 1 inch above the finished dam or threshold. In no case shall the depth of a shower receptor be less than 2 inches or more than 9 inches measured from the top of the finished dam or threshold to the top of the drain. The wall area shall be constructed of smooth, noncorrosive, and nonabsorbent waterproof materials to a height not less than 6 feet above the bathroom floor level. Such walls shall form a watertight joint with each other and with the bathtub, receptor or shower floor. The floor of the compartment shall slope uniformly to the drain at not less than one-fourth nor more than one-half inch per foot.

(ii) The joint around the drain connection shall be made watertight by a flange, clamping ring, or other approved listed means.

(iii) Shower doors and tub and shower enclosures shall be constructed so as to be waterproof and, if glazed, glazing shall comply with the Standard for Safety Glazing Materials used in Buildings—Safety Performance Specifications and Methods of Test, ANSI Z97.1–2004 (incorporated by reference, see § 3280.4).

(iv) Prefabricated plumbing fixtures shall be approved or listed.

(v) Shower and tub-shower combination valves must be balanced pressure, thermostatic, or combination mixing valves that conform to the requirements of ASSE 1016–2005, Performance Requirements for Automatic Compensating Valves for Individual Shower and Tub/Shower Combinations (incorporated by reference, see § 3280.4). Such valves must be equipped with handle position stops that are adjustable in accordance with the valve manufacturer's instructions and to a maximum setting of 120 °F. Hot water supplied to bathtubs and whirlpool bathtubs are to be limited to a temperature of not greater than 120 °F by a water temperature limiting device that conforms to the requirements of ASSE 1070–2004, Performance Requirements for Water Temperature Limiting Devices (incorporated by reference, see § 3280.4).

(4) *Dishwashing machines.* (i) A dishwashing machine must discharge its waste through a fixed air gap installed above the machine, through a high loop as specified by the dishwashing machine manufacturer, or into an open standpipe receptor with a height greater than the washing compartment of the machine. When a standpipe is used, it must be at least 18 inches, but not more than 30 inches, above the trap weir. The drain connections from the air gap or high loop are permitted to connect to an individual trap to a directional fitting installed in the sink tailpiece or to an opening provided on the inlet side of a food waste disposal unit.

(ii) Drain from a dishwashing machine shall not be connected to a sink tailpiece, continuous waste line, or trap on the discharge side of a food waste disposal unit.

(5) *Clothes washing machines.* (i) Clothes washing machines shall drain either into a properly vented trap, into a laundry tub tailpiece with watertight connections, into an open standpipe receptor, or over the rim of a laundry tub.

(ii) Standpipes must be either 1½ inch diameter minimum nominal iron pipe size, 1½ inch diameter nominal brass tubing of not less than No. 20 Brown and Sharp gauge, or 1½ inch diameter approved plastic materials. Receptors must discharge into a vented trap or must be connected to a laundry tub appliance by means of an approved or listed directional fitting. Each standpipe must extend not less than 18 inches or more than 42 inches above its trap and must terminate in an accessible location no lower than the top of the clothes washing machine. A removable, tight-fitting cap or plug must be installed on the standpipe when the clothes washer is not provided.

(iii) Clothes washing machine drain shall not be connected to the tailpiece, continuous waste, or trap of any sink or dishwashing machine.

(c) *Installation*—(1) *Access.* Each plumbing fixture and standpipe receptor shall be located and installed in a manner to be accessible for usage, cleaning, repair and replacement. Access to diverter valves and other connections from the fixture hardware is not required.

(2) *Alignment.* Fixtures shall be set level and in true alignment with adjacent walls. Where practical, piping from fixtures shall extend to nearest wall.

(3) *Brackets.* Wall-hung fixtures shall be rigidly attached to walls by metal brackets or supports without any strain being transmitted to the piping connections. Flush tanks shall be securely fastened to toilets or to the wall with corrosive-resistant materials.

(4) *Tub supports.* Bathtub rims at wall shall be supported on metal hangers or on end-grain wood blocking attached to the wall unless otherwise recommended by the manufacturer of the tub.

(5) *Fixture fittings.* Faucets and diverters shall be installed so that the flow of hot water from the fittings corresponds to the left-hand side of the fitting.

(6) *Hydromassage bathtub*—(i) *Access panel.* A door or panel of sufficient size must be installed to provide access to the pump for repair or replacement.

(ii) *Piping drainage.* The circulation pump must be accessibly located above the crown weir of the trap. The pump drain line must be properly sloped to drain the volute after fixture use.

(iii) *Piping.* Hydromassage bathtub circulation piping must be installed to be self-draining.

(iv) *Electrical.* Wiring must comply with Articles 680.70, 680.71, and 680.72 of the National Electrical Code, NFPA No. 70–2005.

[40 FR 58752, Dec. 18, 1975, as amended at 42 FR 961, Jan. 4, 1977. Redesignated at 44 FR 20679, Apr. 6, 1979, as amended at 52 FR 4586, Feb. 12, 1987; 58 FR 55014, Oct. 25, 1993; 70 FR 72049, Nov. 30, 2005; 71 FR 19639, Apr. 17, 2006; 78 FR 73985, Dec. 9, 2013; 79 FR 31863, June 3, 2014]

§ 3280.608 **Hangers and supports.**

(a) *Strains and stresses.* Piping in a plumbing system shall be installed without undue strains and stresses, and provision shall be made for expansion, contraction, and structural settlement.

(b) *Piping supports.* Piping shall be secured at sufficiently close intervals to keep the pipe in alignment and carry the weight of the pipe and contents. Unless otherwise stated in the standards for specific materials shown in the table in § 3280.604(a), or unless specified by the pipe manufacturer, plastic drainage piping shall be supported at intervals not to exceed 4 feet and plastic water piping shall be supported at intervals not to exceed 3 feet.

(c) *Hangers and anchors.* (1) Hangers and anchors shall be of sufficient strength to support their proportional share of the pipe alignments and prevent rattling.

(2) Piping shall be securely attached to the structure by hangers, clamps, or brackets which provide protection against motion, vibration, road shock, or torque in the chassis.

(3) Hangers and straps supporting plastic pipe shall not compress, distort, cut or abrade the piping and shall allow free movement of the pipe.

§ 3280.609 Water distribution systems.

(a) *Water supply*—(1) *Supply piping.* Piping systems shall be sized to provide an adequate quantity of water to each plumbing fixture at a flow rate sufficient to keep the fixture in a clean and sanitary condition without any danger of backflow or siphonage. (See table in § 3280.609(f)(1)). The manufacturer shall include in his written installation instructions that the manufactured home has been designed for an inlet water pressure of 80 psi, and a statement that when the manufactured home is to be installed in areas where the water pressure exceeds 80 psi, a pressure reducing valve should be installed.

(2) *Hot water supply.* Each manufactured home equipped with a kitchen sink, and bathtub and/or shower shall be provided with a hot water supply system including a listed water heater.

(b) *Water outlets and supply connections*—(1) *Water connection.* Each manufactured home with a water distribution system shall be equipped with a ¾ inch threaded inlet connection. This connection shall be tagged or marked "Fresh Water Connection" (or marked "Fresh Water Fill"). A matching cap or plug shall be provided to seal the water inlet when it is not in use, and shall be permanently attached to the manufactured home or water supply piping. When a master cold water shutoff full flow valve is not installed on the main feeder line in an accessible location, the manufacturer's installation instructions shall indicate that such a valve is to be installed in the water supply line adjacent to the home. When a manufactured home includes expandable rooms or is composed of two or more units, fittings or connectors designed for such purpose shall be provided to connect any water piping. When not connected, the water piping shall be protected by means of matching threaded caps or plugs.

(2) *Prohibited connections.* (i) The installation of potable water supply piping or fixture or appliance connections shall be made in a manner to preclude the possibility of backflow.

(ii) No part of the water system shall be connected to any drainage or vent piping.

(3) *Rim outlets.* The outlets of faucets, spouts, and similar devices shall be spaced at least 1 inch above the flood level of the fixture.

(4) *Appliance connections.* Water supplies connected to clothes washing or dishwashing machines shall be protected by an approved or listed fixed air gap provided within the appliance by the manufacturer.

(5) *Flushometer valves or manually operated flush valves.* An approved or listed vacuum breaker shall be installed and maintained in the water supply line on the discharge side of a water closet flushometer valve or manually operated flush valve. Vacuum breakers shall have a minimum clearance of 6 inches above the flood level of the fixture to the critical level mark unless otherwise permitted in their approval.

(6) *Flush tanks.* Water closet flush tanks shall be equipped with an approved or listed anti-siphon ball cock which shall be installed and maintained with its outlet or critical level mark not less than 1 inch above the full opening of the overflow pipe.

(7) *Hose bibbs.* When provided, all exterior hose bibbs and laundry sink hose

connections must be protected by a listed nonremovable backflow prevention device. This requirement is not applicable to hose connections provided for automatic washing machines with built-in backflow prevention or water heater drain valves.

(8) *Flushometer tanks.* Flushometer tanks must be equipped with an approved air gap or vacuum breaker assembly that is located above the flood-level rim above the fixture.

(c) *Water heater safety devices—*(1) *Relief valves.* (i) All water heaters shall be installed with approved and listed fully automatic valve or valves designed to provide temperature and pressure relief.

(ii) Any temperature relief valve or combined pressure and temperature relief valve installed for this purpose shall have the temperature sensing element immersed in the hottest water within the upper 6 inches of the tank. It shall be set to start relieving at a pressure of 150 psi or the rated working pressure of the tank whichever is lower and at or below a water temperature of 210 °F.

(iii) Relief valves shall be provided with full-sized drains, with cross sectional areas equivalent to that of the relief valve outlet, which shall be directed downward and discharge beneath the manufactured home. Drain lines shall be of a material listed for hot water distribution and shall drain fully by gravity, shall not be trapped, and shall not have their outlets threaded, and the end of the drain shall be visible for inspection.

(d) *Materials—*(1) *Piping material.* Water pipe shall be of standard weight brass, galvanized wrought iron, galvanized steel, Type K, L or M copper tubing, approved or listed plastic or other approved or listed material.

(i) *Plastic piping.* All plastic water piping and fittings in manufactured homes must be listed for use with hot water.

(ii) [Reserved]

(2) *Fittings.* Appropriate fittings shall be used for all changes in size and where pipes are joined. The material and design of fittings shall conform to the type of piping used. Special consideration shall be given to prevent corrosion when dissimilar metals are joined.

(i) Fittings for screw piping shall be standard weight galvanized iron for galvanized iron and steel pipe, and of brass for brass piping. They shall be installed where required for change in direction, reduction of size, or where pipes are joined together.

(ii) Fittings for copper tubing shall be cast brass or drawn copper (sweat-soldered) or shall be approved or listed fittings for the purpose intended.

(3) *Prohibited material.* Used piping materials shall not be permitted. Those pipe dopes, solder, fluxes, oils, solvents, chemicals, or other substances that are toxic, corrosive, or otherwise detrimental to the water system shall not be used. In addition, for those manufactured homes to be connected to a public water system, all water piping shall be lead-free (as defined in section 109(c)(2) of the Safe Drinking Water Act Amendments of 1986) with solders and flux containing not more than 0.2 percent lead and pipes and pipe fittings containing not more than 8.0 percent lead.

(e) *Installation of piping—*(1) *Minimum requirement.* All piping equipment, appurtenances, and devices shall be installed in workmanlike manner and shall conform with the provisions and intent of this standard.

(2) *Screw pipe.* Iron pipe-size brass or galvanized iron or steel pipe fittings shall be joined with approved or listed standard pipe threads fully engaged in the fittings. Pipe ends shall be reamed to the full bore of the pipe. Pipe-joint compound shall be insoluble in water, shall be nontoxic and shall be applied to male threads only.

(3) *Solder fittings.* Joints in copper water tubes shall be made by the appropriate use of approved cast brass or wrought copper fittings, properly soldered together. The surface to be soldered shall be thoroughly cleaned bright mechanically. The joints shall be properly fluxed and made with a solder that contains no more than 0.2 percent lead.

(4) *Flared fittings.* A flaring tool shall be used to shape the ends of flared tubing to match the flare of fittings.

(5) *Plastic pipe and fittings.* Plastic pipe and fittings shall be joined by installation methods recommended by

101

the manufacturer or in accordance with provisions of a listed standard.

(f) *Size of water supply piping*—(1) *Minimum size.* The size of water supply piping and branch lines shall not be less than sizes shown in the following table:

MINIMUM SIZE TUBING AND PIPE FOR WATER DISTRIBUTION SYSTEMS

| Number of fixtures | Tubing (nominal) | | Pipe iron pipe size (inches) |
	Diameter (inches)	Outer diameter (inches)	
1	*¼	⅜	½
2	⅜	½	½
3	½	⅝	½
4	½	⅝	½
5 or more	¾	⅞	¾

*6 ft maximum length.

Exceptions to table: ⅜ inch nominal diameter or ½ inch OD minimum size for clothes washing or dishwashing machines, unless larger size is recommended by the fixture manufacturer. ½ inch nominal diameter or ⅝ inch OD minimum size for flushometer or metering type valves unless otherwise specified in their listing. No galvanized screw piping shall be less than ½ inch iron pipe size.

(2) *Sizing procedure.* Both hot and cold water piping systems shall be computed by the following method:

(i) *Size of branch.* Start at the most remote outlet on any branch of the hot or cold water piping and progressively count towards the water service connection, computing the total number of fixtures supplied along each section of piping. Where branches are joined together, the number of fixtures on each branch shall be totalled so that no fixture is counted twice. Following down the left-hand column of the preceding table a corresponding number of fixtures will be found. The required pipe or tubing size is indicated in the other columns on the same line.

(ii) A water heater, food waste disposal unit, evaporative cooler or ice maker shall not be counted as a water-using fixture when computing pipe sizes.

(g) *Line valves.* Valves, when installed in the water supply distribution system (except those immediately controlling one fixture supply) and when fully opened, shall have a cross-sectional area of the smallest orifice or opening, through which the water flows, at least equal to the cross-sectional area of the nominal size of the pipe in which the valve is installed.

[40 FR 58752, Dec. 18, 1975. Redesignated at 44 FR 20679, Apr. 6, 1979, as amended at 52 FR 4586, Feb. 12, 1987; 53 FR 23611, June 23, 1988; 58 FR 55014, Oct. 25, 1993; 78 FR 73986, Dec. 9, 2013]

§ 3280.610   Drainage systems.

(a) *General.* (1) Each fixture directly connected to the drainage system shall be installed with a water seal trap (§ 3280.606(a)).

(2) The drainage system shall be designed to provide an adequate circulation of air in all piping with no danger of siphonage, aspiration, or forcing of trap seals under conditions of ordinary use.

(b) *Materials*—(1) *Pipe.* Drainage piping must be standard weight galvanized steel, brass, copper tube DWV, listed Scheduled 40 ABS plastic, listed Scheduled 40 PVC plastic, cast iron, or other listed or approved materials.

(2) *Fittings.* Drainage fittings shall be recessed drainage pattern with smooth interior waterways of the same diameter as the piping and shall be of a material conforming to the type of piping used. Drainage fittings shall be designed to provide for a ¼ inch per foot grade in horizontal piping.

(i) Fittings for screw pipe shall be cast iron, malleable iron, brass, or listed plastic with standard pipe threads.

(ii) Fittings for copper tubing shall be cast brass or wrought copper.

(iii) Socket-type fittings for plastic piping shall comply with listed standards.

(iv) Brass or bronze adaptor or wrought copper fittings shall be used to join copper tubing to threaded pipe.

(c) *Drain outlets.* (1) Each manufactured home shall have only one drain outlet.

(2) *Clearance from drain outlet.* The drain outlet shall be provided with a minimum clearance of 3 inches in any direction from all parts of the structure or appurtenances and with not less than 18 inches unrestricted clearance directly in front of the drain outlet.

(3) *Drain connector.* The drain connector shall not be smaller than the

piping to which it is connected and shall be equipped with a water-tight cap or plug matching the drain outlet. The cap or plug shall be permanently attached to the manufactured home or drain outlet.

(4) The drain outlet and drain connector shall not be less than 3 inches inside diameter.

(5) *Preassembly of drain lines.* Section(s) of the drain system, designed to be located underneath the home, are not required to be factory installed when the manufacturer designs the system for site assembly and also provides all materials and components, including piping, fittings, cement, supports, and instructions necessary for proper site installation.

(d) *Fixture connections.* Drainage piping shall be provided with approved or listed inlet fittings for fixture connections, correctly located according to the size and type of fixture to be connected.

(1) *Water closet connection.* The drain connection for each water closet shall be 3 inches minimum inside diameter and shall be fitted with an iron, brass, or listed plastic floor flange adaptor ring securely screwed, soldered or otherwise permanently attached to the drain piping, in an approved manner and securely fastened to the floor.

(2) [Reserved]

(e) *Size of drainage piping.* Fixture drains must be sized as follows:

(1) Fixture drains serving a single lavatory must be a minimum of 1¼ inches in diameter.

(2) Fixture drains serving two or three fixtures must be a minimum of 1½ inches in diameter.

(3) Fixture drains serving four or more fixtures that are individually vented must be a minimum of 2 inches in diameter.

(4) Fixture drains for water closets must be a minimum of 3 inches in diameter.

(f) *Wet-vented drainage system.* Plumbing fixture traps may connect into a wet-vented drainage system which shall be designed and installed to accommodate the passage of air and waste in the same pipe.

(1) *Horizontal piping.* All parts of a wet-vented drainage system, including the connected fixture drains, shall be horizontal except for wet-vented vertical risers which shall terminate with a 1½ inch minimum diameter continuous vent. Where required by structural design, wet-vented drain piping may be offset vertically when other vented fixture drains or relief vents are connected to the drain piping at or below the vertical offsets.

(2) *Size.* A wet-vented drain pipe shall be 2 inches minimum diameter and at least one pipe size larger than the largest connected trap or fixture drain. Not more than three fixtures may connect to a 2-inch diameter wet-vented drain system.

(3) *Length of trap arm.* Fixture traps shall be located within the distance given in §3280.611(c)(5). Not more than one trap shall connect to a trap arm.

(g) *Offsets and branch fittings*—(1) *Changes in direction.* Changes in direction of drainage piping shall be made by the appropriate use of approved or listed fittings, and shall be of the following angles: 11¼, 22½, 45, 60, or 90 degrees; or other approved or listed fittings or combinations of fittings with equivalent radius or sweep.

(2) *Horizontal to vertical.* Horizontal drainage lines, connecting with a vertical pipe shall enter through 45-degree "Y" branches, 60-degree "Y" branches, long-turn "TY" branches, sanitary "T" branches, or other approved or listed fittings or combination of fittings having equivalent sweep. Fittings having more than one branch at the same level shall not be used, unless the fitting is constructed so that the discharge from any one branch cannot readily enter any other branch. However, a double sanitary "T" may be used when the drain line is increased not less than two pipe sizes.

(3) *Horizontal to horizontal and vertical to horizontal.* Horizontal drainage lines connecting with other horizontal drainage lines or vertical drainage lines connected with horizontal drainage lines shall enter through 45-degree "Y" branches, long-turn "TY" branches, or other approved or listed fittings or combination of fittings having equivalent sweep.

(h) *Grade of horizontal drainage piping.* Except for fixture connections on the inlet side of the trap, horizontal drainage piping shall be run in practical

103

alignment and have a uniform grade of not less than ¼ inch per foot toward the manufactured home drain outlet. Where it is impractical, due to the structural features or arrangement of any manufactured home, to obtain a grade of ¼ inch per foot, the pipe or piping may have a grade of not less than ⅛ inch per foot, when a full size cleanout is installed at the upper end.

[40 FR 58752, Dec. 18, 1975. Redesignated at 44 FR 20679, Apr. 6, 1979, as amended at 52 FR 4586, Feb. 12, 1987; 58 FR 55015, Oct. 25, 1993; 78 FR 73986, Dec. 9, 2013]

§ 3280.611　Vents and venting.

(a) *General.* Each plumbing fixture trap shall be protected against siphonage and back pressure, and air circulation shall be ensured throughout all parts of the drainage system by means of vents installed in accordance with the requirements of this section and as otherwise required by this standard.

(b) *Materials*—(1) *Pipe.* Vent piping must be standard weight galvanized steel, brass, copper tube DWV, listed Scheduled 40 ABS plastic, listed Scheduled 40 PVC plastic, cast iron, or other listed or approved materials.

(2) *Fittings.* Appropriate fittings shall be used for all changes in direction or size and where pipes are joined. The material and design of vent fittings shall conform to the type of piping used.

(i) Fittings for screw pipe shall be cast iron, malleable iron, plastic, or brass, with standard pipe threads.

(ii) Fittings for copper tubing shall be cast brass or wrought copper.

(iii) Fittings for plastic piping shall be made to approved applicable standards.

(iv) Brass adaptor fittings or wrought copper shall be used to join copper tubing to threaded pipe.

(v) Listed rectangular tubing may be used for vent piping only providing it has an open cross section at least equal to the circular vent pipe required. Listed transition fittings shall be used.

(c) *Size of vent piping*—(1) *Main vent.* The drain piping for each toilet shall be vented by a 1½ inch minimum diameter vent or rectangular vent of venting cross section equivalent to or greater than the venting cross section of a 1½ inch diameter vent, connected

to the toilet drain by one of the following methods:

(i) A 1½ inch diameter (min.) individual vent pipe or equivalent directly connected to the toilet drain within the distance allowed in § 3280.611(c)(5), for 3-inch trap arms undiminished in size through the roof,

(ii) A 1½ inch diameter (min.) continuous vent or equivalent, indirectly connected to the toilet drain piping within the distance allowed in § 3280.611(c)(5) for 3 inch trap arms through a 2-inch wet vented drain that carries the waste of not more than one fixture, or,

(iii) Two or more vented drains when at least one is wet-vented, or 2-inch diameter (minimum), and each drain is separately connected to the toilet drain. At least one of the drains shall connect within the distance allowed in § 3280.611(c)(5) for 3-inch trap arms.

(2) *Vent pipe areas.* Each individually vented fixture with a 1½ inch or smaller trap shall be provided with a vent pipe equivalent in area to a 1¼ inch nominal pipe size. The main vent, toilet vent and relief vent, and the continuous vent of wet-vented systems shall have an area equivalent to 1½ inch nominal pipe size.

(3) *Common vent.* When two fixture traps located within the distance allowed from their vent have their trap arms connected separately at the same level into an approved double fitting, an individual vent pipe may serve as a common vent without any increase in size.

(4) *Intersecting vents.* Where two or more vent pipes are joined together, no increase in size shall be required; however, the largest vent pipe shall extend full size through the roof.

(5) Distance of fixture trap from vent shall not exceed the values given in the following table:

MAXIMUM DISTANCE OF FIXTURES FROM VENT TRAP

Size of fixture drain (inches)	Distance trap to vent
1¼	4 ft. 6 in.
1½	4 ft 6 in.
2	5 ft.
3	6 ft.

(d) *Mechanical Vents.* Where mechanical vents are used as a secondary vent system for plumbing fixtures that are protected by traps, the mechanical vents must comply with paragraphs (d)(1) or (2) of this section.

(1) Spring-operated mechanical (anti-siphon) vents must comply with the following:

(i) No more than two fixtures individually protected by the spring-operated mechanical vent may be drained by a common 1½ inch diameter drain.

(ii) The drain size for three or more fixtures individually protected by a spring-operated mechanical vent must be at least 2 inches in diameter.

(iii) Spring-operated mechanical vents are restricted to venting fixtures with 1½ inch traps.

(iv) A spring-operated mechanical vent must be installed in a location that allows a free flow of air and is accessible for inspection, maintenance, and replacement. The sealing function must be at least 6 inches above the top of the trap arm.

(v) Materials for the spring-operated mechanical vents must be as follows:

(A) Cap and housing must be listed acrylonitrile-butadiene-styrene, DWV grade;

(B) Stem must be DWV grade nylon or acetal;

(C) Spring must be stainless steel wire, Type 302; and

(D) Sealing disc must be either:

(1) Neoprene, conforming to CISPI–HSN–85, Specification for Neoprene Rubber Gaskets for HUB and Spigot Cast Iron Soil Pipe and Fittings (incorporated by reference, see §3280.4), and to ASTM C564–97, Standard Specification for Rubber Gaskets for Cast Iron Soil Pipe and Fittings (incorporated by reference, see §3280.4); or

(2) Other material, conforming to ASTM C920–02, Standard Specification for Elastomeric Joint Sealants (incorporated by reference, see §3280.4), and to ASTM D4635–01, Standard Specification for Polyethylene Films Made from Low-Density Polyethylene for General Use and Packaging Applications (incorporated by reference, see §3280.4).

(2) Gravity-operated mechanical (air admittance valves) vents must comply with the following:

(i) Where installed to vent any fixture, the drain system must have a minimum 1½ inch diameter vent that terminates outside the manufactured home.

(ii) Where gravity-operated mechanical vent devices terminate in the attic cavity, the following requirements must be met:

(A) The attic cavity must be accessible;

(B) The sealing device must be installed a minimum of 6 inches above the insulation materials; and

(C) The attic must be vented in accordance with §3280.504(c)(1)(i);

(3) Mechanical vents must be installed in accordance with the vent manufacturer's instructions.

(e) *Grade and connections*—(1) *Horizontal vents.* Each vent shall extend vertically from its fixture "T" or point of connection with the waste piping to a point not less than 6 inches above the extreme flood level of the fixture it is venting before offsetting horizontally or being connected with any other vent pipe. Vents for horizontal drains shall connect above the centerline of the drain piping ahead (downstream) of the trap. Where required by structural conditions, vent piping may offset below the rim of the fixture at the maximum angle or height possible.

(f) *Vent terminal.* Vents must terminate through the roof or wall, or to a mechanical vent device in accordance with paragraph (d) of this section.

(1) *Roof extension.* Each vent pipe must extend through its flashing and terminate vertically. Vents that extend through the roof must extend undiminished in size, not less than 2 inches above the roof. Vent openings must be at least 3 feet away from any motor-driven air intake that opens into any habitable area.

(2) *Wall extensions.* Extensions through exterior walls must terminate downward, have a screen to prevent entrance of birds and rodents, and be located as follows:

(i) Extensions must not be located beneath a door, window, or other opening;

(ii) Extensions must be a minimum of 10 feet above the finished floor;

(iii) Extensions must be located a minimum of 2 feet above any building opening that is within 10 feet horizontally of any extension; and

105

(iv) Extensions must not terminate under an overhang with soffit vents.

(3) *Flashing.* The opening around each vent pipe shall be made watertight by an adequate flashing or flashing material.

(g) *Vent caps.* Vent caps, if provided, shall be of the removable type (without removing the flashing from the roof). When vent caps are used for roof space ventilation and the caps are identical to vent caps used for the plumbing system, plumbing system caps shall be identified with permanent markings.

[40 FR 58752, Dec. 18, 1975, as amended at 42 FR 961, Jan. 4, 1977. Redesignated at 44 FR 20679, Apr. 6, 1979, as amended at 58 FR 55015, Oct. 25, 1993; 78 FR 73986, Dec. 9, 2013]

§ 3280.612   Tests and inspection.

(a) *Water system.* All water piping in the water distribution system shall be subjected to a pressure test. The test shall be made by subjecting the system to air or water at 100 psi for 15 minutes without loss of pressure.

(b) *Drainage and vent system and plumbing fixtures.* The waste and vent system shall be tested by one of the three following alternate methods for evidence or indication of leakage:

(1) *Water test.* Before plumbing fixtures are connected, all of the openings into the piping shall be plugged and the entire piping system subjected to a static water test for 15 minutes by filling it with water to the top of the highest vent opening. There shall be no evidence of leakage.

(2) *Air test.* After all fixtures have been installed, the traps filled with water, and the remaining openings securely plugged, the entire system shall be subjected to a 2-inch (manometer) water column air pressure test. If the system loses pressure, leaks may be located with smoke pumped into the system, or with soap suds spread on the exterior of the piping (Bubble test).

(3) *Flood level test.* The manufactured home shall be in a level position, all fixtures shall be connected, and the entire system shall be filled with water to the rim of the water closet bowl. (Tub and shower drains shall be plugged). After all trapped air has been released, the test shall be sustained for not less than 15 minutes without evidence of leaks. Then the system shall

be unplugged and emptied. The waste piping above the level of the water closet bowl shall then be tested and show no indication of leakage when the high fixtures are filled with water and emptied simultaneously to obtain the maximum possible flow in the drain piping.

(c) *Fixture test.* The plumbing fixtures and connections shall be subjected to a flow test by filling them with water and checking for leaks and retarded flow while they are being emptied.

(d) *Shower compartments.* Shower compartments and receptors shall be tested for leaks prior to being covered by finish material. Each pan shall be filled with water to the top of the dam for not less than 15 minutes without evidence of leakage.

[40 FR 58752, Dec. 18, 1975, as amended at 42 FR 961, Jan. 4, 1977; 42 FR 54383, Oct. 5, 1977. Redesignated at 44 FR 20679, Apr. 6, 1979, as amended at 58 FR 55015, Oct. 25, 1993]

Subpart H—Heating, Cooling and Fuel Burning Systems

§ 3280.701   Scope.

Subpart H of this standard covers the heating, cooling and fuel burning equipment installed within, on, or external to a manufactured home.

§ 3280.702   Definitions.

The definitions in this subpart apply to subpart H only.

Accessible, when applied to a fixture, connection, appliance or equipment, means having access thereto, but which may require the removal of an access panel, door or similar obstruction.

Air conditioner blower coil system means a comfort cooling appliance where the condenser section is placed external to the manufactured home and evaporator section with circulating blower attached to the manufactured home air supply duct system. Provision must be made for a return air system to the evaporator/blower section. Refrigerant connection between the two parts of the system is accomplished by tubing.

Air conditioner split system means a comfort cooling appliance where the condenser section is placed external to the manufactured home and the evaporator section incorporated into the heating appliance or with a separate blower/coil section within the manufactured home. Refrigerant connection between the two parts of the system is accomplished by tubing.

Air conditioning condenser section means that portion of a refrigerated air cooling or (in the case of a heat pump) heating system which includes the refrigerant pump (compressor) and the external heat exchanger.

Air conditioning evaporator section means a heat exchanger used to cool or (in the case of a heat pump) heat air for use in comfort cooling (or heating) the living space.

Air conditioning self contained system means a comfort cooling appliance combining the condenser section, evaporator and air circulating blower into one unit with connecting ducts for the supply and return air systems.

Air duct means conduits or passageways for conveying air to or from heating, cooling, air conditioning or ventilation equipment, but not including the plenum.

Automatic pump (oil lifter) means a pump, not an integral part of the oil-burning appliance, that automatically pumps oil from the supply tank and delivers the oil under a constant head to an oil-burning appliance.

Btu. British thermal units means the quantity of heat required to raise the temperature of one pound of water one degree Fahrenheit.

Btuh means British thermal units per hour.

Burner means a device for the final conveyance of fuel or a mixture of fuel and air to the combustion zone.

Central air conditioning system means either an air conditioning split system or an external combination heating/cooling system.

Class 0 air ducts and air connectors means air ducts and air connectors having a fire hazard classification of zero when tested in accordance with UL 181–2003, Factory-Made Air Ducts and Air Connectors (incorporated by reference, see § 3280.4).

Class 1 air ducts and air connectors means air ducts and air connectors having a flame spread rating of not over 25 without evidence of continued progressive combustion and a smoke developed rating of not over 50 when tested in accordance with UL 181–2003, Standard for Safety Factory-Made Air Ducts and Air Connectors (incorporated by reference, see § 3280.4).

Clearance means the distance between the appliance, chimney, vent, chimney or vent connector or plenum and the nearest surface.

Combination space heating and water heating appliance means a listed unit that is designed to provide space heating and water heating from a single primary energy source.

Connector-Gas appliance: means a flexible or semi-rigid connector used to convey fuel gas between a gas outlet and a gas appliance.

Direct-vent system means a system or method of construction where all air for combustion is derived directly from the outside atmosphere and all flue gases are discharged to the outside atmosphere.

Direct-vent system appliance means an appliance that is installed with a direct vent system.

External combination heating/cooling system means a comfort conditioning system placed external to the manufactured home with connecting ducts to the manufactured home for the supply and return air systems.

Factory-built fireplace means a hearth, fire chamber and chimney assembly composed of listed factory-built components assembled in accordance with the terms of listing to form a complete fireplace.

Fireplace stove means a chimney connected solid fuel-burning stove having part of its fire chamber open to the room.

Fuel gas piping system means the arrangement of piping, tubing, fittings, connectors, valves and devices designed and intended to supply or control the flow of fuel gas to the appliance(s).

Fuel oil piping system means the arrangement of piping, tubing, fittings, connectors, valves and devices designed and intended to supply or control the flow of fuel oil to the appliance(s).

Gas clothes dryer means a device used to dry wet laundry by means of heat derived from the combustion of fuel gases.

Gas refrigerator means a gas-burning appliance which is designed to extract heat from a suitable chamber.

Gas supply connection means the terminal end or connection to which a gas supply connector is attached.

Gas supply connector, manufactured home means a listed flexible connector designed for connecting the manufactured home to the gas supply source.

Gas vents means factory-built vent piping and vent fittings listed by an approved testing agency, that are assembled and used in accordance with the terms of their listings, for conveying flue gases to the outside atmosphere.

(1) *Type B gas vent* means a gas vent for venting gas appliances with draft hoods and other gas appliances listed for use with Type B gas vents.

(2) *Type BW gas vent* means a gas vent for venting listed gas-fired vented wall furnaces.

Heat producing appliance means all heating and cooking appliances and fuel burning appliances.

Heating appliance means an appliance for comfort heating, domestic water heating, or a combination of comfort heating and domestic water heating.

Liquefied petroleum gases. The terms *Liquefied petroleum gases, LPG* and *LP-Gas* as used in this standard shall mean and include any material which is composed predominantly of any of the following hydrocarbons, or mixtures of them: propane, propylene butanes (normal butane or isobutane), and butylenes.

Plenum means an air compartment which is part of an air-distributing system, to which one or more ducts or outlets are connected.

(1) Furnace supply plenum is a plenum attached directly to, or an integral part of, the air supply outlet of the furnace.

(2) Furnace return plenum is a plenum attached directly to, or an integral part of, the return inlet of the furnace.

Quick-disconnect device means a hand-operated device which provides a means for connecting and disconnecting a gas supply or connecting gas systems and which is equipped with an automatic means to shut off the gas supply when the device is disconnected.

Readily accessible means direct access without the necessity of removing any panel, door, or similar obstruction.

Roof jack means that portion of a manufactured home heater flue or vent assembly, including the cap, insulating means, flashing, and ceiling plate, located in and above the roof of a manufactured home.

Sealed combustion system appliance means an appliance which by its inherent design is constructed so that all air supplied for combustion, the combustion system of the appliance, and all products of combustion are completely isolated from the atmosphere of the space in which it is installed.

Water heater means an appliance for heating water for domestic purposes.

[40 FR 58752, Dec. 18, 1975. Redesignated at 44 FR 20679, Apr. 6, 1979, as amended at 52 FR 4586, Feb. 12, 1987; 58 FR 55015, Oct. 25, 1993; 78 FR 73987, Dec. 9, 2013]

§ 3280.703 Minimum standards.

Heating, cooling and fuel burning appliances and systems in manufactured homes shall be free of defects, and shall conform to applicable standards in the following table unless otherwise specified in this standard. (See § 3280.4) When more than one standard is referenced, compliance with any one such standard shall meet the requirements of this standard.

APPLIANCES

Heating and Cooling Equipment, Second Edition, with 1999 revisions—UL 1995, 1995.

Liquid Fuel-Burning Heating Appliances for Manufactured Homes and Recreational Vehicles, Seventh Edition, with 1997 revisions—UL 307A-1995.

Fixed and Location-Dedicated Electric Room Heaters, Second Edition, with 1998 revisions—UL 2021-1997.

Electric Baseboard Heating Equipment, Fourth Edition, with 1998 revisions—UL 1042-1994.

Electric Central Air Heating Equipment—UL 1096-Fourth Edition-1986 with revisions July 16, 1986, and January 30, 1988.

Gas Burning Heating Appliances for Manufactured Homes and Recreational Vehicles, Fourth Edition, with 1998 revisions—UL 307B-1995.

Gas Clothes Dryers Volume 1, Type 1 Clothes Dryers—ANSI Z21.5.1-/CSA 7.1—M99—1999 with Addendum Z21.5.1a—1999.

Gas Fired Absorption Summer Air Conditioning Appliances—ANSI Z21.40.1/CGA 2.91—M961996.

Gas-Fired Central Furnaces (Except Direct Vent System Central Furnaces)—ANSI Z21.47–1990 with Addendum Z21.47a–1990 and Z21.47b–1992.

Decorative Gas Appliances for Installation in Solid Fuel Burning Fireplaces—RADCO DS–010–91 (incorporated by reference, see § 3280.4).

Household Cooking Gas Appliances—ANSI Z21.1–2000.

Refrigerators Using Gas Fuel—ANSI Z21.19–1990, with Addendum ANSI Z21.19a–1992 and Z21.19b–1995.

Gas Water Heaters—Volume 1, Storage Water Heaters with Input Ratings of 75,000 BTU per hour or Less—ANSI Z21.10.1–1998 with Addendum Z21.10.1a–2000.

Household Electric Storage Tank Water Heaters, Tenth Edition—UL 174–1996, with 1997 revisions.

FERROUS PIPE AND FITTINGS

Standard Specification for Pipe, Steel, Black and Hot-Dipped, Zinc-Coated, Welded and Seamless—ASTM A53–93.

Standard Specification for Electric-Resistance-Welded Coiled Steel Tubing for Gas and Fuel Oil Lines—ASTM A539–1999.

Pipe Threads, General Purpose (Inch)—ANSI/ASME B1.20.1–1983.

Welding and Seamless Wrought Steel Pipe—ANSI/ASME B36.10–1979.

NONFERROUS PIPE, TUBING, AND FITTINGS

Standard Specification for Seamless Copper Water Tube—ASTM B88–93.

Standard Specification for Seamless Copper Tube for Air Conditioning and Refrigeration Field Service—ASTM B280–95a.

Connectors for Gas Appliances—ANSI Z21.24/CGA 6.10–M97–1997.

Manually Operated Gas Valves for Appliances, Appliance Connector Valves and Hose End Valves—ANSI Z21.15/CGA 9.1–M97–1997.

Standard for Gas Supply Connectors for Manufactured Homes—IAPMO TSC 9–1997.

Standard Specification for General Requirements for Wrought Seamless Copper and Copper-Alloy Tubes—ASTM B251–93.

Standard Specification for Seamless Copper Pipe, Standard Sizes—ASTM B42–93.

MISCELLANEOUS

Factory-Made Air Ducts and Air Connectors, UL 181, Ninth Edition, April 4, 1996, with revisions through May 15, 2003 (incorporated by reference, see § 3280.4).

Standard for Safety Closure Systems for use with Rigid Air Ducts and Air Connectors, UL 181A, 1994, with 1998 revisions.

Standard for Safety Closure Systems for use with Flexible Air Ducts and Air Connectors, First Edition—UL 181B, 1995, with 1998 revisions.

Tube Fittings for Flammable and Combustible Fluids, Refrigeration Service, and Marine Use, Sixth Edition—UL 109–1997, with 2001 revisions.

Pigtails and Flexible Hose Connectors for LP-Gas, Seventh Edition—UL 569, 1995 with 2001 revisions.

Roof Jacks for Manufactured Homes and Recreational Vehicles, Eighth Edition—UL 311, 1994, with 1998 revisions.

Relief Valves for Hot Water Supply Systems, ANSI Z21.22–1999, (incorporated by reference, see § 3280.4).

Automatic Gas Ignition Systems and Components—ANSI Z21.20 with Addendum Z21.20a–2000.

Automatic Valves for Gas Appliances—ANSI Z21.21/CSA 6.5–2000.

Gas Appliance Thermostats—ANSI Z21.23–93 (incorporated by reference, see § 3280.4).

Gas Vents, Ninth Edition—UL 441, 1996 with 1999 revisions.

Standard for the Installation of Oil-Burning Equipment, NFPA 31–01 (incorporated by reference, see § 3280.4).

National Fuel Gas Code—NFPA 54–2002/ANSI Z223.1–2002.

Warm Air Heating and Air Conditioning Systems, NFPA 90B, 1996 Edition.

Liquefied Petroleum Gas Code, NFPA 58–2001 Edition.

Flares for Tubing—SAE–J533b–1992.

Factory-Built Chimneys for Residential Type and Building Heating Appliances, Ninth Edition—UL 103, 1995, with 1999 revisions.

Factory-Built Fireplaces, Seventh Edition—UL 127–1996, with 1999 revisions.

Solid-Fuel Type Room Heaters, Fifth Edition—UL 1482, 1995, with 2000 revisions.

Fireplace Stoves, Eight Edition, with 2000 revisions—UL 737, 1996.

Unitary Air-Conditioning and Air-Source Heat Pump Equipment—ANSI/ARI 210/240–89.

AGA Requirements for Gas Connectors for Connection of Fixed Appliances for Outdoor Installation, Park Trailers, and Manufactured (Mobile) Homes to the Gas Supply—No. 3–87.

[58 FR 55015, Oct. 25, 1993, as amended at 70 FR 72046, Nov. 30, 2005; 78 FR 73987, Dec. 9, 2013]

§ 3280.704   [Reserved]

§ 3280.705   Gas piping systems.

(a) *General.* The requirements of this section shall govern the installation of all fuel gas piping attached to any manufactured home. The gas piping supply system shall be designed for a pressure not exceeding 14 inch water column (½ psi) and not less than 7 inch water column (¼ psi). The manufacturer shall indicate in his written installation instructions the design pressure limitations for safe and effective operation of the gas piping system. None of the requirements listed in this section shall apply to the piping supplied as a part of an appliance. All exterior openings around piping, ducts, plenums or vents shall be sealed to resist the entrance of rodents.

(b) *Materials.* All materials used for the installation, extension, alteration, or repair of any gas piping system shall be new and free from defects or internal obstructions. It shall not be permissible to repair defects in gas piping or fittings. Inferior or defective materials shall be removed and replaced with acceptable material. The system shall be made of materials having a melting point of not less than 1,450 F, except as provided in § 3280.705(e). They shall consist of one or more of the materials described in § 3280.705(b) (1) through (4).

(1) Steel or wrought-iron pipe shall comply with ANSI Standard B36.10–1979, Welded and Seamless Wrought Steel Pipe. Threaded brass pipe in iron pipe sizes may be used. Threaded brass pipe shall comply with ASTM B43–91, Standard Specification for Seamless Red Brass Pipe, Standard Sizes.

(2) Fittings for gas piping shall be wrought iron, malleable iron, steel, or brass (containing not more than 75 percent copper).

(3) Copper tubing must be annealed type, Grade K or L, conforming to the Standard Specification for Seamless Copper Water Tube, ASTM B88–93, or must comply with the Standard Specification for Seamless Copper Tube for Air Conditioning and Refrigeration Service, ASTM B280–1995. Copper tubing must be internally tinned.

(4) Steel tubing must have a minimum wall thickness of 0.032 inch for tubing of ½ inch diameter and smaller and 0.049 inch for diameters ½ inch and larger. Steel tubing must be in accordance with ASTM Standard Specification for Electric-Resistance-Welded Coiled Steel Tubing for Gas and Fuel Oil Lines, ASTM A539–1999, and must be externally corrosion protected.

(5) Corrugated stainless steel tubing (CSST) systems must be listed and installed in accordance with ANSI/IAS LC–1–1997, Fuel Gas Piping Systems Using Corrugated Stainless Steel Tubing (CSST) (incorporated by reference, see § 3280.4), and the requirements of this section.

(c) *Piping design.* Each manufactured home requiring fuel gas for any purpose shall be equipped with a natural gas piping system acceptable for LP-gas. Where fuel gas piping is to be installed in more than one section of an expandable or multiple unit home, the design and construction of the crossover(s) shall be as follows:

(1) All points of crossover shall be readily accessible from the exterior of the home.

(2) The connection(s) between units must be made with a connector(s) listed for exterior use or direct plumbing sized in accordance with § 3280.705(d). A shutoff valve of the non-displaceable rotor type conforming to ANSI Z21.15–1997, Manually Operated Gas Valves for Appliances, Appliances Connector Valves, and Hose End Valves, suitable for outdoor use must be installed at each crossover point upstream of the connection.

(3) The connection(s) may be made by a listed quick disconnect device which shall be designed to provide a positive seal of the supply side of the gas system when such device is separated.

(4) The flexible connector, direct plumbing pipe, or "quick disconnect" device shall be provided with protection from mechanical and impact damage and located to minimize the possibility of tampering.

(5) For gas line cross over connections made with either hard pipe or flexible connectors, the crossover point(s) shall be capped on the supply side to provide a positive seal and covered on the other side with a suitable protective covering.

(6) Suitable protective coverings for the connection device(s) when separated, shall be permanently attached to the device or flexible connector.

(7) When a quick disconnect device is installed, a 3 inch by 1¾ inch minimum size tag made of etched, metal-stamped or embossed brass, stainless steel, anodized or alcalde aluminum not less than 0.020 inch thick or other approved

material (e.g., 0.005 inch plastic laminates) shall be permanently attached on the exterior wall adjacent to the access to the "quick disconnect" device. Each tag shall be legibly inscribed with the following information using letters no smaller than ¼ inch high:

Do Not Use Tools To Separate the "Quick-Disconnect" Device

(d) *Gas pipe sizing.* Gas piping systems shall be sized so that the pressure drop to any appliance inlet connection from any gas supply connection, when all appliances are in operation at maximum capacity, is not more than 0.5 inch water column as determined on the basis of test, or in accordance with table 3280.705(d). When determining gas pipe sizing in the table, gas shall be assumed to have a specific gravity of 0.65 and rated at 1000 B.T.U. per cubic foot. The natural gas supply connection(s) shall be not less than the size of the gas piping but shall be not smaller than ¾ inch nominal pipe size.

TABLE TO PARAGRAPH (d)—MAXIMUM CAPACITY OF DIFFERENT SIZES OF PIPE AND TUBING IN THOUSANDS OF BTU/HR OF NATURAL GAS FOR GAS PRESSURES OF 0.5 PSIG OR LESS, AND A MAXIMUM PRESSURE DROP OF ½ IN. WATER COLUMN

ID (in.)	10 ft	20 ft	30 ft	40 ft	50 ft	60 ft	70 ft	80 ft	90 ft	100 ft
Iron Pipe Sizes—Length										
¼	43	29	24	20	18	16	15	14	13	12
⅜	95	65	52	45	40	36	33	31	29	27
½	175	120	97	82	73	66	61	57	53	50
¾	360	250	200	170	151	138	125	118	110	103
1	680	465	375	320	285	260	240	220	215	195

EHD[2]	ID (in.)	10 ft	20 ft	30 ft	40 ft	50 ft	60 ft	70 ft	80 ft	90 ft	100 ft
Corrugated Stainless Steel Tubing—Length [1]											
13	⅜	31	21	17	14	13	12	11	10	10	9
15	⅜	42	30	24	20	18	16	15	14	13	12
18	½	79	56	45	39	36	33	30	28	27	25
19	½	91	64	52	45	40	36	35	32	31	29
23	¾	155	111	92	80	72	65	60	58	55	52
25	¾	184	132	108	93	84	77	71	66	62	60
30	1	317	222	180	156	138	126	116	108	103	97
31	1	368	258	209	180	161	147	135	127	120	113
37	1¼	598	426	350	304	273	250	231	217	205	195

OD (in.)	10 ft	20 ft	30 ft	40 ft	50 ft	60 ft	70 ft	80 ft	90 ft	100 ft
Copper Tubing—Length										
¼	27	18	15	13	11	10	9	9	8	8
⅜	56	38	31	26	23	21	19	18	17	16
½	113	78	62	53	47	43	39	37	34	33
¾	197	136	109	93	83	75	69	64	60	57
1	280	193	155	132	117	106	98	91	85	81

[1] Includes losses for four 90-degree bends and two end fittings. Tubing runs with larger numbers of bend and/or fittings shall be increased by an equivalent length of tubing according to the following equation: $L = 1.3n$, where L is actual length (ft) of tubing and n is the number of additional fittings and/or bends.
[2] EHD (Equivalent Hydraulic Diameter)—A measure of the hydraulic efficiency between different tubing sizes.

(e) *Joints for gas pipe.* All pipe joints in the piping system, unless welded or brazed, shall be threaded joints that comply with Pipe Threads, General Purpose (Inch), adopted 25 October 1984, ANSI/ASME B1.20.1–1983. Right and left nipples or couplings shall not be used. Unions, if used, shall be of ground joint type. The material used for welding or brazing pipe connections shall have a melting temperature in excess of 1,000 F.

(f) *Joints for tubing.* (1) Tubing joints shall be made with either a single or a double flare of 45 degrees in accordance with Flares For Tubing, SAE–J533b–1992 or with other listed vibration-resistant fittings, or joints may be brazed with material having a melting point exceeding 1,000 °F. Metallic ball

111

sleeve compression-type tubing fittings shall not be used.

(2) Steel tubing joints shall be made with a double-flare in accordance with Flares For Tubing, SAE-J533b-1972.

(g) *Pipe joint compound.* Screw joints shall be made up tight with listed pipe joint compound, insoluble in liquefied petroleum gas, and shall be applied to the male threads only.

(h) *Concealed tubing.* (1) Copper tubing must not be run inside walls, floors, partitions, or roofs. Corrugated stainless steel tubing (CSST) may be run inside walls, floors, partitions, and roofs under the following conditions:

(i) The CSST is protected from accidental puncture by a steel strike barrier not less than 0.058 inch thick, or the barrier's equivalent, installed between the tubing and the finished wall and extending 4 inches beyond concealed penetrations of plates, firestops, and wall studs, or specified by the tubing manufacturer's instructions; and

(ii) The CSST is installed in single runs and is not rigidly secured.

(2) Where tubing passes through exterior walls, floors, partitions, or similar construction, the tubing must be protected by the use of weather-resistant grommets that snugly fit both the tubing and the hole through which the tubing passes, or protected as specified in the tubing manufacturer's instructions.

(3) Concealed joints: Piping or tubing joints must not be located in any wall, floor, partition, or similar concealed construction space.

(i) *Concealed joints.* Piping or tubing joints shall not be located in any floor, wall partition, or similar concealed construction space.

(j) *Gas supply connections.* When gas appliances are installed, at least one gas supply connection shall be provided on each home. The connection shall not be located beneath an exit door. Where more than one connection is provided, the piping system shall be sized to provide adequate capacity from each supply connection.

(k) *Identification of gas supply connections.* Each manufactured home shall have permanently affixed to the exterior skin at or near each gas supply connection or the end of the pipe, a tag of 3 inches by 1¾ inches minimum size,

made of etched, metal-stamped or embossed brass, stainless steel, anodized or alcalde aluminum not less than 0.020 inch thick, or other approved material (e.g., 0.005 inch plastic laminates), which reads as follows. The connector capacity indicated on this tag shall be equal to or greater than the total Btuh rating of all intended gas appliances.

COMBINATION LP-GAS AND NATURAL GAS SYSTEM

This gas piping system is designed for use of either liquefied petroleum gas or natural gas.

NOTICE: BEFORE TURNING ON GAS BE CERTAIN APPLIANCES ARE DESIGNED FOR THE GAS CONNECTED AND ARE EQUIPPED WITH CORRECT ORIFICES. SECURELY CAP THIS INLET WHEN NOT CONNECTED FOR USE.

When connecting to lot outlet, use a listed gas supply connector for mobile homes rated at ☐ 100,000 Btuh or more; ☐ 250,000 Btuh or more.

Before turning on gas, make certain all gas connections have been made tight, all appliance valves are turned off, and any unconnected outlets are capped.

After turning on gas, test gas piping and connections to appliances for leakage with soapy water or bubble solution, and light all pilots.

The connector capacity indicated on this tag shall be equal to or greater than the total Btuh rating of all intended gas appliances.

(1) *LP-gas supply connectors.* (1) A listed LP-Gas flexible connection conforming to UL 569–1995, Pigtails and Flexible Hose Connectors for LP Gas, or equal must be supplied when LP-Gas cylinders(s) and regulator(s) are supplied.

(2) *Appliance connections.* All gas burning appliances shall be connected to the fuel piping. Materials as provided in § 3280.705(b) or listed appliance connectors shall be used. Listed appliance connectors when used shall not run through walls, floors, ceilings or partitions, except for cabinetry, and shall be 3 feet or less in length or 6 feet or less for cooking appliances. Connectors of aluminum shall not be used outdoors. A manufactured home containing a combination LP-natural-gas-

system may be provided with a gas outlet to supply exterior appliances when installed in accordance with the following:

(i) No portion of the completed installation shall project beyond the wall of the manufactured home.

(ii) The outlet must be provided with an approved quick-disconnect device, which must be designed to provide a positive seal on the supply side of the gas system when the appliance is disconnected. A shutoff valve of the non-displaceable rotor type conforming to ANSI Z21.15–1997, Manually Operated Gas Valves, must be installed immediately upstream of the quick-disconnect device. The complete device must be provided as part of the original installation.

(iii) Protective caps or plugs for the "quick-disconnect" device, when disconnected, shall be permanently attached to the manufactured home adjacent to the device.

(iv) A tag shall be permanently attached to the outside of the exterior wall of the manufactured home as close as possible to the gas supply connection. The tag shall indicate the type of gas and the Btuh capacity of the outlet and shall be legibly inscribed as follows:

THIS OUTLET IS DESIGNED FOR USE WITH GAS PORTABLE APPLIANCES WHOSE TOTAL INPUT DO NOT EXCEED ____ BTUH. REPLACE PROTECTIVE COVERING OVER CONNECTOR WHEN NOT IN USE.

(3) *Valves.* A shutoff valve must be installed in the fuel piping at each appliance inside the manufactured home structure, upstream of the union or connector in addition to any valve on the appliance and so arranged to be accessible to permit servicing of the appliance and removal of its components. The shutoff valve must be located within 6 feet of any cooking appliance and within 3 feet of any other appliance. A shutoff valve may serve more than one appliance if located as required by this paragraph (3). The shutoff valve must be of the non-displaceable rotor type and conform to ANSI Z21.15–1997, Manually Operated Gas Valves.

(4) *Gas piping system openings.* All openings in the gas piping system shall be closed gas-tight with threaded pipe plugs or pipe caps.

(5) *Electrical ground.* Gas piping shall not be used for an electrical ground.

(6) *Couplings.* Pipe couplings and unions shall be used to join sections of threaded piping. Right and left nipples or couplings shall not be used.

(7) *Hangers and supports.* All gas piping shall be adequately supported by galvanized or equivalently protected metal straps or hangers at intervals of not more than 4 feet, except where adequate support and protection is provided by structural members. Solid-iron-pipe gas supply connection(s) shall be rigidly anchored to a structural member within 6 inches of the supply connection(s).

(8) *Testing for leakage.* (i) Before appliances are connected, piping systems shall stand a pressure of at least six inches mercury or three PSI gage for a period of not less than ten minutes without showing any drop in pressure. Pressure shall be measured with a mercury manometer or slope gage calibrated so as to be read in increments of not greater than one-tenth pound, or an equivalent device. The source of normal operating pressure shall be isolated before the pressure tests are made. Before a test is begun, the temperature of the ambient air and of the piping shall be approximately the same, and constant air temperature be maintained throughout the test.

(ii) After appliances are connected, the piping system shall be pressurized to not less than 10 inches nor more than 14 inches water column and the appliance connections tested for leakage with soapy water or bubble solution.

[40 FR 58752, Dec. 18, 1975, as amended at 42 FR 54383, Oct. 5, 1977. Redesignated at 44 FR 20679, Apr. 6, 1979, as amended at 52 FR 4587, Feb. 12, 1987; 58 FR 55016, Oct. 25, 1993; 70 FR 72050, Nov. 30, 2005; 78 FR 73987, Dec. 9, 2013]

§3280.706 Oil piping systems.

(a) *General.* The requirements of this section shall govern the installation of all liquid fuel piping attached to any manufactured home. None of the requirements listed in this section shall apply to the piping in the appliance(s).

(b) *Materials.* All materials used for the installation extension, alteration, or repair, of any oil piping systems shall be new and free from defects or internal obstructions. The system shall be made of materials having a melting point of not less than 1,450 F, except as provided in § 280.706(d) and (e). They shall consist of one or more of the materials described in § 3280.706(b) (1) through (4).

(1) Steel or wrought-iron pipe shall comply with ANSI B 36.10–1979, Welded and Seamless Wrought Steel Pipe. Threaded copper or brass pipe in iron pipe sizes may be used.

(2) Fittings for oil piping shall be wrought-iron, malleable iron, steel, or brass (containing not more than 75 percent copper).

(3) Copper tubing must be annealed type, Grade K or L conforming to the Standard Specification for Seamless Copper Water Tube, ASTM B88–93, or shall comply with ASTM B280–1995, Standard Specification for Seamless Copper Tube for Air Conditioning and Refrigeration Field Service.

(4) Steel tubing shall have a minimum wall thickness of 0.032 inch for diameters up to ½ inch and 0.049 inch for diameters ½ inch and larger. Steel tubing shall be constructed in accordance with the Specification for Electric-Resistance-Welded Coiled Steel Tubing for Gas and Field Oil Lines, ASTM, A539–90a, and shall be externally corrosion protected.

(c) *Size of oil piping.* The minimum size of all fuel oil tank piping connecting outside tanks to the appliance shall be no smaller than ⅜ inch OD copper tubing or ¼ inch IPS. If No. 1 fuel oil is used with a listed automatic pump (fuel lifter), copper tubing shall be sized as specified by the pump manufacturer.

(d) *Joints for oil piping.* All pipe joints in the piping system, unless welded or brazed, shall be threaded joints which comply with ANSI/ASME B1.20.1–1983, Pipe Threads, General Purpose (Inch). The material used for brazing pipe connections shall have a melting temperature in excess of 1,000 F.

(e) *Joints for tubing.* Joints in tubing shall be made with either a single or double flare of the proper degree, as recommended by the tubing manufacturer, by means of listed tubing fit-

tings, or brazed with materials having a melting point in excess of 1,000 F.

(f) *Pipe joint compound.* Threaded joints shall be made up tight with listed pipe joint compound which shall be applied to the male threads only.

(g) *Couplings.* Pipe couplings and unions shall be used to join sections of threaded pipe. Right and left nipples or couplings shall not be used.

(h) *Grade of piping.* Fuel oil piping installed in conjunction with gravity feed systems to oil heating equipment shall slope in a gradual rise upward from a central location to both the oil tank and the appliance in order to eliminate air locks.

(i) *Strap hangers.* All oil piping shall be adequately supported by galvanized or equivalently protected metal straps or hangers at intervals of not more than 4 feet, except where adequate support and protection is provided by structural members. Solid-iron-pipe oil supply connection(s) shall be rigidly anchored to a structural member within 6 inches of the supply connection(s).

(j) *Testing Tag.* A tag must be affixed to each oil-fired appliance stating: "Before setting the system in operation, tank installations and piping must be checked for oil leaks with fuel oil of the same grade that will be burned in the appliance. No other material may be used for testing fuel oil tanks and piping. Tanks must be filled to maximum capacity for the final check for oil leakage."

[40 FR 58752, Dec. 18, 1975. Redesignated at 44 FR 20679, Apr. 6, 1979, as amended at 52 FR 4588, Feb. 12, 1987; 58 FR 55017, Oct. 25, 1993; 70 FR 72050, Nov. 30, 2005; 78 FR 73988, Dec. 9, 2013]

§ 3280.707 Heat producing appliances.

(a) Heat-producing appliances and vents, roof jacks and chimneys necessary for their installation in manufactured homes shall be listed or certified by a nationally recognized testing agency for use in manufactured homes.

(1) A manufactured home shall be provided with a comfort heating system.

(i) When a manufactured home is manufactured to contain a heating appliance, the heating appliance shall be installed by the manufacturer of the manufactured home in compliance with applicable sections of this subpart.

(ii) When a manufactured home is manufactured for field application of an external heating or combination heating/cooling appliance, preparation of the manufactured home for this external application shall comply with the applicable sections of this part.

(2) Each gas and oil burning comfort heating appliance must have an Annual Fuel Utilization Efficiency of not less than that specified in 10 CFR part 430, Energy Conservation Program for Consumer Products: Test Procedures for Furnaces/Boilers, Vented Home Heating Equipment and Pool Heaters.

(b) Fuel-burning heat-producing appliances and refrigeration appliances, except ranges and ovens, shall be of the vented type and vented to the outside.

(c) Fuel-burning appliances shall not be converted from one fuel to another fuel unless converted in accordance with the terms of their listing and the appliance manufacturer's instructions.

(d) *Performance efficiency.* Each automatic storage water heater must comply with the efficiency requirements of 10 CFR part 430, Energy Conservation Program for Consumer Products: Energy Conservation Standards for Water Heaters.

(1) All automatic electric storage water heaters installed in manufactured homes shall have a standby loss not exceeding 43 watts/meter^2 (4 watts/ft^2) of tank surface area. The method of test for standby loss shall be as described in section 4.3.1 of Household Automatic Electric Storage Type Water Heaters, ANSI C72.1–1972.

(2) All gas and oil-fired automatic storage water heaters shall have a recovery efficiency, E, and a standby loss, S, as described below. The method of test of E and S shall be as described in section 2.7 of Gas Water heaters, Vol. I, Storage Water Heaters with Input/Ratings of 75,000 BTU per hour or less, ANSI Z21.10.1–1998 with addendums Z21.10.1a–2000, and Z21.10.1b–1992, except that for oil-fired units. CF = 1.0, Q = total gallons of oil consumed and H = total heating value of oil in BTU/gallon.

Storage capacity in gallons	Recovery efficiency	Standby loss
Less than 25	At least 75 percent..	Not more than 7.5 percent.
25 up to 35 ..	00	Not more than 7 percent.
35 or more ...	00	Not more than 6 percent.

(e) Each space heating, cooling or combination heating and cooling system shall be provided with at least one readily adjustable automatic control for regulation of living space temperature. The control shall be placed a minimum of 3 feet from the vertical edge of the appliance compartment door. It shall not be located on an exterior wall or on a wall separating the appliance compartment from a habitable room.

(f) *Oil-fired heating equipment.* All oil-fired heating equipment must conform to Liquid Fuel-burning Heating Appliances for Manufactured Homes and Recreational Vehicles, UL 307A–1995, with 1997 revisions, and be installed in accordance with Standard for the Installation of Oil Burning Equipment, NFPA 31–01 (incorporated by reference, see § 3280.4). Regardless of the requirements of the above-referenced standards, or any other standards referenced in this part, the following are not required:

(1) External switches or remote controls which shut off the burner or the flow of oil to the burner, or

(2) An emergency disconnect switch to interrupt electric power to the equipment under conditions of excessive temperature.

[40 FR 58752, Dec. 17, 1975, as amended at 42 FR 54383, Oct. 5, 1977. Redesignated at 44 FR 20679, Apr. 6, 1979, as amended at 47 FR 49391, Nov. 1, 1982; 52 FR 4588, Feb. 12, 1987; 52 FR 47553, Dec. 15, 1987; 58 FR 55017, Oct. 25, 1993; 70 FR 72050, Nov. 30, 2005; 78 FR 73988, Dec. 9, 2013]

§ 3280.708 Exhaust duct system and provisions for the future installation of a clothes dryer.

(a) *Clothes dryers.* (1) All gas and electric clothes dryers shall be exhausted to the outside by a moisture-lint exhaust duct and termination fitting. When the clothes dryer is supplied by the manufacturer, the exhaust duct and termination fittings shall be completely installed by the manufacturer. However, if the exhaust duct system is subject to damage during transportation, it need not be completely installed at the factory when:

(i) The exhaust duct system is connected to the clothes dryer, and

(ii) A moisture lint exhaust duct system is roughed in and installation instructions are provided in accordance with paragraph (b)(3) or (c) of this section.

(2) A clothes dryer moisture-lint exhaust duct shall not be connected to any other duct, vent or chimney.

(3) The exhaust duct shall not terminate beneath the manufactured home.

(4) Moisture-lint exhaust ducts shall not be connected with sheet metal screws or other fastening devices which extend into the interior of the duct.

(5) Moisture-lint exhaust duct and termination fittings shall be installed in accordance with the appliance manufacturer's printed instructions.

(b) *Provisions for future installation of a gas clothes dryer.* A manufactured home may be provided with "stubbed in" equipment at the factory to supply a gas clothes dryer for future installation by the owner provided it complies with the following provisions:

(1) The "stubbed in" gas outlet shall be provided with a shutoff valve, the outlet of which is closed by threaded pipe plug or cap;

(2) The "stubbed in" gas outlet shall be permanently labeled to identify it for use only as the supply connection for a gas clothes dryer;

(3) A moisture lint duct system consisting of a complete access space (hole) through the wall or floor cavity with a cap or cover on the interior and exterior of the cavity secured in such a manner that they can be removed by a common household tool shall be provided. The cap or cover in place shall limit air infiltration and be designed to resist the entry of water or rodents. The manufacturer is not required to provide the moisture-lint exhaust duct or the termination fitting. The manufacturer shall provide written instructions to the owner on how to complete the exhaust duct installation in accordance with provisions of § 3280.708(a)(1) through (5).

(c) *Provisions for future installation of electric clothes dryers.* When wiring is installed to supply an electric clothes

dryer for future installation by the owner, the manufacturer shall:

(1) Provide a roughed in moisture-lint exhaust duct system consisting of a complete access space (hole) through the wall or floor cavity with a cap or cover on the interior and exterior of the cavity which are secured in such a manner that they can be removed by the use of common household tools. The cap or cover in place shall limit air filtration and be designed to resist the entry of water or rodents into the home. The manufacturer is not required to provide the moisture-lint exhaust duct or the termination fitting;

(2) Install a receptacle for future connection of the dryer;

(3) Provide written instructions on how to complete the exhaust duct installation in accordance with the provisions of paragraphs (a)(1) through (5) of this section.

[42 FR 54383, Oct. 5, 1977. Redesignated at 44 FR 20679, Apr. 6, 1979, as amended at 58 FR 55018, Oct. 25, 1993]

§ 3280.709 Installation of appliances.

(a) The installation of each appliance shall conform to the terms of its listing and the manufacturer's instructions. The installer shall leave the manufacturer's instructions attached to the appliance. Every appliance shall be secured in place to avoid displacement. For the purpose of servicing and replacement, each appliance shall be both accessible and removable.

(b) Heat-producing appliances shall be so located that no doors, drapes, or other such material can be placed or swing closer to the front of the appliance than the clearances specified on the labeled appliances.

(c) Clearances surrounding heat producing appliances shall not be less than the clearances specified in the terms of their listings.

(1) Prevention of storage. The area surrounding heat producing appliances installed in areas with interior or exterior access shall be framed-in or guarded with noncombustible material such that the distance from the appliance to the framing or guarding material is not greater than three inches unless the appliance is installed in compliance with paragraph (c)(2), of this section. When clearance required by the listing

116

is greater than three inches, the guard or frame shall not be closer to the appliance than the distance provided in the listing.

(2) Clearance spaces surrounding heat producing appliances are not required to be framed-in or guarded when:

(i) A space is designed specifically for a clothes washer or dryer;

(ii) Dimensions surrounding the appliance do not exceed three inches; or

(iii) The manufacturer affixes either to a side of an alcove or compartment containing the appliance, or to the appliance itself, in a clearly visible location, a 3″ × 5″ adhesive backed plastic laminated label or the equivalent which reads as follows:

"Warning"

This compartment is not to be used as a storage area. Storage of combustible materials or containers on or near any appliance in this compartment may create a fire hazard. Do not store such materials or containers in this compartment.

(d) All fuel-burning appliances, except ranges, ovens, illuminating appliances, clothes dryers, solid fuel-burning fireplaces and solid fuel-burning fireplace stoves, shall be installed to provide for the complete separation of the combustion system from the interior atmosphere of the manufactured home. Combustion air inlets and flue gas outlets shall be listed or certified as components of the appliance. The required separation may be obtained by:

(1) The installation of direct vent system (sealed combustion system) appliances, or

(2) The installation of appliances within enclosures so as to separate the appliance combustion system and venting system from the interior atmosphere of the manufactured home. There shall not be any door, removable access panel, or other opening into the enclosure from the inside of the manufactured home. Any opening for ducts, piping, wiring, etc., shall be sealed.

(e) A forced air appliance and its return-air system shall be designed and installed so that negative pressure created by the air-circulating fan cannot affect its or another appliance's combustion air supply or act to mix products of combustion with circulating air.

(1) The air circulating fan of a furnace installed in an enclosure with another fuel-burning appliance shall be operable only when any door or panel covering an opening in the furnace fan compartment or in a return air plenum or duct is in the closed position. This does not apply if both appliances are direct vent system (sealed combustion system) appliances.

(2) If a warm air appliance is installed within an enclosure to conform to §3280.709(d)(2), each warm-air outlet and each return air inlet shall extend to the exterior of the enclosure. Ducts, if used for that purpose, shall not have any opening within the enclosure and shall terminate at a location exterior to the enclosure.

(3) Cooling coils installed as a portion of, or in connection with, any forced-air furnace shall be installed on the downstream side unless the furnace is specifically otherwise listed.

(4) An air conditioner evaporator section shall not be located in the air discharge duct or plenum of any forced-air furnace unless the manufactured home manufacturer has complied with certification required in §3280.511.

(5) If a cooling coil is installed with a forced-air furnace, the coil shall be installed in accordance with its listing. When a furnace-coil unit has a limited listing, the installation must be in accordance with that listing.

(6) When an external heating appliance or combination cooling/heating appliance is to be field installed, the home manufacturer shall make provision for proper location of the connections to the supply and return air systems. The manufacturer is not required to provide said appliance(s). The preparation by the manufacturer for connection to the home's supply and return air system shall include all fittings and connection ducts to the main duct and return air system such that the installer is only required to provide:

(i) The appliance;

(ii) Any appliance connections to the home; and

(iii) The connecting duct between the external appliance and the fitting installed on the home by the manufacturer. The above connection preparations by the manufacturer do not apply

117

to supply or return air systems designed only to accept external cooling (i.e., self contained air conditioning systems, etc.)

(7) The installation of a self contained air conditioner comfort cooling appliance shall meet the following requirements:

(i) The installation on a duct common with an installed heating appliance shall require the installation of an automatic damper or other means to prevent the cooled air from passing through the heating appliance unless the heating appliance is certified or listed for such application and the supply system is intended for such an application.

(ii) The installation shall prevent the flow of heated air into the external cooling appliance and its connecting ducts to the manufactured home supply and return air system during the operation of the heating appliance installed in the manufactured home.

(iii) The installation shall prevent simultaneous operation of the heating and cooling appliances.

(f) *Vertical clearance above cooking top.* Ranges shall have a vertical clearance above the cooking top of not less than 24 inches. (See § 3280.204).

(g) Solid fuel-burning factory-built fireplaces and fireplace stoves listed for use in manufactured homes may be installed in manufactured homes provided they and their installation conform to the following paragraphs. A fireplace or fireplace stove shall not be considered as a heating facility for determining compliance with subpart F.

(1) A solid fuel-burning fireplace or fireplace stove shall be equipped with integral door(s) or shutter(s) designed to close the fireplace or fireplace stove fire chamber opening and shall include complete means for venting through the roof, a combustion air inlet, a hearth extension, and means to securely attach the fireplace or the fireplace stove to the manufactured home structure. The installation shall conform to the following paragraphs (g)(1) (i) to (vii) inclusive:

(i) A listed factory-built chimney designed to be attached directly to the fireplace or fireplace stove shall be used. The listed factory built chimney shall be equipped with and contain as part of its listing a termination device(s) and a spark arrester(s).

(ii) A fireplace or fireplace stove, air intake assembly, hearth extension and the chimney shall be installed in accordance with the terms of their listings and their manufacturer's instructions.

(iii) The combustion air inlet shall conduct the air directly into the fire chamber and shall be designed to prevent material from the hearth dropping onto the area beneath the manufactured home.

(iv) The fireplace or fireplace stove shall not be installed in a sleeping room.

(v) Hearth extension shall be of noncombustible material not less than ⅜-inch thick. The hearth shall extend at least 16 inches in front or and at least 8 inches beyond each side of the fireplace or fireplace stove opening. Furthermore the hearth shall extend over the entire surface beneath a fireplace stove and beneath an elevated or overhanging fireplace.

(vi) The label on each solid fuel-burning fireplace and solid fuel-burning fireplace stove shall include the following wording: For use with solid fuel only.

(vii) The chimney shall extend at least three feet above the part of the roof through which it passes and at least two feet above the highest elevation of any part of the manufactured home within 10 feet of the chimney. Portions of the chimney and termination that exceed an elevation of 13½ ft. above ground level may be designed to be removed for transporting the manufactured home.

(h) A corrosion resistant water drip collection and drain pan must be installed under each water heater that will allow water leaking from the water heater to drain to the exterior of the manufactured home, or to a drain.

[40 FR 58752, Dec. 18, 1975. Redesignated at 44 FR 20679, Apr. 6, 1979, as amended at 44 FR 66195, Nov. 19, 1979; 58 FR 55018, Oct. 25, 1993; 70 FR 72050, Nov. 30, 2005]

§ 3280.710 Venting, ventilation and combustion air.

(a) The venting as required by § 3280.707(b) shall be accomplished by one or more of the methods given in (a)(1) and (2) of this section:

(1) An integral vent system listed or certified as part of the appliance.

(2) A venting system consisting entirely of listed components, including roof jack, installed in accordance with the terms of the appliance listing and the appliance manufacturer's instructions.

(b) Venting and combustion air systems shall be installed in accordance with the following:

(1) Components shall be securely assembled and properly aligned at the factory in accordance with the appliance manufacturer's instructions except vertical or horizontal sections of a fuel fired heating appliance venting system that extend beyond the roof line or outside the wall line may be installed at the site. Sectional venting systems shall be listed for such applications and installed in accordance with the terms of their listings and manufacturers' instructions. In cases where sections of the venting system are removed for transportation, a label shall be permanently attached to the appliance indicating the following:

Sections of the venting system have not been installed. Warning-do not operate the appliance until all sections have been assembled and installed in accordance with the manufacturer's instructions.

(2) Draft hood connectors shall be firmly attached to draft hood outlets or flue collars by sheet metal screws or by equivalent effective mechanical fasteners.

(3) Every joint of a vent, vent connector, exhaust duct and combustion air intake shall be secure and in alignment.

(c) Venting systems shall not terminate underneath a manufactured home.

(d) Venting system terminations shall be not less than three feet from any motor-driven air intake discharging into habitable areas.

(e) The area in which cooking appliances are located shall be ventilated by a metal duct which may be single wall, not less than 12.5 square inches in cross-sectional area (minimum dimension shall be two inches) located above the appliance(s) and terminating outside the manufactured home, or by listed mechanical ventilating equipment

discharging outside the home, that is installed in accordance with the terms of listing and the manufacturer's instructions. Gravity or mechanical ventilation shall be installed within a horizontal distance of not more than ten feet from the vertical front of the appliance(s).

(f) Mechanical ventilation which exhausts directly to the outside atmosphere from the living space of a home shall be equipped with an automatic or manual damper. Operating controls shall be provided such that mechanical ventilation can be separately operated without directly energizing other energy consuming devices.

[49 FR 32012, Aug. 9, 1984, as amended at 58 FR 55018, Oct. 25, 1993]

§3280.711 Instructions.

Operating instructions must be provided with each appliance. The operating and installation instructions for each appliance must be provided with the homeowner's manual.

[78 FR 73989, Dec. 9, 2013]

§3280.712 Marking.

(a) Information on clearances, input rating, lighting and shutdown shall be attached to the appliances with the same permanence as the nameplate, and so located that it is easily readable when the appliance is properly installed or shutdown for transporting of manufactured home.

(b) Each fuel-burning appliance shall bear permanent marking designating the type(s) of fuel for which it is listed.

§3280.713 Accessibility.

Every appliance shall be accessible for inspection, service, repair, and replacement without removing permanent construction. For those purposes, inlet piping supplying the appliance shall not be considered permanent construction. Sufficient room shall be available to enable the operator to observe the burner, control, and ignition means while starting the appliance.

[58 FR 55018, Oct. 25, 1993]

§3280.714 Appliances, cooling.

(a) Every air conditioning unit or a combination air conditioning and heating unit shall be listed or certified by a nationally recognized testing agency for the application for which the unit is intended and installed in accordance with the terms of its listing.

(1) Mechanical air conditioners shall be rated in accordance with the ARI Standard 210/240–89 Unitary Air Conditioning and Air Source Unitary Heat Pump Equipment (incorporated by reference, see § 3280.4) and certified by ARI or other nationally recognized testing agency capable of providing follow-up service.

(i) Electric motor-driven unitary air-cooled air conditioners and heat pumps in the cooling mode with rated capacity less than 65,000 BTU/hour (19,045 watts), when rated at ARI standard rating conditions in ARI Standard 210/240–89, Unitary Air-Conditioning and Air-Source Heat Pump Equipment, must have seasonal energy efficiency (SEER) values not less than as specified in 10 CFR Part 430, Energy Conservation Program for Consumer Products: Central Air Conditioners and Heat Pumps Energy Conservation Standards.

(ii) Heat pumps must be certified to comply with all requirements of the ARI Standard 210/240–89, Unitary Air Conditioning and Air-Source Heat Pump Equipment. Electric motor-driven vapor compression heat pumps with supplemental electrical resistance heat must be sized to provide by compression at least 60 percent of the calculated annual heating requirements for the manufactured home being served. A control must be provided and set to prevent operation of supplemental electrical resistance heat at outdoor temperatures above 40 °F (4 °C), except for defrost conditions. Electric motor-driven vapor compression heat pumps with supplemental electric resistance heat conforming to ARI Standard 210/240–89, Unitary Air-Conditioning and Air-Source Heat Pump Equipment, must have Heating Season Performance Factor (HSPF) efficiencies not less than as specified in the 10 CFR Part 430, Energy Conservation Program for Consumer Products: Central Air Conditioners and Heat Pumps Energy Conservation Standards.

(iii) Electric motor-driven vapor compression heat pumps with supple-

mental electric resistance heat conforming to ARI Standard 210/240–89 Unitary Air-Conditioning and Air-Source Heat Pump Equipment shall show coefficient of performance ratios not less than shown below:

COP

Temperature degrees fahrenheit	Coefficient of performance
47	2.5
17	1.7
0	1.0

(2) Gas fired absorption air conditioners must be listed or certified in accordance with ANSI Z21.40.1–1996, Gas Fired, Heat Activated, Air Conditioning and Heat Pump Appliances (incorporated by reference, see § 3280.4), and certified by a nationally recognized testing agency capable of providing follow-up service.

(3) Direct refrigerating systems serving any air conditioning or comfort-cooling system installed in a manufactured home shall employ a type of refrigerant that ranks no lower than Group 5 in the Underwriters' Laboratories, Inc. "Classification of Comparative Life Hazard of Various Chemicals."

(4) When a cooling or heat pump coil and air conditioner blower are installed with a furnace or heating appliance, they shall be tested and listed in combination for heating and safety performance by a nationally recognized testing agency.

(5) Cooling or heat pump indoor coils and outdoor sections shall be certified, listed and rated in combination for capacity and efficiency by a nationally recognized testing agency(ies). Rating procedures shall be based on U.S. Department of Energy test procedures.

(b) *Installation and instructions.* (1) The installation of each appliance shall conform to the terms of its listing as specified on the appliance and in the manufacturer's instructions. The installer shall include the manufacturer's installation instructions in the manufactured home. Appliances shall be secured in place to avoid displacement and movement from vibration and road shock.

(2) Operating instructions shall be provided with the appliance.

120

(c) Fuel-burning air conditioners shall also comply with §280.707.

(d) The appliance rating plate shall be so located that it is easily readable when the appliance is properly installed.

(e) Every installed appliance shall be accessible for inspection, service, repair and replacement without removing permanent construction.

[40 FR 58752, Dec. 18, 1975. Redesignated at 44 FR 20679, Apr. 6, 1979, as amended at 58 FR 55018, Oct. 25, 1993; 70 FR 72051, Nov. 30, 2005; 78 FR 73989, Dec. 9, 2013]

§3280.715 Circulating air systems.

(a) *Supply system.* (1) Supply air ducts, fittings, and any dampers contained therein must be made of galvanized steel, tin-plated steel, or aluminum, or must be listed as Class 0 or Class 1 air ducts and air connectors in accordance with UL 181–2003, Factory-Made Air Ducts and Air Connectors (incorporated by reference, see §3280.4). Class 1 air ducts and air connectors must be located at least 3 feet from the furnace bonnet or plenum. Air connectors must not be used for exterior manufactured home duct connection. A duct system integral with the structure must be of durable construction that can be demonstrated to be equally resistant to fire and deterioration as required by this section. Furnace supply plenums must be constructed of metal that extends a minimum of 3 feet from the heat exchanger measured along the centerline of airflow. Ducts constructed from sheet metal must be in accordance with the following table:

MINIMUM METAL THICKNESS FOR DUCTS [1]

Duct type	Diameter 14 in. or less	Width over 14 in.
Round	0.013	0.016
Enclosed rectangular	.013	.016
Exposed rectangular	.016	.019

[1] When "nominal" thicknesses are specified, 0.003 in. shall be added to these "minimum" metal thicknesses.

(2) *Sizing of ducts for heating.* (i) Ducts shall be so designed that when a labeled forced-air furnace is installed and operated continuously at its normal heating air circulating rate in the manufactured home, with all registers in the full open position, the static pressure measured in the casing shall

not exceed 90% of that shown on the label of the appliance. For upflow furnaces the static pressure shall be taken in the duct plenum. For external heating or combination heating/cooling appliances the static pressure shall be taken at the point used by the agency listing or certifying the appliance.

(ii) When an evaporator-coil specifically designed for the particular furnace is installed between the furnace and the duct plenum, the total static pressure shall be measured downstream of the coil in accordance with the appliance label and shall not exceed 90 percent of that shown on the label of the appliance.

(iii) When any other listed air-cooler coil is installed between the furnace and the duct plenum, the total static pressure shall be measured between the furnace and the coil and it shall not exceed 90 percent of that shown on the label of the furnace.

(iv) The minimum dimension of any branch duct shall be at least 1½ inches, and of any main duct, 2½ inches.

(3) *Sizing of ducts.* (i) The manufactured home manufacturer shall certify the capacity of the air cooling supply duct system for the maximum allowable output of ARI certified central air conditioning systems. The certification shall be at operating static pressure of 0.3 inches of water or greater. (See §3280.511).

(ii) The refrigerated air cooling supply duct system including registers must be capable of handling at least 300 cfm per 10,000 btuh with a static pressure no greater than 0.3 inches of water when measured at room temperature. In the case of application of external self contained comfort cooling appliances or the cooling mode of combination heating/cooling appliances, either the external ducts between the appliance and the manufactured home supply system shall be considered part of, and shall comply with the requirements for the refrigerated air cooling supply duct system, or the connecting duct between the external appliance and the mobile supply duct system shall be a part of the listed appliance. The minimum dimension of any branch duct shall be at least 1½ inches, and of any main duct, 2½ inches.

(4) *Airtightness of supply duct systems.* A supply duct system shall be considered substantially airtight when the static pressure in the duct system, with all registers sealed and with the furnace air circulator at high speed, is at least 80 percent of the static pressure measured in the furnace casing, with its outlets sealed and the furnace air circulator operating at high speed. For the purpose of this paragraph and § 3280.715(b) pressures shall be measured with a water manometer or equivalent device calibrated to read in increments not greater than ¹⁄₁₀ inch water column.

(5) *Expandable or multiple manufactured home connections.* (i) An expandable or multiple manufactured home may have ducts of the heating system installed in the various units. The points of connection must be so designed and constructed that when the manufactured home is fully expanded or coupled, the resulting duct joint will conform to the requirements of this part.

(ii) The manufacturer must provide installation instructions for supporting, mechanically fastening, sealing, and insulating each crossover duct. The instructions must indicate that no portion of the crossover duct is to be in contact with the ground, and must describe the means to support the duct without compressing the insulation and restricting airflow.

(6) Air supply ducts shall be insulated with material having an effective thermal resistance (R) of not less than 4.0 unless they are within manufactured home insulation having a minimum effective value of R–4.0 for floors or R–6.0 for ceilings.

(7) Unless installed in a basement, supply and return ducts, fittings, and crossover duct plenums exposed directly to outside air, such as those under-chassis crossover ducts or ducts connecting external heating, cooling, or combination heating/cooling appliances, must be insulated with material having a minimum thermal resistance of R–8 in all Thermal Zones. All such insulating materials must have a continuous vapor barrier retarder having a perm rating of not more than 1 perm. Where ducts are exposed underneath the manufactured home, they must comply with paragraph (a)(5)(ii) of this

section, and shall be listed for exterior use.

(b) *Return air systems—(1) Return air openings.* Provisions shall be made to permit the return of circulating air from all rooms and living spaces, except toilet room(s), to the circulating air supply inlet of the furnace.

(2) *Duct material.* Return ducts and any diverting dampers contained therein shall be in accordance with the following:

(i) Portions of return ducts directly above the heating surfaces, or closer than 2 feet from the outer jacket or casing of the furnace shall be constructed of metal in accordance with § 3280.715(a)(1) or shall be listed Class 0 or Class 1 air ducts.

(ii) Return ducts, except as required by paragraph (a) of this section, shall be constructed of one-inch (nominal) wood boards (flame spread classification of not more than 200), other suitable material no more flammable than one-inch board or in accordance with § 3280.715(a)(1).

(iii) The interior of combustible ducts shall be lined with noncombustible material at points where there might be danger from incandescent particles dropped through the register or furnace such as directly under floor registers and the bottom return.

(iv) Factory made air ducts used for connecting external heating, cooling or combination heating/cooling appliances to the supply system and return air system of a manufactured home shall be listed by a nationally recognized testing agency. Ducts applied to external heating appliances or combination heating/cooling appliances supply system outlets shall be constructed of metal in accordance with § 3280.715(a)(1) or shall be listed Class 0 or Class 1 air ducts for those portions of the duct closer than 2 feet from the outer casing of the appliance.

(v) Ducts applied to external appliances shall be resistant to deteriorating environmental effects, including but not limited to ultraviolet rays, cold weather, or moisture and shall be resistant to insects and rodents.

(3) *Sizing.* The cross-sectional areas of the return air duct shall not be less than 2 square inches for each 1,000 Btu per hour input rating of the appliance.

Dampers shall not be placed in a combination fresh air intake and return air duct so arranged that the required cross-sectional area will not be reduced at all possible positions of the damper.

(4) *Permanent uncloseable openings.* Living areas not served by return air ducts or closed off from the return opening of the furnace by doors, sliding partitions, or other means shall be provided with permanent uncloseable openings in the doors or separating partitions to allow circulated air to return to the furnace. Such openings may be grilled or louvered. The net free area of each opening shall be not less than 1 square inch for every 5 square feet of total living area closed off from the furnace by the door or partition serviced by that opening. Undercutting doors connecting the closed-off space may be used as a means of providing return air area. However, in the event that doors are undercut, they shall be undercut a minimum of 2 inches and not more than 2½ inches, as measured from the top surface of the floor decking to the bottom of the door and no more than one half of the free air area so provided shall be counted as return air area.

(c) *Joints and seams.* Joints and seams of sheet metal and factory-made flexible ducts, including trunks, branches, risers, crossover ducts, and crossover duct plenums, shall be mechanically secured and made substantially airtight. Slip joints in sheet metal ducts shall have a lap of at least one inch and shall be mechanically fastened. Tapes or caulking compounds shall be permitted to be used for sealing mechanically secure joints. Sealants and tapes shall be applied only to surfaces that are dry and dust-, dirt-, oil-, and grease-free. Tapes and mastic closure systems for use with factory-made rigid fiberglass air ducts and air connectors shall be listed in accordance with UL Standard 181A–1994, with 1998 revisions. Tapes and mastic closure systems used with factory-made flexible air ducts and air connectors shall be listed in accordance with UL Standard 181B–1995, with 1998 revisions.

(d) *Supports and protection.* Ducts must be securely supported. Nails or other fasteners must not be driven or penetrate through duct walls. Where vertical ducts are installed within closets or rooms, they must be enclosed with materials equivalent to those used in the closet or room construction.

(e) *Registers and grilles.* Fittings connecting the registers and grilles to the duct system must be constructed of metal or material that complies with the requirements of Class 1 or 2 ducts under UL 181–1996 with 1998 revisions, Factory Made Air Ducts and Connectors. Air supply terminal devices (registers) when installed in kitchen, bedrooms, and bathrooms must be equipped with adjustable closeable dampers. Registers or grilles must be constructed of metal or conform with the following:

(1) Be made of a material classified 94V–0 or 94V–1, when tested as described in UL 94–1996, with 2001 revisions, Test for Flammability of Plastic Materials for Parts in Devices and Appliances, Fifth Edition; and

(2) Floor registers or grilles shall resist without structural failure a 200 lb. concentrated load on a 2-inch diameter disc applied to the most critical area of the exposed face of the register or grille. For this test the register or grille is to be at a temperature of not less than 165 °F and is to be supported in accordance with the manufacturer's instructions.

[40 FR 58752, Dec. 18, 1975. Redesignated at 44 FR 20679, Apr. 6, 1979, as amended at 52 FR 4589, Feb. 12, 1987; 58 FR 55019, Oct. 25, 1993; 70 FR 72051, Nov. 30, 2005; 78 FR 73989, Dec. 9, 2013]

Subpart I—Electrical Systems

§3280.801 Scope.

(a) Subpart I of this part and Part II of Article 550 of the National Electrical Code (NFPA No. 70–2005) cover the electrical conductors and equipment installed within or on manufactured homes and the conductors that connect manufactured homes to a supply of electricity.

(b) In addition to the requirements of this part and Part II of Article 550 of the National Electrical Code (NFPA No. 70–2005), the applicable portions of other Articles of the National Electrical Code must be followed for electrical installations in manufactured homes. The use of arc-fault breakers under Articles 210.12(A) and (B), 440.65, and 550.25(A) and (B) of the National Electrical Code, NFPA No. 70–2005 is not required. However, if arc-fault breakers are provided, such use must be in accordance with the National Electrical Code, NFPA No. 70–2005. Wherever the requirements of this standard differ from the National Electrical Code, these standards apply.

(c) The provisions of this standard apply to manufactured homes intended for connection to a wiring system nominally rated 120/240 volts, 3-wire AC, with grounded neutral.

(d) All electrical materials, devices, appliances, fittings and other equipment shall be listed or labeled by a nationally recognized testing agency and shall be connected in an approved manner when in service.

(e) Aluminum conductors, aluminum alloy conductors, and aluminum core conductors such as copper clad aluminum; are not acceptable for use in branch circuit wiring in manufactured homes.

[40 FR 58752, Dec. 18, 1975. Redesignated at 44 FR 20679, Apr. 6, 1979, as amended at 58 FR 55019, Oct. 25, 1993; 70 FR 72051, Nov. 30, 2005; 71 FR 19639, Apr. 17, 2006]

§ 3280.802 Definitions.

(a) The following definitions are applicable to subpart I only.

(1) *Accessible* (i) (*As applied to equipment*) means admitting close approach because not guarded by locked doors, elevation, or other effective means. (See *readily accessible*.)

(ii) (*As applied to wiring methods*) means capable of being removed or exposed without damaging the manufactured home structure or finish, or not permanently closed-in by the structure or finish of the manufactured home (see *concealed* and *exposed*).

(2) *Air conditioning or comfort cooling equipment* means all of that equipment intended or installed for the purpose of processing the treatment of air so as to control simultaneously its temperature, humidity, cleanliness, and distribution to meet the requirements of the conditioned space.

(3)(i) *Appliance* means utilization equipment, generally other than industrial, normally built in standardized sizes or types, which is installed or connected as a unit to perform one or more functions, such as clothes washing, air conditioning, food mixing, deep frying, etc.

(ii) *Appliance, fixed* means an appliance which is fastened or otherwise secured at a specific location.

(iii) *Appliance, portable* means an appliance which is actually moved or can easily be moved from one place to another in normal use. For the purpose of this Standard, the following major appliances are considered portable if cord-connected: refrigerators, clothes washers, dishwashers without booster heaters, or other similar appliances.

(iv) *Appliance, stationary* means an appliance which is not easily moved from one place to another in normal use.

(4) *Attachment plug (plug cap) (cap)* means a device which, by insertion in a receptacle, establishes connection between the conductors of the attached flexible cord and the conductors connected permanently to the receptacle.

(5) *Bonding* means the permanent joining of metallic parts to form an electrically conductive path which will assure electrical continuity and the capacity to conduct safely any current likely to be imposed.

(6) *Branch circuit* (i) means the circuit conductors between the final overcurrent device protecting the circuit and the outlet(s). A device not approved for branch circuit protection, such as a thermal cutout or motor overload protective device, is not considered as the overcurrent device protecting the circuit.

(ii) *Branch circuit—appliance* means a branch circuit supplying energy to one or more outlets to which appliances are to be connected, such circuits to have no permanently connected lighting fixtures not a part of an appliance.

(iii) *Branch circuit—general purpose* means a circuit that supplies a number of outlets for lighting and appliances.

(iv) *Branch circuit—individual* means a branch circuit that supplies only one utilization equipment.

(7) *Cabinet* means an enclosure designed either for surface or flush mounting, and provided with a frame, mat, or trim in which swinging doors are hung.

(8) *Circuit breaker* means a device designed to open and close a circuit by nonautomatic means, and to open the circuit automatically on a predetermined overload of current without injury to itself when properly applied within its rating.

(9) *Concealed* means rendered inaccessible by the structure or finish of the manufactured home. Wires in concealed raceways are considered concealed, even though they may become accessible by withdrawing them. (See *accessible (As applied to wiring methods)*)

(10) *Connector, pressure (solderless)* means a device that establishes a connection between two or more conductors or between one or more conductors and a terminal by means of mechanical pressure and without the use of solder.

(11) *Dead front (as applied to switches, circuit-breakers, switchboards, and distribution panelboard)* means so designed, constructed, and installed that no current-carrying parts are normally exposed on the front.

(12) *Demand factor* means the ratio of the maximum demand of a system, or part of a system, to the total connected load of a system or the part of the system under consideration.

(13) *Device* means a unit of an electrical system that is intended to carry but not utilize electrical energy.

(14) *Disconnecting means* means a device, or group of devices, or other means by which the conductors of a circuit can be disconnected from their source of supply.

(15) *Distribution panelboard* means a single panel or a group of panel units designed for assembly in the form of a single panel, including buses, and with or without switches or automatic overcurrent protective devices or both, for the control of light, heat, or power circuits of small individual as well as aggregate capacity; designed to be placed in a cabinet placed in or against a wall or partition and accessible only from the front.

(16) *Enclosed* means surrounded by a case that will prevent a person from accidentally contacting live parts.

(17) *Equipment* means a general term, including material, fittings, devices, appliances, fixtures, apparatus, and the like used as a part of, or in connection with, an electrical installation.

(18) *Exposed* (i) (As applied to live parts) means capable of being inadvertently touched or approached nearer than a safe distance by a person. It is applied to parts not suitably guarded, isolated, or insulated. (See *accessible* and *concealed*.)

(ii) (As applied to *wiring method*) means on or attached to the surface or behind panels designed to allow access. (See *Accessible (as applied to wiring methods)*)

(19) *Externally operable* means capable of being operated without exposing the operator to contact with live parts.

(20) *Feeder assembly* means the overhead or under-chassis feeder conductors, including the grounding conductor, together with the necessary fittings and equipment, or a power supply cord approved for manufactured home use, designed for the purpose of delivering energy from the source of electrical supply to the distribution panelboard within the manufactured home.

(21) *Fitting* means an accessory, such as a locknut, bushing, or other part of a wiring system, that is intended primarily to perform a mechanical rather than an electrical function.

(22) *Ground* means a conducting connection, whether intentional or accidental, between an electrical circuit or equipment and earth, or to some conducting body that serves in place of the earth.

(23) *Grounded* means connected to earth or to some conducting body that serves in place of the earth.

(24) *Grounded conductor* means a system or circuit conductor that is intentionally grounded.

(25) *Grounding conductor* means a conductor used to connect equipment or the grounded circuit of a wiring system to a grounding electrode or electrodes.

(26) *Guarded* means covered, shielded, fenced, enclosed, or otherwise protected by means of suitable covers, casings, barriers, rails, screens, mats or platforms to remove the likelihood of approach or contact by persons or objects to a point of danger.

(27) *Isolated* means not readily accessible to persons unless special means for access are used.

(28) *Laundry area* means an area containing or designed to contain either a

laundry tray, clothes washer and/or clothes dryer.

(29) *Lighting outlet* means an outlet intended for the direct connection of a lampholder, a lighting fixture, or a pendant cord terminating in a lampholder.

(30) *Manufactured home accessory building or structure* means any awning, cabana, ramada, storage cabinet, carport, fence, windbreak or porch established for the use of the occupant of the manufactured home upon a manufactured home lot.

(31) *Manufactured home service equipment* means the equipment containing the disconnecting means, overcurrent protective devices, and receptacles or other means for connecting a manufactured home feeder assembly.

(32) *Outlet* means a point on the wiring system at which current is taken to supply utilization equipment.

(33) *Panelboard* means a single panel or group of panel units designed for assembly in the form of a single panel; including buses, automatic overcurrent protective devices, and with or without switches for the control of light, heat, or power circuits; designed to be placed in a cabinet or cutout box placed in or against a wall or partition and accessible only from the front.

(34) *Raceway* means any channel for holding wires, cables, or busbars that is designed expressly for, and used solely for, this purpose. Raceways may be of metal or insulating material, and the term includes rigid metal conduit, rigid nonmetallic conduit, flexible metal conduit, electrical metallic tubing, underfloor raceways, cellular concrete floor raceways, cellular metal floor raceways, surface raceways, structural raceways, wireways, and busways.

(35) *Raintight* means so constructed or protected that exposure to a beating rain will not result in the entrance of water.

(36) *Readily accessible* means capable of being reached quickly for operation, renewal, or inspection, without requiring those to whom ready access is requisite to climb over or remove obstacles or to resort to portable ladders, chairs, etc. (See *Accessible*.)

(37) *Receptacle* means a contact device installed at the outlet for the connection of an attachment plug. A single receptacle is a single contact device with no other contact device on the same yoke. A multiple receptacle is a device with two or more contact devices on the same yoke.

(38) *Receptacle outlet* means an outlet where one or more receptacles are installed.

(39) *Utilization equipment* means equipment that utilizes electric energy for electronic, electromechanical, chemical, heating, lighting, or similar purposes.

(40) *Voltage (of a circuit)* means the greatest root-mean-square (effective) difference of potential between any two conductors of the circuit concerned. Some systems, such as 3-phase 4-wire, single-phase 3-wire, and 3-wire direct-current may have various circuits of various voltages.

(41) *Weatherproof* means so constructed or protected that exposure to the weather will not interfere with successful operation. Rainproof, raintight, or watertight equipment can fulfill the requirements for weatherproof where varying weather conditions other than wetness, such as snow, ice, dust, or temperature extremes, are not a factor.

[40 FR 58752, Dec. 18, 1975. Redesignated at 44 FR 20679, Apr. 6, 1979, as amended at 78 FR 73989, Dec. 9, 2013]

§ 3280.803   Power supply.

(a) The power supply to the manufactured home shall be a feeder assembly consisting of not more than one listed 50 ampere manufactured home power-supply cords, or a permanently installed circuit. A manufactured home that is factory-equipped with gas or oil-fired central heating equipment and cooking appliances shall be permitted to be provided with a listed manufactured home power-supply cord rated 40 amperes.

(b) If the manufactured home has a power-supply cord, it shall be permanently attached to the distribution panelboard or to a junction box permanently connected to the distribution panelboard, with the free end terminating in an attachment plug cap.

(c) Cords with adapters and pigtail ends, extension cords, and similar items shall not be attached to, or shipped with, a manufactured home.

(d) A suitable clamp or the equivalent must be provided at the distribution panelboard knockout to afford strain relief for the cord to prevent strain from being transmitted to the terminals when the power supply cord is handled in its intended manner.

(e) The cord shall be of an approved type with four conductors, one of which shall be identified by a continuous green color or a continuous green color with one or more yellow stripes for use as the grounding conductor.

(f) The attachment plug cap must be a 3-pole, 4-wire, grounding type, rated 50 amperes, 125/250 volts, intended for use with the 50-ampere, 125/250-volt receptacle configuration, as shown below. The cap must be listed, by itself or as part of a power-supply cord assembly, for the purpose, and must be molded to or installed on the flexible cord so that it is secured tightly to the cord at the point where the cord enters the attachment plug cap. If a right-angle cap is used, the configuration must be so oriented that the grounding member is farthest from the cord.

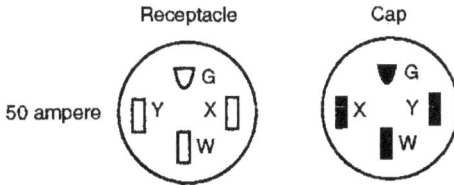

Note: 50-ampere 125/250-volt receptacle and attachment plug cap configurations, 3-pole, 4-wire, grounding types used for manufactured home supply cords and manufactured home parks. Complete details of the 50-ampere cap and receptacle can be found *Wiring Device Dimensional Requirements* (ANSI/NEMA WD-6-1997).

Figure 1 to paragraph (f)

(g) The overall length of a power-supply cord, measured from the end of the cord, including bared leads, to the face of the attachment-plug cap shall not be less than 21 feet and shall not exceed 36½ feet. The length of cord from the face of the attachment-plug cap to the point where the cord enters the manufactured home shall not be less than 20 feet.

(h) The power supply cord shall bear the following marking: "For use with manufactured homes—40 amperes" or "For use with manufactured homes—50 amperes."

(i) Where the cord passes through walls or floors, it must be protected by means of conduits and bushings or the equivalent. The cord is permitted to be installed within the manufactured home walls, provided that a continuous raceway having a maximum size of 1¼ inch is installed from the branch-circuit panelboard to the underside of the manufactured home floor.

(j) Permanent provisions shall be made for the protection of the attachment-plug cap of the power supply cord and any connector cord assembly or receptacle against corrosion and mechanical damage if such devices are in an exterior location while the manufactured home is in transit.

(k) Where the calculated load exceeds 50 amperes or where a permanent feeder is used, the supply shall be by means of:

(1) One mast weatherhead installation installed in accordance with Article 230 of the National Electrical Code, NFPA No. 70–2005, containing four continuous insulated, color-coded, feeder conductors, one of which shall be an equipment grounding conductor; or

127

(2) A listed metal raceway or listed rigid nonmetallic conduit from the disconnecting means in the manufactured home to the underside of the manufactured home, with provisions for the attachment of a suitable junction box or fitting to the raceway on the underside of the manufactured home. The manufacturer must provide written installation instructions stating the proper feeder conductor sizes for the raceway and the size of the junction box to be used; or

(3) Service equipment installed in or on the manufactured home, provided that all of the following conditions are met:

(i) In its written installation instructions, the manufacturer must include information indicating that the home must be secured in place by an anchoring system or installed on and secured to a permanent foundation;

(ii) The installation of the service equipment complies with Article 230 of the National Electrical Code, NFPA 70–2005 (incorporated by reference, see § 3280.4). Exterior service equipment or the enclosure in which it is to be installed must be weatherproof, and conductors must be suitable for use in wet locations;

(iii) Means are provided for the connection of the grounding electrode conductor to the service equipment and routing it to the conductor outside the structure;

(iv) Bonding and grounding of the service must be in accordance with Article 250, NFPA 70–2005, National Electrical Code (incorporated by reference, see § 3280.4);

(v) The manufacturer must include in its installation instructions one method of grounding the service equipment at the installation site. The instructions must clearly state that other methods of grounding are found in Article 250 of NFPA 70–2005, National Electrical Code;

(vi) The minimum size grounding electrode conductor must be specified in the instructions; and

(vi) A red warning label must be mounted on or adjacent to the service equipment. The label must state the following: WARNING—DO NOT PROVIDE ELECTRICAL POWER UNTIL THE GROUNDING ELECTRODE(S) IS INSTALLED AND CONNECTED (SEE INSTALLATION INSTRUCTIONS).

[40 FR 58752, Dec. 18, 1975. Redesignated at 44 FR 20679, Apr. 6, 1979, as amended at 52 FR 4589, Feb. 12, 1987; 58 FR 55019, Oct. 25, 1993; 70 FR 72051, Nov. 30, 2005; 78 FR 73990, Dec. 9, 2013]

§ 3280.804 Disconnecting means and branch-circuit protective equipment.

(a) The branch-circuit equipment is permitted to be combined with the disconnecting means as a single assembly. Such a combination is permitted to be designated as a distribution panelboard. If a fused distribution panelboard is used, the maximum fuse size for the mains shall be plainly marked, with the lettering at least 1/4-inch high and visible when fuses are changed. See Article 110–22 of NFPA 70–2005, National Electrical Code (incorporated by reference, see § 3280.4), concerning the identification of each disconnecting means and each service, feeder, or branch circuit at the point where it originated, and the type of marking needed.

(b) Plug fuses and fuseholders shall be tamper-resistant, Type "S," enclosed in dead-front fuse panelboards. Electrical distribution panels containing circuit breakers shall also be dead-front type.

(c) *Disconnecting means.* A single disconnecting means must be provided in each manufactured home, consisting of a circuit breaker, or a switch and fuses and its accessories, installed in a readily accessible location near the point of entrance of the supply cord or conductors into the manufactured home. The main circuit breakers or fuses must be plainly marked "Main." This equipment must contain a solderless type of grounding connector or bar for the purposes of grounding, with sufficient terminals for all grounding conductors. The neutral bar termination of the grounded circuit conductors must be insulated in accordance with § 3280.809(b).

(d) The disconnecting equipment shall have a rating suitable for the connected load. The distribution equipment, either circuit breaker or fused type, shall be located a minimum of 24 inches from the bottom of such equipment to the floor level of the manufactured home.

(e) A distribution panelboard employing a main circuit breaker must be rated not less than 50 amperes and employ a 2-pole circuit breaker rated 40 amperes for a 40-ampere supply cord, or 50 amperes for a 50-ampere supply cord. A distribution panelboard employing a disconnect switch and fuses must be rated not less than 60 amperes and must employ a single, 2-pole fuseholder rated not less than 60-amperes with 40- or 50-ampere main fuses for 40- or 50-ampere supply cords, respectively. The outside of the distribution panelboard must be plainly marked with the fuse size.

(f) The distribution panelboard must be located in an accessible location, and must not be located in a bathroom or a clothes closet. A clear working space at least 30 inches wide and 30 inches in front of the distribution panelboard must be provided. This space must extend from the floor to the top of the distribution panelboard. Where used as switches, circuit breakers must be installed so that the center of the grip of the operating handle of the circuit breaker, when in its highest position, will not be more than 6 feet, 7 inches above the floor.

(g) Branch-circuit distribution equipment shall be installed in each manufactured home and shall include overcurrent protection for each branch circuit consisting of either circuit breakers or fuses.

(1) The branch circuit overcurrent devices shall be rated:

(i) Not more than the circuit conductors; and

(ii) Not more than 150 percent of the rating of a single appliance rated 13.3 amperes or more which is supplied by an individual branch circuit; but

(iii) Not more than the fuse size marked on the air conditioner or other motor-operated appliance.

(h) A 15-ampere multiple receptacle shall be acceptable when connected to a 20-ampere laundry circuit.

(i) When circuit breakers are provided for branch-circuit protection 240 circuits shall be protected by 2-pole common or companion trip, or handle-tied paired circuit breakers.

(j) A 3 inch by 1-3/4 inch minimum size tag made of etched, metal-stamped or embossed brass, stainless steel, anodized or alclad aluminum not less than 0.020 inch thick, or other approval material (e.g., 0.005 inch plastic laminates) shall be permanently affixed on the outside adjacent to the feeder assembly entrance and shall read: This connection for 120/240 Volt, 3–Pole, 4–Wire, 60 Hertz, _____ Ampere Supply. The correct ampere rating shall be marked on the blank space.

(k) When a home is provided with installed service equipment, a single disconnecting means for disconnecting the branch circuit conductors from the service entrance conductors must be provided in accordance with Article 230, Part VI of the National Electrical Code, NFPA No. 70–2005. The disconnecting means shall be listed for use as service equipment. The disconnecting means may be combined with the disconnect required by § 3280.804(c). The disconnecting means shall be rated not more than the ampere supply or service capacity indicated on the tag required by paragraph (l) of this section.

(l) When a home is provided with installed service equipment, the electrical nameplate required by § 3280.804(j) shall read: "This connection for 120/240 volt, 3 pole, 3 wire, 60 Hertz, _____ Ampere Supply." The correct ampere rating shall be marked in the blank space.

[40 FR 58752, Dec. 18, 1975, as amended at 42 FR 961, Jan. 4, 1977. Redesignated at 44 FR 20679, Apr. 6, 1979, as amended at 52 FR 4589, Feb. 12, 1987; 58 FR 55019, Oct. 25, 1993; 70 FR 72051, Nov. 30, 2005; 78 FR 73990, Dec. 9, 2013]

§ 3280.805 Branch circuits required.

(a) The number of branch circuits required shall be determined in accordance with the following:

(1) Lighting, based on 3 volt-amperes per square foot times outside dimensions of the manufactured home (coupler excluded) divided by 120 volts times amperes to determine number of 15 or 20 ampere lighting area circuits. e.g. [3 × length × width—[120 × (15 or 20)] = number of 15 or 20 ampere circuits. Lighting circuits are permitted to serve built-in gas ovens with electric service for lights, clocks, or timers, or

for listed cord-connected garbage disposal units.

(2) *Small Appliances.* For the small appliance load in kitchens, pantries, dining rooms, and breakfast rooms of manufactured homes, two or more 20-ampere appliance branch circuits, in addition to the branch circuit specified in paragraph (a)(1) of this section, must be provided for all receptacle outlets in these rooms, and such circuits must have no other outlets. Countertop receptacle outlets installed in the kitchen must be supplied by not less than two small appliance branch circuits. One or more of the small appliance branch circuits may also supply other receptacle outlets in the kitchen, pantry, dining room, and breakfast room. Receptacles installed solely for the electrical supply to an electric clock and receptacles installed to provide power for supplemental equipment and lighting on gas-fired ranges, ovens, or counter-mounted cooking units are not subject to the requirements of this paragraph (a)(2).

(3) *General appliances (Including furnace, water heater, range, and central or room air conditioner, etc.).* There shall be one or more circuits of adequate rating in accordance with the following:

(i) The ampere rating of fixed appliances must not exceed 50 percent of the circuit rating if lighting outlets are on the same circuit (receptacles in the kitchen, dining area, and laundry are not considered to be lighting outlets);

(ii) For fixed appliances on a circuit without lighting outlets, the sum of rated amperes shall not exceed the branch-circuit rating. Motor loads or other continuous duty loads shall not exceed 80 percent of the branch circuit rating.

(iii) The rating of a single cord and plug connected appliances on a circuit having no other outlets, shall not exceed 80 percent of the circuit rating.

(iv) The rating of the range branch circuit is based on the range demand as specified for ranges in § 3280.811(a)(5). For central air conditioning, see Article 440 of the National Electrical Code, NFPA No. 70–2005.

(v) Where a laundry area is provided, a 20 ampere branch circuit shall be provided to supply laundry receptacle outlets. This circuit shall have no other outlets. See § 3280.806(a)(7).

(vi) Bathroom receptacle outlets must be supplied by at least one 20-ampere branch circuit. Such circuits must have no other outlets, except that it is permissible to place the receptacle outlet for a heat tape or pipe heating cable required by § 3280.806(d)(10) on a bathroom circuit. (See § 3280.806(b).)

(b) [Reserved]

[40 FR 58752, Dec. 18, 1975. Redesignated at 44 FR 20679, Apr. 6, 1979, as amended at 58 FR 55020, Oct. 25, 1993; 70 FR 72051, Nov. 30, 2005; 78 FR 73991, Dec. 9, 2013]

§ 3280.806   **Receptacle outlets.**

(a) All receptacle outlets shall be:

(1) Of grounding type;

(2) Installed according to Article 406.3 of the National Electrical Code, NFPA No. 70–2005.

(3) Except when supplying specific appliances, be parallel-blade, 15-ampere, 125-volt, either single or duplex.

(b) All 125-volt, single-phase, 15- and 20-ampere receptacle outlets installed outdoors, or in compartments accessible from outside the manufactured home, and in bathrooms, including receptacles in light fixtures, must have ground-fault circuit-interrupter protection for personnel. Ground-fault circuit-interrupter protection for personnel must be provided for receptacles serving countertops in kitchens and receptacle outlets located within 6 feet of a wet bar sink, except for receptacles installed for appliances in dedicated spaces, such as dishwashers, disposals, refrigerators, freezers, and laundry equipment.

(c) There shall be an outlet of the grounding type for each cord-connected fixed appliance installed.

(d) *Receptacle outlets required.* Except in the bath, closet, and hall areas, receptacle outlets must be installed at wall spaces 2 feet or more wide, so that no point along the floor line is more than 6 feet, measured horizontally, from an outlet in that space. Receptacle outlets in floors shall not be counted as part of the required number of receptacle outlets, unless located within 18 inches of the wall. In addition, a receptacle outlet must be installed in the following locations:

(1) Over or adjacent to counter tops in the kitchen (at least one on each side of the sink if counter tops are on each side and 12 inches or over in width).

(2) Adjacent to the refrigerator and free-standing gas-range space. A duplex receptacle may serve as the outlet for a countertop and a refrigerator.

(3) At counter top spaces for built-in vanities.

(4) At counter top spaces under wall-mounted cabinets.

(5) In the wall, at the nearest point where a bar type counter attaches to the wall.

(6) In the wall at the nearest point where a fixed room divider attaches to the wall.

(7) In laundry areas within 6 feet of the intended location of the appliance(s).

(8) At least one receptacle outlet shall be installed outdoors.

(9) At least one wall receptacle outlet shall be installed in bathrooms within 36 inches (914 mm) of the outside edge of each basin. The receptacle outlet must be located on a wall that is adjacent to the basin location. This receptacle is in addition to any receptacle that is part of a lighting fixture or appliance. The receptacle must not be enclosed within a bathroom cabinet or vanity.

(10) On the underside of the home for the connection of pipe heating cable(s) or heat tape(s), and the outlet must:

(i) Be located within 2 feet of the cold water inlet;

(ii) Be connected to an interior branch circuit, other than a small appliance branch circuit;

(iii) Be located on a circuit where all of the outlets are on the load side of the ground-fault circuit-interrupter protection for personnel; and

(iv) Not be considered as the receptacle outlet required by paragraph (8) of this section.

(11) Receptacle outlets are not required in the following locations:

(i) Wall space occupied by built-in kitchen or wardrobe cabinets,

(ii) Wall space behind doors which may be opened fully against a wall surface,

(iii) Room dividers of the lattice type, less than 8 feet long, not solid within 6 inches of the floor,

(iv) Wall space afforded by bar type counters.

(e) Receptacle outlets shall not be installed in or within reach (30 inches) of a shower or bathtub space.

(f) Receptacle outlets shall not be installed above electric baseboard heaters.

(g) Receptacles must not be in a face-up position in any countertop.

[40 FR 58752, Dec. 18, 1975. Redesignated at 44 FR 20679, Apr. 6, 1979, as amended at 58 FR 55020, Oct. 25, 1993; 70 FR 72052, Nov. 30, 2005; 78 FR 73991, Dec. 9, 2013]

§3280.807   Fixtures and appliances.

(a) Electrical materials, devices, appliances, fittings, and other equipment installed, intended for use in, or attached to the manufactured home shall be approved for the application and shall be connected in an approved manner when in service. Facilities shall be provided to securely fasten appliances when the manufactured home is in transit. (See §3280.809.)

(b) Specifically listed pendant-type fixtures or pendant cords shall be permitted in manufactured homes.

(c) Where a lighting fixture is installed over a bathtub or in a shower stall, it must be listed for wet locations. [See also Article 410.4(D) of the National Electrical Code NFPA No. 70–2005.]

(d) The switch for shower lighting fixtures and exhaust fans located over a tub or in a shower stall shall be located outside the tub shower space. (See §3280.806(e).)

(e) Any combustible wall or ceiling finish exposed between the edge of a fixture canopy, or pan and an outlet box shall be covered with non-combustible or limited combustible material.

(f) Every appliance shall be accessible for inspection, service, repair, or replacement without removal of permanent construction.

[40 FR 58752, Dec. 18, 1975. Redesignated at 44 FR 20679, Apr. 6, 1979, as amended at 52 FR 35543, Sept. 22, 1987; 58 FR 55020, Oct. 25, 1993; 70 FR 72052, Nov. 30, 2005; 78 FR 73991, Dec. 9, 2013]

§ 3280.808 Wiring methods and materials.

(a) Except as specifically permitted by this part, the wiring methods and materials specified in the National Electrical Code, NFPA No. 70–2005, must be used in manufactured homes.

(b) Nonmetallic outlet boxes shall be acceptable only with nonmetallic cable.

(c) Nonmetallic cable located 15 inches or less above the floor, if exposed, shall be protected from physical damage by covering boards, guard strips, or conduit. Cable likely to be damaged by stowage shall be so protected in all cases.

(d) Nonmetallic sheathed cable shall be secured by staples, straps, or similar fittings so designed and installed as not to injure any cable. Cable shall be secured in place at intervals not exceeding 4½ feet and within 12 inches from every cabinet, box or fitting.

(e) Metal-clad and nonmetallic cables shall be permitted to pass through the centers of the wide side of 2-inch by 4-inch studs. However, they shall be protected where they pass through 2-inch by 2-inch studs or at other studs or frames where the cable or armor would be less than 1½ inches from the inside or outside surface of the studs when the wall covering materials are in contact with the studs. Steel plates on each side of the cable, or a tube, with not less than No. 16 MSG wall thickness shall be required to protect the cable. These plates or tubes shall be securely held in place.

(f) Where metal faceplates are used, they must be effectively grounded.

(g) If the range, clothes dryer, or similar appliance is connected by metalclad cable or flexible conduit, a length of not less than three feet of free cable or conduit shall be provided to permit moving the appliance. Type NM or Type SE cable shall not be used to connect a range or a dryer. This shall not prohibit the use of Type NM or Type SE cable between the branch circuit overcurrent protective device and a junction box or range or dryer receptacle.

(h) Where rigid metal conduit or intermediate metal conduit is terminated at an enclosure with a locknut and bushing connection, two locknuts must be provided, one inside and one outside of the enclosure. Rigid nonmetallic conduit or electrical nonmetallic tubing is permitted. All cut ends of conduit and tubing must be reamed or otherwise finished to remove rough edges.

(i) Switches must be rated as follows:

(1) For lighting circuits, switches must be rated not less than 10 amperes, 120 to 125 volts, and in no case less than the connected load.

(2) For motors or other loads, switches shall have ampere or horsepower ratings, or both, adequate for loads controlled. (An "AC general-use" snap switch shall be permitted to control a motor 2 horsepower or less with full-load current not over 80 percent of the switch ampere rating).

(j) At least 4 inches of free conductor shall be left at each outlet box except where conductors are intended to loop without joints.

(k) When outdoor or under-chassis line-voltage (120 volts, nominal or higher) wiring is exposed to moisture or physical damage, it must be protected by rigid metal conduit or intermediate metal conduit. The conductors must be suitable for wet locations. Electrical metallic tubing or rigid nonmetallic conduit is permitted to be used when closely routed against frames and equipment enclosures.

(l) Outlet boxes of dimensions less than those required in Table 314.16(A) of the National Electrical Code, NFPA No. 70–2005, are permitted provided the box has been tested and approved for that purpose.

(m) Boxes, fittings, and cabinets shall be securely fastened in place, and shall be supported from a structural member of the home, either directly or by using a substantial brace. Snap-in type boxes provided with special wall or ceiling brackets that securely fasten boxes in walls or ceilings shall be permitted.

(n) Outlet boxes must fit closely to openings in combustible walls and ceilings and must be flush with the finished surface or project therefrom. In walls and ceilings of noncombustible material, outlet boxes and fittings must be installed so that the front edge of the box or fitting will not be set back from the finished surface more than ¼ inch.

Plaster, drywall, or plasterboard surfaces that are broken or incomplete must be repaired so that there will be no gaps or open spaces greater than ⅛ inch at the edge of the box or fitting.

(o) Appliances having branch-circuit terminal connections which operate at temperatures higher than 60 °C (140 °F) shall have circuit conductors as described in paragraphs (p) (1) and (2) of this section:

(1) Branch-circuit conductors having an insulation suitable for the temperature encountered shall be permitted to run directly to the appliance.

(2) Conductors having an insulation suitable for the temperature encountered may be run from the appliance terminal connections to a readily accessible outlet box placed at least one foot from the appliance. If provided, these conductors must be in a suitable raceway or Type AC or MC cable, of at least 18 inches but not more than 6 feet in length.

(p) A substantial brace for securing a box, fitting, or cabinet must be as described in the National Electrical Code, NFPA 70–2005, Article 314.23(B), or the brace, including the fastening mechanism to attach the brace to the home structure, must withstand a force of 50 lbs. applied to the brace at the intended point(s) of attachment for the box in a direction perpendicular to the surface on which the box is installed.

(q) Where the sheathing of NM cable has been cut or damaged and visual inspection reveals that the conductor and its insulation has not been damaged, it shall be permitted to repair the cable sheath with electrical tape which provides equivalent protection to the sheath.

[40 FR 58752, Dec. 18, 1975. Redesignated at 44 FR 20679, Apr. 6, 1979, as amended at 58 FR 55020, Oct. 25, 1993; 70 FR 72052, Nov. 30, 2005; 78 FR 73991, Dec. 9, 2013]

§3280.809 Grounding.

(a) *General.* Grounding of both electrical and nonelectrical metal parts in a manufactured home shall be through connection to a grounding bus in the manufactured home distribution panelboard. The grounding bus shall be grounded through the green-colored conductor in the supply cord or the feeder wiring to the service ground in the service-entrance equipment located adjacent to the manufactured home location. Neither the frame of the manufactured home nor the frame of any appliance shall be connected to the neutral conductor in the manufactured home.

(b) *Insulated neutral.* (1) The grounded circuit conductor (neutral) shall be insulated from the grounding conductors and from equipment enclosures and other grounded parts. The grounded (neutral) circuit terminals in the distribution panelboard and in ranges, clothes dryers, counter-mounted cooking units, and wall-mounted ovens shall be insulated from the equipment enclosure. Bonding screws, straps, or buses in the distribution panelboard or in appliances shall be removed and discarded. However, when service equipment is installed on the manufactured home, the neutral and the ground bus may be connected in the distribution panel.

(2) Connection of ranges and clothes dryers with 120/240 volt, 3-wire ratings shall be made with 4 conductor cord and 3 pole, 4-wire grounding type plugs, or by type AC metal clad conductors enclosed in flexible metal conduit. For 120 volt rated devices a 3-conductor cord and a 2-pole, 3-wire grounding type plug shall be permitted.

(c) *Equipment grounding means.* (1) The green-colored grounding wire in the supply cord or permanent feeder wiring shall be connected to the grounding bus in the distribution panelboard or disconnecting means.

(2) In the electrical system, all exposed metal parts, enclosures, frames, lamp fixture canopies, etc., shall be effectively bonded to the grounding terminal or enclosure of the distribution panelboard.

(3) Cord-connected appliances, such as washing machines, clothes dryers, refrigerators, and the electrical system of gas ranges, etc., shall be grounded by means of an approved cord with grounding conductor and grounding-type attachment plug.

(d) *Bonding of noncurrent-carrying metal parts.* (1) All exposed noncurrent-carrying metal parts that may become energized shall be effectively bonded to the grounding terminal or enclosure of the distribution panelboard. A bonding conductor shall be connected between each distribution panelboard and an accessible terminal on the chassis.

(2) Grounding terminals shall be of the solderless type and approved as pressure-terminal connectors recognized for the wire size used. Star washers or other approved paint-penetrating fitting shall be used to bond terminals to chassis or other coated areas. The bonding conductor shall be solid or stranded, insulated or bare and shall be No. 8 copper minimum, or equal. The bonding conductor shall be routed so as not to be exposed to physical damage. Protection can be afforded by the configuration of the chassis.

(3) Metallic gas, water and waste pipes and metallic air-circulating ducts shall be considered bonded if they are connected to the terminal on the chassis (see § 3280.809) by clamps, solderless connectors, or by suitable grounding-type straps.

(4) Any metallic roof and exterior covering shall be considered bonded if (i) the metal panels overlap one another and are securely attached to the wood or metal frame parts by metallic fasteners, and (ii) if the lower panel of the metallic exterior covering is secured by metallic fasteners at a cross member of the chassis by two metal straps per manufactured home unit or section at opposite ends. The bonding strap material shall be a minimum of 4 inches in width of material equivalent to the skin or a material of equal or better electrical conductivity. The straps shall be fastened with paint-penetrating fittings (such as screws and star washers or equivalent).

[40 FR 58752, Dec. 18, 1975. Redesignated at 44 FR 20679, Apr. 6, 1979, as amended at 58 FR 55020, Oct. 25, 1993]

§ 3280.810 Electrical testing.

(a) *Dielectric strength test.* The wiring of each manufactured home shall be subjected to a 1-minute, 900 to 1079 volt dielectric strength test (with all switches closed) between live parts and the manufactured home ground, and neutral and the manufactured home ground. Alternatively, the test may be performed at 1080 to 1250 volts for 1 second. This test shall be performed after branch circuits are complete and after fixtures or appliances are installed.

Fixtures or appliances which are listed shall not be required to withstand the dielectric strength test.

(b) Each manufactured home shall be subject to:

(1) A continuity test to assure that metallic parts are properly bonded;

(2) Operational test to demonstrate that all equipment, except water heaters, electric furnaces, dishwashers, clothes washers/dryers, and portable appliances, is connected and in working order; and

(3) Polarity checks to determine that connections have been properly made. Visual verification shall be an acceptable check.

[58 FR 55020, Oct. 25, 1993]

§ 3280.811 Calculations.

(a) The following method shall be employed in computing the supply cord and distribution-panelboard load for each feeder assembly for each manufactured home and shall be based on a 3-wire, 120/240 volt supply with 120 loads balanced between the two legs of the 3-wire system. The total load for determining power supply by this method is the summation of:

(1) Lighting and small appliance load as calculated below:

(i) Lighting volt-amperes: Length time width of manufactured home (outside dimensions exclusive of coupler) times 3 volt-amperes per square foot; e.g. Length × width × 3 = lighting volt-amperes.

(ii) Small appliance volt-amperes: Number of circuits time 1,500 volt-amperes for each 20-ampere appliance receptacle circuit (see definition of "Appliance Portable" with Note): e.g. Number of circuits × 1,500 = small appliance volt-amperes.

(iii) Total volts-amperes: Lighting volts-amperes plus small appliance = total volt-amperes.

(iv) First 3,000 total volts-amperes at 100 percent plus remainder at 35 percent = watts to be divided by 240 volts to obtain current (amperes) per leg.

(2) Nameplate amperes for motors and heater loads (exhaust fans, air conditioners, electric, gas, or oil heating). Omit smaller of air conditioning and heating except include blower motor if used as air conditioner evaporator motor. When an air conditioner is not

installed and a 40-ampere power supply cord is provided, allow 15 amperes per leg for air conditioning.

(3) 25 percent of current of largest motor in paragraph (a)(2) of this section.

(4) Total of nameplate amperes for: Disposal, dishwasher, water heater, clothes dryer, wall-mounted oven, cooking units. Where number of these appliances exceeds three, use 75 percent of total.

(5) Derive amperes for free-standing range (as distinguished from separate ovens and cooking units) by dividing values below by 240 volts.

Nameplate rating (in watts)	Use (in watts)
10,000 or less	80 percent of rating.
10,001 to 12,500	8,000.
12,501 to 13,500	8,400.
13,501 to 14,500	8,800.
14,501 to 15,500	9,200.
15,501 to 16,500	9,600.
16,501 to 17,500	10,000.

(6) If outlets or circuits are provided for other than factory-installed appliances, include the anticipated load. The following example is given to illustrate the application of this Method of Calculation:

Example: A manufactured home is 70 × 10 feet and has two portable appliance circuits, a 1000 volt-ampere 240 volt heater, a 200 volt-ampere 120 volt exhaust fan, a 400 volts-ampere 120 volt dishwasher and a 7000 volt-ampere electric range.

Lighting and small appliance load	Volt-ampheres
Lighting 70 × 10 × 3	2,100
Small Appliance	3,000
Total	5,100
1st. 3,000 Volt-Ampheres at 100%	3,000
Remainder (5,100 − 3,000 = 2,100, at 35%	735
Total	3,735

	Amperes per leg A	Amperes per leg B
Lighting and small Appliance	15.5	15.5
Heater 240 volt	4.1	4.1
Fan 120 volt	1.7	
Dishwasher 120 volt		3.3
Range	23.3	23.3
Total	44.6	46.2

Note: Based on the higher current calculated for either leg, use one 50–A supply cord.

(b) The following is an optional method of calculation for lighting and appliance loads for manufactured homes served by single 3-wire 120/240 volt set of feeder conductors with an ampacity of 100 or greater. The total load for determining the feeder ampacity may be computed in accordance with the following table instead of the method previously specified. Feeder conductors whose demand load is determined by this optional calculation are permitted to have the neutral load determined by Article 220.61 of the National Electrical Code, NFPA No. 70–2005. The loads identified in the table as "other load" and as "Remainder of other load" must include the following:

(1) 1500 volt-amperes for each 2-wire, 20-ampere small appliance branch circuit and each laundry branch circuit specified.

(2) 3 volt-amperes per square foot for general lighting and general-use receptacles.

(3) The nameplate rating of all fixed appliances, ranges, wall-mounted ovens, counter-mounted cooking units, and including 4 or more separately controlled space heating loads.

(4) The nameplate ampere or kVA rating of all motors and of all low-power-factor loads.

(5) The largest of the following:

(i) Air conditioning load;

(ii) The 65 percent diversified demand of the central electric space heating load;

(iii) The 65 percent diversified demand of the load of less than four separately-controlled electric space heating units.

(iv) The connected load of four or more separately-controlled electric space heating units.

OPTIONAL CALCULATION FOR MANUFACTURED HOMES WITH 110-AMPERE OR LARGER SERVICE

Load (in kilowatt or kilovoltampere)	Demand factor (percent)
Air-conditioning and cooling including heat pump compressors	100
Central electric space heating	65
Less than 4 separately controlled electric space heating units	65
1st 10 kW of all other load	100
Remainder of other load	40

[40 FR 58752, Dec. 18, 1975. Redesignated at 44 FR 20679, Apr. 6, 1979, as amended at 58 FR 55021, Oct. 25, 1993; 70 FR 72052, Nov. 30, 2005]

§ 3280.812 **Wiring of expandable units and dual units.**

(a) Expandable or multiple unit manufactured homes shall use fixed-type wiring methods and materials for connecting such units to each other.

(b) Expandable or multiple unit manufactured homes not having permanently installed feeders and which are to be moved from one location to another, shall be permitted to have disconnecting means with branch circuit protective equipment in each unit when so located that after assembly or joining together of units the requirements of § 3280.803 will be met.

§ 3280.813 **Outdoor outlets, fixtures, air-conditioning equipment, etc.**

(a) Outdoor fixtures and equipment shall be listed for use in wet locations, except that if located on the underside of the home or located under roof extensions or similarly protected locations, they may be listed for use in damp locations.

(b) A manufactured home provided with a branch circuit designed to energize outside heating equipment or air-conditioning equipment, other than room air conditioners, or both, located outside the manufactured home, other than room air conditioners, must have such branch-circuit conductors terminate in a listed outlet box, or disconnecting means, located on the outside of the manufactured home.

(1) A label must be permanently affixed adjacent to the outlet box. The label must be not less than 0.020-inches thick etched brass, stainless steel, anodized or alclad aluminum, or equivalent, and must not be less than 3 inches × 1¾ inches in size.

(2)(i) The label must include the correct voltage and ampere rating and the following information:

THIS CONNECTION IS FOR HEATING AND/OR AIR-CONDITIONING EQUIPMENT. THE BRANCH CIRCUIT IS RATED AT NOT MORE THAN____AMPERES, AT____VOLTS, 60–HERTZ,____CONDUCTOR AMPACITY. A DISCONNECTING MEANS IS LOCATED WITHIN SIGHT OF THE EQUIPMENT.

(ii) The correct voltage and ampere rating shall be given. The tag must be not less than 0.020-inches thick etched brass, stainless steel, anodized or alclad aluminum, or equivalent. The tag must have a minimum size of not less than 3 inches × 1¾ inches.

[40 FR 58752, Dec. 18, 1975, as amended at 42 FR 961, Jan. 4, 1977. Redesignated at 44 FR 20679, Apr. 6, 1979, as amended at 58 FR 55021, Oct. 25, 1993; 78 FR 73992, Dec. 9, 2013]

§ 3280.814 **Painting of wiring.**

During painting or staining of the manufactured home, it shall be permitted to paint metal raceways (except where grounding continuity would be reduced) or the sheath of the nonmetallic cable. Some arrangement, however, shall be made so that no paint shall be applied to the individual wires, as the color coding may be obliterated by the paint.

§ 3280.815 **Polarization.**

(a)(1) Except as provided in paragraph (a)(2) of this section, the white conductor must be employed for the grounded (neutral) circuit conductors only and must be connected to the white terminal or lead on receptacle outlets and fixtures. The grounded conductor must be the unswitched wire in switched circuits.

(2) A cable containing an insulated conductor with a white or natural gray outer finish or a marking of three continuous white stripes may be used for single-pole, three-way, or four-way switch loops, where this conductor is used for the supply to the switch, but not as a return conductor from the switch to the switched outlet. In these applications, the conductor with white or natural gray insulation or with three continuous white stripes must be permanently re-identified to indicate its use by painting or other effective means at its terminations and at each location where the conductor is visible and accessible.

(b) If the identified (white) conductor of a cable is used for other than grounded conductors or for other than switch loops as explained above (for a 240 volt circuit for example), the conductor shall be finished in a color other than white at each outlet where the conductors are visible and accessible.

(c) Green-colored wires or green with yellow stripe shall be used for grounding conductors only.

[40 FR 58752, Dec. 18, 1975. Redesignated at 44 FR 20679, Apr. 6, 1979, as amended at 58 FR 55021, Oct. 25, 1993; 78 FR 73992, Dec. 9, 2013]

§3280.816 Examination of equipment for safety.

The examination or inspection of equipment for safety, according to this standard, shall be conducted under uniform conditions and by organizations properly equipped and qualified for experimental testing, inspections of the run of goods at factories, and service-value determinations through field examinations.

Subpart J—Transportation

§3280.901 Scope.

Subpart J of this standard covers the general requirement for designing the structure of the manufactured home to fully withstand the adverse effects of transportation shock and vibration without degradation of the integrated structure or of its component parts and the specific requirements pertaining to the transportation system and its relationship to the structure.

§3280.902 Definitions.

(a) *Chassis* means the entire transportation system comprising the following subsystems: drawbar and coupling mechanism, frame, running gear assembly, and lights.

(b) *Drawbar and coupling mechanism* means the rigid assembly, (usually an *A* frame) upon which is mounted a coupling mechanism, which connects the manufactured home's frame to the towing vehicle.

(c) *Frame* means the fabricated rigid substructure which provides considerable support to the affixed manufactured home structure both during transport and on-site; and also provides a platform for securement of the running gear assembly, the drawbar and coupling mechanism.

(d) *Running gear assembly* means the subsystem consisting of suspension springs, axles, bearings, wheels, hubs, tires, and brakes, with their related hardware.

(e) *Lights* means those safety lights and associated wiring required by applicable U.S. Department of Transportation regulations.

(f) *Transportation system*, (Same as chassis, above).

(g) *Highway*, includes all roads and streets to be legally used in transporting the manufactured home.

[40 FR 58752, Dec. 18, 1975. Redesignated at 44 FR 20679, Apr. 6, 1979, as amended at 47 FR 28093, June 29, 1982]

§3280.903 General requirements for designing the structure to withstand transportation shock and vibration.

(a) The cumulative effect of highway transportation shock and vibration upon a manufactured home structure may result in incremental degradation of its designed performance in terms of providing a safe, healthy and durable dwelling. Therefore, the manufactured home shall be designed, in terms of its structural, plumbing, mechanical and electrical systems, to fully withstand such transportation forces during its intended life. (See §§3280.303(c) and 3280.305(a)).

(b) Particular attention shall be given to maintaining watertight integrity and conserving energy by assuring that structural components in the roof and walls (and their interfaces with vents, windows, doors, etc.) are capable of resisting highway shock and vibration forces during primary and subsequent secondary transportation moves.

(c) In place of an engineering analysis, either of the following may be accepted:

(1) Documented technical data of suitable highway tests which were conducted to simulate transportation loads and conditions; or

(2) Acceptable documented evidence of actual transportation experience which meets the intent of this subpart.

§3280.904 Specific requirements for designing the transportation system.

(a) *General.* The entire system (frame, drawbar and coupling mechanism, running gear assembly, and lights) shall be designed and constructed as an integrated, balanced and durable unit

137

which is safe and suitable for its specified use during the intended life of the manufactured home. In operation, the transportation system (supporting the manufactured home structure and its contents) shall effectively respond to the control of the braking, while traveling at applicable towing vehicle in terms of tracking and highway speeds and in normal highway traffic conditions.

NOTE: While the majority of manufactured homes utilize a fabricated steel frame assembly, upon which the manufactured home structure is constructed, it is not the intent of this standard to limit innovation. Therefore, other concepts, such as integrating the frame function into the manufactured home structure, are acceptable provided that such design meets the intent and requirements of this part).

(b) *Specific requirements*—(1) *Drawbar.* The drawbar shall be constructed of sufficient strength, rigidity and durability to safely withstand those dynamic forces experienced during highway transportation. It shall be securely fastened to the manufactured home frame by either a continuous weld or by bolting.

(2) *Coupling mechanism.* The coupling mechanism (which is usually of the socket type) shall be securely fastened to the drawbar in such a manner as to assure safe and effective transfer of the maximum loads, including dynamic loads, between the manufactured home structure and the hitch-assembly of the towing vehicle. The coupling shall be equipped with a manually operated mechanism so adapted as to prevent disengagement of the unit while in operation. The coupling shall be so designed that it can be disconnected regardless of the angle of the manufactured home to the towing vehicle. With the manufactured home parked on level ground, the center of the socket of the coupler shall not be less than 20 inches nor more than 26 inches from ground level.

(3) *Chassis.* The chassis, in conjunction with the manufactured home structure, shall be designed and constructed to effectively sustain the designed loads consisting of the dead load plus a minimum of 3 pounds per square foot floor load, (example: free-standing range, refrigerator, and loose furniture) and the superimposed dynamic load resulting from highway movement but shall not be required to exceed twice the dead load. The integrated design shall be capable of insuring rigidity and structural integrity of the complete manufactured home structure and to insure against deformation of structural or finish members during the intended life of the home.

(4) *Running gear assembly.* (i) The running gear assembly, as part of the chassis, shall be designed to perform, as a balanced system, in order to effectively sustain the designed loads set forth in § 3280.904(b)(3) and to provide for durable dependable safe mobility of the manufactured home. It shall be designed to accept shock and vibration, both from the highway and the towing vehicle and effectively dampen these forces so as to protect the manufactured home structure from damage and fatigue. Its components shall be designed to facilitate routine maintenance, inspection and replacement.

(ii) Location of the running gear assembly shall be determined by documented engineering analysis, taking into account the gross weight (including all contents), total length of the manufactured home, the necessary coupling hitch weight, span distance, and turning radius. The coupling weight shall be not less than 12 percent nor more than 25 percent of the gross weight.

(5) *Spring assemblies.* Spring assemblies (springs, hangers, shackles, bushings and mounting bolts) shall be capable of withstanding all the design loads as outlined in § 3280.904(b)(3) without exceeding maximum allowable stresses for design spring assembly life as recommended by the spring assembly manufacturer. The capacity of the spring system shall assure, that under maximum operating load conditions, sufficient clearance shall be maintained between the tire and manufactured home frame or structure to permit unimpeded wheel movement and for changing tires.

(6) *Axles.* Axles, and their connecting hardware, shall be capable of withstanding all of the design loads outlined in § 3280.904(b)(3) without exceeding maximum allowable stresses for design axle life as recommended by the axle manufacturer. The number of

axles required to provide a safe tow and good ride characteristics shall be determined and documented by engineering analysis. Those alternatives listed in § 3280.903(c) may be accepted in place of such an analysis.

(7) *Hubs and bearings.* Hubs and bearings shall meet the requirements of § 3280.904(b)(3) and good engineering practice. Both of these components shall be accessible for inspection, routine maintenance and replacement of parts.

(8) *Tires, wheels and rims.* Tires, wheels and rims shall meet the requirements of § 3280.904(b)(3). Tires shall be selected for anticipated usage.

(9) *Brake assemblies.* (i) The number, type, size and design of brake assemblies required to assist the towing vehicle in providing effective control and stopping of the manufactured home shall be determined and documented by engineering analysis. Those alternatives listed in § 3280.903(c) may be accepted in place of such an analysis.

(ii) Brakes on the towing vehicle and the manufactured home shall be capable of assuring that the maximum stopping distance from an initial velocity of 20 miles per hour does not exceed 40 feet (U.S. Department of Transportation Regulations).

(10) *Lights and associated wiring.* Highway safety electrical lights and associated wiring shall conform to applicable Federal requirements in terms of location and performance. The manufacturer shall have the option of meeting this requirement by utilizing a temporary light/wiring harness provided by the manufactured home transportation carrier.

PART 3282—MANUFACTURED HOME PROCEDURAL AND ENFORCEMENT REGULATIONS

Subpart A—General

AUTHORITY: 28 U.S.C. 2461; 42 U.S.C. 3535(d), 5403, and 5424.

EFFECTIVE DATE NOTE: At 83 FR 9454, Mar. 15, 2019, the authority citation was revised, effective Apr. 15, 2019. For the convenience of the user, the revised text is set forth as follows:

AUTHORITY: 28 U.S.C. 1 note; 28 U.S.C. 2461 note; 42 U.S.C. 3535(d) and 5424.

SOURCE: 41 FR 19852, May 13, 1976, unless otherwise noted.

EDITORIAL NOTE: Nomenclature changes to part 3282 appear at 78 FR 60199, Oct. 1, 2013.

Subpart A—General

§ 3282.1 Scope and purpose.

(a) The National Manufactured Housing Construction and Safety Standards Act of 1974 (title VI of Pub. L. 93–383, 88 Stat. 700, 42 U.S.C. 5401, *et seq.*) (hereinafter referred to as the Act), requires the Secretary of the Department of Housing and Urban Development to establish Federal manufactured home construction and safety standards and to issue regulations to carry out the purpose of the Act. The standards promulgated pursuant to the Act appear at part 3280 of chapter XX of this title, and apply to all manufactured homes manufactured for sale to purchasers in the United States on or after the effective date of the standards (June 15, 1976). A manufactured home is manufactured on or after June 15, 1976, if it enters the first stage of production on or after that date.

(b) The Secretary is also authorized by the Act to conduct inspections and investigations necessary to enforce the standards, to determine that a manufactured home fails to comply with an applicable standard or contains a defect or an imminent safety hazard, and to direct the manufacturer to furnish notification thereof, and in some cases, to remedy the defect or imminent safety hazard. The purpose of this part is to prescribe procedures for the implementation of these responsibilities of the Secretary under the Act through the use of private and State inspection organizations and cooperation with State manufactured home agencies. It is the policy of the Department to involve State agencies in the enforcement of the Federal manufactured home standards to the maximum extent possible consistent with the capabilities of such agencies and the public interest. The procedures for investigations and investigational proceedings are set forth in 24 CFR part 3800.

[41 FR 19852, May 13, 1976, as amended at 61 FR 10442, Mar. 13, 1996]

§ 3282.6 Separability of provisions.

If any clause, sentence, paragraph, section or other portion of part 3282 shall, for any reason, be adjudged by any court of competent jurisdiction to be invalid, such judgment shall not affect, impair, or invalidate the remainder thereof, but shall be confined by its operation to the clause, sentence, paragraph, or part thereof directly involved in the controversy in which such judgment shall have been rendered.

§ 3282.7 Definitions.

The terms *Department, HUD,* and *Secretary* are defined in 24 CFR part 5.

(a) *Act* means the National Manufactured Housing Construction and Safety Standards Act of 1974, title VI of the Housing and Community Development Act of 1974 (42 U.S.C. 5401 *et seq.*)

(b) *Add-on* means any structure (except a structure designed or produced as an integral part of a manufactured home) which, when attached to the basic manufactured home unit, increases the area, either living or storage, of the manufactured home.

(c) *Alteration* means the replacement, addition, and modification, or removal of any equipment or installation after sale by a manufacturer to a retailer or distributor but prior to sale by a retailer to a purchaser which may affect the construction, fire safety, occupancy, plumbing, heat-producing or electrical system. It includes any modification made in the manufactured home that may affect the compliance of the home with the standards, but it does not include the repair or replacement of a component or appliance requiring plug-in to an electrical receptacle where the replaced item is of the same configuration and rating as the one being replaced. It also does not include the addition of an appliance requiring *plug-in* to an electrical receptacle, which appliance was not provided with the manufactured home by the manufacturer, if the rating of the appliance does not exceed the rating of the receptacle to which it is connected.

(d) *Certification label* see *label.*

(e) *Certification report* means the report prepared by an IPIA (see definition z) for each manufactured home manufacturing plant under § 3282.203 in which the IPIA provides a complete description of the initial comprehensive inspection of the plant, an evaluation of the quality assurance program under the approved quality assurance manual, and the identity of the DAPIA (see definition z) which approved the designs and quality assurance manual used in the plant. Where appropriate under § 3282.362(b)(5), the certification report may be made by a DAPIA.

(f) *Component* means any part, material or appliance which is built in as an integral part of the manufactured home during the manufacturing process.

(g) *Cost information* means information submitted by a manufacturer under section 607 of the Act with respect to alleged cost increases resulting from action by the Secretary, in such form as to permit the public and the Secretary to make an informed judgment on the validity of the manufacturer's statements. Such term includes both the manufacturer's cost and the cost to retail purchasers.

(h) *Date of manufacture* means the date on which the label required by § 3282.205(c) is affixed to the manufactured home.

(i) [Reserved]

(j) *Defect* means a failure to comply with an applicable Federal manufactured home safety and construction standard that renders the manufactured home or any part or component thereof not fit for the ordinary use for which it was intended, but does not result in an unreasonable risk of injury or death to occupants of the affected manufactured home. See related definitions of *imminent safety hazard* (definition q), *noncompliance* (definition x), and *serious defect* (definition ff).

(k) *Design* means drawings, specifications, sketches and the related engineering calculations, tests and data in support of the configurations, structures and systems to be incorporated in manufactured homes manufactured in a plant.

(l) [Reserved]

(m) *Distributor* means any person engaged in the sale and distribution of manufactured homes for resale.

(n) *Failure to conform* means an imminent safety hazard related to the standards, a serious defect, defect, or noncompliance and is used as a substitute for all of those terms.

(o) [Reserved]

(p) *Imminent safety hazard* means a hazard that presents an imminent and unreasonable risk of death or severe personal injury that may or may not be related to failure to comply with an applicable Federal manufactured home construction or safety standard. See related definitions of *defect* (definition j), *noncompliance* (paragraph x) and *serious defect* (paragraph ff).

(q) *Joint monitoring team* means a monitoring inspection team composed of personnel provided by the various State Administrative Agencies, or by HUD or its contract agent, operating under a contract with HUD for the purpose of monitoring, or otherwise aiding in the enforcement of the Federal standards.

(r) *Label* or *certification label* means the approved form of certification by the manufacturer that, under § 3282.362(c)(2)(i), is permanently affixed to each transportable section of each manufactured home manufactured for sale to a purchaser in the United States.

(s) (Same as § 3280.2(a)(13).)

(t) *Manufacturer* means any person engaged in manufacturing or assembling manufactured homes, including any person engaged in importing manufactured homes for resale.

(u) (Same as § 3280.2(a)(16).)

(v) *Manufactured home construction* means all activities relating to the assembly and manufacture of a manufactured home including, but not limited to, those relating to durability, quality, and safety, but does not include those activities regulated under the installation standards in this chapter.

(w) *Manufactured home safety* means the performance of a manufactured home in such a manner that the public is protected against any unreasonable risk of the occurrence of accidents due to the design or construction of such manufactured home, or any unreasonable risk of death or injury to the user or to the public if such accidents do occur.

(x) *Noncompliance* means a failure of a manufactured home to comply with a Federal manufactured home construction or safety standard that does not constitute a defect, serious defect, or imminent safety hazard. See related definitions or *defect* (definition j), *imminent safety hazard* (definition q), and *serious defect* (definition ff).

(y) *Owner* means any person purchasing a manufactured home from any other person after the first purchase of the manufactured home, in good faith, for purposes other than resale.

(z) *Primary Inspection Agency* (PIA) means a State/or private organization that has been accepted by the Secretary in accordance with the requirement of subpart H of this part. There are two types of PIA:

(1) Design Approval PIA (DAPIA), which evaluates and approves or disapproves manufactured home designs and quality control procedures, and

(2) Production Inspection PIA (IPIA), which evaluates the ability of manufactured home manufacturing plants to follow approved quality control procedures and provides ongoing surveillance of the manufacturing process. Organizations may act as one or both of these types.

(aa) *Purchaser* means the first person purchasing a manufactured home in good faith for purposes other than resale.

(bb) *Quality Assurance Manual* means a manual, prepared by each manufacturer for its manufacturing plants and approved by a DAPIA which contains: a statement of the manufacturer's quality assurance program, a chart of the organization showing, by position, all personnel accountable for quality assurance, a list of tests and test equipment required, a station-by-station description of the manufacturing process, a list of inspections required at each station, and a list by title of personnel in the manufacturer's organization to be held responsible for each inspection. Where necessary, the quality assurance manual used in a particular plant shall contain information specific to that plant.

(cc) *To red tag* means to affix a notice to a manufactured home which has been found to contain an imminent safety hazard or a failure to conform with any applicable standard. A *red tag* is the notice so affixed to the manufactured home.

(dd) *Retailer* means any person engaged in the sale, leasing, or distribution of new manufactured homes primarily to persons who in good faith purchase or lease a manufactured home for purposes other than resale.

(ee) *Secretary's agent* means a party operating as an independent contractor under a contract with HUD.

(ff) *Serious defect* means any failure to comply with an applicable Federal manufactured home construction and safety standard that renders the manufactured home or any part thereof not fit for the ordinary use for which it was intended and which results in an unreasonable risk of injury or death to occupants of the affected manufactured home.

(gg) *Standards* means the Federal manufactured home construction and safety standards promulgated under section 604 of the Act, 42 U.S.C. 5403, as part 3280 of these regulations.

(hh) *State* includes each of the several States, the District of Columbia, the Commonwealth of Puerto Rico, Guam, the Virgin Islands, the Canal Zone, and American Samoa.

(ii) *State Administrative Agency* (SAA) means an agency of a State which has been approved or conditionally approved to carry out the State plan for enforcement of the standards pursuant to section 623 of the Act, 42 U.S.C. 5422, and subpart G of this part.

(jj) *State plan application* means the application of any State organization which is submitted to the Secretary for approval as a State Administrative Agency under subpart G.

(kk) *Substantial completion.* A manufactured home is substantially completed if all aspects of construction that can be finished in the manufacturer's plant are completed, except as provided in § 3282.603.

(ll) *System* means a set or arrangement of materials or components related or connected as to form an operating entity, i.e., heating, ventilating and air-conditioning systems, evaporative coolers.

(mm) *United States District Courts* means the Federal district courts of the United States and the United States courts of the Commonwealth of Puerto Rico, Guam, the Virgin Islands, the Canal Zone, and American Samoa.

(nn) (Same as § 3280.2(a)(22).)

[41 FR 19852, May 13, 1976, as amended at 41 FR 24971, June 21, 1976; 47 FR 28093, June 29, 1982; 61 FR 5216, Feb. 9, 1996; 61 FR 10859, Mar. 15, 1996; 78 FR 60199, Oct. 1, 2013; 80 FR 53727, Sept. 8, 2015]

§ 3282.8 Applicability.

(a) *Manufactured homes.* This part applies to all manufactured homes that enter the first stage of production on or after June 15, 1976, and to all manufactured homes that enter the first stage of production before June 15, 1976, to which labels are applied under § 3282.205(d).

(b) *States.* This part applies to States that desire to assume responsibility under the Federal manufactured home construction and safety standards enforcement program. It includes requirements which must be met in order for State agencies to be approved by the Secretary under section 623(c) of the Act, 42 U.S.C. 5422(c). It also includes requirements for States wishing to act as primary inspection agencies, as defined in § 3282.7, or to participate in monitoring activities under § 3282.308.

(c) *Primary inspection and engineering organizations.* This part applies to each private inspection and engineering organization that wishes to qualify as a primary inspection agency under subpart H.

(d) *Manufactured home manufacturers.* This part applies to all manufacturers producing manufactured homes for sale in the United States. It includes:

(1) Inspection procedures to be carried out in the manufacturing plants.

(2) Procedures by which a manufacturer obtains approval of manufactured home designs.

(3) Procedures by which a manufacturer obtains approval of manufacturing quality control and assurance programs.

(4) Procedures by which a manufacturer may obtain production inspections and certification labels for its manufactured homes.

(e) *Manufactured home retailers and distributors.* This part applies to any person selling, leasing, or distributing new manufactured homes for use in the United States. It includes prohibitions of the sale of new manufactured homes to which labels have not been affixed pursuant to subpart H of these regulations or that have been altered, damaged, or otherwise caused not to be in compliance with the Federal standards.

(f) *Purchasers, owners and consumers.* This part applies to purchasers, owners and consumers of manufactured homes in that it sets out procedures to be followed when purchasers, owners and consumers complain to manufacturers, States, the Secretary or others concerning problems in manufactured homes for which remedies are provided under the Act.

(g) [Reserved]

(h) *Imported manufactured homes.* Imported manufactured homes are covered by the regulations except as modified by regulations promulgated jointly by the Secretary and the Secretary of the Treasury.

(i) *Export manufactured homes.* Manufactured Homes intended solely for export are not governed by this part or by part 3280 of this title if a label or tag stating that the manufactured home is intended solely for export is placed on the manufactured home or the outside of the container, if any, in which it is to be exported. However, any manufactured home so tagged or labeled that is not exported but is sold to a purchaser in the United States is subject to this part and part 3280 of this title.

(j) *Add-on.* An add-on added by the retailer or some other party not the manufacturer (except where the manufacturer acts as a retailer) as part of a simultaneous transaction involving the sale of a new manufactured home, is not governed by the standards and is not subject to these regulations. However, the addition of the add-on must not affect the ability of the basic manufactured home to comply with the standards. If the addition of an add-on causes the basic manufactured home to fail to conform to the standards, sale, lease, and offer for sale or lease of the home is prohibited until the manufactured home is brought into conformance with the standards. While the standards do not govern add-ons, the Secretary has the authority to promulgate standards for add-ons and may do so in the future.

(k) A structure (including an expandable room, tip-out, or tag-along unit) which is designed and produced as an integral part of a manufactured home when assembled on site, is governed by the standards and these regulations regardless of the dimensions of such structure.

(1) *Multifamily homes.* Mobile homes designed and manufactured with more than one separate living unit are not covered by the standards and these regulations.

[41 FR 19852, May 13, 1976, as amended at 41 FR 24970, June 21, 1976; 42 FR 35013, July 7, 1977; 44 FR 68733, Nov. 29, 1979; 47 FR 28093, June 29, 1982; 80 FR 53727, Sept. 8, 2015; 83 FR 57688, Nov. 16, 2018]

§ 3282.9 Computation of time.

(a) In computing any period of time prescribed by the regulations in this part, refer to § 26.16(a) of this title.

(b) Extensions of any of the time periods set out in these regulations may be granted by the Secretary or, as appropriate, by a State Administrative Agency, upon a showing of good cause by the party governed by the time period.

[42 FR 2580, Jan. 12, 1977, as amended at 61 FR 10859, Mar. 15, 1996]

§ 3282.10 Civil and criminal penalties.

Failure to comply with these regulations may subject the party in question to the civil and criminal penalties provided for in section 611 of the Act, 42 U.S.C. 5410. The maximum amount of penalties imposed under section 611 of the Act shall be $2,852 for each violation, up to a maximum of $3,565,045 for any related series of violations occurring within one year from the date of the first violation.

[83 FR 32794, July 16, 2018]

EFFECTIVE DATE NOTE: At 84 FR 9454, Mar. 15, 2019, § 3282.10 was revised, effective Apr. 15, 2019. For the convenience of the user, the revised text is set forth as follows:

§ 3282.10 Civil and criminal penalties.

Failure to comply with this part may subject the party in question to the civil and criminal penalties provided for in section 611 of the Act, 42 U.S.C. 5410. The maximum amount of penalties imposed under section 611 of the Act shall be $2,924 for each violation, up to a maximum of $3,654,955 for any related series of violations occurring within one year from the date of the first violation.

§ 3282.11 Preemption and reciprocity.

(a) No State manufactured home standard regarding manufactured home construction and safety which covers aspects of the manufactured home governed by the Federal standards shall be established or continue in effect with respect to manufactured homes subject to the Federal standards and these regulations unless it is identical to the Federal standards.

(b) No State may require, as a condition of entry into or sale in the State, a manufactured home certified (by the application of the label required by § 3282.362(c)(2)(i)) as in conformance with the Federal standards to be subject to State inspection to determine compliance with any standard covering any aspect of the manufactured home covered by the Federal standards. Nor may any State require that a State label be placed on the manufactured home certifying conformance to the Federal standard or an identical standard. Certain actions that States are permitted to take are set out in § 3282.303.

(c) States may participate in the enforcement of the Federal standards enforcement program under these regulations either as SAAs or PIAs or both. These regulations establish the exclusive system for enforcement of the Federal standards. No State may establish or keep in effect through a building code enforcement system or otherwise, procedures or requirements which constitute systems for enforcement of the Federal standards or of identical State standards which are outside the system established in these regulations or which go beyond this system to require remedial actions which are not required by the Act and these regulations. A State may establish or continue in force consumer protections, such as warranty or warranty performance requirements, which respond to individual consumer complaints and so do not constitute systems of enforcement of the Federal standards, regardless of whether the State qualifies as an SAA or PIA.

(d) No State or locality may establish or enforce any rule or regulation or take any action that stands as an obstacle to the accomplishment and execution of the full purposes and objectives of Congress. The test of whether a State rule or action is valid or must give way is whether the State rule can be enforced or the action taken without impairing the Federal superintendent of the manufactured home industry as established by the Act.

[42 FR 2580, Jan. 12, 1977, as amended at 56 FR 65186, Dec. 16, 1991; 61 FR 10859, Mar. 15, 1996]

§ 3282.12 Excluded structures—modular homes.

(a) The purpose of this section is to provide the certification procedure authorized by section 604(h) of the National Manufactured Housing Construction and Safety Standards Act under which modular homes may be excluded from coverage of the Act if the manufacturer of the structure elects to have them excluded. If a manufacturer wishes to construct a structure that is both a manufactured home and a modular home, the manufacturer need not make the certification provided for by this section and may meet both the Federal manufactured home requirements and any modular housing requirements. When the certification is not made, all provisions of the Federal requirements shall be met.

(b) Any structure that meets the definition of *manufactured home* at 24 CFR 3282.7(u) is excluded from the coverage of the National Manufactured Housing Construction and Safety Standards Act, 42 U.S.C. 5401 *et seq.*, if the manufacturer certifies as prescribed in paragraph (c) of this section that:

(1) The structure is designed only for erection or installation on a site-built permanent foundation;

(i) A structure meets this criterion if all written materials and communications relating to installation of the structure, including but not limited to designs, drawings, and installation or erection instructions, indicate that the structure is to be installed on a permanent foundation.

(ii) A site-built permanent foundation is a system of supports, including piers, either partially or entirely below grade which is:

(A) Capable of transferring all design loads imposed by or upon the structure into soil or bedrock without failure,

(B) Placed at an adequate depth below grade to prevent frost damage, and

(C) Constructed of concrete, metal, treated lumber or wood, or grouted masonry; and

(2) The structure is not designed to be moved once erected or installed on a site-built permanent foundation;

(i) A structure meets this criterion if all written materials and communications relating to erection or installation of the structure, including but not limited to designs, drawings, calculations, and installation or erection instructions, indicate that the structure is not intended to be moved after it is erected or installed and if the towing hitch or running gear, which includes axles, brakes, wheels and other parts of the chassis that operate only during transportation, are removable and designed to be removed prior to erection or installation on a site-built permanent foundation; and

(3) The structure is designed and manufactured to comply with the currently effective version of one of the following:

(i) One of the following nationally recognized building codes:

(A) That published by Building Officials and Code Administrators (BOCA) and the National Fire Protection Association (NFPA) and made up of the following:

(*1*) BOCA Basic Building Code,

(*2*) BOCA Basic Industrialized Dwelling Code,

(*3*) BOCA Basic Plumbing Code,

(*4*) BOCA Basic Mechanical Code, and

(*5*) National Electrical Code, or

(B) That published by the Southern Building Code Congress (SBCC) and the NFPA and made up of the following:

(*1*) Standard Building Code,

(*2*) Standard Gas Code,

(*3*) Standard Mechanical Code,

(*4*) Standard Plumbing Code, and

(*5*) National Electrical Code, or

(C) That published by the International Conference of Building Officials (ICBO), the International Association of Plumbing and Mechanical Officials (IAPMO), and the NFPA and made up of the following:

(*1*) Uniform Building Code,

(*2*) Uniform Mechanical Code,

(*3*) Uniform Plumbing Code, and

(*4*) National Electrical Code or

(D) The codes included in paragraphs (b)(3)(i)(A), (B), or (C) in connection with the One- and Two-Family Dwelling Code, or

(E) Any combination of the codes included in paragraphs (b)(3)(i)(A), (B), (C), and (D), that is approved by the Secretary, including combinations using the National Standard Plumbing Code published by the National Association of Plumbing, Heating and Cooling Contractors (PHCC), or

(F) Any other building code accepted by the Secretary as a nationally recognized model building code, or

(ii) Any local code or State or local modular building code accepted as generally equivalent to the codes included under paragraph (b)(3)(i), (the Secretary will consider the manufacturer's certification under paragraph (c) of this section to constitute a certification that the code to which the structure is built is generally equivalent to the referenced codes. This certification of equivalency is subject to the provisions of paragraph (f) of this section) or

(iii) The minimum property standards adopted by the Secretary pursuant to title II of the National Housing Act; and

(4) To the manufacturer's knowledge, the structure is not intended to be used other than on a site-built permanent foundation.

(c) When a manufacturer makes a certification provided for under paragraph (b) of this section, the certification shall state as follows:

The manufacturer of this structure, Name _____; Address _____; (location where structure was manufactured).

Certifies that this structure (Ser. No. _____) is not a manufactured home subject to the provisions of the National Manufactured Housing Construction and Safety Standards Act and is—

(1) designed only for erection or installation on a site-built permanent foundation,

(2) not designed to be moved once so erected or installed,

(3) designed and manufactured to comply with _____ (Here state which code included in paragraph (b)(3) of this section has been followed), and

(4) to the manufacturer's knowledge is not intended to be used other than on a site-built permanent foundation.

(d) This certification shall be affixed in a permanent manner near the electrical panel, on the inside of a kitchen cabinet door, or in any other readily accessible and visible location.

(e) As part of this certification, the manufacturer shall identify each certified structure by a permanent serial number placed on the structure during the first stage of production. If the manufacturer also manufactures manufactured homes that are certified under §§ 3282.205 and 3282.362(c), the series of serial numbers for structures certified under this section shall be distinguishable on the structures and in the manufacturer's records from the series of serial numbers for the manufactured homes that are certified under §§ 3282.205 and 3282.362(c).

(1) If a manufacturer wishes to certify a structure as a manufactured home under §§ 3282.205 and 3282.362(c) after having applied a serial number identifying it as exempted under this section, the manufacturer may do so only with the written consent of the Production Inspection Primary Inspection Agency (IPIA) after thorough inspection of the structure by the IPIA at at least one stage of production and such removal or equipment, components, or materials as the IPIA may require to perform inspections to assure that the structure conforms to the Federal manufactured home standards. The manufacturer shall remove the original serial number and add the serial number required by § 3280.6.

(2) A manufacturer may not certify a structure under this section after having applied the manufactured home serial number under § 3280.6.

(f) All certifications made under this section are subject to investigation by the Secretary to determine their accuracy. If a certification is false or inaccurate, the certification for purposes of this section is invalid and the structures that have been or may be the subject of the certification are not excluded from the coverage of the Act, the Federal Manufactured Home Construction and Safety Standards, or these Regulations.

(1) If the Secretary has information that a certification may be false or inaccurate, the manufacturer will be given written notice of the nature of this information by certified mail and

the procedure of this subparagraph will be followed.

(i) The manufacturer must investigate this matter and report its findings in writing as to the validity of this information to the Secretary within 15 days from the receipt of the Secretary's notice.

(ii) If a written report is received within the time prescribed in paragraph (f)(1)(i) of this section, the Secretary will review this report before determining whether a certification is false or inaccurate. If a report is not received within 15 days from the receipt of the Secretary's notice, the Secretary will make the determination on the basis of the information presented.

(iii) If the Secretary determines that a certification is false or inaccurate, the manufacturer will be given written notice and the reasons for this determination by certified mail.

(2) The Secretary may seek civil and criminal penalties provided for in section 611 of the Act, 42 U.S.C. 5410, if the party in question in the exercise of due care has reason to know that such certification is false or misleading as to any material fact.

[44 FR 68733, Nov. 29, 1979, as amended at 49 FR 10666, Mar. 22, 1984]

§ 3282.13 Voluntary certification.

(a) The purpose of this section is to provide a procedure for voluntary certification of non-conforming manufactured homes as required by 42 U.S.C. 5402(6) as amended by section 308(d)(B) of the Housing and Community Development Act of 1980.

(b) Structures which meet all of the requirements of a *manufactured home* as set out in § 3282.7(u), except the size requirements, shall be *manufactured homes* if the manufacturer files with the Secretary a certification in the following form:

[Name of manufacturer and address where structures are to be manufactured] certifies that it intends to manufacture structures that meet all of the requirements of manufactured homes set forth at 42 U.S.C. 5402(6) except the size requirements. Such structures are to be treated as manufactured homes for the purposes of the National Manufactured Housing Construction and Safety Standards Act of 1974 and the regulations

promulgated pursuant thereto. Such structures will be built in conformance with the Standards. [Name of manufacturer] further certifies that if, at any time it manufactures structures which are not manufactured homes, it will identify each such structure by a permanent serial number placed on the structure during the first stage of production and that the series of serial numbers for such structures shall be distinguishable on the structures and in its records from the series of serial numbers used for manufactured homes.

(c) Whenever a manufacturer which has filed a certification pursuant to § 3282.13(b) produces structures which are not manufactured homes, it must identify each such structure by placing a permanent serial number on the structure during the first stage of production. The series of serial numbers placed on these structures shall be distinguishable on the structure and in the manufacturer's records from the series of serial numbers used for manufactured homes.

(d) A manufacturer may certify a structure as a manufactured home after having applied a serial number identifying it as a structure which is not a manufactured home. To do so, the manufacturer must secure the written consent of the IPIA. This consent may only be given after a DAPIA has approved the manufacturer's design and quality assistance manual in accordance with § 3282.361, and after the IPIA has thoroughly inspected the structure in at least one stage of production and after such removal of equipment, components or materials as the IPIA may require to assure that the structure conforms to the standards. After certification as a manufactured home has been approved, the manufacturer shall remove the original serial number and add the serial number required by § 3280.6.

(e) Once a manufacturer has certified under § 3282.13(b) that it intends to build structures which are manufactured homes in all respects except size, the manufacturer must then, with respect to those structures, comply with all of the requirements of the Act and its regulations. The structures may not thereafter be exempted under any other section of these regulations.

[47 FR 28093, June 29, 1982]

§3282.14 Alternative construction of manufactured homes.

(a) *Policy.* In order to promote the purposes of the Act, the Department will permit the sale or lease of one or more manufactured homes not in compliance with the Standards under circumstances wherein no affirmative action is needed to protect the public interest. The Department encourages innovation and the use of new technology in manufactured homes. Accordingly, HUD will permit manufacturers to utilize new designs or techniques not in compliance with the Standards in cases:

(1) Where a manufacturer proposes to utilize construction that would be prohibited by the Standards;

(2) Where such construction would provide performance that is equivalent to or superior to that required by the Standards; and

(3) Where (i) compliance with the Standards would be unreasonable because of the circumstances of the particular case, or (ii) the alternative construction would be for purposes of research, testing or development of new techniques or designs. If a request for alternative construction is submitted and the facts are consistent with these principles, the Secretary may issue a letter under paragraph (c) of this section stating that no action will be taken under the Act based upon specific failures to conform to the Standards or these regulations, provided that certain conditions are met. The issuance of a letter under paragraph (c) of this section will not affect any right that any purchaser may have under the Act or other applicable law and will not preclude any further agency action that may become necessary.

(b) *Request for alternative construction.* A manufacturer may submit a request for alternative construction of a manufactured home. The request should be sent to the U.S. Department of Housing and Urban Development, Manufactured Housing Standards Division, 451 Seventh Street, SW., Washington, DC 20410. The request must include:

(1) A copy of the manufactured design or plan for each nonconforming model which a manufacturer plans to build;

(2) An explanation of the manner in which the design fails to conform with the Standards, including a list of the specific standards involved;

(3) An explanation of how the design will result in homes that provide the same level of performance, quality, durability and safety as would be provided under the Standards;

(4) A copy of data adequate to support the request, including applicable test data, engineering calculations or certifications from nationally recognized laboratories;

(5) An estimate of the maximum number of manufactured home units affected and the location, if known, to which the units will be shipped;

(6) An indication of the period of time during which the manufacturer proposes to engage in the manufacture, sale or lease of the nonconforming homes;

(7) A copy of the proposed notice to be provided to home purchasers;

(8) A list of the names and addresses of any retailers that would be selling the nonconforming homes; and

(9) A letter from the manufacturer's DAPIA indicating that the design(s) to which any nonconforming homes would be built meet the Standards in all other respects.

(c) *Issuance of the letter by the Secretary*—(1) *Contents of the letter.* If the Secretary issues a letter in response to a request for alternative construction, the letter shall include the specific standards affected, an explanation of the proposed activity or design, an explanation of how the request is consistent with the objectives of the Act, and any conditions that the manufacturer must meet.

(2) *Letter sent to IPIA, DAPIA and SAA.* The Secretary shall forward a copy of the letter to the manufacturer's IPIA and DAPIA along with a letter authorizing the DAPIA to approve plans containing the alternative construction, and authorizing the IPIA to permit use of the alternative construction, provided that the conditions set forth in the letter are met. The Secretary shall also forward a copy of the letter to the SAAs in the State of manufacture and the State(s) in which the homes are to be located, if known.

(3) *Alternative construction in additional models.* In cases where the Secretary grants a letter under this paragraph that is not model-specific, the Secretary may permit the manufacturer to include the alternative construction in additional models. In such cases, the DAPIA shall notify the Department of additional models that incorporate the alternative construction.

(d) *Revocation.* The Secretary may revoke or amend a letter issued under paragraph (c) of this section at any time. Such revocation or amendment will be prospective only. Where manufacturers have requested alternative construction for research, testing or development such alternative construction may not achieve the anticipated results. Therefore, the Secretary may require a manufacturer to bring those homes into compliance with the standards if, after the alternative construction has been in use for a period of time specified by the Secretary, these homes are not, in the Secretary's judgment, providing the levels of safety, quality and durability which would have been provided had the homes been built in compliance with the Standards.

(e) *Notice to prospective purchasers.* Manufacturers receiving letters under paragraph (c) of this section shall provide notice to prospective purchasers that the home does not conform to the Standards. Such notice shall be delivered to each prospective purchase before he or she enters into an agreement to purchase the home. The notice shall be in the following form or in such other form as may be approved by the Secretary:

NOTICE TO PURCHASERS

The Department of Housing and Urban Development has issued a letter to (Name of Manufacturer) concerning the homes in (location if known). As designed, the homes do not meet Federal Manufactured Home Construction and Safety Standards regarding (brief statement of manufacturer's nonconformance).

HUD has evaluated the alternative construction and believes that it provides an equivalent level of quality, durability and safety to that provided by the Standards.

For further information about the specific Federal Standards involved, a copy of the letter issued pursuant to 24 CFR 3282.14(c) is

available from this retailer or manufacturer upon request.

(f) *Serial numbers of homes constructed using alternative construction.* Manufacturers shall provide the Department with the serial numbers assigned to each home produced in conformance with the letter issued under paragraph (c) of this section within 90 days of their date of manufacture. Each serial number shall include the letters "AC" to indicate that the homes was produced under alternative construction procedures.

[49 FR 1967, Jan. 16, 1984]

§ 3282.15 Exemption for recreational vehicles.

(a) *Exemption.* A recreational vehicle that meets the requirements of this section is exempt from 24 CFR parts 3280 and 3282.

(b) *Definition.* A recreational vehicle is:

(1) A vehicle or vehicular structure not certified as a manufactured home;

(2) Designed only for recreational use and not as a primary residence or for permanent occupancy; and is either:

(i) Built and certified in accordance with either NFPA 1192 (incorporated by reference, see § 3282.16) or ANSI A119.5 (incorporated by reference, see § 3282.16) as provided by paragraph (c) of this section; or

(ii) Any vehicle which is self-propelled.

(c) *Notice and certification requirements.* In order for the exemption to apply to an ANSI A119.5–15 certified recreational vehicle, a Manufacturer's Notice must be delivered to the consumer prior to the completion of the sales transaction. The Manufacturer's Notice must also be prominently displayed in a temporary manner in the kitchen (*i.e.*, countertop or exposed cabinet face). The Manufacturer's Notice must meet the following requirements:

(1) *Title of Manufacturer's Notice.* The title of the Manufacturer's Notice shall be "*****MANUFACTURER'S NOTICE*****" which shall be legible and typed using bold letters at least 1 inch in size.

(2) *Content of Notice.* The content of the Manufacturer's Notice text shall be as follows:

The Manufacturer of this unit certifies that it is a Park Model Recreational Vehicle designed only for recreational use, and not for use as a primary residence or for permanent occupancy. The manufacturer of this unit further certifies that this unit has been built in accordance with the ANSI A119.5–15 consensus standard for Park Model Recreational Vehicles.

(3) *Text of Notice.* The text of the Manufacturer's Notice, aside from the Manufacturer's Notice's title shall be legible and typed using letters at least ½ inch in size.

(4) *Removal of Manufacturer's Notice.* The Manufacturer's Notice shall not be removed by any party until the entire sales transaction has been completed.

(5) *Completion of sales transaction.* A sales transaction with a Park Model Recreational Vehicle purchaser is considered completed when all the goods and services that the dealer agreed to provide at the time the contract was formed have been provided. Completion of a retail sale will be at the time the dealer completes installation of the Park Model Recreational Vehicle, if the dealer has agreed to provide the installation, or at the time the dealer delivers the recreational vehicle to a transporter, if the dealer has not agreed to transport or install the Park Model Recreational Vehicle. The sale is also complete upon delivery to the site if the dealer has not agreed to provide installation as completion of sale.

[83 FR 57688, Nov. 16, 2018]

§3282.16 Incorporation by reference

(a) Certain material is incorporated by reference into this part with the approval of the Director of the Federal Register under 5 U.S.C. 552(a) and 1 CFR part 51. To enforce any edition other than that specified in this section, the Department must publish a document in the FEDERAL REGISTER and the material must be available to the public. All approved material is available for inspection at the Office of Manufactured Housing Programs, Manufactured Housing and Construction Standards Division, U.S. Department of Housing and Urban Development, 451 7th Street SW, Room B–133, Washington, DC 20410, 202–402–5216, and is available from the sources listed below.

Copies of incorporated standards that are not available from their producer organizations may be obtained from the Office of Manufactured Housing Programs. These standards are also available for inspection at the National Archives and Records Administration (NARA). For more information on the availability of this material at NARA, call 202–741–6030 or go to *http://www.archives.gov/federal-register/cfr/ibr-locations.html.*

(b) National Fire Protection Association (NFPA), 1 Batterymarch Park, Quincy, MA 02169, telephone number 800–344–3555, website *http://www.nfpa.org.*

(1) NFPA 1192, Standard on Recreational Vehicles, 2015 Edition, issued August 14, 2014, IBR approved for §3282.15(b).

(2) [Reserved]

(c) Recreational Vehicle Industry Association (RVIA), 1896 Preston White Drive, Reston, VA 20191, telephone number 703–620–6003, website *http://www.rvia.org.*

(1) ANSI A119.5: Park Model Recreational Vehicle Standard, 2015 Edition, ANSI-approved April 7, 2015, IBR approved for §3282.15(b).

(2) [Reserved]

[83 FR 57688, Nov. 16, 2018]

Subpart B—Formal Procedures

§3282.51 Scope.

This subpart contains rules of procedure generally applicable to the transaction of official business under the National Manufactured Housing Construction and Safety Standards Act, including the rules governing public availability of information.

§3282.52 Address of communications.

Unless otherwise specified, communications shall be addressed to the Administrator, Office of Manufactured Housing Programs, Office of Housing, Department of Housing and Urban Development, 451 7th Street SW., Washington, DC 20410.

[78 FR 60199, Oct. 1, 2013]

§ 3282.53 Service of process on foreign manufacturers and importers.

The designation of an agent required by section 612(e) of the Act, 42 U.S.C. 5411(e), shall be in writing, dated, and signed by the manufacturer and the designated agent.

[61 FR 10860, Mar. 15, 1996]

§ 3282.54 Public information.

(a) *General.* Subject to the provisions of 24 CFR part 15 covering the production or disclosure of material or information and the provisions of 24 CFR part 16 at 40 FR 39729 relating to the Privacy Act, and except as otherwise provided by paragraphs (b), (c), (d), and (e) of this section, the Secretary may make available to the public:

(1) Any information which may indicate the existence of an imminent safety hazard, and

(2) Any information which may indicate the failure of a manufactured home to comply with applicable manufactured home construction and safety standards, and

(3) Such other information as the Secretary determines is necessary to carry out the Secretary's functions under the Act.

(b) *Protected information.* Data and information submitted or otherwise provided to the Secretary or an agent of the Secretary or a PIA or SAA which fall within the definitions of a trade secret or confidential commercial or financial information are exempt from disclosure under this section, only if the party submitting or providing the information so requests under paragraph (c) of this section. However, the Secretary may disclose such information to any person requesting it after deletion of the portions which are exempt, or in such combined or summary form as does not disclose the portions which are exempt from disclosure or in its entirety in accordance with section 614 of the Act, U.S.C. 5413.

(c) *Obtaining exemption.* Any party submitting any information to the Secretary in any form under this part, or otherwise in relation to the program established by the Act shall, if the party desires the information to be exempt from disclosure, at the time of submittal of the information or at any time thereafter, request that the information or any part thereof be protected from disclosure. The request for nondisclosure shall include the basis for the request under the Act or other authority and complete justification supporting the claim that the material should be exempt from disclosure. The request should also include a statement of the information in such combined or summary form that alleged trade secrets or other protected information and the identity of the submitting party would not be disclosed. This request need not be made with respect to information which was submitted to the Secretary, an SAA or a PIA prior to the effective date of these regulations.

(d) *Request for information from PIAs or SAAs.* Whenever a PIA or SAA receives requests for disclosure of information, it shall disclose the information unless the party from which the information was originally obtained has submitted to the PIA or SAA a request that the information not be disclosed under paragraph (c) of this section, except that the PIA or SAA shall be governed by the provisions of 24 CFR part 16 (40 FR 39729) relating to the Privacy Act which may limit the disclosure of information. If a request for nondisclosure under paragraph (c) of this section has been received with respect ʲto information whose disclosure is requested, the PIA or SAA shall refer the matter to the Secretary within 5 days of the request for disclosure. If a PIA or SAA receives a request for disclosure of information related to this program, which information was submitted to the PIA or SAA prior to the effective date of these regulations, the PIA or SAA shall refer the request for nondisclosure and required information to the Secretary.

[41 FR 19852, May 13, 1976, as amended at 61 FR 10860, Mar. 15, 1996]

Subpart C—Rules and Rulemaking Procedures

§ 3282.101 Generally.

Procedures that apply to the formulation, issuance, amendment, and revocation of rules pursuant to the Act are governed by the Act, the Administrative Procedure Act, 5 U.S.C. 551 *et seq.*, and part 10 of this title, except that the Secretary shall respond to a petition for rulemaking by an interested party within 180 days of receipt of the petition.

[61 FR 10860, Mar. 15, 1996]

§ 3282.111 Petitions for reconsideration of final rules.

(a) *Definition.* A petition for reconsideration of a final rule issued by the Secretary is a request in writing from any interested person which must be received not later than 60 days after publication of the rule in the FEDERAL REGISTER. The petition shall state that it is a petition for reconsideration of a final rule, and shall contain an explanation as to why compliance with the rule is not practicable, is unreasonable, or is not in the public interest. If the petitioner requests the consideration of additional facts, the petitioner shall state the reason they were not presented to be treated as petitions for rulemaking.

(b) *Proceedings on petitions for reconsideration.* The Secretary may grant or deny, in whole or in part, any petition for reconsideration without further proceedings. The Secretary may issue a final decision on reconsideration without further proceeding, or may provide such opportunity to submit comments or information and data as the Secretary deems appropriate.

(c) Unless the Secretary determines otherwise, the filing of a petition under this section does not stay the effectiveness of the rule in question.

(d) Any party seeking to challenge any rule or regulation issued under the Act, except orders issued under section 604 42 U.S.C. 5403, if the challenge is brought before the expiration of the 60 day period set out in paragraph (a) of this section, shall file a timely petition for reconsideration under this section prior to seeking any other remedy.

§ 3282.113 Interpretative bulletins.

When appropriate, the Secretary shall issue interpretative bulletins interpreting the standards under the authority of § 3280.9 of this chapter or interpreting the provisions of this part. Issuance of interpretative bulletins

shall be treated as rulemaking under this subpart C unless the Secretary deems such treatment not to be in the public interest and the interpretation is not otherwise required to be treated as rulemaking. All interpretative bulletins shall be indexed and made available to the public at the Manufactured Housing Standards Division and a copy of the index shall be published periodically in the FEDERAL REGISTER.

[61 FR 10860, Mar. 15, 1996]

Subpart D—Informal and Formal Presentations of Views, Hearings and Investigations

§ 3282.151 Applicability and scope.

(a) This subpart sets out procedures to be followed when an opportunity to present views provided for in the Act is requested by an appropriate party. Section 3282.152 provides for two types of procedures that may be followed, one informal and nonadversary, and one more formal and adversary. Section 3282.152 also sets out criteria to govern which type of procedure will be followed in particular cases.

(b) The procedures of § 3282.152 also apply to:

(1) Proceedings held by the Secretary whenever the suspension or disqualification of a primary inspection agency, which has been granted final approval, is recommended under § 3282.356 of these regulations, and

(2) Resolution of disputes where an SAA or manufacturer disagrees with a determination of a DAPIA under § 3282.361 that a manufactured home design does or does not conform to the standards or that a quality assurance manual is or is not adequate with a decision by an IPIA to red tag or not to red tag or to provide or not to provide a certification label for a manufactured home under § 3282.362 when the IPIA believes that the manufactured home does or does not conform to the standards.

(c) The procedures set out in § 3282.152 shall also be followed whenever State Administrative Agencies hold Formal or Informal Presentations of Views under § 3282.309.

(d) To the extent that these regulations provide for Formal or Informal

153

Presentations of Views for parties that would otherwise qualify for hearings under 2 CFR part 2424, the procedures of 2 CFR part 2424 shall not be available and shall not apply.

[41 FR 19852, May 13, 1976, as amended at 51 FR 34467, Sept. 29, 1986; 61 FR 10442, Mar. 13, 1996; 72 FR 73497, Dec. 27, 2007]

§ 3282.152 Procedures to present views and evidence.

(a) *Policy.* All Formal and Informal Presentations of Views under this subpart shall be public, unless, for good cause, the Secretary determines it is in the public interest that a particular proceeding should be closed. If the Secretary determines that a proceeding should be closed, the Secretary shall state and make publicly available the basis for that determination.

(b) *Request.* Upon receipt of a request to present views and evidence under the Act, the Secretary shall determine whether the proceeding will be a Formal or an Informal Presentation of Views, and shall issue a notice under paragraph (c) of this section.

(c) *Notice.* When the Secretary decides to conduct a Formal or an Informal Presentation of Views under this section, the Secretary shall provide notice as follows:

(1) Except where the need for swift resolution of the question involved prohibits it, notice of a proceeding hereunder shall be published in the FEDERAL REGISTER at least 10 days prior to the date of the proceeding. In any case, notice shall be provided to interested persons to the maximum extent practicable. Direct notice shall be sent by certified mail to the parties involved in the hearing.

(2) The notice, whether published or mailed, shall include a statement of the time, place and nature of the proceeding; reference to the authority under which the proceeding will be held; a statement of the subject matter of the proceeding, the parties and issues involved; and a statement of the manner in which interested persons shall be afforded the opportunity to participate in the hearing.

(3) The notice shall designate the official who shall be the presiding officer for the proceedings and to whom all inquiries should be directed concerning such proceedings.

(4) The notice shall state whether the proceeding shall be held in accordance with the provisions of paragraph (f)—(Informal Presentation of Views) or paragraph (g)—(Formal Presentation of Views) of this section, except that when the Secretary makes the determinations provided for in sections 623 (d) and (f) of the Act, the requirements of paragraph (g) of this section shall apply. In determining whether the requirements of paragraph (f) or those of paragraph (g) of this section shall apply the Secretary shall consider the following:

(i) The necessity for expeditious action;

(ii) The risk of injury to affected members of the public;

(iii) The economic consequences of the decisions to be rendered; and

(iv) Such other factors as the Secretary determines are appropriate.

(d) *Department representative.* If the Department is to be represented by Counsel, such representation shall be by a Department hearing attorney designated by the General Counsel.

(e) *Reporting and transcription.* Oral proceedings shall be stenographically or mechanically reported and transcribed under the supervision of the presiding officer, unless the presiding officer and the parties otherwise agree, in which case a summary approved by the presiding officer shall be kept. The original transcript or summary shall be a part of the record and the sole official transcript, or summary. A copy of the transcript or summary shall be available to any person at a fee established by the Secretary, which fee the Secretary may waive in the public interest. Any information contained in the transcript or summary which would be exempt from required disclosure under § 3282.54 of these regulations may be protected from disclosure if appropriate under that section upon a request for such protection under § 3282.54(c).

(f) *Informal presentation of views.* (1) An Informal Presentation of Views may be written or oral, and may include an opportunity for an oral presentation, whether requested or not, whenever the Secretary concludes that an oral presentation would be in the public interest, and so states in the notice. A presiding officer shall preside over all oral presentations held under this subsection. The purpose of any such presentation shall be to gather information to allow fully informed decision making. Informal Presentations of Views shall not be adversary proceedings. Oral presentations shall be conducted in an informal but orderly manner. The presiding officer shall have the duty and authority to conduct a fair proceeding, to take all necessary action to avoid delay, and to maintain order. In the absence of extraordinary circumstances, the presiding officer at an oral Informal Presentation of Views shall not require that testimony be given under an oath or affirmation, and shall not permit either cross-examination of witnesses by other witnesses or their representatives, or the presentation of rebuttal testimony by persons who have already testified. The rules of evidence prevailing in courts of law or equity shall not control the conduct of oral Informal Presentations of Views.

(2) Within 10 days after an Informal Presentation of Views, the presiding officer shall refer to the Secretary all documentary evidence submitted, the transcript, if any, a summary of the issues involved and information presented in the Informal Presentation of Views and the presiding official's recommendations, with the rationale therefor. The presiding officer shall make any appropriate statements concerning the apparent veracity of witnesses or the validity of factual assertions which may be within the competence of the presiding officer. The Secretary shall issue a Final Determination concerning the matters at issue within 30 days of receipt of the presiding officer's summary. The Final Determination shall include:

(i) A statement of findings, with specific references to principal supporting items of evidence in the record and conclusions, as well as the reasons or bases therefor, upon all of the material issues of fact, law, or discretion as presented on the record, and

(ii) An appropriate order. Notice of the Final Determination shall be given in writing and transmitted by certified mail, return receipt requested, to all

participants in the presentation of views. The Final Determination shall be conclusive, with respect to persons whose interests were represented.

(g) *Formal presentation of views.* (1) A Formal Presentation of Views is an adversary proceeding and includes an opportunity for the oral presentation of evidence. All witnesses shall testify under oath or affirmation, which shall be administered by the presiding officer. Participants shall have the right to present such oral or documentary evidence and to conduct such cross-examination as the presiding officer determines is required for a full and true disclosure of facts. The presiding officer shall receive relevant and material evidence, rule upon offers of proof and exclude all irrelevant, immaterial or unduly repetitious evidence. However, the technicalities of the rules of evidence prevailing in courts of law or equity shall not control the conduct of a Formal Presentation of Views. The presiding officer shall take all necessary action to regulate the course of the Formal Presentation of Views to avoid delay and to maintain order. The presiding officer may exclude the attorney or witness from further participation in the particular Formal Presentation of Views and may render a decision adverse to the interests of the excluded party in his absence.

(2) *Decision.* The presiding officer shall make and file an initial written decision on the matter in question. The decision shall be filed within 10 days after completion of the oral presentation. The decision shall include:

(i) A statement of findings of fact, with specific references to principal supporting items of evidence in the record and conclusions, as well as the reasons or bases therefor, upon all of the material issues of law or discretion presented on the record, and

(ii) An appropriate order.

The presiding officer's decision shall be final and shall constitute the Final Determination of the Secretary unless reversed or modified within 30 days by the Secretary. Notice of the Final Determination shall be given in writing, and transmitted by registered or certified mail, return receipt requested, to all participants in the proceeding. The

Final Determination shall be conclusive with respect to persons whose interests were represented.

[41 FR 19852, May 13, 1976, as amended at 51 FR 34467, Sept. 29, 1986]

§ 3282.153 Public participation in formal or informal presentation of views.

(a) Any interested persons may participate, in writing, in any Formal or Informal Presentation of Views held under the provisions of paragraph (f) or (g) of § 3282.152. The presiding officer shall, to the extent practicable, consider any such written materials.

(b) Any interested person may participate in the oral portion of any Formal or Informal Presentation of Views held under paragraphs (f) and (g) of § 3282.152 unless the presiding officer determines that participation should be limited or barred so as not unduly to prejudice the rights of the parties directly involved or unnecessarily to delay the proceedings.

[51 FR 34468, Sept. 29, 1986]

§ 3282.154 Petitions for formal or informal presentations of views, and requests for extraordinary interim relief.

Any person entitled to a Formal or an Informal Presentation of Views under paragraph (f) or paragraph (g) of § 3282.152 in order to address issues as provided for in § 3282.151(a) may petition the Secretary to initiate such a Presentation of Views. The petition may be accompanied by a request that the Secretary provide appropriate interim relief pending the issuance of the final determination or decision. No interim relief will be granted unless there is a showing of extraordinary cause. Upon receipt of a petition, the Secretary shall grant the petition and issue the notice provided for in § 3282.152(b) for Formal or Informal Presentation of Views, and may grant, deny or defer decision on any request for interim relief.

[51 FR 34468, Sept. 29, 1986]

§ 3282.155 Investigations.

The procedures for investigations and investigational proceedings are set forth in part 3800 of this chapter.

[61 FR 10442, Mar. 13, 1996]

§ 3282.156 Petitions for investigations.

(a) Any person may petition the Secretary in writing to open an investigation into whether noncompliances, defects, serious defects, or imminent safety hazards exist in manufactured homes. A petition shall include the reasons that the petitioner believes warrant an investigation, and it shall state any steps which have previously been taken to remedy the situation. The petition shall include all information known to the petitioner concerning the identity of manufactured homes which may be affected and where those manufactured homes were manufactured. The Secretary shall respond to petitions concerning alleged imminent safety hazards and serious defects within 60 days and to petitions alleging the existence of defects or noncompliances within 120 days.

(b) Any person may petition the Secretary in writing to undertake an investigation for the purpose of determining whether a primary inspection agency should be disqualified. The petition shall set out all facts and information on which the petition is based and a detailed statement of why such information justifies disqualification. The Secretary shall consider such petitions when making determinations on final acceptance and continued acceptance. The Secretary shall respond to such petition within 120 days.

Subpart E—Manufacturer Inspection and Certification Requirements

§ 3282.201 Scope and purpose.

(a) This subpart sets out requirements which must be met by manufacturers of manufactured homes for sale to purchasers in the United States with respect to certification of manufactured home designs, inspection of designs, quality assurance programs, and manufactured home production, and certification of manufactured homes.

Other than references and a general description of responsibilities, this subpart does not set out requirements with respect to remedial actions or reports which must be taken or filed under the Act and these regulations.

(b) The purpose of this subpart is to require manufacturers to participate in a system of design approvals and inspections which serve to assist them in assuring that manufactured homes which they manufacture will conform to Federal standards. Such approvals and inspections provide significant protection to the public by decreasing the number of manufactured homes with possible defects in them, and provide protection to manufacturers by reducing the number of instances in which costly remedial actions must be undertaken after manufactured homes are sold.

§3282.202 Primary inspection agency contracts.

Each manufacturer shall enter into a contract or other agreement with as many Design Inspection Primary Inspection Agencies (DAPIAs) as it wishes and with enough Production Inspection Primary Inspection Agencies (IPIAs) to provide IPIA services for each manufacturing plant as set out in this subpart and in subpart H of this part. In return for the services provided by the DAPIAs and IPIAs, each manufacturer shall pay such reasonable fees as are agreed upon between the manufacturer and the primary inspection agency or, in the case of a State acting as an exclusive IPIA under §3282.3 such fees as may be established by the State.

§3282.203 DAPIA services.

(a) Each manufacturer shall have each manufactured home design and each quality assurance manual which it intends to follow approved by a DAPIA under §3282.361. The manufacturer is free to choose which DAPIA will evaluate and approve its designs and quality assurance materials manufacturer may obtain design and quality assurance manual approval from a single DAPIA regardless of the number of plants in which the design and quality assurance manual will be followed. A manufacturer may also obtain approval

for the same design and quality assurance manual from more than one DAPIA. The choice of which DAPIA or DAPIAs to employ is left to the manufacturer.

(b) The manufacturer shall submit to the DAPIA such information as the DAPIA may require in order to carry out design approvals. This information shall, except where the manufacturer demonstrates to the DAPIA that it is not necessary, include the following:

(1) Construction drawings and/or specifications showing structural details and layouts of frames, floors, walls and roofs, and chassis; material specifications, framing details, door locations, etc., for each floor plan proposed to be manufactured,

(2) Structural analysis and calculations, test data and/or other accepted engineering practices used by the manufacturer to validate the design,

(3) Complete heat loss calculations for each significant variation of home design,

(4) Floor plans showing room arrangement and sizes, window sizes, emergency exists and locations, locations of smoke alarms, fixed appliance range hoods, and other standards related aspects of the manufactured home that can be shown on the floor plans,

(5) Diagrams of the fuel supply system, potable water system and drain, waste and vent systems. The diagrams shall specify the types of materials used, types of fittings and methods of installing required safety equipment,

(6) Wiring diagrams, including circuit allocation of electrical load and branch circuit calculations, a table of the branch circuit protection provided, the type of wiring used, and wiring methods,

(7) Details showing the design of air supply and return systems,

(8) Details of chassis construction, components, connections and running gear including rating capacities of tires,

(9) A list of fixed and portable appliances furnished with the manufactured home, including type of appliance, rating of appliance, and applicable minimum and maximum performance ratings and/or energy requirements,

(10) Detailed manufacturer installation instructions including specifications and procedures for the erection and hook-up of the home at its permanent location, and

(11) Reports of all tests that were run to validate the conformance of the design to the standards.

(c) The manufacturer shall submit to the DAPIA such information as the DAPIA may require in order to carry out quality assurance manual approvals. At a minimum, this information shall include the quality assurance manual for which approval is sought. That manual shall include the manufacturer's quality assurance program, an organizational chart showing the accountability, by position, of the manufacturer's quality control personnel, a description of production tests and test equipment required for compliance with the standards, a station-by-station description of the manufacturing process, a list of quality control inspections required by the manufacturer at each station, and identification by title of each person who will be held accountable for each quality control inspection.

(d) Manufacturers may be required to furnish supplementary information to the DAPIA if the design information or the quality assurance manual is not complete or if any information is not in accordance with accepted engineering practice.

(e) When a manufacturer wishes to make a change in an approved design or quality assurance manual, the manufacturer shall obtain the approval of the DAPIA which approved the design or manual prior to production for sale. The procedures for obtaining such approval are set out in § 3282.361. When applicable under § 3282.605, the IPIA must concur in the change before it can be approved by the DAPIA.

(f) The information to be submitted to a DAPIA under § 3282.203 (b) and (c) may be prepared by the manufacturer's staff or outside consultants, including other DAPIAs. However, a DAPIA may not perform design or quality assurance manual approvals for any manufacturer whose design or manual has been created or prepared in whole or in part by members of the DAPIA's organization or of any affiliated organization.

(g) Each manufacturer shall maintain a copy of the drawings, specifications, and sketches from each approved design received from a DAPIA under § 3282.361(b)(4) in each plant in which manufactured homes are being produced to the design. Each manufacturer shall also maintain in each manufacturing plant a copy of the approved quality assurance manual received from a DAPIA under § 3282.361(c)(3) that is being followed in the plant. These materials shall be kept current and shall be readily accessible for use by the Secretary or other parties acting under these regulations.

[41 FR 19852, May 13, 1976, as amended at 67 FR 12818, Mar. 19, 2002; 80 FR 53727, Sept. 8, 2015]

§ 3282.204 IPIA services.

(a) Each manufacturer shall obtain the services of an IPIA as set out in § 3282.362 for each manufacturing plant operated by the manufacturer.

(b) The manufacturer shall make available to the IPIA operating in each of its plants a copy of the drawings and specifications from the DAPIA approved design and the quality assurance manual for that plant, and the IPIA shall perform an initial factory inspection as set out in § 3282.362(b). If the IPIA issues a deviation report after the initial factory inspection, the manufacturer shall make any corrections or adjustments which are necessary to conform with the DAPIA approved designs and manuals. After the corrections required by the deviation report are completed to the satisfaction of the IPIA, the IPIA shall issue the certification report as described in § 3282.362(b)(2). In certain instances a DAPIA may provide the certification report. (See § 3282.362) The manufacturer shall maintain a current copy of each certification report in the plant to which the certification report relates.

(c) After the certification report has been signed by the IPIA, the manufacturer shall obtain labels from the IPIA and shall affix them to completed manufactured homes as set out in § 3282.362(c)(2). During the initial factory certification, the IPIA may apply labels to manufactured homes which it knows to be in compliance with the standards if it is performing complete inspections of all phases of production of each manufactured home and the manufacturer authorizes it to apply labels.

(d) During the course of production the manufacturer shall maintain a complete set of approved drawings, specifications, and approved design changes for the use of the IPIA's inspector and always available to that inspector when in the manufacturing plant.

(e) If during the course of production, an IPIA finds a failure to conform to a standard exists in a manufactured home under production, the manufacturer must correct the failure to conform in any manufactured home still in the factory and held by distributors or retailers and shall carry out remedial actions under § 3282.416(a) with respect to any other manufactured homes which may contain the same failure to conform.

[41 FR 19852, May 13, 1976, as amended at 78 FR 60199, Oct. 1, 2013]

§ 3282.205 Certification requirements.

(a) Every manufacturer shall make a record of the serial number of each manufactured home produced, and a duly authorized representative of the manufacturer shall certify that each manufactured home has been constructed in accordance with the Federal standards. The manufacturer shall furnish a copy of that certification to the IPIA for the purpose of determining which manufactured homes are subject to the notification and correction requirements of subpart I of this part.

(b) Every manufacturer of manufactured homes shall certify on the data plate as set out in § 3280.5 of chapter XX of 24 CFR and § 3282.362(c)(3) that the manufactured home is designed to comply with the Federal manufactured home construction and safety standards in force at the time of manufacture in addition to providing other information required to be completed on the data plate.

(c) Every manufacturer of manufactured homes shall furnish to the retailer or distributor of each of its man-ufactured homes a certification that such manufactured home, to the best of the manufacturer's knowledge and belief, conforms to all applicable Federal construction and safety standards. This certification shall be in the form of the label provided by the IPIA under § 3282.362(c)(2). The label shall be affixed only at the end of the last stage of production of the manufactured home.

(d) The manufacturer shall apply a label required or allowed by the regulations in this part only to a manufactured home that the manufacturer knows by its inspections to be in compliance with the standards.

[41 FR 19852, May 13, 1976, as amended at 41 FR 24970, June 21, 1976; 61 FR 10860, Mar. 15, 1996]

§ 3282.206 Disagreement with IPIA or DAPIA.

Whenever a manufacturer disagrees with a finding by a DAPIA or an IPIA acting in accordance with subpart H of this part, the manufacturer may request a Formal or Informal Presentation of Views as provided in § 3282.152. The manufacturer shall not, however, produce manufactured homes pursuant to designs which have not been approved by a DAPIA or produce manufactured homes which the relevant IPIA believes not to conform to the standards unless and until:

(a) The Secretary determines that the manufacturer is correct in believing the design of the manufactured home conforms to the standards; or

(b) Extraordinary interim relief is granted under § 3282.154; or

(c) The DAPIA or IPIA otherwise resolves the disagreement.

[41 FR 19852, May 13, 1976, as amended at 51 FR 34468, Sept. 29, 1986; 61 FR 10860, Mar. 15, 1996]

§ 3282.207 Manufactured home consumer manual requirements.

(a) The manufacturer shall provide a consumer manual with each manufactured home that enters the first stage of production on or after July 31, 1977, pursuant to section 617 of the National Manufactured Housing Construction and Safety Standards Act, 42 U.S.C. 5416.

(b) The manufacturer shall provide the consumer manual by placing a manual in each such manufactured home before the manufactured home leaves the manufacturing plant. The manual shall be placed in a conspicuous location in a manner likely to assure that it is not removed until the purchaser removes it.

(c) If a manufacturer is informed that a purchaser did not receive a consumer manual, the manufacturer shall provide the appropriate manual to the purchaser within 30 days of being so informed.

(d) No retailer or distributor may interfere with the distribution of the consumer manual. When necessary, the retailer or distributor shall take any appropriate steps to assure that the purchaser receives a consumer manual from the manufacturer.

(e) *Dispute resolution information.* (1) The manufacturer must include the following language under a heading of "Dispute Resolution Process" in the consumer manual:

Many states have a consumer assistance or dispute resolution program that homeowners may use to resolve problems with manufacturers, retailers, or installers concerning defects in their manufactured homes that render part of the home unfit for its intended use. Such state programs may include a process to resolve a dispute among a manufacturer, a retailer, and an installer about who will correct the defect. In states where there is not a dispute resolution program that meets the federal requirements, the HUD Manufactured Home Dispute Resolution Program will operate. These are "HUD-administered states." The HUD Manufactured Home Dispute Resolution Program is not for cosmetic or minor problems in the home. You may contact the HUD Manufactured Housing Program Office at (202) 708–6423 or (800) 927–2891, or visit the HUD website at *www.hud.gov* to determine whether your state has a state program or whether you should use the HUD Manufactured Home Dispute Resolution Program. Contact information for state programs is also available on the HUD website. If your state has a state program, please contact the state for information about the program, how it operates, and what steps to take to request dispute resolution. When there is no state dispute resolution program, a homeowner may use the HUD Manufactured Home Dispute Resolution Program to resolve disputes among the manufacturer, retailer, and installer about responsibility for the correction or repair of defects in the manufactured home

that were reported during the 1-year period starting on the date of installation. Even after the 1-year period, manufacturers have continuing responsibility to review certain problems that affect the intended use of the manufactured home or its parts, but for which correction may no longer be required under federal law.

(2) The manufacturer must include the following language under a heading of "Additional Information " HUD Manufactured Home Dispute Resolution Program" in the consumer manual:

The steps and information outlined below apply only to the HUD Manufactured Home Dispute Resolution Program that operates in HUD-administered states, as described under the heading "Dispute Resolution Information" in this manual. Under the HUD Manufactured Home Dispute Resolution Program, homeowners must report defects to the manufacturer, retailer, installer, a State Administrative Agency, or HUD within 1 year after the date of the first installation. Homeowners are encouraged to report defects in writing, including, but not limited to, email, written letter, certified mail, or fax, but they may also make a report by telephone. To demonstrate that the report was made within 1 year after the date of installation, homeowners should report defects in a manner that will create a dated record of the report: for example, by certified mail, by fax, or by email. When making a report by telephone, homeowners are encouraged to make a note of the phone call, including names of conversants, date, and time. No particular format is required to submit a report of an alleged defect, but any such report should at a minimum include a description of the alleged defect, the name of the homeowner, and the address of the home.

Homeowners are encouraged to send reports of an alleged defect first to the manufacturer, retailer, or installer of the manufactured home, or a State Administrative Agency. Reports of alleged defects may also be sent to HUD at: HUD, Office of Regulatory Affairs and Manufactured Housing, Attn: Dispute Resolution, 451 Seventh Street, SW., Washington, DC 20410–8000; faxed to (202) 708–4213; e-mailed to *mhs@hud.gov*, or reported telephonically at (202) 708–6423 or (800) 927–2891.

If, after taking the steps outlined above, the homeowner does not receive a satisfactory response from the manufacturer, retailer, or installer, the homeowner may file a dispute resolution request with the dispute resolution provider in writing, or by making a request by phone. No particular format is required to make a request for dispute resolution, but the request should generally include the following information:

(1) The name, address, and contact information of the homeowner;

(2) The name and contact information of the manufacturer, retailer, and installer of the manufactured home;

(3) The date or dates the report of the alleged defect was made;

(4) Identification of the entities or persons to whom each report of the alleged defect was made and the method that was used to make the report;

(5) The date of installation of the manufactured home affected by the alleged defect; and

(6) A description of the alleged defect.

Information about the dispute resolution provider and how to make a request for dispute resolution is available at *http://www.hud.gov* or by contacting the Office of Manufactured Housing Programs at (202) 708–6423 or (800) 927–2891.

A screening agent will review the request and, as appropriate, forward the request to the manufacturer, retailer, installer, and mediator. The mediator will mediate the dispute and attempt to facilitate a settlement. The parties to a settlement include, as applicable, the manufacturer, retailer, and installer. If the parties are unable to reach a settlement that results in correction or repair of the alleged defect, any party or the homeowner may request nonbinding arbitration. Should any party refuse to participate, the arbitration shall proceed without that party's input. Once the arbitrator makes a non-binding recommendation, the arbitrator will forward it to the parties and HUD. HUD will have the option of adopting, modifying, or rejecting the recommendation when issuing an order requiring the responsible party or parties to make any corrections or repairs in the home. At any time before HUD issues a final order, the parties may submit an offer of settlement to HUD that may, at HUD's discretion, be incorporated into the order.

In circumstances where the parties agree that one or more of them, and not the homeowner, is responsible for the alleged defect, the parties will have the opportunity to resolve the dispute outside of the HUD Mediation and Arbitration process by using the Alternative Process. Homeowners will maintain the right to be informed in writing of the outcome when the Alternative Process is used, within 5 days of the outcome. At any time after 30 days of the Alternative Process notification, any participant or the homeowner may invoke the HUD Manufactured Home Dispute Resolution Program and proceed to mediation.

The HUD Manufactured Home Dispute Resolution Program is not a warranty program and does not replace the manufacturer's or any other warranty program.

(f) If a consumer manual or a change or revision to a manual does not substantially comply with the guidelines issued by HUD, the manufacturer shall cease distribution of the consumer manual and shall provide a corrected manual for each manufactured home for which the inadequate or incorrect manual or revision was provided. A manual substantially complies with the guidelines if it includes the language in paragraph (e) of this section and presents current material on each of the subjects covered in the guidelines in sufficient detail to inform consumers about the operation, maintenance, and repair of manufactured homes. An updated copy of guidelines published in the FEDERAL REGISTER on March 15, 1996, can be obtained by contacting the Office of Manufactured Housing and Regulatory Functions, Department of Housing and Urban Development, 451 Seventh Street, SW., Washington, DC, 20410; the Information Center, Department of Housing and Urban Development, Room 1202, 451 Seventh Street, SW., Washington, DC, 20410; or any HUD Area or State Office.

[61 FR 10860, Mar. 15, 1996, as amended at 72 FR 27228, May 14, 2007]

§ 3282.208 Remedial actions—general description.

(a) *Notification.* A manufacturer may be required to provide formal notice to manufactured home owners and retailers, as set out in subpart I of this part, if the manufacturer, the Secretary, or a State Administrative Agency determines under that subpart that an imminent safety hazard, serious defect, defect, or noncompliance exists or may exist in a manufactured home produced by that manufacturer.

(b) *Correction.* A manufacturer may be required to correct imminent safety hazards and serious defects which the manufacturer or the Secretary determines under subpart I exist in manufactured homes produced by the manufacturer. This correction would be carried out in addition to the sending of formal notice as described in paragraph (a) of this section.

(c) *Cooperation.* The manufacturer shall be responsible for working with the DAPIA, IPIA, any SAA, the Secretary, and the Secretary's agent as necessary in the course of carrying out investigations and remedial actions under subpart I.

(d) *Avoidance of formalities.* The provisions for notification and required correction outlined in paragraphs (a) and (b) of this section and described more fully in subpart I may be waived or avoided in certain circumstances under that subpart.

§ 3282.209 Report requirements.

The manufacturer shall submit reports to the PIAs, SAAs, and the Secretary as required by subpart L of these regulations.

§ 3282.210 Payment of monitoring fee.

(a) Each manufacturer shall pay the monitoring fee established under §§ 3282.307 and 3282.454 for each transportable section of each manufactured housing unit that it manufactures under the Federal standards.

(b) The monitoring fee shall be paid in the form of a check made payable to the Secretary or the Secretary's agent. The manufacturer shall give to the IPIA (or to any other person or agency designated in writing by the Secretary) the required check in the amount of the number of labels, as required by § 3282.365, multiplied by the amount of the fee per transportable section of each manufactured housing unit.

[50 FR 28398, July 12, 1985]

§ 3282.211 Record of purchasers.

(a) *Information requirements for purchasers.* (1) Every manufacturer of manufactured homes shall, for each manufactured home manufactured under the Federal standards, provide with the manufactured home a booklet containing at least 3 detachable cards as described in paragraph (a)(2) of this section. On the front of the booklet, in bold faced type, shall be printed the following language:

"Keep this booklet with your manufactured home. Title VI of the Housing and Community Development Act of 1974 provides you with protection against certain construction and safety hazards in your manufactured home. To help assure your protection, the manufacturer of your manufactured home needs the information which these cards, when completed and mailed, will supply. If you bought your home from a re-tailer, please be sure that your retailer has completed and mailed a card for you. If you acquired your home from someone who is not a retailer, you should promptly fill out and send a card to the manufacturer. It is important that you keep this booklet and give it to any person who buys the manufactured home from you."

(2) The detachable cards shall contain blanks for the following information:

(i) Name and address of the retailer or other person selling the manufactured home to the purchaser;

(ii) Name and complete mailing address of the manufactured home purchaser;

(iii) Address where the manufactured home will be located, if not the same as item (a)(2)(ii) of this section.

(iv) Date of sale to the purchaser;

(v) Month, day and year of manufacture;

(vi) Identification number of the manufactured home;

(vii) Model and/or type designation of the manufactured home as provided by the manufacturer; and

(viii) A designation of the zones for which the manufactured home is equipped, as set forth in § 3280.305 in this title.

Additionally, the cards shall have the name and address of the manufacturer printed clearly on the reverse side and shall contain adequate postage or business reply privileges to ensure return to the manufacturer. The manufacturer shall have the responsibility for filing in the blanks on the cards for paragraphs (a)(2) (v), (vi), (vii), and (viii) of this section. The manufacturer shall maintain all cards received so that the manufacturer has a readily accessible record of the current purchaser or owner and the current address of all manufactured homes manufactured by it for which a card has been received.

Subpart F—Retailer and Distributor Responsibilities

§ 3282.251 Scope and purpose.

(a) This subpart sets out the responsibilities which shall be met by distributors and retailers with respect to manufactured homes manufactured after the effective date of the standards for sale to purchasers in the United States. It prohibits the sale, lease, or offer for sale or lease of manufactured homes known by the distributor or retailer not to be in conformance with the standards, and it includes responsibilities for maintaining certain records and assisting in the gathering of certain information.

(b) The purpose of this subpart is to inform distributors and retailers when they may sell manufactured homes, when they are prohibited from selling manufactured homes, and what they may do in order to prepare a manufactured home for sale if it is not in conformance with the standards.

(c) For purposes of this part, any manufacturer or distributor who sells, leases, or offers for sale or lease a manufactured home to a purchaser shall be a retailer for purposes of that transaction.

§3282.252 Prohibition of sale.

(a) No distributor or retailer shall make use of any means of transportation affecting interstate or foreign commerce or the mails to sell, lease, or offer for sale or lease in the United States any manufactured home manufactured on or after the effective date of an applicable standard unless:

(1) There is affixed to the manufactured home a label certifying that the manufactured home conforms to applicable standards as required by §3282.205(c), and

(2) The distributor or retailer, acting as a reasonable distributor or retailer, does not know that the manufactured home does not conform to any applicable standards.

(b) This prohibition applies to any affected manufactured homes until the completion of the entire sales transaction. A sales transaction with a purchaser is considered completed when all the goods and services that the retailer agreed to provide at the time the contract was entered into have been provided. Completion of a retail sale will be at the time the retailer completes installation of the manufactured home, if the retailer has agreed to provide the installation, or at the time the retailer delivers the home to a transporter, if the retailer has not agreed to transport or install the manufactured

home. The sale is also complete upon delivery to the site if the retailer has not agreed to provide installation as completion of sale, except that any sale or lease under subpart M and as provided in §3286.117(a) will not be considered complete until the purchaser or lessor, as applicable, has been provided with a final site inspection report.

(c) This prohibition of sale does not apply to manufactured homes which are placed in production prior to the effective date of the standards, and it does not apply to "used" manufactured homes which are being sold or offered for sale after the first purchase in good faith for purposes other than the resale.

[41 FR 19852, May 13, 1976, as amended at 80 FR 53727, Sept. 8, 2015]

§3282.253 Removal of prohibition of sale.

(a) If a distributor or retailer has a manufactured home in its possession or a manufactured home with respect to a sales transaction has not yet been completed, and a distributor or retailer knows as a result of notification by the manufacturer or otherwise that the manufactured home contains a failure to conform or imminent safety hazard, the distributor or retailer may seek the remedies available under §3282.415.

(b) When, in accordance with §3282.415, a manufacturer corrects a failure to conform to the applicable standard or an imminent safety hazard, the distributor or retailer, acting as a reasonable distributor or retailer, may accept the remedies provided by the manufacturer as having corrected the failure to conform or imminent safety hazard. The distributor or retailer, therefore, may sell, lease, or offer for sale or lease any manufactured home so corrected by the manufacturer.

(c) When a distributor or retailer is authorized by a manufacturer to correct a failure to conform to the applicable standard or an imminent safety hazard and completes the correction in accordance with the manufacturer's instructions, the distributor or retailer may sell, or lease or offer for sale or lease the manufactured home in question, provided that the distributor or retailer, acting as a reasonable distributor or retailer knows that the manufactured home conforms to the standards. A distributor or retailer and a manufacturer, at the manufacturer's option, may agree in advance that the distributor or retailer is authorized to make such corrections as the manufacturer believes are within the expertise of the dealer.

(d) If the corrections made under paragraphs (b) and (c) of this section do not bring the manufactured home into conformance or correct the imminent safety hazard, the provisions of § 3282.415 will continue in effect prior to completion of the sales transaction.

[41 FR 19852, May 13, 1976, as amended at 78 FR 60199, Oct. 1, 2013]

§ 3282.254 Distributor and retailer alterations.

(a) If a distributor or retailer alters a manufactured home in such a way as to create an imminent safety hazard or to create a condition which causes a failure to conform with applicable Federal standards, the manufactured home affected may not be sold, leased, or offered for sale or lease.

(b) After correction by the distributor or retailer of the failure to conform or imminent safety hazard, the corrected manufactured home may be sold, leased, or offered for sale or lease.

(c) Distributors and retailers shall maintain complete records of all alterations made under paragraphs (a) and (b) of this section.

§ 3282.255 Completion of information card.

(a) Whenever a distributor or retailer sells a manufactured home subject to the standards to a purchaser, the distributor or retailer shall fill out the card with information provided by the purchaser and shall send the card to the manufacturer. (See § 3282.211.)

(b) Whenever a distributor or retailer sells a manufactured home to an owner which was originally manufactured under the standards, the distributor or retailer shall similarly use one of the detachable cards which was originally provided with the manufactured home. If such a card is no longer available, the distributor or retailer shall obtain the information which the card would require and send it to the manufacturer of the manufactured home in an appropriate format.

§ 3282.256 Distributor or retailer complaint handling.

(a) When a distributor or retailer believes that a manufactured home in its possession which it has not yet sold to a purchaser contains an imminent safety hazard, serious defect, defect, or noncompliance, the distributor or retailer shall refer the matter to the manufacturer for remedial action under § 3282.415. If the distributor or retailer is not satisfied with the action taken by the manufacturer, it may refer the matter to the SAA in the state in which the manufactured home is located, or to the Secretary if there is no such SAA.

(b) Where a distributor or retailer receives a consumer complaint or other information concerning a manufactured home sold by the distributor or retailer, indicating the possible existence of an imminent safety hazard, serious defect, defect, or noncompliance in the manufactured home, the distributor or retailer shall refer the matter to the manufacturer.

Subpart G—State Administrative Agencies

§ 3282.301 General—scope.

This subpart sets out procedures to be followed and requirements to be met by States which wish to participate as State Administrative Agencies (SAA) under the Federal standards enforcement program. Requirements relating to States which wish to participate as primary inspection agencies under the Federal standards enforcement program are set out in subpart H of this part. Requirements which States must meet in order to receive full or conditional approval as SAAs and the responsibilities of such agencies are set out in § 3282.302. Reporting requirements for approved and conditionally approved SAAs are set out in subpart L.

§ 3282.302 State plan.

A State wishing to qualify and act as an SAA under this subpart shall make a State Plan Application under this section. The State Plan Application shall be made to the Administrator, Office of Manufactured Housing Programs, Office of Housing, Department of Housing and Urban Development, 451 7th Street SW., Washington, DC 20410, and shall include:

(a) An original and one copy of a cover sheet which shall show the following:

(1) The name and address of the State agency designated as the sole agency responsible for administering the plan throughout the State,

(2) The name of the administrator in charge of the agency,

(3) The name, title, address, and phone number of the person responsible for handling consumer complaints concerning standards related problems in manufactured homes under subpart I of this part,

(4) A list of personnel who will carry out the State plan,

(5) The number of manufactured home manufacturing plants presently operating in the State,

(6) The estimated total number of manufactured homes manufactured in the State per year,

(7) The estimated total number of manufactured homes set up in the State per year, and

(8) A certification signed by the administrator in charge of the designated State agency stating that, if it is approved by the Secretary, the State plan will be carried out in full, and that the regulations issued under the Act shall be followed,

(b) An original and one copy of appropriate materials which:

(1) Demonstrate how the designated State agency shall ensure effective handling of consumer complaints and other information referred to it that relate to noncompliances, defects, serious defects or imminent safety hazards as set out in subpart I of this part, including the holding of Formal and Informal Presentations of Views and the fulfilling of all other responsibilities of SAAs as set out in this subpart G,

(2) Provide that personnel of the designated agency shall, under State law or as agents of HUD, have the right at any reasonable time to enter and inspect all factories, warehouses, or establishments in the State in which manufactured homes are manufactured,

(3) Provide for the imposition under State authority of civil and criminal penalties which are identical to those set out in section 611 of the Act, 42 U.S.C. 5410 except that civil penalties shall be payable to the State rather than to the United States,

(4) Provide for the notification and correction procedures under subpart I of this part where the SAA is to act under that subpart by providing the required approval by the SAA of the plan for notification and correction described in §§3282.408, 3282.409, and 3282.410, including approval of the number of units that may be affected and the proposed repairs, and by providing for approval of corrective actions where appropriate under subpart I,

(5) Provide for oversight by the SAA of:

(i) Remedial actions carried out by manufacturers for which the SAA approved the plan for notification and correction or for which the SAA has waived formal notification under subpart I.

(ii) A manufacturer's handling of consumer complaints and other information under subpart I as to plants located in the State.

(6) Provide for the setting of monitoring inspection fees in accordance with guidelines established by the Secretary and provide for participation in the fee distribution system set out in §3282.307.

(7) Contain satisfactory assurances in whatever form is appropriate under State law that the designated agency has or will have the legal authority necessary to carry out the State plan as submitted for full or conditional approval,

(8) Contain satisfactory assurances that the designated agency has or will have, in its own staff or provided by other agencies of the state or otherwise, the personnel, qualified by education or experience necessary to carry out the State plan,

(9) Include the resumes of administrative personnel in policy making positions and of all inspectors and engineers to be utilized by the designated agency in carrying out the State plan,

(10) Include a certification that none of the personnel who may be involved in carrying out the State plan in any way are subject to any conflict of interest of the type discussed in § 3282.359 or otherwise, except that members of councils, committees, or similar bodies providing advice to the designated agency are not subject to the requirement,

(11) Include an estimate of the cost to the State of carrying out all activities called for in the State plan, under this section and § 3282.303, which estimate shall be broken down by particular function and indicate the correlation between the estimate and the number of manufactured homes manufactured in the State and the number of manufactured homes imported into the State, and the relationship of these factors to any fees currently charged and any fees charged during the preceding two calendar years. A description of all current and past State activities with respect to manufactured homes shall be included with this estimate.

(12) Give satisfactory assurances that the State shall devote adequate funds to carrying out its State plan,

(13) Indicate that State Law requires manufacturers, distributors, and retailers in the State to make reports pursuant to section 614 of the Act 42 U.S.C. 5413 and this chapter of these regulations in the same manner and to the same extent as if the State plan were not in effect,

(14) Provide that the designated agency shall make reports to the Secretary as required by subpart L of this part in such form and containing such information as the Secretary shall from time to time require,

(c) A state plan may be granted conditional approval if all of the requirements of § 3282.302 (a) and (b) are met except paragraphs (b)(2), (b)(3), (b)(6) or (b)(13). When conditional approval is given, the state shall not be considered approved under section 623 of the Act, 42 U.S.C. 5422, but it will participate in all phases of the program as called for in its State plan. Conditional approval shall last for a maximum of five years, by which time all requirements shall be met for full approval, or conditional approval shall lapse. However, the Sec-

retary may for good cause grant an extension of conditional approval upon petition by the SAA.

(d) If a State wishes to discontinue participation in the Federal enforcement program as an SAA, it shall provide the Secretary with a minimum of 90 days notice.

(e) *Exclusive IPIA status.* (1) A State that wishes to act as an exclusive IPIA under § 3282.352 shall so indicate in its State Plan and shall include in the information provided under paragraph (b)(11) of this section the fee schedule for the State's activities as an IPIA and the relationship between the proposed fees and the other information provided under paragraph (b)(11) of this section. If the Secretary determines that the fees to be charged by a State acting as an IPIA are unreasonable, the Secretary shall not grant the State status as an exclusive IPIA.

(2) The State shall also demonstrate in its State Plan that it has the present capability to act as an IPIA for all plants operating in the State.

[41 FR 19852, May 13, 1976, as amended at 47 FR 5888, Feb. 9, 1982; 51 FR 34468, Sept. 29, 1986; 61 FR 10860, Mar. 15, 1996; 78 FR 60199, Oct. 1, 2013]

§ 3282.303 State plan—suggested provisions.

The following are not required to be included in the State plan, but they are urged as necessary to provide full consumer protection and assurances of manufactured home safety:

(a) Provision for monitoring of retailers' lots within the State for transit damage, seal tampering, and retailer performance generally,

(b) Provision of approvals of all alterations made to certified manufactured homes by retailer in the State. Under this program, the State would assure that alterations did not result in the failure of the manufactured home to comply with the standards.

(c) Provision for monitoring of the installation of manufactured homes set up in the State to assure that the homes are properly installed and, where necessary, tied down,

(d) Provision for inspection of used manufactured homes and requirements under State authority that used manufactured homes meet a minimal level of safety and durability at the time of sale, and,

(e) Provision for regulation of manufactured home transportation over the road to the extent that such regulation is not preempted by Federal authority.

§3282.304 Inadequate State plan.

If the Secretary determines that a State plan submitted under this subpart is not adequate, the designated State agency shall be informed of the additions and corrections required for approval. A revised State plan shall be submitted within 30 days of receipt of such determination. If the revised State plan is inadequate or if the State fails to resubmit within the 30 day period or otherwise indicates that it does not intend to change its State plan as submitted, the Secretary shall notify the designated State agency that the State plan is not approved and that it has a right to a hearing on the disapproval in accordance with subpart D of this part.

§3282.305 State plan approval.

The Secretary's approval or conditional approval of a State plan Application shall qualify that State to perform the functions for which it has been approved.

§3282.306 Withdrawal of State approval.

The Secretary shall, on the basis of reports submitted by the State, and on the basis of HUD monitoring, make a continuing evaluation of the manner in which each State is carrying out its State plan and shall submit the reports of such evaluation to the appropriate committees of the Congress. Whenever the Secretary finds, after affording due notice and opportunity for a hearing in accordance with subpart D of this part, that in the administration of the State program there is a failure to comply substantially with any provision of the State plan or that the State plan has become inadequate, the Secretary shall notify the State of withdrawal of approval or conditional approval of the State program. The State program shall cease to be in effect at such time as the Secretary may establish.

§3282.307 Monitoring inspection fee establishment and distribution.

(a) Each approved State shall establish a monitoring inspection fee in an amount required by the Secretary. This fee shall be an amount paid by each manufactured home manufacturer in the State for each transportable section of each manufactured housing unit produced by the manufacturer in that State. In non-approved and conditionally-approved States, the fee shall be set by the Secretary.

(b) The monitoring inspection fee shall be paid by the manufacturer to the Secretary or to the Secretary's Agent, who shall distribute a portion of the fees collected from all manufactured home manufacturers among the approved and conditionally-approved States in accordance with an agreement between the Secretary and the States and based upon the following formula:

(1) $9.00 of the monitoring inspection fee collected for each transportable section of each new manufactured housing unit that, after leaving the manufacturing plant, is first located on the premises of a retailer, distributor, or purchaser in that State; plus

(2) $2.50 of the monitoring inspection fee collected for each transportable section of each new manufactured housing unit produced in a manufacturing plant in that State.

(c) A portion of the monitoring inspection fee collected also shall be distributed by the Secretary or the Secretary's Agent based on the extent of participation of the State in the Joint Team Monitoring Program set out in §3282.308.

(d) To assure that a State devotes adequate funds to carry out its State Plan, a State may impose an additional reasonable inspection fee to offset expenses incurred by that State in conducting inspections. Such fee shall not exceed that amount which is the difference between the amount of funds distributed to the State as provided in paragraph (b) of this section and the amount necessary to cover the costs of inspections. Such fee shall be part of the State Plan pursuant to §3282.302(b) (11) and (12) and shall be subject to the approval of the Secretary pursuant to §3282.305.

(e) The Secretary may establish by notice in the FEDERAL REGISTER a monitoring inspection fee which is to be paid by manufacturers for each transportable section of each manufactured housing unit manufactured in nonapproved and conditionally approved States as described in § 3282.210. To determine the amount of the inspection fee to be paid for each transportable section of each manufactured home, the Secretary shall divide the (estimated) number of transportable sections of manufactured homes (based on recent industry production figures) into the anticipated aggregate cost of conducting the inspection program in the foreseeable feature. The time period selected for projecting the Department's inspection-related costs and number of transportable sections need not always be the same, but must be for a period of sufficient duration to provide for access to reasonable underlying data. To determine the aggregate cost of conducting the inspection program, the Secretary shall calculate the sum necessary to support:

(1) Inspection-related activities of State Administrative Agencies;

(2) Inspection-related activities performed by the Department of Housing and Urban Development;

(3) Inspection-related activities performed by monitoring inspection contractors;

(4) Miscellaneous activities involving the performance of inspection-related activities by the Department, including on-site inspections on an ad hoc basis; and

(5) Maintenance of adequate funds to offset short-term fluctuations in costs that do not warrant revising the fee under the authority of this section.

(f) The Secretary may at any time revise the amount of the fees established under paragraph (a) or (e) of this section by placing a notice of the amount of the revised fee in the FEDERAL REGISTER.

[50 FR 28398, July 12, 1985, as amended at 56 FR 65186, Dec. 16, 1991]

§ 3282.308 State participation in monitoring of primary inspection agencies.

(a) An SAA may provide personnel to participate in joint team monitoring of primary inspection agencies as set out in subpart J. If an SAA wishes to do so, it must include in its State plan a list of what personnel would be supplied for the teams, their qualifications, and how many person-years the State would supply. All personnel will be subject to approval by the Secretary or the Secretary's agent. A person-year is 2,080 hours of work.

(b) If an SAA wishes to monitor the performance of primary inspection agencies acting within the State, it must include in its State plan a description of how extensively, how often, and by whom this will be carried out. This monitoring shall be coordinated by the Secretary, or the Secretary's agent with monitoring carried out by joint monitoring teams, and in no event shall an SAA provide monitoring where the State is also acting as a primary inspection agency.

§ 3282.309 Formal and informal presentations of views held by SAAs.

(a) When an SAA is the appropriate agency to hold a Formal or Informal Presentation of Views under § 3282.412 of subpart I, the SAA shall follow the procedures set out in §§ 3282.152 and 3282.153, with the SAA acting as the Secretary otherwise would under that section. Where § 3282.152 requires publication of notice in the FEDERAL REGISTER, the SAA shall, to the maximum extent possible, provide equivalent notice throughout the State by publication in the newspaper or newspapers having statewide coverage or otherwise. The determination of whether to provide an Informal Presentation of Views under § 3282.152(f), or a Formal Presentation of Views under § 3282.152(g), is left to the SAA.

(b) Notwithstanding the provisions of § 3282.152(f)(2) and (g)(2) relating to the conclusive effect of a final determination, any party, in a proceeding held at an SAA under this section, including specifically the owners of affected manufactured homes, States in which affected manufactured homes are located, consumer groups representing affected owners and manufacturers (but limited to parties with similar substantial interest) may appeal to the Secretary in writing any Final Determination by an SAA which is adverse to the interest of that party. This appeal on the record shall be made within 30 days of the date on which the Final Determination was made by the SAA.

[41 FR 19852, May 13, 1976, as amended at 51 FR 34468, Sept. 29, 1986; 78 FR 60199, Oct. 1, 2013]

Subpart H—Primary Inspection Agencies

§3282.351 General.

(a) This subpart sets out the requirements which must be met by States or private organizations which wish to qualify as primary inspection agencies under these regulations. It also sets out the various functions which will be carried out by primary inspection agencies.

(b) There are four basic functions which are performed by primary inspection agencies:

(1) Approval of the manufacturer's manufactured home design to assure that it is in compliance with the standard;

(2) Approval of the manufacturer's quality control program to assure that it is compatible with the design;

(3) Approval of the manufacturer's plant facility and manufacturing process to assure that the manufacturer can perform its approved quality control program and can produce manufactured homes in conformance with its approved design, and

(4) Performance of ongoing inspections of the manufacturing process in each manufacturing plant to assure that the manufacturer is continuing to perform its approved quality control program and, with respect to those aspects of manufactured homes inspected, is continuing to produce manufactured homes in performance with its approved designs and in conformance with the standards (see §3282.362(c)(1)).

(c) There are two types of primary inspection agencies which perform these functions:

(1) Those which approve designs and quality control programs (Design Approval Primary Inspection Agencies—DAPIAs) and

(2) Those which approve plants and perform ongoing inspections in the manufacturing plants (Production Inspection Primary Inspection Agencies—IPIAs).

(d) States and private organizations whose submissions under this subpart are acceptable shall be granted provisional acceptance. Final acceptance shall be conditioned upon adequate performance, which will be determined through monitoring of the actions of the primary inspection agencies. Monitoring of all primary inspection agencies shall be carried out as set out in subpart J. HUD accepted agencies can perform DAPIA functions for any manufacturer in any State and IPIA functions in any State except those in which the State has been approved to act as the exclusive IPIA under §3282.352.

(e) Primary inspection agencies approved under this subpart may contract with manufactured home manufacturers (see §3282.202) to provide the services set out in this subpart. Any PIA which charges fees which are excessive in relation to the services rendered shall be subject to disqualification under §3282.356.

§3282.352 State exclusive IPIA functions.

(a) Any State which has an approved State Administrative Agency may, if accepted as an IPIA, act as the exclusive IPIA within the State. A State which acts as an IPIA but is not approved as an SAA may not act as the exclusive IPIA in the State. A State which acts as an exclusive IPIA shall be staffed to provide IPIA services to all manufacturers within the state and may not charge unreasonable fees for those services.

(b) States which wish to act as exclusive IPIAs shall apply for approval to do so in their State plan applications. They shall specify the fees they will charge for IPIA services and shall submit proposed fee revisions to the Secretary prior to instituting any change in fees. If at any time the Secretary finds that those fees are not commensurate with the fees generally being charged for similar services, the Secretary will withhold or revoke approval to act as an exclusive IPIA. States acting as DAPIAs and also as exclusive IPIAs shall establish separate fees for the two functions and shall specify

169

what additional services (such as approval of design changes and full time inspections) these fees cover. As provided in § 3282.302(b)(11), each State shall submit fee schedules for its activities and, where appropriate, the fees presently charged for DAPIA and IPIA services, and any fees charged for DAPIA and IPIA services during the preceding two calendar years.

(c) A State's status as an exclusive IPIA shall commence upon approval of the State Plan Application and acceptance of the State's submission under § 3282.355. Where a private organization accepted or provisionally accepted as an IPIA under this subpart H is operating in a manufacturing plant within the State on the date the State's status as an exclusive IPIA commences, the private organization may provide IPIA services in that plant for 90 days after that date.

[61 FR 10861, Mar. 15, 1996]

§ 3282.353 Submission format.

States and private organizations that wish to act as primary inspection agencies shall submit to the Administrator, Office of Manufactured Housing Programs, Office of Housing, Department of Housing and Urban Development, 451 7th Street SW., Washington, DC 20410, an application that includes the following:

(a) A cover sheet which shall show the following:

(1) Name and address of the party making the application;

(2) The capacity (DAPIA, IPIA) in which the party wishes to be approved to act;

(3) A list of the key personnel who will perform the various functions required under these regulations;

(4) The number of manufactured home manufacturers and manufacturing plants for which the submitting party proposes to act in each of the capacities for which it wishes to be approved to act;

(5) The estimated total number of manufactured homes produced by those manufacturers and in those plants per year;

(6) The number of years the proposed primary inspection agency has been actively engaged in the enforcement of manufactured home standards; and

(7) A certification by the party applying that it will follow the Federal manufactured home construction and safety standards set out at 24 CFR part 3280 and any interpretations of those standards which may be made by the Secretary.

(b) A detailed schedule of fees to be charged broken down by the services for which they will be charged.

(c) A detailed description of how the submitting party intends to carry out all of the functions for which it wishes to be approved under this subpart, with appropriate cross-references to sections of this subpart, including examples and complete descriptions of all reports, tests, and evaluations which the party would be required to make. Where appropriate, later sections of this subpart identify particular items which must be included in the submission. The Secretary may request further detailed information, when appropriate.

(d) A party wishing to be approved as a DAPIA shall submit a copy of a manufactured home design that it has approved (or if it has not approved a design, one that it has evaluated and a deviation report showing where the design is not in conformance with the standards) and a copy of a quality assurance manual that it has approved (or if it was not approved a manual, one that it has evaluated and a deviation report showing where the manual is inadequate).

(e) A party wishing to be approved as an IPIA shall submit a copy of a certification report which it has prepared for a manufactured home plant or, if it has not prepared such a report, an evaluation of a manufacturing plant which it has inspected with a description of what changes shall be made before a certification report can be issued. A party that has not previously inspected manufactured homes may nevertheless be accepted on the basis of the qualifications of its personnel and its commitment to perform the required functions.

[41 FR 19852, May 13, 1976, as amended at 61 FR 10861, Mar. 15, 1996; 78 FR 60199, Oct. 1, 2013]

§ 3282.354 Submittal of false information or refusal to submit information.

The submittal of false information or the refusal to submit information required under this subpart may be sufficient cause for the Secretary to revoke or withhold acceptance.

§ 3282.355 Submission acceptance.

(a) A party whose submission is determined by the Department to be adequate shall be granted provisional acceptance until December 15, 1976, or for a six month period from the date of such determination, whichever is later.

(b) Final acceptance of a party to act as a primary inspection agency will be contingent upon adequate performance during the period of provisional acceptance as determined through monitoring carried out under subpart J and upon satisfactory acceptance under § 3282.361(e) or § 3282.362(e). Final acceptance shall be withheld if performance is inadequate.

(c) Continued acceptance as a primary inspection agency shall be contingent upon continued adequacy of performance as determined through monitoring carried out under subpart J. If the Secretary determines that a primary inspection agency that has been granted final acceptance is performing inadequately, the Secretary shall suspend the acceptance, and the primary inspection agency shall be entitled to a Formal or Informal Presentation of Views as set out in subpart D of this part.

[41 FR 19852, May 13, 1976, as amended at 51 FR 34468, Sept. 29, 1986; 61 FR 10861, Mar. 15, 1996]

§ 3282.356 Disqualification and requalification of primary inspection agencies.

(a) The Secretary, based on monitoring reports or on other reliable information, may determine that a primary inspection agency which has been accepted under this subpart is not adequately carrying out one or more of its required functions. In so determining, the Secretary shall consider the impact of disqualification on manufacturers and other affected parties and shall seek to assure that the manufacturing process is not disrupted unnecessarily.

Whenever the Secretary disqualifies a primary inspection agency under this section, the primary inspection agency shall have a right to a Formal or Informal Presentation of Views under subpart D of this part.

(b) Interested persons may petition the Secretary to disqualify a primary inspection agency under the provisions of § 3282.156(b).

(c) A primary inspection agency which has been disqualified under paragraph (a) may resubmit an application under § 3282.353. The submission shall include a full explanation of how problems or inadequacies which resulted in disqualifications have been rectified and how the primary inspection agency shall assure that such problems shall not recur.

(d) When appropriate, the Secretary shall publish in the FEDERAL REGISTER or otherwise make available to the public for comment a disqualified PIA's application for requalification, subject to the provisions of § 3282.54.

(e) Both provisional and final acceptance of any IPIA (or DAPIA) automatically expires at the end of any period of one year during which it has not acted as an IPIA (or DAPIA). An IPIA (or DAPIA) has not acted as such unless it has actively performed its services as an IPIA (or DAPIA) for at least one manufacturer by which it has been selected. An IPIA (or DAPIA) whose acceptance has expired pursuant to this section may resubmit an application under § 3282.353 in order to again be qualified as an IPIA (or DAPIA), when it can show a bona fide prospect of performing IPIA (or DAPIA) services.

[41 FR 19852, May 13, 1976, as amended at 45 FR 59311, Sept. 9, 1980; 51 FR 34468, Sept. 29, 1986]

§ 3282.357 Background and experience.

All private organizations shall submit statements of the organizations' experience in the housing industry, including a list of housing products, equipment, and structures for which evaluation, testing and follow-up inspection services have been furnished. They shall also submit statements regarding the length of time these services have been provided by them. In addition, all such submissions shall include a list of other products for which the submitting party provides evaluation, inspection, and listing or labeling services and the standard applied to each product, as well as the length of time it has provided these additional services.

§ 3282.358   Personnel.

(a) Each primary inspection agency shall have qualified personnel capable of carrying out all of the functions for which the primary inspection agency is seeking to be approved or disapproved. Where a State intends to act as the exclusive IPIA in the State, it shall show that it has adequate personnel to so act in all plants in the State.

(b) Each submission shall indicate the total number of personnel employed by the submitting party, the number of personnel available for this program, and the locations of the activities of the personnel to be used in the program.

(c) Each submission shall include the names and qualifications of the administrator and the supervisor who will be directly responsible for the program, and résumés of their experience.

(d) Each submission shall contain the information set out in paragraphs (d)(1) through (d)(9) of this section. Depending upon the functions (DAPIA or IPIA) to be undertaken by a particular primary inspection agency, some of the categories of personnel listed may not be required. In such cases, the submission should indicate which of the categories of information are not required and explain why they are not needed. The submission should identify which personnel will carry out each of the functions the party plans to perform. The qualifications of the personnel to perform one or more of the functions will be judged in accordance with the requirements of ASTM Standard E–541 except that the requirement for registration as a professional engineer or architect may be waived for personnel whose qualifications by experience or education equal those of a registered engineer or architect. The categories of personnel to be included in the submission are as follows:

(1) The names of engineers practicing structural engineering who will be involved in the evaluation, testing, or followup inspection services, and résumés of their experience.

(2) The names of engineers practicing mechanical engineering who will be involved in the evaluation, testing, or followup, inspection services and résumés of their experience.

(3) The names of engineers practicing electrical engineering who will be involved in the evaluation, testing, or followup inspection services and résumés of their experience.

(4) The names of engineers practicing fire protection engineering who will be involved in the evaluation, testing, or followup inspection services, and résumés of their experience.

(5) The names of all other engineers assigned to this program, the capacity in which they will be employed, and résumés of their experience.

(6) The names of all full-time and part-time consulting architects and engineers, their registration, and résumés of their experience.

(7) The names of inspectors and other technicians along with résumés of experience and a description of the type of work each will perform.

(8) A general outline of the applicant agency's training program for assuring that all inspectors and other technicians are properly trained to do each specific job assigned.

(9) The names and qualifications of individuals serving on advisory panels that assist the applicant agency in making its policies conform with the public interest in the field of public health and safety.

(e) All information required by this section shall be kept current. The Secretary shall be notified of any change in personnel or management or change of ownership or State jurisdiction within 30 days of such change.

§ 3282.359   Conflict of interest.

(a) All submissions by private organizations shall include a statement that the submitting party is independent in that it does not have any actual or potential conflict of interest and is not affiliated with or influenced or controlled by any producer, supplier, or vendor of products in any manner which might affect its capacity to render reports of findings objectively and without bias.

(b) A private organization shall be judged to be free of conflicting affiliation, influence, and control if it demonstrates compliance with all of the following criteria:

(1) It has no managerial affiliation with any producer, supplier, or vendor of products for which it performs PIA services, and is not engaged in the sale or promotion of any such product or material;

(2) The results of its work do not accrue financial benefits to the organization via stock ownership of any producer, supplier or vendor of the products involved;

(3) Its directors and other management personnel and its engineers and inspectors involved in certification activities hold no stock in and receive no stock option or other benefits, financial, or otherwise, from any producer, supplier, or vendor of the product involved, other than compensation under § 3282.202 of this part;

(4) The employment security status of its personnel is free of influence or control of any producer, supplier, or vendor, and

(5) It does not perform design or quality assurance manual approval services for any manufacturer whose design or manual has been created or prepared in whole or in part by engineers of its organization or engineers of any affiliated organization.

(c) All submissions by States shall include a statement that personnel who will be in any way involved in carrying out the State plan or PIA function are free of any conflict of interest except that with respect to members of councils, committees or similar bodies providing advice to the designated agency are not subject to this requirement.

§ 3282.360 PIA acceptance of product certification programs or listings.

In determining whether products to be included in a manufactured home are acceptable under the standards set out in part 3280 of 24 CFR, all PIAs shall accept all product verification programs, labelings, and listings unless the PIA has reason to believe that a particular certification is not acceptable, in which case, the PIA shall so inform the Secretary and provide the

Secretary with full documentation and information on which it bases its belief. Pending a determination by the Secretary, the PIA shall provisionally accept the certification. The Secretary's determination shall be binding on all PIAs.

§ 3282.361 Design Approval Primary Inspection Agency (DAPIA).

(a) *General.* (1) The DAPIA selected by a manufacturer under § 3282.203 shall be responsible for evaluating all manufactured home designs submitted to it by the manufacturer and for assuring that they conform to the standards. It shall also be responsible for evaluating all quality control programs submitted to it by the manufacturer by reviewing the quality assurance manuals in which the programs are set out to assure that the manuals reflect programs which are compatible with the designs to be followed and which commit the manufacturer to make adequate inspections and tests of every part of every manufactured home produced.

(2) A design or quality assurance manual approved by a DAPIA shall be accepted by all IPIAs acting under § 3282.362 who deal with the design, quality assurance manual, or manufactured homes built to them, and by all other parties, as, respectively, being in conformance with the Federal standards or as providing for adequate quality control to assure conformance. However, each design and quality assurance manual is subject to review and verification by the Secretary or the Secretary's agent at any time.

(b) *Designs.* (1) In evaluating designs for compliance with the standards, the DAPIA will not allow any deviations from accepted engineering practice standards for design calculations or any deviations from accepted test standards, except that the DAPIA, for good cause, may request the Secretary to accept innovations which are not yet accepted practices. Acceptances by the Secretary shall be published in the form of interpretative bulletins, where appropriate.

(2) The DAPIA shall require the manufacturer to submit floor plans and specific information for each manufactured home design or variation which the DAPIA is to evaluate. It shall also

require the submission of drawings, specifications, calculations, and test records of the structural, electrical and mechanical systems of each such manufactured home design or variation. The manufacturer need not supply duplicate information where systems are common to several floor plans. Each DAPIA shall develop and carry out procedures for evaluating original manufactured home designs by requiring manufacturers to submit necessary drawings and calculations and carry out such verifications and calculations as it deems necessary. Where compliance with the standards cannot be determined on the basis of drawings and calculations, the DAPIA shall require any necessary tests to be carried out at its own facility, at separate testing facilities or at the manufacturer's plant.

(3) *Design deviation report.* After evaluating the manufacturer's design, the DAPIA shall furnish the manufacturer with a design deviation report which specifies in detail, item by item with appropriate citations to the standards, the specific deviations in the manufacturer's design which must be rectified in order to produce manufactured homes which comply with the standards. The design deviation report may acknowledge the possibility of alternative designs, tests, listings, and certifications and state the conditions under which they will be acceptable. The design deviation report shall, to the extent practicable, be complete for each design evaluated in order to avoid repeated rejections and additional costs to the manufacturer.

(4) *Design approval.* The DAPIA shall signify approval of a design by placing its stamp of approval or authorized signature on each drawing and each sheet of test results. The DAPIA shall clearly cross-reference the calculations and test results to applicable drawings. The DAPIA may require the manufacturer to do the cross-referencing if it wishes. It shall indicate on each sheet how any deviations from the standards have been or shall be resolved. Within 5 days after approving a design, the DAPIA shall forward a copy of the design to the manufacturer and the Secretary or the Secretary's agent (prior to the effective date of the standards the latter copy shall go to the Secretary.)

The DAPIA shall maintain a complete up-to-date set of approved designs and design changes approved under paragraph (b)(5) of this section which it can duplicate and copies of which it can furnish to interested parties as needed when disputes arise.

(5) *Design change approval.* The DAPIA shall also be responsible for approving all changes which a manufacturer wishes to make in a design approved by the DAPIA. In reviewing design changes, the DAPIA shall respond as quickly as possible to avoid disruption of the manufacturing process. Within 5 days after approving a design change, the DAPIA shall forward a copy of this change to the manufacturer and the Secretary or the Secretary's agent as set out in paragraph (b)(4) of this section to be included in the design to which the change was made.

(c) *Quality assurance manuals.* (1) In evaluating a quality assurance manual, the DAPIA shall identify any aspects of designs to be manufactured under the manual which require special quality control procedures. The DAPIA shall determine whether the manual under which a particular design is to be manufactured reflects those special procedures, and shall also determine whether the manuals which it evaluates provide for such inspections and testing of each manufactured home so that the manufacturer, by following the manual, can assure that each manufactured home it manufactures will conform to the standards. The manual shall, at a minimum, include the information set out in § 3282.203(c).

(2) *Manual deviation report.* After evaluating a manufacturer's quality assurance manual, the DAPIA shall furnish the manufacturer with a manual deviation report which specifies in detail any changes which a manufacturer must make in order for the quality assurance manual to be acceptable. The manual deviation report shall, to the extent practicable, be complete for each design in order to avoid repeated rejections and additional costs to the manufacturer.

(3) *Manual approval.* The DAPIA shall signify approval of the manufacturer's quality assurance manual by placing

its stamp of approval or authorized signature on the cover page of the manual. Within 5 days of approving a quality assurance manual, the DAPIA shall forward a copy of the quality assurance manual to the manufacturer and the Secretary or the Secretary's agent (prior to the effective date of the standards, the latter copy shall go to the Secretary). The DAPIA shall maintain a complete up-to-date set of approved manuals and manual changes approved under paragraph (c)(4) of this section which it can duplicate and copies of which it can furnish to interested parties as needed when disputes arise.

(4) *Manual change approval.* Each change the manufacturer wishes to make in its quality assurance manual must be approved by the DAPIA, and, when subject to §3282.604, concurred in by the IPIA. Within 5 days after approving a manual change, the DAPIA shall forward a copy of the change to the manufacturer and the Secretary or the Secretary's agent as set out in paragraph (c)(3) of this section to be included in the manual to which the change was made.

(d) *Requirements for full acceptance—DAPIA.* (1) Before granting full acceptance to a DAPIA, the Secretary or the Secretary's agent shall review and evaluate at least one complete design and one quality assurance manual which has been approved by the DAPIA. These shall be designs and manuals approved to the Federal standards, and they shall be chosen at random from those approved by the DAPIA during the period of provisional acceptance.

(2) If the Secretary determines that a design or quality assurance manual shows an inadequate level of performance, the Secretary or the Secretary's agent shall carry out further evaluations. If the Secretary finds the level of performance to be unacceptable, the Secretary shall not grant full acceptance. If full acceptance has not been granted by the end of the provisional acceptance period, provisional acceptance shall lapse unless the Secretary determines that the failure to obtain full acceptance resulted from the fact that the Secretary or her agent has not

had adequate time in which to complete an evaluation.

[41 FR 19852, May 13, 1976, as amended at 61 FR 10861, Mar. 15, 1996; 80 FR 53727, Sept. 8, 2015]

§3282.362 Production Inspection Primary Inspection Agencies (IPIAs).

(a) *General—(1) IPIA responsibilities.* An IPIA selected by a manufacturer under §3282.204 to act in a particular manufacturing plant shall be responsible for assuring:

(i) That the plant is capable of following the quality control procedures set out in the quality assurance manual to be followed in that plant;

(ii) That the plant continues to follow the quality assurance manual;

(iii) That any part of any manufactured home that it actually inspects conforms with the design, or where the design is not specific with respect to an aspect of the standards, to the standards;

(iv) That whenever it finds a manufactured home in production which fails to conform to the design or where the design is not specific, to the standards, the failure to conform is corrected before the manufactured home leaves the manufacturing plant; and

(v) That if a failure to conform to the design, or where the design is not specific, to the standards, is found in one manufactured home, all other homes still in the plant which the IPIA's records or the records of the manufacturer indicate might not conform to the design or to standards are inspected and, if necessary, brought up to the standards before they leave the plant.

(2) No more than one IPIA shall operate in any one manufacturing plant, except that where a manufacturer decides to change from one IPIA to another, the two may operate in the plant simultaneously for a limited period of time to the extent necessary to assure a smooth transition.

(b) *Plant approval.* (1) Each IPIA shall, with respect to each manufacturing plant for which it is responsible, evaluate the quality control procedures being followed by the manufacturer in the plant to determine whether those procedures are consistent with and fulfill the procedures set out in the

DAPIA approved quality assurance manual being followed in the plant. As part of this evaluation, and prior to the issuance of any labels to the manufacturer, the IPIA shall make a complete inspection of the manufacture of at least one manufactured home through all of the operations in the manufacturer's plant. The purpose of this initial factory inspection is to determine whether the manufacturer is capable of producing manufactured homes in conformance with the approved design and, to the extent the design is not specific with respect to an aspect of the standards, with the standards and to determine whether the manufacturer's quality control procedures as set out in the quality assurance manual, plant equipment, and personnel, will assure that such conformance continues. This inspection should be made by one or more qualified engineers who have reviewed the approved design and by an inspector who has been carefully briefed by the engineers on the restrictive aspects of the design. The manufactured home shall be inspected to the approved design for the home except that where the design is not specific with respect to any aspect of the standards, the inspection shall be to the standards as to that aspect of the manufactured home. If the first manufactured home inspected fails to conform to the design or, with respect to any aspect of the standards not specifically covered by the design, to the standards, additional units shall be similarly inspected until the IPIA is satisfied that the manufacturer is conforming to the approved design, or where the design is not specific with respect to any aspect of the standards, to the standards and quality assurance manual.

(2) *Certification report.* If, on the basis of the initial comprehensive factory inspection required by paragraph (b)(1) of this section, the IPIA determines that the manufacturer is performing adequately, the IPIA shall prepare and forward to the manufacturer, to HUD, and to HUD's agent a certification report as described in this paragraph (b)(2) of this section. The issuance of the certification report is a prerequisite to the commencement of production surveillance under paragraph (c) of this section in the plant for which the report is issued. At the time the certification report is issued, the IPIA may provide the manufacturer with a two to four week supply of labels to be applied to manufactured homes produced in the plant. The IPIA shall maintain a copy of each certification report which it issues.

(3) The certification report shall include:

(i) The name of the DAPIA which approved the manufacturer's design and quality assurance manual and the dates of those approvals,

(ii) The names and titles of the IPIA engineers and inspectors who performed the initial comprehensive inspection,

(iii) A full report of inspections made, serial numbers inspected, any failures to comply which were observed, corrective actions taken, and dates of inspections, and

(iv) A certification that at least one manufactured home has been completely inspected in all phases of its production in the plant, that the manufacturer is performing in conformance with the approved designs and quality assurance manual and, to the extent the design is not specific with respect to any aspects of the standards, with the standards, and the IPIA is satisfied that the manufacturer can produce manufactured homes in conformance with the designs, and where the designs are not specific, with the standards on a continuing basis.

(4) *Inadequate manufacturer performance.* Where an IPIA determines that the performance of a manufacturer is not yet adequate to justify the issuance of a certification report and labels to the manufacturer, the IPIA may label manufactured homes itself by using such of its personnel as it deems necessary to perform complete inspections of all phases of production of each manufactured home being produced and labeling only those determined after any necessary corrections to be in conformance with the design and, as appropriate, with the standards. This procedure shall continue until the IPIA determines that the manufacturer's performance is adequate to justify the issuance of a certification report.

(c) *Production surveillance.* (1) After it has issued a certification report under paragraph (b) of this section, the IPIA shall carry out ongoing surveillance of the manufacturing process in the plant. The IPIA shall be responsible for conducting representative inspections to assure that the manufacturer is performing its quality control program pursuant to and consistent with its approved quality assurance manual and to assure that whatever part of a manufactured home is actually inspected by the IPIA is fully in conformance with the design and, as appropriate under paragraph (a)(1)(iii) of this section, with the standards before a label is issued for or placed on that manufactured home. The surveillance visits shall commence no later than that date on which the IPIA determines they must commence so that the IPIA can assure that every manufactured home to be produced after the effective date of the standards to which a label provided for in paragraph (c)(2) of this section is affixed, is inspected in at least one stage of its production. The frequency of subsequent visits to the plant shall continue to be such that every manufactured home is inspected at some stage in its production. In the course of each visit, the IPIA shall make a complete inspection of every phase of production and of every visible part of every manufactured home which is at each stage of production. The inspection shall be made to the approved design except where the design is not specific with respect to an aspect of the standards, in which case the inspection of that aspect of the manufactured home shall be made to the standards. The IPIA shall assure that no label is placed on any manufactured home which it finds fails to conform with the approved design or, as appropriate, the standards in the course of these inspections and shall assure that no labels are placed on other manufactured homes still in the plant which may also not conform until those homes are inspected and if necessary corrected to the design or the standards. If an IPIA finds a manufactured home that fails to conform to the design, or as appropriate under paragraph (a)(1)(iii) of this section, to the standards, the IPIA may, in addition to

withholding the label for the unit, proceed to red tag the home until the failure to conform is corrected. Only the IPIA is authorized to remove a red tag. When manufactured homes repeatedly fail to conform to the design, or as appropriate under paragraph (a)(1)(iii) of this section, to the standards in the same assembly station or when there is evidence that the manufacturer is ignoring or not performing under its approved quality assurance manual, the IPIA shall increase the frequency of these inspections until it is satisfied that the manufacturer is performing to its approved quality assurance manual. Failure to perform to the approved manual justifies withholding labels until an adequate level of performance is attained. As part of its function of assuring quality control, the IPIA shall inspect materials in storage and test equipment used by the manufacturer at least once a month, and more frequently if unacceptable conditions are observed. With the prior approval of the Secretary, an IPIA may decrease the frequency of any inspections.

(2) *Labeling*—(i) *Labels required.* (A) The IPIA shall continuously provide the manufacturer with a two- to four-week supply (at the convenience of the IPIA and the manufacturer) of the labels described in this subsection, except that no labels shall be issued for use when the IPIA is not present if the IPIA is not satisfied that the manufacturer can and is producing manufactured homes which conform to the design and, as appropriate, to the standards. Where necessary, the IPIA shall reclaim labels already given to the manufacturer. In no event shall the IPIA allow a label to be affixed to a manufactured home if the IPIA believes that the manufactured home fails to conform to the design, or, where the design is not specific with respect to an aspect of the standards, to the standards. Labels for such manufactured homes shall be provided only after the failure to conform has been remedied, or after the Secretary has determined that there is no failure to conform.

(B) A permanent label shall be affixed to each transportable section of each manufactured home for sale or lease to a purchaser or lessor in the

United States in such a manner that removal will damage the label so that it cannot be reused. This label is provided by the IPIA and is separate and distinct from the data plate that the manufacturer is required to provide under § 3280.5.

(C) The label shall read as follows:

"As evidenced by this label No. ABC 000 001, the manufacturer certifies to the best of the manufacturer's knowledge and belief that this manufactured home has been inspected in accordance with the requirements of the Department of Housing and Urban Development and is constructed in conformance with the Federal Manufactured Home Construction and Safety Standards in effect on the date of manufacture. See data plate."

(D) The label shall be 2 in. by 4 in. in size and shall be permanently attached to the manufactured home by means of 4 blind rivets, drive screws, or other means that render it difficult to remove without defacing it. It shall be etched on .032 in. thick aluminum plate. The label number shall be etched or stamped with a 3 letter IPIA designation which the Secretary shall assign and a 6 digit number which the label supplier shall stamp sequentially on labels supplied to each IPIA.

(E) The label shall be located at the tail-light end of each transportable section of the manufactured home approximately one foot up from the floor and one foot in from the road side, or as near that location on a permanent part of the exterior of the manufactured home as practicable. The roadside is the right side of the manufactured home when one views the manufactured home from the tow bar end of the manufactured home. It shall be applied to the manufactured home unit in the manufacturing plant by the manufacturer or the IPIA, as appropriate.

(F) The label shall be provided to the manufacturer only by the IPIA. The IPIA shall provide the labels in sequentially numbered series. The IPIA may obtain labels from the Secretary or the Secretary's agent, or where the IPIA obtains the prior approval of the Secretary, from a label manufacturer. However, if the IPIA obtains labels directly from a label supplier, those labels must be sequentially numbered without any duplication of label numbers.

(G) Whenever the IPIA determines that a manufactured home which has been labeled, but which has not yet been released by the manufacturer may not conform to the design or, as appropriate under paragraph (a)(1)(iii) of this section, to the standards, the IPIA by itself or through an agent shall red tag the manufactured home. Where the IPIA determines that a manufactured home which has been labeled and released by the manufacturer, but not yet sold to a purchaser (as described in § 3282.252(b)) may not conform, the IPIA may, in its discretion, proceed to red tag the manufactured home. Only the IPIA is authorized to remove red tags, though it may do so through agents which it deems qualified to determine that the failure to conform has been corrected. Red tags may be removed when the IPIA is satisfied, through inspections, assurances from the manufacturer, or otherwise, that the affected homes conform.

(H) Labels that are damaged, destroyed, or otherwise made illegible or removed shall be replaced by the IPIA, after determination that the manufactured home is in compliance with the standards, by a new label of a different serial number. The IPIA's labeling record shall be permanently marked with the number of the replacement label and a corresponding record of the replacement label.

(ii) *Label control.* The labels used in each plant shall be under the direct control of the IPIA acting in that plant. Only the IPIA shall provide the labels to the manufacturer. The IPIA shall assure that the manufacturer does not use any other label to indicate conformance to the standards.

(A) The IPIA shall be responsible for obtaining labels. Labels shall be obtained from HUD or its agent, or with the approval of the Secretary, from a label manufacturer. The labels shall meet the requirements of this section. Where the IPIA obtains labels directly from a label manufacturer, the IPIA shall be responsible for assuring that the label manufacturer does not provide labels directly to the manufacturer of manufactured homes. If the label manufacturer fails to supply correct labels or allows labels to be released to parties other than the IPIA, the IPIA shall cease dealing with the label manufacturer.

(B) The labels shall be shipped to and stored by the IPIA's at a location which permits ready access to manufacturing plants under its surveillance. The labels shall be stored under strict security and inventory control. They shall be released only by the IPIA to the manufacturer under these regulations.

(C) The IPIA shall be able to account for all labels which it has obtained through the date on which the manufactured home leaves the manufacturing plant, and it shall be able to identify the serial number of the manufactured home to which each particular label is affixed.

(D) The IPIA shall keep in its central record office a list of the serial numbers of labels issued from the label producer to the IPIA and by the IPIA to the manufacturing plant.

(E) Failure to maintain control of labels through the date the manufactured home leaves the manufacturing plant and failure to keep adequate records of which label is on which manufactured home shall render the IPIA subject to disqualification under §3282.356.

(3) *Data plate.* (i) The IPIA shall assure that each manufactured home produced in each manufacturing plant under its surveillance is supplied with a data plate which meets the requirements of this section and of §3280.5 of chapter XX of 24 CFR. The data plate shall be furnished by the manufacturer and affixed inside the manufactured home on or near the main electrical distribution panel. The data plate shall contain the following information:

(A) The name and address of the manufacturing plant in which the manufactured home was manufactured,

(B) The serial number and model designation of the unit and the date the unit was manufactured,

(C) The statement "This manufactured home is designed to comply with the Federal Manufactured Home Construction and Safety Standards in force at the time of manufacture.",

(D) A list of major factory-installed equipment including the manufacturer's name and the model designation of each appliance,

(E) Reference to the roof load zone and wind load zone for which the home is designed and duplicates of the maps as set forth in §3280.305. This information may be combined with the heating/cooling certificate and insulation zone map required by §§3280.510 and 3280.511. The Wind Zone Map on the Data Plate shall also contain the statement:

This home has not been designed for the higher wind pressures and anchoring provisions required for ocean/coastal areas and should not be located within 1500' of the coastline in Wind Zones II and III, unless the home and its anchoring and foundation system have been designed for the increased requirements specified for Exposure D in ANSI/ASCE 7–88.

(F) The statement:

This home has ___ has not ___ (appropriate blank to be checked by manufacturer) been equipped with storm shutters or other protective coverings for windows and exterior door openings. For homes designed to be located in Wind Zones II and III, which have not been provided with shutters or equivalent covering devices, it is strongly recommended that the home be made ready to be equipped with these devices in accordance with the method recommended in the manufacturers printed instructions.

(G) The statement: "Design Approval by", followed by the name of the agency that approved the design.

(ii) A copy of the data plate shall be furnished to the IPIA, and the IPIA shall keep a permanent record of the data plate as part of its labeling record so that the information is available during the life of the manufactured home in case the data plate in the manufactured home is defaced or destroyed.

(d) *Permanent records.* The IPIA shall maintain the following records as appropriate:

(1) Records of all labels issued, applied, removed, and replaced by label number, manufactured home serial number, manufactured home type, manufacturer's name, retailer destination, and copies of corresponding data plates.

(2) Records of all manufactured homes which are red tagged, and the status of each home.

(3) Records of all inspections made at each manufacturing plant on each manufactured home serial number,

each failure to conform found, and the action taken in each case.

(4) Records of all inspections made at other locations of manufactured homes identified by manufacturer and serial number, all manufactured homes believed to contain the same failure to conform, and the action taken in each case.

All records shall specify the precise section of the standard which is in question and contain a clear and concise explanation of the process by which the IPIA reached any conclusions. All records shall be traceable to specific manufactured home serial numbers and through the manufacturer's records to retailers and purchasers.

(5) Records of all site inspections made as required under procedures applicable to approval of AC or on-site completion pursuant to §§ 3282.14 or 3282.610.

(e) *Requirements for full acceptance— IPIA.* (1) Before granting full acceptance to an IPIA, the Secretary or the Secretary's agent shall review and evaluate at least one certification report which has been prepared by the IPIA during the period of provisional acceptance. The Secretary or the Secretary's agent shall also review in depth the IPIA's administrative capabilities and otherwise review the IPIA's performance of its responsibilities under these regulations.

(2) Where the Secretary determines on the basis of these reviews that an IPIA is not meeting an adequate level of performance, the Secretary or the Secretary's agent shall carry out further evaluations. If the Secretary finds the level of performance to be unacceptable, the Secretary shall not grant full acceptance. If full acceptance has not been granted by the end of the provisional acceptance period, provisional acceptance shall lapse unless the Secretary determines that the failure to obtain full acceptance resulted from the fact that the Secretary or the Secretary's agent has not had adequate time in which to complete an evaluation.

[41 FR 19852, May 13, 1976, as amended at 42 FR 2580, Jan. 12, 1977; 42 FR 35157, July 8, 1977; 59 FR 2474, Jan. 14, 1994; 61 FR 10861, Mar. 15, 1996; 80 FR 53727, Sept. 8, 2015]

§ 3282.363 **Right of entry and inspection.**

Each primary inspection agency shall secure from each manufacturer and manufacturing plant under its surveillance an agreement that the Secretary, the State Administrative Agency and the primary inspection agency have the right to inspect the plant and its manufactured home inspection, labeling, and delivery records, and any of its manufactured homes in the hands of retailers or distributors at any reasonable time.

§ 3282.364 **Inspection responsibilities and coordination.**

All primary inspection agencies shall be responsible for acting as necessary under their contractual commitment with the manufacturer to determine whether alleged failures to conform to the standards may exist in manufactured homes produced under their surveillance and to determine the source of the problems. The DAPIA may be required to examine the designs in question or the quality assurance manual under which the manufactured homes were produced. The IPIA may be required to reexamine the quality control procedures which it has approved to determine if they conform to the quality assurance manual, and the IPIA shall have primary responsibility for inspecting actual units produced and, where necessary, for inspecting units released by the manufacturer. All primary inspection agencies acting with respect to particular manufacturer or plant shall act in close coordination so that all necessary functions are performed effectively and efficiently.

§ 3282.365 **Forwarding monitoring fee.**

The IPIA shall, whenever it provides labels to a manufacturer, obtain from the manufacturer the monitoring fee to be forwarded to the Secretary or the Secretary's agent as set out in § 3282.210. If a manufacturer fails to provide the monitoring fee as required by § 3282.210 to be forwarded by the IPIA under this section, the IPIA shall immediately inform the Secretary; or the Secretary's Agent.

§3282.366 Notification and correction campaign responsibilities.

(a) Both IPIAs and DAPIAs are responsible for assisting the Secretary or an SAA in identifying the class of manufactured homes that may have been affected where the Secretary or an SAA makes or is contemplating making a preliminary determination of imminent safety hazard, serious defect, defect, or noncompliance under §3282.412 with respect to manufactured homes for which the IPIA and DAPIA provided either plant inspection or design approval services.

(b) The IPIA must in each manufacturing plant review at least monthly the manufacturer's service and inspection records to verify if appropriate determinations are being made by the manufacturer under §3282.404 and, if not, take the actions required by this section and §3282.404.

(c) The IPIA in each manufacturing plant is also responsible for reviewing manufacturer determinations of the class of manufactured homes affected when the manufacturer is acting under subpart I. The IPIA must concur in the method used to determine the class of potentially affected manufactured homes or is to state why it finds the method to be inappropriate, inadequate, or incorrect.

[78 FR 60200, Oct. 1, 2013]

Subpart I—Consumer Complaint Handling and Remedial Actions

SOURCE: 78 FR 60200, Oct. 1, 2013, unless otherwise noted.

§3282.401 Purpose and scope.

(a) *Purpose.* The purpose of this subpart is to establish a system of protections provided by the Act with respect to imminent safety hazards and failures to conform to the construction and safety standards with a minimum of formality and delay, while protecting the rights of all parties.

(b) *Scope.* This subpart sets out the procedures to be followed by manufacturers, retailers, and distributors, SAAs, primary inspection agencies, and the Secretary to assure that notification and correction are provided with respect to manufactured homes when required under this subpart. Notification and correction may be required with respect to manufactured homes that have been sold or otherwise released by the manufacturer to another party.

§3282.402 General provisions.

(a) *Purchaser's rights.* Nothing in this subpart shall limit the rights of the purchaser under any contract or applicable law.

(b) *Manufacturer's liability limited.* A manufacturer is not responsible for failures that occur in any manufactured home or component as the result of normal wear and aging, consumer abuse, or neglect of maintenance. The life of a component warranty may be one of the indicators used to establish normal wear and aging. A failure of any component may not be attributed by the manufacturer to normal wear and aging under this subpart during the term of any applicable warranty provided by the original manufacturer of the affected component.

§3282.403 Consumer complaint and information referral.

(a) *Retailer responsibilities.* When a retailer receives a consumer complaint or other information about a home in its possession, or that it has sold or leased, that likely indicates a noncompliance, defect, serious defect, or imminent safety hazard, the retailer must forward the complaint or information to the manufacturer of the manufactured home in question as early as possible, in accordance with §3282.256.

(b) *SAA and HUD responsibilities.* (1) When an SAA or the Secretary receives a consumer complaint or other information that likely indicates a noncompliance, defect, serious defect, or imminent safety hazard in a manufactured home, the SAA or HUD must:

(i) Forward the complaint or information to the manufacturer of the home in question as early as possible; and

(ii) Send a copy of the complaint or other information to the SAA of the State where the manufactured home was manufactured or to the Secretary if there is no such SAA.

(2) When it appears from the complaint or other information that an imminent safety hazard or serious defect may be involved, the SAA of the State where the home was manufactured must also send a copy of the complaint or other information to the Secretary.

(c) *Manufacturer responsibilities.* Whenever the manufacturer receives information from any source that the manufacturer believes in good faith relates to a noncompliance, defect, serious defect, or imminent safety hazard in any of its manufactured homes, the manufacturer must, for each such occurrence, make the determinations required by § 3282.404.

§ 3282.404 Manufacturers' determinations and related concurrences.

(a) *Initial determination.* (1) Not later than 30 days after a manufacturer receives information that it believes in good faith may indicate a noncompliance, defect, serious defect, or imminent safety hazard, the manufacturer must make a specific initial determination that there is a noncompliance, defect, serious defect, or imminent safety hazard, or that the information requires no further action under this subpart. If a manufacturer makes a final determination of noncompliance for an individual home (see § 3282.412(b)) and a class of homes is not involved, no further action is needed by the manufacturer other than to keep a record of its determination as required by § 3282.417. If the manufacturer determines that it is not the cause of the problem, but a problem still exists, the manufacturer must forward the information in its possession to the appropriate retailer (see § 3282.254), and, if known, to the installer (see §§ 3286.115 and 3286.811) for their consideration. Alternatively, the manufacturer, retailer, or installer may choose to submit the issue for resolution under dispute resolution (see 24 CFR part 3288).

(2) When a manufacturer makes an initial determination that there is a serious defect or an imminent safety hazard, the manufacturer must immediately notify the Secretary, the SAA in the state of manufacture, and the manufacturer's IPIA.

(3) In making the determination of noncompliance, defect, serious defect,

or imminent safety hazard, or that no further action is required under this subpart, the manufacturer must review the information it received and carry out investigations, including, a review of service records, IPIA inspection records, and, as appropriate, inspections of homes in the class. The manufacturer must review the information, the known facts, and the circumstances relating to the complaint or information, including service records, approved designs, and audit findings, as applicable, to decide what investigations are reasonable.

(b) *Class determination.* (1) When the manufacturer makes an initial determination of defect, serious defect, or imminent safety hazard, the manufacturer must also make a good-faith determination of the class that includes each manufactured home in which the same defect, serious defect, or imminent safety hazard exists or likely exists. Multiple occurrences of defects may be considered the same defect if they have the same cause, are related to a specific workstation description, or are related to the same failure to follow the manufacturer's approved quality assurance manual. Good faith may be used as a defense to the imposition of a penalty, but does not relieve the manufacturer of its responsibilities for notification or correction under this subpart I. The manufacturer must make this class determination not later than 20 days after making a determination of defect, serious defect, or imminent safety hazard.

(2) Paragraph (c) of this section sets out methods for a manufacturer to use in determining the class of manufactured homes. If the manufacturer can identify the precise manufactured homes affected by the defect, serious defect, or imminent safety hazard, the class of manufactured homes may include only those manufactured homes actually affected by the same defect, serious defect, or imminent safety hazard. The manufacturer is also permitted to exclude from the class those manufactured homes for which the manufacturer has information that indicates the homes were not affected by the same cause. If it is not possible to identify the precise manufactured homes affected, the class must include

every manufactured home in the group of homes that is identifiable, since the same defect, serious defect, or imminent safety hazard exists or likely exists in some homes in that group of manufactured homes.

(3) For purposes related to this section, a defect, a serious defect, or an imminent safety hazard likely exists in a manufactured home if the cause of the defect, serious defect, or imminent safety hazard is such that the same defect, serious defect, or imminent safety hazard would likely have been introduced systematically into more than one manufactured home. Indications that the defect, serious defect, or imminent safety hazard would likely have been introduced systematically may include, but are not limited to, complaints that can be traced to the same faulty design or faulty construction, problems known to exist in supplies of components or parts, information related to the performance of a particular employee or use of a particular process, and information signaling a failure to follow quality control procedures with respect to a particular aspect of the manufactured home.

(4) If the manufacturer must determine the class of homes pursuant to paragraph (b) of this section, the manufacturer must obtain from the IPIA, and the IPIA must provide, either:

(i) The IPIA's written concurrence on the methods used by the manufacturer to identify the homes that should be included in the class of homes; or

(ii) The IPIA's written statement explaining why it believes the manufacturer's methods for determining the class of homes were inappropriate or inadequate.

(c) *Methods for determining class.* (1) In making a class determination under paragraph (b) of this section, a manufacturer is responsible for carrying out reasonable investigations. In carrying out investigations, the manufacturer must review the information, the known facts, and the relevant circumstances, and generally must establish the cause of the defect, serious defect, or imminent safety hazard. Based on the results of such investigations and all information received or developed, the manufacturer must use an appropriate method or appropriate

methods to determine the class of manufactured homes in which the same defect, serious defect, or imminent safety hazard exists or likely exists.

(2) Methods that may be used in determining the class of manufactured homes include, but are not limited to:

(i) Inspection of the manufactured home in question, including its design, to determine whether the defect, serious defect, or imminent safety hazard resulted from the design itself;

(ii) Physical inspection of manufactured homes of the same design or construction, as appropriate, that were produced before and after a home in question;

(iii) Inspection of the service records of a home in question and of homes of the same design or construction, as appropriate, produced before and after that home, if it is clear that the cause of the defect, serious defect, or imminent safety hazard is such that the defect, serious defect, or imminent safety hazard would be visible to and reportable by consumers or retailers;

(iv) Inspection of manufacturer quality control records to determine whether quality control procedures were followed and, if not, the time frame during which they were not;

(v) Inspection of IPIA records to determine whether the defect, serious defect, or imminent safety hazard was either detected or specifically found not to exist in some manufactured homes;

(vi) Identification of the cause as relating to a particular employee whose work, or to a process whose use, would have been common to the production of the manufacturer's homes for a period of time; and

(vii) Inspection of records relating to components supplied by other parties and known to contain or suspected of containing a defect, a serious defect, or an imminent safety hazard.

(3) When the Secretary or an SAA decides the method chosen by the manufacturer to conduct an investigation in order to make a class determination is not the most appropriate method, the Secretary or SAA must explain in writing to the manufacturer why the chosen method is not the most appropriate.

(d) *Documentation required.* The manufacturer must comply with the recordkeeping requirements in § 3282.417 as applicable to its determinations and any IPIA concurrence or statement that it does not concur.

§ 3282.405 Notification pursuant to manufacturer's determination.

(a) *General requirement.* Every manufacturer of manufactured homes must provide notification, as set out in this section, with respect to any manufactured home produced by the manufacturer in which the manufacturer determines, in good faith, that there exists or likely exists in more than one home, the same defect introduced systematically, a serious defect, or an imminent safety hazard.

(b) *Requirements by category.* (1) *Noncompliance.* A manufacturer must provide notification of a noncompliance only when ordered to do so by the Secretary or an SAA, pursuant to §§ 3282.412 and 3282.413.

(2) *Defects.* When a manufacturer has made a class determination in accordance with § 3282.404 that a defect exists or likely exists in more than one home, the manufacturer must prepare a plan for notification in accordance with § 3282.408, and must provide notification with respect to each manufactured home in the class of manufactured homes.

(3) *Serious defects and imminent safety hazards.* When a manufacturer has made an initial determination in accordance with § 3282.404(a) that a serious defect or imminent safety hazard exists or likely exists, the manufacturer must prepare a plan for notification in accordance with § 3282.408, must provide notification with respect to all manufactured homes in which the serious defect or imminent safety hazard exists or likely exists, and must correct the home or homes in accordance with § 3282.406.

(c) *Plan for notification required.* (1) If a manufacturer determines that it is responsible for providing notification under this section, the manufacturer must prepare and receive approval on a plan for notification as set out in § 3282.408, unless the manufacturer meets alternative requirements established in § 3282.407.

(2) If the Secretary or SAA orders a manufacturer to provide notification in accordance with the procedures in §§ 3282.412 and 3282.413, the Secretary or SAA has the option of requiring a manufacturer to prepare and receive approval on a plan for notification.

(d) *Method of notification.* When a manufacturer provides notification as required under this section, notification must be:

(1) By certified mail or other more expeditious means that provides a receipt to each retailer or distributor to whom any manufactured home in the class of homes containing the defect, serious defect, or imminent safety hazard was delivered;

(2) By certified mail or other more expeditious means that provides a receipt to the first purchaser of each manufactured home in the class of manufactured homes containing the defect, serious defect, or imminent safety hazard, and, to the extent feasible, to any subsequent owner to whom any warranty provided by the manufacturer or required by federal, state, or local law on such manufactured home has been transferred, except that notification need not be sent to any person known by the manufacturer not to own the manufactured home in question if the manufacturer has a record of a subsequent owner of the manufactured home; and

(3) By certified mail or other more expeditious means that provides a receipt to each other person who is a registered owner of a manufactured home in the class of homes containing the defect, serious defect, or imminent safety hazard and whose name has been ascertained pursuant to § 3282.211 or is known to the manufacturer.

§ 3282.406 Required manufacturer correction.

(a) *Correction of noncompliances and defects.* (1) Section 3282.415 sets out requirements with respect to a manufacturer's correction of any noncompliance or defect that exists in each manufactured home that has been sold or otherwise released to a retailer but that has not yet been sold to a purchaser.

(2) In accordance with section 623 of the Act and Part 3288, "Manufactured

Home Dispute Resolution Program," of this chapter, the manufacturer, retailer, or installer of a manufactured home deemed responsible for correction of repairs or defects must correct, at its expense, each failure in the performance, construction, components, or material of the home that renders the home or any part of the home not fit for the ordinary use for which it was intended and that is reported during the one-year period beginning on the date of installation of the home (see § 3286.115).

(b) *Correction of serious defects and imminent safety hazards.* (1) A manufacturer required to furnish notification under § 3282.405 or § 3282.413 must correct, at its expense, any serious defect or imminent safety hazard that can be related to an error in design or assembly of the manufactured home by the manufacturer, including an error in design or assembly of any component or system incorporated into the manufactured home by the manufacturer.

(2) If, while making corrections under any of the provisions of this subpart, the manufacturer creates an imminent safety hazard or serious defect, the manufacturer shall correct the imminent safety hazard or serious defect.

(3) Each serious defect or imminent safety hazard corrected under this paragraph (b) must be brought into compliance with applicable construction and safety standards or, where those standards are not specific, with the manufacturer's approved design.

(c) *Inclusion in plan.* (1) In the plan required by § 3282.408, the manufacturer must provide for correction of those homes that are required to be corrected pursuant to paragraph (b) of this section.

(2) If the Secretary or SAA orders a manufacturer to provide correction in accordance with the procedures in § 3282.413, the Secretary or SAA has the option of requiring a manufacturer to prepare and receive approval on a plan for correction.

(d) *Corrections by owners.* A manufacturer that is required to make corrections under paragraph (b) of this section, or that elects to make corrections in accordance with § 3282.407, must reimburse any owner of an affected manufactured home who choses to make the correction before the manufacturer did so, for the reasonable cost of correction.

(e) *Correction of appliances, components, or systems.* (1) If any appliance, component, or system in a manufactured home is covered by a product warranty, the manufacturer, retailer, or installer that is responsible under this section for correcting a noncompliance, defect, serious defect, or imminent safety hazard in the appliance, component, or system may seek the required correction directly from the producer. The SAA that approves any plan of notification required pursuant to § 3282.408 or the Secretary, as applicable, may establish reasonable time limits for the manufacturer of the home and the producer of the appliance, component, or system to agree on who is to make the correction and for completing the correction.

(2) Nothing in this section shall prevent the manufacturer, retailer, or installer from seeking indemnification from the producer of the appliance, component, or system for correction work done on any appliance, component, or system.

§ 3282.407 **Voluntary compliance with the notification and correction requirements under the Act.**

A manufacturer that takes corrective action that complies with one of the following three alternatives to the requirement in § 3282.408 for preparing a plan will be deemed to have provided any notification required by § 3282.405:

(a) *Voluntary action—one home.* When a manufacturer has made a determination that only one manufactured home is involved, the manufacturer is not required to provide notification pursuant to § 3282.405 or to prepare or submit a plan if:

(1) The manufacturer has made a determination of defect; or

(2) The manufacturer has made a determination of serious defect or imminent safety hazard and corrects the home within the 20-day period. The manufacturer must maintain, in the plant where the manufactured home was manufactured, a complete record of the correction. The record must describe briefly the facts of the case and any known cause of the serious defect

or imminent safety hazard, state what corrective actions were taken, and be maintained in the service records in a form that will allow the Secretary or an SAA to review all such corrections.

(b) *Voluntary action—multiple homes.* Regardless of whether a plan has been submitted under § 3282.408, the manufacturer may act prior to obtaining approval of the plan. Such action is subject to review and disapproval by the SAA of the state where the home was manufactured or by the Secretary, unless the manufacturer obtains the written agreement of the SAA or the Secretary that the corrective action is adequate. If such an agreement is obtained, the correction must be accepted as adequate by all SAAs and the Secretary, if the manufacturer makes the correction as agreed to and any imminent safety hazard or serious defect is eliminated.

(c) *Waiver.* (1) A manufacturer may obtain a waiver of the notification requirements in § 3282.405 and the plan requirements in § 3282.408 either from the SAA of the state of manufacture, when all of the manufactured homes that would be covered by the plan were manufactured in that state, or from the Secretary. As of the date of a request for a waiver, the notification and plan requirements are deferred pending timely submission of any additional documentation as the SAA or the Secretary may require and final resolution of the waiver request. If a waiver request is not granted, the plan required by § 3282.408 must be submitted within 5 days after the expiration of the time frame established in § 3282.408, if the manufacturer is notified that the request was not granted.

(2) The waiver may be approved if, not later than 20 days after making the determination that notification is required, the manufacturer presents evidence that it, in good faith, believes would show to the satisfaction of the SAA or the Secretary that:

(i) The manufacturer has identified all homes that would be covered by the plan in accordance with § 3282.408;

(ii) The manufacturer will correct, at its expense, all of the identified homes, either within 60 days of being informed that the request for waiver has been

granted or within another time limit approved in the waiver;

(iii) The proposed repairs are adequate to remove the defect, serious defect, or imminent safety hazard that gave rise to the determination that correction is required; and

(3) The manufacturer must correct all affected manufactured homes within 60 days of being informed that the request for waiver has been granted or within the time limit approved in the waiver, as applicable. The manufacturer must record the known cause of the problem and the correction in the service records, in an approved form that will allow the Secretary or SAA to review the cause and correction.

§ 3282.408 Plan of notification required.

(a) *Manufacturer's plan required.* Except as provided in § 3282.407, if a manufacturer determines that it is responsible for providing notification under § 3282.405, the manufacturer must prepare a plan in accordance with this section and § 3282.409. The manufacturer must, as soon as practical, but not later than 20 days after making the determination of defect, serious defect, or imminent safety hazard, submit the plan for approval to one of the following, as appropriate:

(1) The SAA of the State of manufacture, when all of the manufactured homes covered by the plan were manufactured in that State; or

(2) The Secretary, when the manufactured homes were manufactured in more than one State or there is no SAA in the State of manufacture.

(b) *Implementation of plan.* Upon approval of the plan, including any changes for cause required by the Secretary or SAA after consultation with the manufacturer, the manufacturer must carry out the approved plan within the agreed time limits.

§ 3282.409 Contents of plan.

(a) *Purpose of plan.* This section sets out the requirements that must be met by a manufacturer in preparing any plan it is required to submit under § 3282.408. The underlying requirement is that the plan show how the manufacturer will fulfill its responsibilities with respect to notification and correction.

(b) *Contents of plan.* The plan must:

(1) Identify, by serial number and other appropriate identifying criteria, all manufactured homes for which notification is to be provided, as determined pursuant to § 3282.404;

(2) Include a copy of the notice that the manufacturer proposes to use to provide the notification required by § 3282.405;

(3) Provide for correction of those manufactured homes that are required to be corrected pursuant to § 3282.406(b);

(4) Include the IPIA's written concurrence or statement on the methods used by the manufacturer to identify the homes that should be included in the class of homes, as required pursuant to § 3282.404(b); and

(5) Include a deadline for completion of all notifications and corrections.

(c) *Contents of notice.* Except as otherwise agreed by the Secretary or the SAA reviewing the plan under § 3282.408, the notice to be approved as part of the plan must include the following:

(1) An opening statement that reads: "This notice is sent to you in accordance with the requirements of the National Manufactured Housing Construction and Safety Standards Act."

(2) The following statement: "[choose one, as appropriate: Manufacturer's name, or the Secretary, or the (insert State) SAA] has determined that [insert identifying criteria of manufactured home] may not comply with an applicable Federal Manufactured Home Construction or Safety Standard."

(3) Except when the manufacturer is providing notice pursuant to an approved plan or agreement with the Secretary or an SAA under § 3282.408, each applicable statement must read as follows:

(i) "An imminent safety hazard may exist in (identifying criteria of manufactured home)."

(ii) "A serious defect may exist in (identifying criteria of manufactured home)."

(iii) "A defect may exist in (identifying criteria of manufactured home)."

(4) A clear description of the defect, serious defect, or imminent safety hazard and an explanation of the risk to the occupants, which must include:

(i) The location of the defect, serious defect, or imminent safety hazard in the manufactured home;

(ii) A description of any hazards, malfunctions, deterioration, or other consequences that may reasonably be expected to result from the defect, serious defect, or imminent safety hazard;

(iii) A statement of the conditions that may cause such consequences to arise; and

(iv) Precautions, if any, that the owner can, should, or must take to reduce the chance that the consequences will arise before the manufactured home is repaired;

(5) A statement of whether there will be any warning that a dangerous occurrence may take place and what that warning would be, and of any signs that the owner might see, hear, smell, or feel that might indicate danger or deterioration of the manufactured home as a result of the defect, serious defect, or imminent safety hazard;

(6) A statement that the manufacturer will correct the manufactured home, if the manufacturer will correct the manufactured home under this subpart or otherwise;

(7) A statement in accordance with whichever of the following is appropriate:

(i) Where the manufacturer will correct the manufactured home at no cost to the owner, the statement must indicate how and when the correction will be done, how long the correction will take, and any other information that may be helpful to the owner; or

(ii) When the manufacturer does not bear the cost of repair, the notification must include a detailed description of all parts and materials needed to make the correction; a description of all steps to be followed in making the correction, including appropriate illustrations; and an estimate of the cost of the purchaser or owner of the correction;

(8) A statement informing the owner that the owner may submit a complaint to the SAA or Secretary if the owner believes that:

(i) The notification or the remedy described therein is inadequate;

(ii) The manufacturer has failed or is unable to remedy the problem in accordance with its notification; or

(iii) The manufacturer has failed or is unable to remedy the problem within a reasonable time after the owner's first attempt to obtain remedy; and

(9) A statement that any actions taken by the manufacturer under the Act in no way limit the rights of the owner or any other person under any contract or other applicable law and that the owner may have further rights under contract or other applicable law.

§ 3282.410 Implementation of plan.

(a) *Deadline for notifications.* (1) The manufacturer must complete the notifications carried out under a plan approved by an SAA or the Secretary under § 3282.408 on or before the deadline approved by the SAA or Secretary. In approving each deadline, an SAA or the Secretary will allow a reasonable time to complete all notifications, taking into account the number of manufactured homes involved and the difficulty of completing the notifications.

(2) The manufacturer must, at the time of dispatch, furnish to the SAA or the Secretary a true or representative copy of each notice, bulletin, and other written communication sent to retailers, distributors, or owners of manufactured homes regarding any serious defect or imminent safety hazard that may exist in any homes produced by the manufacturer, or regarding any noncompliance or defect for which the SAA or Secretary requires, under § 3282.413(c), the manufacturer to submit a plan for providing notification.

(b) *Deadline for corrections.* A manufacturer that is required to correct a serious defect or imminent safety hazard pursuant to § 3282.406(b) must complete implementation of the plan required by § 3282.408 on or before the deadline approved by the SAA or the Secretary. The deadline must be no later than 60 days after approval of the plan. In approving the deadline, the SAA or the Secretary will allow a reasonable amount of time to complete the plan, taking into account the seriousness of the problem, the number of manufactured homes involved, the immediacy of any risk, and the difficulty of completing the action. The serious-

ness and immediacy of any risk posed by the serious defect or imminent safety hazard will be given greater weight than other considerations.

(c) *Extensions.* An SAA that approved a plan or the Secretary may grant an extension of the deadlines included in a plan, if the manufacturer requests such an extension in writing and shows good cause for the extension, if the SAA or the Secretary decides that the extension is justified and not contrary to the public interest. When the Secretary grants an extension for completion of any corrections, the Secretary will notify the manufacturer and must publish notice of such extension in the FEDERAL REGISTER. When an SAA grants an extension for completion of any corrections, the SAA must notify the Secretary and the manufacturer.

(d) *Recordkeeping.* The manufacturer must provide the report and maintain the records that are required by § 3282.417 for all notification and correction actions.

§ 3282.411 SAA initiation of remedial action.

(a) *SAA review of information.* Whenever an SAA has information indicating the possible existence of a noncompliance, defect, serious defect, or imminent safety hazard in a manufactured home, the SAA may initiate administrative review of the need for notification and correction. An SAA initiates administrative review by either:

(1) Referring the matter to another SAA in accordance with paragraph (b) of this section or to the Secretary; or

(2) Taking action itself, in accordance with § 3282.412, when it appears that all of the homes affected by the noncompliance, defect, serious defect, or imminent safety hazard were manufactured in the SAA's State.

(b) *SAA referral of matter.* If at any time it appears that the affected manufactured homes were manufactured in more than one State, an SAA that decides to initiate such administrative review must refer the matter to the Secretary for possible action pursuant to § 3282.412. If it appears that all of the affected manufactured homes were manufactured in another State, an SAA that decides to initiate administrative review must refer the matter to the SAA in the State of manufacture or to the Secretary, for possible action pursuant to § 3282.412.

§ 3282.412 Preliminary and final administrative determinations.

(a) *Grounds for issuance of preliminary determination.* The Secretary or, in accordance with § 3282.411, an SAA in the State of manufacture, may issue a Notice of Preliminary Determination when:

(1) The manufacturer has not provided to the Secretary or SAA the necessary information to make a determination that:

(i) A noncompliance, defect, serious defect, or imminent safety hazard possibly exists; or

(ii) A manufacturer had information that likely indicates a noncompliance, defect, serious defect, or imminent safety hazard for which the manufacturer failed to make the determinations required under § 3282.404;

(2) The Secretary or SAA has information that indicates a noncompliance, defect, serious defect, or imminent safety hazard possibly exists, and, in the case of the SAA, the SAA believes that:

(i) The affected manufactured home has been sold or otherwise released by a manufacturer to a retailer or distributor, but there is no completed sale of the home to a purchaser;

(ii) Based on the same factors that are established for a manufacturer's class determination in § 3282.404(b), the information indicates a class of homes in which a noncompliance or defect possibly exists; or

(iii) The information indicates one or more homes in which a serious defect or an imminent safety hazard possibly exists;

(3) The Secretary or SAA is reviewing a plan under § 3282.408 and the Secretary or SAA disagree with the manufacturer on proposed changes to the plan;

(4) The Secretary or SAA believes that the manufacturer has failed to fulfill the requirements of a waiver granted under § 3282.407(c); or

(5) There is information that a manufacturer failed to make the determinations required under § 3282.404.

(b) *Additional requirements—SAA issuance.* (1) An SAA that receives information that indicates a serious defect or an imminent safety hazard possibly exists in a home manufactured in that SAA's State must notify the Secretary about that information.

(2) An SAA that issues a preliminary determination must provide a copy of the preliminary determination to the Secretary at the time of its issuance. Failure to comply with this requirement does not affect the validity of the preliminary determination.

(c) *Additional requirements—Secretary issuance.* The Secretary will notify the SAA of each State where the affected homes were manufactured, and, to the extent reasonable, the SAA of each State where the homes are located, of the issuance of a preliminary determination. Failure to comply with this requirement does not affect the validity of the preliminary determination.

(d) *Notice of Preliminary Determination.* (1) The Notice of Preliminary Determination must be sent by certified mail or express delivery and must:

(i) Include the factual basis for the determination;

(ii) Include the criteria used to identify any class of homes in which the noncompliance, defect, serious defect, or imminent safety hazard possibly exists;

(iii) If applicable, indicate that the manufacturer may be required to make corrections on a home or in a class of homes; and

(iv) If the preliminary determination is that the manufacturer failed to make an initial determination required under § 3282.404(a), include an allegation that the manufacturer failed to act in good faith.

(2) The Notice of Preliminary Determination must inform the manufacturer that the preliminary determination will become final unless the manufacturer requests a hearing or presentation of views under subpart D of this part.

(e) *Presentation of views.* (1) If a manufacturer elects to exercise its right to a hearing or presentation of views, the Secretary or the SAA, as applicable, must receive the manufacturer's request for a hearing or presentation of views:

(i) Within 15 days of delivery of the Notice of Preliminary Determination of serious defect, defect, or noncompliance; or

(ii) Within 5 days of delivery of the Notice of Preliminary Determination of imminent safety hazard.

(2) A Formal or an Informal Presentation of Views will be held in accordance with § 3282.152 promptly upon receipt of a manufacturer's request under paragraph (c) of this section.

(f) *Issuance of Final Determination.* (1) The SAA or the Secretary, as appropriate, may make a Final Determination that is based on the allegations in the preliminary determination and adverse to the manufacturer if:

(i) The manufacturer fails to respond to the Notice of Preliminary Determination within the time period established in paragraph (c)(2) of this section; or

(ii) The SAA or the Secretary decides that the views and evidence presented by the manufacturer or others are insufficient to rebut the preliminary determination.

(2) At the time that the SAA or Secretary makes a Final Determination that an imminent safety hazard, serious defect, defect, or noncompliance exists, the SAA or Secretary, as appropriate, must issue an order in accordance with § 3282.413.

§ 3282.413 Implementation of Final Determination.

(a) *Issuance of orders.* (1) The SAA or the Secretary, as appropriate, must issue an order directing the manufacturer to furnish notification if:

(i) The SAA makes a Final Determination that a defect or noncompliance exists in a class of homes;

(ii) The Secretary makes a Final Determination that an imminent safety hazard, serious defect, defect, or noncompliance exists; or

(iii) The SAA makes a Final Determination that an imminent safety hazard or a serious defect exists in any home, and the SAA has received the Secretary's concurrence on the issuance of the Final Determination and order.

(2) The SAA or the Secretary, as appropriate, must issue an order directing the manufacturer to make correc-

tions in any affected manufactured home if:

(i) The SAA or the Secretary makes a Final Determination that a defect or noncompliance exists in a manufactured home that has been sold or otherwise released by a manufacturer to a retailer or distributor but for which the sale to a purchaser has not been completed;

(ii) The Secretary makes a Final Determination that an imminent safety hazard or serious defect exists; or

(iii) The SAA makes a Final Determination that an imminent safety hazard or serious defect exists in any home, and the SAA has received the Secretary's concurrence on the issuance of the Final Determination and order.

(3) Only the Secretary may issue an order directing a manufacturer to repurchase or replace any manufactured home already sold to a purchaser, unless the Secretary authorizes an SAA to issue such an order.

(4) An SAA that has a concurrence or authorization from the Secretary on any order issued under this section must have the Secretary's concurrence on any subsequent changes to the order. An SAA that has issued a Preliminary Determination must have the Secretary's concurrence on any waiver of notification or any settlement when the concerns addressed in the Preliminary Determination involve a serious defect or an imminent safety hazard.

(5) If an SAA or the Secretary makes a Final Determination that the manufacturer failed to make, in good faith, an initial determination required under § 3282.404(a):

(i) The SAA may impose any penalties or take any action applicable under State law and may refer the matter to the Secretary for appropriate action; and

(ii) The Secretary may take any action permitted by law.

(b) *Decision to order replacement or repurchase.* The SAA or the Secretary will order correction of any manufactured home covered by an order issued in accordance with paragraph (a)(2) of this section, unless any requirements and factors applicable under § 3282.414 and § 3282.415 indicate that the SAA or the Secretary should order replacement or repurchase of the home.

(c) *Time for compliance with order.* (1) The SAA or the Secretary may require the manufacturer to submit a plan for providing any notification and any correction, replacement, or repurchase remedy that results from an order under this section. The manufacturer's plan must include the method and date by which notification and any corrective action will be provided.

(2) The manufacturer must provide any such notification and correction, replacement, or repurchase remedy as early as practicable, but not later than:

(i) Thirty days after issuance of the order, in the case of a Final Determination of imminent safety hazard or when the SAA or Secretary has ordered replacement or repurchase of a home pursuant to § 3282.414; or

(ii) Sixty days after issuance of the order, in the case of a Final Determination of serious defect, defect, or noncompliance.

(3) Subject to the requirements of paragraph (a)(3) of this section, the SAA that issued the order or the Secretary may grant an extension of the deadline for compliance with an order if:

(i) The manufacturer requests such an extension in writing and shows good cause for the extension; and

(ii) The SAA or the Secretary is satisfied that the extension is justified in the public interest.

(4) When the SAA grants an extension, it must notify the manufacturer and forward to the Secretary a draft of a notice of the extension for the Secretary to publish in the FEDERAL REGISTER. When the Secretary grants an extension, the Secretary must notify the manufacturer and publish notice of such extension in the FEDERAL REGISTER.

(d) *Appeal of SAA determination.* Within 10 days of a manufacturer receiving notice that an SAA has made a Final Determination that an imminent safety hazard, a serious defect, a defect, or noncompliance exists or that the manufacturer failed to make the determinations required under § 3282.404, the manufacturer may appeal the Final De-

termination to the Secretary under § 3282.309.

(e) *Settlement offers.* A manufacturer may propose in writing, at any time, an offer of settlement and shall submit it for consideration by the Secretary or the SAA that issued the Notice of Preliminary Determination. The Secretary or the SAA has the option of providing the manufacturer making the offer with an opportunity to make an oral presentation in support of such offer. If the manufacturer is notified that an offer of settlement is rejected, the offer is deemed to have been withdrawn and will not constitute a part of the record in the proceeding. Final acceptance by the Secretary or an SAA of any offer of settlement automatically terminates any proceedings related to the matter involved in the settlement.

(f) *Waiver of notification.* (1) At any time after the Secretary or an SAA has issued a Notice of Preliminary Determination, the manufacturer may ask the Secretary or SAA to waive any formal notification requirements. When requesting a waiver, the manufacturer must certify that:

(i) The manufacturer has made a class determination in accordance with § 3282.404(b);

(ii) The manufacturer will correct, at the manufacturer's expense, all affected manufactured homes in the class within a time period specified by the Secretary or SAA, but not later than 60 days after the manufacturer is notified of the acceptance of the request for waiver or the issuance of any Final Determination, whichever is later; and

(iii) The proposed repairs are adequate to correct the noncompliance, defect, serious defect, or imminent safety hazard that gave rise to the issuance of the Notice of Preliminary Determination.

(2) If the Secretary or SAA grants a waiver, the manufacturer must reimburse any owner of an affected manufactured home who chose to make the correction before the manufacturer did so, for the reasonable cost of correction.

(g) *Recordkeeping.* The manufacturer must provide the report and maintain the records that are required by § 3282.417 for all notification and correction actions.

§ 3282.414 Replacement or repurchase of homes after sale to purchaser.

(a) *Order to replace or repurchase.* Whenever a manufacturer cannot correct or remove an imminent safety hazard or a serious defect in a manufactured home, for which there is a completed sale to a purchaser, within 60 days of the issuance of an order under § 3282.413 or any extension of the 60-day deadline that has been granted by the Secretary in accordance with § 3282.413(c)(3), the Secretary or, if authorized in writing by the Secretary in accordance with § 3282.413(a)(3), the SAA may require that the manufacturer:

(1) Replace the manufactured home with a home that:

(i) Is substantially equal in size, equipment, and quality; and

(ii) Either is new or is in the same condition that the defective manufactured home would have been in at the time of discovery of the imminent safety hazard or serious defect had the imminent safety hazard or serious defect not existed; or

(2) Take possession of the manufactured home, if the Secretary or the SAA so orders, and refund the purchase price in full, except that the amount of the purchase price may be reduced by a reasonable amount for depreciation if the home has been in the possession of the owner for more than one year and the amount of depreciation is based on:

(i) Actual use of the home; and

(ii) An appraisal system approved by the Secretary or the SAA that does not take into account damage or deterioration resulting from the imminent safety hazard or serious defect.

(b) *Factors affecting order.* In determining whether to order replacement or refund by the manufacturer, the Secretary or the SAA will consider:

(1) The threat of injury or death to manufactured home occupants;

(2) Any costs and inconvenience to manufactured-home owners that will result from the lack of adequate repair within the specified period;

(3) The expense to the manufacturer;

(4) Any obligations imposed on the manufacturer under contract, or other applicable law of which the Secretary or the SAA has knowledge; and

(5) Any other relevant factors that may be brought to the attention of the Secretary or the SAA.

(c) *Owner's election of remedy.* When under contract or other applicable law the owner has the right of election between replacement and refund, the manufacturer must inform the owner of such right of election and must inform the Secretary of the election, if any, made by the owner.

(d) *Recordkeeping.* The manufacturer must provide the report that is required by § 3282.417 when a manufactured home has been replaced or repurchased under this section.

§ 3282.415 Correction of homes before sale to purchaser.

(a) *Sale or lease prohibited.* Manufacturers, retailers, and distributors must not sell, lease, or offer for sale or lease any manufactured home that they have reason to know, in the exercise of due care, contains a noncompliance, defect, serious defect, or imminent safety hazard. The sale of a home to a purchaser is complete when all contractual obligations of the manufacturer, retailer, and distributor to the purchaser and conditions specified in § 3282.252 have been met.

(b) *Retailer/distributor notification to manufacturer.* When a retailer, acting as a reasonable retailer, or a distributor, acting as a reasonable distributor, believes that a manufactured home that has been sold to the retailer or distributor, but for which there is no completed sale to a purchaser, likely contains a noncompliance, defect, serious defect, or imminent safety hazard, the retailer or distributor must notify the manufacturer of the home in a timely manner.

(c) *Manufacturer's remedial responsibilities.* Upon a Final Determination pursuant to § 3282.412(f) by the Secretary or an SAA, a determination by a court of appropriate jurisdiction, or a manufacturer's own determination that a manufactured home that has been sold to a retailer but for which there is no completed sale to a purchaser contains a noncompliance, defect, serious defect, or imminent safety hazard, the manufacturer must do one of the following:

(1) Immediately repurchase such manufactured home from the retailer or distributor at the price paid by the retailer or distributor, plus pay all transportation charges involved, if any, and a reasonable reimbursement of not less than one percent per month of such price paid, prorated from the date the manufacturer receives notice by certified mail of the noncompliance, defect, serious defect, or imminent safety hazard; or

(2) At its expense, immediately furnish to the retailer or distributor all required parts or equipment for installation in the home by the retailer or distributor, and the manufacturer must reimburse the retailer or distributor for the reasonable value of the retailer's or distributor's work, plus a reasonable reimbursement of not less than one percent per month of the manufacturer's or distributor's selling price, prorated from the date the manufacturer receives notice by certified mail to the date the noncompliance, defect, serious defect, or imminent safety hazard is corrected, so long as the retailer or distributor proceeds with reasonable diligence with the required work; or

(3) Carry out all needed corrections to the home.

(d) *Establishing costs.* The value of reasonable reimbursements as specified in paragraph (c) of this section will be fixed by either:

(1) Mutual agreement of the manufacturer and retailer or distributor; or

(2) A court in an action brought under section 613(b) of the Act (42 U.S.C. 5412(b)).

(e) *Records required.* The manufacturer and the retailer or distributor must maintain records of their actions taken under this section in accordance with §3282.417.

(f) *Exception for leased homes.* This section does not apply to any manufactured home purchased by a retailer or distributor that has been leased by such retailer or distributor to a tenant for purposes other than resale. Other remedies that may be available to a retailer or distributor under subpart I of this part continue to be applicable.

(g) *Indemnification.* A manufacturer may indemnify itself through agreements or contracts with retailers, distributors, transporters, installers, or others for the costs of repurchase, parts, equipment, and corrective work incurred by the manufacturer pursuant to paragraph (c).

§3282.416 Oversight of notification and correction activities.

(a) *IPIA responsibilities.* The IPIA in each manufacturing plant must:

(1) Assure that notifications required under this subpart I are sent to all owners, purchasers, retailers, and distributors of whom the manufacturer has knowledge;

(2) Audit the certificates required by §3282.417 to assure that the manufacturer has made required corrections;

(3) Whenever a manufacturer is required to determine a class of homes pursuant to §3282.404(b), provide either:

(i) The IPIA's written concurrence on the methods used by the manufacturer to identify the homes that should be included in the class of homes; or

(ii) The IPIA's written statement explaining why it believes the manufacturer's methods for determining the class of homes were inappropriate or inadequate; and

(4) Conduct, at least monthly, a review the manufacturer's service records of determinations under §3282.404 and take appropriate action in accordance with §§3282.362(c) and 3282.364.

(b) *SAA and Secretary's responsibilities.* (1) SAA oversight of manufacturer compliance with this subpart will be done primarily by periodically checking the records that manufacturers are required to keep under §3282.417.

(2) The SAA or Secretary to which the report required by §3282.417(a) is sent is responsible for assuring, through oversight, that remedial actions have been carried out as described in the report. The SAA of the State in which an affected manufactured home is located may inspect that home to determine whether any correction required under this subpart I is carried out in accordance with the approved plan or, if there is no plan, with the construction and safety standards or other approval obtained by the manufacturer.

§ 3282.417 Recordkeeping requirements.

(a) *Manufacturer report on notifications and corrections.* Within 30 days after the deadline for completing any notifications, corrections, replacement, or repurchase required pursuant to this subpart, the manufacturer must provide a complete report of the action taken to, as appropriate, the Secretary or the SAA that approved the plan under § 3282.408, granted a waiver, or issued the order under § 3282.413. If any other SAA or the Secretary forwarded the relevant consumer complaint or other information to the manufacturer in accordance with § 3282.403, the manufacturer must send a copy of the report to that SAA or the Secretary, as applicable.

(b) *Records of manufacturer's determinations.* (1) A manufacturer must record each initial and class determination required under § 3282.404, in a manner approved by the Secretary or an SAA and that identifies who made each determination, what each determination was, and all bases for each determination. Such information must be available for review by the IPIA.

(2) The manufacturer records must include:

(i) The information it received that likely indicated a noncompliance, defect, serious defect, or imminent safety hazard;

(ii) All of the manufacturer's determinations and each basis for those determinations;

(iii) The methods used by the manufacturer to establish any class, including, when applicable, the cause of the defect, serious defect, or imminent safety hazard; and

(iv) Any IPIA concurrence or statement that it does not concur with the manufacturer's class determination, in accordance with § 3282.404(b).

(3) When the records that a manufacturer is required to keep in accordance with this paragraph (b) involve a class of manufactured homes that have the same noncompliance, defect, serious defect, or imminent safety hazard, the manufacturer has the option of meeting the requirements of this paragraph by establishing a class determination file, instead of including the same information in the file required by para-graph (e) of this section for each affected home. Such class determination file must contain the records of each class determination, notification, and correction, as applicable. For each class determination, the manufacturer must record once in each class determination file the information common to the class, and must identify by serial number all of the homes that the class comprises and that are subject to notification and correction, as applicable.

(c) *Manufacturer records of notifications.* When a manufacturer is required to provide notification under this subpart, the manufacturer must maintain a record of each type of notice sent and a complete list of the persons notified and their addresses. The manufacturer must maintain these records in a manner approved by the Secretary or an SAA to identify each notification campaign.

(d) *Manufacturer records of corrections.* When a manufacturer is required to provide or provides correction under this subpart, the manufacturer must maintain a record of one of the following, as appropriate, for each manufactured home involved:

(1) If the correction is made, a certification by the manufacturer that the repair was made to conform to the federal construction and safety standards in effect at the time the home was manufactured and that each identified imminent safety hazard or serious defect has been corrected; or

(2) If the owner refuses to allow the manufacturer to repair the home, a certification by the manufacturer that:

(i) The owner has been informed of the problem that may exist in the home;

(ii) The owner has been provided with a description of any hazards, malfunctions, deterioration, or other consequences that may reasonably be expected to result from the defect, serious defect, or imminent safety hazard; and

(iii) An attempt has been made to repair the problems, but the owner has refused the repair.

(e) *Maintenance of manufacturer's records.* (1) Except as provided in paragraph (b)(3) of this section, for each manufactured home produced by a manufacturer, the manufacturer must maintain in a printed or electronic format all of the information required by paragraphs (b), (c), and (d) of this section, and must consolidate the information in a readily accessible file or in a readily accessible combination of a printed file and an electronic file. For each home, the manufacturer also must include in such file a copy of the homes data plate; all information related to manufacture, handling, and assembly of the home; any checklist or similar documentation used by the manufacturer in the transport of the home; the name and address of the retailer; the original or a copy of each purchaser's registration record received by the manufacturer; all correspondence with the retailer and homeowner that is related to the home; any information received by the manufacturer regarding setup of the home; all work orders for servicing the home; and the information that the manufacturer is required to keep pursuant to §3282.211. The manufacturer must organize all such files in order of the serial numbers of the homes produced.

(2) The manufacturer must maintain each of these manufactured-home records at the plant where the home was produced. If that plant is no longer in existence, the manufacturer must keep the records at its nearest production plant in the same State, or, if such a plant does not exist, at the manufacturer's corporate headquarters.

§3282.418 Factors for appropriateness and amount of civil penalties.

In determining whether to seek a civil penalty for a violation of the requirements of this subpart, and the amount of such penalty to be recommended, the Secretary will consider the provisions of the Act and the following factors:

(a) The gravity of the violation;

(b) The degree of the violator's culpability, including whether the violator had acted in good faith in trying to comply with the requirements;

(c) The injury to the public;

(d) Any injury to owners or occupants of manufactured homes

(e) The ability to pay the penalty;

(f) Any benefits received by the violator;

(g) The extent of potential benefits to other persons;

(h) Any history of prior violations;

(i) Deterrence of future violations; and

(j) Such other factors as justice may require.

Subpart J—Monitoring of Primary Inspection Agencies

§3282.451 General.

The actions of all primary inspection agencies accepted under subpart H shall be monitored by the Secretary or the Secretary's agent to determine whether the PIAs are fulfilling their responsibilities under these regulations. This monitoring shall be carried out primarily through joint monitoring teams made up of personnel supplied by SAAs and by the Secretary or the Secretary's agent. Monitoring parties shall make recommendations to the Secretary with respect to final acceptance of PIAs under §§3282.361(e) and 3282.362(e), continued acceptance, and disqualification or requalification under §3282.356, and with respect to any changes which PIAs should make in their operations in order to continue to be approved. Based on this monitoring, the Secretary shall determine whether PIAs should continue to be approved under these regulations.

§3282.452 Participation in monitoring.

(a) *Joint monitoring teams.* (1) The Secretary or the Secretary's agent shall develop and coordinate joint monitoring teams which shall be made up of qualified personnel provided by SAAs and by the Secretary or the Secretary's agent. The Secretary or the Secretary's agent shall determine whether personnel are qualified based on education or experience.

(2) The joint monitoring teams will operate generally on a regional basis. To the extent possible, the teams shall be so scheduled that personnel provided by an SAA will be monitoring operations in manufactured home plants from which manufactured homes are shipped into their State.

(3) Personnel from an SAA shall not participate on joint monitoring teams operating within their State.

(4) States are encouraged but not required to participate on joint monitoring teams.

(b) *State monitoring.* A State may carry out monitoring of IPIA functions at plant facilities within the State if the State is not acting as an IPIA. Where a State wishes to carry out monitoring activities it shall do so in coordination with the Secretary and the Secretary's agent. To the extent that the State is performing adequate monitoring, the frequency of the joint team monitoring may be reduced to one visit per year consistent with the requirements of § 3282.453.

(c) *Review of staff capability.* The monitoring party shall review the capability of the PIA's staff to perform the functions it is required to perform.

(d) *Review of interpretations.* The monitoring party shall review all records of interpretations of the standards made by the PIA to determine whether they are consistent and to determine whether there are any conflicts which should be referred to the Secretary for determination.

(e) *DAPIA.* Monitoring parties shall review on a random basis at least 10 percent of the design and quality assurance manual approvals made by each DAPIA in each year.

(f) *IPIA.* The monitoring parties shall assure that the IPIAs are carrying out all of the functions for which they have been accepted. In particular, they shall assure that the manufacturing process is as stated in the certification reports, that the IPIAs are carrying out the required number of inspections, that inspections are effective, and that the IPIAs are maintaining complete label control as required by § 3282.362. A monitoring team shall monitor the IPIA's office procedures, files, and label control and the monitoring team shall send copies of its report to the Secretary or the Secretary's agent, which shall send copies to all monitoring teams which monitor the operations of the subject IPIA.

(g) *Remedial actions.* The monitoring parties shall review the remedial action records of the manufacturers and of the primary inspection agencies closely to determine whether the primary inspection agencies have been carrying out their responsibilities with respect to remedial actions.

§ 3282.453   Frequency and extent of monitoring.

(a) The actions of all primary inspection agencies shall be monitored at a frequency adequate to assure that they are performing consistently and fulfilling their responsibilities under these regulations. Every aspect of the primary inspection agencies' performance shall be monitored.

(b) Frequency of monitoring. The performance of each primary inspection agency shall be monitored during its period of provisional acceptance by a complete review of its records and, in the case of IPAs, by a complete inspection of the operations of at least one manufacturing plant which it has approved or in which it is operating. After the initial inspection, the performance of each primary inspection agency shall be monitored four times per year, except that the number of monitoring visits may be decreased to a minimum of one per year if the performance of the primary inspection agency is deemed by the Secretary or the Secretary's agent to be superior, and it may be increased as necessary if performance is suspect. There shall be a minimum of one review per year of the records of each primary inspection agency, and there shall be more reviews as needed.

Subpart K—Departmental Oversight

§ 3282.501   General.

The Secretary shall oversee the performance of SAAs, the Secretary's agent, and primary inspection agencies as follows:

(a) The Secretary shall review SAA reports to ensure that States are taking appropriate actions with regard to the enforcement of the standards and with respect to the functions for which they are approved under these regulations.

(b) The Secretary shall review monitoring reports submitted by the Secretary's agent to determine that it is performing in accordance with the contract between it and the Secretary.

(c) The Secretary shall review monitoring reports to determine whether PIAs are fulfilling their responsibilities under these regulations.

(d) The Secretary shall make random visits for the purpose of overseeing the activities of SAAs and the Secretary's agent.

(e) The Secretary shall take such other actions to oversee the system established by these regulations as it deems appropriate.

(f) All records maintained by all parties acting under these regulations with respect to those actions shall be available to the Secretary, the Secretary's agent, and where appropriate, SAAs and PIAs for review at any reasonable time.

§ 3282.502 Departmental implementation.

To the extent that SAAs or any parties contracting with the Secretary do not perform functions called for under these regulations, those functions shall be carried out by the Secretary with its own personnel or through other appropriate parties.

§ 3282.503 Determinations and hearings.

The Secretary shall make all the determinations and hold such hearings as are required by these regulations, and the Secretary shall resolve all disputes arising under these regulations.

Subpart L—Manufacturer, IPIA and SAA Reports

§ 3282.551 Scope and purpose.

This subpart describes the reports which shall be submitted by manufacturers, PIAs and SAAs as part of the system of enforcement established under these regulations. Additional reports described in subpart I are required when corrective actions are taken under that subpart.

§ 3282.552 Manufacturer reports for joint monitoring fees.

The manufacturer must submit to the IPIA in each of its manufacturing plants, and to HUD or to the Secretary's agent, a monthly production report that includes the serial numbers of each manufactured home manufactured and labeled at that plant during the preceding month. The report must also include the date of manufacture, State of first location of these manufactured homes after leaving the plant, type of unit, and any other information required under this part. For all homes to be completed pursuant to subpart M of these regulations, the production report must also include a brief description of the work to be completed on site. The State of first location is the State of the premises of the retailer or purchaser to whom the manufactured home is first shipped. The monthly report must be submitted by the 10th day of each month and contain information describing the manufacturer's previous month's activities. The manufacturer is encouraged to submit the report electronically, when feasible.

[80 FR 53727, Sept. 8, 2015]

§ 3282.553 IPIA reports.

Each IPIA shall submit by the twentieth day of each month to each SAA, or if no SAA to the Secretary, in each state where it is engaged in the inspection of manufacturing plants, a report of the operations of each manufacturer in that State for the preceding month which includes the following information:

(a) The number of single-wide and double-wide manufactured homes labeled in the preceding month;

(b) The number of inspection visits made to each manufacturing plant in the preceding month; and

(c) The number of manufactured homes with a failure to conform to the standards or an imminent safety hazard during the preceding month found in the manufacturing plant.

The manufacturers report for the preceding month described in § 3282.552 shall be attached to each such IPIA report as an appendix thereto.

§ 3282.554 SAA reports.

Each SAA shall submit, prior to the last day of each month, to the Secretary a report covering the preceding month which includes:

(a) The description and status of all presentations of views, hearings and other legal actions during the preceding month; and

(b) The description of the SAA's oversight activities and findings regarding consumer complaints, notification, and correction actions during the preceding month. The IPIA report for the preceding month described in § 3282.553, as well as any orders issued pursuant to 3282.413 and manufacturer reports under § 3282.417(a), which were received during the preceding month, are to be attached to each such SAA report as an Appendix thereto.

[41 FR 19852, May 13, 1976, as amended at 78 FR 60208, Oct. 1, 2013]

Subpart M—On-Site Completion of Construction of Manufactured Homes

SOURCE: 80 FR 53727, Sept. 8, 2015, unless otherwise noted.

§ 3282.601 Purpose and applicability.

(a) *Purpose of section.* Under HUD oversight, this section establishes the procedure for limited on-site completion of some aspects of construction that cannot be completed at the factory.

(b) *Applicability.* This section may be applied when all requirements of this subpart are met. To be applicable a manufactured home must:

(1) Be substantially completed in the factory;

(2) Meet the requirements of the Construction and Safety Standards upon completion of the site work; and

(3) Be inspected by the manufacturer's IPIA as provided in this subpart, unless specifically exempted as installation under HUD's Model Installation Standards, 24 CFR part 3285. This subpart does not apply to Alternative Construction (see § 3282.14) that does not comply with the Manufactured Home Construction and Safety Standards.

§ 3282.602 Construction qualifying for on-site completion.

(a) The manufacturer, the manufacturer's DAPIA acting on behalf of HUD, and the manufacturer's IPIA acting on behalf of HUD may agree to permit certain aspects of construction of a manufactured home to be completed to the Construction and Safety Standards on-site in accordance with the require-

ments of this subpart. The aspects of construction that may be approved to be completed on-site are the partial completion of structural assemblies or systems (*e.g.,* electrical, plumbing, heating, cooling, fuel burning, and fire safety systems) and components built as an integral part of the home, when the partial completion on-site is warranted because completion of the partial structural assembly or system during the manufacturing process in the factory would not be practicable (*e.g.,* because of the home design or which could result in transportation damage or if precluded because of road restrictions). Examples of construction that may be completed on-site include:

(1) Hinged roof and eave construction, unless exempted as installation by § 3285.801(f) of the Model Manufactured Home Installation Standards and completed and inspected in accordance with the Manufactured Home Installation Program;

(2) Any work required by the home design that cannot be completed in the factory, or when the manufacturer authorizes the retailer to provide an add-on, not including an attached garage, to the home during installation, when that work would take the home out of conformance with the construction and safety standards and then bring it back into conformance;

(3) Appliances provided by the manufacturer, installer, retailer, or purchaser, including fireplaces to be installed on site;

(4) Components or parts that are shipped loose with the manufactured home and that will be installed on-site, unless exempted as installation by the installation standards;

(5) Exterior applications such as brick siding, stucco, or tile roof systems; and

(6) Other construction such as roof extensions (dormers), site-installed windows in roofs, removable or open floor sections for basement stairs, and sidewall bay windows.

(b) The manufacturer or a licensed contractor or similarly qualified professional with prior authorization from the manufacturer may perform the on-site work in accordance with the DAPIA approvals and site completion instructions. However, the manufacturer is responsible for the adequacy of all on-site completion work regardless of who does the work, and must prepare and provide all site inspection reports, as well as the certification of completion, and must fulfill all of its responsibilities and maintain all records at the factory of origin as required by § 3282.609.

§ 3282.603 Request for approval; DAPIA review, notification, and approval.

(a) *Manufacturer's request for approval.* The manufacturer must request, in writing, and obtain approval of its DAPIA for any aspect of construction that is to be completed on-site under this subpart. The manufacturer, its IPIA, and its DAPIA must work together to reach agreements necessary to enable the request to be reviewed and approved.

(b) *DAPIA notification.* The DAPIA, acting on behalf of HUD, must notify the manufacturer of the results of the DAPIA's review of the manufacturer's request, and must retain a copy of the notification in the DAPIA's records. The DAPIA shall also forward a copy of the approval to HUD or the Secretary's agent as provided under § 3282.361(a)(4). The notification must either:

(1) Approve the request if it is consistent with this section and the objectives of the Act; or

(2) Deny the proposed on-site completion and set out the reasons for the denial.

(c) *Manner of DAPIA approval.* Notification of DAPIA approval must include, by incorporation or by listing, the information required by paragraph (d) of this section, and must be indicated by the DAPIA placing its stamp of approval or authorized signature on each page of the manufacturer's designs submitted with its request for approval. The DAPIA must include an "SC" designation on each page that includes an element of construction that is to be completed on-site and must include those pages as part of the approved design package.

(d) *Contents of DAPIA approval.* Any approval by the DAPIA under this section must:

(1) Include a unique site completion numeric identification for each approval for each manufacturer (*i.e.*, manufacturer name or abbreviation, SC–XX);

(2) Identify the work to be completed on-site;

(3) List all models to which the approval applies, or indicate that the approval is not model-specific;

(4) Include acceptance by the DAPIA of a quality assurance manual for on-site completion meeting the requirements of paragraph (e) of this section;

(5) Include the IPIA's written agreement to accept responsibility for completion of the necessary on-site inspections and accompanying records;

(6) Identify instructions authorized for completing the work on-site that meet the requirements of paragraph (f) of this section;

(7) Include the manufacturer's system for tracking the status of homes built under the approval until the on-site work and necessary inspections have been completed, to assure that the work is being performed properly;

(8) Include a quality control checklist to be used by the manufacturer and IPIA and approved by the DAPIA to verify that all required components, materials, labels, and instructions needed for site completion are provided in each home prior to shipment;

(9) Include an inspection checklist developed by the IPIA and manufacturer and approved by the DAPIA, that is to be used by the final site inspectors;

(10) Include a Consumer Information Notice developed by the manufacturer and approved by the DAPIA that explains the on-site completion process and identifies the work to be completed on-site; and

(11) Include any other requirements and limitations that the DAPIA deems necessary or appropriate to accomplish the purposes of the Act.

(e) *Quality assurance manual for on-site completion requirements.* The portion of the quality assurance manual for on-site completion required by paragraph (d)(3) of this section must receive the written concurrence of the manufacturer's IPIA with regard to its acceptability and applicability to the on-site completion of the affected manufactured homes. It must include a commitment by the manufacturer to prepare a final site inspection report that will be submitted to the IPIA for its review. When appropriate, this portion of the quality assurance manual for on-site completion will be deemed a change in the manufacturer's quality assurance manual for the applicable models, in accordance with §§ 3282.203 and 3282.361.

(f) *Instructions for completion on-site.* The DAPIA must include instructions authorized for completing the work on-site as a separate part of the manufacturer's approved design package. The manufacturer must provide a copy of these instructions and the inspection checklist required by paragraph (d)(9) of this section to the IPIA for monitoring and inspection purposes.

§ 3282.604 DAPIA responsibilities.

The DAPIA, acting on behalf of HUD, for any manufacturer proceeding under this section is responsible for:

(a) Verifying that all information required by § 3282.603 has been submitted by the manufacturer;

(b) Reviewing and approving the manufacturer's designs, quality control checklist, site inspection checklist, site completion instructions, and quality assurance manuals for site work to be performed;

(c) Maintaining all records and approvals for at least 5 years;

(d) Revoking or amending its approvals in accordance with § 3282.609; and

(e) Reviewing its approvals under this section at least every 3 years or more frequently if there are changes made to the Manufactured Home Construction and Safety Standards, 24 CFR part 3280, to verify continued compliance with the Standards.

§ 3282.605 Requirements applicable to completion of construction.

(a) *Serial numbers of homes completed on-site.* The serial number of each home completed in conformance with this section must include the prefix or suffix "SC".

(b) *Labeling.* A manufacturer that has received a DAPIA approval under § 3282.604 may certify and label a manufactured home that is substantially completed in the manufacturer's plant at the proper completion of the in-plant production phase, even though some aspects of construction will be completed on-site in accordance with the DAPIA's approval. Any such homes or sections of such homes must have a label affixed in accordance with § 3282.362(c)(2) and be shipped with a Consumer Information Notice that meets the requirements of § 3282.606.

(c) *Site inspection.* Prior to occupancy, the manufacturer must ensure that each home is inspected on-site. The manufacturer is responsible for inspecting all aspects of construction that are completed on-site as provided in its approved designs and quality assurance manual for on-site completion.

(d) *Site inspection report.* (1) In preparing the site inspection report, the manufacturer must use the inspection checklist approved by the DAPIA in accordance with § 3282.603(d)(9), and must prepare a final site inspection report and provide a copy to the IPIA within 5 business days of completing the report. Within 5 business days after the date that the IPIA notifies the manufacturer of the IPIA's approval of the final site inspection report, the manufacturer must provide a copy of the approved report to the lessor or purchaser prior to occupancy and, as applicable, the appropriate retailer and any person or entity other than the manufacturer that performed the on-site construction work.

(2) Each approved final site inspection report must include:

(i) The name and address of the manufacturer;

(ii) The serial number of the manufactured home;

(iii) The address of the home site;

(iv) The name of the person and/or agency responsible for the manufacturer's final site inspection;

(v) The name of each person and/or agency who performs on-site inspections on behalf of the IPIA, the name of the person responsible for acceptance of the manufacturer's final on-site inspection report on behalf of the IPIA, and the IPIA's name, mailing address, and telephone number;

(vi) A description of the work performed on-site and the inspections made;

(vii) When applicable, verification that any problems noted during inspections have been corrected prior to certification of compliance; and

(viii) Certification by the manufacturer of completion in accordance with the DAPIA-approved instructions and that the home conforms with the approved design or, as appropriate under §3282.362(a)(1)(iii), the construction and safety standards.

(3) The IPIA must review each manufacturer's final on-site inspection report and determine whether to accept that inspection report.

(i) Concurrent with the manufacturer's final site inspection, the IPIA or the IPIA's agent must inspect all of the on-site work for homes completed using an approval under this section. The IPIA must use the inspection checklist approved by the DAPIA in accordance with §3282.603(d)(9).

(ii) If the IPIA determines that the manufacturer is not performing adequately in conformance with the approval, the IPIA must redtag and reinspect until it is satisfied that the manufacturer is conforming to the conditions included in the approval. The home may not be occupied until the manufacturer and the IPIA have provided reports, required by this section, confirming compliance with the Construction and Safety Standards.

(iii) The IPIA must notify the manufacturer of the IPIA's acceptance of the manufacturer's final site inspection report. The IPIA may indicate acceptance by issuing its own final site inspection report or by indicating, in writing, its acceptance of the manufacturer's site inspection report showing that the work completed on-site is in compliance with the DAPIA approval and the Construction and Safety Standards.

(4) Within 5 business days of the date of IPIA's notification to the manufacturer of the acceptance of its final site inspection report, the manufacturer must provide to the purchaser or lessor, as applicable, the manufacturer's final site inspection report. For purposes of establishing the manufacturer's and retailer's responsibilities under the Act and subparts F and I of this part, the sale or lease of the manufactured home will not be considered complete until the purchaser or lessor, as applicable, has been provided with the report.

(e) *Report to HUD.* (1) The manufacturer must report to HUD through its IPIA, on the manufacturer's monthly production report required in accordance with §3282.552, the serial number and site completion numeric identification (see §3282.603(d)(1)) of each home produced under an approval issued pursuant to this section.

(2) The report must be consistent with the DAPIA approval issued pursuant to this section.

(3) The manufacturer must submit a copy of the report, or a separate listing of all information provided on each report for homes that are completed under an approval issued pursuant to this section, to the SAAs of the States where the home is substantially completed in the factory and where the home is sited, as applicable.

§3282.606 Consumer information.

(a) *Notice.* Any home completed under the procedures established in this section must be shipped with a temporary notice that explains that the home will comply with the requirements of the construction and safety standards only after all of the site work has been completed and inspected. The notice must be legible and typed, using letters at least ¼ inch high in the text of the notice and ¾ inch high for the title. The notice must read as follows:

IMPORTANT CONSUMER INFORMATION NOTICE

WARNING: DO NOT LIVE IN THIS HOME UNTIL THE ON–SITE WORK HAS BEEN COMPLETED AND THE MANUFACTURER HAS PROVIDED A COPY OF THE INSPECTION REPORT THAT CERTIFIES THAT THE HOME HAS BEEN INSPECTED AND IS CONSTRUCTED IN ACCORDANCE WITH APPROVED INSTRUCTIONS FOR MEETING THE CONSTRUCTION AND SAFETY STANDARDS.

This home has been substantially completed at the factory and certified as having been constructed in conformance with the Federal Manufactured Home Construction and Safety Standards when specified work is performed and inspected at the home site. This on-site work must be performed in accordance with manufacturer's instructions that have been approved for this purpose. The work to be performed on-site is [insert description of all work to be performed in accordance with the construction and safety standards].

This notice may be removed by the purchaser or lessor when the manufacturer provides the first purchaser or lessor with a copy of the manufacturer's final site inspection report, as required by regulation. This final report must include the manufacturer's certification of completion. All manufactured homes may also be subject to separate regulations requiring approval of items not covered by the Federal Manufactured Home Construction and Safety Standards, such as installation and utility connections.

(b) *Placement of notice in home.* The notice required by paragraph (a) of this section must be displayed in a conspicuous and prominent location within the manufactured home and in a manner likely to assure that it is not removed until, or under the authorization of, the purchaser or lessor. The notice is to be removed only by the first purchaser or lessor. No retailer, installation or construction contractor, or other person may interfere with the required display of the notice.

(c) *Providing notice before sale.* The manufacturer or retailer must also provide a copy of the Consumer Information Notice to prospective purchasers of any home to which the approval applies before the purchasers enter into an agreement to purchase the home.

(d) *When sale or lease of home is complete.* For purposes of establishing the manufacturer's and retailer's responsibilities for on-site completion under the Act and subparts F and I of this part, the sale or lease of the manufactured home will not be considered complete until the purchaser or lessor, as applicable, has been provided with a copy of the final site inspection report required under § 3282.605(d) and a copy of the manufacturer's certification of completion required under § 3282.609(k) and (l). For 5 years from the date of the sale or lease of each home, the manufacturer must maintain in its records an indication that the final on-site inspection report and certification of completion has been provided to the lessor or purchaser and, as applicable, the appropriate retailer.

§ 3282.607 IPIA responsibilities.

The IPIA, acting on behalf of HUD, for any manufacturer proceeding under this section is responsible for:

(a) Working with the manufacturer and the manufacturer's DAPIA to incorporate into the DAPIA-approved quality assurance manual for on-site completion any changes that are necessary to ensure that homes completed on-site conform to the requirements of this section;

(b) Providing the manufacturer with a supply of the labels described in this section, in accordance with the requirements of § 3282.362(c)(2)(i)(A);

(c) Overseeing the effectiveness of the manufacturer's quality control system for assuring that on-site work is completed to the DAPIA-approved designs, which must include:

(1) Verifying that the manufacturer's quality control manual at the installation site is functioning and being followed;

(2) Monitoring the manufacturer's system for tracking the status of each home built under the approval until the on-site work and necessary inspections have been completed;

(3) Reviewing all of the manufacturer's final on-site inspection reports; and

(4) Inspecting all of the on-site construction work for each home utilizing an IPIA inspector or an independent qualified third-party inspector acceptable to the IPIA and acting as the designee or representative:

(i) Prior to close-up, unless access panels are provided to allow the work to be inspected after all work is completed on-site; and

(ii) After all work is completed on-site, except for close-up;

(d) Designating an IPIA inspector or an independent qualified third-party inspector acceptable to the IPIA, as set forth under § 3282.358(d), who is not associated with the manufacturer and is not involved with the site construction or completion of the home and is free of any conflict of interest in accordance with § 3282.359, to inspect the work done on-site for the purpose of determining compliance with:

(1) The approved design or, as appropriate under § 3282.362(a)(1)(iii), the

Construction and Safety Standards; and

(2) The DAPIA-approved quality assurance manual for on-site completion applicable to the labeling and completion of the affected manufactured homes;

(e) Notifying the manufacturer of the IPIA's acceptance of the manufacturer's final site inspection report (see §3282.605(d)(3)(iii));

(f) Preparing final site inspection reports and providing notification to the manufacturer of its acceptance of the manufacturer's final site inspection report within 5 business days of preparing its report. The IPIA is to maintain its final site inspection reports and those of the manufacturer for a period of at least 5 years. All reports must be available for HUD and SAA review in the IPIA's central record office as part of the labeling records; and

(g) Reporting to HUD, the DAPIA, and the manufacturer if one or more homes has not been site inspected prior to occupancy or when arrangements for one or more manufactured homes to be site inspected have not been made.

§3282.608 Manufacturer responsibilities.

A manufacturer proceeding under this section is responsible for:

(a) Obtaining DAPIA approval for completion of construction on-site, in accordance with §3282.603;

(b) Obtaining the IPIA's agreement to perform on-site inspections as necessary under this section and the terms of the DAPIA's approval;

(c) Notifying the IPIA that the home is ready for inspection;

(d) Paying the IPIA's costs for performing on-site inspections of work completed under this section;

(e) Either before or at the time on-site work commences, providing the IPIA with a copy of any applicable DAPIA-approved quality assurance manual for on-site completion, the approved instructions for completing the construction work on-site, and an approved inspection checklist, and maintaining this information on the job site until all on-site work is completed and accepted by the IPIA;

(f) Satisfactorily completing all on-site construction and required repairs

or authorizing a licensed contractor or similarly qualified person to complete all site construction and any needed repairs;

(g) Providing a written certification to the lessor or purchaser, when all site construction work is completed, that each home, to the best of the manufacturer's knowledge and belief, is constructed in conformance with the Construction and Safety Standards;

(h) Ensuring that the consumer notification requirements of §3282.606 are met for any home completed under this subpart;

(i) Maintaining a system for tracking the status of homes built under the approval until the on-site work and necessary inspections have been completed, such that the system will assure that the work is performed in accordance with the quality control manual and other conditions of the approval;

(j) Ensuring performance of all work as necessary to assure compliance with the Construction and Safety Standards upon completion of the site work, including §3280.303(b) of this chapter, regardless of who does the work or where the work is completed;

(k) Preparing a site inspection report upon completion of the work on-site, certifying completion in accordance with DAPIA-approved instruction and that the home conforms with the approved design or, as appropriate under §3282.362(a)(1)(iii), the construction and safety standards;

(l) Arranging for an on-site inspection of each home upon completion of the on-site work by the IPIA or its authorized designee prior to occupancy to verify compliance of the work with the DAPIA-approved designs and the Construction and Safety Standards;

(m) Providing its final on-site inspection report and certification of completion to the IPIA and, after approval, to the lessor or purchaser and, as applicable, the appropriate retailer, and to the SAA upon request;

(n) Maintaining in its records the approval notification from the DAPIA, the manufacturer's final on-site inspection report and certification of completion, and the IPIA's acceptance of the final site inspection report and certification, and making all such records available for review by HUD in the factory of origin;

(o) Reporting to HUD or its agent the serial numbers assigned to each home completed in conformance with this section and as required by § 3282.552; and

(p) Providing cumulative quarterly production reports to HUD or its agent that include the site completion numeric identification number(s) for each home (see § 3282.603(d)(1)); the serial number(s) for each home; the HUD label number(s) assigned to each home; the retailer's name and address for each home; the name, address, and phone number for each home purchaser; the dates of the final site completion inspection for each home; and whether each home was inspected prior to occupancy.

(q) Maintaining copies of all records for on-site completion for each home, as required by this section, in the unit file to be maintained by the manufacturer.

§ 3282.609 Revocation or amendment of DAPIA approval.

(a) The DAPIA that issued an approval or the Secretary may revoke or amend, prospectively, an approval notification issued under § 3282.603. The approval may be revoked or amended whenever the DAPIA or HUD determines that:

(1) The manufacturer is not complying with the terms of the approval or the requirements of this section;

(2) The approval was not issued in conformance with the requirements of § 3282.603;

(3) A home produced under the approval fails to comply with the Federal construction and safety standards or contains an imminent safety hazard; or

(4) The manufacturer fails to make arrangements for one or more manufactured homes to be inspected by the IPIA prior to occupancy.

(b) The DAPIA must immediately notify the manufacturer, the IPIA, and HUD of any revocation or amendment of DAPIA approval.

§ 3282.610 Failure to comply with the procedures of this subpart.

In addition to other sanctions available under the Act and this part, HUD may prohibit any manufacturer or PIA found to be in violation of the requirements of this section from carrying out their functions of this Subpart in the future, after providing an opportunity for an informal presentation of views in accordance with § 3282.152(f). Repeated infractions of the requirements of this section may be grounds for the suspension or disqualification of a PIA under §§ 3282.355 and 3282.356.

§ 3282.611 Compliance with this subpart.

If the manufacturer and IPIA, as applicable, complies with the requirements of this section and the home complies with the construction and safety standards for those aspects of construction covered by the DAPIA approval, then HUD will consider a manufacturer or retailer that has permitted a manufactured home approved for on-site completion under this section to be sold, leased, offered for sale or lease, introduced, delivered, or imported to be in compliance with the certification requirements of the Act and the applicable implementing regulations in this part 3282 for those aspects of construction covered by the approval.

PART 3284—MANUFACTURED HOUSING PROGRAM FEE

Sec.
3284.1 Applicability.
3284.5 Amount of fee.
3284.10 Payments to States.

AUTHORITY: 42 U.S.C. 3535(d), 5419 and 5424.

SOURCE: 67 FR 52835, Aug. 13, 2002, unless otherwise noted.

§ 3284.1 Applicability.

This part applies to manufacturers that are subject to the requirements of the National Manufactured Housing Construction and Safety Standards Act of 1974 (the Act), and to States having State plans approved in accordance with the Act. The amounts established under this part for any fee collected from manufacturers will be used, to the extent approved in advance in an annual appropriations Act, to offset the expenses incurred by HUD in connection with the manufactured housing program authorized by the Act.

§ 3284.5 Amount of fee.

Each manufacturer, as defined in § 3282.7 of this chapter, must pay a fee of $100 per transportable section of each manufactured housing unit that it manufactures under the requirements of part 3280 of this chapter.

[79 FR 47377, Aug. 13, 2014]

§ 3284.10 Payments to States.

Each calendar year HUD will pay each State that, on December 27, 2000, had a State plan approved pursuant to subpart G of part 3282 of this chapter a total amount that is not less than the amount paid to that State for the 12 months ending at the close of business on December 26, 2000.

PART 3285—MODEL MANUFAC-TURED HOME INSTALLATION STANDARDS

Subpart A—General

Subpart B—Pre-Installation Considerations

Subpart C—Site Preparation

Subpart D—Foundations

Subpart E—Anchorage Against Wind

Subpart F—Optional Features

Subpart G—Ductwork and Plumbing and Fuel Supply Systems

Subpart H—Electrical Systems and Equipment

Subpart I—Exterior and Interior Close-Up

Subpart J—Optional Information for Manufacturer's Installation Instructions

3285.907 Manufacturer additions to installation instructions.

AUTHORITY: 42 U.S.C. 3535(d), 5403, 5404, and 5424.

SOURCE: 72 FR 59362, Oct. 19, 2007, unless otherwise noted.

Subpart A—General

§ 3285.1 Administration.

(a) *Scope.* These Model Installation Standards provide minimum requirements for the initial installation of new manufactured homes, in accordance with section 605 of the Act (42 U.S.C. 5404). The Model Installation Standards are one component of the Manufactured Home Installation Program in Part 3286 of this chapter, upon effect, and serve as the basis for developing the manufacturers' installation instructions required by § 3285.2 of this subpart. The manufacturer's installation instructions, including specific methods for performing a specific operation or assembly, will be deemed to comply with these Model Installation Standards, provided they meet or exceed the minimum requirements of these Model Installation Standards and do not take the home out of compliance with the Manufactured Home Construction and Safety Standards (24 CFR part 3280). Work necessary to join all sections of a multi-section home specifically identified in Subparts G, H, and I of this part, or work associated with connecting exterior lights, chain-hung light fixtures, or ceiling-suspended fans, as specifically identified in Subpart I, is not considered assembly or construction of the home, although the design of those elements of a manufactured home must comply with the Manufactured Home Construction and Safety Standards (MHCSS). However, work associated with the completion of hinged roofs and eaves in § 3285.801 and other work done on-site and not specifically identified in this part as close-up is considered construction and assembly and is subject to the requirements of the Manufactured Home Construction and Safety Standards (24 CFR part 3280) and the Manufactured Home Procedural and Enforcement Regulations (24 CFR part 3282).

(1) States that choose to operate an installation program for manufactured homes in lieu of the federal program must implement installation standards that provide protection to its residents that equals or exceeds the protection provided by these Model Installation Standards.

(2) In states that do not choose to operate their own installation program for manufactured homes, these Model Installation Standards serve as the minimum standards for manufactured home installations.

(b) *Applicability.* The standards set forth herein have been established to accomplish certain basic objectives and are not to be construed as relieving manufacturers, retailers, installers, or other parties of responsibility for compliance with other applicable ordinances, codes, regulations, and laws. The manufactured homes covered by this standard must comply with requirements of the U.S. Department of Housing and Urban Development's (HUD) MHCSS Program, as set forth in 24 CFR part 3280, Manufactured Home Construction and Safety Standards, and 24 CFR part 3282, Manufactured Home Procedural and Enforcement Regulations, as well as with, upon effect, the Manufactured Home Installation Program, 24 CFR part 3286, and the Dispute Resolution Program, 24 CFR part 3288. The requirements of this part do not apply to homes installed on site-built permanent foundations when the manufacturer certifies the home in accordance with § 3282.12 of this chapter.

(c) *Consultation with the Manufactured Housing Consensus Committee.* The Secretary will seek input from the Manufactured Housing Consensus Committee (MHCC) when revising the installation standards in this part 3285. Before publication of a proposed rule to revise the installation standards, the Secretary will provide the MHCC with a 120-day opportunity to comment on such revision. The MHCC may send to the Secretary any of the MHCC's own recommendations to adopt new installation standards or to modify or repeal any of the installation standards in this part. Along with each recommendation, the MHCC must set forth pertinent data and arguments in support of the action sought. The Secretary will either:

(1) Accept or modify the recommendation and publish it for public comment in accordance with section 553 of the Administrative Procedure Act (5 U.S.C. 553), along with an explanation of the reasons for any such modification; or

(2) Reject the recommendation entirely, and provide to the MHCC a written explanation of the reasons for the rejection.

§ 3285.2 Manufacturer installation instructions.

(a) *Instructions required.* A manufacturer must provide with each new manufactured home, installation designs and instructions that have been approved by the Secretary or DAPIA. The approved installation instructions must include all topics covered in the Model Installation Standards for the installation of manufactured homes. These installation instructions and any variations thereto that are prepared to comply with paragraph (c) of this section must provide protection to residents of the manufactured homes that equals or exceeds the protection provided by these Model Installation Standards and must not take the manufactured home out of compliance with the MHCSS. These instructions must insure that each home will be supported and anchored in a manner that is capable of meeting or exceeding the design loads required by the MHCSS.

(b) *Professional engineer or registered architect certification.* A professional engineer or registered architect must prepare and certify that the manufacturer's installation instructions meet or exceed the Model Installation Standards for foundation support and anchoring whenever:

(1) The manufacturer's installation instructions do not conform in their entirety to the minimum requirements or tables or their conditions for foundation support and anchoring of this Standard; or

(2) An alternative foundation system or anchoring system is employed, including designs for basements and perimeter support foundation systems, whether or not it is included in the installation instructions; or

(3) Materials such as metal piers or alternatives to concrete footing materials are required by the installation instructions; or

(4) Foundation support and anchoring systems are designed for use in areas subject to freezing or for use in areas subject to flood damage or high seismic risk; or

(5) Foundations support and anchoring systems are designed to be used in special snow load conditions or in severe wind design areas; or

(6) Site conditions do not allow the use of the manufacturer's installation instructions; or

(7) There are any other circumstances in which the manufacturer's installation instructions would not permit the home to be installed in conformance with the Installation Standards or the MHCSS.

(c) *Variations to installation instructions.* (1) Before an installer provides support or anchorage that are different than those methods specified in the manufacturer's installation instructions, or when the installer encounters site or other conditions (such as areas that are subject to flood damage or high seismic risk) that prevent the use of the instructions, the installer must:

(i) First attempt to obtain DAPIA-approved designs and instructions prepared by the manufacturer; or

(ii) If designs and instructions are not available from the manufacturer, obtain an alternate design prepared and certified by a registered professional engineer or registered architect for the support and anchorage of the manufactured home that is consistent with the manufactured home design, conforms to the requirements of the MHCSS, and has been approved by the manufacturer and the DAPIA.

(2) The manufacturer's installation instructions must include an explanation of the requirement in paragraph (c)(1) of this section.

(d) *Installer certification.* In making the certification of the installation required under part 3286 of this chapter, upon effect, an installer must certify that it completed the installation in compliance with either the manufacturer's instructions or with an alternate installation design and instructions that have been prepared by the manufacturer or prepared in compliance with paragraph (c) of this section.

(e) *Temporary storage.* The installation instructions must provide at least one method for temporarily supporting each transportable section of a manufactured home, to prevent structural and other damage to the structure, when those section(s) are temporarily sited at the manufacturer's facility, retailer's lot, or the home site.

§ 3285.3 Alterations during initial installation.

Additions, modifications, or replacement or removal of any equipment that affects the installation of the home made by the manufacturer, retailer, or installer prior to completion of the installation by an installer must equal or exceed the protections and requirements of these Model Installation Standards, the MHCSS (24 CFR part 3280) and the Manufactured Home Procedural and Enforcement Regulations (24 CFR part 3282). An alteration, as defined in § 3282.7 of this chapter, must not affect the ability of the basic manufactured home to comply with the MHCSS, and the alteration must not impose additional loads to the manufactured home or its foundation, unless the alteration is included in the manufacturer's DAPIA-approved designs and installation instructions, or is designed by a registered professional engineer or architect consistent with the manufacturer's design and that conforms to the requirements of the MHCSS.

§ 3285.4 Incorporation by reference (IBR).

(a) The materials listed in this section are incorporated by reference in the corresponding sections noted. These incorporations by reference were approved by the Director of the Federal Register, in accordance with 5 U.S.C. 552(a) and 1 CFR part 51. The materials are available for purchase at the corresponding addresses noted below, and all are available for inspection at the Office of Manufactured Housing Programs, U.S. Department of Housing and Urban Development, 451 Seventh Street, SW., Room 9164, Washington, DC 20410; or the National Archives and Records Administration (NARA). For information on the availability of this material at NARA, call (202) 741-6030, or go to: *http://www.archives.gov/federal-register/cfr/ibr-locations.html.*

(b) The materials listed below are available for purchase from the Air Conditioning Contractors of America (ACCA), 2800 Shirlington Road, Suite 300, Arlington, Virginia 22206.

(1) ACCA Manual J, Residential Load Calculation, 8th Edition, IBR approved for § 3285.503(a)(1)(i)(A).

(2) [Reserved]

(c) The materials listed below are available for purchase from APA—The Engineered Wood Association, 7011 South 19th Street, Tacoma, Washington 98411, telephone number (253) 565-6600, fax number (253) 565-7265.

(1) PS1-95, Construction and Industrial Plywood (with typical APA trademarks), 1995 edition, IBR approved for § 3285.312(a)(2)(i).

(2) [Reserved]

(d) The materials listed below are available for purchase from American Society of Heating, Refrigerating and Air Conditioning Engineers (ASHRAE), 1791 Tullie Circle, NE., Atlanta, Georgia 30329-2305.

(1) ASHRAE Handbook of Fundamentals, 1997 Inch-Pound Edition, IBR approved for § 3285.503(a)(1)(i)(A).

(2) [Reserved]

(e) The materials listed below are available for purchase from American Society for Testing and Materials (ASTM), 100 Barr Harbor Drive, West Conshohocken, Pennsylvania 19428-2959.

(1) ASTM C 90-02a, Standard Specification for Loadbearing Concrete Masonry Units, 2002, IBR approved for § 3285.312(a)(1)(i).

(2) ASTM D 1586-99, Standard Test Method for Penetration Test and Split-Barrel Sampling of Soils, 1999, IBR approved for the table at § 3285.202(c).

(3) ASTM D 2487-00, Standard Practice for Classification of Soils for Engineering Purposes (Unified Soil Classification System), 2000, IBR approved for the table at § 3285.202(c).

(4) ASTM D 2488-00, Standard Practice for Description and Identification of Soils (Visual-Manual Procedure), 2000, IBR approved for the table at § 3285.202(c).

(5) ASTM D 3953-97, Standard Specification for Strapping, Flat Steel and Seals, 1997, IBR approved for

§ 3285.402(b)(2) and Note 10 to Table 1 to § 3285.402.

(f) The materials listed below are available for purchase from American Wood-Preservers' Association (AWPA), P.O. Box 388, Selma, Alabama 36702.

(1) AWPA M4–02, Standard for the Care of Preservative-Treated Wood Products, 2002, IBR approved for § 3285.312(a)(2)(iii).

(2) AWPA U1–04, Use Category System; User Specification for Treated Wood, 2004, IBR approved for §§ 3285.303(b)(1), 3285.312(a)(2)(ii), and 3285.504(c).

(g) The materials listed below are available for purchase from the Federal Emergency Management Administration (FEMA), 500 C Street, SW., Washington, DC 20472.

(1) FEMA 85/September 1985, Manufactured Home Installation in Flood Hazard Areas, 1985, IBR approved for § 3285.102(d)(3).

(2) [Reserved]

(h) The materials listed below are available for purchase from the National Fire Protection Association (NFPA), 1 Batterymarch Park, Quincy, Massachusetts 02169–7471.

(1) NFPA 31, Standard for the Installation of Oil Burning Equipment, 2001 edition, IBR approved for §§ 3285.905(a) and 3285.905(d)(3).

(2) NFPA 70, National Electrical Code, 2005 edition, IBR approved for §§ 3285.702(e)(1) and 3285.906.

(3) NFPA 501A, Standard for Fire Safety Criteria for Manufactured Home Installations, Sites, and Communities, 2003 edition, IBR approved for § 3285.101.

(i) The materials listed below are available for purchase from the Structural Engineering Institute/American Society of Civil Engineers (SEI/ASCE), 1801 Alexander Bell Drive, Reston, Virginia 20191.

(1) SEI/ASCE 32–01, Design and Construction of Frost-Protected Shallow Foundations, 2001, IBR approved for §§ 3285.312(b)(2)(ii) and 3285.312(b)(3)(ii).

(2) [Reserved]

(j) The materials listed below are available for purchase from Underwriters Laboratories (UL), 333 Pfingsten Road, Northbrook, Illinois 60062.

(1) UL 181A, Closure Systems for Use With Rigid Air Ducts and Air Connec-tors, 1994, with 1998 revisions, IBR approved for § 3285.606(a).

(2) UL 181B, Closure Systems for Use With Flexible Air Ducts and Air Connectors, 1995, with 1998 revisions, IBR approved for § 3285.606(a).

§ 3285.5 Definitions.

The definitions contained in this section apply to the terms used in these Model Installation Standards. Where terms are not included, common usage of the terms applies. The definitions are as follows:

Act. The National Manufactured Housing Construction and Safety Standards Act of 1974, 42 U.S.C. 5401–5426.

Anchor assembly. Any device or other means designed to transfer home anchoring loads to the ground.

Anchoring equipment. Ties, straps, cables, turnbuckles, chains, and other approved components, including tensioning devices that are used to secure a manufactured home to anchor assemblies.

Anchoring system. A combination of anchoring equipment and anchor assemblies that will, when properly designed and installed, resist the uplift, overturning, and lateral forces on the manufactured home and on its support and foundation system.

Approved. When used in connection with any material, appliance or construction, means complying with the requirements of the Department of Housing and Urban Development.

Arid region. An area subject to 15 inches or less of annual rainfall.

Base flood. The flood having a one percent chance of being equaled or exceeded in any given year.

Base flood elevation (BFE). The elevation of the base flood, including wave height, relative to the datum specified on a LAHJ's flood hazard map.

Comfort cooling certificate. A certificate permanently affixed to an interior surface of the home specifying the factory design and preparations for air conditioning the manufactured home.

Crossovers. Utility interconnections in multi-section homes that are located where the sections are joined. Crossover connections include heating and cooling ducts, electrical circuits, water pipes, drain plumbing, and gas lines.

Design Approval Primary Inspection Agency (DAPIA). A state or private organization that has been accepted by the Secretary in accordance with the requirements of Part 3282, Subpart H of this chapter, which evaluates and approves or disapproves manufactured home designs and quality control procedures.

Diagonal tie. A tie intended to resist horizontal or shear forces, but which may resist vertical, uplift, and overturning forces.

Flood hazard area. The greater of either: The special flood hazard area shown on the flood insurance rate map; or the area subject to flooding during the design flood and shown on a LAHJ's flood hazard map, or otherwise legally designated.

Flood hazard map. A map delineating the flood hazard area and adopted by a LAHJ.

Footing. That portion of the support system that transmits loads directly to the soil.

Foundation system. A system of support that is capable of transferring all design loads to the ground, including elements of the support system, as defined in this section, or a site-built permanent foundation that meets the requirements of 24 CFR 3282.12.

Ground anchor. A specific anchoring assembly device designed to transfer home anchoring loads to the ground.

Installation instructions. DAPIA-approved instructions provided by the home manufacturer that accompany each new manufactured home and detail the home manufacturer requirements for support and anchoring systems, and other work completed at the installation site to comply with these Model Installation Standards and the Manufactured Home Construction and Safety Standards in 24 CFR part 3280.

Installation standards. Reasonable specifications for the installation of a new manufactured home, at the place of occupancy, to ensure proper siting; the joining of all sections of the home; and the installation of stabilization, support, or anchoring systems.

Labeled. A label, symbol, or other identifying mark of a nationally recognized testing laboratory, inspection agency, or other organization concerned with product evaluation that maintains periodic inspection of production of labeled equipment or materials, and by whose labeling is indicated compliance with nationally recognized standards or tests to determine suitable usage in a specified manner.

Listed or certified. Included in a list published by a nationally recognized testing laboratory, inspection agency, or other organization concerned with product evaluation that maintains periodic inspection of production of listed equipment or materials, and whose listing states either that the equipment or material meets nationally recognized standards or has been tested and found suitable for use in a specified manner.

Local authority having jurisdiction (LAHJ). The state, city, county, city and county, municipality, utility, or organization that has local responsibilities and requirements that must be complied with during the installation of a manufactured home.

Lowest floor. The floor of the lowest enclosed area of a manufactured home. An unfinished or flood-resistant enclosure, used solely for vehicle parking, home access, or limited storage, must not be considered the lowest floor, provided the enclosed area is not constructed so as to render the home in violation of the flood-related provisions of this standard.

Manufactured home. A structure, transportable in one or more sections, which in the traveling mode is 8 body feet or more in width or 40 body feet or more in length, or which when erected on site is 320 or more square feet, and which is built on a permanent chassis and designed to be used as a dwelling with or without a permanent foundation when connected to the required utilities, and includes the plumbing, heating, air-conditioning, and electrical systems contained in the structure. This term includes all structures that meet the above requirements, except the size requirements and with respect to which the manufacturer voluntarily files a certification, pursuant to § 3282.13 of this chapter, and complies with the MHCSS set forth in part 3280 of this chapter. The term does not include any self-propelled recreational vehicle. Calculations used to determine the number of square feet in a structure will include the total of square feet for each transportable section comprising the completed structure and will be based on the structure's exterior dimensions measured at the largest horizontal projections when erected on-site. These dimensions will include all expandable rooms, cabinets, and other projections containing interior space, but do not include bay windows. Nothing in this definition should be interpreted to mean that a manufactured home necessarily meets the requirements of HUD's Minimum Property Standards (HUD Handbook 4900.1) or that it is automatically eligible for financing under 12 U.S.C. 1709(b) certification.

Manufactured Home Construction and Safety Standards or MHCSS. The Manufactured Home Construction and Safety Standards established in part 3280 of this chapter, pursuant to section 604 of the Act, 42 U.S.C. 5403.

Manufactured home gas supply connector. A listed connector designed for connecting the manufactured home to the gas supply source.

Manufactured home site. A designated parcel of land designed for the installation of one manufactured home for the exclusive use of the occupants of the home.

Manufactured Housing Consensus Committee or MHCC. The consensus committee established pursuant to section 604(a)(3) of the Act, 42 U.S.C. 5403(a)(3).

Model Installation Standards. The installation standards established in part 3285 of this chapter, pursuant to section 605 of the Act, 42 U.S.C. 5404.

Peak cap construction means any roof peak construction that is either shipped loose or site constructed and is site installed to complete the roof ridge/peak of a home.

Peak flip construction means any roof peak construction that requires the joining of two or more cut top chord members on site. The cut top chords must be joined at the factory by straps, hinges, or other means.

Pier. That portion of the support system between the footing and the manufactured home, exclusive of shims. Types of piers include, but are not limited to: Manufactured steel stands;

pressure-treated wood; manufactured concrete stands; concrete blocks; and portions of foundation walls.

Ramada. Any freestanding roof or shade structure, installed or erected above a manufactured home or any portion thereof.

Secretary. The Secretary of Housing and Urban Development, or an official of HUD delegated the authority of the Secretary with respect to the Act.

Site. An area of land upon which a manufactured home is installed.

Skirting. A weather-resistant material used to enclose the perimeter, under the living area of the home, from the bottom of the manufactured home to grade.

Stabilizing devices. All components of the anchoring and support systems, such as piers, footings, ties, anchoring equipment, anchoring assemblies, or any other equipment, materials, and methods of construction, that support and secure the manufactured home to the ground.

State. Each of the several states, the District of Columbia, the Commonwealth of Puerto Rico, Guam, the Virgin Islands, and American Samoa.

Support system. Pilings, columns, footings, piers, foundation walls, shims, and any combination thereof that, when properly installed, support the manufactured home.

Tie. Straps, cable, or securing devices used to connect the manufactured home to anchoring assemblies.

Ultimate load. The absolute maximum magnitude of load that a component or system can sustain, limited only by failure.

Utility connection. The connection of the manufactured home to utilities that include, but are not limited to, electricity, water, sewer, gas, or fuel oil.

Vertical tie. A tie intended to resist uplifting and overturning forces.

Wind zone. The areas designated on the Basic Wind Zone Map, as further defined in § 3280.305(c) of the Manufactured Home Construction and Safety Standards in this chapter, which delineate the wind design load requirements.

Working load. The maximum recommended load that may be exerted on a component or system determined by

211

dividing the ultimate load of a component or system by an appropriate factor of safety.

[72 FR 59362, Oct. 19, 2007, as amended at 79 FR 53614, Sept. 10, 2014; 80 FR 53731, Sept. 8, 2015]

§ 3285.6 Final leveling of manufactured home.

The manufactured home must be adequately leveled prior to completion of the installation, so that the home's performance will not be adversely affected. The home will be considered adequately leveled if there is no more than ¼ inch difference between adjacent pier supports (frame or perimeter) and the exterior doors and windows of the home do not bind and can be properly operated.

Subpart B—Pre-Installation Considerations

§ 3285.101 Fire separation.

Fire separation distances must be in accordance with the requirements of Chapter 6 of NFPA 501A, 2003 edition (incorporated by reference, see § 3285.4) or the requirements of the LAHJ. The installation instructions must clearly indicate this requirement in a separate section and must caution installers to take into account any local requirements on fire separation.

§ 3285.102 Installation of manufactured homes in flood hazard areas.

(a) *Definitions.* Except to the extent otherwise defined in Subpart A, the terms used in this subpart are as defined in 44 CFR 59.1 of the National Flood Insurance Program (NFIP) regulations.

(b) *Applicability.* The provisions of this section apply to the initial installation of new manufactured homes located wholly or partly within a flood hazard area.

(c) *Pre-installation considerations.* Prior to the initial installation of a new manufactured home, the installer is responsible for determining whether the manufactured home site lies wholly or partly within a special flood hazard area as shown on the LAHJ's Flood Insurance Rate Map, Flood Boundary and Floodway Map, or Flood Hazard Boundary Map, or if no LAHJ, in accordance

with NFIP regulations. If so located, and before an installation method is agreed upon, the map and supporting studies adopted by the LAHJ must be used to determine the flood hazard zone and base flood elevation at the site.

(d) *General elevation and foundation requirements*—(1) *Methods and practices.* Manufactured homes located wholly or partly within special flood hazard areas must be installed on foundations engineered to incorporate methods and practices that minimize flood damage during the base flood, in accordance with the requirements of the LAHJ, 44 CFR 60.3(a) through (e), and other provisions of 44 CFR referenced by those paragraphs.

(2) *Outside appliances.* (i) Appliances installed on the manufactured home site in flood hazard areas must be anchored and elevated to or above the same elevation as the lowest elevation of the lowest floor of the home.

(ii) Appliance air inlets and exhausts in flood hazard areas must be located at or above the same elevation as the lowest elevation of the lowest floor of the home.

(3) *Related guidance.* Refer to FEMA 85/September 1985, Manufactured Home Installation in Flood Hazard Areas, 1985 (incorporated by reference, see § 3285.4).

§ 3285.103 Site suitability with design zone maps.

Prior to the initial installation of a new manufactured home and as part of making the certification of the installation required under part 3286, upon effect, the installer is to verify that the design and construction of the manufactured home, as indicated on the design zone maps provided with the home, are suitable for the site location where the home is to be installed. The design zone maps are those identified in part 3280 of this chapter.

(a) *Wind zone.* Manufactured homes must not be installed in a wind zone that exceeds the design wind loads for which the home has been designed, as evidenced by the wind zone indicated on the home's data plate and as further defined by counties or local governments within affected states, as applicable, in § 3280.305(c)(2) of the Manufactured Home Construction and Safety Standards in this chapter.

(b) *Roof load zone.* Manufactured homes must not be located in a roof load zone that exceeds the design roof load for which the home has been designed, as evidenced by the roof load zone indicated on the home's data plate and as further defined by counties or local governments within affected states, as applicable, in § 3280.305(c)(3) of the Manufactured Home Construction and Safety Standards in this chapter. Refer to § 3285.315 for Special Snow Load Conditions.

(c) *Thermal zone.* Manufactured homes must not be installed in a thermal zone that exceeds the thermal zone for which the home has been designed, as evidenced by the thermal zone indicated on the heating/cooling certificate and insulation zone map and as further defined by counties or local governments within affected states, as applicable, in § 3280.504(b)(5) of the Manufactured Home Construction and Safety Standards in this chapter. The manufacturer may provide the heating/cooling information and insulation zone map on the home's data plate.

§ 3285.104 Moving manufactured home to location.

Refer to § 3285.902 for considerations related to moving the manufactured home to the site of installation.

§ 3285.105 Permits, other alterations, and on-site structures.

Refer to § 3285.903 for considerations related to permitting, other alterations, and on-site structures.

Subpart C—Site Preparation

§ 3285.201 Soil conditions.

To help prevent settling or sagging, the foundation must be constructed on firm, undisturbed soil or fill compacted to at least 90 percent of its maximum relative density. All organic material such as grass, roots, twigs, and wood scraps must be removed in areas where footings are to be placed. After removal of organic material, the home site must be graded or otherwise prepared to ensure adequate drainage, in accordance with § 3285.203.

§ 3285.202 Soil classifications and bearing capacity.

The soil classification and bearing capacity of the soil must be determined before the foundation is constructed and anchored. The soil classification and bearing capacity must be determined by one or more of the following methods, unless the soil bearing capacity is established as permitted in paragraph (f) of this section:

(a) *Soil tests.* Soil tests that are in accordance with generally accepted engineering practice; or

(b) *Soil records.* Soil records of the applicable LAHJ; or

(c) *Soil classifications and bearing capacities.* If the soil class or bearing capacity cannot be determined by test or soil records, but its type can be identified, the soil classification, allowable pressures, and torque values shown in Table to § 3285.202 may be used.

(d) A pocket penetrometer; or

(e) In lieu of determining the soil bearing capacity by use of the methods shown in the table, an allowable pressure of 1,500 psf may be used, unless the site-specific information requires the use of lower values based on soil classification and type.

(f) If the soil appears to be composed of peat, organic clays, or uncompacted fill, or appears to have unusual conditions, a registered professional geologist, registered professional engineer, or registered architect must determine the soil classification and maximum allowable soil bearing capacity.

TABLE TO § 3285.202

Soil classification		Soil description	Allowable soil bearing pressure (psf) [1]	Blow count ASTM D 1586-99	Torque probe [3] value [4] (inch-pounds)-
Classification number	ASTM D 2487–00 or D 2488–00 (incorporated by reference, see § 3285.4)				
1	....	Rock or hard pan	4000 + ...		

213

TABLE TO § 3285.202—Continued

Soil classification		Soil description	Allowable soil bearing pressure (psf) [1]	Blow count ASTM D 1586–99	Torque probe [3] value [4] (inch-pounds)-
Classi-fication number	ASTM D 2487–00 or D 2488–00 (incorporated by reference, see § 3285.4)				
2	GW, GP, SW, SP, GM, SM	Sandy gravel and gravel; very than dense and/orcemented sands;coursegravel/cobbles;preloaded silts,clays and coral.	2000	40 +	More than 550.
3	GC, SC, ML, CL	Sand; silty sand; clayey sand; siltygravel; medium dense course sands; sandygravel; and very stiff silt, sand clays.	1500	24–39	351–550.
4A	CG, MH [2]	Loose to medium dense sands; firm to stiff clays and silts; alluvial fills.	1000	18–23	276–350.
4B	CH, MH [2]	Loose sands; firm clays; alluvial fills	1000	12–17	175–275.
5	OL, OH, PT	Uncompacted fill; peat; organic clays	Refer to 3285.202(e).	0–11	Less than 175.

Notes:
[1] The values provided in this table have not been adjusted for overburden pressure, embedment depth, water table height, or settlement problems.
[2] For soils classified as CH or MH, without either torque probe values or blow count test results, selected anchors must be rated for a 4B soil.
[3] The torque test probe is a device for measuring the torque value of soils to assist in evaluating the holding capacity of the soil in which the ground anchor is placed. The shaft must be of suitable length for the full depth of the ground anchor.
[4] The torque value is a measure of the load resistance provided by the soil when subject to the turning or twisting force of the probe.

§ 3285.203 Site Drainage.

(a) *Purpose.* Drainage must be provided to direct surface water away from the home to protect against erosion of foundation supports and to prevent water build-up under the home, as shown in Figure to § 3285.203.

(b) The home site must be graded as shown in Figure to § 3285.203, or other methods, such as a drain tile and automatic sump pump system, must be provided to remove any water that may collect under the home.

(c) All drainage must be diverted away from the home and must slope a minimum of one-half inch per foot away from the foundation for the first ten feet. Where property lines, walls, slopes, or other physical conditions prohibit this slope, the site must be provided with drains or swales or otherwise graded to drain water away from the structure, as shown in Figure to § 3285.203.

(d) *Sloped site considerations.* The home, where sited, must be protected from surface runoff from the surrounding area.

(e) Refer to § 3285.902 regarding the use of drainage structures to drain surface runoff.

(f) *Gutters and downspouts.* Manufacturers must specify in their installation instructions whether the home is suitable for the installation of gutters and downspouts. If suitable, the installation instructions must indicate that when gutters and downspouts are installed, the runoff must be directed away from the home.

Figure to § 3285.203 - Grading and drainage.

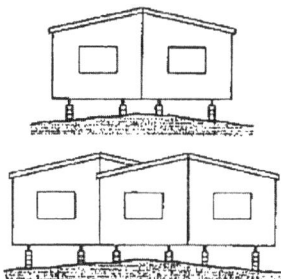

Crown and grade site to slope away from the home

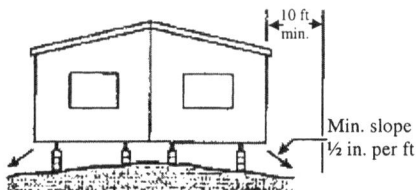

Home sites must be prepared so that there will be no depressions in which surface water may accumulate beneath the home. The area of the site covered by the manufactured home must be graded, sloped, or designed to provide drainage from beneath the home or to the property line.

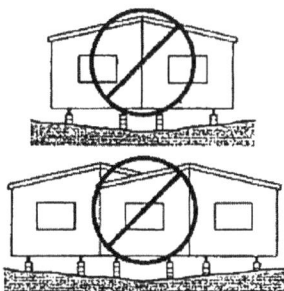

Do not grade site or set the home so that water collects beneath the home.

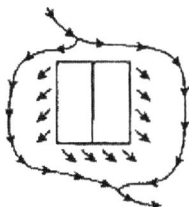

Natural drainage must be diverted around and away from the home.

§ 3285.204 Ground moisture control.

(a) *Vapor retarder.* If the space under the home is to be enclosed with skirting or other materials, a vapor retarder must be installed to cover the ground under the home, unless the home is installed in an arid region with dry soil conditions.

(b) *Vapor retarder material.* A minimum of six mil polyethylene sheeting or its equivalent must be used.

(c) *Proper installation.* (1) The entire area under the home must be covered with the vapor retarder, as noted in § 3285.204(a), except for areas under open porches, decks, and recessed entries. Joints in the vapor retarder must be overlapped at least 12 inches.

(2) The vapor retarder may be placed directly beneath footings, or otherwise installed around or over footings placed at grade, and around anchors or other obstructions.

(3) Any voids or tears in the vapor retarder must be repaired. At least one repair method must be provided in the manufacturer's installation instructions.

Subpart D—Foundations

§ 3285.301 General.

(a) Foundations for manufactured home installations must be designed and constructed in accordance with this subpart and must be based on site conditions, home design features, and the loads the home was designed to withstand, as shown on the home's data plate.

(b) Foundation systems that are not pier and footing type configurations may be used when verified by engineering data and designed in accordance with § 3285.301(d), consistent with the design loads of the MHCSS. Pier and footing specifications that are different than those provided in this subpart, such as block size, metal piers, section width, loads, and spacing, may be used when verified by engineering data that comply with §§ 3285.301(c) and (d) and are capable of resisting all design loads of the MHCSS.

(c) All foundation details, plans, and test data must be designed and certified by a registered professional engineer or registered architect, and must

not take the home out of compliance with the MHCSS. (See 3285.2)

(d) Alternative foundation systems or designs are permitted in accordance with either of the following:

(1) Systems or designs must be manufactured and installed in accordance with their listings by a nationally recognized testing agency, based on a nationally recognized testing protocol; or

(2) System designs must be prepared by a professional engineer or a registered architect or tested and certified by a professional engineer or registered architect in accordance with acceptable engineering practice and must be manufactured and installed so as not to take the home out of compliance with the Manufactured Home Construction and Safety Standards (part 3280 of this chapter).

§ 3285.302 Flood hazard areas.

In flood hazard areas, foundations, anchorings, and support systems must be capable of resisting loads associated with design flood and wind events or combined wind and flood events, and homes must be installed on foundation supports that are designed and anchored to prevent floatation, collapse, or lateral movement of the structure. Manufacturer's installation instructions must indicate whether:

(a) The foundation specifications have been designed for flood-resistant considerations, and, if so, the conditions of applicability for velocities, depths, or wave action; or

(b) The foundation specifications are not designed to address flood loads.

§ 3285.303 Piers.

(a) *General.* The piers used must be capable of transmitting the vertical live and dead loads to the footings or foundation.

(b) *Acceptable piers—materials specification.* (1) Piers are permitted to be concrete blocks; pressure-treated wood with a water borne preservative, in accordance with AWPA Standard U1-04 (incorporated by reference, see § 3285.4) for Use Category 4B ground contact applications; or adjustable metal or concrete piers.

(2) Manufactured piers must be listed or labeled for the required vertical load

capacity, and, where required by design, for the appropriate horizontal load capacity.

(c) *Design requirements.* (1) *Load-bearing capacity.* The load bearing capacity for each pier must be designed to include consideration for the dimensions of the home, the design dead and live loads, the spacing of the piers, and the way the piers are used to support the home.

(2) Center beam/mating wall support must be required for multi-section homes and designs must be consistent with Tables 2 and 3 to § 3285.303 and Figures A, B, and C to § 3285.310.

(d) *Pier loads.* (1) Design support configurations for the pier loads, pier spacing, and roof live loads must be in accordance with Tables 1, 2, and 3 to § 3285.303 and the MHCSS. Other pier designs are permitted in accordance with the provisions of this subpart.

(2) Manufactured piers must be rated at least to the loads required to safely support the dead and live loads, as required by § 3285.301, and the installation instructions for those piers must be consistent with Tables 1, 2, and 3 to this section.

TABLE 1 TO § 3285.303—FRAME BLOCKING ONLY/PERIMETER SUPPORT NOT REQUIRED EXCEPT AT OPENINGS

Pier spacing	Roof live load (psf)	Location	Load (lbs.)
4 ft. 0 in.	20	Frame	2,900
	30	Frame	3,300
	40	Frame	3,600
6 ft. 0 in.	20	Frame	4,200
	30	Frame	4,700
	40	Frame	5,200
8 ft. 0 in.	20	Frame	5,500
	30	Frame	6,200
	40	Frame	6,900
10 ft. 0 in.	20	Frame	6,800
	30	Frame	7,600
	40	Frame	8,500

NOTES: 1. See Table to § 3285.312 for cast-in-place footing design by using the noted loads.

2. Table 1 is based on the following design assumptions: maximum 16 ft. nominal section width (15 ft. actual width), 12" eave, 10" I-beam size, 300 lbs. pier dead load, 10 psf roof dead load, 6 psf floor dead load, 35 plf wall dead load, and 10 plf chassis dead load.

3. Interpolation for other pier spacing is permitted.

4. The pier spacing and loads shown in the above table do not consider flood or seismic loads and are not intended for use in flood or seismic hazard areas. In those areas, the foundation support system is to be designed by a professional engineer or architect.

5. See Table to § 3285.312 for sizing of footings.

TABLE 2 TO § 3285.303—FRAME PLUS PERIMETER BLOCKING/PERIMETER BLOCKING REQUIRED

Maximum pier spacing	Roof live load(psf)	Location	Load (lbs.)
4 ft. 0 in.	20	Frame	1,400
		Perimeter	1,900
		Mating	3,200
4 ft. 0 in.	30	Frame	1,400
		Perimeter	2,300
		Mating	3,800
4 ft. 0 in.	40	Frame	1,400
		Perimeter	2,600
		Mating	4,400
6 ft. 0 in.	20	Frame	1,900
		Perimeter	2,700
		Mating	4,700
6 ft. 0 in.	30	Frame	1,900
		Perimeter	3,200
		Mating	5,600
6 ft. 0 in.	40	Frame	1,900
		Perimeter	3,700
		Mating	6,500
8 ft. 0 in.	20	Frame	2,400
		Perimeter	3,500
		Mating	6,100
8 ft. 0 in.	30	Frame	2,400
		Perimeter	4,200
		Mating	7,300
8 ft. 0 in.	40	Frame	2,400
		Perimeter	4,800
		Mating	8,500
10 ft. 0 in.	20	Frame	2,900
		Perimeter	4,300
		Mating	7,600
10 ft. 0 in.	30	Frame	2,900
		Perimeter	5,100
		Mating	9,100
10 ft. 0 in.	40	Frame	2,900
		Perimeter	6,000
		Mating	10,600

NOTES: 1. See Table to § 3285.312 for cast-in-place footing design by using the noted loads.

2. Mating wall perimeter piers and footings only required under full height mating walls supporting roof loads. Refer to Figures A and B to § 3285.310.

3. Table 2 is based on the following design assumptions: maximum 16 ft. nominal section width (15 ft. actual width), 12" eave, 10"

I-beam size, 300 lbs. pier dead load, 10 psf roof dead load, 6 psf floor dead load, 35 plf wall dead load, and 10 plf chassis dead load.

4. Interpolation for other pier spacing is permitted.

5. The pier spacing and loads shown in the above table do not consider flood or seismic loads and are not intended for use in flood or seismic hazard areas. In those areas, the foundation support system is to be designed by a professional engineer or architect.

6. See Table to § 3285.312 for sizing of footings.

TABLE 3 TO § 3285.303—RIDGE BEAM SPAN FOOTING CAPACITY

Mating wall opening (ft)	Roof live load (psf)	Pier and footing load (lbs.)
5	20	1,200
	30	1,600
	40	1,900
10	20	2,300
	30	3,100
	40	3,800
15	20	3,500
	30	4,700
	40	5,800
20	20	4,700
	30	6,200
	40	7,500
25	20	5,800
	30	7,800
	40	9,700
30	20	7,000
	30	9,300
	40	11,600
35	20	8,100
	30	10,900
	40	13,600

NOTES: 1. See Table to § 3285.312 for cast-in-place footing design by using the noted loads.

2. Table 3 is based on the following design assumptions: maximum 16 ft. nominal section width (15 ft. actual width), 10″ I-beam size, 300 lbs. pier dead load, 10 psf roof dead load, 6 psf floor dead load, 35 plf wall dead load, and 10 plf chassis dead load.

3. Loads listed are maximum column loads for each section of the manufactured home.

4. Interpolation for maximum allowable pier and column loads is permitted for mateline openings between those shown in the table.

5. The pier spacing and loads shown in the above table do not consider flood or seismic loads and are not intended for use in flood or seismic hazard areas. In those areas, the foundation support system must be designed by a professional engineer or registered architect.

6. See Table to § 3285.312 for sizing of footings.

§ 3285.304   Pier configuration.

(a) *Concrete blocks.* Installation instructions for concrete block piers must be developed in accordance with the following provisions and must be consistent with Figures A and B to § 3285.306.

(1) Load-bearing (not decorative) concrete blocks must have nominal dimensions of at least 8 inches × 8 inches × 16 inches;

(2) The concrete blocks must be stacked with their hollow cells aligned vertically; and

(3) When piers are constructed of blocks stacked side-by-side, each layer must be at right angles to the preceding one, as shown in Figure B to § 3285.306.

(b) *Caps.* (1) Structural loads must be evenly distributed across capped-hollow block piers, as shown in Figures A and B to § 3285.306.

(2) Caps must be solid concrete or masonry at least 4 inches in nominal thickness, or hardboard lumber at least 2 inches nominal in thickness; or be corrosion-protected minimum one-half inch thick steel; or be of other listed materials.

(3) All caps must be of the same length and width as the piers on which they rest.

(4) When split caps are used on double-stacked blocks, the caps must be installed with the long dimension across the joint in the blocks below.

(c) *Gaps.* Any gaps that occur during installation between the bottom of the main chassis beam and foundation support system must be filled by:

(1) Nominal 4 inch × 6 inch × 1 inch shims to level the home and fill any gaps between the base of the main chassis beam and the top of the pier cap;

(2) Shims must be used in pairs, as shown in Figures A and B to § 3285.306, and must be driven in tightly so that they do not occupy more than one inch of vertical height; and

(3) Hardwood plates no thicker than 2 inches nominal in thickness or 2 inch or 4 inch nominal concrete block must be used to fill in any remaining vertical gaps.

(d) *Manufactured pier heights.* Manufactured pier heights must be selected so that the adjustable risers do not extend more than 2 inches when finally positioned.

§ 3285.305   Clearance under homes.

A minimum clearance of 12 inches must be maintained between the lowest member of the main frame (I-beam or channel beam) and the grade under all areas of the home.

§ 3285.306   Design procedures for concrete block piers.

(a) *Frame piers less than 36 inches high.* (1) Frame piers less than 36 inches high are permitted to be constructed of single, open, or closed-cell concrete blocks, 8 inches ʺ 8 inches ʺ 16 inches, when the design capacity of the block is not exceeded.

(2) The frame piers must be installed so that the long sides are at right angles to the supported I-beam, as shown in Figure A to this section.

(3) The concrete blocks must be stacked with their hollow cells aligned vertically and must be positioned at right angles to the footings.

(4) Horizontal offsets from the top to the bottom of the pier must not exceed one-half inch.

(5) Mortar is not required, unless specified in the installation instructions or required by a registered professional engineer or registered architect.

(b) *Frame piers 36 inches to 67 inches high and corner piers.* (1) All frame piers between 36 inches and 67 inches high and all corner piers over three blocks high must be constructed out of double, interlocked concrete blocks, as shown in Figure B to this section, when the design capacity of the block is not exceeded. Mortar is not required for concrete block piers, unless otherwise specified in the installation instructions or required by a professional engineer or registered architect.

(2) Horizontal offsets from the top to the bottom of the pier must not exceed one inch.

(c) *All piers over 67 inches high.* Piers over 67 inches high must be designed by a registered professional engineer or registered architect, in accordance with acceptable engineering practice. Mortar is not required for concrete block piers, unless otherwise specified in the manufacturer installation instructions or by the design.

Figure A to § 3285.306 Typical Footing and Pier Design, Single Concrete Block.

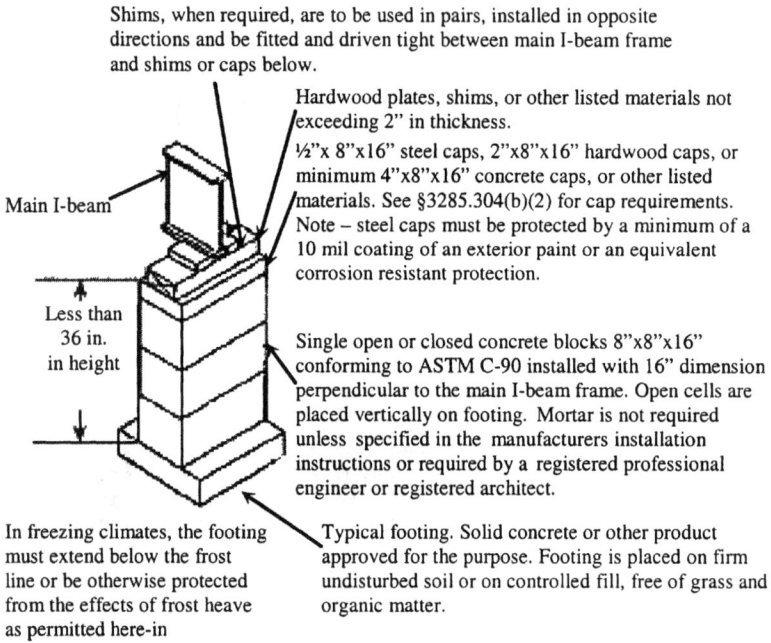

Shims, when required, are to be used in pairs, installed in opposite directions and be fitted and driven tight between main I-beam frame and shims or caps below.

Hardwood plates, shims, or other listed materials not exceeding 2" in thickness.

½"x 8"x16" steel caps, 2"x8"x16" hardwood caps, or minimum 4"x8"x16" concrete caps, or other listed materials. See §3285.304(b)(2) for cap requirements. Note – steel caps must be protected by a minimum of a 10 mil coating of an exterior paint or an equivalent corrosion resistant protection.

Main I-beam

Less than 36 in. in height

Single open or closed concrete blocks 8"x8"x16" conforming to ASTM C-90 installed with 16" dimension perpendicular to the main I-beam frame. Open cells are placed vertically on footing. Mortar is not required unless specified in the manufacturers installation instructions or required by a registered professional engineer or registered architect.

In freezing climates, the footing must extend below the frost line or be otherwise protected from the effects of frost heave as permitted here-in

Typical footing. Solid concrete or other product approved for the purpose. Footing is placed on firm undisturbed soil or on controlled fill, free of grass and organic matter.

Figure B to 3285.306(b) Typical Footing and Pier Installation, Double Concrete Block.

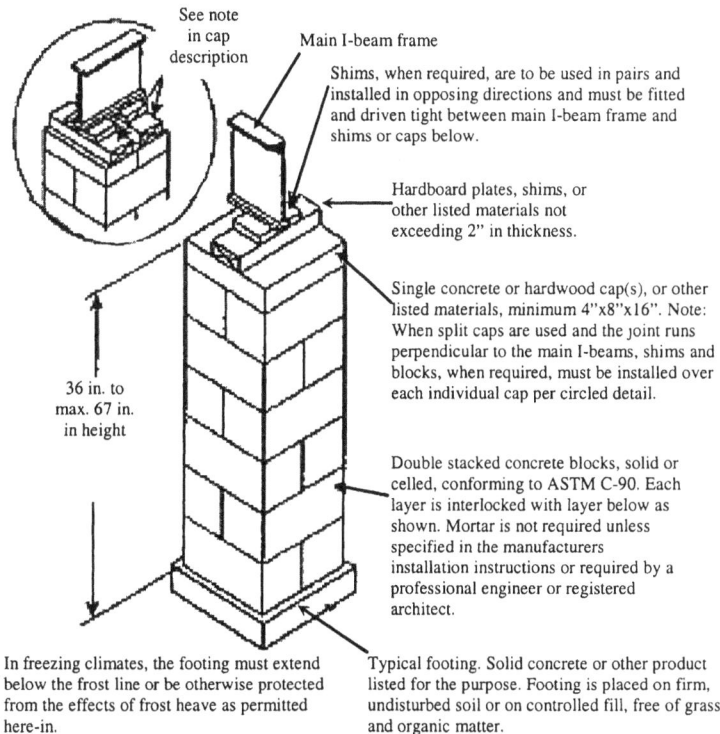

See note in cap description

Main I-beam frame

Shims, when required, are to be used in pairs and installed in opposing directions and must be fitted and driven tight between main I-beam frame and shims or caps below.

Hardboard plates, shims, or other listed materials not exceeding 2" in thickness.

Single concrete or hardwood cap(s), or other listed materials, minimum 4"x8"x16". Note: When split caps are used and the joint runs perpendicular to the main I-beams, shims and blocks, when required, must be installed over each individual cap per circled detail.

36 in. to max. 67 in. in height

Double stacked concrete blocks, solid or celled, conforming to ASTM C-90. Each layer is interlocked with layer below as shown. Mortar is not required unless specified in the manufacturers installation instructions or required by a professional engineer or registered architect.

In freezing climates, the footing must extend below the frost line or be otherwise protected from the effects of frost heave as permitted here-in.

Typical footing. Solid concrete or other product listed for the purpose. Footing is placed on firm, undisturbed soil or on controlled fill, free of grass and organic matter.

§ 3285.307   Perimeter support piers.

(a) Piers required at mate-line supports, perimeter piers, and piers at exterior wall openings are permitted to be constructed of single open-cell or closed-cell concrete blocks, with nominal dimensions of 8 inches × 8 inches × 16 inches, to a maximum height of 54 inches, as shown in Figure A to this section, when the design capacity of the block is not exceeded.

(b) Piers used for perimeter support must be installed with the long dimension parallel to the perimeter rail.

§ 3285.308   Manufactured piers.

(a) Manufactured piers must be listed and labeled and installed to the pier manufacturer's installation instruc-

tions. See § 3285.303(d)(2) for additional requirements.

(b) Metal or other manufactured piers must be provided with protection against weather deterioration and corrosion at least equivalent to that provided by a coating of zinc on steel of .30 oz./ft.^{2} of surface coated.

§ 3285.309   [Reserved]

§ 3285.310   Pier location and spacing.

(a) The location and spacing of piers depends upon the dimensions of the home, the live and dead loads, the type of construction (single-or multi-section), I-beam size, soil bearing capacity, footing size, and such other factors as the location of doors or other openings.

(b) Mate-line and column pier supports must be in accordance with this subpart and consistent with Figures A through C to this section, unless the pier support and footing configuration is designed by a registered professional engineer or registered architect.

(c) Piers supporting the frame must be no more than 24 inches from both ends and not more than 120 inches center to center under the main rails.

(d) *Pier support locations.* Pier support locations and spacing must be presented to be consistent with Figures A and B to § 3285.312, as applicable, unless alternative designs are provided by a professional engineer or registered architect in accordance with acceptable engineering practice.

Figure A to § 3285.310 Typical Mate-Line Column Pier and Mating Wall Support when Frame Only Blocking is Required.

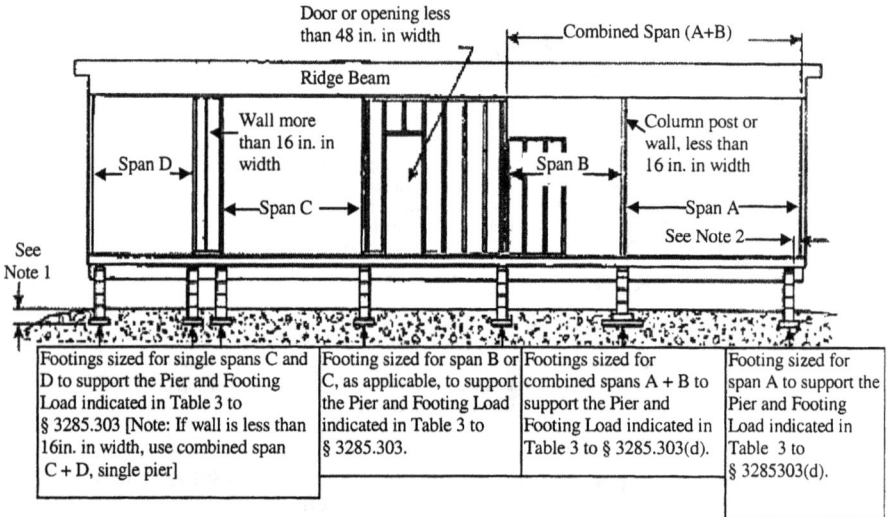

NOTES: 1. Bottom of footings must extend below frost line depth, unless designed for placement above the frost line. (See § 3285.312(b)).

2. Piers may be offset up to 6 in. in either direction along the supported members to allow for plumbing, electrical, mechanical, equipment, crawlspaces, or other devices.

3. Single-stack concrete block pier loads must not exceed 8,000 lbs.

4. Prefabricated piers must not exceed their approved or listed maximum vertical or horizontal design loads.

5. When a full-height mating wall does not support the ridge beam, this area is considered an unsupported span—Span B.

6. Piers are not required at openings in the mating wall that are less than 48 inches in width. Place piers on both sides of mating wall openings that are 48 inches or greater in width. For roof loads of 40 psf or greater, a professional engineer or registered architect must determine the maximum mating wall opening permitted without pier or other supports.

Figure B to § 3285.310(b) Typical Mate-Line Column Pier and Mating Wall Support When Perimeter Blocking is Required.

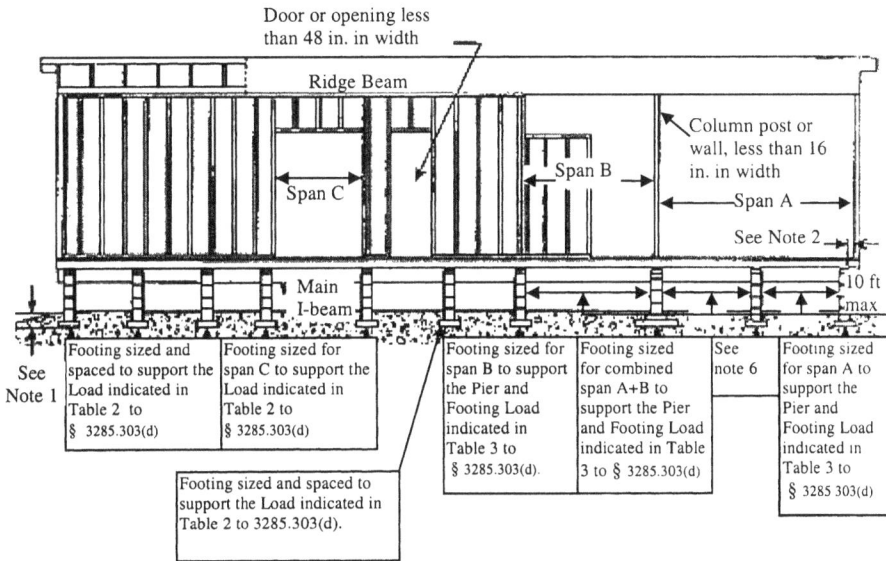

NOTES: 1. Bottom of footings must be below the frost line depth, unless designed for placement above the frost line. (See § 3285.312(b)).

2. Piers may be offset 6 in. in either direction along supported members to allow for plumbing electrical, mechanical equipment, crawlspaces, or other devices.

3. Single stack concrete block pier loads must not exceed 8,000 lbs.

4. Piers are not required at openings in the mating wall that are less than 48 inches in width. Place piers on both sides of mating wall openings that are 48 inches or greater in width. For roof loads of 40 psf or greater, a professional engineer or registered architect must determine the maximum mating wall opening permitted without pier or other supports.

5. When a full-height mating wall does not support the ridge beam, this area is considered an unsupported span—Span B.

6. In areas where the open span is greater than 10 ft., intermediate piers and footings must be placed at maximum 10 ft. on center.

7. Prefabricated piers must not exceed their approved or listed maximum horizontal or vertical design loads.

8. Column piers are in addition to piers required under full-height mating walls.

Figure C to § 3285.310 Typical Mate-Line Column and Piers.

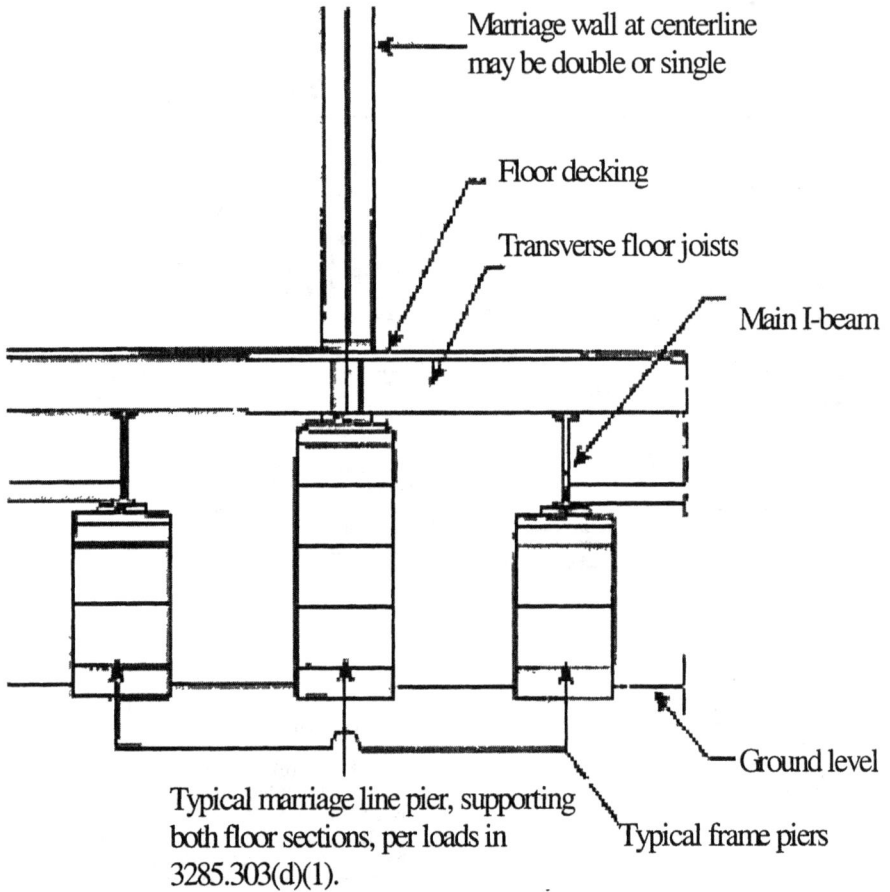

Marriage wall at centerline may be double or single

Floor decking

Transverse floor joists

Main I-beam

Ground level

Typical marriage line pier, supporting both floor sections, per loads in 3285.303(d)(1).

Typical frame piers

NOTES: 1. Mate-line column support piers are installed with the long dimension of the concrete block perpendicular to the rim joists.

2. Pier and footing designed to support both floor sections. Loads as listed in Table 3 to § 3285.303 are total column loads for both sections.

§ 3285.311   Required   perimeter   supports.

(a) Perimeter pier or other supports must be located as follows:

(1) On both sides of side wall exterior doors (such as entry, patio, and sliding glass doors) and any other side wall openings of 48 inches or greater in width, and under load-bearing porch posts, factory installed fireplaces, and fireplace stoves).

(2) Other perimeter supports must be:

(i) Located in accordance with Table 2 to § 3285.303; or

(ii) Provided by other means such as additional outriggers or floor joists. When this alternative is used, the designs required by § 3285.301 must consider the additional loads in sizing the pier and footing supports under the main chassis beam.

(b) For roof live loads of 40 psf or greater, a professional engineer or architect must determine the maximum sidewall opening permitted without perimeter pier or other supports.

(c) The location and installation of any perimeter pier support must not take the home out of compliance with the Manufactured Home Construction and Safety Standards (part 3280 of this chapter).

§3285.312 Footings.

(a) Materials approved for footings must provide equal load-bearing capacity and resistance to decay, as required by this section. Footings must be placed on undisturbed soil or fill compacted to 90 percent of maximum relative density. A footing must support every pier. Footings are to be either:

(1) *Concrete.*

(i) Four inch nominal precast concrete pads meeting or exceeding ASTM C 90–02a, Standard Specification for Loadbearing Concrete Masonry Units (incorporated by reference, see §3285.4), without reinforcement, with at least a 28-day compressive strength of 1,200 pounds per square inch (psi); or

(ii) Six inch minimum poured-in-place concrete pads, slabs, or ribbons with at least a 28-day compressive strength of 3,000 pounds per square inch (psi). Site-specific soil conditions or design load requirements may also require the use of reinforcing steel in cast-in-place concrete footings.

(2) *Pressure-treated wood.*

(i) Pressure-treated wood footings must consist of a minimum of two layers of nominal 2-inch thick pressure-treated wood, a single layer of nominal ¾-inch thick, pressure-treated plywood with a maximum size of 16 inches by 16 inches, or at least two layers of ¾-inch thick, pressure-treated plywood for sizes greater than 16 inches by 16 inches. Plywood used for this purpose is to be rated exposure 1 or exterior sheathing, in accordance with PS1–95, Construction and Industrial Plywood (incorporated by reference, see §3285.4).

(ii) Pressure treated lumber is to be treated with a water-borne adhesive, in accordance with AWPA Standard U1–04 (incorporated by reference, see §3285.4) for Use Category 4B ground contact applications.

(iii) Cut ends of pressure treated lumber must be field-treated, in accordance with AWPA Standard M4–02 (incorporated by reference, see §3285.4).

(3) *ABS footing pads.*

(i) ABS footing pads are permitted, provided they are installed in accordance with the pad manufacturer installation instructions and certified for use in the soil classification at the site.

(ii) ABS footing pads must be listed or labeled for the required load capacity.

(4) Other Materials. Footings may be of other materials than those identified in this section, provided they are listed for such use and meet all other applicable requirements of this subpart.

(b) *Placement in freezing climates.* Footings placed in freezing climates must be designed using methods and practices that prevent the effects of frost heave by one of the following methods:

(1) Conventional footings. Conventional footings must be placed below the frost line depth for the site unless an insulated foundation or monolithic slab is used (refer to §§3285.312(b)(2) and 3285.312(b)(3)). When the frost line depth is not available from the LAHJ, a registered professional engineer, registered architect, or registered geologist must be consulted to determine the required frost line depth for the manufactured home site. This is not subject to the provisions in §3285.2(c) that also require review by the manufacturer and approval by its DAPIA for any variations to the manufacturer's installation instructions for support and anchoring.

(2) *Monolithic slab systems.* A monolithic slab is permitted above the frost line when all relevant site-specific conditions, including soil characteristics, site preparation, ventilation, and insulative properties of the under floor enclosure, are considered and anchorage requirements are accommodated as set out in §3285.401. The monolithic slab system must be designed by a registered professional engineer or registered architect:

(i) In accordance with acceptable engineering practice to prevent the effects of frost heave; or

(ii) In accordance with SEI/ASCE 32–01 (incorporated by reference, see § 3285.4).

(3) *Insulated foundations.* An insulated foundation is permitted above the frost line, when all relevant site-specific conditions, including soil characteristics, site preparation, ventilation, and insulative properties of the under floor enclosure, are considered, and the foundation is designed by a registered professional engineer or registered architect:

(i) In accordance with acceptable engineering practice to prevent the effects of frost heave; or

(ii) In accordance with SEI/ASCE 32–01 (incorporated by reference, see § 3285.4).

(c) *Sizing of footings.* The sizing and layout of footings depends on the load-bearing capacity of the soil, footings, and the piers. See §§ 3285.202 and 3285.303, and Table to 3285.312.

Figure A to § 3285.312 Typical Blocking Diagram for Single Section Homes

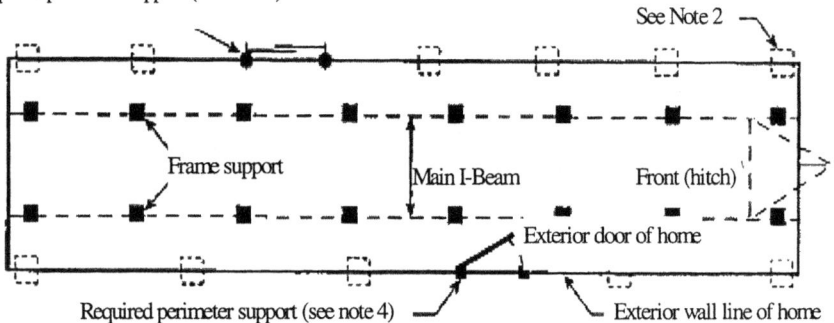

NOTES: 1. Refer to Table 1 of § 3285.303 for pier and footing requirements when frame blocking only is used.

2. In addition to blocking required by § 3285.311, see Table 2 to § 3285.303 for maximum perimeter blocking loads.

3. End piers under main I-beams may be set back a maximum of 24 inches, as measured from the outside edge of the floor to the center of the pier.

4. Place piers on both sides of sidewall exterior doors, patio doors, and sliding glass doors; under porch posts, factory-installed fireplaces, and fireplace stoves; under jamb studs at multiple window openings; and at any other sidewall openings 48 inches or greater in width. For roof loads of 40 psf or greater, a professional engineer or registered architect must determine the maximum sidewall opening permitted without perimeter supports. See §§ 3285.307 and 3285.311 for additional requirements and for locating perimeter supports.

Figure B to § 3285.312 Typical Blocking Diagram for Multi-section Home.

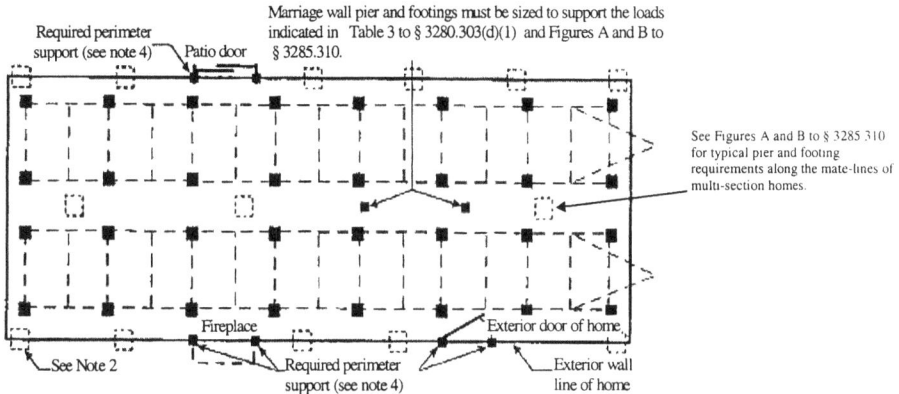

NOTES: 1. Refer to Table 1 to §3285.303 for pier and footing requirements when frame blocking only is used.

2. In addition to blocking required by §3285.311, see Tables 2 and 3 to §3285.303 for maximum perimeter blocking loads.

3. End piers under main I-beams may be set back a maximum of 24 inches, as measured from the outside edge of the floor to the center of the pier.

4. Place piers on both sides of sidewall exterior doors, patio doors, and sliding glass doors; under porch posts, factory-installed fireplaces, and fireplace stoves; under jamb studs at multiple window openings; and at any other sidewall openings of 48 inches or greater in width. For roof loads of 40 psf or greater, a professional engineer or registered architect must determine the maximum side wall opening permitted without perimeter supports or mating wall opening permitted without pier or other supports. See §§3285.307 and 3285.311 for additional information on requirements and for locating perimeter supports.

5. When an end pier under the mate-line also serves as a column pier, it may be set back a maximum of 6 in., as measured from the inside edge of the exterior wall to the center of the pier.

TABLE TO § 3285.312—THE SIZE AND CAPACITY FOR UNREINFORCED CAST-IN-PLACE FOOTINGS

Soil capacity (psf)	Minimum footing size (in.)	8 in. × 16 in. pier		16 in. × 16 in. pier	
		Maximum footing capacity (lbs.)	Unreinforced cast-in-place minimum thickness (in.)	Maximum footing capacity (lbs.)	Unreinforced cast-in-place minimum thickness (in.)
1,000	16 × 16	1,600	6	1,600	6
	20 × 20	2,600	6	2,600	6
	24 × 24	3,700	6	3,700	6
	30 × 30	5,600	8	5,800	6
	36 × 36	7,900	10	8,100	8
	42 × 42	4 10,700	10	10,700	10
	48 × 48	4 13,100	12	13,600	10
1,500	16 × 16	2,500	6	2,500	6
	20 × 20	4,000	6	4,000	6
	24 × 24	5,600	8	5,700	6
	30 × 30	4 8,500	10	8,900	8
	36 × 36	4 12,400	10	12,600	8
	42 × 42	4 16,500	12	4 16,800	10
	48 × 48	4 21,200	14	4 21,600	12
2,000	16 × 16	3,400	6	3,400	6
	20 × 20	5,300	6	5,300	6
	24 × 24	7,600	8	7,700	6
	30 × 30	4 11,700	10	11,900	8
	36 × 36	4 16,700	15	4 16,900	10
	42 × 42	4 21,700	18	4 22,700	12

227

TABLE TO § 3285.312—THE SIZE AND CAPACITY FOR UNREINFORCED CAST-IN-PLACE FOOTINGS—Continued

Soil capacity (psf)	Minimum footing size (in.)	8 in. × 16 in. pier		16 in. × 16 in. pier	
		Maximum footing capacity (lbs.)	Unreinforced cast-in-place minimum thickness (in.)	Maximum footing capacity (lbs.)	Unreinforced cast-in-place minimum thickness (in.)
2,500	16 × 16	4,300	6	4,300	6
	20 × 20	6,700	6	6,700	6
	24 × 24	4 9,600	8	9,700	6
	30 × 30	4 14,800	10	15,000	8
	36 × 36	4 20,700	12	4 21,400	10
3,000	16 × 16	5,200	6	5,200	6
	20 × 20	8,100	8	8,100	6
	24 × 24	4 11,500	10	11,700	6
	30 × 30	4 17,800	12	4 18,100	8
	36 × 36	4 25,400	14	4 25,900	10
4,000	16 × 16	7,000	6	7,000	6
	20 × 20	4 10,800	8	10,900	6
	24 × 24	4 15,500	10	15,600	8
	30 × 30	4 23,300	12	4 24,200	10

NOTES: 1. The footing sizes shown are for square pads and are based on the area (in.²), shear and bending required for the loads shown. Other configurations, such as rectangular or circular configurations, can be used, provided the area and depth is equal to or greater than the area and depth of the square footing shown in the table, and the distance from the edge of the pier to the edge of the footing is not less than the thickness of the footing.

2. The 6 in. cast-in-place values can be used for 4 in. unreinforced precast concrete footings.

3. The capacity values listed have been reduced by the dead load of the concrete footing.

4. Concrete block piers must not exceed their design capacity of 8,000 lbs. for 8″ × 16″ single stack block and 16,000 lbs. for 16″ × 16″ double stack block.

5. A registered professional engineer or registered architect must prepare the design, if the design loads exceed the capacity for single or double stack concrete block piers shown in footnote 4.

§ 3285.313   Combination systems.

Support systems that combine both load-bearing capacity and uplift resistance must also be sized and designed for all applicable design loads.

§ 3285.314   [Reserved]

§ 3285.315   Special snow load conditions.

(a) *General.* Foundations for homes designed for and located in areas with roof live loads greater than 40 psf must be designed by the manufacturer for the special snow load conditions, in accordance with acceptable engineering practice. Where site or other conditions prohibit the use of the manufacturer's instructions, a registered professional engineer or registered architect must design the foundation for the special snow load conditions.

(b) *Ramadas.* Ramadas may be used in areas with roof live loads greater than 40 psf. Ramadas are to be self-supporting, except that any connection to the home must be for weatherproofing only.

Subpart E—Anchorage Against Wind

§ 3285.401   Anchoring instructions.

(a) After blocking and leveling, the manufactured home must be secured against the wind by use of anchor assembly type installations or by connecting the home to an alternative foundation system. See § 3285.301.

(b) For anchor assembly type installations, the installation instructions must require the home to be secured against the wind, as described in this section. The installation instructions and design for anchor type assemblies must be prepared by a registered professional engineer or registered architect, in accordance with acceptable engineering practice, the design loads of the MHCSS, and § 3285.301(d).

(c) All anchoring and foundation systems must be capable of meeting the loads that the home was designed to withstand required by part 3280, subpart D of this chapter, as shown on the home's data plate. Exception: Manufactured homes that are installed in less restrictive roof load zone and wind zone areas may have foundation or anchorage systems that are capable of meeting the lower design load provisions of the Standards, if the design for the lower requirements is either provided in the installation instructions or the foundation and anchorage system is designed by a professional engineer or registered architect.

(d) The installation instructions are to include at least the following information and details for anchor assembly-type installations:

(1) The maximum spacing for installing diagonal ties and any required vertical ties or straps to ground anchors;

(2) The minimum and maximum angles or dimensions for installing diagonal ties or straps to ground anchors and the main chassis members of the manufactured home;

(3) Requirements for connecting the diagonal ties to the main chassis members of the manufactured home. If the diagonal ties are attached to the bottom flange of the main chassis beam, the frame must be designed to prevent rotation of the beam;

(4) Requirements for longitudinal and mating wall tie-downs and anchorage;

(5) The method of strap attachment to the main chassis member and ground anchor, including provisions for swivel-type connections;

(6) The methods for protecting vertical and diagonal strapping at sharp corners by use of radius clips or other means; and

(7) As applicable, the requirements for sizing and installation of stabilizer plates.

§ 3285.402 Ground anchor installations.

(a) *Ground anchor certification and testing.* (1) Each ground anchor assembly must be manufactured and provided with installation instructions, and must be labeled or otherwise identified and subject to an on-going quality assurance surveillance program in accordance with its listing or certification (see 24 CFR 3285.5) by a nationally recognized testing laboratory. A registered professional engineer or architect must certify that each ground anchor assembly is capable of resisting all loads in paragraph (c) of this section based on the test methods in paragraph (b) of this section for use in soil(s) classified in accordance with § 3285.202.

(2) Each ground anchor assembly that has been listed prior to November 10, 2014 is not subject to paragraph (b) of this section, provided it has been previously tested in accordance with this paragraph. A professional engineer or registered architect must have certified the testing. The ground anchor must be listed by a nationally recognized testing agency and the listing or certification includes or has met all of the following requirements:

(i) A minimum of three tests meeting all of the requirements of this section were conducted for each ground anchor assembly design;

(ii) Each of the ground anchor assembly designs tested must have met or exceeded a working load of 3,150 pounds and sustained an ultimate load of 4,725 pounds in the weakest soil classification for which the anchors were tested and certified;

(iii) The soil in which the anchor was certified has been classified by one of the methods indicated in § 3285.202 of these Standards and the anchor is not listed for use in a weaker/higher soil classification than tested and identified in the Table to § 3285.202;

(iv) A test report was provided for each ground anchor assembly design that identifies the soil classification in which the ground anchor was tested and listed and includes complete specifications and dimensions for the ground anchor assembly;

(v) For each of the ground anchor assemblies tested, the maximum deflection at 3,150 pounds did not exceed two inches vertically or three inches horizontally;

(vi) For each of the ground anchor assemblies tested, the maximum deflection at 4,725 pounds did not exceed two inches vertically or three inches horizontally;

(vii) For the stabilizer plate test method, at least three tests were performed at the minimum angle of pull to the horizontal specified in the listing and the minimum angle of pull to the horizontal must have been at least 30 degrees. Any existing ground anchor assembly tests and certifications where the angle of pull was less than 30 degrees will need to be re-evaluated in accordance with paragraph (b) of this section; and

(viii) For the stabilizer plate test method, the minimum angle of pull to the horizontal is specified in the listing.

(b) *Standard test methods for establishing working load design values of ground anchor assemblies used for new manufactured home installations*—(1) *Scope.* (i) These testing procedures provide standard test methods for establishing both ultimate loads and load resistance design values.

(ii) Each assembly or component of an anchor assembly must be tested by the methods established by this section, and therefore be suitable, as listed or certified for installation in an appropriately classified soil, for installation of manufactured homes.

(iii) To secure approval of ground anchor assembly products and components, ground anchor manufacturers must have their products tested and listed by a nationally recognized testing laboratory, or tested and certified by an independent registered professional engineer.

(iv) The testing laboratory or independent registered engineer must be free from any conflict of interest from the product manufacturer and any of the product manufacturer's affiliates.

(2) *Definitions.* The definitions contained in this section apply to the terms used in subpart E of this part.

Allowable displacement limits. Criteria establishing the maximum amount of displacement of a material, assembly, or component under load.

Certification test site. A site used for the purpose of anchor assembly qualification testing in accordance with this section.

Cohesive soil. A soil with sufficient clay content to exhibit substantial plastic behavior when moist or wet (i.e., able to be readily molded or rolled into a ⅛ -inch thread at a wide range of moisture contents).

Ground anchor manufacturer. Any person or company engaged in manufacturing or importing ground anchor assemblies.

Non-Cohesive soil. Sand, gravel, and similar soils that are predominantly granular and lack a sufficient quantity of fine, clay-sized particles to exhibit the behavior of cohesive soil as defined in this section.

Ultimate anchor load. The lower of either the highest load achieved during an individual test prior to failure due to exceeding allowable displacement limits or the load at failure of the anchoring equipment or its attachment point to the testing apparatus.

Working anchor load. The ultimate anchor load in pounds divided by a factor of safety of 1.5.

(3) *Determination of soil classification*—(i) *General description of soil classification.* The general description of soil classification is to be determined in accordance with the methods specified in the Table to § 3285.202.

(ii) *Standards for identification of soil and soil classification.* The soil test torque probe method must be used at the certification test site for soil classification. At a minimum, the soil test torque probe must be used at three sample locations representative of the extent of the certification site test area. Soil characteristics must be measured at a depth below ground surface of not greater than the anchor helix depth and not less than ⅔ of the anchor helix depth for each ground anchor depth evaluated within the test area. The lowest torque probe value resulting in the highest soil classification number must be used. Additional guidance regarding the soil test torque probe method is available at the Appendix to this section and at § 3282.202.

(iii) *Classification in non-cohesive soils.* Ground anchor assemblies must be tested and listed or certified, and labeled for use in non-cohesive soil. Ground anchor assemblies are permitted to be tested, listed or certified, and labeled for use in cohesive soil.

(4) *Field testing apparatus.* (i) The testing equipment for conducting tests to list or certify a ground anchor assembly for use in a classified soil must

be capable of meeting the requirements of paragraph (b)(7) of this section as determined by the testing agency.

(ii) The testing equipment shall be calibrated to meet the testing requirements of paragraph (b)(7) of this section as determined by the testing agency.

(5) *Test specimens details and selection.* (i) Test specimens are to be examined by the independent testing, listing, or certifying entity for conformance with engineered drawings, specifications, and other information provided by the ground anchor manufacturer or producer including:

(A) Dimensions and specifications on all welds and fasteners;

(B) Dimensions and specifications of all metal or material;

(C) Model number and its location on the ground anchor; and

(ii) Necessary test specimens and products for the installed anchor assembly tests must be randomly selected by the independent testing, listing, or certifying entity.

(6) *Test requirements.* (i) Field tests must be performed on each anchor assembly installed in a classified soil as defined in paragraph (b)(3) of this section.

(ii) Field test apparatuses must be as specified in paragraph (b)(4) of this section, and must conform to the testing requirements of paragraph (b)(7) of this section.

(iii) Testing equipment shall be adequate for testing as determined by the testing agency.

NOTE TO PARAGRAPH (b)(6): As a recommended practice, the test rig soil reactions (bearing pads) should not be located closer to the center of the anchor assembly (anchor head) than the lesser of D, 4d, or 32 inches where D is the depth of the anchor helix and d is the diameter of the anchor helix, both in inches. However, experience with a particular test rig, types of anchors, and soil conditions may justify other acceptable dimensional tolerances.

(7) *Field tests of anchor assemblies.* (i) The soil characteristics at the certification test site must be identified and recorded according to paragraph (b)(3) of this section. The date, approximate time, and names of persons conducting and witnessing the anchor assembly tests must also be recorded at each certification test site.

(ii) Connection of the testing apparatus to the anchor assembly head must provide loading conditions to the anchor head, similar to actual site conditions. Adequacy of the connection must be determined by the testing agency or test engineer.

(iii) For soil classifications 3, 4A, and 4B, testing must be performed in the lower 50 percentile torque probe value of the soil classification being tested. For soil classifications 1 and 2 the torque probe value must not exceed 750 inch-pounds.

(iv) A minimum of three tests must be performed and the result of each test must meet or exceed 4,725 pounds pull (3,150 × 1.5 factor of safety) in the direction of pull.

(v) Special-purpose anchor assemblies, including those needed to accommodate unique design loads identified by manufacturers in their installation instructions, may be certified under this section or to more stringent requirements such as higher working loads, more restrictive anchor head displacements and/or tested angle limitations.

(vi) *Angle of pull.* Where the test apparatus configuration results in a changing angle of pull due to anchor assembly displacement during a lateral angle pull test, the angle of pull at the ultimate anchor load is to be recorded as the load angle for the test. Load angles are to be measured relative to the plane of the ground surface and shall be permitted to be rounded to the nearest 5-degree increment.

(vii) *Displacement measurement.* Vertical displacement (for all tests) and horizontal displacement (for lateral angle pull tests) must be measured relative to the centerline of the test apparatus' connection to the ground anchor assembly (anchor head) and the ground. A stable ground reference point for displacement measurements must be located independent of the test apparatus and not closer to the anchor assembly than the soil reaction points of the test apparatus. Displacement measurements shall be taken using a device with not less than ⅛-inch reading increments. Measurements shall be permitted to be rounded to the nearest ⅛-inch increment.

231

(8) *Anchor assembly field test methods.* (i) An anchor assembly must be tested in accordance with one or more of the assembly configurations addressed in paragraphs (b)(8)(iii), (iv) and (v) of this section. The as-tested configuration of any anchor assembly is a condition of the listing or certification. Alternate configurations are acceptable provided test conditions appropriately simulate actual end-use conditions and the as-tested configuration is addressed in the manufacturer's installation instructions.

(ii) Anchor assemblies designed for multiple connections to the manufactured home must be individually tested as specified in paragraphs (b)(8)(iii) and (iv) of this section.

(iii) Anchor assembly/stabilizer plate method. The following anchor assembly installation and testing must be consistently applied for all tests:

(A) The ground anchor is to be installed at an angle of 10–15 degrees from vertical to a depth of one-half (½) to two-thirds (⅔) of the anchor length.

(B) A stabilizer plate is to be driven vertically on the side of the ground anchor shaft facing the tensioning equipment three inches (3″) from the shaft and the top of the plate must be installed flush with the soil surface or not more than one inch below the soil surface.

(C) The ground anchor is to be driven to its full depth into the soil with the bottom of the anchor head not more than ¾ inch (¾″) above the stabilizer plate.

(D) The ground anchor head is to be attached to the tensioning equipment such that the tension load and displacement can be recorded. The tensioning equipment must be positioned to load the ground anchor and stabilizer plate at the minimum angle to the test site ground surface for which the anchor is being evaluated.

(E) The ground anchor is to be pre-tensioned to 500 pounds so that the anchor shaft contacts the stabilizer plate. If the anchor shaft does not come into contact with the stabilizer plate an anchor setting load not to exceed 1,000 pounds is permitted to be applied and then released prior to re-application of the 500-pound pre-tension force.

(F) The location of the ground anchor head is to be marked after it is pre-tensioned for measuring subsequent movement under test loading.

(G) Increase the load throughout the test. The recommended rate of load application must be such that the loading to not less than 4725 pounds is reached in not less than 2 minutes from the time the 500 pound pre-tension load is achieved.

(H) Record the load and displacement, at a minimum of 500–1000 pound increments, such that a minimum of five data points will be obtained to determine a load deflection curve. For each datum, the applied load and the ground anchor head displacement is to be recorded. In addition, the load and displacement is to be recorded at the Failure Mode identified in paragraph (b)(10) of this section. It is permissible to halt the addition of load at each loading increment for up to 60 seconds to facilitate taking displacement readings. The ultimate anchor load of the ground anchor assembly and corresponding displacement is to be recorded. The pre-tension load of 500 pounds should be included in the 4725 pound ultimate anchor load test. It is permissible to interpolate between displacement and load measurements to determine the ultimate anchor load.

(I) All ground anchor assemblies must be tested to the following:

(1) Failure due to displacement of the ground anchor assembly as established in paragraph (b)(9) of this section, or

(2) Failure of either the anchoring equipment or its attachment point to the testing apparatus, or to a minimum of 4725 pounds (when possible tests should be taken to 6000 pounds to provide additional data but this is not required).

(iv) Vertical in-line anchor assembly method. Anchor assembly installation and withdrawal procedures for test purposes are to be as follows, and be used consistently throughout all tests;

(A) The ground anchor must be installed vertically.

(B) The ground anchor must be driven to its full depth into the soil.

(C) The ground anchor head must be attached to the tensioning equipment such that the load and ground anchor head displacement can be recorded.

(D) The ground anchor must be pulled in line with the ground anchor shaft.

(E) The ground anchor shall be pre-tensioned to 500 pounds.

(F) The location of the ground anchor head must be marked after it is pre-tensioned for measuring subsequent movement under test loading.

(G) Increase the load throughout the test. The recommended rate of load application shall be such that the loading to not less than 4725 pounds is reached in not less than 2 minutes from the time the 500 pound pre-tension load is achieved.

(H) Record the load and displacement, at a minimum of 500–1000 pound increments, such that a minimum of five data points will be obtained to determine a load deflection curve. For each datum, the applied load and the ground anchor head displacement is to be recorded. In addition, the load and displacement is to be recorded at the Failure Mode identified in paragraph (b)(10) of this section. It is permissible to halt the addition of load at each loading increment for up to 60 seconds to facilitate taking displacement readings. The ultimate anchor load of the ground anchor assembly and corresponding displacement is to be recorded. The pre-tension load of 500 pounds should be included in the 4725 pound ultimate anchor load test. It shall be permissible to interpolate between displacement and load measurements to determine the Ultimate anchor load.

(I) All ground anchor assemblies must be tested to the following:

(1) Failure due to displacement of the ground anchor assembly as established in paragraph (b)(9) of this section, or

(2) Failure of either the anchoring equipment or its attachment point to the testing apparatus, or to a minimum of 4725 pounds (when possible tests should be taken to 6000 pounds to provide additional data but this is NOT required).

(v) In line ground anchor assembly method. Ground anchor assembly installation and withdrawal procedures for test purposes must be as follows, and must be used consistently throughout all tests.

(A) The ground anchor must be installed at an angle from the horizontal ground surface at which it is to be rated.

(B) The ground anchor must be driven to its full depth into the soil.

(C) The ground anchor head must be attached to the tensioning equipment such that tension and displacement can be recorded.

(D) The anchor must be pulled in line with the ground anchor shaft.

(E) The ground anchor shall be pre-tensioned 500 pounds.

(F) The location of the ground anchor head is to be marked after it is pre-tensioned for measuring subsequent movement under test loading.

(G) Increase the load throughout the test. The recommended rate of load application must be such that the loading to not less than 4725 pounds is reached in not less than 2 minutes from the time the 500 pound pre-tension load is achieved.

(H) Record the load and displacement, at a minimum of 500–1000 pound increments, such that a minimum of five data points will be obtained to determine a load deflection curve. For each datum, the applied load and the ground anchor head displacement is to be recorded. In addition, the load and displacement is to be recorded at the Failure Mode identified in paragraph (b)(10) of this section. It shall be permissible to halt the addition of load at each loading increment for up to 60 seconds to facilitate taking displacement readings. The ultimate anchor load of the ground anchor assembly and corresponding displacement must be recorded. The pre-tension load of 500 pounds should be included in the 4725 pound ultimate anchor load test. It is permissible to interpolate between displacement and load measurements to determine the Ultimate anchor load.

(I) All ground anchor assemblies must be tested to the following:

(1) failure due to displacement of the ground anchor assembly as established in paragraph (b)(9) of this section, or

(2) Failure of either the anchoring equipment or its attachment point to the testing apparatus, or to a minimum of 4725 pounds (when possible tests should be taken to 6000 pounds to

provide additional data but this is NOT required)

Note to paragraph (b)(8). Additional testing at angles of pull greater than the minimum angle of pull may be used to provide design values for specific angles of pull greater than the minimum angle for which evaluation is sought.

(9) *Failure criteria.* The following conditions constitute failure of the ground anchor test assembly:

(i) When the ground anchor head, or its attachment point, displaces 2 inches in the vertical or horizontal direction from its pre-tensioned measurement position prior to reaching a total load of 3150 pounds (including any pretension load).

(ii) When the ground anchor head, or its attachment point, displaces 2 inches (2″) in the vertical direction or 3 inches (3″) in the horizontal direction from its pre-tensioned measurement position prior to reaching a total load of 4725 pounds (including any pretension load).

(iii) When breakage of any component of the ground anchor shaft occurs prior to reaching a total load of 4725 pounds.

(10) *Use of ultimate anchor loads to establish the working load design value.* (i) The working load design value is the lowest ultimate anchor load determined by testing, divided by a 1.5 factor of safety.

(ii) The working load design value, for each installation method and soil classification, shall be stated in the ground anchor assembly listing or certification. An anchor tested in a given soil classification number must not be approved for use in a higher/weaker soil classification number. For example an anchor tested in soil classification 3 must not be approved for soil classification 4A or 4B unless it is also tested in those soils. The 500 pound pre-tension is included in the ultimate anchor load.

(11) *Test report.* The test report to support the listing or certification for each ground anchor assembly tested is to include all conditions under which the ground anchor assembly was tested, including the following:

(i) A copy of all test data accumulated during the testing.

(ii) The soil characteristics including moisture content and methods for determining soil characteristics for each type of soil for which the ground anchoring assembly was evaluated.

(iii) The model of the ground anchor assembly tested.

(iv) The ground anchor assembly test method used.

(v) Detailed drawings including all dimensions of the ground anchor assembly and its components.

(vi) Method of installation at the test site.

(vii) Date of installation and date of testing.

(viii) Location of the certification test site.

(ix) Test equipment used.

(x) For each anchor specimen tested: For each load increment the load in pounds and resultant displacements in inches in chart or graph form.

(xi) The working load design value and ultimate anchor load determined in accordance with paragraph (b)(10) of this section.

(xii) If required, a description of the stabilizer plate used in each ground anchor assembly/stabilizer plate test, including the name of the manufacturer.

(xiii) Angle(s) of pull for which the anchor has been tested.

(xiv) Embedment depth of the ground anchor assembly.

(xv) The application and orientation of the applied load.

(xvi) A description of the mode and location of failure for each ground anchor assembly tested.

(xvii) Name and signature of the nationally recognized testing agency or registered professional engineer certifying the testing and evaluation.

(xviii) The soil classification(s) for which each ground anchor assembly is certified for use and the working load design value and minimum ultimate load capacity for those soil classification(s).

(12) *Approved ground anchor assemblies.* Each ground anchor manufacturer or producer must provide the following information for use of approved ground anchor assemblies and this information must also be included in the listing or certification for each ground anchor assembly:

(i) Drawings showing ground anchor installation.

(ii) Specifications for the ground anchor assembly including:

(A) Soils classifications listed or certified for use;

(B) The working load and minimum ultimate anchor load capacity for the anchor assembly in the soil classification(s) it is listed or certified for use;

(C) Model number and its location on the anchor;

(D) Instructions for use, including pre-tensioning;

(E) Angle(s) of pull for which the anchor has been listed and certified; and

(F) Manufacturer, size and type of stabilizer plate required.

(c) *Specifications for tie-down straps and ground anchors*—(1) *Ground anchors.* Ground anchors must be installed in accordance with their listing or certification, be installed to their full depth, be provided with protection against weather deterioration and corrosion at least equivalent to that provided by a coating of zinc on steel of not less than 0.30 oz./ft.^{2} of surface coated, and be capable of resisting a minimum ultimate load of 4,725 lbs. and a working load of 3,150 lbs., as installed, unless reduced capacities are noted in accordance with note 11 of Table 1 to this section or note 12 of Tables 2 and 3 to this section. The ultimate load and working load of ground anchors and anchoring equipment must be determined by a registered professional engineer, registered architect, or tested by a nationally recognized third-party testing agency in accordance with a nationally recognized testing protocol.

(2) *Tie-down straps.* A 1¼ inch × 0.035 inch or larger steel strapping conforming to ASTM D 3953—97, Standard Specification for Strapping, Flat Steel and Seals (incorporated by reference, see § 3285.4), Type 1, Grade 1, Finish B, with a minimum total capacity of 4,725 pounds (lbs.) and a working capacity of 3,150 pounds (lbs.) must be used. The tie-down straps must be provided with protection against weather deterioration and corrosion at least equivalent to that provided by a coating of zinc on steel of not less than 0.30 oz./ft.^{2} of surface coated. Slit or cut edges of coated strapping need not be zinc coated.

(d) *Number and location of ground anchors.* (1) Ground anchor and anchor strap spacing must be:

(i) No greater than the spacing shown in Tables 1 through 3 to this section and Figures A and B to this section; or

(ii) Designed by a registered engineer or architect, in accordance with acceptable engineering practice and the requirements of the MHCSS for any conditions that are outside the parameters and applicability of the Tables 1 through 3 to this section.

(2) The requirements in paragraph (c) of this section must be used to determine the maximum spacing of ground anchors and their accompanying anchor straps, based on the soil classification determined in accordance with § 3285.202:

(i) The installed ground anchor type and size (length) must be listed for use in the soil class at the site and for the minimum and maximum angle permitted between the diagonal strap and the ground; and

(ii) All ground anchors must be installed in accordance with their listing or certification and the ground anchor manufacturer installation instructions; and

(iii) If required by the ground anchor listing or certification, the correct size and type of stabilizer plate is installed. If metal stabilizer plates are used, they must be provided with protection against weather deterioration and corrosion at least equivalent to that provided by a coating of zinc on steel of not less than 0.30 oz./ft.2 of surface coated. Alternatively, ABS stabilizer plates may be used when listed and certified for such use.

(3) *Longitudinal anchoring.* Manufactured homes must also be stabilized against wind in the longitudinal direction in all Wind Zones. Manufactured homes located in Wind Zones II and III must have longitudinal ground anchors installed on the ends of the manufactured home transportable section(s) or be provided with alternative systems that are capable of resisting wind forces in the longitudinal direction. See Figure C to § 3285.402 for an example of one method that may be used to

provide longitudinal anchoring. A professional engineer or registered architect must certify the longitudinal anchoring method or any alternative system used as adequate to provide the required stabilization, in accordance with acceptable engineering practice.

Figure A to § 3285.402 Ground Anchor Locations and Spacing – Plan View.

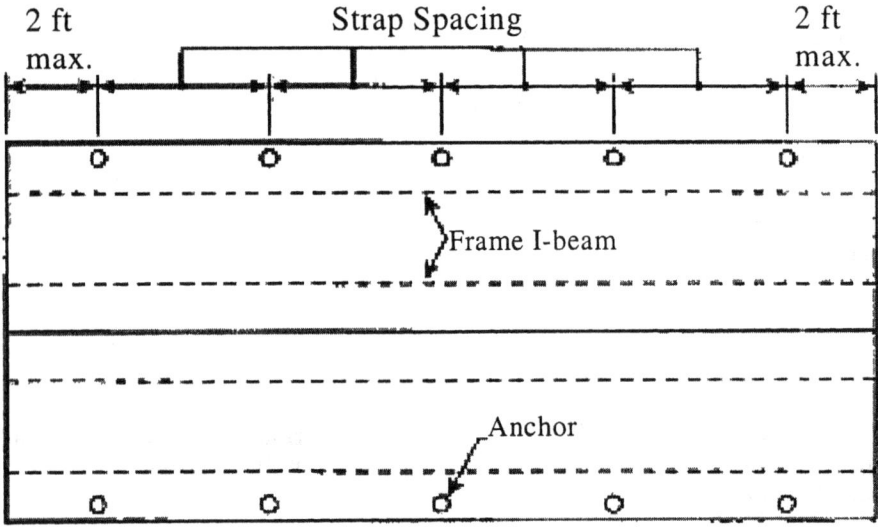

NOTES: 1. Refer to Tables 1, 2, and 3 to this section for maximum ground anchor spacing.

2. Longitudinal anchors not shown for clarity; refer to 3285.402(b)(2) for longitudinal anchoring requirements.

Figure B to § 3285.402 Anchor Strap and Pier Relationship.

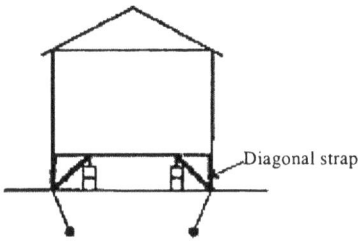

Near Beam Method

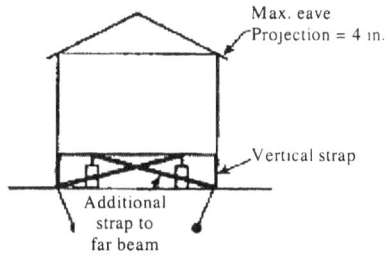

Second Beam Method
(Vertical tie down straps required)

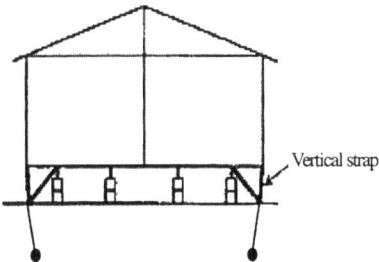

Near Beam Method
(Mate-line piers and anchors omitted for clarity)

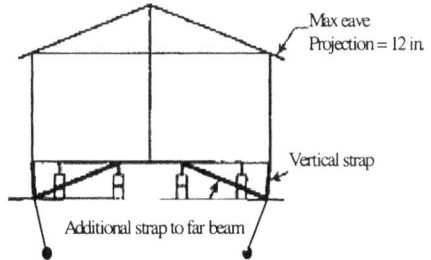

Second Beam Method
(Mate-line piers and anchors omitted for clarity)

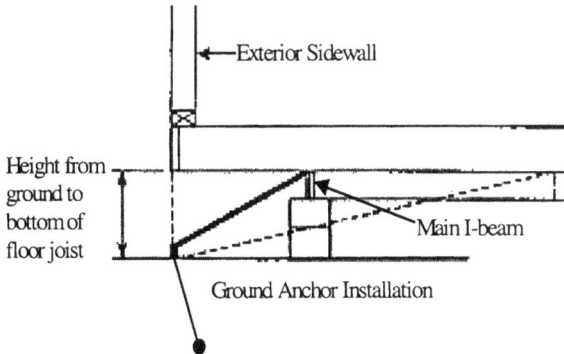

NOTES: 1. Vertical Straps are not required in Wind Zone I.

2. The frame must be designed to prevent rotation of the main chassis beam, when the diagonal ties are not attached to the top flange of the beam. See § 3285.401(d)(3).

Figure C to § 3285.402 Longitudinal Anchoring

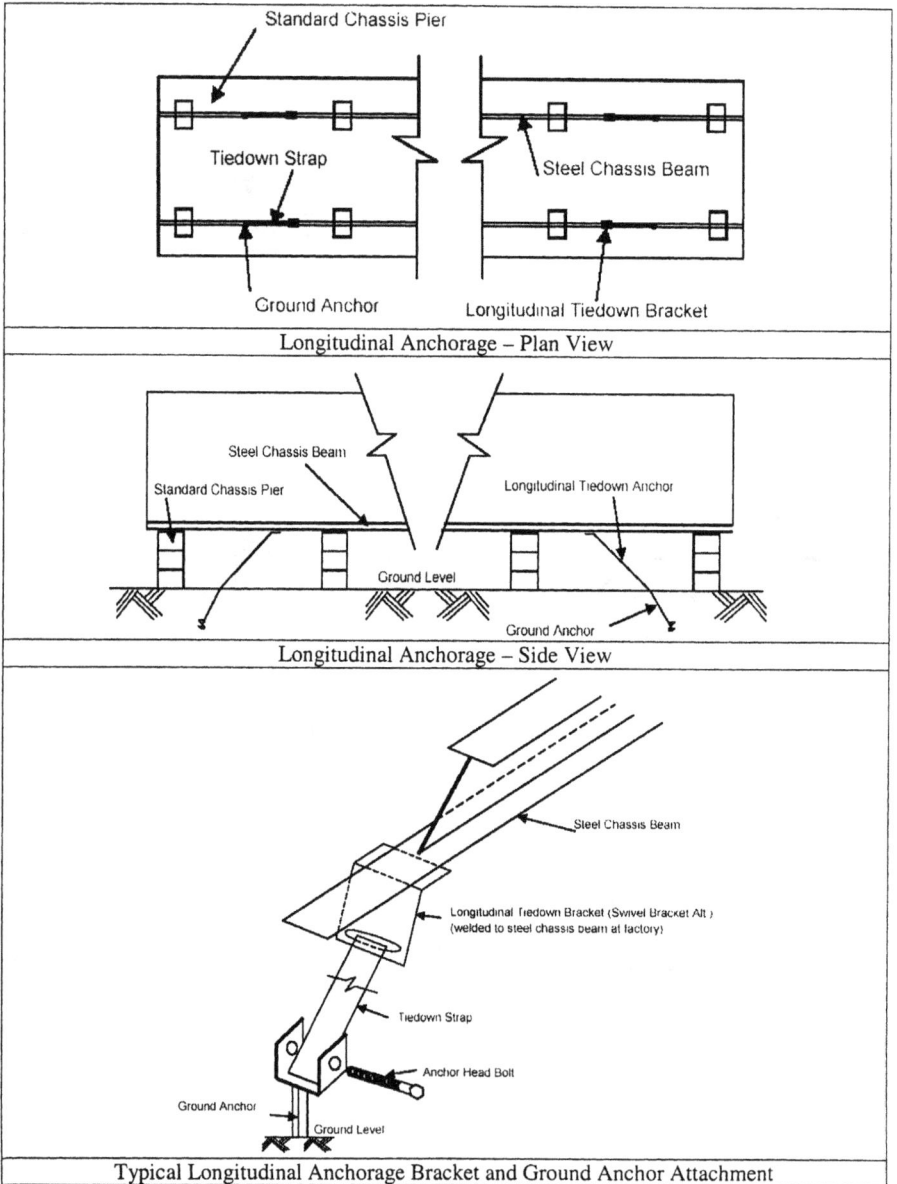

Standard Chassis Pier

Tiedown Strap

Steel Chassis Beam

Ground Anchor

Longitudinal Tiedown Bracket

Longitudinal Anchorage – Plan View

Steel Chassis Beam

Standard Chassis Pier

Longitudinal Tiedown Anchor

Ground Level

Ground Anchor

Longitudinal Anchorage – Side View

Steel Chassis Beam

Longitudinal Tiedown Bracket (Swivel Bracket Alt.)
(welded to steel chassis beam at factory)

Tiedown Strap

Anchor Head Bolt

Ground Anchor

Ground Level

Typical Longitudinal Anchorage Bracket and Ground Anchor Attachment

TABLE 1 TO § 3285.402—MAXIMUM DIAGONAL TIE-DOWN STRAP SPACING, WIND ZONE I

Nominal floor width, single section/multi-section	Max. height from ground to diagonal strap attachment	I-beam spacing 82.5 in.	I-beam spacing 99.5 in.
12/24 ft. 144 in. nominal section(s)	25 in	14 ft. 2 in	N/A.
	33 in	11 ft. 9in	N/A.

238

TABLE 1 TO § 3285.402—MAXIMUM DIAGONAL TIE-DOWN STRAP SPACING, WIND ZONE I— Continued

Nominal floor width, single section/multi-section	Max. height from ground to diagonal strap attachment	I-beam spacing 82.5 in.	I-beam spacing 99.5 in.
	46 in	9 ft. 1in	N/A.
	67 in	N/A	N/A.
14/28 ft. 168 in. nominal section(s)	25 in	18 ft. 2in	15 ft. 11 in.
	33 in	16 ft. 1 in	13 ft. 6 in.
	46 in	13 ft. 3 in	10 ft. 8in.
	67 in	10 ft. 0 in	N/A.
16/32 ft. 180 in. to 192 in. nominal section(s)	25 in	N/A	19 ft. 5in.
	33 in	19 ft. 0 in	17 ft. 5 in.
	46 in	16 ft. 5 in	14 ft. 7 in.
	67 in	13 ft. 1 in	11 ft. 3 in.

NOTES: 1. Table is based on maximum 90 in. sidewall height.

2. Table is based on maximum 4 in. inset for ground anchor head from edge of floor or wall.

3. Table is based on main rail (I-beam) spacing per given column.

4. Table is based on maximum 4 in. eave width for single-section homes and maximum 12 in. for multi-section homes.

5. Table is based on maximum 20-degree roof pitch (4.³⁄₁₂).

6. Table is based upon the minimum height between the ground and the bottom of the floor joist being 18 inches. Interpolation may be required for other heights from ground to strap attachment.

7. Additional tie-downs may be required per the home manufacturer instructions.

8. Ground anchors must be certified for these conditions by a professional engineer, architect, or listed by a nationally recognized testing laboratory.

9. Ground anchors must be installed to their full depth, and stabilizer plates, if required by the ground anchor listing or certification, must also be installed in accordance with the listing or certification and in accordance with the ground anchor and home manufacturer instructions.

10. Strapping and anchoring equipment must be certified by a registered professional engineer or registered architect, or listed by a nationally recognized testing agency to resist these specified forces, in accordance with testing procedures in ASTM D 3953–97, Standard Specification for Strapping, Flat Steel and Seals (incorporated by reference, see § 3285.4).

11. A reduced ground anchor or strap working load capacity will require reduced tie-down strap and anchor spacing.

12. Ground anchors must not be spaced closer than the minimum spacing permitted by the listing or certification.

13. Table is based on a 3,150 lbs. working load capacity, and straps must be placed within 2 ft. of the ends of the home.

14. Table is based on a minimum angle of 30 degrees and a maximum angle of 60 degrees between the diagonal strap and the ground.

15. Table does not consider flood or seismic loads and is not intended for use in flood or seismic hazard areas. In those areas, the anchorage system is to be designed by a professional engineer or architect.

TABLE 2 TO § 3285.402—MAXIMUM DIAGONAL TIE-DOWN STRAP SPACING, WIND ZONE II.

Nominal floor width, single section/multi-section	Max. height from ground to diagonal strap attachment	Near beam method I–beam spacing		Second beam method I–beam spacing	
		82.5 in.	99.5 in.	82.5 in.	99.5 in.
12 ft/24 ft. 144 in. nominal section(s).	25 in	6 ft. 2 in	4 ft. 3 in	N/A	N/A
	33 in	5 ft. 2 in	N/A	N/A	N/A
	46 in	4 ft. 0 in	N/A	N/A	N/A
	67 in	N/A	N/A	6 ft 1 in	6 ft 3 in
14 ft/28 ft. 168 in. nominal section(s).	25 in	7 ft. 7 in	6 ft. 9 in	N/A	N/A
	33 in	6 ft. 10 in	5 ft. 9 in	N/A	N/A
	46 in	5 ft. 7 in	4 ft. 6 in	N/A	N/A
	67 in	4 ft. 3 in	N/A	N/A	N/A
16 ft/32 ft. 180 in. to 192 in. nominal section(s).	25 in	N/A	7 ft. 10 in	N/A	N/A

239

TABLE 2 TO § 3285.402—MAXIMUM DIAGONAL TIE-DOWN STRAP SPACING, WIND ZONE II.—
Continued

Nominal floor width, single section/multi-section	Max. height from ground to diagonal strap attachment	Near beam method I–beam spacing		Second beam method I–beam spacing	
		82.5 in.	99.5 in.	82.5 in.	99.5 in.
	33 in	7 ft. 6 in	7 ft. 2 in	N/A	N/A
	46 in	6 ft. 9 in	6 ft. 0 in	N/A	N/A
	67 in	5 ft. 4 in	4 ft. 7 in	N/A	N/A

NOTES: 1. Table is based on maximum 90 in. sidewall height.

2. Table is based on maximum 4 in. inset for ground anchor head from edge of floor or wall.

3. Tables are based on main rail (I-beam) spacing per given column.

4. Table is based on maximum 4 in. eave width for single-section homes and maximum 12 in. for multi-section homes.

5. Table is based on maximum 20-degree roof pitch (4.3/12).

6. All manufactured homes designed to be located in Wind Zone II must have a vertical tie installed at each diagonal tie location.

7. Table is based upon the minimum height between the ground and the bottom of the floor joist being 18 inches. Interpolation may be required for other heights from ground to strap attachment.

8. Additional tie downs may be required per the home manufacturer instructions.

9. Ground anchors must be certified by a professional engineer, or registered architect, or listed by a nationally recognized testing laboratory.

10. Ground anchors must be installed to their full depth, and stabilizer plates, if required by the ground anchor listing or certification, must also be installed in accord-ance with the listing or certification and in accordance with the ground anchor and home manufacturer instructions.

11. Strapping and anchoring equipment must be certified by a registered professional engineer or registered architect or must be listed by a nationally recognized testing agency to resist these specified forces, in accordance with testing procedures in ASTM D 3953—97, Standard Specification for Strapping, Flat Steel and Seals (incorporated by reference, see § 3285.4).

12. A reduced ground anchor or strap working load capacity will require reduced tie-down strap and anchor spacing.

13. Ground anchors must not be spaced closer than the minimum spacing permitted by the listing or certification.

14. Table is based on a 3,150 lbs. working load capacity, and straps must be placed within 2 ft. of the ends of the home.

15. Table is based on a minimum angle of 30 degrees and a maximum of 60 degrees between the diagonal strap and the ground.

16. Table does not consider flood or seismic loads and is not intended for use in flood or seismic hazard areas. In those areas, the anchorage system is to be designed by a professional engineer or architect.

TABLE 3 TO § 3285.402—MAXIMUM DIAGONAL TIE-DOWN STRAP SPACING, WIND ZONE III.

Nominal floor width, single section/multi-section	Max. height from ground to diagonal strap attachment	Near beam method I-beam spacing		Second beam method I-beam spacing	
		82.5 in.	99.5 in.	82.5 in.	99.5 in.
12 ft./24 ft. 144 in. nominal section(s).	25 in	5 ft. 1 in	N/A	N/A	N/A
	33 in	4 ft. 3 in	N/A	N/A	N/A
	46 in	N/A	N/A	N/A	N/A
	67 in	N/A	N/A	N/A	N/A
14 ft./28 ft. 168 in. nominal section(s).	25 in	6 ft. 2 in.	5 ft. 7 in	N/A	N/A
	33 in	5 ft. 8 in	4 ft. 9 in	N/A	N/A
	46 in	4 ft. 8 in	N/A	N/A	N/A
	67 in	N/A	N/A	N/A	N/A
16 ft./32 ft. 180 in. to 192 in. nominal sections.	25 in	N/A	6 ft. 3 in	N/A	N/A
	33 in	6 ft. 1 in	5 ft. 11 in	N/A	N/A
	46 in	5 ft. 7 in	5 ft. 0 in	N/A	N/A
	67 in	4 ft. 5 in	N/A	N/A	N/A

NOTES: 1. Table is based on maximum 90 in. sidewall height.

2. Table is based on maximum 4 in. inset for ground anchor head from edge of floor or wall.

3. Table is based on main rail (I-beam) spacing per given column.

4. Table is based on maximum 4 in. eave width for single-section homes and maximum 12 in. for multi-section homes.

5. Table is based on maximum 20-degree roof pitch (4.3/12).

6. All manufactured homes designed to be located in Wind Zone III must have a vertical tie installed at each diagonal tie location.

7. Table is based upon the minimum height between the ground and the bottom of the floor joist being 18 inches. Interpolation may be required for other heights from ground to strap attachment.

8. Additional tie downs may be required per the home manufacturer instructions.

9. Ground anchors must be certified by a professional engineer, or registered architect, or listed by a nationally recognized testing laboratory.

10. Ground anchors must be installed to their full depth, and stabilizer plates, if required by the ground anchor listing or certification, must also be installed in accordance with the listing or certification and per the ground anchor and home manufacturer instructions.

11. Strapping and anchoring equipment must be certified by a registered professional engineer or registered architect or must be listed by a nationally recognized testing agency to resist these specified forces, in accordance with testing procedures in ASTM D 3953–97, Standard Specification for Strapping, Flat Steel and Seals (incorporated by reference, see § 3285.4).

12. A reduced ground anchor or strap working load capacity will require reduced tiedown strap and anchor spacing.

13. Ground anchors must not be spaced closer than the minimum spacing permitted by the listing or certification.

14. Table is based on a 3,150 lbs. working load capacity, and straps must be placed within 2 ft. of the ends of the home.

15. Table is based on a minimum angle of 30 degrees and a maximum angle of 60 degrees between the diagonal strap and the ground.

16. Table does not consider flood or seismic loads and is not intended for use in flood or seismic hazard areas. In those areas, the anchorage system is to be designed by a professional engineer or architect.

APPENDIX TO § 3285.402

Torque Probe Method for determining soil classification: This kit contains a 5-foot long steel earth-probe rod, with a helix at the end. It resembles a wood-boring bit on a larger scale. The tip of the probe is inserted as deep as the bottom helix of the ground anchor assembly that is being considered for installation. The torque wrench is placed on the top of the probe. The torque wrench is used to rotate the probe steadily so one can read the scale on the wrench. If the torque wrench reads 551 inch-pounds or greater, then a Class 2 soil is present according to the Table to 24 CFR 3285.202(a)(3). A Class 3 soil is from 351 to 550 inch-pounds. A Class 4A soil is from 276 to 350 inch-pounds, and a Class 4B soil is from 175 to 275 inch-pounds. When the torque wrench reading is below 175 inch-pounds, a professional engineer should be consulted.

[72 FR 59362, Oct. 19, 2007, as amended at 79 FR 53614, Sept. 10, 2014]

§ 3285.403 Sidewall, over-the-roof, mate-line, and shear wall straps.

If sidewall, over-the-roof, mate-line, or shear wall straps are installed on the home, they must be connected to an anchoring assembly.

§ 3285.404 Severe climatic conditions.

In frost-susceptible soil locations, ground anchor augers must be installed below the frost line, unless the foundation system is frost-protected to prevent the effects of frost heave, in accordance with acceptable engineering practice and § 3280.306 of this chapter and § 3285.312.

§ 3285.405 Severe wind zones.

When any part of a home is installed within 1,500 feet of a coastline in Wind Zones II or III, the manufactured home must be designed for the increased requirements, as specified on the home's data plate (refer to § 3280.5(f) of this chapter) in accordance with acceptable engineering practice. Where site or other conditions prohibit the use of the manufacturer's instructions, a registered professional engineer or registered architect, in accordance with acceptable engineering practice, must design anchorage for the special wind conditions.

§ 3285.406 Flood hazard areas.

Refer to § 3285.302 for anchoring requirements in flood hazard areas.

Subpart F—Optional Features

§ 3285.501 Home installation manual supplements.

Supplemental instructions for optional equipment or features must be approved by the DAPIA as not taking the home out of conformance with the requirements of this part, or part 3280 of this chapter, and included with the manufacturer installation instructions.

§ 3285.502 Expanding rooms.

The support and anchoring systems for expanding rooms must be installed in accordance with designs provided by the home manufacturer or prepared by a registered professional engineer or registered architect, in accordance with acceptable engineering practice.

§ 3285.503 Optional appliances.

(a) *Comfort cooling systems.* When not provided and installed by the home manufacturer, any comfort cooling systems that are installed must be installed according to the appliance manufacturer's installation instructions.

(1) *Air conditioners.* Air conditioning equipment must be listed or certified by a nationally recognized testing agency for the application for which the unit is intended and installed in accordance with the terms of its listing or certification (see § 3280.714 of this chapter).

(i) *Energy efficiency.* (A) Site-installed central air conditioning equipment must be sized to meet the home's heat gain requirement, in accordance with Chapter 28 of the 1997 ASHRAE Handbook of Fundamentals (incorporated by reference, see § 3285.4) or ACCA Manual J, Residential Cooling Load, 8th Edition (incorporated by reference, see § 3285.4). Information necessary to calculate the home's heat gain can be found on the home's comfort cooling certificate.

(B) The BTU/hr. rated capacity of the site-installed air conditioning equipment must not exceed the air distribution system's rated BTU/hr. capacity as shown on the home's compliance certificate.

(ii) *Circuit rating.* If a manufactured home is factory-provided with an exterior outlet to energize heating and/or air conditioning equipment, the branch circuit rating on the tag adjacent to this outlet must be equal to or greater than the minimum circuit amperage identified on the equipment rating plate.

(iii) *A-coil units.* (A) A-coil air conditioning units must be compatible and listed for use with the furnace in the home and installed in accordance with the appliance manufacturer's instructions.

(B) The air conditioner manufacturer instructions must be followed.

(C) All condensation must be directed beyond the perimeter of the home by means specified by the equipment manufacturer.

(2) *Heat pumps.* Heat pumps must be listed or certified by a nationally recognized testing agency for the application for which the unit is intended and installed in accordance with the terms of its listing or certification. (See § 3280.714 of this chapter).

(3) *Evaporative coolers.* (i) A roof-mounted cooler must be listed or certified by a nationally recognized testing agency for the application for which the unit is intended and installed in accordance with the terms of its listing (see § 3280.714 of this chapter).

(A) Any discharge grill must not be closer than three feet from a smoke alarm.

(B) Before installing a roof-mounted evaporative cooler on-site, the installer must ensure that the roof will support the weight of the cooler.

(C) A rigid base must be provided to distribute the cooler weight over multiple roof trusses to adequately support the weight of the evaporative cooler.

(ii) An evaporative cooler that is not roof-mounted is to be installed in accordance with the requirements of its listing or the equipment manufacturer's instructions, whichever is the more restrictive.

(b) *Fireplaces and wood-stoves.* When not provided by the home manufacturer, fireplaces and wood-stoves including chimneys and air inlets for fireplaces and wood stoves must be listed for use with manufactured homes and must be installed in accordance with their listings.

(c) *Appliance venting.* (1) All fuel burning heat producing appliances of the vented type except ranges and ovens must be vented to the exterior of the home.

(2) Upon completion, the venting system must comply with all requirements of §§ 3280.707(b) and 3280.710 of the Manufactured Home Construction and Safety Standards in this chapter.

(3) When the vent exhausts through the floor, the vent must not terminate under the home and must extend to the home's exterior and through any skirting that may be installed.

(d) *Clothes dryer exhaust duct system.* A clothes dryer exhaust duct system must conform with and be completed in accordance with the appliance manufacturer instructions and § 3280.708 of this chapter. The vents must exhaust to the exterior of the home, beyond any perimeter skirting installed around it, as shown in Figure to § 3285.503.

Figure A to § 3285.503 Dryer Exhaust System.

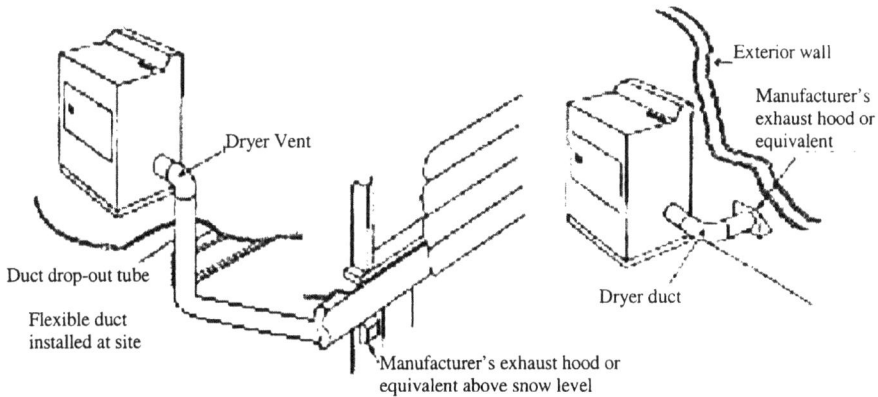

Exterior wall

Manufacturer's exhaust hood or equivalent

Dryer Vent

Dryer duct

Duct drop-out tube

Flexible duct installed at site

Manufacturer's exhaust hood or equivalent above snow level

NOTES: 1. Installation of the exhaust system must be in accordance with the dryer manufacturer instructions.

2. Dryer exhaust system must not contain reverse slope or terminate under the home.

§ 3285.504 Skirting.

(a) Skirting, if used, must be of weather-resistant materials or provided with protection against weather deterioration at least equivalent to that provided by a coating of zinc on steel of not less than 0.30 oz./ft.^{2} of surface coated.

(b) Skirting must not be attached in a manner that can cause water to be trapped between the siding and trim or forced up into the wall cavities trim to which it is attached.

(c) All wood skirting within 6 inches of the ground must be pressure-treated in accordance with AWPA Standard U1 (incorporated by reference, see § 3285.4) for Use Category 4A, Ground Anchor Contact Applications, or be naturally resistant to decay and termite infestations.

(d) Skirting must not be attached in a manner that impedes the contraction and expansion characteristics of the home's exterior covering.

§ 3285.505 Crawlspace ventilation.

(a) A crawlspace with skirting must be provided with ventilation openings. The minimum net area of ventilation openings must not be less than one square foot (ft.^{2}) for every 150 square feet (ft.^{2}) of the home's floor area. The total area of ventilation openings may be reduced to one square foot (ft.^{2}) for every 1,500 square feet (ft.^{2}) of the home's floor area, where a uniform 6-mil polyethylene sheet material or other acceptable vapor retarder is installed, according to § 3285.204, on the ground surface beneath the entire floor area of the home.

(b) Ventilation openings must be placed as high as practicable above the ground.

(c) Ventilation openings must be located on at least two opposite sides to provide cross-ventilation.

(d) Ventilation openings must be covered for their full height and width with a perforated corrosion and weather-resistant covering that is designed to prevent the entry of rodents. In areas subject to freezing, the coverings for the ventilation openings must also be of the adjustable type, permitting them to be in the open or closed position, depending on the climatic conditions.

(e) Access opening(s) not less than 18 inches in width and 24 inches in height and not less than three square feet (ft.²) in area must be provided and must be located so that any utility connections located under the home are accessible.

(f) Dryer vents and combustion air inlets must pass through the skirting to the outside. Any surface water run-off from the furnace, air conditioning, or water heater drains must be directed away from under the home or collected by other methods identified in § 3285.203.

Subpart G—Ductwork and Plumbing and Fuel Supply Systems

§ 3285.601 Field assembly.

Home manufacturers must provide specific installation instructions for the proper field assembly of manufacturer-supplied and shipped loose ducts, plumbing, and fuel supply system parts that are necessary to join all sections of the home and are designed to be located underneath the home. The installation instructions must be designed in accordance with applicable requirements of part 3280, subparts G and H, of this chapter, as specified in this subpart.

§ 3285.602 Utility connections.

Refer to § 3285.904 for considerations for utility system connections.

§ 3285.603 Water supply.

(a) *Crossover.* Multi-section homes with plumbing in both sections require water-line crossover connections to join all sections of the home. The crossover design requirements are located in, and must be designed in accordance with, § 3280.609 of this chapter.

(b) *Maximum supply pressure and reduction.* When the local water supply pressure exceeds 80 psi to the manufactured home, a pressure-reducing valve must be installed.

(c) *Mandatory shutoff valve.* (1) An identified and accessible shutoff valve must be installed between the water supply and the inlet.

(2) The water riser for the shutoff valve connection must be located underneath or adjacent to the home.

(3) The shutoff valve must be a full-flow gate or ball valve, or equivalent valve.

(d) *Freezing protection.* Water line crossovers completed during installation must be protected from freezing. The freeze protection design requirements are located in, and must be designed in accordance with, § 3280.603 of this chapter.

(1) If subject to freezing temperatures, the water connection must be wrapped with insulation or otherwise protected to prevent freezing.

(2) In areas subject to freezing or subfreezing temperatures, exposed sections of water supply piping, shutoff valves, pressure reducers, and pipes in water heater compartments must be insulated or otherwise protected from freezing.

(3) *Use of pipe heating cable.* Only pipe heating cable listed for manufactured home use is permitted to be used, and it must be installed in accordance with the cable manufacturer installation instructions.

(e) *Testing procedures.* (1) The water system must be inspected and tested for leaks after completion at the site. The installation instructions must provide testing requirements that are consistent with § 3280.612 of this chapter.

(2) The water heater must be disconnected when using an air-only test.

§3285.604 Drainage system.

(a) *Crossovers.* Multi-section homes with plumbing in more than one section require drainage system crossover connections to join all sections of the home. The crossover design requirements are located in, and must be designed in accordance with, §3280.610 of this chapter.

(b) *Assembly and support.* If portions of the drainage system were shipped loose because they were necessary to join all sections of the home and designed to be located underneath the home, they must be installed and supported in accordance with §3280.608 of this chapter.

(c) *Proper slopes.* Drains must be completed in accordance with §3280.610 of this chapter.

(1) Drain lines must not slope less than one-quarter inch per foot, unless otherwise noted on the schematic diagram, as shown in Figure to §3285.604.

(2) A slope of one-eight inch per foot may be permitted when a clean-out is installed at the upper end of the run.

(d) *Testing procedures.* The drainage system must be inspected and tested for leaks after completion at the site. The installation instructions must provide testing requirements that are consistent with §3280.612 of this chapter.

Figure A to § 3285.604 Drain Pipe Slope and Connections.

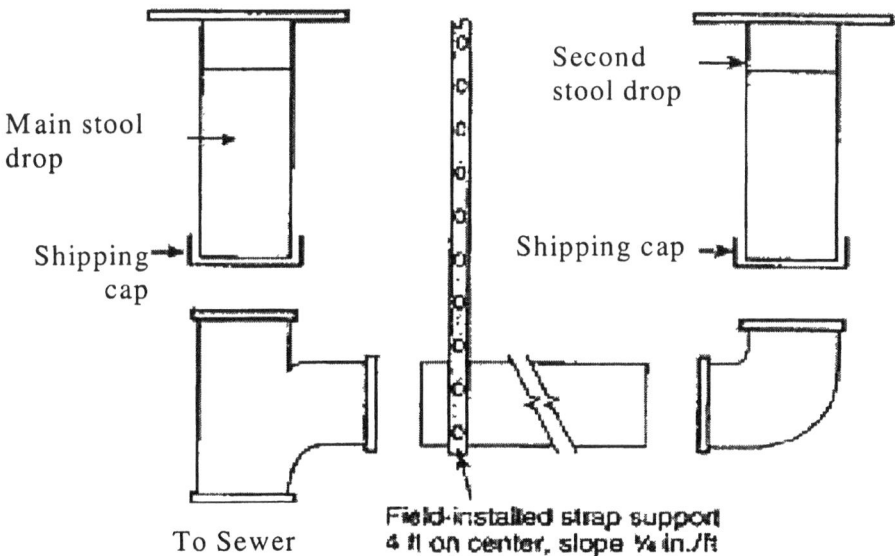

§3285.605 Fuel supply system.

(a) *Proper supply pressure.* The gas piping system in the home is designed for a pressure that is at least 7 inches of water column [4oz./in.^{2} or 0.25 psi] and not more than 14 inches of water column [8 oz./in.^{2} or 0.5 psi]. If gas from any supply source exceeds, or could exceed this pressure, a regulator must be installed if required by the LAHJ.

(b) *Crossovers.* (1) Multi-section homes with fuel supply piping in both sections require crossover connections to join all sections of the home. The crossover design requirements are located in, and must be designed in accordance with, §3280.705 of this chapter.

(2) Tools must not be required to connect or remove the flexible connector quick-disconnect.

(c) *Testing procedures.* The gas system must be inspected and tested for leaks after completion at the site. The installation instructions must provide testing requirements that are consistent with § 3280.705 of this chapter.

§ 3285.606 Ductwork connections.

(a) Multi-section homes with ductwork in more than one section require crossover connections to complete the duct system of the home. All ductwork connections, including duct collars, must be sealed to prevent air leakage. Galvanized metal straps or tape and mastics listed to UL 181A (incorporated by reference, see § 3285.4), for closure systems with rigid air ducts and connectors, or UL 181B (incorporated by reference, see § 3285.4), for closure systems with flexible air ducts and connectors, must be used around the duct collar and secured tightly to make all connections.

(b) If metal straps are used, they must be secured with galvanized sheet metal screws.

(c) Metal ducts must be fastened to the collar with a minimum of three galvanized sheet metal screws equally spaced around the collar.

(d) Air conditioning or heating ducts must be installed in accordance with applicable requirements of the duct manufacturer installation instructions.

(e) The duct must be suspended or supported above the ground by straps or other means that are spaced at a maximum distance not to exceed 4′-0″ or as otherwise permitted by the installation instructions. When straps are used to support a flexible type duct, the straps must be at least ½″ wider than the spacing of the metal spirals encasing the duct. The ducts must be installed such that the straps cannot slip between any two spirals and arranged under the floor to prevent compression or kinking in any location, as shown in Figures A and B to this section. In-floor crossover ducts are permitted, in accordance with § 3285.606(g).

(f) Crossover ducts outside the thermal envelope must be insulated with materials that conform to designs consistent with part 3280, subpart F of this chapter.

(g) In-floor or ceiling crossover duct connections must be installed and sealed to prevent air leakage.

Figure A to §3285.606 – Crossover Duct Installation with Two Connecting Ducts.

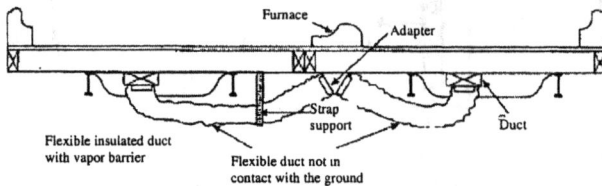

NOTES: 1. This system is typically used when a crossover duct has not been built into the floor and the furnace is outside the I-Beam. With this type of installation, it is necessary for two flexible ducts to be installed.

2. The crossover duct must be listed for exterior use.

Figure B to §3285.606 Crossover Duct Installation with One Connecting Duct.

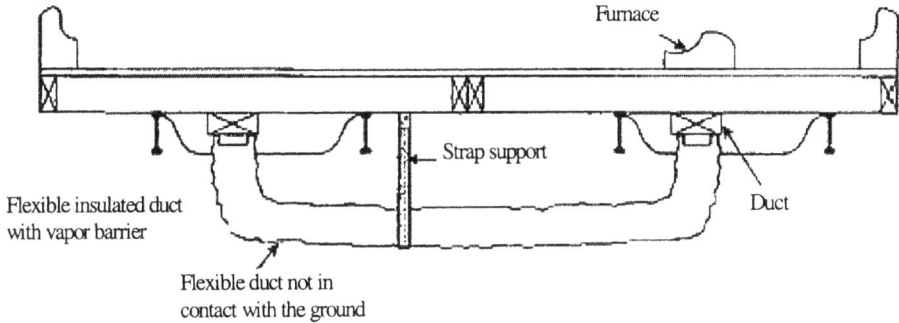

NOTES: 1. This system is typically used when a crossover duct has not been built into the floor and the furnace is situated directly over the main duct in one section of the home. A single flexible duct is then used to connect the two sections to each other.

2. The crossover duct must be listed for exterior use.

Subpart H—Electrical Systems and Equipment

§3285.701   Electrical crossovers.

Multi-section homes with electrical wiring in more than one section require crossover connections in all sections of the home. The crossover must be designed in accordance with part 3280, subpart I of this chapter, and completed in accordance with the directions provided in the installation instructions.

§3285.702   Miscellaneous lights and fixtures.

(a) When the home is installed, exterior lighting fixtures, ceiling-suspended (paddle) fans, and chain-hung lighting fixtures are permitted to be installed in accordance with their listings and part 3280, subpart I of this chapter.

(b) *Grounding.* (1) All the exterior lighting fixtures and ceiling fans installed per §3285.702(a) must be grounded by a fixture-grounding device or by a fixture-grounding wire.

(2) For chain-hung lighting fixtures, as shown in Figure A to this section, both a fixture-grounding device and a fixture-grounding wire must be used. The identified conductor must be the neutral conductor.

(c) Where lighting fixtures are mounted on combustible surfaces such as hardboard, a limited combustible or noncombustible ring, as shown in Figures A and B to this section, must be installed to completely cover the combustible surface exposed between the fixture canopy and the wiring outlet box.

(d) *Exterior lights.* (1) The junction box covers must be removed and wire-to-wire connections must be made using listed wire connectors.

(2) Wires must be connected black-to-black, white-to-white, and equipment ground-to-equipment ground.

(3) The wires must be pushed into the box, and the lighting fixture must be secured to the junction box.

(4) The lighting fixture must be caulked around its base to ensure a watertight seal to the sidewall.

(5) The light bulb must be installed and the globe must be attached.

(e) *Ceiling fans.* (1) Ceiling-suspended (paddle) fans must be connected to junction box listed and marked for ceiling fan application, in accordance with Article 314.27(b) of the National Electrical Code, NFPA No. 70–2005 (incorporated by reference, see §3285.4); and

(2) The ceiling fan must be installed with the trailing edges of the blades at least 6 feet 4 inches above the finished floor; and

(3) The wiring must be connected in accordance with the product manufacturer installation instructions.

(f) *Testing.* (1) After completion of all electrical wiring and connections, including crossovers, electrical lights, and ceiling fans, the electrical system must be inspected and tested at the site, in accordance with the testing requirements of § 3280.810(b) of this chapter.

(2) The installation instructions must indicate that each manufactured home must be subjected to the following tests:

(i) An electrical continuity test to ensure that metallic parts are effectively bonded;

(ii) Operational tests of all devices and utilization equipment, except water heaters, electric ranges, electric furnaces, dishwashers, clothes washers/dryers, and portable appliances, to demonstrate that they are connected and in working order; and

(iii) For electrical equipment installed or completed during installation, electrical polarity checks must be completed to determine that connections have been made properly. Visual verification is an acceptable electrical polarity check.

Figure A to § 3285.702 Typical Installation of Chain-Hung Lighting Fixture.

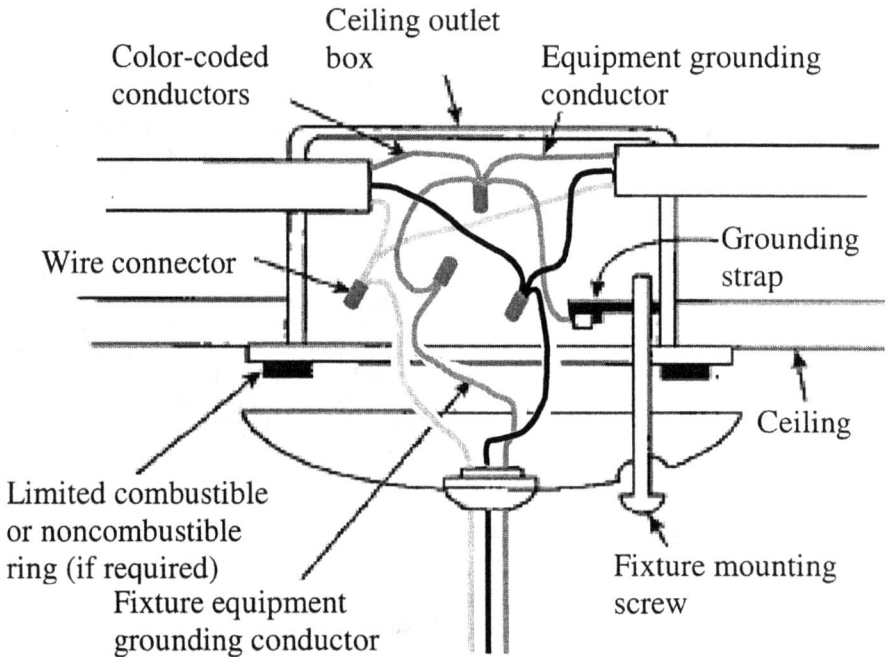

Figure B to § 3285.702 Typical Installation of Surface-Mounted Exterior Lighting Fixture.

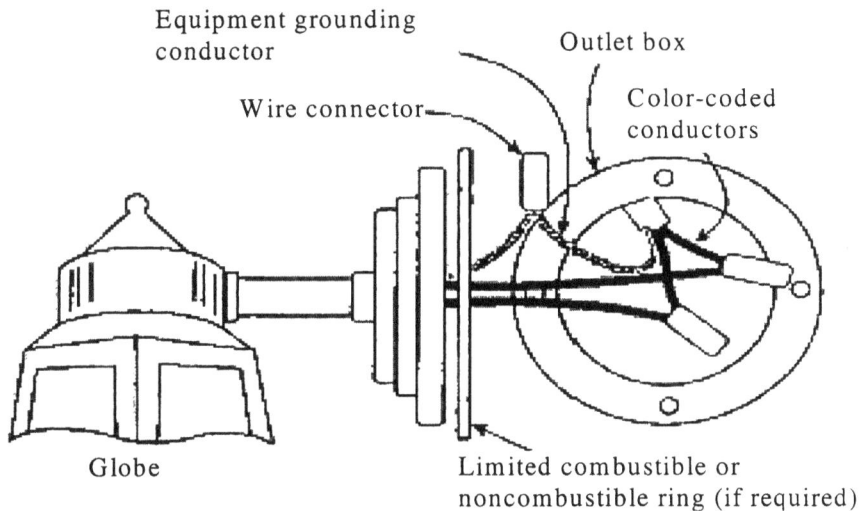

[72 FR 59362, Oct. 19, 2007; 72 FR 62308, Nov. 2, 2007]

§ 3285.703 Smoke alarms.

Smoke alarms must be functionally tested in accordance with applicable requirements of the smoke alarm manufacturer instructions and must be consistent with §3280.208 of this chapter.

§ 3285.704 Telephone and cable TV.

Refer to § 3285.906 for considerations pertinent to installation of telephone and cable TV.

Subpart I—Exterior and Interior Close-Up

§ 3285.801 Exterior close-up.

(a) Exterior siding and roofing necessary to join all sections of the home must be installed according to the product manufacturer installation instructions and must be fastened in accordance with designs and manufacturer instructions, consistent with §§ 3280.305 and 3280.307 of this chapter. Exterior close-up strips/trim must be fastened securely and sealed with exterior sealant (see figure A to this section).

(b) *Joints and seams.* All joints and seams in exterior wall coverings that were disturbed during location of the home must be made weatherproof.

(c) Prior to installing the siding, the polyethylene sheeting covering exterior walls for transit must be completely removed.

(d) Prior to completing the exterior close-up, any holes in the roofing must be made weatherproof and sealed with a sealant or other material that is suitable for use with the roofing in which the hole is made.

(e) *Mate-line gasket.* The home manufacturer must provide materials and designs for mate-line gaskets or other methods designed to resist the entry of air, water, water vapor, insects, and rodents at all mate-line locations exposed to the exterior (see Figure B to this section).

(f) *Hinged roofs and eaves.* Hinged roofs and eaves must be completed during installation in compliance with all requirements of the Manufactured Home Construction and Safety Standards (24 CFR part 3280) and the Manufactured Home Procedural and Enforcement Regulations (24 CFR part 3282). Unless exempted by the following provisions, hinged roofs are also subject to a final inspection for compliance with the Manufactured Home Construction and Safety Standards (24 CFR part 3280) by the IPIA or a qualified independent inspector acceptable to the IPIA. Homes with hinged roofs that are exempted from IPIA inspection are instead to be completed and inspected in accordance with the Manufactured Home Installation Program (24 CFR part 3286). This includes homes:

(1) That are designed to be located in Wind Zone I;

(2) In which the roof pitch of the hinged roof is less than 7:12, including designs incorporating peak cap construction or peak flip construction; and

(3) In which fuel burning appliance flue penetrations are not above the hinge.

FIGURE A to §3285.801 Installation of Field-Applied Horizontal Lap Siding

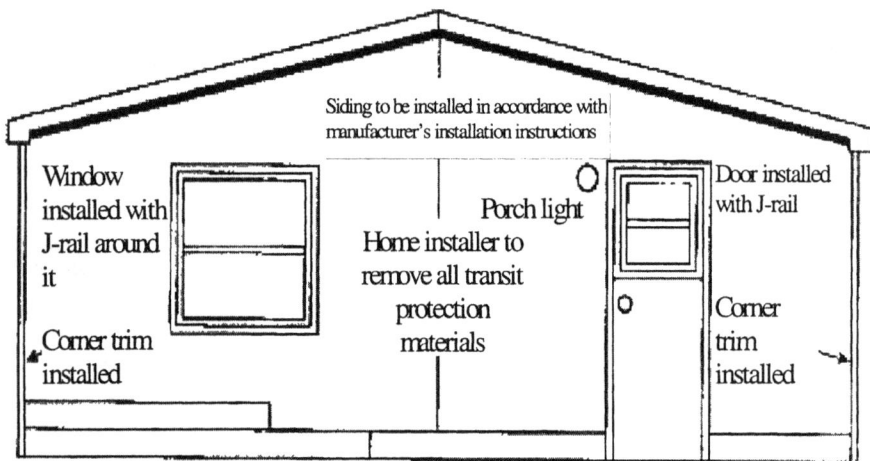

NOTES: 1. Multi-section homes with horizontal-lap siding can be shipped with no siding on the front and rear end walls.

2. The manufacturer must install doors/windows trimmed with J-rail or the equivalent and protect all exposed materials not designed for exposure to the weather with plastic sheeting for transport. Siding, starter trim, and vents may be shipped loose in the home for installation on set-up.

3. All home installers must ensure that all field installed trim, windows, doors, and other openings are properly sealed according to the siding manufacturer installation instructions.

Figure B to § 3285.801 Mate-Line Gasket.

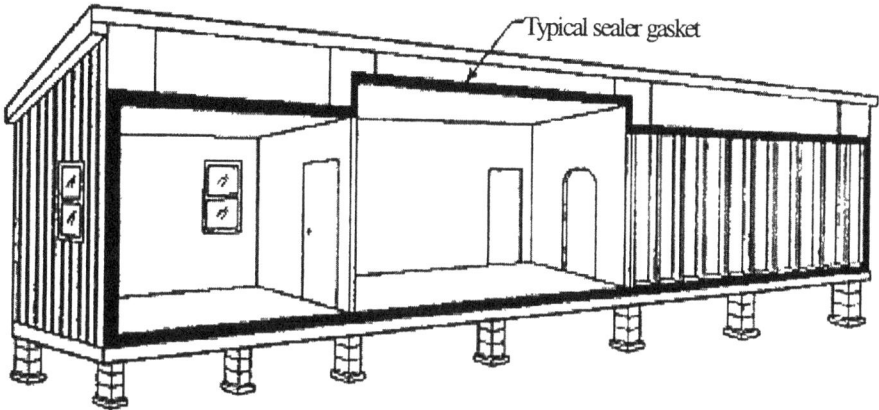

Typical sealer gasket

NOTE: On multi-section manufactured homes, install the sealer gasket on the ceiling, end walls, and floor mate-line prior to joining the sections together.

[72 FR 59362, Oct. 19, 2007, as amended at 80 FR 53731, Sept. 8, 2015]

§ 3285.802 Structural interconnection of multi-section homes.

(a) For multi-section homes, structural interconnections along the interior and exterior at the mate-line are necessary to join all sections of the home.

(b) Structural interconnection must be designed in accordance with the requirements located in § 3280.305 of this chapter to ensure a completely integrated structure.

(c) Upon completion of the exterior close-up, no gaps are permitted between the structural elements being interconnected along the mate-line of multi-section homes. However, prior to completion of the exterior close-up, gaps that do not exceed one inch are permitted between structural elements provided:

(1) The gaps are closed before completion of close-up;

(2) The home sections are in contact with each other; and

(3) The mating gasket is providing a proper seal. All such gaps must be shimmed with dimensional lumber, and fastener lengths used to make connections between the structural elements must be increased to provide adequate penetration into the receiving member.

§ 3285.803 Interior close-up.

(a) All shipping blocking, strapping, or bracing must be removed from appliances, windows, and doors.

(b) Interior close up items necessary to join all sections of the home or items subject to transportation damage may be packaged or shipped with the home for site installation.

(c) Shipped-loose wall paneling necessary for the joining of all sections of the home must be installed by using polyvinyl acetate (PVA) adhesive on all framing members and fastened with minimum 1½ inch long staples or nails at 6 inches on center panel edges and 12 inches on center in the field, unless alternative fastening methods are permitted in the installation instructions (see Figure A to § 3285.803).

251

FIGURE A to §3285.803 - Installation of Interior Field-Applied Panels.

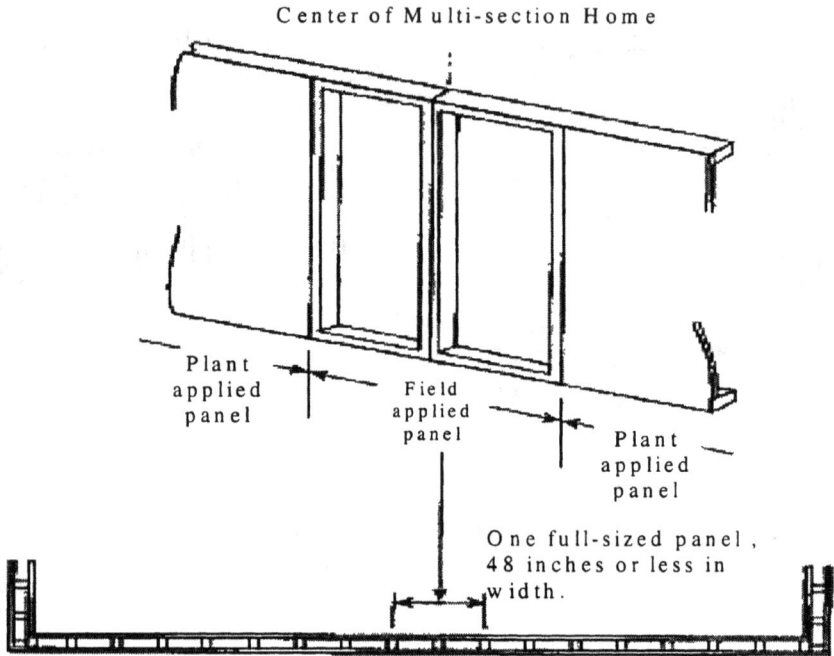

NOTE: Specific designs must be approved by a DAPIA and included in the home manufacturer installation instructions.

§ 3285.804 Bottom board repair.

(a) The bottom board covering must be inspected for any loosening or areas that might have been damaged or torn during installation or transportation. Any missing insulation is to be replaced prior to closure and repair of the bottom board.

(b) Any splits or tears in the bottom board must be resealed with tape or patches in accordance with methods provided in the manufacturers installation instructions.

(c) Plumbing P-traps must be checked to be sure they are well-insulated and covered.

(d) All edges of repaired areas must be taped or otherwise sealed.

Subpart J—Optional Information for Manufacturer's Installation Instructions

§ 3285.901 General.

The planning and permitting processes, as well as utility connection, access, and other requirements, are outside of HUD's authority and may be governed by LAHJs. These Model Installation Standards do not attempt to comprehensively address such requirements. However, HUD recommends that the manufacturer's installation instructions include the information and advisories in this Subpart J, in order to protect the manufactured home, as constructed in accordance with the MHCSS.

§ 3285.902 Moving manufactured home to location.

It is recommended that the installation instructions indicate that the LAHJ be informed before moving the manufactured home to the site. It is also recommended that the installation instructions indicate that the manufactured home is not to be moved to the site until the site is prepared in accordance with subpart C of this part and when the utilities are available as required by the LAHJ. Examples of related areas that might be addressed in the installation instructions for meeting this recommendation include:

(a) *Access for the transporter.* Before attempting to move a home, ensure that the transportation equipment and home can be routed to the installation site and that all special transportation permits required by the LAHJ have been obtained.

(b) *Drainage structures.* Ditches and culverts used to drain surface runoff meet the requirements of the LAHJ and are considered in the overall site preparation.

§ 3285.903 Permits, alterations, and on-site structures.

It is recommended that the installation instructions include the following information related to permits, alterations, and on-site structures:

(a) *Issuance of permits.* All necessary LAHJ fees should be paid and permits should be obtained, which may include verification that LAHJ requirements regarding encroachments in streets, yards, and courts are obeyed and that permissible setback and fire separation distances from property lines and public roads are met.

(b) *Alterations.* Prior to making any alteration to a home or its installation, contact the LAHJ to determine if plan approval and permits are required.

(c) *Installation of on-site structures.* Each accessory building and structure is designed to support all of its own live and dead loads, unless the structure, including any attached garage, carport, deck, and porch, is to be attached to the manufactured home and is otherwise included in the installation instructions or designed by a registered professional engineer or registered architect.

§ 3285.904 Utility system connections.

(a) It is recommended that the manufacturer's installation instructions indicate the following procedures be used prior to making any utility system connection:

(1) Where an LAHJ and utility services are available, that the LAHJ and all utility services each be consulted before connecting the manufactured home to any utilities, or

(2) Where no LAHJ exists and utility services are available, that the utilities be consulted before connecting the manufactured home to any utility service; or

(3) In rural areas where no LAHJ or utility services are available, that a professional be consulted prior to making any system connections.

(b) *Qualified personnel.* Only qualified personnel familiar with local requirements are permitted to make utility site connections and conduct tests.

(c) *Drainage system.* The main drain line must be connected to the site's sewer hookup, using an elastomeric coupler or by other methods acceptable to the LAHJ, as shown in Figure A to this section.

(d) *Fuel supply system.* (1) *Conversion of gas appliances.* A service person acceptable to the LAHJ must convert the appliance from one type of gas to another, following instructions by the manufacturer of each appliance.

(2) *Orifices and regulators.* Before making any connections to the site supply, the inlet orifices of all gas-burning appliances must be checked to ensure they are correctly set up for the type of gas to be supplied.

(3) *Connection procedures.* Gas-burning appliance vents must be inspected to ensure that they are connected to the appliance and that roof jacks are properly installed and have not come loose during transit.

(4) *Gas appliance start-up procedures.* The LAHJ should be consulted concerning the following gas appliance startup procedures:

(i) One at a time, opening equipment shutoff valves, lighting pilot lights when provided, and adjusting burners and spark igniters for automatic ignition systems, in accordance with each appliance manufacturer instructions.

(ii) Checking the operation of the furnace and water heater thermostats.

Figure A to § 3285.904 – Connection to Site Sewer.

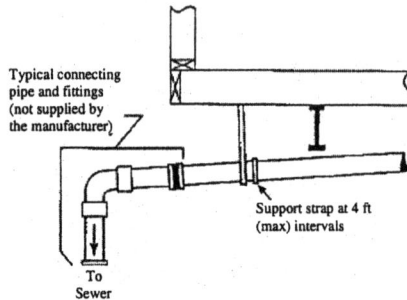

NOTE: Fittings in the drainage system that are subject to freezing, such as P-traps in the floor, are protected with insulation by the manufacturer. Insulation must be replaced if it is removed for access to the P-trap.

§ 3285.905   Heating oil systems.

It is recommended that the installation instructions include the following information related to heating oil systems, when applicable:

(a) Homes equipped with oil burning furnaces should have their oil supply tank and piping installed and tested on-site, in accordance with NFPA 31, Standard for the Installation of Oil Burning Equipment, 2001 (incorporated by reference, see § 3285.4) or the LAHJ, whichever is more stringent.

(b) The oil burning furnace manufacturer's instructions should be consulted for pipe size and installation procedures.

(c) Oil storage tanks and pipe installations should meet all applicable local regulations.

(d) *Tank installation requirements.* (1) The tank should be located where it is accessible to service and supply and where it is safe from fire and other hazards.

(2) In flood hazard areas, the oil storage tank should be anchored and elevated to or above the design flood elevation, or anchored and designed to prevent flotation, collapse, or permanent lateral movement during the design flood.

(3) *Leak test procedure.* Before the system is operated, it should be checked for leaks in the tank and supply piping, in accordance with NFPA 31, Standard

for the Installation of Oil Burning Equipment, 2001 (incorporated by reference, see § 3285.4) or the requirements of the LAHJ, whichever is more stringent.

§ 3285.906   Telephone and cable TV.

It is recommended that the installation instructions explain that telephone and cable TV wiring should be installed in accordance with requirements of the LAHJ and the National Electrical Code, NFPA No. 70–2005 (incorporated by reference, see § 3285.4).

§ 3285.907   Manufacturer additions to installation instructions.

A manufacturer may include in its installation instructions items that are not required by this chapter as long as the items included by the manufacturer are consistent with the Model Installation Standards in this part and do not take the manufactured home out of compliance with the MHCSS.

PART 3286—MANUFACTURED HOME INSTALLATION PROGRAM

Subpart A—Generally Applicable Provisions and Requirements

AUTHORITY: 42 U.S.C. 3535(d), 5404, and 5424.

SOURCE: 73 FR 35292, June 20, 2008, unless otherwise noted.

Subpart A—Generally Applicable Provisions and Requirements

§ 3286.1 Purpose.

(a) *Purpose.* The purpose of this part is to establish the regulations that are applicable to HUD's administration of an installation program that meets the requirements of sections 602 (42 U.S.C. 5401) and 605 (42 U.S.C. 5404) of the National Manufactured Housing Construction and Safety Standards Act of 1974. The purpose of this subpart A is to establish the regulations that are applicable with respect to all manufactured homes before they are sold to a purchaser. The requirements in subpart A apply regardless of whether the actual installation of a manufactured home is regulated by HUD or a state with a qualifying installation program.

(b) *Implementation.* This part is effective on October 20, 2008. Implementation will be undertaken in accordance

255

with the phased-in schedule provided by notice published in the FEDERAL REGISTER.

§ 3286.2 Applicability.

(a) *All states.* The requirements in subpart A are applicable in all states.

(b) *States without installation programs.* The requirements in subparts B through H of this part are applicable only in those states where HUD is administering an installation program in accordance with this part.

(c) *States with installation programs.* The requirements in subpart I of this part are applicable to only those states that want to administer their own installation programs in lieu of the installation program administered by HUD in accordance with this part.

(d) *Exclusion.* None of the requirements of this part apply to:

(1) Any structure that a manufacturer certifies as being excluded from the coverage of the Act in accordance with § 3282.12 of this chapter; or

(2) Temporary housing units provided under the Robert T. Stafford Disaster Relief and Emergency Assistance Act (42 U.S.C. 5121 *et seq.*) to victims of Presidentially declared disasters, when the manufactured home is installed by persons holding an emergency contractor license issued by the state in which the home is sited or installed by the Federal Emergency Management Agency; or

(3) Any manufactured home after the initial installation of the home following the first purchase of the home in good faith for purposes other than resale. State installation programs may regulate subsequent installations of manufactured homes.

(4) Any manufactured home installed on Indian reservations.

§ 3286.3 Definitions.

The following definitions apply in this part, except as otherwise noted in the regulations in this part:

Act means the National Manufactured Housing Construction and Safety Standards Act of 1974, 42 U.S.C. 5401–5425.

Certification of installation means the certification, provided by an installer under the HUD-administered installation program in accordance with § 3286.111, that indicates that the manufactured home has been installed in compliance with the appropriate design and instructions and has been inspected as required by this part.

Defect means any defect in the performance, construction, components, or material of a manufactured home that renders the home or any part thereof not fit for the ordinary use for which it was intended.

Design Approval Primary Inspection Agency (DAPIA) means a state agency or private organization that has been accepted by the Secretary, in accordance with the requirement of subpart H of part 3282, to evaluate and either approve or disapprove manufactured home designs and quality control procedures.

Distributor means any person engaged in the sale and distribution of manufactured homes for resale.

HUD means the United States Department of Housing and Urban Development.

HUD-administered installation program means the installation program to be administered by HUD, in accordance with this part, in those states that do not have a qualifying installation program.

Installation means completion of work done specified in § 3286.505 to stabilize, support, anchor, and close up a manufactured home and to join sections of a multi-section manufactured home, when any such work is governed by the federal installation standards in part 3285 of this chapter or by state installation standards that are certified as part of a qualifying installation program.

Installation defect means any defect in the performance, installation, installation components, installation material, or close-up of a manufactured home that renders the home or any part thereof not fit for the ordinary use for which it was intended or otherwise takes the home out of compliance with the Manufactured Home Construction and Safety Standards in 24 CFR part 3280.

Installation design means drawings, specifications, sketches, and the related engineering calculations, tests, and data in support of the installation configurations and systems to be incorporated in the installation of manufactured homes.

Installation instructions means DAPIA-approved instructions provided by the home manufacturer that accompany each new manufactured home and detail the home manufacturer requirements for support and anchoring systems and other work completed at the installation site to comply with the Model Manufactured Home Installation Standards in 24 CFR part 3285 and the Manufactured Home Construction and Safety Standards in 24 CFR part 3280.

Installation standards means the standards established by HUD in 24 CFR part 3285, or any set of state standards that the Secretary has determined provide protection to the residents of manufactured homes that equals or exceeds the protection provided by the standards in 24 CFR part 3285.

Installer means the person or entity who is retained to engage in, or who engages in, the business of directing, supervising, controlling, or correcting the initial installation of a manufactured home, as governed by part 3285 of this chapter.

Installer's license or *installation license* means the evidence that an installer has met the requirements for installing manufactured homes under the HUD-administered installation program. The term does not incorporate a state-issued installation license or certification, except to the extent provided in this part. The term does not imply that HUD approves or recommends an installer or warrants the work of an installer, and should not be used in any way that indicates HUD approval in violation of 18 U.S.C. 709.

Lessee means the first person who leases a manufactured home from a retailer after the initial installation.

Manufactured home means a structure, transportable in one or more sections, which, in the traveling mode, is 8 body feet or more in width or 40 body feet or more in length, or, when erected on-site, is 320 or more square feet, and which is built on a permanent chassis and designed to be used as a dwelling with or without a permanent foundation when connected to the required utilities, and includes the plumbing,

heating, air-conditioning, and electrical systems contained therein. The term also includes any structure that meets all the requirements of this paragraph except the size requirements and with respect to which the manufacturer voluntarily files a certification pursuant to § 3282.13 of this chapter and complies with the installation standards established under part 3285 and the construction and safety standards in part 3280 of this chapter, but such term does not include any self-propelled recreational vehicle. Calculations used to determine the number of square feet in a structure will include the total of square feet for each transportable section comprising the completed structure and will be based on the structure's exterior dimensions measured at the largest horizontal projections when erected on-site. These dimensions will include all expandable rooms, cabinets, and other projections containing interior space, but do not include bay windows. Nothing in this definition should be interpreted to mean that a manufactured home necessarily meets the requirements of HUD's Minimum Property Standards (HUD Handbook 4900.1) or that it is automatically eligible for financing under 12 U.S.C. 1709(b).

Manufactured Housing Consensus Committee, or *MHCC*, means the consensus committee established pursuant to section 604(a)(3) of the Act, 42 U.S.C. 5403(a)(3).

Manufacturer means any person engaged in manufacturing or assembling manufactured homes, including any person engaged in importing manufactured homes for resale.

Manufacturer's certification label means the permanent label that is required by § 3280.11 of this chapter to be affixed to each transportable section of each manufactured home.

Person includes, unless the context indicates otherwise, corporations, companies, associations, firms, partnerships, societies, and joint stock companies, as well as individuals, but does not include any agency of government or tribal government entity.

Professional engineer or registered architect means an individual or entity: licensed to practice engineering or architecture in a state; and subject to all laws and limitations imposed by the state agency that regulates the applicable profession, and who is engaged in the professional practice of rendering service or creative work requiring education, training, and experience in architecture or engineering sciences and the application of special knowledge of the mathematical, physical, and engineering sciences in such professional or creative work as consultation, investigation, evaluation, planning or design, and supervision of construction for the purpose of securing compliance with specifications and design for any such work.

Purchaser means the first person purchasing a manufactured home in good faith for purposes other than resale.

Qualified trainer means a person who has met the requirements established in subpart D of this part to be recognized as qualified to provide training to installers for purposes of the HUD-administered installation program.

Qualifying installation program means an installation program that a state certifies, in accordance with the requirements set out in subpart I of this part, as meeting the requirements of 42 U.S.C. 5404(c)(3).

Resident means any person residing in the manufactured home.

Retailer means any person engaged in the sale, leasing, or distribution of new manufactured homes primarily to persons who in good faith purchase or lease a manufactured home for purposes other than resale, and, for purposes of this part, the term includes any manufacturer or distributor that sells a manufactured home directly to a purchaser.

Secretary means the Secretary of Housing and Urban Development.

Set up means any assembly or installation of a manufactured home on-site that includes aspects of work that are governed by parts 3280 or 3285 of this chapter.

State includes each of the 50 states, the District of Columbia, the Commonwealth of Puerto Rico, Guam, the Virgin Islands, and American Samoa.

§ 3286.5 Overview of installation program.

(a) *HUD-administered installation program.* HUD will administer the installation program, as established and set out in subparts A through H of this part, in a state unless that state administers its own qualifying installation program. The states in which HUD administers an installation program can be identified under this part by referring to a list on a Web site maintained by HUD or by calling HUD. For convenience only, the current URL of the Web site is *http://www.hud.gov/offices/hsg/sfh/mhs/mhshome.cfm* and the current toll-free telephone number to contact the HUD Office of Manufactured Housing Programs is 1–800–927–2891, extension 57.

(b) *State-administered installation programs.* States that have qualifying installation programs, as established through the procedures set out in subpart I of this part, will administer their own programs, except for generally applicable requirements in this subpart A.

(c) *Manufacturer and retailer requirements.* (1) Manufacturers and retailers are responsible for compliance of the home with the construction and safety standards in part 3280 of this chapter, in accordance with the Act and applicable regulations. Manufacturers and retailers must also comply with applicable requirements in this part relating to the installation of the manufactured home.

(2) In the installation instructions required pursuant to part 3285 of this chapter, the manufacturer must include instructions for supporting the manufactured home or sections of homes temporarily and protecting the interior of the manufactured home or sections of homes from damage, pending the first siting of the home for occupancy. The instructions must be adequate to assure that the temporary supports and weatherization used will be sufficient to prevent the home and its transportable sections from being brought out of conformance with the construction and safety standards in part 3280 of this chapter if the home or its sections is either:

(i) Stored at any location for more than 30 days; or

(ii) In the possession of any entity for more than 30 days.

(d) *HUD oversight.* The Secretary may take such actions as are authorized by the Act to oversee the system established by the regulations in this part, as the Secretary deems appropriate.

§3286.7 Consumer information.

(a) *Manufacturer's consumer manual.* In each consumer manual provided by a manufacturer as required in §3282.207 of this chapter, the manufacturer must include a recommendation that any home that has been reinstalled after its original installation should be inspected after it is set up, in order to assure that it has not been damaged and is properly installed.

(b) *Retailer disclosures before sale or lease.* Prior to execution of the sales contract to purchase or agreement to lease a manufactured home, the retailer must provide the purchaser or lessee with a consumer disclosure. This disclosure must be in a document separate from the sales or lease agreement. The disclosure must include the following information, as applicable:

(1) When the installation of the home is in a state that administers its own qualifying installation program, the consumer disclosure must clearly state that the home will be required to comply with all state requirements for the installation of the home;

(2) When the installation of the home is in a state that does not administer its own qualifying installation program, the consumer disclosure must clearly state that the home will be required to comply with federal requirements, including installation in accordance with federal installation standards set forth in 24 CFR part 3285 and certification by a licensed installer of installation work, regardless of whether the work is performed by the homeowner or anyone else, and when certification includes inspection by an appropriate person;

(3) For all homes, the home may also be required to comply with additional state and local requirements for its installation;

(4) For all homes, additional information about the requirements disclosed under paragraphs (b)(1) through (b)(4) of this section is available from the retailer and, in the case of the federal requirements, is available in part 3286 of Title 24 of the Code of Federal Regulations and from the U.S. Department of Housing and Urban Development;

(5) For all homes, compliance with any additional federal, state, and local requirements, including a requirement for inspection of the installation of the home, may involve additional costs to the purchaser or lessee; and

(6) For all homes, a recommendation that any home that has been reinstalled after its original installation should be professionally inspected after it is set up, in order to assure that it has not been damaged in transit and is properly installed.

§3286.9 Manufacturer shipment responsibilities.

(a) *Providing information to HUD.* At or before the time that each manufactured home is shipped by a manufacturer, the manufacturer must provide HUD, through the Production Inspection Primary Inspection Agency (IPIA), in accordance with §3282.552 of this chapter, with information, as applicable, about:

(1) The serial number and manufacturer's certification label number of the home;

(2) The manufacturer of the home; and

(3) The name and address of the retailer or distributor that has arranged for the home to be shipped.

(b) *Manufacturer's installation instructions.* The manufacturer is required to provide with each manufactured home, installation designs and instructions for the installation of the manufactured home that have been approved by a DAPIA. A DAPIA must give approval only if the installation designs and instructions provide equal or greater protection than the protection provided under the installation standards.

§3286.11 Temporary storage of units.

Pursuant to §3286.5(c), the manufacturer is required to provide instructions for the temporary support and protection of the interior from damage of its manufactured homes or sections of homes. Every manufacturer, distributor, retailer, or installer that has possession of a home is required to support each transportable section of a manufactured home that is temporarily located on a site used by that manufacturer, distributor, retailer, or installer in accordance with the manufacturer's instructions.

§ 3286.13 Waiver of rights invalid.

Any provision of a contract or agreement entered into by a manufactured home purchaser that seeks to waive any recourse to either the HUD installation program or a state-qualifying installation program is void.

§ 3286.15 Consultation with the Manufactured Housing Consensus Committee (MHCC).

The Secretary will seek input from the MHCC when revising the installation program regulations in this part 3286. Before publication of a proposed rule to revise these regulations, the Secretary will provide the MHCC with a 120-day opportunity to comment on such revision. The MHCC may send to the Secretary any of the MHCC's own recommendations to adopt new installation program regulations or to modify or repeal any of the regulations in this part. Along with each recommendation, the MHCC must set forth pertinent data and arguments in support of the action sought. The Secretary will either: Accept or modify the recommendation and publish it for public comment in accordance with section 553 of the Administrative Procedure Act (5 U.S.C. 553), along with an explanation of the reasons for any such modification; or reject the recommendation entirely, and provide to the MHCC a written explanation of the reasons for the rejection. This section does not supersede section 605 of the National Manufactured Housing Construction and Safety Standards Act.

Subpart B—Certification of Installation in HUD-Administered States

§ 3286.101 Purpose.

The purpose of this subpart B is to establish the systems for tracking and certifying a manufactured home installation that is to be completed in accordance with the HUD-administered installation program.

§ 3286.102 Information provided by manufacturer.

(a) *Shipment of home to retailer or distributor.* At the time the manufactured home is shipped to a retailer or distributor, the manufacturer must provide notice to the retailer or distributor that tracking information for the home is being provided to HUD, and the information must be updated by the retailer or distributor in accordance with the requirements in § 3286.113. Such notice must include all of the information required in § 3286.9(a). The manufacturer is also encouraged to provide notice to the retailer that reminds the retailer of its other responsibilities under this part.

(b) *Manufacturer's installation instructions.* The manufacturer is required to include in its installation instructions for the home a notice that the home is required to be installed in accordance with:

(1) An installation design and instructions that have been provided by the manufacturer and approved by the Secretary directly or through review by the DAPIA; or

(2) An installation design and instructions that have been prepared and certified by a professional engineer or registered architect, that have been approved by the manufacturer and the DAPIA as providing a level of protection for residents of the home that equals or exceeds the protection provided by the federal installation standards in part 3285 of this chapter.

§ 3286.103 DAPIA-approved installation instructions.

(a) *Providing instructions to purchaser or lessee.* (1) For each manufactured home sold or leased to a purchaser or lessee, the retailer must provide the purchaser or lessee with a copy of the manufacturer's DAPIA-approved installation instructions for the home.

(2) If the installation requires a design that is different from that provided by the manufacturer in paragraph (a)(1) of this section, the installation design and instructions must be prepared and certified by a professional engineer or registered architect, that have been approved by the manufacturer and the DAPIA as providing a level of protection for residents of the

home that equals or exceeds the protection provided by the federal installation standards in part 3285 of this chapter.

(b) *Providing instructions to installer.* When the retailer or manufacturer agrees to provide any set up in connection with the sale of the home, the retailer or manufacturer must provide a copy of the approved installation instructions required in paragraph (a)(1) of this section or, as applicable, installation design and instructions required in paragraph (a)(2) of this section to each company or, in the case of sole proprietor, to each individual who performs set up or installation work on the home.

§3286.105 Requirement for installer licensing.

(a) *Installer Licensing.* The installer that installs a manufactured home in a state that does not have a qualifying installation program must be certified or licensed in accordance with the requirements in subpart C of this part.

(b) *Use of licensed installer.* When the retailer or manufacturer agrees to provide any set up in connection with the sale or lease of the home, the retailer or manufacturer must ensure that the installer is licensed in accordance with these regulations.

§3286.107 Installation in accordance with standards.

(a) *Compliance with installation requirements.* (1) For purposes of determining installer compliance, a manufactured home that is subject to the requirements of this subpart B must be installed in accordance with:

(i) An installation design and instructions that have been provided by the manufacturer and approved by the Secretary directly or through review by the DAPIA; or

(ii) An installation design and instructions that have been prepared and certified by a professional engineer or registered architect, that have been approved by the manufacturer and the DAPIA as providing a level of protection for residents of the home that equals or exceeds the protection provided by the federal installation standards in part 3285 of this chapter.

(2) If the installation instructions do not comply with the installation standards, the manufacturer is responsible for any aspect of installation that is completed in accordance with the installation instructions and that does not comply with the installation standards.

(3) All installation work must be in conformance with accepted practices to ensure durable, livable, and safe housing, and must demonstrate acceptable workmanship reflecting, at a minimum, journeyman quality of work of the various trades.

(4) Except as set out in paragraph (a)(2) of this section, all installation defects due to the work of the installer are the responsibility of the installer or retailer or manufacturer that retained the installer and must be corrected.

(5) If the manufacturer or retailer retains the installer, they are jointly and severally responsible with the installer for correcting installation defects.

(6) Installation defects must be corrected within 60 days after the date of discovery of the installation defect.

(b) *Secretarial approval of manufacturer's designs.* A manufacturer that seeks a Secretarial determination under paragraph (a) of this section that its installation designs and instructions provide protection to residents of manufactured homes that equals or exceeds the protection provided by the HUD federal installation standards in part 3285 of this chapter must send the request for such determination and a copy of the applicable designs and instructions to: Administrator, Office of Manufactured Housing Programs, HUD, 451 Seventh Street, SW., Room 9164, Washington, DC 20410–8000, or to a fax number or e-mail address obtained by calling the Office of Manufactured Housing Programs at the toll-free telephone number 1–800–927–2891, extension 57.

(c) *Compliance with construction and safety standards.* The installer must not take the home out of compliance with the construction and safety standards applicable under part 3280 of this chapter.

(d) *Homeowner installations.* The purchaser of a home sited in a state in which HUD administers the installation program may perform installation work on the home that is in accordance with paragraph (a) of this section, provided that the work is certified in accordance with § 3286.111.

(e) *Compliance with construction and safety standards.* This rule does not alter or affect the requirements of the Act concerning compliance with the construction and safety standards, and the implementing regulations in parts 3280 and 3282 of this chapter, which apply regardless of where the work is completed.

§ 3286.109 Inspection requirements—generally.

The installer or the retailer must arrange for the inspection of the installation work on any manufactured home that is sited in a state without a qualifying installation program. Before the home can be occupied, the installer must certify, and the inspector must verify, the home as having been installed in conformance with the requirements of § 3286.107(a). The requirements for installer certification are set out in subpart E of this part.

§ 3286.111 Installer certification of installation.

(a) *Certification required.* When the installation work is complete, a licensed installer must visit the jobsite and certify that:

(1) The manufactured home has been installed in accordance with:

(i) An installation design and instructions that have been provided by the manufacturer and approved by the Secretary directly or through review by the DAPIA; or

(ii) An installation design and instructions that have been prepared and certified by a professional engineer or registered architect, that have been approved by the manufacturer and the DAPIA as providing a level of protection for residents of the home that equals or exceeds the protection provided by the federal installation standards in part 3285 of this chapter.

(2) The installation of the home has been inspected as required by § 3286.503 and an inspector has verified the installation as meeting the requirements of this part.

(3) All installation defects brought to the installer's attention have been corrected.

(b) *Recipients of certification.* The installer must provide a signed copy of its certification to the retailer that contracted with the purchaser or lessee for the sale or lease of the home, and to the purchaser or other person with whom the installer contracted for the installation work.

§ 3286.113 Information provided by retailer.

(a) *Tracking information.* Within 30 days from the time a purchaser or lessee enters into a contract to purchase or lease a manufactured home, the retailer or distributor of the home must provide HUD with the following information:

(1) The home's serial number and manufacturer's certification label number;

(2) The name and address of the retailer or distributor that is selling or leasing the home;

(3) The state and address where the home is to be sited, and, if known, the name of the local jurisdiction; and

(4) The name of the purchaser or lessee.

(b) *Installation information.* Within 30 days from the date of installation, the retailer or distributor of the home must provide HUD with the following information:

(1) The name, address, telephone number, and license number of the licensed installer;

(2) The date of installer certification of completion of the installation;

(3) The date a qualified inspector verified the installation as being in compliance with the requirements of this part; and

(4) The name, address, and telephone number of the qualified inspector who performed the inspection of the installation as required by § 3286.109.

(c) *Method of providing information.* (1) The retailer or distributor must provide a copy of the information set forth in paragraphs (a) and (b) of this section to HUD by providing a copy of the information to HUD by facsimile, e-mail, or first-class or overnight delivery.

(2) The information must be sent to: Administrator, Office of Manufactured

Housing Programs, HUD, 451 Seventh Street, SW., Room 9164, Washington, DC 20410–8000, or to a fax number or e-mail address obtained by calling the Office of Manufactured Housing Programs. For convenience only, the URL of the Web site is *http://www.hud.gov/offices/hsg/sfh/mhs/mhshome.cfm* and the toll-free telephone number to contact the Office of Manufactured Housing Programs is 1–800–927–2891, extension 57.

(d) *Correcting information.* If the information provided by the retailer changes after it has been provided to HUD, the retailer must correct the information within 10 business days after the retailer learns of the change.

(e) *Record retention requirements.* The retailer or distributor must maintain a copy of the records required in paragraphs (a) and (b) of this section for 3 years from the date of installation, as under §3286.115.

§3286.115 Date of installation.

The date of installation will be the date the installer has certified that all required inspections have been completed, all utilities are connected, and the manufactured home is ready for occupancy as established, if applicable, by a certificate of occupancy, except as follows: If the manufactured home has not been sold to the first person purchasing the home in good faith for purposes other than resale by the date the home is ready for occupancy, the date of installation is the date of the purchase agreement or sales contract for the manufactured home.

§3286.117 Completion of sale date.

(a) *Date of sale defined.* For purposes of determining the responsibilities of a manufacturer, retailer, or distributor under subpart I of part 3282 of this chapter, the sale of a manufactured home will not be considered complete until all the goods and services that the manufacturer, retailer, or distributor agreed to provide at the time the contract was entered into have been provided.

(b) *Compliance with construction and safety standards.* When a retailer or manufacturer is providing the installation and an installer installs a home in such a way as to create an imminent safety hazard or cause the home to not comply with the construction and safety standards in part 3280 of this chapter, and those issues are discovered during the installation of the home, the sale or lease of the home is not complete until the home is corrected.

Subpart C—Installer Licensing in HUD-Administered States

§3286.201 Purpose.

The purpose of this subpart C is to establish the requirements for a person to qualify to install a manufactured home in accordance with the HUD-administered installation program. Installers will be required to meet licensing, training, and insurance requirements established in this part. Licensed installers will self-certify their installations of manufactured homes to be in compliance with the Model Manufactured Home Installation Standards in part 3285 of this chapter. In order for such an installer to self-certify compliance with the installation standards, the installer will have to assure that acceptable inspections, as required in subpart F of this part, are performed.

§3286.203 Installation license required.

(a) *Installation license required.* (1) Any individual or entity that engages in the business of directing, supervising, or controlling initial installations of new manufactured homes in a state without a qualifying installation program must itself have, or must employ someone who has, a valid manufactured home installation license issued in accordance with the requirements of this subpart C. For each installation covered under these requirements, the licensed installer, and any company that employs the licensed installer, will be responsible for the proper and competent performance of all employees working under the licensed installer's supervision and for assuring that the installation work complies with this part.

(2) A business that employs a licensed installer to represent the business and hold the installer's license retains primary responsibility for performance of the installation work in

compliance with the requirements of this part.

(3) A license is not required for individuals working as direct employees of a licensed installer or for the company that employs a licensed installer, provided that those individuals are supervised by a licensed installer.

(4) The installer must display an original or a copy of a valid installation license at the site of the installation while performing work related to the installation of the home.

(5) The installer is responsible for understanding and following, as applicable, the approved manufacturer installation instructions and any alternative installation design and instructions that have been certified by a professional engineer or registered architect, that have been approved by the manufacturer and DAPIA as providing a level of protection for residents of the home that equals or exceeds the protection provided by the federal installation standards in part 3285 of this chapter.

(b) *Installation license not required.* An installation license is not required for:

(1) Site preparation that is not subject to the requirements of part 3285 of this chapter;

(2) Connection of utilities to the manufactured home;

(3) Add-ons subject to the requirements of § 3282.8(j) of this chapter;

(4) Temporary installations on dealer, distributor, manufacturer, or other sales or storage lots, when the manufactured home is not serving as an occupied residence;

(5) Home maintenance, repairs, or corrections, or other noninstallation-related work performed by the home manufacturer under warranty or other obligations or service agreements;

(6) Installations performed by authorized representatives of the Federal Emergency Management Agency in order to provide emergency housing after a natural disaster; or

(7) Work performed at the home site that is not covered by the federal installation standards in part 3285 of this chapter or the requirements of this part.

§ 3286.205 Prerequisites for installation license.

(a) *Required experience.* (1) In order to obtain an installation license to perform manufactured home installations under the HUD-administered installation program, an individual must meet at least one of the following minimum experience requirements:

(i) 1,800 hours of experience installing manufactured homes;

(ii) 3,600 hours of experience in the construction of manufactured homes;

(iii) 3,600 hours of experience as a building construction supervisor;

(iv) 1,800 hours as an active manufactured home installation inspector;

(v) Completion of one year of a college program in a construction-related field; or

(vi) Any combination of experience or education from paragraphs (a)(1)(i) through (a)(1)(v) of this section that totals 3,600 hours.

(2) An installer who is certified or licensed to perform manufactured home installations in a state with a qualifying installation program may be exempted by the Secretary from complying with these experience requirements, if the Secretary determines that the state requirements are substantially equal to the HUD experience requirements.

(b) *Required training*—(1) *Initial applicant.* An applicant for an installation license must complete 12 hours of training, at least 4 hours of which must consist of training on the federal installation standards in part 3285 of this chapter and the installation program regulations in this part. An installer who is licensed to perform installations in a state with a qualified installation program may postpone the training requirements of this section until October 20, 2009.

(2) *Renewal applicant.* In order to qualify for renewal of an installation license, the licensed installer must complete 8 hours of continuing education during the 3-year license period, including in any particular subject area that may be required by HUD to be covered in order to assure adequate understanding of installation requirements.

(3) The training required under this paragraph (b) must be conducted by

trainers who meet the requirements of subpart D of this part and must meet the curriculum requirements established in §3286.308 or §3286.309, as applicable.

(c) *Testing.* An applicant for an installation license must have successfully received a passing grade of 70 percent on a HUD-administered or HUD-approved examination covering the Manufactured Home Installation Program and the federal installation standards in part 3285.

(d) *Surety bond or insurance.* An applicant for an installation license must provide evidence of and must maintain, when available in the state of installation, a surety bond or insurance that will cover the cost of repairing all damage to the home and its supports caused by the installer during the installation up to and including replacement of the home. HUD may require the licensed installer to provide proof of the surety bond or insurance at any time. The licensed installer must notify HUD of any changes or cancellations with the surety bond or insurance coverage.

§3286.207 **Process for obtaining installation license.**

(a) *Where to apply.* An applicant for an initial or renewed installation license must provide the applicant's legal name, address, and telephone number to HUD. The application, with all required information, must be sent to: Administrator, Office of Manufactured Housing Programs, HUD, 451 Seventh Street, SW., Room 9164, Washington, DC 20410–8000, or to a fax number or e-mail address obtained by calling the Office of Manufactured Housing Programs. For convenience only, the current URL of the Web site is *http://www.hud.gov/offices/hsg/sfh/mhs/mhshome.cfm*, and the current toll-free telephone number to contact the Office of Manufactured Housing Programs is 1–800–927–2891, extension 57.

(b) *Proof of experience.* Every applicant for an initial installation license must submit verification of the experience required in §3286.205(a). This verification may be in the form of statements by past or present employers or a self-certification that the applicant meets those experience require-

ments, but HUD may contact the applicant for additional verification at any time. The applicant must also provide to HUD employment information relevant to the applicant's experience as an installer, including the dates and type of such employment. An installer who is certified or licensed to perform manufactured home installations in a state with a qualifying installation program may seek an exemption from the experience requirement by submitting proof of such certification or license.

(c) *Proof of training.* Every applicant for an initial installation license, or the renewal of an installation license, must submit verification of successful completion of the training required in §3286.205(b). This verification must be in the form of a certificate of completion from a qualified trainer that the applicant has completed the requisite number of hours of a qualifying curriculum, as set out in §3286.308 or §3286.309.

(d) *Proof of surety bond or insurance.* Every applicant for an installation license must submit the name of the applicant's surety bond or insurance carrier and the number of the policy required in §3286.205(d).

(e) *Other application submissions.* (1) Every applicant for an installation license must submit a list of all states in which the applicant holds a similar installation certification or license, and a list of all states in which the applicant has had such a certification or license revoked, suspended, or denied.

(2) When the examination is not administered by HUD, every applicant for an initial installation license must submit certification of a passing grade on the examination required by §3286.205(c).

(f) *Issuance or denial of an installation license.* (1) When HUD confirms that an applicant has met the requirements in this subpart C, HUD will either:

(i) Provide an installation license to the applicant that, as long as the installation license remains in effect, establishes the applicant's qualification to install manufactured homes in a state subject to the HUD-administered installation program; or

(ii) Provide a written explanation of why HUD deems the applicant to not qualify for an installation license, including on grounds applicable under § 3286.209 for suspension or revocation of an installation license and any other specified evidence of inability to adequately meet the requirements of this part.

(2) An applicant who is denied an installation license under this subpart C, other than for failure to pass the installation license test, may request from HUD an opportunity for a presentation of views, in accordance with subpart D of part 3282 of this chapter, for the purpose of establishing the applicant's qualifications to obtain an installation license.

(g) *Assignment of license prohibited.* An installation license issued under this part may not be transferred, assigned, or pledged to another entity or individual.

§ 3286.209 Denial, suspension, or revocation of installation license.

(a) *Oversight.* The Secretary may make a continuing evaluation of the manner in which each licensed installer is carrying out his or her responsibilities under this subpart C.

(b) *Denial, suspension, or revocation.* After notice and an opportunity for a presentation of views in accordance with subpart D of part 3282 of this chapter, the Secretary may deny, suspend, or revoke an installation license under this part. An installation license may be denied, suspended, or revoked for, among other things:

(1) Providing false records or information to any party;

(2) Refusing to submit information that the Secretary requires to be submitted;

(3) Failure to comply with applicable requirements of parts 3285, 3286, or 3288 of this chapter;

(4) Failure to take appropriate actions upon a failed inspection, as provided in § 3286.509;

(5) Fraudulently obtaining or attempting to obtain an installation license, or fraudulently or deceptively using an installation license;

(6) Using or attempting to use an expired, suspended, or revoked installation license;

(7) Violating state or federal laws that relate to the fitness and qualifica-

tion or ability of the applicant to install homes; or

(8) Engaging in poor conduct or workmanship as evidenced by one or more of the following:

(i) Installing one or more homes that fail to meet the requirements of § 3286.107;

(ii) An unsatisfied judgment in favor of a consumer;

(iii) Repeatedly engaging in fraud, deception, misrepresentation, or knowing omissions of material facts relating to installation contracts;

(iv) Having a similar state installation license or certification denied, suspended, or revoked;

(v) Having the renewal of a similar state installation license or certification denied for any cause other than failure to pay a renewal fee; or

(vi) Failure to maintain the surety bond or insurance required by § 3286.205(d).

(c) *Other criteria.* In deciding whether to suspend or revoke an installation license, the Secretary will consider the impact of the suspension or revocation on other affected parties and will seek to assure that the sales and siting of manufactured homes are not unduly disrupted.

(d) *Reinstating an installation license.* An installer whose installation license has been denied, suspended, or revoked may submit a new application in accordance with this subpart C. Installers whose installation licenses have been suspended may also reinstate their installation licenses in any manner provided under the terms of their suspensions.

§ 3286.211 Expiration and renewal of installation licenses.

(a) *Expiration.* Each installation license issued or renewed under this subpart C will expire 3 years after the date of its issuance or renewal.

(b) *Renewal.* An application for the renewal of an installation license must include the information required by, and must be submitted to, HUD in accordance with § 3286.207, and must be submitted at least 60 days before the date the license expires. Any person applying for a license renewal after the date the license expires must apply for a new installation license following the requirements established under this subpart C for application for an initial installation license.

Subpart D—Training of Installers in HUD-Administered States

§3286.301 Purpose.

The purpose of this subpart D is to establish the requirements for a person to qualify to provide the training required under subpart C of this part. This training is required for manufactured home installers who want to be licensed in accordance with the HUD-administered installation program.

§3286.303 Responsibilities of qualified trainers.

(a) *Curriculum and hours.* In providing training to installers for the purpose of qualifying installers under the HUD-administered installation program, qualified trainers must adequately address the curriculum and instruction-time requirements established in subparts C and D of this part.

(b) *Attendance records.* Qualified trainers must maintain records of the times, locations, names of attendees at each session, and content of all courses offered. When an attendee misses a significant portion of any training session, the trainer must assure that the attendee makes up the missed portion of the instruction.

(c) *Certificates of completion of training.* Qualified trainers must provide certificates of completion to course attendees that indicate the level of compliance with the applicable curriculum and time requirements under subparts C and D of this part.

(d) *Record retention.* All records maintained by trainers and continuing education providers must be retained for 3 years, and must be made available to HUD upon request.

(e) *Testing of installers.* Qualified trainers may be authorized to administer the installation license testing required for initial licensing of installers, as set forth in §3286.205(c).

§3286.305 Installation trainer criteria.

(a) *Trainer qualification required.* (1) All classes that provide manufactured home installation education classes used to satisfy the requirements for

the initial issuance and renewal of installation licenses under subpart C of this part must be taught by trainers who are registered with HUD as qualified trainers. In order to register with HUD as a qualified trainer, a person must meet the experience requirements of this section.

(2) Any entity other than a natural person may also provide initial training and continuing education, as long as such entity establishes its qualification as a trainer by providing evidence and assurance that the entity's individual trainers meet the requirements of this section.

(b) *Experience prerequisites.* In order to qualify as a trainer, an individual or other training entity must provide to HUD evidence that each individual who will be responsible for providing training:

(1) Has a minimum of 3,600 hours of experience in one or more of the following:

(i) As a supervisor of manufactured home installations;

(ii) As a supervisor in the building construction industry;

(iii) In design work related to the building construction industry; or

(2) Has completed a 2-year educational program in a construction-related field.

(c) *Certification of curriculum.* In order to register as a qualified trainer, an individual or other training entity must submit to HUD certification that training provided in accordance with this subpart D will meet the curriculum requirements established in §3286.308 or §3286.309, as applicable.

§3286.307 Process for obtaining trainer's qualification.

(a) *Where to apply.* An applicant for qualification as a trainer must provide the applicant's legal name, address, and telephone number to HUD. The application, with all required information, must be sent to: Administrator, Office of Manufactured Housing Programs, HUD, 451 Seventh Street, SW., Room 9164, Washington DC 20410–8000, or to a fax number or e-mail address obtained by calling the Office of Manufactured Housing Programs. For convenience only, the URL of the Web site is *http://www.hud.gov/offices/hsg/sfh/mhs/*

mhshome.cfm, and the toll-free telephone number to contact the Office of Manufactured Housing Programs is 1–800–927–2891, extension 57.

(b) *Proof of experience.* (1) Every individual applicant for initial qualification as a trainer must submit verification of the experience required in § 3286.305. This verification may be in the form of statements by past or present employers or a self-certification that the applicant meets those experience requirements, but HUD may contact the applicant for additional verification at any time. The applicant must also provide to HUD employment information relevant to the applicant's experience as a trainer, including the dates and type of such employment. A trainer who is licensed, or otherwise certified, to provide manufactured home installation training in a state with a qualifying installation program may seek an exemption from the experience requirement by submitting proof of such license or other certification. An individual who applies for renewal qualification as a trainer is not required to submit additional proof of experience.

(2) An entity that seeks to be designated as a qualified trainer must provide evidence and assurance that the entity's individual trainers meet the experience requirements in § 3286.305.

(c) *Other qualification information.* (1) An applicant for initial or renewal qualification as a trainer must submit to HUD a list of all states in which the applicant has had a similar training qualification revoked, suspended, or denied.

(2) An applicant also must submit to HUD a certification that training provided in accordance with this subpart D will meet the curriculum requirements established in § 3286.308 or § 3286.309, as applicable.

(d) *Confirmation or denial of qualification.* (1) When HUD confirms that an applicant has met the experience and curriculum requirements in this section, HUD will either:

(i) Provide to the applicant a written confirmation that the applicant is a qualified trainer under this part, and will add the applicant's name to a list maintained by HUD of qualified trainers; or

(ii) Provide a written explanation of why HUD deems the applicant to not qualify as a trainer, including on grounds applicable under § 3286.311 for suspension or revocation of a qualification and any other specified evidence of inability to meet the requirements of this part.

(2) An applicant whose qualification is denied by HUD may request an opportunity for a presentation of views, in accordance with subpart D of part 3282 of this chapter, for the purpose of establishing the applicant's qualifications to be a qualified trainer or the adequacy of any training curriculum that is challenged by HUD.

(e) *Assignment of qualification prohibited.* A qualification issued under this subpart D may not be transferred, assigned, or pledged to another entity or individual.

§ 3286.308 Training curriculum.

(a) *Curriculum for initial installer licensing.* The training provided by qualified trainers to installers to meet the initial requirements of the HUD-administered installation program must include at least 12 hours of training, at least 4 hours of which must consist of training on the federal installation standards in part 3285 of this chapter and the installation program regulations in this part. The curriculum must include, at a minimum, training in the following areas:

(1) An overview of the Act and the general regulatory structure of the HUD manufactured housing program;

(2) An overview of the manufactured home installation standards and regulations established in parts 3285 and 3286 of this chapter, and specific instruction including:

(i) Preinstallation considerations;

(ii) Site preparation;

(iii) Foundations;

(iv) Anchorage against wind;

(v) Optional features, including comfort cooling systems;

(vi) Ductwork and plumbing and fuel supply systems;

(vii) Electrical systems; and

(viii) Exterior and interior close-up work;

(3) An overview of the construction and safety standards and regulations

found in parts 3280 and 3282 of this chapter;

(4) Licensing requirements applicable to installers;

(5) Installer responsibilities for correction of improper installation, including installer obligations under applicable state and HUD manufactured housing dispute resolution programs;

(6) Inspection requirements and procedures;

(7) Problem-reporting mechanisms;

(8) Operational checks and adjustments; and

(9) Penalties for any person's failure to comply with the requirements of this part 3286 and parts 3285 and 3288 of this chapter.

(b) *Updating curriculum.* Qualified trainers must revise and modify course curriculum as needed to include, at a minimum, any relevant modifications to the Act or the implementing standards and regulations in this chapter, as well as to provide any training further mandated by HUD.

§ 3286.309 **Continuing education-trainers and curriculum.**

(a) *HUD-mandated elements.* Only qualified trainers are permitted to provide any training on particular subject areas that are required by HUD to be an element of the continuing education requirement set out in § 3286.205(b)(2) for the renewal of an installer's license. In implementing this requirement, HUD will:

(1) Establish the minimum number of hours and the required curriculum for such subject areas, according to experience with the program and changes in program requirements; and

(2) Provide information about the hours and curriculum directly to qualified trainers and licensed installers, or through general publication of the information.

(b) *Other training.* (1) The remainder of the 8 hours required to meet the continuing education requirement may be met through training provided either by qualified trainers or by any combination of the following:

(i) Accredited educational institutions, including community colleges and universities;

(ii) A provider of continuing education units who is certified by the

International Association for Continuing Education and Training;

(iii) Agencies at any level of government; and

(iv) State or national professional associations.

(2) The curriculum for the remainder of the 8 hours of continuing education training must relate to any aspect of manufactured home installation or construction, or to the general fields of building construction or contracting.

§ 3286.311 **Suspension or revocation of trainer's qualification.**

(a) *Oversight.* The Secretary may make a continuing evaluation of the manner in which each qualified trainer is carrying out the trainer's responsibilities under this subpart D.

(b) *Suspension or revocation of qualification.* After notice and an opportunity for a presentation of views in accordance with subpart D of part 3282 of this chapter, the Secretary may suspend or revoke a trainer's qualification under this part. A trainer's qualification may be suspended or revoked for cause, which may include:

(1) Providing false records or information to HUD;

(2) Refusing to submit information required to be submitted by the Secretary in accordance with the Act;

(3) Certifying, or improperly assisting certification of, a person as having met the training requirements established in this part when that person has not completed the required training;

(4) Failing to appropriately supervise installation training that is used to meet the requirements of this part and that is provided by other persons; and

(5) Any other failures to comply with the requirements of this part.

(c) *Other criteria.* In deciding whether to suspend or revoke a trainer's qualification, the Secretary will consider the impact of the suspension or revocation on other affected parties and will seek to assure that the sales and siting of manufactured homes are not unduly disrupted.

(d) *Reinstating qualification.* A trainer whose qualification has been suspended or revoked may submit a new application to be qualified in accordance with this subpart D no sooner than 6 months after the date of suspension or revocation. A trainer whose qualification has been suspended may also reinstate the qualification in any manner provided under the terms of the suspension.

§ 3286.313 Expiration and renewal of trainer qualification.

(a) *Expiration.* Each notice of qualification issued or renewed under this subpart D will expire 5 years after the date of its issuance or renewal.

(b) *Renewal.* An application for the renewal of a trainer qualification must be submitted to HUD in accordance with § 3286.307, and must be submitted at least 60 days before the date the trainer's term of qualification expires. Any person applying for a qualification renewal after the date the qualification expires must apply for a new qualification, following the requirements established under this subpart D for application for initial qualification as an installation trainer.

Subpart E—Installer Responsibilities of Installation in HUD-Administered States

§ 3286.401 Purpose.

The purpose of this subpart E is to set out the responsibilities of the installer who is accountable for the installation of a manufactured home in compliance with the requirements of the HUD-administered installation program.

§ 3286.403 Licensing requirements.

An installer of manufactured homes must comply with the licensing requirements set forth in subpart C of this part.

§ 3286.405 Installation suitability.

(a) *Site appropriateness.* Before installing a manufactured home at any site, the installer must assure that the site is suitable for installing the home by verifying that:

(1) The site is accessible;

(2) The site is appropriate for the foundation or support and stabilization system that is to be used to install the home in accordance with the federal installation standards or alternative requirements in part 3285 of this chapter;

(3) The data plate required by § 3280.5 of this chapter is affixed to the home, that the home is designed for the roof load, wind load, and thermal zones that are applicable to the intended site; and

(4) The installation site is protected from surface run-off and can be graded in accordance with part 3285.

(b) *Installer notification of unsuitable site.* If the installer determines that the home cannot be installed properly at the site, the installer must:

(1) Notify the purchaser or other person with whom the installer contracted for the installation work, identifying the reasons why the site is unsuitable;

(2) Notify the retailer that contracted with the purchaser for the sale of the home, identifying the reasons why the site is unsuitable;

(3) Notify HUD, identifying the reasons why the site is unsuitable;

(4) Decline to install the home until the site and the home are both verified by the installer as suitable for the site under this section; and

(5) Ensure that all unique characteristics of the site have been fully addressed.

(c) *Installer notification of failures to comply with the construction and safety standards.* If the installer notices and recognizes failures to comply with the construction and safety standards in part 3280 of this chapter prior to beginning any installation work, during the course of the installation work, or after the installation work is complete, the installer must notify the manufacturer and retailer of each failure to comply.

(d) *Retailer notification.* The retailer must provide a copy of the notification received in paragraphs (b) and (c) of this section to any subsequent installer.

§ 3286.407 Supervising work of crew.

The installer will be responsible for the work performed by each person engaged to perform installation tasks on a manufactured home, in accordance with the HUD-administered installation program.

§ 3286.409 Obtaining inspection.

(a) *Inspection obligations.* Ten business days prior to the completion of installation, the installer must arrange for a third-party inspection of the work performed, in accordance with subpart F of this part, unless the installer and retailer who contracted with the purchaser for the sale of the home agree, in writing, that during the same time period the retailer will arrange for the inspection. Such inspection must be performed as soon as practicable by an inspector who meets the qualifications set forth in § 3286.511. The scope of the inspections that are required to be performed is addressed in § 3286.505.

(b) *Contract rights not affected.* Failure to arrange for an inspection of a home within 5 business days will not affect the validity or enforceability of any sale or contract for the sale of any manufactured home.

(c) *State or local permits.* The licensed installer should obtain all necessary permits required under state or local laws.

§ 3286.411 Certifying installation.

(a) *Certification required.* When the installation work is complete, a licensed installer must visit the jobsite and certify that:

(1) The manufactured home has been installed in accordance with:

(i) An installation design and instructions that have been provided by the manufacturer and approved by the Secretary directly or through review by the DAPIA; or

(ii) An installation design and instructions that have been prepared and certified by a professional engineer or registered architect, that have been approved by the manufacturer and the DAPIA as providing a level of protection for residents of the home that equals or exceeds the protection provided by the federal installation standards in part 3285 of this chapter.

(2) The installation of the home has been inspected as required by § 3286.503, and an inspector has verified the installation as meeting the requirements of this part.

(3) All installation defects brought to the installer's attention have been corrected.

(b) *Recipients of certification.* The installer must provide a signed copy of its certification to the retailer that contracted with the purchaser or lessee for the sale or lease of the home, and to the purchaser or other person with whom the installer contracted for the installation work.

§ 3286.413 Recordkeeping.

(a) *Records to be retained.* The installer must retain:

(1) A record of the name and address of the purchaser or other person with whom the installer contracted for the installation work and the address of the home installed;

(2) A copy of the contract pursuant to which the installer performed the installation work;

(3) A copy of any notice from an inspector disapproving the installation work;

(4) A copy of the qualified inspector's verification of the installation work;

(5) A copy of the installer's certification of completion of installation in accordance with the requirements of this part; and

(6) A copy of foundation designs used to install the home, if different from the designs provided by the manufacturer, including evidence that the foundation designs and instructions were certified by a professional engineer or registered architect, including the name, address, and telephone number of the professional engineer or architect certifying the designs.

(b) Retention requirement. The records listed in paragraph (a) of this section must be maintained for a period of 3 years after the installer certifies completion of installation.

Subpart F—Inspection of Installations in HUD-Administered States

§ 3286.501 Purpose.

The purpose of this subpart F is to provide additional detail about the inspection that must be performed by a qualified third-party inspector before the installation of a manufactured home may be verified by the inspector and certified by the installer under the HUD-administered installation program.

§ 3286.503　Inspection required.

(a) *Timing of requirements.* Ten business days prior to the completion of the installation of each manufactured home, the installer must arrange for a third-party inspection of the work performed, unless the installer and retailer who contracted with the purchaser for the sale of the home agree, in writing, that during the same time period the retailer will arrange for the inspection. Such inspection must be performed as soon as practicable by an inspector that meets the qualifications set out in § 3286.511. The scope of the inspections that are required to be performed is addressed in § 3286.505.

(b) *Disclosure of requirement.* At the time of sale, the retailer must disclose to the purchaser, in a manner provided in § 3286.7, that the manufactured home must be installed in accordance with applicable federal and state law, including requirements for a third-party inspection of the installation. If the cost of inspection of the home's installation is not included in the sales price of the home, the sales contract must include a clear disclosure about whether the purchaser will be charged separately for the inspection of the home's installation and the amount of such charge.

(c) *Providing instructions to inspectors.* Installation instructions must be made available to the inspector at the installation site by the installer.

§ 3286.505　Minimum elements to be inspected.

The installation of every manufactured home that is subject to the HUD-administered installation program is required to be inspected for each of the installation elements included in a checklist. The checklist must include assurance that each of the following elements complies with the requirements of part 3285 of this chapter:

(a) Site location with respect to home design and construction;

(b) Consideration of site-specific conditions;

(c) Site preparation and grading for drainage;

(d) Foundation construction;

(e) Anchorage including verification that the ground anchors have been installed in accordance with the manufacturer's instructions, in a soil classification permitted by the anchor listing or certification, with the required size and type of stabilizer plate, if required by the listing or certification, and at an orientation and angle of pull permitted by its listing or certification.

(f) Installation of optional features;

(g) Completion of ductwork, plumbing, and fuel supply systems;

(h) Electrical systems;

(i) Exterior and interior close-up;

(j) Skirting, if installed; and

(k) Completion of operational checks and adjustments.

[73 FR 35292, June 20, 2008, as amended at 79 FR 53618, Sept. 10, 2014]

§ 3286.507　Verifying installation.

(a) *Verification by inspector.* When an inspector is satisfied that the manufactured home has been installed in accordance with the requirements of this part, the inspector must provide verification of the installation in writing and return the evidence of such verification to the installer.

(b) *Certification by installer.* (1) Once an installation has been inspected and verified, the installer is permitted to certify the installation as provided in § 3286.111. The installer must provide a signed copy of the certification to:

(i) The retailer that contracted with the purchaser for the sale of the home;

(ii) The purchaser; and

(iii) Any other person that contracted to obtain the services of the installer for the installation work on the home.

(2) The installer must retain records in accordance with § 3286.413.

§ 3286.509　Reinspection upon failure to pass.

(a) *Procedures for failed inspection.* If the inspector cannot verify the installation of the manufactured home, the inspector must immediately notify the installer of any failures to comply with the installation standards and explain the reasons why the inspector cannot issue verification that the installation complies with the requirements of this part. After the installation is corrected, it must be reinspected before verification can be issued.

(b) *Cost of reinspection.* If there is any cost for the reinspection of an installation that an inspector has refused to verify, that cost must be paid by the installer or the retailer and, absent a written agreement with the purchaser that specifically states otherwise, that cost cannot be charged to the purchaser of the manufactured home.

§ 3286.511 Inspector qualifications.

(a) Qualifications. Any individual or entity who meets at least one of the following qualifications is permitted to review the work and verify the installation of a manufactured home that is subject to the requirements of the HUD-administered installation program:

(1) A manufactured home or residential building inspector employed by the local authority having jurisdiction over the site of the home, provided that the jurisdiction has a residential code enforcement program;

(2) A professional engineer;

(3) A registered architect;

(4) A HUD-accepted Production Inspection Primary Inspection Agency (IPIA) or a Design Approval Primary Inspection Agency (DAPIA); or

(5) An International Code Council certified inspector.

(b) *Independence required.* The inspector must be independent of the manufacturer, the retailer, the installer, and any other person that has a monetary interest, other than collection of an inspection fee, in the completion of the sale of the home to the purchaser.

(c) *Suspension or revocation of inspection authority.* After notice and an opportunity for a presentation of views in accordance with subpart D of part 3282 of this chapter, the Secretary may suspend or revoke an inspector's authority to inspect manufactured home installations under this part in HUD-administered states. An inspector's authority may be suspended or revoked for cause. In deciding whether to suspend or revoke an inspector's authority to conduct such installation inspections, the Secretary will consider the impact of the suspension or revocation on other affected parties and will seek to assure that the sales and siting of manufactured homes are not unduly disrupted.

(d) *Reinstating inspection authority.* An inspector whose authority to inspect manufactured home installations in HUD-administered states has been suspended or revoked under this section may apply for reauthorization by contacting: Administrator, Office of Manufactured Housing Programs, HUD, 451 Seventh Street, SW., Room 9164, Washington, DC 20410–8000, or to a fax number or e-mail address obtained by calling the Office of Manufactured Housing Programs at the toll-free telephone number 1–800–927–2891, extension 57.

Subpart G—Retailer Responsibilities in HUD-Administered States

§ 3286.601 Purpose.

The purpose of this subpart G is to set out the requirements that apply to a retailer with respect to the federal installation requirements applicable to new manufactured homes that the retailer sells or leases and that will be installed in states that do not have qualifying installation programs. These requirements are in addition to other requirements that apply to retailers of manufactured homes pursuant to other parts of this chapter.

§ 3286.603 At or before sale.

(a) *Before contract.* (1) The retailer is required to support each transportable section of a manufactured home that is temporarily or permanently located on a site used by a retailer in accordance with the manufacturer's instructions.

(2) Before a purchaser or lessee signs a contract of sale or lease for a manufactured home, the retailer must:

(i) Provide the purchaser or lessee with a copy of the consumer disclosure statement required in § 3286.7(b); and

(ii) Verify that the wind, thermal, and roof load zones of the home being purchased or leased are appropriate for the site where the purchaser or lessee plans to install the home for occupancy; and

(iii) If the cost of inspection of the home's installation is not included in the sales price of the home, provide the disclosure required in § 3286.7(b).

(b) *Occupancy site not known.* When at the time of purchase the purchaser does not know the locale for the initial siting of the home for occupancy, the retailer must advise the purchaser that:

(1) The home was designed and constructed for specific wind, thermal, and roof load zones; and

(2) If the home is sited in a different zone, the home may not pass the required installation inspection because the home will have been installed in a manner that would take it out of compliance with the construction and safety standards in part 3280 of this chapter.

(c) *Verification of installer license.* When the retailer or manufacturer agrees to provide any set up in connection with the sale or lease of the home, the retailer or manufacturer must verify that the installer is licensed in accordance with these regulations.

§ 3286.605   After sale.

(a) *Tracking installation information.* The retailer is responsible for providing to HUD the information required pursuant to § 3286.113.

(b) *Other tracking and compliance requirements.* The retailer continues to be responsible for compliance with the tracking and compliance requirements set out in subpart F of part 3282 of this chapter, which are related to HUD construction and safety standards.

§ 3286.607   Recordkeeping.

The retailer is responsible for the reporting and recordkeeping requirements under § 3286.113.

Subpart H—Oversight and Enforcement in HUD-Administered States

§ 3286.701   Purpose.

The purpose of this subpart H is to set out the mechanisms by which manufacturers, retailers, distributors, installers, and installation inspectors will be held accountable for assuring the appropriate installation of manufactured homes. The requirements in subpart A of this part are applicable in all states, the requirements in subparts B through H are applicable in states where the HUD-administered installation program operates, and the requirements in subpart I are applicable in states with qualifying installation programs. It is the policy of the Secretary, regarding manufactured home installation program enforcement matters, to cooperate with state or local agencies having authority to regulate the installation of manufactured homes. In addition to actions expressly recognized under this subpart H and other provisions in this part, however, HUD may take any actions authorized by the Act in order to oversee the system established by the regulations in this part.

§ 3286.703   Failure to comply.

(a) *Penalties and injunctive relief.* Failure to comply with the requirements of this part is a prohibited act under section 610(a)(7) of the Act, 42 U.S.C. 5409(a). Any person who fails to comply with the requirements of this part is subject to civil and criminal penalties, and to actions for injunctive relief, in accordance with sections 611 and 612 of the Act, 42 U.S.C. 5410 and 5411.

(b) *Presentation of views.* When practicable, the Secretary will provide notice to any person against whom an action for injunctive relief is contemplated and will afford such person an opportunity to request a presentation of views. The procedures set forth in §§ 3282.152 through 3282.154 of this chapter shall apply to each request to present views and to each presentation of views authorized in accordance with this section.

(c) *Investigations.* The procedures for investigations and investigational proceedings are set forth in part 3800 of this chapter.

§ 3286.705   Applicability of dispute resolution program.

(a) *Generally.* Regardless of any action taken under § 3286.703, for any defect in a manufactured home that is reported during the one-year period beginning on the date of installation, as specified in § 3286.115, any rights and remedies available under the HUD dispute resolution program, as implemented in part 3288 of this chapter, continue to apply as provided in that part.

(b) *Waiver of rights invalid.* Any provision of a contract or agreement entered into by a manufactured home purchaser that seeks to waive any recourse to either HUD or a state dispute resolution program is void.

Subpart I—State Programs

§3286.801 Purpose.

The purpose of this subpart I is to establish the requirements that must be met by a state to implement and administer its own installation program, either as part of its approved state plan or under this subpart, in such a way that the state would not be covered by the HUD-administered installation program. This subpart I also establishes the procedure for determining whether a state installation program meets the requirements of the Act for a qualifying installation program that will operate in lieu of the HUD-administered installation program.

§3286.803 State qualifying installation programs.

(a) *Qualifying installation program supersedes.* The HUD-administered installation program will not be implemented in any state that is identified as fully or conditionally accepted under the requirements and procedures of this subpart I or in accordance with part 3282 of this chapter.

(b) *Minimum elements.* To be accepted as a fully qualifying installation program, a state installation program must include the following elements:

(1) Installation standards that meet or exceed the requirements of §3286.107(a) and that apply to every initial installation of a new manufactured home within the state;

(2) The training of manufactured home installers;

(3) The licensing of, or other method of certifying or approving, manufactured home installers to perform the initial installations of new manufactured homes in the state;

(4) A method for inspecting the initial installations of new manufactured homes in the state that is implemented and used to hold installers responsible for the work they perform; and

(5) Provision of adequate funding and personnel to administer the state installation program.

(c) *Conditional acceptance.* (1) A state installation program that meets the minimum requirements set forth under paragraphs (b)(1), (4), and (5) of this section may be conditionally accepted by the Secretary if the state provides assurances deemed adequate by the Secretary that the state is moving to meet all of the requirements for full acceptance. If the Secretary conditionally accepts a state's installation program, the Secretary will provide to the state an explanation of what is necessary to obtain full acceptance.

(2) A conditionally accepted state will be permitted to implement its own installation program in lieu of the HUD-administered program for a period of not more than 3 years. The Secretary may for good cause grant an extension of conditional approval upon petition by the state.

(d) *Limited exemptions from requirements.* A state installation program may be accepted by the Secretary as a qualifying installation program if the state can demonstrate that it lacks legal authority, as a matter of federal law, to impose the minimum requirements set forth under paragraph (b) of this section in certain geographic areas of the state, but that the minimum requirements do apply in all other geographic areas of the state.

§3286.805 Procedures for identification as qualified installation program.

(a) *Submission of certification.* (1) A state seeking identification as having a qualified installation program must submit a completed State Installation Program Certification form to the Secretary for review and acceptance and indicate if the installation program will be part of its approved state plan in accordance with part 3282 of this chapter.

(2) A state must include a qualified installation program as part of any state plan application submitted for approval under §3282.302 of this chapter, if the state does not have a fully or conditionally approved state plan in effect at the time of submission of the state plan application. In all other cases, a qualified installation program is permitted, but is not required, to be

275

submitted as a part of a state plan approved in accordance with § 3282.305 of this chapter.

(b) *HUD review and action.* (1) The Secretary will review the State Installation Program Certification form submitted by a state and may request that the state submit additional information as necessary. Unless the Secretary has contacted the state for additional information or has conditionally accepted or rejected the state installation program, the state installation program will be considered to have been accepted by the Secretary as a fully qualifying installation program as of the earlier of:

(i) Ninety days after the Secretary receives the state's completed State Installation Program Certification form; or

(ii) The date that the Secretary issues notification to the state of its full acceptance.

(2) A notice of full or conditional acceptance will include the effective date of acceptance.

(c) *Rejection of state installation program.* (1) If the Secretary intends to reject a state's installation program, the Secretary will provide to the state an explanation of what is necessary to obtain full or conditional acceptance. The state will be given 90 days from the date the Secretary provides such explanation to submit a revised State Installation Program Certification form.

(2) If the Secretary decides that any revised State Installation Program Certification form is inadequate, or if the state fails to submit a revised form within the 90-day period or otherwise indicates that it does not intend to change its form, the Secretary will notify the state that its installation program is not accepted.

(3) A state whose State Installation Program Certification form is rejected has a right to a presentation of views on the rejection using the procedures set forth under subpart D of part 3282 of this chapter. The state's request for a presentation of views must be submitted to the Secretary within 60 days after the Secretary has provided notification that the state's installation program has been rejected.

§ 3286.807 **Recertification required.**

(a) *Recertification.* To maintain its status as a qualified installation program when the installation program is not part of the approved state plan in accordance with part 3282 of this chapter, a state must submit a new State Installation Program Certification form to the Secretary for review and action as follows:

(1) Every 5 years after the state's most recent certification as a qualified installation program; and

(2) Whenever there is a change to the state's installation program or a change in the HUD requirements applicable to qualifying installation programs such that the state's installation program no longer complies with the minimum requirements set forth in § 3286.803(b), regardless of when the state's next regular recertification of its installation program would be due.

(b) *Due date of recertification.* (1) A state's recertification required in paragraph (a) of this section must be filed within 90 days of, as applicable:

(i) The 5-year anniversary of the effective date of the Secretary's acceptance of the state's most recent certification as a qualified installation program; and

(ii) The effective date of the state or HUD action that makes a significant change to the state's installation program.

(2) Upon petition by the state, the Secretary may for good cause grant an extension of the deadline for recertification.

(c) *Failure to Recertify.* (1) A state whose certification of its installation program, when the installation program is not part of the approved state plan in accordance with part 3282 of this chapter, has been accepted by the Secretary is permitted to administer its installation program in lieu of the HUD-administered installation program until the effective date of a notification by the Secretary that the state's certification of its installation program is no longer approved.

(2) A state whose recertification of its installation program is rejected by the Secretary has a right to a presentation of views on the rejection using the procedures set forth under subpart D of part 3282 of this chapter. The

state's request for a presentation of views must be submitted to the Secretary within 60 days after the Secretary has provided notification that the state's recertification of its installation program has been rejected.

§ 3286.809 Withdrawal of qualifying installation program status.

(a) *Voluntary withdrawal.* Any state that intends to withdraw from its responsibilities to administer a qualifying installation program should provide the Secretary with a minimum of 90 days notice.

(b) *Involuntary withdrawal.* Whenever the Secretary finds, after affording notice and an opportunity for a hearing in accordance with subpart D of part 3282 of this chapter, that a state installation program fails to comply substantially with any provision of the installation program requirements or that the state program has become inadequate, the Secretary will notify the state of withdrawal of acceptance or conditional acceptance of the state installation program. The HUD-administered installation program will begin to operate in such state at such time as the Secretary establishes in issuing the finding.

§ 3286.811 Effect on other manufactured housing program requirements.

A state with a qualifying installation program will operate in lieu of HUD with respect to only the installation program established under subparts B through H of this part. No state may permit its installation program, even if it is a qualified installation program under this part, to supersede the requirements applicable to HUD's Manufactured Housing Construction and Safety Standards and enforcement programs. Regardless of whether a state has a qualified installation program:

(a) *Construction and safety standards.* Any responsibilities, rights, and remedies applicable under the Manufactured Home Construction and Safety Standards Act in part 3280 of this chapter and the Manufactured Home Procedural and Enforcement Regulations in part 3282 of this chapter continue to apply as provided in those parts; and

(b) *Dispute resolution.* For any defect in a manufactured home that is reported during the one-year period beginning on the date of installation defined in § 3286.115, any responsibilities, rights, and remedies applicable under the HUD dispute resolution program as implemented in part 3288 of this chapter continue to apply as provided in that part.

§ 3286.813 Inclusion in state plan.

If a state installation program is included in a state plan approved in accordance with § 3282.302 of this chapter, the state installation program is subject to all of the requirements for such a state plan, including annual review by HUD.

PART 3288—MANUFACTURED HOME DISPUTE RESOLUTION PROGRAM

277

Subpart E—Dispute Resolution Program Rulemaking Procedures

3288.300 Applicability.
3288.305 Consultation with the Manufactured Housing Consensus Committee.

AUTHORITY: 42 U.S.C. 3535(d), 5422 and 5424.

SOURCE: 72 FR 27229, May 14, 2007, unless otherwise noted.

Subpart A—General

§ 3288.1 Purpose and scope.

(a) *Purpose.* The Act is intended, in part, to protect the quality, safety, durability, and affordability of manufactured homes. Section 623(c)(12) of the Act (42 U.S.C. 5422 (c)(12)) requires the implementation of "a dispute resolution program for the timely resolution of disputes between manufacturers, retailers, and installers of manufactured homes regarding responsibility, and for the issuance of appropriate orders, for the correction or repair of defects in manufactured homes that are reported during the 1-year period beginning on the date of installation." The purpose of this part is to provide a dispute resolution program for the timely resolution of disputes among manufacturers, retailers, and installers regarding the responsibility for correction or repair of defects reported by the homeowner or others and reported in the 1-year period after the first installation of the manufactured home.

(b) *Scope*—(1) *Applicability.* In carrying out this purpose, it is presumed that if a manufactured home contains an alleged defect that is reported in the first year after installation and was not caused by the homeowner, then the manufacturer, retailer, or installer is responsible for the alleged defect and the dispute resolution process recognized in this part is an appropriate means for resolving disputes about responsibility for correction and repair of the alleged defect. For purposes of the dispute resolution process recognized in this part, only alleged defects reported in the first year after the first installation are covered by the process. The state where the home is sited determines whether the HUD Manufactured Home Dispute Resolution Program or a state program applies. Subpart A of this part establishes general

provisions applicable to HUD's implementation of a dispute resolution program as required by the Act. Subpart B of this part establishes the HUD Manufactured Home Dispute Resolution Program that HUD will administer in any state that does not establish a program that complies with the Act and been accepted by HUD as provided in subpart D of this part. Subpart C of this part provides an Alternative Process for manufacturers, retailers, and installers who agree that a homeowner is not responsible for the alleged defect to resolve their disputes about responsibility for correction or repair outside of the HUD Mediation and Arbitration Process under subpart B. Subpart D of this part establishes the minimum requirements that must be met by a state applying to implement its own dispute resolution program that complies with the Act, and the procedure for determining whether the requirements for complying have been met. Subpart E of this part establishes special rulemaking procedures that apply to the issuance of new regulations that implement the dispute resolution requirements set forth in section 623 of the Act (42 U.S.C. 5422).

(2) *Warranties not affected.* This part is not a warranty program and the requirements established in this part do not replace the manufacturer's or any other warranty program. Such warranty program may have its own requirements.

§ 3288.3 Definitions.

The following definitions apply in this part:

Act means the National Manufactured Housing Construction and Safety Standards Act of 1974, 42 U.S.C. 5401–5426.

Appropriate order means an order issued by HUD or an order that is enforceable under state law.

Date of installation means the date all utilities are connected and the manufactured home is ready for occupancy as established, if applicable, by a certificate of occupancy, except as follows: if the manufactured home has not been sold to the first person purchasing the home in good faith for purposes other than resale by the date the home is ready for occupancy, the date of installation is the date of closing under the purchase agreement or sales contract for the manufactured home.

Day means a calendar day.

Defect means any defect in the performance, construction, components, or material of a manufactured home that renders the home or any part of the home not fit for the ordinary use for which it was intended, including, but not limited to, a defect in the construction, safety, or installation of the home. For purposes of state certification under §3288.205, HUD will find it acceptable if the threshold for the state's program is functionally equivalent to this definition.

Dispute resolution provider means a person or entity providing dispute resolution services for HUD.

Homeowner means a person who purchased or leased the manufactured home in good faith for purposes other than resale.

HUD means the U.S. Department of Housing and Urban Development.

Installer means the person who is retained to engage in, or who engages in, the business of directing, supervising, controlling, or correcting the initial installation of a manufactured home.

Manufactured home has the same meaning as the term "manufactured home" as defined in 24 CFR 3280.2.

Manufactured Housing Consensus Committee or MHCC means the consensus committee established pursuant to section 604(a)(3) of the Act, 42 U.S.C. 5403(a)(3).

Party or parties means, individually or collectively, the manufacturer, retailer, or installer of a manufactured home in which a defect has been reported in accordance with §3288.20.

State Administrative Agency means an agency of a state that has been approved or conditionally approved to carry out the state plan for enforcement of the standards pursuant to section 623 of the Act, 42 U.S.C. 5422.

Timely reporting means the reporting of an alleged defect within 1 year after the date of installation of a manufactured home in accordance with §3288.20.

Timely resolution means the resolution of disputes among manufacturers, retailers, and installers within 120 days of the time a request for dispute resolution is made, except that if the defect presents an unreasonable risk of injury, death, or significant loss or damage to valuable personal property, the resolution must be within 60 days of the time a request for dispute resolution is made.

§3288.5 Retailer notification at sale.

Retailer notice at the time of signing. At the time of signing a contract for sale or lease for a manufactured home, the retailer must provide the purchaser with a retailer notice. This notice may be in a separate document from the sales contract or may be incorporated clearly in a separate section on consumer dispute resolution information at the top of the sales contract. The notice must include the following language:

The U.S. Department of Housing and Urban Development (HUD) Manufactured Home Dispute Resolution Program is available to resolve disputes among manufacturers, retailers, or installers concerning defects in manufactured homes. Many states also have a consumer assistance or dispute resolution program. For additional information about these programs, see sections titled "Dispute Resolution Process" and "Additional Information—HUD Manufactured Home Dispute Resolution Program" in the Consumer Manual required to be provided to the purchaser. These programs are not warranty programs and do not replace the manufacturer's, or any other person's, warranty program.

Subpart B—HUD Manufactured Home Dispute Resolution Program in HUD-Administered States

§3288.10 Applicability.

The requirements of the HUD Manufactured Home Dispute Resolution Program established in this subpart B apply in each state that does not establish a state dispute resolution program that complies with the Act and has been accepted by HUD as provided in subpart D of this part.

§3288.15 Eligibility for dispute resolution.

(a) *Initiation of actions.* Manufacturers, retailers, and installers of manufactured homes are eligible to initiate and participate in the HUD Manufactured Home Dispute Resolution Program. Homeowners may initiate action under, and be observers to, the HUD Manufactured Home Dispute Resolution Program.

(b) *Eligible disputes.* Only disputes concerning alleged defects that have been reported to the manufacturer, retailer, installer, HUD, or a State Administrative Agency within 1 year after the date of the first installation of the manufactured home are eligible for resolution through the HUD Manufactured Home Dispute Resolution Program. The eligible dispute includes the defect alleged in a timely report and any related issues.

§ 3288.20   **Reporting a defect.**

(a) *Making a report.* To preserve the right to request dispute resolution through HUD, alleged defects must be reported to the manufacturer, retailer, installer, HUD, or a State Administrative Agency. An alleged defect may be reported by a homeowner, manufacturer, retailer, or installer.

(b) *Form of report.* It is recommended that alleged defects be reported in writing, including, but not limited to, e-mail, written letter, certified mail, or fax. The existence of an alleged defect may also be reported by telephone.

(c) *Content of report.* No particular form or format is required to report an alleged defect, but any such report must, at a minimum, include a description of the alleged defect, the name of homeowner, and the address of the home.

(d) *Record of report*—(1) *To evidence timeliness.* To establish timely reporting, the report of an alleged defect that is made to the manufacturer, retailer, installer, or a State Administrative Agency of the manufactured home should be done in a manner that will create a dated record of the report that demonstrates that the report was made within 1 year after the date of installation; for example, by certified mail, fax, or email. Persons who report an alleged defect by telephone should make a contemporaneous note of the telephone call, including date, time, the name of the person who received the report, the name of the business contacted, and the telephone number

called. If the matter goes to arbitration, the arbitrator and HUD will review whether there is sufficient evidence to believe the report was made on a timely basis.

(2) *Obligation to retain.* Each report of a defect, including logs of telephonic complaints, received by a manufacturer, retailer, a State Administrative Agency or installer, must be maintained for 3 years from the date of receipt.

(e) *Reports made to a State Administrative Agency.* Reports of defects in the manufactured home that are made in the first year after its installation can be sent to the appropriate State Administrative Agency. Contact information about a State Administrative Agency is available at *http://www.hud.gov.* Contact the appropriate State Administrative Agency to determine the method for making the report.

(f) *Reports made to HUD.* Reports of alleged defects in the manufactured home that are made in the first year after its installation can be sent to HUD. The report to HUD may be made using any of the following methods:

(1) In writing at: HUD, Office of Regulatory Affairs and Manufactured Housing, Attn: Dispute Resolution, 451 Seventh Street, SW., Washington, DC 20410–8000;

(2) By telephone at: (202) 708–6423 or (800) 927–2891;

(3) By fax at: (202) 708–4213; or

(4) By e-mail at *mhs@hud.gov.*

(g) *Effect of report.* The reporting of an alleged defect does not initiate the HUD Manufactured Home Dispute Resolution Program, but only establishes whether the requirement of timely reporting in accordance with § 3288.15(b) has been met. The HUD Manufactured Home Dispute Resolution Process is initiated when a request for dispute resolution is submitted to HUD in accordance with § 3288.25.

§ 3288.25   **Initiation of dispute resolution.**

(a) *Preliminary effort.* HUD strongly encourages the homeowner or party reporting an alleged defect to seek to resolve the dispute directly with any manufacturer, retailer, or installer that the person reporting the defect believes to be responsible before initiating the HUD dispute resolution process.

(b) *Request for dispute resolution.* Any of the parties or the homeowner may initiate the HUD Manufactured Home Dispute Resolution Program at any time after an alleged defect has been reported, by requesting dispute resolution, as follows:

(1) By mailing, e-mailing, or otherwise delivering a written request for dispute resolution to the dispute resolution provider at the address or e-mail address provided either at *http://www.hud.gov,* or by contacting HUD's Office of Regulatory Affairs and Manufactured Housing at (202) 708–6423 or (800) 927–2891;

(2) By faxing a request for dispute resolution to the fax number provided either at *http://www.hud.gov,* or by contacting HUD's Office of Regulatory Affairs and Manufactured Housing at (202) 708–6423 or (800) 927–2891; or

(3) By telephoning a request for dispute resolution to the number provided either at *http://www.hud.gov,* or by contacting HUD's Office of Regulatory Affairs and Manufactured Housing at (202) 708–6423 or (800) 927–2891.

(c) *Requested information.* The dispute resolution provider will request at least the following information when a person seeks to initiate dispute resolution under the HUD Manufactured Home Dispute Resolution Program:

(1) The name, address, and contact information of the homeowner;

(2) The name and contact information of the manufacturer, retailer, and installer of the manufactured home, to the extent available;

(3) The date the report of the alleged defect was made;

(4) The name and contact information of the recipient or recipients of the report of the alleged defect;

(5) The date of installation of the manufactured home affected by the alleged defect; and

(6) A description of the alleged defect.

§3288.30 Screening of dispute resolution request.

(a) *Review for sufficiency.* When the request for dispute resolution has been received by the dispute resolution provider, a screening neutral will review the sufficiency of the information provided in the request for dispute resolution and determine if the dispute resolution process should proceed. If the screening neutral determines that a defect is properly alleged and timely reported, notice of the request will be forwarded, as provided in §3288.33, to the manufacturer, retailer, and installer, as appropriate and to the extent the appropriate parties can be identified based on the information in the request.

(b) *Insufficient information.* If a request for dispute resolution is lacking any information necessary to determine if the dispute resolution process should proceed, the screening neutral will contact the requester or the parties about supplementing the initial request. If information necessary to qualify the matter for the HUD Manufactured Home Dispute Resolution Program is not received within a reasonable time established by the screening neutral, the request for dispute resolution will be considered withdrawn.

(c) *Denial of a dispute.* Denial by all of the parties that there is a dispute does not preclude the dispute resolution process from going forward to mediation. A screening neutral's determination that a defect is properly alleged is prima facie evidence of a dispute. If the defect has not been corrected or repaired, the matter will be referred to mediation.

(d) *Determination of unreasonable risk.* If the screening neutral determines there is sufficient documentation of an alleged defect presenting an unreasonable risk of injury or death, he or she will send a copy of the request to HUD.

§3288.33 Notice of dispute resolution.

(a) Once the screening neutral determines that a defect is properly alleged and timely reported, notice about the request will be forwarded to the parties by overnight delivery, commercial carrier, or fax.

(b) If the parties have not initiated the Alternative Process in accordance with §3288.105 of this part within 7 days of the screening neutral's notification, the screening neutral will refer the matter to mediation.

§ 3288.35 Mediation.

(a) *Mediator.* The dispute resolution provider will provide for the selection of a mediator. The selected mediator will not be the person who screened the dispute resolution request. The selected mediator will mediate the dispute and attempt to facilitate a settlement. If a party identifies any other party that should be included in the mediation, the mediator will contact the other party and provide information about the scheduled mediation meetings.

(b) *Time—*(1) *For reaching settlement.* Except as provided in paragraph (b)(2) of this section, the parties are allowed 30 days from the commencement of the mediation to reach a mediated settlement. In every case, the dispute resolution provider will notify the parties and the homeowner, in writing, of the date of the commencement of the mediation.

(2) *Alleged defects presenting an unreasonable risk of injury, death, or significant loss or damage to valuable personal property.* For mediations involving alleged defects that appear to present an unreasonable risk of injury, death, or significant loss or damage to valuable personal property as determined by the screening neutral, the parties have a maximum 10 days from the commencement of the mediation to reach a settlement.

(3) *For corrective repairs.* Unless a longer period is agreed to in writing by the parties to the mediated settlement and the homeowner, corrective repairs must be completed no later than 30 days after the date the settlement agreement is signed by the applicable parties.

(c) *Denial of dispute.* During mediation, denial of a dispute by all parties without acceptance of responsibility will result in the mediator referring the matter to arbitration for determination of the defect and responsibility for the defect.

(d) *Written settlement agreement.* (1) Upon reaching an agreement, the parties will sign a written settlement agreement. The dispute resolution provider will forward copies of the agreements with the original signatures of the parties to the parties, the homeowner, and to HUD.

(2) Sample agreements will be made available to the parties as drafting guidance by the dispute resolution provider.

(e) *Failure of mediation.* If mediation is not successful, parties or the homeowner may proceed to nonbinding arbitration, as provided in § 3288.40 of this part.

(f) *Confidentiality.* Except for the report of an alleged defect, any request for dispute resolution, and any written settlement agreement, all other documents and communications provided in confidence and used in the mediation will be confidential, in accordance with the Administrative Dispute Resolution Act of 1996 (5 U.S.C. 571 *et seq.*).

§ 3288.40 Nonbinding arbitration.

(a) *When initiated.* (1) If, following mediation under § 3288.35, the parties fail to reach a settlement, any party or the homeowner may, within 15 days of the expiration of the deadline applicable under § 3288.35(b), initiate nonbinding arbitration.

(2) In addition, arbitration may be initiated upon referral by the mediator pursuant to § 3288.35(c).

(b) *Written request—*(1) *Submission to HUD.* A written request for arbitration must be submitted to the dispute resolution provider. Information about the dispute resolution provider and how to make a request for dispute resolution will be available at *http://www.hud.gov* or by contacting HUD's Office of Manufactured Housing Programs at (202) 708–6423 or (800) 927–2891.

(2) *Contents of request.* The written request for arbitration must include:

(i) The name and address of the party making the request;

(ii) A brief description of the alleged defect or a copy of the report of the alleged defect; and

(iii) A copy of the request for dispute resolution.

(c) *Appointment and authority of arbitrator.* Upon receipt of the request, the dispute resolution provider will select an arbitrator. The arbitrator will have the authority to:

(1) Set hearing dates and deadlines;

(2) Conduct on-site inspections;

(3) Issue requests for documentation and information necessary to complete the record;

(4) Dismiss frivolous allegations;

(5) Make proposed findings, including findings of defect and culpability and a disposition recommendation to HUD; and

(6) Recommend apportionment of the responsibility of paying for or providing any correction or repair of the home when recommending that culpability be assessed to more than one party.

(d) *Denial of dispute.* If the parties deny a dispute exists and the arbitrator determines there is a defect, the arbitrator will make a determination of responsibility for the defect.

(e) *Notice to parties.* The dispute resolution provider will provide the parties and the homeowner with a notice setting forth the date, place, and time an arbitration is to be held.

(f) *Proceedings.* (1) If all parties do not request an in-person hearing under paragraph (f)(2) of this section within 5 days of the dispute resolution provider's receipt of the request for arbitration, or if the arbitrator rejects the request for an in-person hearing, the arbitrator may conduct either a record review or a telephonic hearing.

(2) If any party wants to request an in-person hearing, in which the parties or their representatives may personally appear before the arbitrator, the arbitrator will consider such a request if it is made by all of the parties that are participating in the arbitration. Such an in-person hearing will be held at the discretion of the arbitrator, after considering appropriate factors, such as cost.

(g) *Effect on nonparticipating parties.* If a party chooses not to participate in the arbitration, the process will continue without further input from that party. In such a case, the arbitrator may rely on the record developed through the arbitration to find a nonparticipating party responsible for correction or repair of a defect.

(h) *Completion of arbitration.* (1) Unless an extension is granted for good cause by HUD, the arbitrator, within 21 days of the dispute resolution provider's receipt of the request for arbitration, the arbitrator will complete the arbitration process and provide HUD with all background information used during the arbitration and with a written, nonbinding recommendation as to which party or parties are responsible for the defect, and what corrective actions should be taken.

(2) Unless an extension is granted for good cause by HUD, the arbitrator, within 21 days of the dispute resolution provider's receipt of the request for arbitration, will provide the parties with a copy of the nonbinding recommendation that was delivered to HUD, in accordance with §3288.40(h)(1).

(i) *Settlement offers.* At any time before HUD issues a final order, the parties may submit to HUD a proposal to resolve the dispute.

§3288.45 HUD review and order.

(a) *Appropriate order.* HUD will review the arbitrator's recommendation provided in accordance with §3288.40(h), any settlement offers presented by the parties in accordance with §3288.40(i), and the information gathered during the arbitration, and will issue an appropriate order in which HUD may accept, modify, or reject the recommendations. HUD will forward a copy of the order to the arbitrator and to each of the parties and the homeowner, whether or not a party chose to participate in the arbitration.

(b) *Contents of order.* If HUD finds that a defect exists, the order will include the following:

(1) Assignment of responsibility for the correction and repair of all defects and associated costs; and

(2) If the manufacturer, retailer, or installer is responsible for corrective action, a date by which the correction and repair of each defect must be completed, taking into consideration the seriousness of the defect.

(c) *Failure to comply.* Failure to comply with an order issued by HUD is a violation of section 610(a)(5) of the Act (42 U.S.C. 5409(a)(5)).

Subpart C—Alternative Process in HUD-Administered States

§3288.100 Scope and applicability.

The requirements of this subpart C may be followed in lieu of the requirements of subpart B of this part to resolve disputes among manufacturers, retailers, and installers of manufactured homes in any state where subpart B of this part would otherwise apply. In limited circumstances, this subpart C permits manufacturers, retailers, and installers of manufactured homes to use neutrals of their choosing to resolve disputes concerning alleged defects in manufactured homes.

§ 3288.105 Time when Alternative Process is available.

(a) The Alternative Process may be invoked after an alleged defect has been reported, pursuant to § 3288.15(b). However, the Alternative Process may not be invoked more than 7 days after notification of a request for dispute resolution has been received by all of the parties. The notification must be delivered by overnight delivery, commercial carrier, or fax by the screening neutral, in accordance with § 3288.30. If within 7 days of the receipt of notification, the Alternative Process is not initiated, the screening neutral will refer the matter to the mediator. Once the Alternative Process is invoked, neither the parties nor the homeowner may invoke the Mediation and Arbitration Process in the HUD Manufactured Home Dispute Resolution Program for 30 days.

(b) No particular form or format is required to provide notification for the Alternative Process, but the party or parties submitting the notification must include a statement from the parties participating in the Alternative Process stating that the homeowner is not responsible for the alleged defect and that one or more of the parties will correct or repair the defect. All required agreements are set forth in § 3288.110 of this part. The parties must also make reasonable efforts to include the following information in the notification:

(1) Identification of the case; and

(2) Identification of the parties participating in the Alternative Process.

(c) The screening neutral will notify the parties if the case is referred to the Alternative Process for resolution.

§ 3288.110 Alternative Process agreements.

(a) *Required agreement.* To use the Alternative Process, the manufacturer,

retailer, and installer of the manufactured home at issue, as appropriate, must agree:

(1) That there is a defect in the manufactured home;

(2) That the manufacturer, retailer, or installer is responsible for the defect;

(3) That the homeowner is not responsible for the defect;

(4) To engage a neutral to evaluate the dispute and make an assignment of responsibility for correction and repair; and

(5) To notify the homeowner of, and allow the homeowner to be present at, any meetings and to inform the homeowner of the outcome.

(b) *Additional element of agreement.* In addition, the parties should agree to act upon the neutral's assignment of responsibility for correction and repair.

Subpart D—State Dispute Resolution Programs in Non-HUD Administered States

§ 3288.200 Applicability.

This subpart D establishes the minimum requirements that must be met by a state to implement its own dispute resolution program and therefore not be covered by the HUD Manufactured Home Dispute Resolution Program established in accordance with subpart B. The subpart also establishes the procedure for determining whether the state dispute resolution program meets the requirements of the Act for operating in lieu of the HUD Manufactured Home Dispute Resolution Program.

§ 3288.205 Minimum requirements.

(a) *List of requirements.* The HUD Manufactured Home Dispute Resolution Program will not be implemented in any state that complies with the procedures of this subpart D and that has a dispute resolution program that provides for the following minimum requirements:

(1) The timely resolution of disputes among manufacturers, retailers, or installers regarding responsibility for correction and repair of defects in manufactured homes;

(2) The issuance of appropriate orders for correction and repair of defects in such homes;

(3) A coverage period for disputes that includes at least defects that are reported within 1 year after the date of first installation; and

(4) Adequate funding and personnel.

(b) *Applicability to programs in state plans.* (1) In order to include a dispute resolution program in a state plan that on February 8, 2008 is fully or conditionally approved under §3282.302 of this chapter, a state must amend its state plan to provide for the requirements of paragraphs (a)(1) through (3) of this section.

(2) After February 8, 2008, a state that submits a state plan for approval in accordance with §3282.302 of this chapter must provide for the requirements of paragraphs (a)(1) through (3) of this section in its state plan.

§3288.210 Acceptance and recertification process.

(a) *Submission of certification.* A state seeking HUD acceptance of its state dispute resolution program under this subpart must submit to HUD a completed Dispute Resolution Certification Form, which is available by contacting HUD by telephone at (202) 708–6423 or by e-mail at *mhs@hud.gov.* The certification may be submitted as a part of, or independent of, a state plan under §3282.302 of this chapter. If included as part of a state plan, the state does not have to separately certify that it meets the requirements of §3288.205(a)(4).

(b) *HUD review and action.* (1) HUD will review the Dispute Resolution Certification Form submitted by a state and may contact the state to request additional clarification or information as necessary. Upon completing its review, HUD will provide the state with notice of acceptance, conditional acceptance, or rejection of its dispute resolution program.

(2) A notice of acceptance will include the date of acceptance.

(3) If HUD rejects a state's dispute resolution program, HUD will provide an explanation of what is necessary to obtain full acceptance. A revised Dispute Resolution Certification Form may be submitted within 30 days of receipt of such notification. If the revised

Dispute Resolution Certification Form is inadequate or if the state fails to resubmit within the 30-day period or otherwise indicates that it does not intend to change its Dispute Resolution Certification Form, HUD will notify the state that its dispute resolution program is not accepted and that it has a right to a hearing on the rejection using the procedures set forth under subpart D of part 3282 of this chapter.

(c) *Conditional acceptance.* A state meeting three of the four minimum requirements set forth under §3288.205(a)(1) through (4) will be conditionally accepted by HUD. If HUD conditionally accepts a state's dispute resolution program, HUD will provide an explanation of what is necessary to obtain full acceptance. A revised Dispute Resolution Certification Form may be submitted within 30 days of receipt of such notification. Any state conditionally accepted will be permitted to implement its own dispute resolution program for a period of not more than 3 years, absent extension of this period by HUD.

(d) *Revocation.* If HUD becomes aware at any time that a state no longer meets the minimum requirements set forth under §3288.205, HUD may revoke acceptance of the state's certification after an opportunity for a hearing, using the procedures set forth under subpart D of part 3282.

(e) *Recertification of a program not included in state plan.* Except as provided in paragraph (f), to maintain its accepted status, a state whose program is not included in an approved or conditionally approved state plan must submit a current Dispute Resolution Certification Form to HUD for review and acceptance as follows:

(1) Every 3 years within 90 days of the day and month of the most recent date of HUD's acceptance of the state's program or

(2) Whenever there is a significant change to the program.

(f) *Inclusion in state plan.* If a state dispute resolution program is part of a state plan, it will be reviewed annually as part of the state plan and separate recertification of the state's dispute resolution program is not required.

§ 3288.215 Effect on other manufactured home program requirements.

A state with an accepted dispute resolution program will operate in lieu of HUD's Manufactured Home Dispute Resolution Program established under subpart B of this part 3288. A state dispute resolution program, even if it is an accepted dispute resolution program under this part, does not supersede the requirements applicable to any other aspect of HUD's manufactured home program. Any responsibilities, rights, and remedies applicable under the Manufactured Home Construction and Safety Standards in part 3280 of this chapter and the Manufactured Home Procedural and Enforcement Regulations in part 3282 of this chapter continue to apply as provided in those parts in all states.

Subpart E—Dispute Resolution Program Rulemaking Procedures

§ 3288.300 Applicability.

This subpart establishes special regulatory procedures for issuing or revising dispute resolution program regulations as codified in this part.

§ 3288.305 Consultation with the Manufactured Housing Consensus Committee.

HUD will seek input from the MHCC when revising the HUD Manufactured Home Dispute Resolution Program regulations in this part 3288. Before publication of a proposed rule to revise these regulations, HUD will provide the MHCC with an opportunity to comment on such revision. The MHCC may send to HUD any of the MHCC's own recommendations to adopt new dispute resolution program regulations or to modify or repeal any of the regulations in this part. Along with each recommendation, the MHCC must set forth pertinent data and arguments in support of the action sought. HUD will either: accept or modify the recommendation and publish it for public comment in accordance with section 553 of the Administrative Procedure Act (5 U.S.C. 553), along with an explanation of the reasons for any such modification; or reject the recommendation entirely, and provide to the MHCC a written explanation of the

reasons for the rejection. This section does not supersede section 605 of the National Manufactured Housing Construction and Safety Standards Act of 1974 (42 U.S.C. 5404).

PARTS 3289–3799 [RESERVED]

PART 3800—INVESTIGATIONS IN CONSUMER REGULATORY PROGRAMS

Sec.
3800.10 Scope of rules.
3800.20 Subpoenas in investigations.
3800.30 Subpoena enforcement in district court.
3800.40 Investigational proceedings.
3800.50 Rights of witnesses in investigational proceedings.
3800.60 Settlements.

AUTHORITY: 12 U.S.C. 2601 *et seq.*; 15 U.S.C. 1714; 42 U.S.C. 3535(d) and 5413.

SOURCE: 61 FR 10441, Mar. 13, 1996, unless otherwise noted.

§ 3800.10 Scope of rules.

This part applies to investigations and investigational proceedings undertaken by the Secretary, or the Secretary's designee, pursuant to the following:

(a) The Interstate Land Sales Full Disclosure Act, 15 U.S.C. 1701 *et seq.*;

(b) The National Manufactured Housing Construction and Safety Standards Act of 1974, 42 U.S.C. 5401 *et seq.*; and

(c) The Real Estate Settlement Procedures Act of 1974, 12 U.S.C. 2601 *et seq.*

§ 3800.20 Subpoenas in investigations.

(a) The Secretary may issue subpoenas relating to any matter under investigation. A subpoena may:

(1) Require testimony to be taken by interrogatories;

(2) Require the attendance and testimony of witnesses at a specific time and place;

(3) Require access to, examination of, and the right to copy documents; and

(4) Require the production of documents at a specific time and place.

(b) A subpoenaed person may petition the Secretary or the Secretary's designee to modify or withdraw a subpoena by filing the petition within 10 days after service of the subpoena. The petition may be in letter form, but must set forth the facts and law upon which the petition is based.

§ 3800.30 Subpoena enforcement in district court.

In the case of contumacy of a witness or a witness's refusal to obey a subpoena or order of the Secretary, the United States district court for the jurisdiction in which an investigation is carried on may issue an order requiring compliance with the subpoena. HUD headquarters in Washington, DC, is one of the locations in which the Secretary carries on investigations of its consumer regulatory programs.

§ 3800.40 Investigational proceedings.

(a) For the purpose of hearing the testimony of witnesses and receiving documents and other data relating to any subject under investigation, the Secretary, or the Secretary's designee, may conduct an investigational proceeding.

(b) The Secretary, or the Secretary's designee, ("presiding official") shall preside over the investigational proceeding. The proceeding shall be stenographically or mechanically reported. A transcript shall be a part of the record of the investigation.

(c) Unless the presiding official determines otherwise, investigational proceedings shall be public.

(d) The presiding official shall take all necessary action to regulate the course of the proceeding to avoid delay and to maintain order. If necessary to maintain order, the presiding official may exclude a witness or counsel from a proceeding. The Department may also take further action as permitted by statute.

§ 3800.50 Rights of witnesses in investigational proceedings.

(a) Any person who testifies at a public investigational proceeding shall be entitled, on payment of costs, to purchase a copy of a transcript of the testimony the person provided.

(b) In a nonpublic investigational proceeding, the presiding official may for good cause limit a witness to an inspection of the official transcript of that witness's testimony.

(c) Any person subpoenaed to appear at an investigational proceeding may be represented by counsel as follows:

(1) With respect to any question asked of a witness, a witness may obtain confidential advice from counsel;

(2) If a witness refuses to answer a question, counsel for the witness may briefly state the legal grounds for the refusal;

(3) Counsel for the witness may object to a question or a request for production of documents that is beyond the scope of the investigation or for which a privilege of the witness to refuse to answer may be invoked. In so doing, counsel for the witness may state briefly the grounds for the objection. Objections will be deemed continuing throughout the course of the proceeding. Repetitious or cumulative statements of an objection or the grounds for an objection are unnecessary and impermissible; and

(4) After the Department's examination of a witness, counsel for the witness may request that the witness be permitted to clarify any answers to correct any ambiguity, equivocation, or incompleteness in the witness's testimony. The decision to grant or deny this request is within the sole discretion of the presiding official.

§ 3800.60 Settlements.

(a) At any time during an investigation, the Department and the parties subject to an investigation may conduct settlement negotiations.

(b) When the Secretary or Secretary's designee deems it appropriate, the Department may enter into a settlement agreement.

PARTS 3801–3899 [RESERVED]

CHAPTER XXIV—BOARD OF DIRECTORS OF THE HOPE FOR HOMEOWNERS PROGRAM [RESERVED]

PARTS 4000–4099 [RESERVED]

CHAPTER XXV—NEIGHBORHOOD REINVESTMENT CORPORATION

PART 4100—ORGANIZATION AND CHANNELING OF FUNCTIONS

Sec.
4100.1 Functions and activities.
4100.2 General organization.
4100.3 Field activities.
4100.4 Inquiries.

AUTHORITY: Title VI, Pub. L. 95–557, 92 Stat. 2115 (42 U.S.C. 8101 *et seq.*); as amended by sec. 315, Pub. L. 96–399, 94 Stat. 1645; sec. 710, Pub. L. 97–320, 96 Stat. 1544; and sec. 520, Pub. L. 100–242, 101 Stat. 1815.

SOURCE: 49 FR 12700, Mar. 30, 1984, unless otherwise noted.

§ 4100.1 Functions and activities.

(a) *General statement.* The Neighborhood Reinvestment Corporation (referred to in this part as *the Corporation*) was established by Congress in the Neighborhood Reinvestment Corporation Act (title VI of the Housing and Community Development Amendments of 1978, Pub. L. 95–557, October 31, 1978). The Corporation is not a department, agency, or instrumentality of the Federal Government.

(b) The Corporation is authorized to receive and expend Federal appropriations and other public and private revenues to conduct a variety of programs designed primarily to revitalize older urban neighborhoods by mobilizing public, private, and community resources at the neighborhood level. These programs include:

(1) *Neighborhood Housing Services.* The major effort of the Corporation is to assist local communities in the development, expansion and provision of technical services to local Neighborhood Housing Services (NHS) programs. NHS programs are based upon partnerships of community residents, and representatives of local governments and financial institutions. Each local program is administered by an autonomous, private, non-profit corporation, and conducts a comprehensive revitalization effort in locally selected neighborhoods. Services to neighborhood residents include rehabilitation counseling, construction assistance, financial counseling, loan referrals and loans at flexible rates and terms to homeowners who do not meet private lending criteria. Programs and strategies to remove blighting influences, obtain improved public services and amenities, and improve the neighborhood's image and the functioning of its real estate market are also undertaken. To insure the continuing effectiveness of NHS programs, the Corporation provides grants, training, information and technical services to NHS programs.'

(2) *Mutual Housing Associations.* The Corporation also supports the organizational development of, and provides technical assistance to, Mutual Housing Associations. Mutual Housing Associations are private, nonprofit organizations which own, manage and continually develop affordable housing. Mutual Housing residents are members of the Association which owns and manages their buildings; thus they enjoy the security of long-term housing tenure. Mutual Housing developments are capitalized through up-front grants and mortgages in a combination that ensures permanent affordability to low- and moderate-income families. Monthly housing charges to residents are kept at affordable levels on a continuing basis. A key element of Mutual Housing is the Association's commitment to use all resources in excess of operating and maintenance costs for the production of additional units. A Mutual Housing Association's board of directors includes current member-residents, potential residents, and representatives from the community, local government and business. Residents and community members make up the majority on the board. A highly qualified professional staff, employed by the Mutual Housing Association, carries out the day-to-day activities of the organization. In addition to creating new affordable housing opportunities, Mutual Housing Associations offer a creative alternative for subsidized rental housing developments whose subsidies are scheduled to expire.

(3) *Neighborhood preservation projects.* The Corporation identifies, monitors, evaluates and supports through demonstration grants and technical assistance other promising neighborhood preservation strategies based on local, public-private partnerships.

(4) *Programmatic supplements.* Proven, replicable programmatic tools are offered as broadly as resources permit. Often, these selected strategies are supported by Neighborhood Reinvestment grants. The Corporation's major programmatic supplements include the following:

(i) *Neighborhood economic development and commercial revitalization strategies.* The Corporation's neighborhood economic development and commercial revitalization strategies offer NHSs a variety of tools designed to stabilize and enhance the economic base of NHS neighborhoods. They complement NHSs' revitalization mission by focusing the energies and resources of the partnership on the economic issues underlying neighborhood decline. Neighborhood economic development and commercial revitalization assures a viable neighborhood economy by strengthening small businesses and improving the physical environment of the area, thus providing additional goods, services, and employment opportunities for the community.

(ii) *Housing Development Strategies.* The Corporation's Housing Development Strategies program addresses the shortage of affordable, quality housing available to low to moderate income families in NHS neighborhoods, as well as the blighting effect of vacant lots and substandard properties. Home ownership opportunities are created through the planning and implementation of a variety of housing mechanisms by the NHS, which are intended to reverse negative real estate market trends, enhance new residential growth, and create renewed neighborhood pride. The mechanisms being used to achieve these goals include the following.

(A) The Owner Built Housing program is a supervised housing construction process that helps moderate-income homeowners to collectively build their own homes. The NHS provides technical assistance while private lenders and public bodies providing financing.

(B) The Owner Rehab Housing program assists low to moderate income families in collectively rehabilitating existing blighted and vacant structures.

(C) The Infill Housing program provides a mechanism for assisting NHSs in building new units on vacant land to meet the needs of prospective lower income homeowners.

(D) The Urban Subdivisions program focuses on providing low cost, new housing for low-to-moderate income families on tracts of land suitable for the construction of 20 or more units.

(iii) *Problem properties strategies.* This program assists NHSs in addressing specific problem areas beyond the scope of basic NHS services and typical financial resources. Through the implementation of various problem properties strategies, NHS programs are able to assist tenants to purchase, improve the physical condition of target blocks, eliminate vacant neighborhood eyesores, develop housing and service facilities for special populations, and stimulate private reinvestment and new conventional mortgages in the NHS community.

(5) *Apartment Improvement Program.* The goal of the Apartment Improvement Program is to provide an effective, economical means of revitalizing and preserving neighborhoods with multi-family housing for the benefit of the current residents. The program is based upon a partnership of tenants and community representatives, property owners and managers, financial institutions and local government. The program assists in the development of an individually tailored improvement plan of activities from which each building may benefit, including tenant participation, tax assessment reviews, and increased investment or restructured mortgages to improve the economic viability of the buildings and to finance improvements.

(6) *Neighborhood Housing Services of America.* The Corporation also supports Neighborhood Housing Services of America (NHSA), an independent, private, non-profit corporation which provides a variety of services to local NHS programs, including a secondary market for NHS revolving loan fund loans, and the strengthening of private sector resources available to the network of local NHSs.

[49 FR 12700, Mar. 30, 1984, as amended at 54 FR 13061, Mar. 30, 1989]

§4100.2 General organization.

(a) *The Board of Directors.* (1) The Corporation is under the direction of a Board of Directors composed of six members: the Chairman of the Federal Home Loan Bank Board or a member of the Federal Home Loan Bank Board designated by the Chairman; the Secretary of Housing and Urban Development; the Chairman of the Board of Governors of the Federal Reserve System, or a member of the Board of Governors of the Federal Reserve System designated by the Chairman; the Chairman of the Federal Deposit Insurance Corporation or the appointive member of the Board of Directors of the Federal Deposit Insurance Corporation if so designated by the Chairman; the Comptroller of the Currency; and the Chairman of the National Credit Union Administration, or a member of the Board of the National Credit Union Administration designated by the Chairman. Members of the Board serve without additional compensation. The Board elects from among its members a Chairman and Vice-Chairman. The Bylaws of the Corporation provide for the creation of an Audit Committee, and such other committees as the Board may from time to time establish.

(2) The Board holds an Annual Meeting each year during the month of May (or as the Bylaws or the Board may specify). The Board also holds regular meetings at least quarterly and special meetings as required. The meetings of the Board are conducted in accordance with provisions of the Neighborhood Reinvestment Corporation Act, the Government in the Sunshine Act (5 U.S.C. 552b), the Corporation's Bylaws, and when not inconsistent with the foregoing, with Robert's Rules of Order. Every portion of every meeting of the Board is open to public observation except as provided by the Government in the Sunshine Act. Interested members of the public may attend such meetings, but may not participate therein unless invited or permitted to do so by the Board.

(3) The Secretary of the Corporation, in consultation with the Corporation's General Counsel, is responsible for taking such steps as are required to ensure the Corporation's compliance with the Government in the Sunshine Act, as that Act may be amended from time to time. Consistent with this responsibility, the Secretary of the Corporation provides to the Communications Department at the principal office of the Corporation such records as the Act requires to be made available to the public for access during regular office hours on regular business days.

(b) *The Officers.* (1) The officers of the Corporation are the Executive Director, the Deputy Executive Director, the Secretary, the Treasurer, and such other officer positions as the Board may, in consultation with the Executive Director, create. The Board elects the officers of the Corporation annually.

(2) The Neighborhood Reinvestment Corporation Act provides that the Executive Director shall serve as the chief executive officer of the Corporation. Consistent with that authority, the Corporation's Bylaws provide that the Executive Director shall have the responsibility and authority for the day-to-day administration of the affairs of the Corporation under the general supervision of the Board. The Board periodically reviews the activities of the Executive Director and, from time to time, provides guidance and policy direction to the Executive Director in the exercise of his or her authority.

(3) The responsibilities and authorities of the other officers of the Corporation are set forth in the Corporation's Bylaws, resolutions and policies adopted by the Board, duties and authorities delegated to each officer, other statutes and this statement. (See, for example, the Government in the Sunshine Act and paragraph (a)(3) of this section for specific duties of the Secretary and General Counsel.)

(c) *Principal office.* The Corporation maintains its principal office in the District of Columbia. Currently, the principal office is maintained at 1325 G Street NW., Suite 800, Washington, DC 20005.

[49 FR 12700, Mar. 30, 1984, as amended at 54 FR 13062, Mar. 30, 1989]

§4100.3 Field activities.

The Corporation conducts its field activities from district and field offices around the country. District offices provide coordination of field activities in support of local programs within the geographic limits of each district. Field offices within each district provide assistance in the development and support of local programs. A current directory of all district and field offices can be obtained upon request from the Communications Department, Neighborhood Reinvestment Corporation, 1325 G Street NW., Suite 800, Washington, DC 20005.

[49 FR 12700, Mar. 30, 1984, as amended at 54 FR 13061, Mar. 30, 1989]

§4100.4 Inquiries.

(a) *General.* All requests for information, forms, and records should be addressed to: Communications Department, Neighborhood Reinvestment Corporation, 1325 G Street NW., Suite 800, Washington, DC 20005.

(b) *Applications.* Applications for the Corporation's assistance in the development of NHS programs and complementary programs and strategies, or the support of other promising neighborhood strategies are accepted on an ongoing basis. Local governmental or nonprofit entities should submit completed applications (forms are available upon request), including supportive materials, to the Corporation at the address stated in paragraph (a) of this section. The Corporation reviews applications to determine their readiness for development or support. Promising applications are selected for field reviews. Subject to the availability of the Corporation's resources, the Corporation may enter into agreements with top ranking applicants to provide financial and technical assistance in the development or support of selected programs. The application form contains a list of the criteria used for determining the readiness and promise of applications.

(c) *Records.* (1) The Corporation maintains such records and information for public inspection and copying as are required by the Freedom of Information Act (5 U.S.C. 552), as that Act may be amended from time to time. Records are available for public inspection and copying during regular business hours on regular business days at the address stated in paragraph (a) of this section. Requests for records should be sub-

mitted in writing and state the full name and address of the person requesting the records and a description of the records or other information sought that is reasonably sufficient to permit their identification without undue difficulty. A request should be submitted sufficiently in advance of the date inspection or copying is desired, preferably by mail.

(2) Although the Corporation finds that the publication of indexes of statements of policy and interpretations or administrative staff manuals and instructions would be unnecessary and impracticable, such information will be made available upon request.

(d) *Fees for providing copies for records.* Fees shall be assessed pursuant to the Freedom of Information Act (5 U.S.C. 552) in order to recover the full allowable direct costs of providing copies of records. For purposes of this section, the term *direct costs* means those expenditures which the Corporation actually incurs in searching for and duplicating (and in the case of commercial use requesters, reviewing) documents to respond to a Freedom of Information Act ("FOIA") request. Direct costs include, for example, the salaries of the employees performing the work (the basic rate of pay plus 16 percent of that rate to cover benefits) and the cost of operating duplicating equipment. The term *search* includes all time spent looking for material that is responsive to a request, including page-by-page or line-by-line identification of material within documents. Searches may be done manually or by computer using existing programming. The term *duplication* refers to the process of making a copy of a document necessary to respond to a FOIA request. Such copies can take the form of paper copy, microfilm, audiovisual materials, or machine readable documentation (e.g., magnetic tape or disk), among others. The term *review* refers to the process of examining documents located in response to a commercial use request to determine whether any portion of any document is permitted to be withheld. It also includes processing any documents for disclosure, e.g., doing all that is necessary to exise them and otherwise prepare them for release. Review does not include time spent resolving general legal or policy issues regarding the application of exemptions. A schedule based on these principles is set forth in paragraph (d)(9) of this section.

(1) *Categories of requesters.* Fees will be assessed according to the category of the requester. There are four categories:

(i) *Commercial use requesters.* For purposes of this section, the term *commercial use request* refers to a request from or on behalf of one who seeks information for a use or purpose that furthers the commercial, trade, or profit interests of the requester or the person on whose behalf the request is made. In determining whether a requester properly belongs in this category, the Corporation will look to the use to which the requester will put the documents requested. If the use is not clear from the request itself, or if there is reasonable cause to doubt the requester's stated use, the Corporation shall seek additional clarification before assigning the request to a specific category.

(ii) *Educational and noncommercial scientific institution requesters.* For purposes of this section, the term *educational institution* refers to a preschool, a public or private elementary or secondary school, an institution of graduate higher education, an institution of undergraduate higher education, an institution of professional education, or an institution of vocational education, which operates a program or programs of scholarly research. The term *noncommercial scientific institution* refers to an institution that is not operated on a *commercial* basis, as that term is used in paragraph (d)(1)(i) of this section, and which is operated solely for the purpose of conducting scientific research the results of which are not intended to promote any particular product or industry. To be eligible for inclusion in this category, requesters must show that the request is made as authorized by and under the auspices of a qualifying institution, and that the records are not sought for a commercial use, but are sought in furtherance of scholarly (if the request is from an educational institution) or scientific (if the request is from a non-commercial scientific institution) research.

(iii) *Requesters who are representatives of the news media.* For purposes of this section, the term *representative of the news media* refers to any person actively gathering information for an entity that is organized and operated to publish or broadcast news to the public. Examples of news media entities include television or radio stations broadcasting to the public at large, and publishers of periodicals (but only in those instances when they can qualify as disseminators of *news*) who make their products available for purchase or subscription by the general public. These examples are not intended to be all-inclusive. In the case of *freelance* journalists, they may be regarded as working for a news organization if they demonstrate a solid basis for expecting publication through that organization, even though not actually employed by it. A publication contract would be the clearest proof, but the Corporation may also look at the past publication record of a requester in making this determination. To be eligible for inclusion in this category, a requester must meet the criteria above, and his or her request must not be made for a commerical use. In reference to this class of requester, a request for records supporting the news dissemination function of the requester shall not be considered to be a request that is for a commercial use.

(iv) All other requesters.

(2) *Limitations on fees to be charged—* (i) *Commercial use requesters.* Commercial use requesters shall be assessed the full direct costs for searching for, reviewing, and duplicating records, in accordance with the fee schedule at paragraph (d)(9) of this section. Commercial use requesters are not entitled to the free search time or free pages of duplication provided to other categories of requesters.

(ii) *Educational and noncommercial scientific institution requesters.* Requesters in this category may be assessed fees only for duplication of records in excess of the first 100 pages. Requesters in this category may not be assessed fees for search or review.

(iii) *Requesters who are representatives of the news media.* Requesters in this category may be assessed fees only for duplication of records in excess of the first 100 pages. Requesters in this category may not be assessed fees for research or review.

(iv) *All other requesters.* Requesters who do not fit into any of the categories above shall be assessed fees only for searching and duplicating records, except that the first 100 pages of duplication and the first two hours of search time shall be furnished without charge. Requesters in this category may not be assessed fees for review.

(v) *Review of records.* Charges will be assessed only for the initial review of the located documents and not for time spent at the administrative appeal level on an exemption applied at the initial determination level. However, where records or portions of records are withheld in full under an exemption which is subsequently determined not to apply, and these records are reviewed again to determine the applicability of other exemptions not previously considered, charges for review are properly assessable.

(vi) *Additional copies.* The Corporation will normally furnish only one copy of any record. The allowance of 100 free pages of duplication under paragraphs (d)(2) (ii), (iii), and (iv) of this section shall not apply to additional copies furnished at the request of the record requester. Full duplication fees shall be assessed for each page of each such additional copy.

(3) *Charges for unsuccessful search.* Where applicable under paragraph (d)(2) of this section search fees may be assessed for time spent searching, even if the Corporation fails to locate the records or if records located are determined to be exempt from disclosure.

(4) *Notice of anticipated fees in excess of $25.00.* Unless the person making the request states in his or her initial request that he or she will pay all costs regardless of amount, the Corporation will notify him or her as soon as possible if there is reason to believe that the cost for obtaining access to and/or copies of such records will exceed $25. If such notice is given, the time limitations contained in the Freedom of Information Act shall not commence until the person making the intitial request agrees in writing to pay such cost.

(5) *Advance payments.* The Communications Director is authorized to require an advance payment of an amount up to the full estimated charges whenever he or she determines that:

(i) The allowable charges that a requester may be required to pay are likely to exceed $250 and the requester has no history of payment and cannot provide satisfactory assurance that payment will be made; or

(ii) A requester has previously failed to pay a fee charged in a timely manner.

If such a payment is required, the time limitations contained in the Freedom of Information Act shall not commence until payment is made.

(6) *Charging interest.* The Corporation will assess interest charges on any unpaid fees starting on the 31st day following the day on which the billing for fees was sent to the requester. Interest will be at the rate prescribed in 31 U.S.C. 3717 and will accrue from the date of the billing. Receipt of the fee by the Corporation, even if not processed, will stay the accrual of interest. Interest is not chargeable for unpaid advance payments under paragraph (d)(5) of this section.

(7) *Aggregating requests.* A requester may not file multiple requests at the same time, each seeking portions of the document or documents, solely in order to avoid payment of fees. When the Corporation reasonably believes that a requester, or a group of requesters acting in concert, is attempting to break a request down into a series of requests for the purpose of evading the assessment of fees, the Corporation may aggregate any such requests and charge accordingly.

(8) *Waiver or reduction of fee.* The Corporation will furnish documents without charge or at a reduced charge when it is determined that disclosure of the information is in the public interest because it is likely to contribute significantly to public understanding of the operations or activities of the Corporation and is not primarily in the commercial interest of the requester. In making a request for a waiver or reduction of fees, a requester should include a clear statement of his or her interest in the requested documents: The

proposed use for the documents and whether the requester will derive income or other benefit from such use; and a statement of how the public will benefit from such use. Determinations concerning waiver or reduction of fees shall be made by the Executive Director, or his or her designee.

(9) *Schedule of fees*. Fees for searching for, reviewing, duplicating, and providing records and information of the Corporation under this section will be assessed in accordance with the following schedule:

(i) *Manual search*. For each quarter hour or fraction thereof: $3.37.

(ii) *Computer search*. For each quarter hour or fraction thereof: $3.37.

(iii) *Review*. For each quarter hour or fraction thereof: $4.87.

(iv) *Duplication*.

(A) For a paper photocopy of an existing paper record, $.10 per page.

(B) For duplication of records other than existing paper records (such as computer-stored information, audio or video tapes, microfiche or microfilm), the fee shall equal the actual direct cost of production and duplication of the records or information in a form that is reasonably usable by the requester.

(10) *Processing costs*. The Communications Director will waive payment in instances in which the costs of routine collection and processing of the fee are likely to equal or exceed the amount of the fee.

[49 FR 12700, Mar. 30, 1984, as amended at 54 FR 50953, Dec. 19, 1989]

PARTS 4101–4199 [RESERVED]

FINDING AIDS

A list of CFR titles, subtitles, chapters, subchapters and parts and an alphabetical list of agencies publishing in the CFR are included in the CFR Index and Finding Aids volume to the Code of Federal Regulations which is published separately and revised annually.

Table of CFR Titles and Chapters

(Revised as of April 1, 2019)

Title 1—General Provisions

Title 2—Grants and Agreements

Title 2—Grants and Agreements—Continued

Title 3—The President

Title 4—Accounts

Title 5—Administrative Personnel

305

Title 5—Administrative Personnel—Continued

Title 6—Domestic Security

Title 7—Agriculture

Title 7—Agriculture—Continued

308

Title 12—Banks and Banking—Continued

Title 13—Business Credit and Assistance

Title 14—Aeronautics and Space

Title 15—Commerce and Foreign Trade

Title 23—Highways—Continued

Title 24—Housing and Urban Development

Title 25—Indians

Title 26—Internal Revenue

Title 27—Alcohol, Tobacco Products and Firearms

Title 28—Judicial Administration

Title 29—Labor

Title 29—Labor—Continued

Title 30—Mineral Resources

Title 31—Money and Finance: Treasury

Title 34—Education—Continued

Title 35 [Reserved]

Title 36—Parks, Forests, and Public Property

Title 37—Patents, Trademarks, and Copyrights

Title 38—Pensions, Bonuses, and Veterans' Relief

Title 39—Postal Service

Title 40—Protection of Environment

Title 41—Public Contracts and Property Management

Title 41—Public Contracts and Property Management—Continued

Title 42—Public Health

Title 43—Public Lands: Interior

Title 44—Emergency Management and Assistance

Title 45—Public Welfare

Title 49—Transportation

Title 50—Wildlife and Fisheries

Alphabetical List of Agencies Appearing in the CFR

(Revised as of April 1, 2019)

Agency	CFR Title, Subtitle or Chapter
Administrative Conference of the United States	1, III
Advisory Council on Historic Preservation	36, VIII
Advocacy and Outreach, Office of	7, XXV
Afghanistan Reconstruction, Special Inspector General for	5, LXXXIII
African Development Foundation	22, XV
Federal Acquisition Regulation	48, 57
Agency for International Development	2, VII; 22, II
Federal Acquisition Regulation	48, 7
Agricultural Marketing Service	7, I, IX, X, XI
Agricultural Research Service	7, V
Agriculture, Department of	2, IV; 5, LXXIII
Advocacy and Outreach, Office of	7, XXV
Agricultural Marketing Service	7, I, IX, X, XI
Agricultural Research Service	7, V
Animal and Plant Health Inspection Service	7, III; 9, I
Chief Financial Officer, Office of	7, XXX
Commodity Credit Corporation	7, XIV
Economic Research Service	7, XXXVII
Energy Policy and New Uses, Office of	2, IX; 7, XXIX
Environmental Quality, Office of	7, XXXI
Farm Service Agency	7, VII, XVIII
Federal Acquisition Regulation	48, 4
Federal Crop Insurance Corporation	7, IV
Food and Nutrition Service	7, II
Food Safety and Inspection Service	9, III
Foreign Agricultural Service	7, XV
Forest Service	36, II
Grain Inspection, Packers and Stockyards Administration	7, VIII; 9, II
Information Resources Management, Office of	7, XXVII
Inspector General, Office of	7, XXVI
National Agricultural Library	7, XLI
National Agricultural Statistics Service	7, XXXVI
National Institute of Food and Agriculture	7, XXXIV
Natural Resources Conservation Service	7, VI
Operations, Office of	7, XXVIII
Procurement and Property Management, Office of	7, XXXII
Rural Business-Cooperative Service	7, XVIII, XLII
Rural Development Administration	7, XLII
Rural Housing Service	7, XVIII, XXXV
Rural Telephone Bank	7, XVI
Rural Utilities Service	7, XVII, XVIII, XLII
Secretary of Agriculture, Office of	7, Subtitle A
Transportation, Office of	7, XXXIII
World Agricultural Outlook Board	7, XXXVIII
Air Force, Department of	32, VII
Federal Acquisition Regulation Supplement	48, 53
Air Transportation Stabilization Board	14, VI
Alcohol and Tobacco Tax and Trade Bureau	27, I
Alcohol, Tobacco, Firearms, and Explosives, Bureau of	27, II
AMTRAK	49, VII
American Battle Monuments Commission	36, IV
American Indians, Office of the Special Trustee	25, VII
Animal and Plant Health Inspection Service	7, III; 9, I

Agency	CFR Title, Subtitle or Chapter
Appalachian Regional Commission	5, IX
Architectural and Transportation Barriers Compliance Board	36, XI
Arctic Research Commission	45, XXIII
Armed Forces Retirement Home	5, XI
Army, Department of	32, V
Engineers, Corps of	33, II; 36, III
Federal Acquisition Regulation	48, 51
Bilingual Education and Minority Languages Affairs, Office of	34, V
Blind or Severely Disabled, Committee for Purchase from People Who Are	41, 51
Broadcasting Board of Governors	22, V
Federal Acquisition Regulation	48, 19
Career, Technical, and Adult Education, Office of	34, IV
Census Bureau	15, I
Centers for Medicare & Medicaid Services	42, IV
Central Intelligence Agency	32, XIX
Chemical Safety and Hazardous Investigation Board	40, VI
Chief Financial Officer, Office of	7, XXX
Child Support Enforcement, Office of	45, III
Children and Families, Administration for	45, II, III, IV, X, XIII
Civil Rights, Commission on	5, LXVIII; 45, VII
Civil Rights, Office for	34, I
Council of the Inspectors General on Integrity and Efficiency	5, XCVIII
Court Services and Offender Supervision Agency for the District of Columbia	5, LXX
Coast Guard	33, I; 46, I; 49, IV
Coast Guard (Great Lakes Pilotage)	46, III
Commerce, Department of	2, XIII; 44, IV; 50, VI
Census Bureau	15, I
Economic Analysis, Bureau of	15, VIII
Economic Development Administration	13, III
Emergency Management and Assistance	44, IV
Federal Acquisition Regulation	48, 13
Foreign-Trade Zones Board	15, IV
Industry and Security, Bureau of	15, VII
International Trade Administration	15, III; 19, III
National Institute of Standards and Technology	15, II; 37, IV
National Marine Fisheries Service	50, II, IV
National Oceanic and Atmospheric Administration	15, IX; 50, II, III, IV, VI
National Technical Information Service	15, XI
National Telecommunications and Information Administration	15, XXIII; 47, III, IV
National Weather Service	15, IX
Patent and Trademark Office, United States	37, I
Secretary of Commerce, Office of	15, Subtitle A
Commercial Space Transportation	14, III
Commodity Credit Corporation	7, XIV
Commodity Futures Trading Commission	5, XLI; 17, I
Community Planning and Development, Office of Assistant Secretary for	24, V, VI
Community Services, Office of	45, X
Comptroller of the Currency	12, I
Construction Industry Collective Bargaining Commission	29, IX
Consumer Financial Protection Bureau	5, LXXXIV; 12, X
Consumer Product Safety Commission	5, LXXI; 16, II
Copyright Royalty Board	37, III
Corporation for National and Community Service	2, XXII; 45, XII, XXV
Cost Accounting Standards Board	48, 99
Council on Environmental Quality	40, V
Court Services and Offender Supervision Agency for the District of Columbia	5, LXX; 28, VIII
Customs and Border Protection	19, I
Defense Contract Audit Agency	32, I
Defense, Department of	2, XI; 5, XXVI; 32, Subtitle A; 40, VII
Advanced Research Projects Agency	32, I
Air Force Department	32, VII

325

326

327

Agency	CFR Title, Subtitle or Chapter
Indian Arts and Crafts Board	25, II
Indian Health Service	25, V
Industry and Security, Bureau of	15, VII
Information Resources Management, Office of	7, XXVII
Information Security Oversight Office, National Archives and Records Administration	32, XX
Inspector General	
Agriculture Department	7, XXVI
Health and Human Services Department	42, V
Housing and Urban Development Department	24, XII, XV
Institute of Peace, United States	22, XVII
Inter-American Foundation	5, LXIII; 22, X
Interior, Department of	2, XIV
American Indians, Office of the Special Trustee	25, VII
Endangered Species Committee	50, IV
Federal Acquisition Regulation	48, 14
Federal Property Management Regulations System	41, 114
Fish and Wildlife Service, United States	50, I, IV
Geological Survey	30, IV
Indian Affairs, Bureau of	25, I, V
Indian Affairs, Office of the Assistant Secretary	25, VI
Indian Arts and Crafts Board	25, II
Land Management, Bureau of	43, II
National Indian Gaming Commission	25, III
National Park Service	36, I
Natural Resource Revenue, Office of	30, XII
Ocean Energy Management, Bureau of	30, V
Reclamation, Bureau of	43, I
Safety and Enforcement Bureau, Bureau of	30, II
Secretary of the Interior, Office of	2, XIV; 43, Subtitle A
Surface Mining Reclamation and Enforcement, Office of	30, VII
Internal Revenue Service	26, I
International Boundary and Water Commission, United States and Mexico, United States Section	22, XI
International Development, United States Agency for	22, II
Federal Acquisition Regulation	48, 7
International Development Cooperation Agency, United States	22, XII
International Joint Commission, United States and Canada	22, IV
International Organizations Employees Loyalty Board	5, V
International Trade Administration	15, III; 19, III
International Trade Commission, United States	19, II
Interstate Commerce Commission	5, XL
Investment Security, Office of	31, VIII
James Madison Memorial Fellowship Foundation	45, XXIV
Japan–United States Friendship Commission	22, XVI
Joint Board for the Enrollment of Actuaries	20, VIII
Justice, Department of	2, XXVIII; 5, XXVIII; 28, I, XI; 40, IV
Alcohol, Tobacco, Firearms, and Explosives, Bureau of	27, II
Drug Enforcement Administration	21, II
Federal Acquisition Regulation	48, 28
Federal Claims Collection Standards	31, IX
Federal Prison Industries, Inc.	28, III
Foreign Claims Settlement Commission of the United States	45, V
Immigration Review, Executive Office for	8, V
Independent Counsel, Offices of	28, VI
Prisons, Bureau of	28, V
Property Management Regulations	41, 128
Labor, Department of	2, XXIX; 5, XLII
Employee Benefits Security Administration	29, XXV
Employees' Compensation Appeals Board	20, IV
Employment and Training Administration	20, V
Employment Standards Administration	20, VI
Federal Acquisition Regulation	48, 29
Federal Contract Compliance Programs, Office of	41, 60

329

Agency	CFR Title, Subtitle or Chapter
Selective Service System	32, XVI
Small Business Administration	2, XXVII; 13, I
Smithsonian Institution	36, V
Social Security Administration	2, XXIII; 20, III; 48, 23
Soldiers' and Airmen's Home, United States	5, XI
Special Counsel, Office of	5, VIII
Special Education and Rehabilitative Services, Office of	34, III
State, Department of	2, VI; 22, I; 28, XI
Federal Acquisition Regulation	48, 6
Surface Mining Reclamation and Enforcement, Office of	30, VII
Surface Transportation Board	49, X
Susquehanna River Basin Commission	18, VIII
Tennessee Valley Authority	5, LXIX; 18, XIII
Trade Representative, United States, Office of	15, XX
Transportation, Department of	2, XII; 5, L
Commercial Space Transportation	14, III
Emergency Management and Assistance	44, IV
Federal Acquisition Regulation	48, 12
Federal Aviation Administration	14, I
Federal Highway Administration	23, I, II
Federal Motor Carrier Safety Administration	49, III
Federal Railroad Administration	49, II
Federal Transit Administration	49, VI
Maritime Administration	46, II
National Highway Traffic Safety Administration	23, II, III; 47, IV; 49, V
Pipeline and Hazardous Materials Safety Administration	49, I
Saint Lawrence Seaway Development Corporation	33, IV
Secretary of Transportation, Office of	14, II; 49, Subtitle A
Transportation Statistics Bureau	49, XI
Transportation, Office of	7, XXXIII
Transportation Security Administration	49, XII
Transportation Statistics Bureau	49, XI
Travel Allowances, Temporary Duty (TDY)	41, 301
Treasury, Department of the	2, X;5, XXI; 12, XV; 17, IV; 31, IX
Alcohol and Tobacco Tax and Trade Bureau	27, I
Community Development Financial Institutions Fund	12, XVIII
Comptroller of the Currency	12, I
Customs and Border Protection	19, I
Engraving and Printing, Bureau of	31, VI
Federal Acquisition Regulation	48, 10
Federal Claims Collection Standards	31, IX
Federal Law Enforcement Training Center	31, VII
Financial Crimes Enforcement Network	31, X
Fiscal Service	31, II
Foreign Assets Control, Office of	31, V
Internal Revenue Service	26, I
Investment Security, Office of	31, VIII
Monetary Offices	31, I
Secret Service	31, IV
Secretary of the Treasury, Office of	31, Subtitle A
Truman, Harry S. Scholarship Foundation	45, XVIII
United States and Canada, International Joint Commission	22, IV
United States and Mexico, International Boundary and Water Commission, United States Section	22, XI
U.S. Copyright Office	37, II
Utah Reclamation Mitigation and Conservation Commission	43, III
Veterans Affairs, Department of	2, VIII; 38, I
Federal Acquisition Regulation	48, 8
Veterans' Employment and Training Service, Office of the Assistant Secretary for	41, 61; 20, IX
Vice President of the United States, Office of	32, XXVIII
Wage and Hour Division	29, V
Water Resources Council	18, VI
Workers' Compensation Programs, Office of	20, I, VII
World Agricultural Outlook Board	7, XXXVIII

List of CFR Sections Affected

All changes in this volume of the Code of Federal Regulations (CFR) that were made by documents published in the FEDERAL REGISTER since January 1, 2014 are enumerated in the following list. Entries indicate the nature of the changes effected. Page numbers refer to FEDERAL REGISTER pages. The user should consult the entries for chapters, parts and subparts as well as sections for revisions.

For changes to this volume of the CFR prior to this listing, consult the annual edition of the monthly List of CFR Sections Affected (LSA). The LSA is available at *www.govinfo.gov*. For changes to this volume of the CFR prior to 2001, see the "List of CFR Sections Affected, 1949–1963, 1964–1972, 1973–1985, and 1986–2000" published in 11 separate volumes. The "List of CFR Sections Affected 1986–2000" is available at *www.govinfo.gov*.

2018

2019

(Regulations published from January 1, 2019, through April 1, 2019)

○

www.ingramcontent.com/pod-product-compliance
Lightning Source LLC
Chambersburg PA
CBHW061128220326
41599CB00024B/4201